PACIFIC OCEAN

Midway Islands

HAWAIIAN
ISLANDS

Pearl
Harbor

Wake Island

N

GILBERT
ISLANDS

| 0 | 500 | 1000 |

MILES

TENNOZAN

Books by George Feifer

Tennozan: The Battle of Okinawa and the Atomic Bomb (1992)

The Destined Hour, *with Barbara and Barry Rosen* (1982)

To Dance, *with Valery Panov* (1978)

Moscow Farewell (1976)

Our Motherland (1973)

Solzhenitsyn *with David Burg* (1972)

The Girl from Petrovka (1971)

Message from Moscow (1969)

The Challenge of Change (1967)

Justice in Moscow (1964)

TENNOZAN

The Battle of Okinawa and the Atomic Bomb

George Feifer

Ticknor & Fields

New York   1992

For information about permission to reproduce
selections from this book, write to Permissions,
Ticknor & Fields, 215 Park Avenue South, New
York, New York 10003.

———————————◆———————————

Library of Congress Cataloging-in-Publication Data
Feifer, George.
Tennozan : the Battle of Okinawa and the atomic
bomb / George Feifer.
p.   cm.
Includes bibliographical references and index.
ISBN 0-395-59924-5
1. World War, 1939–1945 — Campaigns — Japan — Okinawa
Island.   2. Okinawa Island — History.   3. Atomic bomb.
I. Title.
D767.99.O45F45   1992   91-46913
940.54′25 — dc20   CIP

Printed in the United States of America

Book design by David Ford
Maps by George Ward

TENNOZAN

A site where
a sixteenth-century
Japanese ruler staked
his entire fate on
a single battle.
It has come to mean
any decisive
struggle.

There was never a good war or a bad peace.
— Benjamin Franklin

Nothing is worse than war? Dishonour is worse than war.
Slavery is worse than war.
— Winston Churchill

The cherry is the first among flowers as the warrior is the first among men.
— Old Japanese saying

The fortress of Okinawa now appeared to be the home islands' only pro-
tection from invasion, and its defense was the key to whether Japan would
survive as an independent nation . . . so that Okinawa, Japan's last impor-
tant stand in the war, became virtually synonymous with kamikaze.
— Ivan Morris, *The Nobility of Failure: Tragic Heroes in the History of Japan*

KILL JAPS. KILL JAPS.
KILL MORE JAPS

You will help to kill the yellow bastards
if you do your job well.
— A sign at the headquarters of
Admiral William F. (Bull) Halsey,
commander of the fleet that helped
devastate Okinawa

The Ryukyus were not Kyushu, or Shikoku, or Honshu; Okinawa retained
importance [for the Japanese] only as a potential field of battle, a distant
border area in which the oncoming enemy could be checked, pinned down,
and ultimately destroyed.
— George Kerr

There was a fury, a storm of devastation, to the campaign on Okinawa that surpassed the ground fighting seen anywhere else in the war.
— Geoffrey Perret, historian of U.S. Army operations in World War II

It's a good thing how the Lord helps one to block out unpleasant memories. I don't think one could vividly remember those feelings and still have his sanity.
— An American Marine gravely wounded on Sugar Loaf Hill

The funny thing is I remember more of the amusing incidents than the blood and the gore.
— Another American veteran of the Okinawa campaign

In retrospect, the battle for Okinawa can be described only in the grim superlatives of war. In size, scope and ferocity, it dwarfed the Battle of Britain. Never before had there been, probably never again will there be, such a vicious sprawling struggle of planes against planes, of ships against planes. Never before, in so short a space, had the Navy lost so many ships; never before in land fighting had so much American blood been shed in so short a time in so small an area: probably never before in any three months of the war had the enemy suffered so hugely, and the final toll of American casualties was the highest experienced in any campaign against the Japanese. There have been larger land battles, more protracted air campaigns, but Okinawa was the largest combined operation, a "no quarter" struggle fought on, under and over the sea and land.
— Hanson W. Baldwin, military historian

The real war will never get in the books.
— Walt Whitman, volunteer hospital nurse, Civil War

Contents

Book IV

Introduction

I USED to picture Okinawa as a distant island where an important battle of World War II took place. Like most Americans born before 1940, I knew slightly more about Iwo Jima, a much smaller Pacific island where the battle is remembered as savage. Actually, the savagery on Okinawa three months later and some eight hundred miles southwest was greater, although, for reasons I will discuss, that unhappy distinction never registered in America's national consciousness. The Okinawan campaign and Japanese defensive effort were many times larger and more deadly. In fact, what took place on and around the island in the spring of 1945 was the greatest land, sea and air battle of all time. The Japanese called it a Tennozan, a decisive struggle on which, for a time, they staked everything.

The battle was also a turning point in modern history. That first operation on Japanese soil — Okinawa was politically part of Japan, to which it reverted in 1972 — was also the last battle before the start of the atomic age. Without the essential facts, it is impossible to understand the decision, made some six weeks after the campaign ended, to use the atomic bomb.

Although no precise assessment of the rights and wrongs of that decision is likely to be made, the debate deserves to be conducted with evidence as well as emotion. The deep revulsion still provoked by the horrors at Hiroshima and Nagasaki is of course wholly appropriate. But it is difficult to evaluate the destruction of those cities out of context, without the knowledge that Okinawan civilians, not to mention the fighting men of both armies there, endured worse. The best estimate of the dead in the two obliterated cities is around 200,000. The Okinawan campaign killed fewer noncombatants, some 150,000. But the total number of dead, including servicemen, was significantly higher. And conventional explosives on the island caused far greater damage to Okinawan tradition, culture and well-being than the atomic bombs did to the Japanese. Measured by sheer suffering as well as by devastation of national life, the battle of Okinawa was a greater tragedy. And had the war progressed to the Japanese mainland, the next battleground after Okinawa, the damage would have been incomparable.

I mention this at the start not to stake a claim in some ghoulish competition to crown the greatest catastrophe, but to point out that the Okinawan suffering has never been recognized; proportionately far smaller losses in Japan and America always prompted much greater sorrow. This book was conceived as an account of the fighting men's ordeal that never won rightful gratitude in America. I hope it will convey a hint of the immense exertion, terror, agony and carnage in that battle. But nonmilitary issues that emerged during the course of my research pushed me toward a larger story.

Okinawans' punishment and suffering continue to this day as a direct result of that conflict, although they, the accommodating, exceptionally peaceful islanders, were among its chief victims then. That was one of the war's plentiful ironies — or inevitable consequences: the weakest and poorest usually bear the greatest burdens. Still, present-day Okinawans do not behave like oppressed subjects, at least in their daily lives. Despite grave damage to many bodies and minds, the majority remain largely as they were before the battle, easygoing and amiable. My travels as a journalist have convinced me of the durability of national character. Formed by fundamental factors such as soil, climate and centuries of common memories, most peoples' underlying attitudes and customs change far more slowly than their fortunes. Okinawans conform to the general pattern, having retained their most salient characteristics for ages.

Although it is hard for me to say what has and hasn't changed in the national character of my own country, some of the qualities for which Americans are known — infectious optimism and dismal ignorance of other cultures, rare personal generosity and a lasting inability to recognize the fact of American imperialism — were much in evidence during the Okinawan campaign. In some ways, it seemed a brighter time for the country, despite the hardships of the Depression that colored the childhood of almost every fighting man and despite the fighting itself. Perhaps inevitably, America lost some of her bearings, and also hasn't been genuinely happy, as the world's rich kid, a role World War II awarded her.

As for the Japanese, they were a formidable enemy on Okinawa, as elsewhere in the Pacific War. Their accomplishments despite severe technological inferiority were stunning. I was midway in my research — in fact, conducting interviews on Shikoku — when Theodore White, the distinguished journalist, published a forceful article arguing that the economic struggle between America and Japan was actually an extension of World War II. White's notion struck me as a dangerous fallacy; Japanese VCRs are very different from the Japanese torpedoes and bombs that did the damage at Pearl Harbor. I believe Japan has every right to wage economic war, which she learned the hard way from imperialist Western powers, including

America. (This is not to say that she is yet willing to fight fairly by giving her Western competitors opportunities inside Japan equal to those enjoyed by Japanese businessmen in other countries.) White's article appeared in 1985, just as many Americans were waking to, or trying to explain away, the threat of Japanese industrial and commercial excellence. His warning that the Japanese purpose is nothing less than the "dismantling of American industry" seems to owe more to American paranoia and self-pity — qualities that helped make the Cold War more dominating than it need have been — than to fact or reason.

At the same time, some of the Japanese traits most evident during the country's imperialist conquests fifty and sixty years ago foster her current commercial expansion. Perhaps no army in the world could have labored and fought with such bravery, endurance and sublimation of individual well-being for the sake of a national cause as the Japanese Army demonstrated on Okinawa. Perhaps no people were so driven by a desire to prove themselves, no matter what the hardships and consequences. It seems to me that the Japanese goal was more than mere victory. Some deep national yearning impelled them to make horrific sacrifices and blinded them to what most other peoples considered reality. Although the nature of contemporary Japan lies well outside the scope of this book, the qualities displayed on Okinawa — extraordinary intensity, insularity and a zealous capacity to endure pain in order to serve the nation and obtain rewards in a later life — may help explain the startling Japanese triumphs in manufacture and trade.

There have been great national changes since 1945, but the samurai ethic lives on in board rooms. It is far better to have that country as a commercial rival than a military enemy, but even as a peaceful competitor, she presents a mighty challenge, for reasons that became startlingly clear on Okinawa.

Well over a million people were on the island and in the surrounding seas during the year or so of preparation for and action in the 1945 battle. Nearly a quarter of them — Okinawan, Japanese and American — were killed. It is of course impossible to tell the full story of the living or the dead. At first, I tried to omit no category of participant. But after reading my initial pages about a confusing array of regiments, crews, companies, platoons, and squads, I decided to focus on fewer soldiers and civilians.* The only people more conscious

---

*On the American side, I followed the 6th Marine Division, which took the most casualties while capturing some 75 percent of Okinawa's territory, including many of the best

than I of the categories this approach excludes will be those excluded themselves: whole Army divisions in some cases, together with the entire crews of capital ships and hundreds of thousands of Okinawan farmers. I hope they will recognize themselves in some of the people I have drawn, although I may risk offending some in attempting to convey a sense of the huge, complex whole through greater detail about what is meant to be a representative selection.

War's horror exists partly because outsiders can't know it. "If people really knew, the war would be stopped tomorrow," said Prime Minister David Lloyd George in 1916, when trench warfare was bleeding his Britain white. "But of course they don't know and can't know." Not even most servicemen know, since a minute proportion of them actually fight — and those who do are unlikely to describe their ordeal, partly because few are writers, partly because all rightly believe that no one who hasn't experienced combat can understand. As a historian of battle recently put it, combat is too little related to "anything recognizably human or natural."

It is chiefly infantrymen who are placed in "mortal contact with the enemy," in the same historian's phrase — roughly a quarter of 1 percent of Americans during World War II. Of the eleven million uniformed men in 1945, some 7 percent of the population, about 5 percent served in infantry combat divisions, of which only about 60 percent were in the lines. Those who wore uniforms but never saw combat remained innocent of war's real misery, even if they were stuck on a mosquito-infested atoll. As E. B. Sledge pointed out in a superb account of his fighting on Okinawa, the majority of servicemen behind the lines had almost as little notion as the civilians back home of the infantryman's war of "incredible cruelty," in which "decent men were reduced to a brutish existence in their fight for survival amid the violent death, terror, tension, fatigue and filth." All this was "totally incomprehensible" to the uninitiated, as a man who lived a mere few hundred yards from it discovered on Okinawa.

> After we left the Sugar Loaf Hill area and passed through the shambles of Naha, we reached a rural area that had been under American fire for some time. We passed by a dead horse or mule and three dead Japanese soldiers who were a mess. The unforgettable memory is the stench of the rotting bodies. It's an unbelievably overpowering odor. Artillerymen did not see that part of war often because we did our killing long distance. To see the results

---

defensive fortifications. Japanese losses were far more shocking; the scarcity of survivors narrowed my choice of individuals to interview. The relatively small British naval force did not substantially affect the course of the battle.

was horrible . . . I survived Okinawa because I was artillery,
not infantry.

Not having fought at Okinawa or anywhere else, I too don't know
what is unknowable to outsiders. But the stories I heard during my
research were close enough to horror for me. In any case, this book
does not pretend to be a military history, of which some good ones
exist in English and in Japanese, but sketches of a few elements of
the battle and its background that may suggest what Okinawans,
Americans and Japanese endured. Even now, most survivors have
only a vague, often mistaken, impression of the other participants in
their shared nightmare.

Okinawans suffered most, devastated beyond calculation by the
"typhoon of bombs and steel" in 1945. But all were victims, which
seemed to me another reason for not attempting to provide a conventional account of the fighting, day by day, hill by hill, decimated
platoon by decimated platoon. The Battle of Okinawa involved matters more important than its bloody heroism and anguish in the field
and on the sea.

The causes of the Pacific War were less clear-cut than most Americans believe. During the preceding decades, Washington and individual Americans had sometimes scorned Tokyo and individual Japanese
with haughty insensitivity and racial prejudice, and few Japanese forgot the insults. Resentment nourished their determination to strike
at America in 1941. Still, the attack on Pearl Harbor, not to mention
the earlier aggression against fellow Asians in Manchuria and China,
went beyond anything that could conceivably have been a justifiable
reaction. It was chiefly an expression of national self-interest, a
"need" and "right" to grab other nations' land and food. Even in
defense, as on Okinawa, Japan was a brutal aggressor. It is now
clearer than ever that a Japanese victory in the war — closer to a
right-against-wrong war than most others — would have been a calamity to her possessions and captured territories; probably also to
the militarist homeland itself.

But it goes without saying that not all Japanese soldiers were brutal — and most of those who were, like those who weren't, were
themselves brutalized. Almost all survivors of the Okinawa battle I
interviewed had become deeply suspicious of militarism.* I can't say
they appear to feel much remorse for the immeasurable suffering

---

*Despite the reluctance of most Japanese to say anything they fear may displease a
listener, especially a foreign one, I don't think I was fooled much, although interviewing
through an interpreter is doubly tricky.

Japan caused other peoples in World War II, in particular Okinawans, whose pain many mentioned only when prompted. But they
are appalled by war — and by leaders who take their people to it,
journalists who lie to fire them up — as only people with their experience of hoodwinking and suffering can be. It was almost inevitable
that many of those I saw, among them writers of memoirs and participants in Japanese-American memorial activities, formed a self-
selected group, more likely to be internationally minded and "liberal"
than the average survivor. In any case, those elderly men, some of
whom surely did gruesome things as young men, impressed me as
wise, friendly and kind.

The American survivors are also an inspiring collection, and on
average more troubled than the Japanese by Okinawan suffering. I
would argue that generalizations about those who fought in the front
lines are valid because the battle was the foremost influence on the
young men and molded them all for life. The savage hardship was
indelible, together with love for those who made the experience
bearable by sharing its misery and the profound hope that it won't
be repeated. Yet those unabashed patriots, whose middle-American
lawns fly the Stars and Stripes on holidays, saw enough of real war to
detest it and are close enough to their natural deaths not to feel they
must hide what they know. Anyone who thinks life in the trenches
leaves a man fond of a good fight should talk to the survivors of
Okinawa. They are justly proud of their feats but free of movie warriors' bravado and baloney.

As they dug into the mud trying to stay alive, many Americans
asked themselves what they were doing in that hell, a world from
home. For Okinawans also trying to survive, the blood-soaked mud
was from their own fields and animal pens; it *was* home. They endured far more than the Japanese and the Americans, yet remain as
gentle and hospitable as in the descriptions of them I had read before
visiting the island. Long residence in Russia and other dictatorial
countries has left me impatient with leaders who preach peace and
oppress the weak. But when Okinawans plead for peace, I shut up
and listen.

The quotations of the battle's participants and victims are authentic. (To keep them so, I retained the almost universal American use
during the war of the offensive "Jap" and "Nip.") I also added the
wisdom of some experts, in epigraphs at the start of each chapter
and sometimes within the text. However, skipping the quotes ought
not to detract from following the text. The same should apply to the
footnotes, which can be read for points of supplementary interest.

I made no acknowledgments in previous books but I never needed so much help. Masahide Ota, Dave Evans, Nancy Bray and, especially, the skilled and forbearing Tamako Yorichika aided me greatly with research and explanation. The Okinawa International Foundation funded a second trip to the island so that I could check the surprising observations of my first. John Herman's editing was as good as its reputation. I have borrowed liberally from previous writings, particularly a collection entitled *An Oral History of the Battle of Okinawa.*

A hundred Okinawans, Americans and Japanese deserve my individual thanks. All I can say here that may have meaning to others is that I met people in all three places whose first instinct was to "do good." If only, I kept thinking during my interviews, they would get to know one another. Indifference and patriotism, that bane of mankind still revered in each individual country, have largely kept them from doing so.

But now a handful are actually meeting one another. Although they are far too few, the good thing they are accomplishing was exemplified several years ago when, after long preparation, a memorial to Okinawans, Japanese and Americans killed during the campaign was unveiled in a Garden of Remembrance on Okinawa. Veterans who attended the ceremony, some so scarred by combat's torment and so full of hateful memory of the enemy that they feared returning to the island, put their arms around men of the other side and wept. Together, they mourned all the dead — and felt cleansed and uplifted; some felt a bond.

The inspiring memorial was unveiled in 1987, forty-two years after the event. If the perception that emerged there of the other side as human beings had been shared earlier, much of the horror might have been avoided. "But I also came to realize that if our concept of . . . civilization was to mean anything, we had to acknowledge the humanity of even our misled and murderous enemies," John Hersey, once a war correspondent, wrote recently. Congratulations are not yet in order: to this day, care and concern for the chief victims are insufficient. I will not apologize for repeating in later chapters that more innocent civilians died on Okinawa, and in greater agony, than in Hiroshima and Nagasaki and that the cultural damage was incalculably greater than that of the two atomic bombs. Okinawans are hardly the first people to endure a martyrdom of geography, but few have endured more with less recognition.

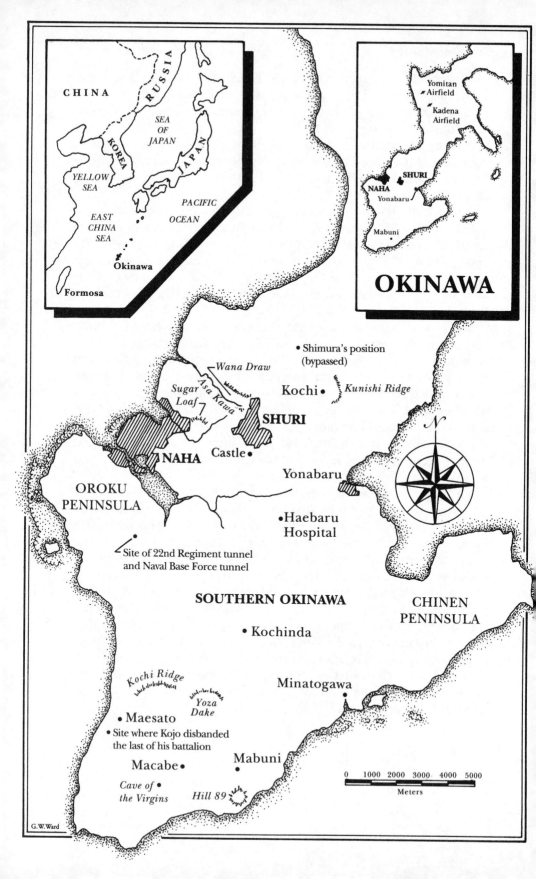

CHINA

RUSSIA

SEA OF JAPAN

KOREA

YELLOW SEA

JAPAN

PACIFIC OCEAN

EAST CHINA SEA

Okinawa

Formosa

Yomitan Airfield

Kadena Airfield

SHURI

NAHA

Yonabaru

Mabuni

OKINAWA

• Shimura's position (bypassed)

Wana Draw

Asa Kawa

Sugar Loaf

Kochi •   *Kunishi Ridge*

SHURI

Castle •

NAHA

Yonabaru

 OROKU PENINSULA

•Haebaru Hospital

Site of 22nd Regiment tunnel and Naval Base Force tunnel

SOUTHERN OKINAWA

CHINEN PENINSULA

• Kochinda

Kochi Ridge

Yoza Dake

Minatogawa

• Maesato

• Site where Kojo disbanded the last of his battalion

Mabuni

Macabe •

Cave of the Virgins •   Hill 89

N

0   1000 2000 3000 4000 5000

Meters

G.W. Ward

Book I

1 · Operation Heaven Number One

What would we have done in olden times? We would have risked everything on one momentous gamble! Have we all become women? Hark back to history! Evoke the spirit of . . . [Admiral Isoroku] Yamamoto at Pearl Harbor . . . A show of spirit, that's what we want! The spirit of our glorious ancestors. The spirit of the Yamato *people. The gods will come to our aid.*

    — The Chief of Operations at Combined Fleet headquarters, urging a sortie
      by *Yamato*

We die for sovereign and country. I understand that. But isn't there more to it than that? My death, my life, the defeat of Japan as a whole: I'd like to link these with something more general, more universal, something to do with values. What the devil is the purpose of all this?

    — A reserve officer aboard *Yamato*

Isn't it enough to wear on your breasts the chrysanthemum emblem of the special attack force and to die with 'long live the Emperor' on your lips?

    — The response of a regular *Yamato* officer

O N MARCH 25, 1945, an immense fleet of American warships closed on Okinawa, the largest pendant in the Ryukyu chain of some 140 islands gently arcing down toward Formosa from the Japanese homeland's southernmost tip. The following day, hundreds of ships began a final week of bombardment before invading the home of the once independent Okinawan dynasty. Four days later, Admiral Koshiro Oikawa prepared for an audience with Emperor Hirohito in Tokyo, some nine hundred miles northeast. Oikawa served as the Emperor's adviser on naval affairs but was not himself well informed, owing to fellow admirals. The rivalrous atmosphere that hindered communications between Japanese Army and Navy brass strained relations within each service too, in this case between Oikawa and the commanders of the Combined Fleet. They kept the Emperor's man, whose principal office was the Imperial Navy's Chief of Staff, at arm's length from the vital decisions about operations.

Current Imperial advisers had an impossible task in any case. The country seemed locked in a death march. The Pacific War could no more be stopped than won. No one could acknowledge that the end was in sight because the only possible end was oblivion.

A joyfully triumphant beginning made that deplorable outcome doubly difficult to accept. Few Japanese generals and fewer admirals had believed a long struggle with America would bring total victory, but many had hoped that swift, stinging blows would persuade Washington to share the Pacific — permit Japan to pursue her interests — rather than subject Americans to more hardship. The attack on Pearl Harbor that initiated the war in December 1941 appeared successful beyond its proponents' wildest dreams. The American brass, including General Douglas MacArthur, had been almost unanimous in doubting that a nation inferior in every way their perceptions recorded would contemplate such a risky, unmanageable gambit, one that would deliver them to speedy destruction. Respected analysts called the notion "utterly stupid" and "almost fantastic." "When the Japs come down here," an Associated Press correspondent allowed, conveying the prewar mood of the American garrison in the Philippines, "they'll be playing in the big leagues for the first time in their lives." That was shortly before the brilliantly daring raid, that Sunday morning of December 7, on the major United States naval base, some twenty miles from Honolulu. Carrier-based Japanese planes killed and wounded four thousand Americans while sinking or severely disabling five of the eight battleships nestled in "battleship row," twenty-one ships in all.

Later it would become an article of faith that the tactical master stroke at Pearl Harbor was a great strategic blunder, serving to shake Americans from their pacifist isolationism — Hitler had invaded Poland two years earlier and now occupied most of Europe — and unite them in hot resolve for vengeance. But virtually every American saw the destruction of so much of the Pacific fleet during those few hours as a national calamity rather than as a Japanese mistake. The near panic it prompted may have revealed more about America's susceptibility to paranoia than about the military situation. Still, if the situation could not fairly be called calamitous, it was certainly gloomy.

Spectacular strikes and lightning landings followed Pearl Harbor, stunning Americans with disaster after disaster. Three months later, Japan had taken vast areas of the Pacific by seizing island territories equivalent in size to half the United States. Her conquests would soon extend to a near circle with a diameter of twenty-eight hundred miles, from Manchuria to China to Burma to the Dutch East Indies to New Guinea, almost to Australia, to five hundred miles west of Hawaii to the Bering Sea. Americans were particularly shocked by the fall of the Philippines despite the long-standing presence of a

U.S. garrison there. The citadel island of Corregidor, its massive fortifications protected by prodigious concrete, had been thought unconquerable. But nothing stopped the enduring, thirsting Japanese.

Their men were tougher and better trained. Many of their weapons were superior. The supposedly backward Orientals had better binoculars, range finders and illumination devices, better planes and much better torpedoes. Their crack ships, relentlessly drilled under the most demanding conditions, were unequaled in seamanship and firepower. Their carrier pilots were probably the world's best, with the most combat experience, acquired in China. But the loss of great numbers of those pilots at the crucial Battle of Midway, in June 1942, was among the circumstances that would turn the tide. Every perceptive Japanese admiral knew immediately after Midway that the huge gamble of hard punches to persuade America to negotiate rather than fight was lost. For the Pearl Harbor strike had achieved the opposite psychological effect to the one intended. Instead of discouraging a people softened by democracy and luxury from shouldering the burdens of all-out warfare, it jolted the world's greatest economic power, whose industrial capacity was roughly ten times greater than Japan's, into unprecedented industrial and military action. Nothing could have kindled righteous American wrath like the shock of the "sneak attack," as generations would know it, even after America began making her own surprise attacks on little countries such as Grenada and Panama.

But the Battle of Midway brought little relief to the Americans fighting in the Pacific. Re-creating the past is always difficult, since events that have occurred are clothed with inevitability. "That was not true at the time," as William Manchester tersely pointed out about what now seems certain American victories in the Pacific War. It was true only that the final outcome was in little doubt once American factories began producing their mountains of arms and equipment. Hopelessly outclassed Japan had no chance against that industrial might. By the start of fighting on Okinawa, America was producing not double or triple but forty times the Japanese tonnage of warships, only one category of items in her colossal output of weaponry. The industrialist Henry Kaiser was turning out an escort aircraft carrier every week and more than a Liberty cargo ship every day. But the certainty, the inevitability, became apparent only after the fact.

The thirty-three months following Midway felt more like three decades to the combat troops in the Pacific. A succession of fierce struggles, one more unimaginable than the next, were required to retake Japanese-held territory. The Solomon Islands, Gilbert Islands, Mariana Islands, Bonin Islands . . . the names evoke images of supremely ferocious combat in wretched conditions. Guadalcanal, Bougainville, Tarawa, Kwajalein, Peleliu, Guam, Tinian, Saipan . . . Not every island and atoll was host to progressively greater savagery, but the trend was clear: the nearer the site to the sacred Japanese homeland, the greater the resistance and blood. Grim slaughter on Pacific beaches had pushed the estimate of casualties high for the landing on Iwo Jima, about seven hundred miles south of Tokyo Bay. The first six days produced ten times the expected number; the total reached nearly twenty-six thousand Americans, most in their teens and early twenties, before some 250 Japanese launched a final suicide attack on the same March day in 1945 when the American warships began the final pre-invasion bombardment of Okinawa.

It was time — as it had been for at least two savage years — for Japan to think of capitulation. But no matter how clear that was to Allied observers, the realization and logic were apparent to few Japanese. Their defense of honor, more important than the defense of any military position, could not be abandoned until many more millions died. Admission of defeat was so inconceivable to the military commanders who ruled the country that Admiral Oikawa would not think to mention it to his Emperor, although the almost certainly futile defense of Okinawa they were to discuss would surely be far costlier than all previous island bloodbaths. American troops headed there joked about "the Golden Gate in '48," the year they hoped to be home after Japan's full defeat. Okinawa was the beginning of the end, but that day of total oblivion was still several years away. The lost war was far from over.

The admiral's audience would take place in the Imperial Palace, which lay in the center of Tokyo and at the heart of national beliefs. The cherished complex might have substituted for a pair of vividly contrasting symbols a Columbia University anthropologist was just then using to explain Japanese behavior to confounded and contemptuous Americans. Ruth Benedict's celebrated study of the enemy's cultural patterns emphasized two outwardly incompatible devotions. Her symbol for the nation's consummate love of stylized beauty was the chrysanthemum, which the Emperor used on his seal and most Japanese held in awe. For their glorification of martial ferocity, Benedict used the much-worshiped sword. The Emperor's centuries-old castle displayed both passions. Elaborate thought and care went to nurturing exquisite gardens within that masterwork of fortress architecture.

With their wide moats, high embankments and concentric circles of massive walls, the Imperial grounds occupied almost a square mile of the overcrowded city. American pilots had been ordered to spare it. Elsewhere, the bombing was less intense than in previous weeks only because so much of the capital had already been leveled. Air-raid sirens were wailing again when Oikawa was driven through the gates on March 29, as wave after swarming wave of American planes joined the American armada in pounding Okinawa. The harried Chief of Staff tried to think how best to accomplish his mission of briefing the Emperor about current operations. He and members of his staff waited in a damp bomb shelter near the Imperial library. They bowed deeply when His Majesty appeared, then seated themselves at a conference table.

Hollywood would not have cast Hirohito for the role. Even in his field marshal's uniform, the "middle-aged guy with glasses," as a student of the period recently described him, looked more the shy academic than a belligerent empire's ceremonial leader. But his people revered him as a direct descendent of the Sun Goddess and of one of her earlier offspring, Hirohito's ancestor, believed to have ascended the throne as Japan's first Emperor twenty-six centuries earlier. When Oikawa and his staff took their places at the table, they sat sideways in order to avert their gaze from the demigod they'd come to advise. Few Japanese permitted themselves to look directly at the slight divine presence, let alone have an opinion about his appearance.

Had it been up to the Emperor, this meeting almost certainly would have been unnecessary: there would have been no war. The conservative introvert probably had no greater personal ambition than to practice his avocation of marine biology. He had even sought to restrain some of Japan's military adventures in the 1930s, but fear that his military commanders would bypass his "interference," diminishing his influence even more, pushed him further into the role of a tight-lipped observer. If he had had any power to stop the war now, in the spring of 1945, he probably would have used it. Certainly he would have wanted to, not because the war had been wrong from the first, but because it had taken such terrible turns. For His Majesty was no less an amalgam of conflicting desires than anyone else. He hadn't always been a disapproving spectator and never, so far as anyone has reported, considered Pearl Harbor an act of shameful aggression. Once the Pacific War had begun as well as it did for Japan, he relished victory no less than his gardeners did. Nor was he quite as powerless or innocent as his postwar defenders would claim. He studied some battle plans attentively, sometimes asking questions that were interpreted as suggestions for altering tactics. Hirohito wanted Japan to lose less than he had wanted her to fight.

On that March 29, the Emperor's questions would directly affect not merely tactics but the lives of thousands of sailors. Oikawa's briefing naturally focused on preparations for the defense of Okinawa. If the enemy landed troops there, the war would enter a stage of almost inconceivable menace. Okinawa was a mere 350 miles from the southern tip of Kyushu, one of the four major Japanese home islands. And it was not an occupied territory but actually part of Japan, at least as a color on the map: the Ryukyus were one of the forty-seven prefectures. That is why the battle there would be the beginning of the end.

The nature of the threat was self-evident; need for what was called "special" measures of the highest degree of sacrifice was clear. The Chief of Staff informed the Emperor about provisions for kamikaze operations, which had already begun in a preliminary way, against the American fleet engaged in the bombardment. The Emperor urged Oikawa to "leave nothing to be desired" in executing those plans "with a hard struggle by all our forces, since [they] will decide the fate of our Empire." Oikawa's assurance that two thousand planes were available for the suicidal attacks left Hirohito clearly concerned. Was that all? he asked in his reedy, high-pitched voice. The admiral's hasty reply that the Army would contribute an additional fifteen hundred aircraft did not dispel His Majesty's puzzlement. "But where is the Navy?" he asked, his tone putting an edge to the question. "Are there no more ships? No surface forces?"

Those questions sealed the fate of six of the Imperial Navy's last small collection of operational warships. Among the half dozen, representing far over half the Navy's fighting strength, was the world's biggest and best battleship, doomed by a horror of loss of face that would grip Combined Fleet headquarters when it learned of the Emperor's meeting with Oikawa. His Majesty's query about why nothing had been planned for the surface ships was enough to send the battleship *Yamato* on a hopeless mission; the most powerful tactical or strategic reason could no longer keep her in port. The same need to save face — in the war in defense of honor and obligation rather than of militarily valuable equipment or territory — would cause much of the terrible waste at Okinawa, of which the six ships would be a fraction. Together with the Imperial system and the Japanese military ethos, it was to multiply the carnage by several times.

The superb naval sculpture called *Yamato* was no mere battleship nor merely "the mightiest engine of destruction afloat," as the U.S. Naval Institute would call her. The masterpiece of naval design and construction was a symbol and legend, a source of immense pride for the Japanese Navy and people.

Her beauty was inspiring even to those lacking a practiced naval eye. *Yamato*'s supremely graceful profile belied her size. Even the most recently commissioned American battlewagons of the *Iowa* class — not to mention older Japanese models, with their top-heavy pagoda superstructures — looked bulky by comparison. A sweeping foredeck made *Yamato* a marine greyhound, eager to leap upon the enemy — and able to, thanks to an innovative hull shape that helped boost her speed well above what was expected from a ship of her size and firepower. Twelve engine and boiler rooms discharged their exhaust through a single funnel that swept back at a rakish 25-degree angle. A streamlined superstructure managed to contain most of her hundred-plus antiaircraft guns of up to 5 inches without cluttering her elegant lines. With her teak weatherdeck unbroken from stem to stern — a distance of 863 feet, slightly less than the length of three football fields — she was a "singularly beautiful ship," as the distinguished naval historian Samuel Eliot Morison called her.

As the Japanese Army seemed to love austerity for its own sake, beyond its contribution to discipline, the Japanese Navy came close to making a virtue of its miserably overcrowded shipboard quarters. The crew's appointments on "Hotel Yamato," as lesser ships' envious sailors nicknamed her, were indulgent by comparison. Eighty cooks manned her main galleys. She even had revolutionary air conditioning in many compartments, an extraordinary luxury in a navy that almost boasted of difficult conditions as an aid to nourishing the commitment to self-sacrifice inherent in *Yamato damashii*, "the Japanese fighting spirit." More to the point, she was not only one of the most intelligent and efficient capital ships ever built but also the most powerful and most heavily armored, fully 40 percent larger than the four ships of the same great *Iowa* class, each of which displaced forty-nine thousand tons compared with her sixty-eight thousand. No warship's protection had ever been as strong or thorough. With main armor of sixteen inches and further protection of vital parts such as magazines by belts up to two feet thick, she was built to withstand the heaviest American naval shells and thousand-pound bombs dropped from eleven thousand feet.

Her own main armament consisted of nine 18.1-inch guns, compared with 16-inchers on the *Iowa*-class "wagons." *Yamato*'s seventy-foot-long cannon fired shells of 3220 pounds — 30 percent heavier than America's new 16-inchers — a distance of nearly thirty miles, which meant it could destroy the best-armed enemy vessels well before they could try to close within their range of her. This peerless ordnance was mounted in three triple turrets, two forward and one aft. The blast of their salvos was so tremendous that the ship's boats had to be stored in the aircraft hangar together with the spotter planes. Although the *Iowa*-class ships had more speed and a more rapid rate of fire from their main turrets, it was universally accepted that heavier guns virtually guaranteed victory in surface battles with lesser ships. Monumental *Yamato*, with her 18.1 shells and other staggering specifications, was almost certain to destroy the best American battleship, even small groups of battleships, if she encountered them without carriers. She was unbeatable against ordinary surface opposition and nearly unsinkable, thanks to her armor and to ingenious damage-control dispositions throughout her five decks. A Japanese passion for offense made some of the Imperial Navy's new ships top-heavy with guns at the expense of protection and seaworthiness. Not *Yamato*.

Her steel would have sufficed for a railroad line between Tokyo and Osaka, 250 miles apart. It said much about national priorities and perceived solutions to national problems that such a superb vessel, with its enormous consumption of resources, had been built at a time when the majority of Japanese panted to feed themselves. Much of the overwhelmingly agricultural country was bent over in rice paddies; some families sold their daughters into prostitution to survive. Only fierce ambition, matching sacrifice and impassioned science permitted such a colossal construction project of such advanced conception, with dozens of major design and engineering triumphs and hundreds of components on the leading edge of naval technology, to be launched on such a relatively slight industrial base.

Yamato's keel had been laid in 1937,* in a drydock heavily screened by bamboo matting and other measures to keep her existence secret. Japan's prowar, antiforeigner fervor accounted for that strict secrecy. The construction did not violate the 1922 Washington and 1930 London treaties, under which Tokyo had joined the other major Pacific powers in restricting naval tonnage, because those treaties lapsed at the end of 1936. But *Yamato* and a sister ship called *Musashi*, begun a year later, were to be the Naval General Staff's ace in the hole in a war with America, which would surely not build battleships too large to use the Panama Canal. (The Japanese also began construction of *Shinano* in 1939, but canceled two other even larger ships of the *Yamato* class, scheduled to be laid in 1942.) American bombs sank *Musashi* in October 1944, five months before the Emperor's fatal questions to Admiral Oikawa. American torpedoes sank *Shinano* the following month, days after her commissioning as a converted aircraft carrier. The submarine that made that extraordinary kill had taken time off from her lifeguard patrol for downed B-29s because

*That year, Japanese military spending reached 70 percent of government expenditure.

no air raids on the Japanese mainland were scheduled that night. The six torpedoes hit the supercarrier as she was on her way in internal waters from the yard that had built her to further fitting out at the great naval port of Kure. She went down a hundred miles south of Tokyo Bay.

But the first of her class was intact and fit. It did not matter to most Japanese that this was because she had done little real fighting: in previous battles, *Yamato* was kept beyond the range of American guns. What everyone could see was that the Imperial Japanese Navy's only surviving operational battleship remained spotless, her silvery paintwork unblemished. *Yamato* was the Navy's "lucky ship," a survivor of the Battle of the Philippine Sea as well as Midway and the only capital ship to emerge from Leyte Gulf with only two insignificant bomb hits. To the Japanese people, it seemed natural, if not prescribed, that she remained magnificent even at that hopeless stage of the war, for the great battleship bore their own name: Japanese often called themselves "the Yamato people," after the ancient kingdom on the Yamato Plain on Honshu, the largest mainland island. Thus the evocative name, nothing less than the poetic word for Japan, rang with symbolic, religious and patriotic significance, the very kind that sustained the Japanese people, especially as the war turned toward disaster. Like the kamikaze planes and pilots, the pride of the fleet was thought to have a special mission.

Her narrower goal that first week of April, the planned foray to Okinawa, had much in common with kamikaze sorties. For despite *Yamato*'s magnificence and crushing power, she was on her way toward obsolescence the moment she was quietly commissioned, several days after the attack on Pearl Harbor. That attack itself would end forever the perception of the battleship as the epitome of naval power. For those with vision, it laid to rest the notion that surface ships would fight it out for control of the Pacific, with victory going to the behemoths with the biggest guns and strongest armor.

One of the strategists with the keenest foresight was "the Japanese Nelson" who planned the tactically and technically masterly Pearl Harbor strike. Isoroku Yamamoto was also called "the reluctant admiral" because he — who had studied at Harvard and served as the naval attaché in Washington — had opposed war against the United States until the eleventh hour. "Do not uncover the teapot and release a typhoon," he warned when a staff officer first suggested the attack on Pearl Harbor. Yamamoto also vigorously opposed the building of the superbattleships. Asked how aircraft could possibly sink the new titans with their prodigious antiaircraft armament, he replied prophetically that torpedo bombers could do the job against any such protection. "The fiercest serpent can be overcome by a swarm of ants." The Pacific War repeatedly confirmed his foresight. As much as *Yamato*'s officers loved her, numerous sinkings of great capital ships by planes since 1941 led some to classify the vessel with the Great Wall of China and the Pyramids as "the world's three great follies, prize examples of uselessness." Airpower had won the day at Pearl Harbor and every subsequent large naval engagement in the Pacific. It had disposed of the greatest, grandest capital ships — and Japanese pilots had started this trend in 1941. Two days after Pearl Harbor, they sank Britain's *Repulse* and *Prince of Wales* off the coast of Singapore, two thousand miles southwest of Okinawa.

Japanese admirals knew those stunning lessons better than anyone. One of the most prominent was Minister of the Navy Mitsumasa Yonai. Yonai, once a deeply admired line officer, had been among the sizable faction of senior admirals who had tried to avert war with America. Now he regretted that the skeptics hadn't opposed the venture with greater determination and honesty by pitting their superior knowledge of world realities against the views of the little-traveled, narrow-minded zealots who had gained control of the Army. They had allowed themselves to be convinced, against their own assessments and better judgment, that quick, smashing defeats would persuade irresolute, comfort-loving Americans not to make the sacrifices required for a total fight. Yonai had become so appalled by the course of the war and his own complicity in extending it to America that he, a former Prime Minister, was holding secret talks, in fear of his life, with a few like-minded officers who hoped against hope to find a way to end hostilities.

The Minister of the Navy was now less concerned with the debate over plans for *Yamato* than with trying to replace the present Prime Minister — himself a replacement for the notorious General Hideki Tojo after the fall of Saipan — with someone who would permit a more open suit for peace. He had asked a trusted admiral to make a study of how to get Japan out of the war, and held secret consultations about the same matter with members of the Imperial household. Yonai felt his political maneuvering bore on the existence of Japan herself, not just on that of one battleship or even a fleet. But to the degree that he concerned himself with the debate about *Yamato*'s mission to Okinawa, he leaned against it. Such a sortie would be as useless, even harmful, as continued resistance in general.

The Navy's senior staff cleaved into factions. Many knew as well as Yonai that the war was lost but were afraid to say so openly. Some argued that the Navy must preserve its few remaining fighting ships for the battle for the home islands. Others yearned for immediate action no matter what the odds or consequences, especially since carrier-based American planes had just begun striking hard at previously protected mainland naval bases. Better that the remnants of the fleet make a glorious final charge than be sunk by those planes at their moorings, with the insufferable humiliation to naval and national self-respect. Although the proportion of "mystical" firebrands was distinctly smaller than in the Army, those in the Navy used the same kinds of emotional appeal to honor and glory, to the Japanese spirit and the obligations to the Emperor. "Even if the odds were only 10 percent in favor, the effort would be worthwhile," argued Captain Shegenori Kami, the Combined Fleet's Chief of Operations. "A true samurai doesn't ask whether his efforts pay. He merely seeks the opportunity to sacrifice himself."

Much lower in the command chain, the skipper of *Yahagi*, a light cruiser that would be in *Yamato*'s screen, thought quite differently. Captain Tameichi Hara was one of the distinguished fighting officers who went against the grain of that Japanese appeal for sacrifice and more sacrifice. Hara pointedly told his men that they should not hesitate to come back alive, a reversal of the more common pep talk to Japanese servicemen.* His key order was: "If the ship should be damaged or sunk, don't hesitate to save yourself" — advice he would follow himself, in a rare refutation of the belief that Japanese commanding officers should not be last to leave their ships only because they must go down with them.

Some argued less ideologically that the overriding consideration was the simple duty to fight. The Army was complaining that it had done all the fighting at Iwo Jima and would be doing it all again on Okinawa. The air forces too had committed themselves to hard action in the crucial new battle, especially in suicidal special-attack raids. The Navy's Commander-in-Chief was swayed by one argument, then another. Of course the Imperial Navy must not lose more face, but which alternative offered less certainty of doing so? This time the Combined Fleet's staff did not ignore Naval Chief of Staff Oikawa. They interpreted the Emperor's questions to him as a reproach. It would have been impossible for the Navy not to carry out what His Majesty appeared to have suggested with characteristic

---

*"As you know," Hara addressed his crew, "hundreds of our comrades have flown bomb-laden planes on one-way missions against the enemy. Thousands more . . . are standing by at every airfield. Hundreds of our comrades are ready in submarines to man one-way torpedoes. Thousands of others will drive explosive torpedo boats or crawl the bottom of the sea to fasten explosive charges against enemy ships. Our job in this mission is part of the same pattern. Our mission appears suicidal and it is. But I wish to emphasize that suicide is not the objective. The objective is victory . . . You are not to be slain merely as sacrifices for the nation."

Japanese indirectness: that surface ships must join the pilots' sacrifice. Even to admit to him the tiny number of fighting ships left would have been an intolerable loss of face.

It is too simple to say that at that stage of the war, the entire nation of Yamato was attempting to do what *Yamato* had been directed to perform at Okinawa or that the same obligation to make a total sacrifice would be expected of the Japanese people as a whole when the home islands were invaded. But the parallels were strong. When nothing was left but a supreme gesture of sacrificial defiance against an overwhelming force, that gesture had to be made. As a senior officer on one of *Yamato*'s escort ships remembered it, Hirohito's questions "implied essentially this: 'Others are dying. Kamikaze pilots are dying gloriously. Why are you doing nothing? You too should die!'"

Pilots were indeed dying in great numbers over Okinawa, which compounded Japan's problems in more ways than one: if planes were available for suicide runs, why not to escort *Yamato*, if necessary in shifts? Forty years later, an English authority on Japanese military affairs would question this waste of the Imperial Navy's sparse remaining power. "The failure to protect that *Yamato* Task Force — totally bereft of air cover whilst Japanese planes [largely kamikaze] filled the skies over Okinawa — seems almost inexplicable." But when news of what had occurred at the Imperial briefing reached the Combined Fleet's staff in 1945, the debate was resolved. Operation *Ten ichigo* — Heaven Number One — was assured, and *Yamato* was as good as sunk.

> *The time has come. Kamikaze Yamato, be a truly divine wind!*
> — *Yamato*'s Executive Officer

> *These days the entire nation shares the fate of having death on the doorstep.*
> — Ensign Mitsuru Yoshida of *Yamato*

> *Now came the first sextet of dive bombers from the* Bennington *under Lt. Cmdr. Ed De Garmo. The clouds lay no more than 3000 feet above the sea, but the Dauntlesses . . . came out of the clouds on radar and dove after the big battleship. The heavy bursts of flack were about 1000 feet short and below the altitude of the oncoming planes.*
> *"In pairs!" De Garmo screamed into his JV. "Let's get the big bastard!"*
> — Lawrence Cortesi, *Valor at Okinawa*

The naval chiefs' urge to act, even at the certain cost of the Navy's last and finest jewel, needed no explanation. The destruction of Japan's major cities distressed them even more than the enemy's imminent landing on Okinawa. Operating from new bases on Saipan, Tinian and Guam, those islands of the earlier bloodbaths, state-of-the-art American aircraft were erasing urban targets with the new tactic of saturation bombing. Osaka, Kobe, Yokohama, Nagoya . . . one after another, one night almost following the next, the industrial centers and their civilian populations were being blasted by hundreds of B-29s loaded to their unprecedented limits with high-explosive and incendiary bombs. The awe-inspiring Superfortresses were commanded by Major General Curtis LeMay, father of the new strategy of saturation bombing. LeMay, who had arrived from Europe in January to take over the 21st Bomber Command, promised that Japan would be "beaten back into the dark ages." Within a month after the landing on Okinawa, incendiaries would make up 75 percent of American bomb loads because urban centers had become the chief targets. The policy shift from precision bombing of strategic sites to the destruction of entire cities would lead a Yokohama observer to report that looting was no problem after an obliterating raid: nothing was left but rubble.

Tokyo's biggest turn had come three weeks before Oikawa's March 26 briefing of the Emperor, while American landing forces for Okinawa were being assembled on staging islands or were en route in troopships. Attacking the capital from low altitude during the night of March 9–10, 334 airplanes incinerated the central districts with ten times the tonnage of the Luftwaffe bombs that had caused "the Great Fire of London" on a September night in 1940. This Great Fire Raid, as it became known, roasted residents on the streets and in their homes as if entire city blocks had been shoveled into ovens. The horror in those congested sixteen square miles of wood and bamboo was unequaled anywhere on the home islands. By the count of charred corpses piled where victims had tried to escape, even the forthcoming atomic devastation of Hiroshima and Nagasaki would be lesser events.* Measured by sheer numbers of torturous deaths or by decibels of human pain, that tragedy would be exceeded only by what awaited the Okinawan people.

That night's strong wind whipped the flames of American incendiary bombs into a wall of fire roiling hundreds of feet in the air. It raced ahead like a tidal wave, sucking whole city sections into the

---

*Casualty statistics for the conventional and atomic bombings are more art than science. But although no single set of commonly accepted figures exists for any of these three cities, prudent average suggests the atomic bomb killed some 140,000 in Hiroshima, half within days, the other half by slower-acting burns and radiation. But the conventional bombs dropped on Tokyo that night of March 9–10 probably left about 197,000 dead and missing — "scorched and boiled and baked to death," as put by General LeMay. And this was far from the climax of LeMay's operations. In late May, when the fighting on Okinawa would reach its apogee, American planes would drop 3200 tons of high explosive on Yokohama, the same on Osaka, and 4000 more on Tokyo, consuming new districts in another sea of flames.

fiery vortex. A quarter of a million buildings were consumed. Before daylight, nearly a fifth of Tokyo's industrial areas and 63 percent of its commercial districts disappeared. The heat burned bodies to ash in an instant, like some industrial furnace disposing of autumn leaves. It ignited hordes at a distance: people running from the flames as fast as they could, who seemed to be escaping, burst into balls of fire. Others jumped into canals for salvation and were cooked alive in boiling water. Scores of thousands died of suffocation, the flames having extracted all oxygen from the air. This was probably the greatest one-night disaster, with the largest sum of suffering, endured by any city in world history. While senior naval personnel debated the pros and cons of *Yamato*'s sortie three weeks later, the Navy Ministry's windows remained caked in black from the smoke and volunteers in face masks were cremating the last piles of carbonized corpses. All Tokyo was suffused with an acrid stench.

Kure, on the Inland Sea about two thirds of the way from Tokyo to the southernmost port city of Kagoshima — and about twenty miles from Hiroshima — had so far been spared major devastation, although it was home to Japan's largest naval base, including the yard where *Yamato* had been launched three years earlier, after over five years of construction and fitting out. Kure's turn for destruction would come six weeks later, during the battle for Okinawa's Sugar Loaf Hill. Meanwhile, civilian food rations were approaching the starvation level — the average Japanese now existed on some fifteen hundred calories a day — and cadets at the Naval Academy on the tiny island of Eta Jima facing the naval port were too busy digging caves and tunnels for refuge from the expected bombing to learn much seamanship. They were jokingly dubbed "moles."

While the enemy fleet's last pre-invasion salvos were pounding Okinawa, *Yamato* was waiting her turn for routine repairs in Kure. Moored to an outer buoy, the great ship seemed to a twenty-two-year-old ensign named Mitsuru Yoshida "like a gigantic rock commanding all around her." Within hours after the enemy landing on Okinawa, five hundred miles south, the rock was ordered under way, and her officers carefully counted their men: anyone who missed a sailing for action could face a firing squad. A detailed chart of Okinawan waters on the chart table showed an arc representing the range of *Yamato*'s big guns to the landing beaches. She did not sail directly there, however, but to a safer anchorage behind an island about fifteen miles from Hiroshima while the plans for her sortie were drawn up. A single bomb dropped near her two days later from a high-flying B-29 while she rode at anchor did no damage.

Combined Fleet headquarters' order to launch her unique operation came in Fleet Signal 607 to Vice Admiral Seiichi Ito, commander of Task Force II, as the Second Fleet battle group to be led by *Yamato* had been designated. Ito, a graduate student at Yale in the late 1920s, had opposed the mission from the start, certain that it held no hope without air cover — without, in fact, any air support at all. Although Combined Fleet headquarters had stopped communicating with the Second Fleet, perhaps out of embarrassment, it ordered its Chief of Staff, Ito's classmate and close friend at the Naval Academy, to fly in to reassure him. Since no naval or military argument could do this, the classmate used moral suasion: Task Force II was being requested to die gloriously, heralding the death of all Japanese who preferred that to surrender. "Sooner or later, it will come to a special [suicide] attack by the entire nation, the hundred million of us." Ito was asked to "die admirably" as a model for the hundred million.

The admiral agreed, but his captains had their say too, some of it heated, when summoned to a conference. Most, including *Yamato*'s captain, were also opposed. The British Royal Navy, the infant Imperial Navy's model and teacher during the century's first decades, had had a strong influence — specifically, the British motto "Fight bravely, but not in vain." After the five-hour conference, the commander of the single cruiser among *Yamato*'s escorts told his crew they were participating in "a suicide mission pure and simple . . . but unlike those our Air Force is carrying out, it hasn't got the slightest chance of destroying an important target." The admiral in command of the entire nine-ship screen — the light cruiser plus eight destroyers — protested that "without air protection, we will needlessly sacrifice the lives of five thousand sailors. We cannot possibly hope to reach Okinawa against massive American air attacks. I would gladly die at this very moment if I thought my death would help save our honorable homeland. But . . . the officers [of the screening ships] believe they can accomplish more if allowed to go out alone as raiders to attack American ships. I agree with them." And the admiral in command of the squadron that included the eight destroyers said, on April 5, that "this isn't even a kamikaze mission, since that implies the chance of chalking up a worthy target." That admiral told the Combined Fleet's Chief of Staff that "our little fleet has no chance against the might of the enemy forces and . . . such an operation would be a genuine suicide sortie."

But in the end, Task Force Commander Ito broke a long silence at a crucial meeting by reflecting that all were being given an appropriate opportunity to perform their highest duty. "A samurai lives so that he is always prepared to die," he said. That unchallengeable statement — although it skirted the salient question of whether this was the right moment to die — ended all argument at the command level. A captain observed that "orders are orders; we now must make the best of the situation." The other skippers and division commanders chorused approval.

Many of *Yamato*'s officers were also aware — even while hoping otherwise — that the mission would be nothing more or less than a suicidal display of useless courage. Few knew precisely that the Americans had fifteen fleet carriers in Okinawan waters, plus a dozen smaller escort carriers and the help, if needed, of five more of the Royal Navy's best, which were operating just a few hundred miles to the west. But even less knowledgeable junior officers recognized the foray as an exercise in fantasy. Those young men accepted that they too had little life remaining; by now, the casualty rate among Naval Academy graduates was over 90 percent. It was not going to their death but going pointlessly that disturbed them. The most unhappy were veterans of such battles as the Coral Sea and Philippine Sea, where they had seen for themselves what enemy airpower did to ships lacking air cover. They did not hope to survive the war, only to die in a battle that might inflict damage on the enemy.

Talking confidentially among themselves, the majority argued that the operation could only fail. The enemy's air reconnaissance was too thorough for them to avoid detection far before their surface guns would be in range to fire a single shot. And once they were spotted, American airpower was too overwhelming, just as American submarines had become too prevalent and efficient, for them to escape destruction by delivery systems their great ship was not designed to counter. "Which country showed the world what airplanes could do by sinking the *Prince of Wales*?" an ironic voice asked. Even if *Yamato* did manage to reach Okinawa, *so* many enemy battleships and heavy cruisers would be waiting for her that she would have no hope against their combined might. "We'll be as vulnerable as a man walking alone on a dark night carrying only a lantern," said the twenty-two-year-old ensign, Mitsuru Yoshida, to himself.

Against this, the chief argument remained, just as it did at higher levels, the duty, glory and joy of dying for Emperor and country. At least one officer said aloud that the men's deaths would find purpose by contributing to defeat rather than victory. "How else can Japan be saved except by losing and coming to its senses? . . . We will lead the way. We'll die as harbingers of Japan's new life. That's where our real satisfaction lies, doesn't it?"

During the ceremonial drinking of sake the evening before the sailing, the ship seemed overwhelmed by the immensity of her mission and impending tragedy, both matching her in size and significance. The men performed their roles like actors trapped in a morality play. A young ensign at one of the solemnly gay "drinking jamborees" dropped a glass raised to toast their departure, an unlucky omen in Japanese tradition. It shattered on the deck.

But there was also joyous drinking at the meeting places of the ship's various divisions. Some young officers affectionately patted the bald head of Captain Kosaku Ariga, one of the Navy's most courageous and popular senior officers. In the knowledge that this would probably be everyone's last social event, the skipper joined the fun instead of punishing that exceedingly uncommon display of liberty. Love for the captain and for his legendary bravery and skill filled the heart of every man and officer; the special circumstance linking them swelled each heart yet further. There were tumultuous, throaty cheers for the Emperor and for the treasured captain and ship. After the gatherings, fifty-odd midshipmen, assigned to *Yamato* for training after their recent graduation from the Naval Academy, were sent ashore over their passionate pleas to stay and fight. (One weeping midshipman on the light cruiser begged to remain aboard so that he could at least clean the latrines. He was put ashore, together with most of the ship's supplies, since shortages were extreme on the homeland and the crew would soon have no more need of them.) Peerless *Yamato* and her nine escorts got under way for Okinawa the following afternoon, VOW TO DIE FOR THE EMPEROR chalked on a blackboard behind a main turret.

April 6 was a glorious spring day. The Captain of the light cruiser saw a soft breeze whipping up small waves on the calm Inland Sea. "A few thousand meters away, radiant cherry blossoms dotted the shore and distant mountains sparkled under the cobalt sky." Captain Hara, who had been among the most critical of the "suicide sortie," now felt that "this beautiful homeland is worthy of our sacrifices." An hour later on that same April 6, all hands assembled in clean uniforms on the foredeck for the executive officer's reading of a farewell message from the Combined Fleet's commander-in-chief. They heard the task force identified as "special," meaning suicidal, and the attack described as "unparalleled in its heroic bravery." Urgings to "exalt the glorious tradition of the Imperial Navy's surface forces" and "transmit its glory to posterity" were intended to uplift spirits — and did. When the executive officer read, "The fate of the Empire truly rests on this one action," all instantly recognized the echo of Admiral Heihachiro Togo's almost identical flag-signal exhortation to obliterate the Russian fleet at Tsushima in 1905. That encouragement had been repeated often enough in the present war — Admiral Yamamoto recited it to the attack planes about to take off for Pearl Harbor — to have become a cliché. The evocation of those glorious moments was almost pathetic now, the message intended not for a powerful fleet with expectations of victory but for a certain victim of an act of desperation. But the celebrated words boosted spirits all the same; stunning victories by naval forces *had* swung the balance for Japan before. "Let each unit, special attack unit or otherwise, fight fiercely, annihilate the enemy task force at every turn, and thereby make secure the Empire's foundations for all eternity . . . Fight gloriously to the death and completely destroy the enemy fleet . . . render this operation the turning point of the war!"

The crew bowed in the direction of the Emperor, sang the national anthem and shouted Banzai three times. The assistant radar officer, young Mitsuru Yoshida was deeply moved, although he had no illusions about victory; he saw the main tower "looming high above us in the bright moonlight . . . Indescribable." The exhilaration of leading the great attack in the prized ship did defy words. At that moment, the incomparable vessel steaming away on her sacred mission seemed the very soul of eternal, exalted Japan. Eyes watered and spines tingled as if the entire nation, present and past, were a military band playing a send-off march — and a recessional hymn.

"Do a good job," officers encouraged. "Die a death worthy of you."

Okinawa was six hundred miles away.

Yamato's official departure report had her sailing with two thousand tons of bunker oil, too little for a round trip. This helped spawn a myth that she had been dispatched as a sacrifice, with enough fuel to reach Okinawa but not to return. The Japanese public, when they finally learned the outcome, would long believe that had been the case. But even if the sortie's planners were that certain of failure, young officers on the Combined Fleet staff could not let the world's best ship go the way of planned extinction. Before she got under way, they rushed around Kure, frantically securing more precious bunker oil from overlooked storage places and from ships not participating in the mission, keeping this secret from higher officers in Kure as well as at Combined Fleet headquarters and among the Naval General Staff. Although Japanese admirals and Western historians would long talk about the anticipated one-way voyage, *Yamato's* bunkers, three-quarters full when she left, held more than enough fuel to bring her home.

The young staff officers who secured those unrecorded extra tons knew the staggering odds as well as anyone. If *Yamato* did have the inconceivably good luck to reach Okinawa undetected, she could sink no more than several American capital ships before the combined firepower of the enemy fleet would blow her out of the water. She would have a fighting chance against any two, possibly even three or four, battleships and cruisers. But magnificent and powerful as she was, she had no hope against the dozen battlewagons with 14- and 16-inch guns that would engage her. And such speculation did not take into account the American carriers and their planes, the most important factor in every major engagement at sea. Not even those who blindly hoped she might somehow stay undetected long enough to close to firing range could hope also that she would remain safe from air attack.

Task Force II's actual operational plan was uncharacteristically ambiguous for Japanese practice, but understandably so. The primary task was to serve as a decoy; it would weaken enemy defenses against a forthcoming mass kamikaze attack by drawing off American carrier-based fighter interceptors. For this purpose, the group was to survive as long and shoot down as many enemy planes as possible. If *Yamato* and some of her screening ships managed to reach Okinawa, they were to charge a large enemy anchorage offshore at daybreak on April 8. *Yamato*'s huge guns would devastate enemy naval and shore targets, perhaps sink enough transports and cause enough shock to force the enemy to leave Okinawa. Finally, the ship would beach herself and continue firing as a kind of floating artillery brigade until all ammunition was expended, whereupon surviving crew members would join the Japanese ground force as foot soldiers, using machine guns and pistols already distributed to each division.

For a few hours, the ship's majesty continued to make the inevitable also unthinkable. "Thanks to the incomparable seaworthiness of [her] construction," Ensign Yoshida recorded about the first hours under way, "there is no pitch or roll; even on the bridge we have the illusion of standing on firm ground." Yet the sea was deadly. With *Yamato* in the center and the light cruiser *Yahagi* bringing up the rear, the force deployed in a formation for night sailing under threat of submarine attack. The Bungo Strait, through which it sortied from the Inland Sea, was considered hostile waters, part of what American submariners had dubbed the "Hit Parade" waters. Yet this narrow passage had to be run because B-29s had just remined safer straits east and west, and here too speed had to be held to twelve knots to enable lookouts to search for mines. The beautiful spring day was ending in a glorious twilight. Like Captain Hara of the light cruiser, sailors gazed at the early cherry blossoms — ancient symbol of Japanese purity and evanescence, modern symbol of suicide tactics and volunteers. Lovingly observing Kyushu, a few miles to starboard, and

Shikoku, a few miles to port, the crew tried not to think that this would be their last sight of the home islands and to forget that "the enemy that controls the sky controls the sea."

It also controlled the radio waves. An American cryptanalysis center in Pearl Harbor had been working hard on secret Fleet Signal 607 and the flurry of intercepted radio messages connected with it. Intelligence analysts had put together an accurate summary of Task Group II's composition and intentions even before it set sail. Partly because of this, *Yamato* got no farther than the Bungo Strait before the first American sightings were made. In the late afternoon of April 6, *Hackleback* and *Threadin,* two submarines patrolling for the Japanese group, radioed an accurate description of it to Task Force 58, still the American strike force at sea in the area. Trailing the formation by five miles, the submarines, which had orders to scout rather than attack, watched in fascination. The contact reports of American planes that took over the surveillance the following morning — a minute-by-minute record of the force's position, course, and speed — were monitored by *Yamato*'s radio personnel, but the captain could do nothing about them short of turning back. It may have been too late even for that. Hours after sailing, the great ship was doomed.

The men who manned their watches on the bridge that night worked with quiet intensity, the highest-ranking officers distinguished by fluorescent initials on their caps. Just before midnight, Ensign Yoshida climbed a ladder to the bridge for lookout duty. Not knowing when he might be alone again, he faced his home in Tokyo, bowed his head and said a brief prayer.

Task Force 58 was roughly a hundred miles northeast of the fighting on Okinawa — some four hundred miles from Task Force II — when the submarine reports told its intelligence section what it had been waiting to hear. A search plane from the carrier *Essex* found the *Yamato* group at dawn the following morning. From that time on, it was relentlessly shadowed by aircraft flying just out of range of Japanese antiaircraft armament, among them flying boats based at Kerama Retto, an island group fifteen miles west of Okinawa that Americans had taken a few days before landing on Okinawa itself. Admiral Raymond Spruance, commander of the Fifth Fleet, had intended to give his battleships first crack at the *Yamato* as a kind of combat training after their months of escorting carriers and bombarding shore targets.* Adrenaline surged through battleship crews

---

*While serving as assistant chief of Naval Intelligence in 1927, Spruance had become very friendly with Seiichi Ito, now Commander of Task Force II, then assistant naval attaché at the Japanese Embassy in Washington (where many top Japanese admirals had served). Some Japanese observers held the romantic notion that Spruance might have

when Spruance signaled them to prepare for a battle of behemoths that would surely be the last major surface action of the war. But Vice Admiral Marc Mitscher, of Task Force 58, wanted to show that his planes could sink the world's most powerful ship, and Spruance yielded to his subordinate in direct command of the fighting unit.

Mitscher ordered all four of Task Force 58's groups into launching positions. (One group, delayed by refueling, would miss the action.) Reconnaissance planes from no less than a dozen carriers, four heavy and eight light, stalked *Yamato* while their strike craft were readied. In the unlikely event that those carriers and their escort of eight fast battleships and a dozen heavy cruisers would be unable to deal with the vastly weaker enemy group, older, more vulnerable ships from the flotilla bombarding Okinawa were also ordered to make ready to engage: six battleships (of the ten in the shore-bombardment force), seven cruisers and twenty-one destroyers.

Ninety minutes after the sighting of *Yamato* from the air that morning, the task groups began launching their strikes from about 250 miles southeast, near a Ryukyuan island north of Okinawa. The first main attack of 280 planes included dive-bombers with thousand- and five-hundred-pound bombs and torpedo bombers with the latest torpedoes. The flying boats, which had been shadowing the prey from a nicely protecting overcast, guided them to their target, now just over halfway to Okinawa.

On board *Yamato*, there was some relief that the force had come so far without damage, despite the enemy search planes that were known to be plotting its position minute by minute. At noon, in the open waters of the East China Sea, a smiling force commander expressed confidence that all had gone well on the morning watch even though a radio report from a lookout on a Ryukyu island north of Okinawa had announced that an estimated 250 enemy planes were headed in the expedition's direction. Half an hour later, a new radar contact was made and a hoarse voice reported the direction and range of the armada of hostile aircraft. The warning was so similar to hundreds of shipboard drills that the crew at first found it hard to accept as real. But the tension quickly surged as lookouts strained to see the enemy. At last two Grummans were spotted, then five, then thirty. *Yamato*'s huge antiaircraft armament had been bolstered by extra guns before her sailing. When Captain Ariga ordered, "Com-

---

favored using battleships rather than aircraft carriers in order to give his old friend Ito the chance to go down fighting in a last surface action.

The Fifth Fleet, so named when commanded by Spruance, became the Third Fleet when commanded by Admiral William Halsey, with whom Spruance alternated in 1945.

mence firing!" six 6-inch secondary batteries, twenty-four 5-inch antiaircraft, and 150 machine guns opened fire at the same instant,
joined by the escorting destroyers' main and secondary batteries. The
roar was as terrible as the sight of *so many* hostile planes.

No Japanese force could come close to putting up so much flak.
Firing a new shell with a time fuse that burst into a cone of six thousand small particles, *Yamato*'s main batteries had once shot down an
entire ten-plane formation. But now the force faced far too many
planes piloted by men with too much skill and determination. A
bomb hit one of the destroyers almost immediately. She exposed
her crimson underbelly, lifted her stern into the air, and sank in less
than a minute, leaving a few dozen survivors. And despite the black
curtain of shellbursts and shrapnel from *Yamato,* despite desperate
evasive maneuvers with her 150,000-horsepower engines straining
mightily at full throttle, two Curtis Helldivers persisted and penetrated the curtain. In minutes, they hit the ship with two bombs near
the aft tower, destroying one of her radar rooms. Four minutes later,
a torpedo bomber scored a hit on the port bow. A hot fragment killed
a sailor near Ensign Yoshida. Through the deafening din of the explosions and antiaircraft fire, he heard "the dull thud of his skull
striking against the bulkhead and sniffed fresh blood in the pall of
smoke" rising from the hits.

The first strike broke off. During the ensuing lull, some sailors assured themselves they'd survived the worst: the enemy carriers had
surely exhausted themselves. Knowing that a single torpedo could
not seriously damage the great ship, her officers tried to make light
of the hit, some telling themselves they would take revenge on
American ships by nightfall. As medical corpsmen removed the body
of the sailor from the bridge, Captain Ariga comforted the others.
"We're still afloat and still fighting," the famous veteran declared.
The chief of staff pronounced the strike very skillful, speculating that
pilots of such fearlessness in bearing down to bomb and torpedo and
such dexterity in the face of the ship's great antiaircraft fire must be
of the enemy elite.

The second wave arrived less than an hour after the first; there
were so many planes that a gunner likened the little spots under the
clouds to sesame seeds. Bullets and shrapnel flew everywhere, as
thick as buckshot. Three sailors toppled simultaneously on young
Yoshida. A fellow ensign tried to rise and bandage his thigh with a
blood-soaked towel. As he was placed on the stretcher — for which
Yoshida had shouted — he turned pale, smiled slightly and fell back
dead. The charred flesh, the smell of human fat heavy in the air, and

the flocks of sailors blown apart by direct hits so that "not even the stench of their deaths [was] left to float in the air" were a kind of phantasmagoria. The same horror had occurred many times before elsewhere in the Pacific, but for those involved, the scale of the hunt and size of the prey made this even harder to register as reality. One of the first two bombs destroyed the compartment that housed the scopes for the air-search radar, a devastating loss but one that, in fact, hastened the end only marginally.

Yamato's antiaircraft fire remained "without parallel" in the Japanese Navy. Her remarkable agility allowed her to dodge torpedoes as if she were a much smaller ship. She fired her 18.1-inch guns into the sea, presumably to down low-flying torpedo planes with the massive waterspouts. Still, the number of planes and their pilots' skill and flexibility in adapting to cloud cover and other conditions unnerved the Japanese gunners. No less than five torpedoes struck the port side during the second wave. "The invulnerable *Yamato*" began listing to port as more bombs rained on her, causing enormous casualties among the gunners. It was "a scene of carnage with no place for the living."

Even the near misses inflicted heavy damage. Their waterspouts were so fierce — a wild force, "ten times more than a torrential shower" — that they threatened to shatter metal high on the bridge. In the almost continuous attacks from 1300 to 1417 hours, the sailors lost track of the waves. The third one, of over a hundred planes, arrived on the heels of the second. Attacking "like a sudden rainshower," the aircraft scored several direct bomb hits near the stack and two more torpedo hits, again port amidships. Not even the least sinkable ship could take infinite damage. The six torpedo hits on the port side caused serious flooding, despite 1150 watertight compartments designed to prevent it. The pressure of the sea water crashing through the bomb and torpedo holes was simply too great.

The list to port weakened morale and threatened fighting capability, which would be cut in half if the tilt went to 5 degrees, playing hell with shell conveyance in the ammunition spaces below. Another ingenious engineering design allowed lists to be corrected by flooding the corresponding spaces on the opposite side. When the skipper ordered this measure, Ensign Yoshida immediately telephoned to warn the crews of the starboard boiler and engine rooms — but too late. Caught between the cold sea water rushing in and the steam of damaged boilers, several hundred men were atomized.

> Until this moment those men have made the ship go, battling sweltering heat and deafening noise, uncomplaining throughout. Confined in the depths of the ship with no way of knowing how the

battle is going, their bodies bathed in sweat and oil, they can converse and communicate only by hand signals . . . In the instant the water rushes in, the black gang on duty are dashed into pieces, turned into drops of spray. In that instant they see nothing and hear nothing; shattered into lumps, they dissolve.

At the price of those several hundred lives, the ship's trim was nearly restored, but her speed and maneuverability were much reduced. Low in the water and moving slowly, *Yamato* was an increasingly easy target, now seriously damaged even by the near misses that further loosened her plates and widened the flooding. But new explosions caused most of the havoc. The fourth wave, of over 150 planes, landed at least ten more bombs topside and gouged out more of the port side with new torpedo hits. The ship lost speed ever more rapidly. Her steering gear disabled, she was almost out of control.

Even amid the blinding light and thunderous noise of the explosions, Japanese professionals marveled at the flying skill that made the American planes so different from practice targets. During the attack on the bridge, Yoshida noticed the flushed faces of the pilots bearing down on him one after another, their eyes opened wide or squeezed tight. "Most have their mouths open and almost ecstatic expressions on their faces . . . Coming in again and again on the ideal approach, precisely, exactly, calmly, they evoke in us a sense of exhilaration. Virtuosi. Theirs is a strength we cannot divine, a force we cannot fathom." The Americans managed to reduce to an absolute minimum the straight segment of their approach courses necessary for bombing and torpedo runs, thus shortening their moments of vulnerability before zigzagging away. At the same time, Japanese officers were surprised that no pilot, even among the few who were hit, thought to crash his plane into the ship, kamikaze-style.

The once peerless vessel was a nightmare of desolation. The gun mounts had been destroyed one by one. Everything topside was a jumble of jagged steel and chunks of human flesh seared to lumps of blackened metal. Torrents of the crew's blood washed body parts along the slanting deck. A brief respite followed the fifth wave. Electrical failure had crippled the giant turrets. The convergence of torpedoes flooded the reputedly impregnable communications department; the supposedly watertight radio room had taken so much water that the ship had to rely entirely on light blinkers and flag signals to communicate with her screen. Without radio capability, the giant vessel seemed to be disintegrating into separate parts while she floated in the water "like a chunk of waterlogged wood." One bomb among hundreds killed all occupants of the emergency dispensary, including medical officers and corpsmen . . .

Hope you will bring back a nice fish for breakfast.
> — Signal from the Commander of the American landing forces to the
> Commander of the Gunfire and Covering Forces just before the sighting
> of *Yamato*

The rivets of the rail are icy against my palms but inside my body I feel a flush of warmth.

Father, mother, older sister, late brother-in-law lost in action a year ago. They stand clearly before me.

And the faces of acquaintances, teachers and friends pass before my mind's eye and face.

People I have met in my short life and cannot forget: their images blanket my sight, and I pay my respects to them as if they really stood in front of me . . .

"I am grateful to you," I whisper repeatedly, instinctively . . .

I have gained the road to an easy death. Death is easy.

You not blessed with death, you who are still forced to live. How will you endure all the days after tomorrow?
> — Mitsuru Yoshida, *Requiem for Battleship* Yamato

When the final attack began at 1400, the list was again so great that it exposed the starboard side of the vulnerable belly. Severe damage to the rudder ended all evasive action, making the ship a nearly stationary target for torpedoes. Seventy degrees of list. An incredible 80 degrees! Most ships sink at half that angle. Two years earlier, Yoshida, then an undergraduate, seemed destined to join Japan's elite from Tokyo Imperial University, its chief training ground. Now the ensign watched his "unsinkable giant ship" writhe in torment, "an ideal target for bombs, nothing more." Overwhelmed by fatigue, the living kept to duty amid the fearful desolation — still firing a few single-mount machine guns — until they joined the corpses strewn about them. Captain Ariga, renowned for his bravery well before he took command of the ship, shouted to the living, "Hold on, men! Hold on!" The encouragement of the burly, beloved Gorilla, as he was nicknamed, did as much and as little as any display could. Great *Yamato* had taken stunning punishment from Avengers, Corsairs, Hellcats and others. Since her fate was certain, her amazing strength served only to prolong her agony.

With the ship helpless and its antiaircraft fire drastically reduced, the battle had become a kind of show for the American planes. So many of the 386 that flew in the four waves were now circling above that they had to wait their turns for new runs, especially when rain squalls joined the low clouds to obscure the targets. Still, their enjoyment had its price: an Avenger's bombing run was so low that *Yamato*'s final explosion set it afire. The pilot bailed out. Two PBM seaplanes that happened to have been among the first to locate Task

Force II and radio its position early that morning spotted his rubber raft. One of the two served as a decoy for Japanese fire while the other neatly landed to pluck the pilot from a seaweed of Japanese corpses and survivors.* Those Japanese still able to see were dumbstruck by American pains to save an individual life, a display of values that would play a full part in their disillusionment with Japanese militarism after the war. Keizo Komura, the rear admiral in command of the escort ships, watched the feat of the PBMs from nearby in the water. Choking with oil as he struggled to stay afloat after the sinking of his flagship, *Yahagi*,† he observed the splendid little maneuver with near awe.

The rescue would be much written about, but it was seldom noted that the two crewmen of the same crippled Avenger had parachute trouble and drowned. If all men are equal in their Creator's eyes and families' hearts, the selection of those who are written about is as unfair as the tiny percentage who are chosen for combat during wartime and killed.

But there were a thousand times more Japanese unsung heroes than American at 1 P.M. that April 7. At the last moment, when it was too late to save *Yamato*, Admiral Seiichi Ito made a brave decision. From his prestigious place on *Yamato*'s bridge, the tall, stooping force commander who had helped devise the strategy of the war's every important naval battle, watched almost silently the destruction and carnage he had foreseen when opposing the operation. Now he ordered it broken off and directed the surviving ships to return to port after rescuing the men from their disabled sisters.

That order required great courage and resolve. Some senior officers in the group resented it bitterly, seeing cowardice in Ito's retreat from "a hundred million deaths rather than surrender!" Perhaps Ito's decision to abandon the operation at that final moment was an expression of "I told you so!" to its proponents, who cared more for

---

*Taking off again, the PBM delivered the pilot to an Okinawan airfield called Yomitan, which Marines would long remember for having taken it within hours of their initial landing on Easter Sunday, a week earlier.

†The attack on the new light cruiser *Yahagi*, the most imposing of the screening ships, was second only to that on the main target. She took twelve bombs and seven torpedoes before going down. Admiral Komura had opposed the sortie as vigorously as anyone. Declaring his happiness to die if it would achieve any result at all, he nevertheless protested that "without aircraft protection, we will needlessly sacrifice the lives of 5000 sailors; we cannot possibly hope to reach Okinawa against massive American air attacks." When *Yahagi* was destroyed, however, he refused to be put in a lifeboat. Going down with her, he bobbed back to the surface in time to see the American seaplanes save the lucky pilot.

the Navy's honor than for its men or ships. The admiral, who long had lobbied for transfer from his desk job to a risky sea command, shook hands with the surviving officers who crawled to him through the slanting deck's wreckage. His final order to those who pleaded to stay with him was to save themselves. Then he retired to his private quarters just under the bridge. His door did not open again.

Universally admired Captain Ariga ordered all hands on deck. Even as the few survivors below struggled out of hatches, water cascaded into the openings, dooming others. Smoke too thick for flags to be seen required that the remaining destroyers be signaled by lamp to come alongside for removal of *Yamato*'s survivors. But the destroyers kept their distance, fearing that the great hulk — 300 yards long, 130 feet in beam — would suck them to the bottom together with herself. Many of the living on *Yamato* did not want rescue in any case. They kept at their watches — in the magazines and some engine rooms too — until the end. The navigation officer and his chief assistant refused fellow officers' exhortations to obey the order to abandon ship. Instead, they bound themselves together to lessen the possibility of floating or involuntarily struggling to the surface, then stared, open-eyed, at the water rushing to submerge them. A sailor who volunteered to stand guard at the battle flag earned an equally proud death by clinging unwaveringly to the staff as the flag dipped below the waves. And when Captain Ariga suddenly remembered the portraits of the Emperor and Empress that had pride of place in the senior wardroom, he was assured they would not suffer the unspeakable disgrace of being captured after floating to the surface. The officer in charge of the sacred images was guarding them in his quarters, his hatch locked from the inside.

Ariga had no more wish to leave the ship than did Admiral Ito. To make certain he would stay, he had a messenger help tie him to the binnacle in the antiaircraft command post atop the bridge. (The messenger could barely keep upright on the steeply slanting deck slippery with blood.) Ariga cried, "Long live the Emperor!" and awaited the end calmly, eating biscuits a grieving lookout pressed into his hand before leaping into the water as ordered. A half-naked officer on deck stabbed the air with his sword while screaming "Banzai!" at squads of enemy planes circling overhead, as if to symbolize the purpose of the mission and of continuing the war.

After her ten torpedo hits, seven on the port side, five bomb hits and hundreds of near misses, the derelict received the coup de grâce from her own munitions. The list now approached 90 degrees, pulling the hull almost vertical in the water. But before it could capsize, shells stored in the magazines slipped from their positions and began knocking their fuses against bulkheads and overheads. *Yamato* had sailed with a full load of ammunition for her every weapon, an armory of explosives. Most of the 1080 18.1-inch monsters for the main batteries remained unused. Had they detonated when she was still on the surface, perhaps not a single member of the crew would have survived. As it was, the sea water into which she had all but sunk deadened the blasts. The largest took place the instant the pride of the Japanese Navy rolled over and plunged toward her grave, 450 fathoms below.*

The convulsion was on a scale with the ship. The flash of light and six thousand-foot pillar of fire could be seen in Kagoshima, two hundred miles away. Thick umber smoke bubbling up from the ocean rose into a mushroom cloud almost four miles high. "The prettiest sight I've ever seen," noted a gunner in one of the American planes that had disposed of the world's biggest and best battleship in well under two hours, just over a hundred miles off the Kyushu coast. There was only a little hyperbole in Samuel Morison's conclusion that this quick dispatch of the world's mightiest warship ended "five centuries of naval warfare" based on competition between surface ships.

Although less passionate about offense over defense than the Imperial Army, the Navy favored speed and firepower over precaution and protection. For all *Yamato*'s superb innovations and construction, her medical facilities had not been designed to cope with heavy casualties. Most of the wounded had to fend for themselves during the battle. Most still alive when the hulk went down were lost immediately: she carried no lifeboats or rafts. Even the relative handful of nonwounded had little chance to escape being sucked down with the enormous weight of metal. Those who fought free or managed to come up struggled in water heavy with oil "as thick as melted caramels" and on fire in many places. So black with it that their blood couldn't be seen, some survivors sang to keep up their courage as they flailed about, swallowing oil. Others went mad and consumed

---

* Paradoxically, the explosion saved several dozen sailors by blowing them from the ship that was taking them to the bottom, a blow hard enough to take them back to the surface. Yoshida was among those lucky few. So was the executive officer, who on his way down in the clear water saw men "dancing about" farther in the depths until sudden flashes of the explosion's red light shot through the endless deep blue. However, the only men saved were those not yet drowned on their way down — who surfaced at the last second before they passed out. Those blown up an instant earlier, desperately gasping to relieve their bursting lungs, were sucked into the stack or killed by the explosion's downpour of fire and hot metal.

their last energy in wild thrashing. Hundreds choked and burned to death. Ensign Yoshida tried to help the wounded, but the explosion that had providentially shot him to the surface at the last instant before he drowned was so great that he could find no debris big enough to make a raft. The ship's residue was in little bits and splinters.

> *Yamato* — support of my life, now gone. Only bubbles, bubbles. The strafing fire of machine guns. Planes that skim past, hugging the water, carefree . . . The faces, the heads near me. Jet black, monstrous. Like balls of charcoal the size of cantaloupes . . . Teeth chattering, I groan with the cold. I ball my fists and strike them together . . . Something presses up on my chest. To endure the pain, I tense up my toes as I tread water.

Several American planes made final strafing runs at the survivors struggling in the oil, some singing the national anthem and others chanting the military song that begins, "If I go away to sea, I'll return a brine-soaked corpse." This was one of the rare times when gallantry lay with the Japanese, whose pilots often murdered Americans descending in parachutes but had refrained from shooting at the survivors of *Repulse* and *Prince of Wales*. Some, like Ensign Yoshida, found bits of wreckage to cling to. Many who had hung on until now, even with their entrails curling into the water from gashes, slipped under one by one.

The three surviving destroyers put boats over the side to salvage what they could of the human wreckage. Believing their duty was to continue with the operation until directly ordered otherwise, the skippers ordered their crews to pull in only those healthy enough to fight on. The highest ranking officer found alive, the admiral in command of the destroyer squadron, washed the oil from himself when pulled aboard, then wrote a signal to Combined Fleet headquarters that he was headed for Okinawa.

The Surface Special Attack Force had accomplished its "most tragic and heroic attack of the war," the Combined Fleet's commander-in-chief summed up. After his miraculous survival, Ensign Mitsuru Yoshida remembered it quite differently — as "an operation that will live in naval annals for its recklessness and stupidity." Operation Heaven Number One cost the American forces twelve fliers and ten of their 386 planes — of which several, according to Yoshida, were lost when *Yamato*'s final explosion engulfed them while they were circling to observe her end. It cost the Japanese seven ships and 4250 men, almost as many as the American Navy's entire losses of killed and missing in action at and around Okinawa, a toll itself far heavier than any previous naval campaign in the war. Not one man on the destroyer *Asashimo* survived. All but 23 officers and 246 sailors of *Yamato*'s complement of 3332 died.

A twenty-two-year-old executive officer of a destroyer in the screen who observed *Yamato*'s end would later grieve for the magnificent ship and for his friends who served on her, then fume at the exorbitant folly he had recognized even before the sortie.* But now the very young exec had no time for even a second's thought about such larger matters. When *Yamato* was gone, the enemy planes immediately turned their attention to the surviving escort vessels, including his own *Kasumi*.

Destroyer *Kasumi* (Spring Mist) had emerged whole from the battles of the Philippine Sea and Leyte Gulf, where much of the Japanese fleet went down. Although a bomb to her engine room mortally wounded her now, half her crew remained lucky; most of them transferred to *Fuyutsuki*, which bravely rushed alongside to save them before sinking the hulk with torpedoes. *Fuyutsuki* (Winter Moon) was one of four destroyers that escaped sinking, even during this courageous rescue of *Kasumi*'s survivors. When she returned to her base in Sasebo the following day, the authorities ordered the crew quartered in a kind of isolation for several weeks in an attempt to keep the debacle of Task Force II from the public. The same reception awaited some of *Yamato*'s complement who survived the last American strafing.

It has often been written that the end of *Yamato* marked the end of the Imperial Japanese Navy, which, apart from its remaining planes, was now but a glorious memory. Actually, a heavy cruiser and

---

*Such folly would help make realists of many who survived it, including a much respected naval historian named Masataka Chihaya. As the Combined Fleet headquarters operations officer, Chihaya was among the younger staff who rushed around to obtain *Yamato*'s additional fuel for a return voyage. His historical studies after the war were prompted by puzzlement over how such a great institution as the Imperial Navy could have come to such a catastrophic end. He concluded that the Navy, although not quite as short-sighted and wrapped in the conceit of its might as the Army, had lost contact with larger realities. Just as many Army units were superb at close combat with bayonets, the Navy was splendid in design, seamanship and many forms of maneuvers and tactics. Man for man, its extremely intelligent, highly motivated officers, especially the Naval Academy graduates, were at least as good as any others in the world. But what they were best at was preparing for a war no longer being fought. They were dismally less good at larger strategy and thinking, including assessment of American industrial production and judgment of the American character. Even when Chihaya attended the War College in 1943, he was taught "the old lessons of sea battles, including much concentration on the so-called decisive battle that would win the war, instead of the larger picture of resources and true national strength that of course would determine the eventual outcome." This narrowness of outlook was what allowed the Navy to make miserable miscalculations about the most important factors — or simply to ignore them.

a destroyer engaged five Royal Navy destroyers the following month, and a submarine sank the cruiser *Indianapolis* in July. Several other capital ships remained intact later but served more as targets for American planes than as offensive threats. Except for aircraft and feeble antisubmarine efforts off the coasts of the home islands, the Navy would contribute nothing of operational significance after this last spasm of "glory" on April 7. (One of Task Force II's four surviving ships would become the 129th and last Japanese destroyer to go down when it hit a mine in the Japan Sea on July 30.) Immobilized by lack of fuel, the handful of surviving heavy ships rode at anchor under heavy camouflage near their bases, relegated to floating antiaircraft batteries. In "a final revenge for Pearl Harbor," as one historian called it, American planes sank them almost to the last one, whereupon their officers and sailors prepared to join the defense, which *Kasumi*'s former executive officer knew to be "hopeless," against the inevitable American landings on the homeland after Okinawa was lost.

When the Emperor was informed of the destruction of *Yamato* and five of her escorts, he raised his hand to his temple and swayed in disbelief. "Gone?" he muttered. "She's gone?" When Admiral Matome Ugaki heard — the commander of the Fifth Air Fleet that was mounting most of the kamikaze attacks on the American fleet off Okinawa — he noted in his diary that battleships were still needed for the day when "we resume the offensive," which would include a "general offensive" by the Japanese Army on Okinawa. When General Mitsuru Ushijima heard — the commander of that army on Okinawa — he snorted about the "infernal waste" and recalled that he had advised the Navy against the adventure, even urged its cancelation. "Banzai charges should be left to soldiers," he said.

When Japanese soldiers on Okinawa were informed — by leaflets dropped by American planes* with the headline BATTLESHIP YAMATO DESTROYED — they admired the quality of the paper but guffawed in disbelief. A photograph of the sinking ship in that day's leaflet prompted some to scoff at the absurd measures desperate American propagandists were taking to try to demoralize them. Some argued down naval officers — from a Naval Base Force participating in Okinawa's defense — who were willing to confirm the silly, subversive rumor. They, the men in the field, knew *Yamato* could never be sunk,

---

*Some eight million American leaflets would be dropped throughout the Okinawa campaign. The practice began before the American landing a week earlier than *Yamato*'s end. Those first efforts announced Allied victories — "British Army Enters Rangoon," "The Red Army Nears the Suburbs of Berlin" — and urged the Japanese to surrender before being destroyed.

and they were the enemy American infantrymen had to face, on Okinawan ground and in subterranean fortifications. Like the sailors in Operation Heaven Number One, Japanese troops would often be committed to actions that were useless for any rational military purpose. The percentage of them who would be killed in action on the island was only slightly smaller than on the *Yamato* mission, although that larger madness would consume three months rather than an hour and a quarter.

2 · American Participants

Maybe it was their training — or brainwashing. Our boys came over wanting to fight bad. They were a bunch of gung-ho kids itching to get into the field and beat the ass off the dirty Japs.

— An American who fought at Okinawa

Kids today would probably call me a sucker or something, but that's the way I am. I love the Corps and my country.

— A Marine who landed on Okinawa after managing to enlist despite being a husband and father of four

That's what I was geared for at the time, adventure I guess you'd call it.

— A Marine who landed on Okinawa two years after running away from home and managing to enlist at sixteen

Maybe there is glory in war but not for anyone fighting it. There's only fear and filth, shock and suffering. You see such blood, so many bashed bodies, so much gore. You're an animal, a barbarian, just like the enemy. No one who fought has illusions about glory.

— Dick Whitaker, another kid itchy for adventure

A LARGE honor roll dominated Main Street in Saugerties, a Hudson River town some fifty miles below Albany. Stalwarts' names were inscribed the moment they answered the call. The 1944 high school yearbook gave corresponding pride of place to photographs of graduates in uniform, with gold stars for the five killed in action since 1941. Admiration also suffused Broome's, a hotel, restaurant, and bowling alley whose clientele did not ordinarily ruminate about civic goals. George Broome kept a private honor roll of his patrons over the fireplace of his saloon.

Broome looked the other way when skinny, under-aged Dick Whitaker savored the bar's company of high school seniors, local workers and servicemen on leave. The national outpouring of patriotism had sharpened the itch of all Whitaker's friends to join Democracy's fight against her enemies. The good war beckoned mightily to would-be heroes who thrilled at John Wayne types relishing the boundless adventure. Whitaker himself yearned to join Saugerties's young recruits already certified as heroes.

He couldn't forget Pearl Harbor or Franklin Roosevelt's Day of Infamy speech, which he heard with his parents on the radio in their modest living room. The tantalized fourteen-year-old had been filling a scrapbook with magazine illustrations of Hitler's Stukas and U-boats. About the new enemy, he knew only that its queer little people bought lots of scrap and made cheap copies of American things. But he wondered whether Roosevelt's outrage over Japan's treachery might somehow speed him into the fighting — which he still pictured in Europe. As panzers seemed a natural step up from cars, war was an exciting step from the best movies, its appeal doubled by his emotional involvement.

The budding valiant in the world's finest cause went on to enlist in the Marines at seventeen, but his father refused to sign the papers. So it was back to time-wasting high school. Despite his father's reduction to part-time work during the Depression, life in Saugerties and in the creek-filled countryside — perfect for fishing in summer, hockey in winter — was full of happiness for a son who loved the outdoors. And although boys' company was mostly boys in that puritan time, girls too liked the easygoing extrovert. Still, he couldn't be entirely happy. He was aging and wars didn't last forever.

His luck changed when he graduated from high school in June 1944 — nine months before *Yamato*'s final mission. Drafted immediately, the just-turned eighteen-year-old took a bus to Albany to join a long line of fellow draftees shuffling slowly toward an Army induction counter in a post office corridor. The Marine recruiter who had arranged Whitaker's vetoed enlistment the previous year hurried past and recognized the avid lad. "Hey, Mac, still want the Marines?" Dick did indeed — and so did the boy with him, an acquaintance from near Saugerties. The sergeant motioned them out of the line.

"But the Army called us up," Whitaker fretted.

"Don't worry, I'll take care of it."

The enterprising recruiter gave the boys a pass for a YMCA room and chits for dinner and breakfast at a cafeteria. "Go to that room and don't leave it. I said *don't leave* except to eat. Report back here at seven in the morning."

Away from home for the first time, Whitaker stared at the ceiling of the tiny room. Apprehension about his soon-to-be-real military romance was compounded by a more specific fear of being caught AWOL from the Army draft. He and his acquaintance grabbed some candy instead of risking dinner and spent a restless night.

At least there was no worry about oversleeping. The boys bolted breakfast and were back at the post office well before seven o'clock, when the sergeant swore Whitaker "back" into the Marines. Hours later, he boarded a train for his great adventure.

When I say fall out, all I want to see is dust and assholes.
— A drill instructor's greeting to Marine Corps recruits arriving at boot camp at Parris Island

I hated being in the Marines. First there was boot camp, a terrible experience for someone just out of high school who had been living at home in a quiet small town community. Boot camp was living in a tent, long hard hours, unreasonable orders and being treated like a criminal. It was like I had broken a law by joining the Marines and had been sent to reform school.
— Thomas Hannaher, a kid from Minnesota

They made you feel like a piece of crap. It was worth it, although you didn't understand that then. They were making sure they could beat you down and you'd come up still able to do the job. The idea was that if you could get through boot camp, you could handle yourself anywhere.
— Norris Buchter, a tough kid from Connecticut

The only redeeming factors were my comrades' incredible bravery and their devotion to each other. Marine Corps training taught us to kill efficiently and try to survive. But it also taught us loyalty to each other — and love.
— E. B. Sledge, who took boot camp in San Diego, July 1943

The train was so crowded that many had to stand. Marine boot camp for East Coast recruits was on Parris Island, fifty miles below Charleston, South Carolina. A Navy coxswain on the barge that ferried them across liked to mention the teeming 'gators there. "Tell you one thing, fellas. They'll gobble you up in about two minutes if you change your mind and try to swim back across."

Heads were shaved and dignity stripped instantly. Every last recruit was a worthless nothing. For washing their new fatigues, a scrub brush and pail were flung at them, and anyone who dropped his "gear" felt his drill instructor's marching boot in his bottom. *"You are not Marines. You are stupid fucking civilian clowns! You are the fucking dregs!"*

Communication between platoons was forbidden but earlier recruits managed to welcome the raw ones without turning their heads. "You'll be *sor*-ry!" Many ardent boys were very sorry before the first sunset.

The training was dehumanizing as well as harsh. Its purpose was to undo everything the recruits had believed about themselves and reconstruct them mentally and emotionally as well as physically — to make them into Marines, the best fighters in the world. That belief was crucial. The best in the world would never be stopped by any defense and never let a buddy down no matter how deadly the enemy fire. If some drill instructors were sadists, as most recruits were convinced about their own, that was coincidental. The dregs could be made the best only by stripping away their individual egos and reassembling them as interchangeable members of fighting units. When a Brooklyn boy in Whitaker's group protested that he couldn't remove his pegged pants as told without taking off his shoes, he was handed a knife. His first lesson was that the Corps was sublime and he contemptible. His second was to follow orders: nothing else mattered.

Strong young men in body, the recruits were still emotional boys — a necessary condition for their remaking into utter subordinates to those who gave the orders. Why else would they feel compelled to undertake combat's otherwise impossible acts such as running up Okinawan hills honeycombed with Japanese gun emplacements? Only total indoctrinates in the glorious traditions they had to uphold would leave their cover to attack the enemy's most murderous positions.

No living person had impressed most recruits, or ever would, as much as their amazingly tyrannical drill instructors. The authority of the boot camp DI seemed like natural, or unnatural, law itself. "Hey, you — shithead. Move your head again in ranks and I'll boot you so far up your fucking ass that you'll have to unbutton your fucking collar for your farts." Communication between units was prohibited partly to deprive new recruits of the confidence that they could survive. Whitaker actually wondered at times whether the drill instructors were trying to kill the eighty members of his Platoon 452. When they incurred the milder wrath of their chief DI, a sergeant named Blackburn, he ordered them to place their scrubbing buckets over their heads and sing the Marine Corps hymn. Bellowing into this curious headgear, they could not hear him stalking the ranks. "Louder, you half-ass bunch of scumbag civilians. *Louder,* you fucking fuck-ups!" Anyone perceived as not shouting beyond the top of his lungs received a swagger stick's deafening whack on his bucket. Many singing more thunderously than they had believed possible got the whack anyway.

Punishment was meted out to the entire bone-weary platoon even for one member's seemingly insignificant error. The point was to eliminate slip-ups in the unity of the group by correcting or weeding out the incompetents. If seventy-nine fucking clowns got it right and one didn't, repeating the entire exercise again and again and again put great pressure on the screwball who didn't until some of the others took care of him privately. In combat, the enemy would break the chain if he found a single weak link. The slightest slip-up would jeopardize the dozens or hundreds who got it right. The recruits did not know it but they were being brainwashed, molded, *never* to let the unit down in the slightest little anything. Each would have to be able to count utterly on every one of the others. Platoon 452 grew smaller. Better to learn on the drill fields that not all were cut out to be Marines than in a foxhole under attack in the dark of night.

Physical hardening was the least of it. Hardy specimens raised on outdoor labor or athletic conditioning, as a majority were, soon took more or less in stride the day-long endurance tests that earlier had made them vomit and pass out. Learning how to kill took finer training. Marine Corps hype aside, the callow youths were made into excellent riflemen. Endlessly field stripping and reassembling their M-1s blindfolded, they came to know them far better than their own bodies. The carbine, Browning automatic rifle and several varieties of machine guns were introduced, but it was in use of "the piece" that they had to become maestros. ("Piece" was obligatory nomenclature. Any dog-tired unfortunate who called his M-1 a "gun" was awarded extra hours of a testicle-centered drill that would keep him from ever making the mistake again.) They learned to compensate for range when there was no time to adjust their sights. They became practiced in the art of "Kentucky windage" — making instant allowance for wind at various ranges. Every recruit came to regard his piece as an extension of himself. He could point it as quickly as his finger and be certain of hitting a head or chest at a hundred yards without kneeling or propping the piece against a support, which gave consistent accuracy at even greater distances. Should his ammunition run out, he knew how to kill quickly with his bayonet.

The men of Platoon 452 graduated knowing they were damn good because that was what the Corps had made them.* The grueling test passed together would link them forever, partly in contempt of lesser men, partly in trust that all other Marines would respond as instantly and unquestioningly to every order. By nature, their admiration of themselves valued the individual only as part of the collective: the reliable cog in the fighting machine. It came from having endured great hardship as a group because that was the only way to do it; from acceptance into a community by whose values alone they had come to measure themselves — and which fueled precisely the elitism they would need to tackle their punishing work. None would let the Corps down because no *Marine* ever did.

*During the last week, Sergeant Blackburn started calling "Fuck-off number one" and "Fuck-off number two" — twin brothers named Salami — by their proper names.

A huge Parris Island sign preached, LET NO MOTHER EVER SAY HER SON DIED IN COMBAT FOR LACK OF TRAINING. Wondering why fathers had been left out, Whitaker thought to himself that neither parent would ever say it about him. Boot camp's overriding lesson — the purpose for the proficiency with weapons, utter reliability in extreme circumstances, and esprit de corps that would conquer fear of death — was how to close with the enemy and kill him, which the new Marines felt proud to have mastered.

> *Battle is . . . to the young. Its physical ordeals — discomfort, loss of sleep, hunger, thirst, burdens — are not only better borne by men under thirty; so too are its terrors, its anxieties, its separations, its bereavements.*
> — Paul Fussell

After Edmund De Mar's father, a Brooklyn truck driver, lost his job during the Depression, the family left its Long Island house for humbler quarters in a Connecticut town inhabited by a well-married, disapproving aunt. Still nothing worked out for them. Ed would not have been fond of school even if his Brooklyn accent hadn't been mocked there. He quit, did even smaller odd jobs than his father, and, with a few spare dollars from cleaning up the mess of the 1938 hurricane, took off for Miami with friends in an old Plymouth. The nineteen-year-olds arrived on Christmas Eve with a nickel each and forewarning of how the local police treated vagrants.

Down to one nickel again two years later after a series of O. Henry adventures, De Mar, now almost twenty-one, saw a Marine in dress blues promising "Adventure!" on a post office poster. On the bus to his physical in Savannah, he told himself that at least he'd be partway back to Connecticut if he failed.

The entry point for Parris Island was a profoundly hick town called Yamassee. When De Mar stepped off the bus there, a Marine in what the recruits thought was a campaign hat was waiting. They didn't yet know what a drill instructor was. One boy extended his hand and politely introduced himself, in response to which the DI slapped him hard in the face. "I don't give a goddam who you think you are. You're a fucking pukey weakling, a *nothing*." De Mar considered getting back on the bus.

Fifteen months later, he was Corporal of the Guard one Sunday afternoon at a naval air station just below Miami when a jeep raced toward him, breaking the base speed limit and peacetime slumber. "The Japs!" bellowed the driver. "Corporal De Mar, the Japs have bombed Pearl Harbor!"

"Those yellow bastards!" De Mar responded. "Where's Pearl Harbor?"

When De Mar was shipped out, it wasn't to one of America's Pacific outposts that were falling to "those yellow bastards" like bowling pins but to security duty in the Panama Canal. Sailing east on one ship one day and west on another the next, he spent two years watching for saboteurs trying to cripple the canal by blowing up the vessel or a lock with an explosive charge. On Okinawa, he would be among the few prewar regulars — and, at the age of twenty-six, one of the fighting Marines' older enlisted men. On the American side, it would never be more true than in the Pacific War's hardest encounter that wars made by older generations are fought by younger.

Thomas Hannaher's father was born in the Dakota Territory. The boy's body didn't accommodate his yearning to impress the girls with athletic feats. He felt even worse as a freshman at North Dakota State when his high school friends went into the services but he was classified 4F. The unlucky eighteen-year-old's second stab at joining the fighting men brought him up against the same medical captain who had uncovered his asthma during his dismal first examination. "What are you doing back here?" he asked. An instant lie came to the ordinarily upright boy: "Because the colonel said I was okay." The captain chose not to dispute the colonel; Hannaher was in — and chose the Corps at the end of the final line. "What are you doing there, trying to commit suicide?" asked a friend from whom he'd been separated during the physical. Hannaher had no idea what he was doing there. Far from hero material, the unathletic teenager had never even fired a gun, something almost a little odd in the Dakotas. It made no sense at all except in terms of his old desire to prove himself. One of the war's million ironies would have Hannaher among the few Marines unwounded during the entire Okinawan campaign, months after his friend was blown to bits during the Battle of the Bulge in Belgium.

John D. Rockefeller, Jr., prudently calculated the danger of Axis bombs. Soon after Pearl Harbor, Rockefeller, one of the five sons of the "original" John D. Rockefeller, decided to move himself and his Park Avenue apartment's art treasures to his country estate. Joseph Bangert's family also made that move to Tarrytown, New York, young Joe's father being John D's personal driver, one of five who served that branch of the family. (Rockefeller's reputation as a penny-pinching son of a bitch had made *père* Bangert reluctant to take the job forty-three years earlier, but decades had drawn driver and passenger close, despite occasional bickering over such matters as who should pay the driver's laundry bills when the two were on the road together. Bangert once heard his father argue with the boss over an expense item of a dime.)

Fearless Joe was the youngest and wildest of eleven Bangert boys, the only one who wouldn't go to college. By 1943, four of that black sheep's elder brothers were in service overseas — and sixteen-year-old Joe, itchy to do something too apart from screwing up in school, enlisted in the Navy. The self-confessed "smartass" and "hell raiser" was directed to report again after he turned seventeen — with his parents' consent, which was needed until the volunteer was eighteen. He obtained it by slipping in the form with others required for playing high school football.

With no medics of their own, Marines were assigned Navy corpsmen. Bangert took his first step toward that hazardous work at his induction, when he was told of a pressing need for medical corpsmen — who were automatically promoted to second-class seamen with a pay of $54 a month instead of $50 for third class. After boot camp and corpsman training, he was assigned to a California naval hospital — and took his second step. An inspection that earned less than a perfect mark in some areas for which he was responsible fired the wrath of his officer, a fastidious nurse.

"Are you through?" the second-class corpsman asked the ensign after her harangue.

"No!" she screamed and continued castigating until she ran out of breath.

"*Now* are you through?" Bangert repeated.

"Yes, I'm through."

The smartass lifted a broom. "Then take this and shove it up your gigi."

He walked out and asked his chief to assign him to combat duty, a request not to be denied, given the Corps's shortage of bodies on the Pacific islands.

Marines reached Okinawa in a variety of ways. A minority came from previous island battles after intervals of rest, rehabilitation and more training. Others were graduates of more specialized schools, from which they were sent to embarkation centers, then on slow boats to Pacific way stations. What all had in common, apart from their spirited training, was patriotic zeal.

Lenly Cotten, the son of separated parents (then a rare arrangement), began running away from home as a child. He managed to fool the examiners and enlist at sixteen, but his first duty disappointed him because there were no Japs to kill on the Aleutian Islands. "You wanted combat because that's what you were trained for from the first day in boot camp. All those months preparing to fight got to you; you wanted to *do* it." Back in the States at eighteen, Cotten had an idea. He knew replacement troops for Iwo Jima were so badly needed that anyone caught AWOL was shipped there immediately. "It didn't matter whether you were two hours or two months over the hill, you got an automatic summary [court-martial] and were on your way to combat." But Cotten was in Camp Lejeune on the East Coast, from which he might go to Europe, where Germany was almost finished. So he hitchhiked west, careful to avoid military police patrols until he had crossed the Mississippi — then gave himself up. "I knew I'd get sent straight to the Pacific from anywhere west of there. My only real worry was that the war would be over before I could get there and be a hero."

The invading force would be made up of over half a million Americans. No more than a handful of them had any real knowledge about Japan. Whitaker knew "absolutely nothing until the sneak attack on Pearl." "If I had any impression of Japs at all," another Marine would remember, "it was that they were funny little people walking around tea gardens in kimonos." A third thought of them as "gooks who were trying to peddle things to the States but didn't have a hope in hell, except for trashy souvenirs." A fourth classified them as "Oriental. Inscrutable. And nothing to do with us, so who cared?"

But virtually the entire half million cared very much that Japan was a sinister place populated by evil people. Those whose troopships stopped at Pearl Harbor on the way to their unknown destination knew even better than the others. The sight of the sunken battleships' hulls and memory of the Japanese treachery fired their rage.

Fred Poppe loved sailing in Long Island Sound and volunteered for the Navy, but flat feet and astigmatism excluded him from all programs leading to a commission. Now he was a quartermaster third class on a brand-new landing craft converted to a floating rocket launcher. "Sometimes my buddies and I would cry when presenting arms to the flag. Actually cry — because of American goodness and virtuousness, all so beautiful and pure, we believed with all our hearts. Against this were the Japs, low-grade monsters who were totally inferior in everything, especially intelligence — we were told in high school that one bomb would set all Tokyo ablaze because those creatures mostly lived in bamboo huts — but who fought savagely and committed terrible atrocities."

About Okinawa, they knew nothing whatever. Most would hear their first something aboard troopships bearing them there.

3 · Japanese Participants

In the Army, complete submissiveness was instilled in a short time. Young men were transformed into monsters of self-abasement, humiliation, and shrewdness by subjecting them to fear of violence in the name of punishment.
— Hiroshi Minami, *The Psychology of the Japanese People*

Basic training caused many more deaths than necessary but it was effective for our way of fighting. Your beatings made you lose your mind and stop thinking even about self-preservation. You only trembled to obey.
— A Japanese soldier on Okinawa

The Japanese soldier was a remarkable man. On Okinawa, he fought — and how he fought! — with no air cover whatever and amazingly little support. His resilience and endurance were tremendous.
— General James Day, who fought on Okinawa as a corporal and returned forty years later as commander of all U.S. forces there

What did I think about Pearl Harbor? As a regular Japanese Army officer, I never thought about anything except my duty and work.
— Tadashi Kojo, former captain

W HILE DICK WHITAKER was downing his pre-induction beers in Broome's, Tadashi Kojo was practicing the martial art of kendo across the Ussuri River from Siberia. Stationed in the bleak barracks settlement of Nishi-Toan, Kojo's 22nd Regiment of the Japanese 24th Infantry Division lived on hot resolve to crush the hated Russians.

In that June of 1944, the proud regiment was guarding Manchuria, the jewel of the Empire. After victory in the Sino-Japanese War of 1895, Tokyo claimed the Liaotung Peninsula, convinced heart and soul that the relatively small tract, tipped by Port Arthur, was among its just spoils. When Japan was forced to back down, patriots vowed to endure any privation — to "lie on kindling wood and lick gall" — to get back their own.

The intervention of France, Germany and Russia forced that humiliating retreat, their own appetites upset by Japan's wish to join their table of Asian snacks. About the upstart Japanese, some European statesmen said "yellow" outright. St. Petersburg's greed hit hardest at Japan. At that time and place, control of railroads meant control of territory. The Russians were determined to keep all others from establishing a power base in resource-rich Manchuria, around whose northern hump their recently begun Trans-Siberian Railway would curve before ending at Vladivostok. Three years later, they would lease the same Liaotung Peninsula, with rights to build railroads to connect with the Trans-Siberian.

The Japanese had reason to believe the Russians wanted Manchuria for themselves and that the other powers had ganged up on them. After all, Tokyo was only trying to follow the trail previously blazed by the European powers on the Asian continent. Ever since Commodore Matthew Perry had ended their deep isolation in 1853, the poor, technologically backward nation worked sacrificially to industrialize and militarize in the pattern of their economic betters. But instead of being welcomed into the imperialist club, as they had naïvely hoped to be, they were given to know they were of the wrong color.

Japanese memories of those insults remained fresh in 1944. The 22nd Regiment's officers revered the Army for its part in defeating the arrogant Russians in the War of 1905. That victory had astonished the West, which had taken for granted that the great bear would maul the foolhardy little upstart. Very few Westerners knew anything about Japanese pluck and dedication. In a mere fifty years after Perry's arrival, feudal, agricultural Nippon had put forth the astonishing effort to make herself at least a partially industrialized country, the proof of which was the defeat of a European power. The triumph brought rich balm to Japan's wounded honor. The West's docile pupil had become a minor world power almost overnight — but remained as sensitive as ever to her rating relative to others.

The Army restored more national honor in 1931 by taking not just the "stolen" Manchurian peninsula but all of it. That conquest, a first step to the catastrophe of the Pacific War, was wildly cheered. With Japan's population soaring to sixty-six million and the Depression crippling the national economy, many believed Manchuria was vital for their survival. Renamed Manchukuo and ruled by a puppet government, it was seen as salvation from the severe overpopulation and underendowment in raw materials that was squeezing the Japanese people and depriving her industry.

The 22nd Regiment, whose long history of distinguished service included the Russo-Japanese War, now kept unblinking watch on Soviet detachments across the river. Manchuria/Manchukuo had been a de facto colony for thirteen years, but the Japanese were convinced Russia's designs on it hadn't changed. Although the war with

America was important, the regiment's officers still saw their chief enemy in Japan's old rapacious competitor for Manchuria. A non-invasion pact with the Soviet Union was no guarantee the great deceiver Stalin would not attack tomorrow.

Actually, the senior officers were certain their own regiment would attack. The fighting units trained relentlessly for an undeclared night strike across the river and through the Soviet marshes on the other side. Russia should have been crushed years ago in a huge Axis pincer movement, Hitler's armies taking Moscow from the west. Avid for the next opportunity, the officers, overachievers in training as in so much else, kept their troops poised and ready.

The isolation helped. The soldiers' chief relief from their extremely Spartan living conditions were prostitutes — some from Korea, another "protectorate." They had little relief from regular beatings. Bullying noncommissioned officers went up and down the ranks, bashing faces. The sport was almost prescribed at evening roll call, when the men lined up at their cots. No one laughed when superiors had to stand on tiptoe to strike the faces of the tallest. Everything from ladles to straps was used, but mostly the base of the palm. The recipients learned to clench their teeth to keep them intact. Some toppled over, dazed and bleeding.

They were hardly the first or last cannon fodder to be both miserably treated and utterly loyal. As in other countries in the grip of feudalistic patriotism, there may even have been a correlation between wretched treatment and devotion to the beloved homeland. The Emperor inspired awe and adoration. Japan's holiness was secure as long as the descendant of the Sun Goddess was in the Imperial Palace. The barracks were full of whispered complaints against individual sadists, but there was virtually no questioning of the Empire's uniqueness, rightness and mission, or of one's duty to suffer and die for it. All had grown up steeped in a belief to which the most respected newspapers contributed irreproachable support.

> We Japanese know that our god, from whom the Emperor is descended, watches over Japan. This deity and the Japanese are related by consanguinity. The whole world searches for God but only Japan possesses Him; Japan is the divine country . . . therefore the Emperor's will is the only key to a new universal order.

All came to instant, unbreathing attention when the Emperor or anything pertaining to him was mentioned, as during the frequent readings of the Imperial Rescript to Soldiers and Sailors, a document that predated the much less relevant and (for officers) less important Constitution. The text of the Rescript identified it as "the Grand Way of Heaven and Earth" and "the universal law of humanity." Those ten minutes of fundamental rules and philosophy had to be memorized to perfection. A recruit bound for Okinawa that June had taken basic training at about the same time as Dick Whitaker on Parris Island. He watched fellow recruits who made the tiniest mistake reciting the Rescript's stilted, archaic phrases beaten bloody, then comforted during renewed attempts to learn the text. It reminded him of good-guy, bad-guy police teams working a suspect. Officers of other units had killed themselves to atone for the disgrace of a slip of the tongue or mispronunciation of key words in their reading of the Rescript to their troops. No one tried to stop them; their shame was understood.

Much more minor infractions also earned blows, often to all members of the units involved. Although this drive to establish collective responsibility had its parallel in American basic training, Japanese intentions differed tellingly. Bruised quarry who tried to supply a reason when asked why they were being hit were hit even harder. The point was that they weren't supposed to know the reason, were never supposed to think. The submissiveness that was as rooted in civilian life as deep bows had to be made supreme and unthinking. A Japanese psychologist concluded shortly after the war that "violence was used to implant the idea of absolute obedience," which was grounded in a lack of all thought, right or wrong. To be hit was part of a soldier's duty, and the more perceptive recruits recognized that the goal was fear, not punishment. "It was sometimes not a matter of obeying or disobeying," remembered a soldier who would fight opposite Dick Whitaker on the Okinawan hill nicknamed Sugar Loaf. "I was beaten for no justifiable reason and quite unexpectedly."

"I was hit almost every evening as a recruit," remembered another infantryman who would also fight on Sugar Loaf. "Utter obedience was demanded. If I was shown a piece of black paper and told it was white, I'd have to agree." Another remembered being slapped every evening "for nothing." When he actually committed a slip-up — forgetting to hang his string-strung purse from his neck — he and two other transgressors were stripped to the waist and a Senior Private whacked his face with an old shoe. The swelling lasted longer than a week.

Many recruits eventually headed for Okinawa lived in constant fear of nightly beatings for "a bad attitude," which also meant for nothing. One man lost so much weight that doctors grew worried during a rare physical and ordered a ration of five raw eggs a week, all instantly confiscated by the veteran soldiers who administered the beatings. One day, the men in his group were asked to jot down their candid thoughts about Army life. "Being neither cats nor dogs, we'd like to be treated like human beings," he wrote naïvely. That triggered more severe beatings.

Fighting units like the 22nd Regiment gave basic training themselves, permitting noncommissioned officers to establish their tyranny from the start. During the dreaded first year, recruits were in complete servitude to everyone above. The word of a superior even one grade up was likened to an Imperial order — an arrangement aided by Article Two of the same Imperial Rescript, instructing that "Inferiors should regard the orders of their superiors as issuing directly from Us."* Scrupulous Japanese attention to the fine points of caste and hierarchy conferred superiority on those with a single day more in service. Noncoms buttressed their tyranny with a warning that disobedience to them, even of an order to scrub latrines, was tantamount to disobedience to the Emperor himself.

With civilian upbringing rooted in Emperor worship and a caste system based on strict submission, all this was far less strange and onerous to Japanese soldiers than it would have been to American. As in all countries, the social order of civilian life in Japan, where conformity, discipline, hierarchy, loyalty, duty and obedience were paramount, was tightly woven into the fabric of military ethics and practices. The concepts of individual rights and challenge to authority were remote to those who had grown up in a bureaucratic dominion where the earliest lessons focused on conforming to the group's expectations and where nonconformist behavior earned instant sharp disapproval. Prewar Japan was so locked in hard work and instinctive bows to seniority and authority — and in a belief that perseverance and endurance to suffering are among the most desirable qualities — that Army life, even in its tormenting first year, represented liberation to some.

In 1933, fourteen-year-old Kuni-ichi Izuchi, whose artillery battery would be annihilated on Okinawa, traveled to the ancient capital of Kyoto to be apprenticed to a respected painter. During the next five years, little Kuni-ichi's hands were permanently covered with chilblains. Although he had already graduated from a trade school, his duties included scrubbing his master's floor with rags and water that often froze in winter. He knew his relatively kind master liked him. The blows for not doing exactly as told were simply in accor-

---

* Article Two also required superiors "never [to] treat their inferiors with contempt or arrogance . . . Except when official duty requires them to be strict and severe, superiors should treat their inferiors with consideration, making kindness their chief aim, so that all grades may unite in their service to the Emperor." In practice, those were nice noises.

dance with the accepted approach to training: lessons were to be literally "beaten into the pupil's head," in the Japanese expression. In addition to the cleaning, which lasted into the night, Izuchi looked after the master's children and saw to a hundred household chores — without a single painting lesson during the full first year. Kyoto was only an hour away from his village by train, but the boy endured four additional years of heavy work and severe discipline without once going home to visit, although he often longed to indulge in that impermissible weakness. By the time he took basic training with his regiment — then fighting in China — military discipline was a snap for him. And although he rated his chances of surviving the American war as only 10 to 20 percent, he was confident Japan would win if everyone did his job as told.

Still, Army life was sufficiently grimmer than the grinding apprenticeships to make many nonprofessional soldiers dream of returning home, especially during the physical training. The grueling tests included "cold endurance" marches in winter and "heat endurance" in summer, both to the extremes of endurance — and beyond: casualties were frequent. The purpose was to build stoical disregard of pain, exhaustion and the elements; a Western expert before the war indeed witnessed "endurance . . . little short of phenomenal." Night movements and attacks figured importantly in Japanese tactics. Rooted out of bed in the dead of night, soldiers were ordered to don very heavy packs and keep going, no matter what. "Why don't you let them sleep?" a British observer asked during a forty-eight-hour marathon. "They already know how to sleep," the training officer answered instantly.

Kojo's Nishi-Toan base had no radios or movies. Day after day of bayonet practice, including sessions before breakfast and after supper, served for sport. Bayonet charges also helped stress the supreme importance of the attack. Officers relentlessly instructed their units that they could defeat the enemy only by putting away all thought of their own lives — and by taking the offensive that had served so well from the Sino-Japanese wars to the Russo-Japanese War to Pearl Harbor and Singapore.

> There is hell
> Under the falling blade.
> Jump into it and
> You may be saved.

and:

> Let your enemy cut your skin,
> You cut his flesh.
> Let your enemy cut your flesh,
> You sever his bones.

True grit helped make the Japanese soldier "Japan's supreme weapon," as a historian recently put it. A manual issued to all recruits on entering the Army made the same point.

> When you encounter the enemy after landing, regard yourself as
> an avenger come face to face at last with your father's murderer.
> The discomforts of the long sea voyage and the rigors of the
> march have all been but months of waiting for this moment when
> you may slay your enemy. Here before you is the man whose death
> will lighten your heart of its burden of brooding anger. Should you
> fail to destroy him, you may never rest in peace — and the first blow
> is always the vital one!

Regular Army field officers saw that opportunity to strike the first, vital blow as the full purpose of their lives. The equals of their men in endurance and bayonet skills, they practiced kendo religiously. The lack of nonmilitary activities in desolate Nishi-Toan did not bother them; they knew little more, wanted nothing more. Evenings, they drank sake and discussed tactics, troop training and preparing for the all-important Staff College examination.

Tadashi Kojo was as tough as nails and as single-minded as his fellow officers. Formerly the regiment's training officer responsible for basic training, the boyish-looking twenty-three-year-old was now its most junior battalion commander and still a stickler for rules. Captain Kojo never hit his men; he left that to his noncoms. The scrupulous patrician merely rapped his junior officers with his riding crop occasionally, and they, in turn, slapped their men's faces. The men admired their dashing battalion commander and were afraid of him. Mistakes triggered his short temper. Arrogance was part of the professionalism of young regular officers.

In Kojo's case, it could draw on high social stature. Almost a thousand years earlier, an important clan in a central region sent a young samurai to put down new roots in a remote, southern frontier called Satsuma. The youth became a minor feudal lord and one of his sons was given the name of Kojo, "Small Castle." The Kojos later pledged allegiance to Satsuma's powerful Shimazu lords. Their prominence extended to Tadashi's youth, when his grandmother acknowledged neighbors' deep bows with a much shallower movement.

The family had its failures too. Some had to sell off land — even, at one point, the gate to the family house. When Tadashi's paternal grandfather traveled to Nagasaki in the 1920s, the passionate womanizer went straight to a famous bordello in the red-light district. To settle his gambling debts, the playboy once sold his son's house, his undisputed right because Japan's current civil law gave the pater-familias control of all family wealth. Tadashi's father could either move out or buy back the house.

He managed to buy it back each time because he was a distinguished surgeon, for which he had been interning in progressive Nagasaki when his father visited. Now his private clinic had one of Kagoshima Prefecture's two x-ray machines, the other belonging to the prefectural hospital. Though he cared for his poorest patients without charge, he earned more than the prefectural governor, and was so keen on education that he did the unheard of, especially in poor, backward Satsuma: sent a daughter to Tokyo to study.

The affluent family tried to hold its two daughters and six sons, three of whom would attend the Imperial Military Academy, to the frugality more expected in spartan Satsuma than elsewhere in Japan. But Tadashi's father, who saw up to 150 patients a day and pored over medical journals when not attending conferences in Tokyo and Kyoto, lacked time to apply the strict discipline also admired in Satsuma. Tadashi's loving mother, the daughter of a rich Nagasaki businessman, matched her husband's professional standing with a cultural refinement apparent in her calligraphy, poetry and playing of the lyre-like *koto*. She devoted herself to her children.

Uncommonly free of rules and with positively indulgent exposure, by Satsuma's standards, to cosmopolitan influences, Tadashi climbed nearby mountains, swam in the local river and rowed boats in Kagoshima Bay opposite the active volcano Sakurajima. The family's bayside village, some fifteen miles from Kagoshima, was even more conservative than the city: the poor farming community was as tradition-bound as Nagasaki was liberal. Most of the legal privileges of samurais, who had been just below aristocrats on feudal Japan's class ladder, were officially abolished in 1873, twenty years after Perry's arrival. But Satsuma schools instilled the old ways of hierarchy, obedience and stringent service. Administrators pointedly segregated the samurai boys during ceremonies and extracurricular activities.

Tadashi often postponed studying for reading, his love of which prompted thoughts of a literary career. But samurai boys were constantly exhorted to prepare for the life of few words and valorous deeds that characterized real Satsuma men. Partly out of warrior tradition, partly because the narrowness of Satsuma childhood retarded education for other professions, many top pupils applied for the military academies. The ardently patriotic director of the Kojos' village school urged this on Tadashi too, an excellent if erratic pupil.

Eventually, he needed no more urging. After all, Army officers were a national elite as well as provincial heroes: most of Japan's prime ministers had been generals. Tadashi's parents championed medicine, pointing out that an Army doctor would have the best of two worlds. But rare as it was in Satsuma, they left the decision to their boy — who now wanted to be a *real* soldier.

Competition to enter the Imperial Military Academy remained intense in the mid-1930s, even while the Academy was greatly expanding for Japan's deeper involvement in war. Kojo's class would accept one of every fifteen applicants. But he easily passed the entrance exam and entered in 1937, at the age of seventeen.

During his years in the Academy, Japan loathed the Western powers less than it would later, partly because confidence was high from 1937 to 1940; the Army was thrashing China and not yet fighting the Pacific Allies. Still, every youth received stiff daily doses of jingoism. The quick, happy gobbling of Manchuria had sharpened appetites. Editorialists espoused further expansion as the only answer to the Depression-caused collapse of western markets and the doubling of population in fifty years. The few who challenged the growing passion for military power were labeled *hikoku-min,* "noncitizens," and accused of endangering national security. Weaving a hold on the country of the samurai spirit and group mentality, prophets of national and self-fulfillment through conquest won more concessions the more violent they became. A growing corps of dreamer-terrorists got their way through the very fury of their belief.

The superpatriots excited poor peasants who yearned for better conditions for themselves and glory for their nation — and who lacked all notion of the wretchedness their aspirations caused other peoples. The most determined used intimidation and assassination to silence disapproving liberals and moderates. Especially after they yanked the country into war with China in 1937, the year Kojo became a cadet, their Imperial Way extremism established the national climate. "War is the father of creativeness and the mother of culture," began an Army pamphlet published three years earlier.

The Academy itself was pervaded by surging, unqualified love for the Army as the source of supreme honor and good, mixed with a joyful determination to sacrifice for Emperor and country. Cadet Kojo's conviction that death in the line was life's finest fulfillment preceded his Academy stint. The population of his rugged native Satsuma — renamed Kagoshima Prefecture after the main city — remained top-heavy in samurai who felt useless in civilian life and happy for the national turn toward their soldierly outlook. Even the influence of Kojo's rich, worldly parents did not shake his acceptance of the axiom that the highest service was military.

The Academy's curriculum was squeezed from four to three years as enrollment rapidly increased. Whole pages of Kojo's textbooks were crossed out, and those texts concerned military matters almost entirely. In this sense, it is misleading to consider the Shikan Gakko the equivalent of West Point, which then offered science and humanities courses similar to those in ordinary colleges. The Imperial Military Academy more resembled a superior Officers' Training School. Cinema and theater were forbidden, even Japanese movies and plays, even on holidays; the same went for correspondence with women. Only a small percentage had pursued serious nonmilitary interests before matriculating: most cadets were bright boys from poor farm families, very grateful for their chance to escape poverty while serving Japan. Those who had indulged in dangerous distractions were cured. It was an article of faith that any thought unrelated to training and fighting could only dull an officer's edge.

After the war, Kojo realized that, far from contributing to the Army's strength, this prized narrowness implanted a fatal weakness. But Cadet Kojo would not have believed that the Imperial Academy — which supplied the backbone for the Japanese Army more than West Point did for the American — actually trained officers to be blind to critical realities on the battlefield. The Academy staff prided itself on having no background knowledge to consider anything nonmilitary, just as the high command was proud of its ignorance of such political and economic factors as America's will to fight the costly war. It taught that discipline, field tactics and skill with arms were what counted, together with inculcation of the crucial, indomitable Japanese spirit that would destroy all enemies.

Kojo was not a zealous student. Even a delay of a second was considered intolerable for cadets. But while others awoke well before reveille, leaping out of bed for a running start on the morning duties, Kojo slept until the last possible moment and was often last to dash for inspection. The Academy was even stricter than he had expected. The teenager missed his family's warmth and luxury, especially during the half hour of evening free time. Fearing he was soft, he tried not to let the trains that ran near the compound near Tokyo — the former residence of one of the Tokugawa family, who ruled Japan as shoguns until the Meiji Restoration — remind him of how much he wanted to go home. He regretted that no book other than military texts and training manuals could be opened without permission. But with time, that restriction seemed natural, then natural not to want permission. His training officers, most of whom had fought in Manchuria or China, impressed him deeply. All Academy graduates themselves, they helped tighten the circle of conformity and contempt for the outside interests. Although sometimes so tired that he dozed in class, his face swollen from slaps for infractions in saluting and in the condition of his shoes and rifle, Kojo was immensely grateful for his destiny. Privilege was merging with the unswerving elite of regular officers and their noble cause. The Academy inspired its cadets to strive for supreme integrity, loyalty and unselfishness.

Kojo's sole goal — the highest purpose — became the one that had been held up to him from his first days in school: unthinking sacrifice for the Emperor and the Imperial family. By now, Hirohito had given up trying to restrain the Army from gobbling Asian territory in his name. His Majesty probably learned to take satisfaction in the conquests; in any case, he conferred a blessing on the Army by attending the Academy's graduation ceremonies. He dismounted from his white horse and stood beside the commandant during the presentation of the diplomas, the August Presence conferring on the graduates the highest conceivable honor in the world. The drill field burned with purpose and desire. Kojo could barely breathe for the awe, affection and devotion that surged through his body like an electric charge.

Some of this sensation returned the first time he held his own sword in his hands. He knew Satsuma families with over a hundred beautifully maintained swords, passed down from when their families armed others in emergencies. Such weapons, made of superb steel, were rightly called the soul of the samurai. Kojo was prepared to pay five months' salary for his, his gambling grandfather having disposed of the family armory to settle more debts. But a friend's grandmother gave him a graduation gift from her family's collection — a Stradivarius of weapons, made by Sukesada, the master thirteenth-century swordsmith. Kojo's resolve to do his duty for sacred Japan was stronger than ever when he was assigned to the 22nd Regiment on the Manchuria-Siberia border.

By the time he reported there, he knew he had the makings of a leader. Academy graduates recognized each other at a glance, supreme military bearing distinguishing them from reserve officers. Rigid Kojo would become the exemplar of this elite with its single-minded purpose. Regular officers even walked differently, as if to demonstrate, with their ramrod stiffness and perfect composure, the absence of interest in anything but military concerns. The Academy had trained them never to show weakness, which included all personal emotion. When very occasional entertainers visited from Japan, the men sat cross-legged on the floor beneath the officers' benches. Comedians told jokes and the regular officers' faces remained granite. They would never indulge in something so unmilitary as laughter in sight of the men.

Later in 1940, Kojo was sent to a combat engineering course in Chiba, a city of military schools near Tokyo. Older classmates took him along to a geisha house, that mainstay of officers' entertainment. Handsomer than ever, and with all the normal instincts, the apprentice officer had hardly spoken to a girl outside his family. Now he found the geishas impossibly beautiful — literally impossible, because he couldn't think of a single word to say to them.

But the tongue-tied twenty-year-old was already learning to drink like an officer. On his return from the toilet after a later evening's surfeit of sake, a lovely geisha leaped from ambush in the corridor. The tremulous excitement of his first kiss grew even greater because he still had no idea of what to say or do. "I liked you from the first party," the geisha declared. "Why didn't you talk to me?" Kojo didn't explain that he hadn't dared to look at the women long enough to distinguish one from the other.

He eventually learned what to do from a prostitute back in Manchuria. But he repeated the pleasure rarely, preferring to sublimate his waxing desire to duty. Young officers were expected to perform all physical tasks better than their men. During the day, there were training exercises, maneuvers and session after session of kendo. Evenings were for Army shoptalk over sake.

Although they rarely discussed more than the military aspects of Japan's enemies, Kojo knew what was daily repeated: that the ABCD encirclement — by America, Britain, China, and the Dutch — threatened to reduce his pitifully poor country to permanent poverty and subservience. It seemed to him the height of anti-Japanese hypocrisy for the European powers, fat on their own colonies, to criticize Japan's modest, "justified" imperial efforts. The Emperor's presence at the center of decisions of course guaranteed their wisdom and justice. He also knew Japan to be utterly right in her foreign policy, with a "holy task" to settle her painful scores. Then she of the ancient traditions of the highest virtue would take her proper place in the world as its leading race (as Japanese referred to themselves throughout the war).

Kojo had no doubt and no capacity to doubt; only contempt for doubt. Pearl Harbor disappointed him even as it exhilarated him, for he feared it might delay the settling of scores with Russia. But if it led to fighting America, he relished the prospect; his troops were invincible in hand-to-hand combat. He could no more believe that his men's ceaseless bayonet practice would be nearly worthless in the only combat awaiting him than that his Army was capable of moral wrongs.

In 1943, Kojo was sent to a school for battalion commanders, normally a major's billet. A severe shortage of field officers had developed in the still-expanding and now hard-pressed Army. He himself was a first lieutenant, and all his classmates in the intense, five-month course were his equally young Academy classmates. When he returned to his regiment the next spring, he found that most of the senior officers had been transferred to fighting units elsewhere. He was promoted to captain and the regiment's youngest battalion commander, in command of fifteen hundred men. Another battalion in his regiment was soon detached and sent to an atoll in the Caroline Islands. But although this told the new captain that the island battles were not going easily, no Academy graduate expected victory without sacrifice and setbacks.

Kojo's men also took that victory almost for granted in that summer of 1944. With virtually no information about the world apart from what the Army told them, they knew next to nothing about the enemy's control of the seas, the Empire's strangulation by submarine, even the loss of Guadalcanal, Tarawa and other Pacific islands. They knew less about the ruinous swing in arms advantage as American plants disgorged dizzying quantities of everything military and Japanese plants faltered for lack of fuel and raw materials. Even the handful of men who considered such larger realities doubted their country could be defeated. Japan had never been invaded. Its armies had not lost a war in twenty-three hundred years. In recent times, the sanctified homeland had prevailed against Portuguese, Spanish, Dutch, British, Chinese and Russian aggressors, teaching all those ill-wishers respect by breaking Western imperialism's "stranglehold" in Asia.

Their belief in Japanese invincibility was rooted in their image of themselves as a unique people whose ideals and values were unattainable by others. Their Japanese fighting spirit — the cherished *Yamato damashii* — far surpassed the moral strength of other countries, particularly the democracies. The *Yamato* in this phrase was almost superfluous, inasmuch as *damashii* — nobility, self-sacrifice, purity — could not apply to foreigners. The vast majority of civilians also believed the press reports about Japan's massive blows to the arrogant enemy, and genuinely accepted their leaders' assurances of eventual triumph. Even the tiny minority not raised in the cocoon of Japanese myths, hurts and isolation, even those who suspected something had gone wrong in the Pacific, could not imagine defeat. The Japanese people transcended all others in the spiritual strength — largely achieved by learning to endure pain — that would determine the final outcome.

Yamato damashii helped explain why punched and slapped Japanese soldiers remained confident; in part, it was precisely because they were punched and slapped. One man who would fight on Sugar Loaf Hill "suffered a very great deal" through his entire Army life, yet was convinced that "the system was the basis of Japan's power. Officers were trained to lead, soldiers to carry out their orders. We all learned not to be discouraged but to persevere despite any hardship." In well-trained units like Kojo's 22nd Regiment, it was axiomatic that harsh discipline was vital to hone the Japanese spirit and keep Japan best. The possibility of defeat never occurred to the captain himself, any more than he speculated that gravity would cease operating.

4 · Okinawa

Okinawans tend to be friendly and nonaggressive.
— *Okinawa: A Tiger by the Tail*

[Okinawa] has primitive industry, an earthy beauty [and] idyllic charm in its people and fields.
— *Life* magazine

The mildness, pliability, acquiescence and agreeableness of the people, commented upon by so many observers, are seen as a product of this long period in which a weak and small people was forced to placate two powerful civilizations.
— *The Great Loochoo: A Study of Okinawan Village Life*

[Japan's] many suppositions that the Okinawan people were primitive . . . is a complete error due to ignorance of their true culture and to Okinawan humility . . . The politicians simply regarded these small islands as a burden — so poor, so backward, so unimportant.
— Soetsu Yanagi

It was as pretty and gentle a sight as you ever saw. It had the softness of antiquity about it and the miniature charm and daintiness that we see in Japanese prints.
— Ernie Pyle, reporting from Okinawa by Navy radio

We will never permit a single enemy to step on the Emperor's soil. The enemy has landed on the Philippines and some South Pacific islands but we will make Okinawa the last decisive battleground and destroy him. Defending Okinawa means defending the land of the Emperor . . . Know that you will accept your fate in order to obey the Emperor's will.
— A Japanese colonel to Okinawan conscripts

I left Okinawa knowing little more about it than when I arrived, except for how to use its terrain to kill Japs and try to stay alive.
— Dick Whitaker

IN A NATIONAL radio address in late 1943, Prime Minister Hideki Tojo called the battle for Leyte a Tennozan. Memory of the sixteenth-century battle on which a feudal leader staked his entire army and fate appealed to a people fond of dramatic gestures. However, many Japanese were disturbed by the need to keep shifting visions of the present war's decisive victory to islands ever closer to home. Okinawa's turn came in March 1944. Until then, most of its small garrison had been manning shore batteries or servicing planes and ships for antisubmarine operations. Now Imperial General Headquarters activated the 32nd Army for its defense — but belatedly and with grudging supplies for the new force. Okinawa was only one of many outlying islands that could not be lost.

The first serious shipments of equipment arrived in April 1944, a year before *Yamato's* end. Their meagerness puzzled schoolchildren raised on tales of Japan's invincible might. The arrival of the first troops — chiefly airfield construction units, for IGHQ still considered Okinawa a base for more forward operations — hardly reassured their parents. They seemed a mere token force.

When American strategists began preparing for the campaign, their problem was ignorance: intelligence discovered the Ryukyus were among the world's least explored inhabited areas. Japan had kept foreigners away for over sixty years. A secret War Department study established that fewer than 280 resided there in 1930, ten Russians and two Americans among Formosans, Chinese and Koreans.

If American agents could have landed on Okinawa in 1944, they would have found an ancient patchwork of tiny fields, sparsely inhabited mountains and thousands of sharp ridges and rises — "escarpments," in the language of the troops soon to be pinned down in them. The overwhelming majority of the people were farmers who lived in thin frame houses with thatched roofs or, for the richer ones, tiles. A Chinese lion protected against ill winds and evil spirits. Stone walls and trees attempted the same against the typhoons.

Clustered into South Sea island–like villages, the miniature houses helped make Okinawa a pastoral delight, little spoiled since Commodore Perry's 1854 notation: "It would be difficult for you to imagine the beauties of this island with respect to the charming scenery and the marvelous perfection of cultivation." Even during the early fighting in 1945, Ernie Pyle would crowd his dispatches with descriptions of lovely vistas radiating an aura of gentle beauty. "It all seemed so quiet and peaceful" when the celebrated war correspondent camped one night on a hill overlooking a small river and the soft grass of terraced bluffs.

> You could come from a dozen parts of America and still find scenery on Okinawa that looked like your country at home. Southern boys say the reddish clay and the pine trees remind them of Georgia. Westerners see California in the green rolling hills, partly

wooded, partly patch-worked with little green fields. And the
farmed plains look like our Mid-west. Okinawa is one of the few
places I've been in this war where our troops don't gripe about
what an awful place it is.

A young sailor on a battleship preparing to join the initial naval
bombardment — which alone would ravage the land with over sixty
thousand 5- to 16-inch shells — gazed at the target and felt "I don't
know, real enchanted by it. I felt I was looking at a really beautiful
painting." A lieutenant on a smaller ship wrote his parents that only
Hawaii had seemed prettier in all the Pacific.

> Rich green hills, rolling and irregular, alternately sunny and
> shaded, jut abruptly out of a calm deep blue sea . . . The air [is]
> warm and mild; the sun bright and refulgent . . . Think I'll ad-
> vertise Travel Tours after the war. "Russet, jade hillsides above
> azure water, neath crimson and gold of setting sun . . ." Oh,
> what a setting!

The memory would soon haunt some Americans. The scene of an
ambush — piles of empty cartridge cases, bloody battle dressings, putrid corpses — would prompt one to reflect on the peaceful land's
hideous scourging. "As I looked at the flotsam of battle scattered
along that little path, I was struck with the utter incongruity of it all.
There the Okinawans had tilled their soil with ancient and crude
farming methods; but the war had come, bringing with it the latest
and most refined technology for killing. It seemed so insane, and I
realized that the war was like some sort of disease afflicting man . . .
There on Okinawa the disease was disrupting a place as pretty as a
pastoral painting."

Sensitive Japanese soldiers agreed. Even those who considered the
natives "little brown monkeys"* and yearned to return to "civilization" on the mainland were moved by the Okinawan "dreamland"
and "paradise." "I thought I'd never see anything so beautiful," one
said with a sigh. "The people welcomed us so warmly. They were
friendly, cooperative. Did they have the slightest idea of what would
happen to them and their lovely homeland?" After six wretched days
on a troopship from Kagoshima, another arrival saw red tile roofs —
Okinawan tiling was among the world's most beautiful — amid dazzlingly vivid greens: "a whole island shimmering like a gem in a
dream world . . . Who thought then that the whole of this fairy island
would be burnt down in the flame of an inferno and turned into a
pile of blackened rocks?"

---

*Most Okinawans were indeed darker and shorter than most Japanese. The average
adult was then about five feet tall, wiry and slightly bowlegged.

Okinawans' mixed origins may have accounted for their legendary hospitality. Although those origins remain undocumented, recent ethnological and botanical research indicates the island was never part of Japan proper. The earliest Ryukyuans probably descended from peoples who crossed a prehistoric land bridge from the Asian continent, then were joined by Malaysians and Micronesians carried north by the prevailing Black Current and by Japanese from the north. In later centuries, Chinese visitors were common, Okinawans being among the Asian peoples in Peking's orbit. Eighteenth-century Chinese observers found the island country very poor — the poorest of all he knew, one concluded — but unfailingly gracious, as their name for it affirmed: *Shurei no kuni,* "the Nation of Constant Courtesy." Another believed that "the absence of crime and the simplicity of punishment betokened an approach to the ideal society set forth in the classics, where all men knew their proper place and none violated the law."

Western visitors were likely to romanticize backward natives whose lives they hardly knew. But enough were experienced travelers to give weight to their reactions, especially since they were nearly unanimous. A Dutch scholar set the pattern in the late seventeenth century. "The inhabitants . . . are a good-natured, merry sort of people leading an agreeable, contented life, diverting themselves after their work is done with a glass of rice beer and playing upon their musical instruments, which they carry out with them into the fields for this purpose."

One of the next European arrivals was a Royal Navy officer charting Far Eastern waters. In 1816, Captain Basil Hall found "an honest, peaceful, unassuming people, with neither money nor arms, kindly, hospitable and without guile, secure within the classes in which their society was originated." Hall's grandson added that Okinawans' most prominent characteristics were "their gentleness of spirit and manner, their yielding and submissive disposition, their hospitality and kindness, their aversion to violence and crime."

Okinawans may have been gentle because they had no choice. Until the establishment of the first lasting dynasty in the thirteenth century, warlords had battled one another much as in Japan, if less fiercely. Now the islanders were squeezed by China and Japan as those powers competed to control them and also helpless against the approach of hungry Portuguese, Dutch, English and other Westerners. Still, observer after observer noted their mildness and acquiescence, even in comparison to other subtropical islands. "Nothing can exceed the honesty of these good and kindhearted people . . . the greatest anxiety and every means [were] used to render our situation comfortable," noted a shipwrecked sailor. A surgeon on a British ship stated that Okinawans "displayed a spirit of intelligence and genius which seemed the more extraordinary, considering the confined circle in which they live . . . the kindness and hospitality of [the] inhabitants have fixed upon every mind a deep and lasting impression of gratitude and esteem." Some visitors wondered how such an open, gracious, good-humored people could exist.*

The absence of arms astonished the visitors. Stopping at St. Helena on his way home, Captain Hall told a thunderstruck Napoleon that Okinawans had no cannon, muskets, bows, arrows or even daggers. The Emperor was scornful of a people who lacked the means of waging war. On the other hand, the Okinawan language, which had a common root with old Japanese but diverged into a separate tongue, was rich in terms of hospitality. The islanders startled ships by provisioning them without charge from their meager stores. "No people we have yet met with have been so friendly, for the moment they came alongside, one handed a jar of water to us, and another a basket of boiled sweet potatoes, without asking or seeming to wish for any recompense," wrote Hall.

Of course there had always been a full share of nasty schemers. But the prevailing tenderness still pervaded the landscape and people in 1944, enough to make men of both armies feel it almost tangibly when they landed. Together with fleas, flies and superstition, the "delightful" island, as *Life* magazine would call it, had a touch of paradise.

It was also a paradise for malaria and other tropical diseases, and the Ryukyus had higher rates of tuberculosis and venereal diseases then all other Japanese prefectures. Okinawans, with their laggard economic development and island sense of time, had a stubborn, southern resistance to industrial discipline. Most were honest and did their work well but at a pace and without a drive to achieve that

---

*Other comments seem exaggerated, unless one remembers the hardships of sea voyages by sail and the delight in landing where natives weren't hostile. "A worthy, friendly, and a happy race of people." ". . . The singular humanity of the natives . . . behaving with a degree of politeness which rendered their company very pleasing." "For gentle dignity of manners, superior advancement in the arts, and general intelligence, the inhabitants . . . are by far the most interesting enlightened nation in the Pacific Ocean."

But Okinawa's tenderness still surprises modern travelers — even at bullfights, which celebrate a kind of reductio ad minimum of violence. A 1991 visitor watched two fat, sloppy and hornless bulls led into a ring of earthen levees. Loving owners made them touch noses, after which the beasts attempted to push each other down. The winner "has ribbons tied around his head, is given a large bottle of Asahi dry beer to guzzle and is then drenched in sake. The audience does much the same — and so the Okinawan evening proceeds, with everyone, four-legged or two, getting pleasantly tipsy, and then going home, to house or to byre."

irritated Japanese. After the battle, a young native would notice a contrast between his prisoner of war camp and scrupulously neat Japanese ones nearby. Japanese amateur shows boasted costumes ingeniously fashioned from old parachutes, whereas Okinawan actors chose to "go back to ancient times," appearing almost naked.*

Okinawa's problems included an internal caste system and vigorous snobbery. As most Japanese looked down at most Okinawans, rich Okinawans, especially from the cities, tended to look down at farming villagers, who did the same to inhabitants of the smaller Ryukyu islands. More painfully, there was overcrowding. The island's southern third, where by far the hardest fighting would take place, was over four times more densely populated than Rhode Island. This would contribute to the coming battle's extraordinary toll in civilian deaths, as it had contributed to centuries of poverty. "When you come to Okinawa," a folk song advised, "please wear straw shoes" — for the coral was as hard on bare feet as it was to cultivation. The majority of the population eked out their existence on thin, harsh soil. Nature took away almost as much as it gave. The chronicle of natural disasters, especially crop-ruining, house-flattening typhoons, reads like the drum rolls of a dirge to a little people also regularly decimated by drought, plague and famine. "The whole fragile, minuscule structure survived throughout the centuries at bare subsistence level," a Western historian summarized. No threat to anyone, the patch of meager land would never be a prize, except for its strategic position in other nations' plans.

Poverty remained widespread in 1944. It was rooted in subtropical lassitude, agricultural backwardness and the typhoons that regularly ravaged housing and crops. The 1940 population, about 475,000 before the battle in 1945, owned 250 motor vehicles, one to every two thousand persons. A quarter were busses. In "poor" Japan, which felt compelled to seize other people's land, the average farmer farmed five *tan*, about one and a quarter acres. It was two *tan* on Okinawa, and per capita income was about half the mainland average.

Farmers usually went without shoes. They planted their tiny fields chiefly with sugar cane, most of the crop now going to the mainland's war-economy alcohol, and with sweet potatoes. The blessed sweet potato, which had arrived on a seventeenth-century ship returning from delivering tribute to the Chinese court, remained the mainstay

---

*The shows themselves revealed the same contrast, skillful Japanese performing with far more refinement than the Okinawans, who presented chiefly "farmers' plays." But Okinawan theater had always been more ribald and accessible than Japanese Kabuki and No plays; also more fun.

of the "poor man's" diet.* A naval research unit that would analyze soil samples after the American landing first discovered that "Okinawa's earth was made of sweet potatoes — everywhere we dug." Next, it found the fields were "generously fertilized with night soil — a rich source . . . of typhoid and paratyphoid bacilli, which a month later [in May 1945, when the fighting was most severe] produced a mild outbreak among our troops."

Despite great hunger for farmland, much of the island remained untilled. The mountain soil was too thin, large tracts were covered with sand and thousands of coral escarpments had no covering at all — thus an even more intense cultivation of the arable land. Although private ownership had replaced an ancient system of common ownership, a long history of village responsibility for the common welfare bound the little hamlets, also tightly linked by family ties, in a deep sense of cooperation and community obligation.

Bean soup, a few garden vegetables and very occasional pork and fish provided relief from the sweet potatoes. Rice was a luxury for many farmers. They considered rain good weather, since water was scarce despite a heavy annual rainfall, most of which ran off the coral. But there was much laughter and song. There was an easygoing attitude toward one's time on earth, far easier than in intense, driven mainland Japan.

Soetsu Yanagi, the "father" of Japanese folk art, visited in 1939 and extolled Okinawa's simplicity, "naturalness," and freedom from the corruption of the machine — all that helped to keep the natives poor. But the careful observer had reason to fall in love with the island's uninhibited literature, music, architecture, sculpture, dancing and decorative arts — and the way in which all were woven, like the vivid local cloth, into daily life. The hand-dyed cloth itself expressed the comic sweetness of most Okinawan art: in carefree disregard of seasonal limitations, bold brilliant flowers were celebrated together with falling snow. "This tiny chain of islands adrift in the ocean has had a singular and independent cultural history of a thousand years," Yanagi concluded. "Okinawans possess a richness of artistic inheritance in arts and crafts such as to put cultural values above the economic."

Much of the amusement came at *mo-ashibi*, a village picnic or "field play-around." Almost everyone danced and sang there — and elsewhere. "Musical life was in the streets, the homes, and the fields . . .

---

*Although the hero who returned with it from China isn't known by name, he "nonetheless is a very celebrated person in Ryukyuan history and life," as Morton Morris wrote. The tuber's role in preventing starvation would never be greater than during the forthcoming battle and its aftermath.

Everybody sings: one starts and at once others gather and join in . . . Songs of innocence, songs of heaven." The innocence was spiritual; sexual mores were distinctly more relaxed than Japan's. A young man who didn't meet his love at a *mo-ashibi* was likely to visit her at night, and bastards weren't scorned as in Japan. Women's supervision of ceremonial and spiritual life gave them more status than in Japan; separate purses provided greater independence.

The relative lack of inhibition and stricture may have nourished Okinawans' ability to survive the coming battle. Struck by the rarity of mental breakdown despite their tremendous physical and mental strains in 1945, an American psychologist later suggested that emotional security from prolonged breast feeding on demand was strong enough to withstand even that holocaust. Another concluded that Okinawa was "of vast significance to those interested in child guidance" because the young were raised in the bosom of community gentleness as well as in abundant parental love. Psychiatrists speculated that absence of fear thanks to emotional stability was the reason that not one of fifteen hundred young children cried when their fingers were pricked for a blood test.

> *Manifestations of extreme nationalism — the mass hysteria which swept Japan along the road to national defeat — were unpopular in Okinawa. The common people could not afford the "voluntary" contributions; they had no traditions glorifying war and the fighting man . . . [But] children at school were subjected to an intensive propaganda campaign and stirred to admiration for heroic deeds reported from the China warfront . . . The youths of Okinawa were prepared to do their duty.*
> — George Kerr, about the late 1930s

> *Throughout the Sino-Japanese War, the Russo-Japanese War and the China Incident to the Pacific War, Okinawans' thought patterns and activities very well reflected their idea that the more they sacrifice themselves for the Japanese cause, the quicker they will reach their goal of attaining identity with Japan. Okinawan sacrifice in the . . . Pacific War disclosed the cruel result of this thought pattern more than sufficiently.*
> — Masahide Ota, one of the youths eager to do his duty

The Otas of Kume Island were even poorer than their counterparts on Okinawa, fifty miles west. Like many of the lesser inhabited Ryukyus, little Kume lagged behind Okinawa economically as Okinawa lagged behind the Japanese mainland. Masahide Ota grew up with the children who rose at dawn to help their mothers on tiny farms before setting off for school. Masahide's mother raised him and three older children alone: her husband was among the sixty thousand Ryukyuans who emigrated in search of relief for their families during the decades following World War I, in his case to Brazil, just after Masahide's birth.

Masahide was a tough lad, his little body hardened by the work of feeding the family horse, cow and handful of goats. His robust health was threatened only by teeth decayed from his chewing black sugar, but they toughened him further: in the absence of dentists and drugs, he learned to endure the pain of his cavities. He grew to adolescence without movies or thoughts of girls but enjoyed baseball on days when he didn't have to hurry from school to his duties on the farm. The bat was whittled from a fence post. There were no gloves or masks. Masahide played catcher until a foul tip smashed the bridge of his nose.

The ocean was visible from his little house. Gazing at it, the poor young villager with the round face and big eyes thought of his father, of joining him in Brazil, of crossing the water to the larger world. The village school, a modest building beside a stand of towering old pine trees, had no library, and the Otas had never had books at home, but older boys of neighbors returned from schools on Okinawa with a few. Groping through a work of a well-known Japanese philosopher, Masahide was surprised by the notion that people thought about life's meaning and purpose. Until then, he had lived and farmed with no questions about why and no suspicion that questions existed.

In school, he learned that America practiced racial discrimination against Asians as well as blacks and that it was corrupted by something ugly and weak called democracy. The only Japanese he saw were school inspectors, to whom the student body bowed so deeply that they might have kneeled. On Japanese national holidays, such as the Emperor's birthday, they also bowed in the direction of the Imperial Palace in Tokyo, a thousand miles northeast. The principal donned white gloves to hold and read the Imperial Rescript on Education.

In 1941, sixteen-year-old Masahide boarded a ferry for the eight-hour trip covering the fifty miles to Okinawa. Top students in outer island elementary schools were awarded free places in Okinawa's Normal School, chief training ground for Ryukyuan schoolteachers. Top in his Kume elementary school, Masahide arrived in his school uniform, nervous and very curious. He hadn't considered engineering or some other profession because that would have been pointless. The scholarship was his one lucky chance to be educated.

The Normal School stood at the foot of Shuri Castle in Okinawa's former capital. It was the highest educational institution in the Ryukyus, the only Japanese prefecture of the forty-seven lacking a uni-

versity. Ota learned that baseball had a third base; on Kume, they
had played with two. The dazzled farm boy heard recorded music
for the first time — patriotic music, for Okinawa was being milita-
rized, although not to the extent of the Japanese mainland. Village
festivals and the singing of nonmilitary songs had been prohibited.
Ota learned a new ditty: "Monday, Monday, Tuesday, Wednesday,
Thursday, Friday, Friday." It was sung by middle-school boys who
had no weekends or half days: they were put to work restoring an
old system of tunnels beneath Shuri Castle and helping with other
military projects, in Ota's case the construction of new airfields at
Kadena and Yomitan, over twenty miles north. The boys walked
there and stayed overnight, digging and carting earth during every
spare moment.

Strict as the segregation of the sexes had become in ordinary
middle schools — a cardinal rule of Japanese administration — it was
much more so in the Normal School for future holders of the high
title of native teachers. Movies were prohibited. (Ota sneaked in just
once.) Boys were forbidden to exchange a word with girls. But young
Ota had no such interest to suppress. The prestigious Normal
School, half of whose teachers were mainland Japanese, was the realization of his dream. He loved learning and again did so well that
he was appointed one of the three adjutants to the principal (who
held a colonel's rank in the Army). The elevation moved him from
his dormitory to a little room next to the principal's in Government
House.

In that official residence, every attempt was made to practice the
most solemn mainland ways, which flattered the intensely dedicated
Ota even as he struggled to complete everything on time and correctly. He fairly ached with desire to be worthy of his honors and to
prove himself to his superiors. The great pride he took in his school's
geographical and political position at the heart of Okinawan affairs
swelled further after Pearl Harbor. The exciting war with America
made every little duty more important; it promised a chance for full
approval for something supremely loyal and demanding for Japan.
In short, he was the picture of a teenager bursting with patriotism —
but with the difference common to many nations recently taken over
or absorbed by a larger one. In fact, Ota represented two of Okinawa's problems. The native elite was more moved to prove itself to
a mother country or occupying power than to consider its people's
needs — and the ordinary people had long been too trusting and
submissive.

In 1944, the upper crust, into which Ota would soon graduate, saw
the war largely as an opportunity at last to win acceptance by their

former conquerers. That small caste included toadies to rich and powerful Japanese on Okinawa itself. It also embraced the whole range of Uncle Toms who appeared under colonialism and oppression — inevitably, since most good jobs and professional careers could be won only by shining in the Japanese-regulated schools, then going to the mainland for higher education or business opportunities. In any case, Ota and, more important, his Okinawan teachers in the predominantly Japanese Normal School were far from typical.

This showed most clearly in their attitudes toward the war. When it tightened around Japan in 1942 and 1943 and she tightened her hold on Okinawa, most natives felt a jumble of contradictions rather than the grateful patriotism of the elite eager to compensate for the disadvantage of not being Japanese. It almost went without saying that the Okinawan majority wanted victory for the Rising Sun. Yet they could not easily forget their history, little of which endeared Japan to them.

Okinawans had not always been so poor. In the fifteenth and sixteenth centuries, their ships ranged to China, Korea, Java, the South Sea islands and Japan. They were welcomed as honest traders; sailors and artifacts of a dozen nationalities enlivened their principal port of Naha. Sporadic raids and incursions by Japanese pirates were only a minor threat to the melting-pot culture. Open to the world, at peace with their neighbors, Okinawans flourished like Far Eastern Venetians, in control of their own commerce and destiny.

They drank too much — especially awamori, a potent liquor distilled from Thai rice. Too much of their trading profits went to rich town dwellers and to the court's elaborate ceremonies, derived from Peking's. The Chinese observer who spoke of all Okinawans knowing their "proper place" was describing a society of great hardship for the farming majority stuck at the bottom — on whose backs Ryukyu kings built and maintained their castle in Shuri, the hilltop capital four miles above Naha. But in addition to its beguiling crafts and culture, the "toy state" had essential decency and unusual tolerance. Even its farmers prospered, compared with those in later eras.

Near the end of the sixteenth century, Japan's most powerful feudal ruler ordered Okinawa to contribute men and arms to an invasion of China. But Shuri Castle disliked military campaigns. It is generally believed that Okinawans refused to support a huge Mongol invasion of Japan in the thirteenth century, after which Mongol forces ravaged the island in punishment. Now Japan was the aggressor, and Shuri still disliked invasions.

It did not want to spoil its trade with Korea, through which the invaders would attack. It was even more reluctant to offend China, its cultural model and most valued trading partner. The Loochoo Islands — Chinese for the characters pronounced "Ryukyu" in Japanese — were officially recognized as a client state of the Empire and paid tribute to the Emperor.* The King's respectful answer apologized that great distance and lack of funds had kept his "small and humble island kingdom" from rendering due reverence to the Japanese ruler, but now he was sending some gifts "with the sole desire to show our sincerity and courtesy and not because we think [these articles] of any great value."

This didn't work. And the death of the Japanese ruler (who attacked Korea without Okinawa's help) was even worse for the islanders. This was because Shuri, probably misinformed about the amazingly bloody events in Japan, declined to send respects to the feudal lord who won the struggle to succeed him.

A powerful family named Shimazu had fought with the losers in that fierce clash for succession. The Shimazus were lords of the remote, mountainous province where Tadashi Kojo's ancestor had settled, a curiosity on the nation's geographical and psychological extremities, somewhat like the place of Wales in Great Britain. Satsuma's closed, clannish people spoke a dialect that puzzled other Japanese. As those others became westernized with astonishing speed after Perry's arrival, Satsuma's 600,000 inhabitants clung to their traditions. Roughly 40 percent — over 70 percent in the city of Kagoshima — were samurai, many as poor as ordinary farmers in more prosperous provinces. Stoicism, obedience and service to one's rulers — when not rebelling against them — were admired everywhere in Japan, but more so there. In that sense, the generally more narrow and militaristic Satsuma people were right to consider themselves the most Japanese Japanese. It was Okinawans' bad luck that those lovers of arms were their closest Japanese neighbors.

The Shimazu lord coveted the island's profitable maritime trade as much as he wanted to ingratiate himself with the new regime in Edo (the former name of Tokyo), which he had failed to support. He requested permission to punish Shuri for not having paid respects to the same new regime — the one that would soon close Japan. The new rulers in Edo were surely happy to divert warlike Satsuma to a harmless enterprise at sea, in the opposite direction from themselves.

In 1609, the Shimazu lord dispatched three thousand men in over a hundred war junks from Kagoshima Bay. Satsuma warriors were renowned for their skill and ferocity. A scattering of Okinawan arms

*Other transliterations for the Loochoos — "bubbles floating on the water" — are Luchu, Lew Chew, Loo Choo and Liu Ch'iu.

had been stored since their last use over two centuries earlier. The untrained islanders' frantic resistance was easily overcome; Shuri Castle was taken and looted. Irreplaceable national treasures were taken off to Kagoshima, together with the King. The devastating expedition that ended the small country's separate development grew out of the very conditions that had made that development so promising: the refusal of the Nation of Constant Courtesy to join bigpower military conflicts.

Skillfully applying his overwhelming force, the Shimazu lord forced Okinawans to bear responsibility for their own pitiless persecution. After three years of imprisonment, the King pledged an oath recognizing an (imagined) "ancient" dependency on Satsuma, apologizing for the recent troubles and swearing indebtedness and obedience for himself and his heirs "forever." A royal adviser who refused to sign the documents specifying those terms was beheaded. Okinawa's Golden Age was over. She would never again control her own destiny.

Satsuma control explained the lack of arms on Okinawa: its overlords permitted none.* Shimazu exploitation was so drastic that when the King returned and saw its effects, he ordered that he not be buried in the royal tombs, a gesture of supreme significance where the highest spiritual goal was reunion with one's ancestors.

Satsuma's taxes, roughly an eighth of the kingdom's annual revenues, reduced most of the people to terrible poverty. Men paid in rice, in some cases up to 80 percent of the annual yield. Women paid in their beautifully patterned cloth, so much of which had to be woven for Japanese kimonos that some may have felt forced to suffocate their infant daughters to save them from a life of misery like their own. Much of the scant food left after paying the tributes was lost to the droughts, fires and earthquakes that continued to ravage the is-

---

*This prompted cultivation of the activity for which Okinawa is better known to Americans and Europeans than anything else. The martial art of unarmed self-defense called karate is not strictly Okinawan, having been originally borrowed, like so much else in its culture, from China. Combining Chinese kung-fu with the new weapons — forged by repeated pounding — of their own hands (*te*) and feet, some Okinawans trained in secret on what they hoped would be a new means of resistance. The aim was to penetrate the Japanese armor of lacquered bamboo and to use farm poles and threshing sticks — anything solid — to counter the steel of samurai swords. Although those methods proved useless in driving away the oppressors, Okinawans "passed down the legacy of their art," as a devotee recently wrote, "developed by the small and weak to deal with a larger, better-armed adversary . . . In time it came to be known as *kara-te*, meaning both 'China hand' and 'emptyhanded.'"

Okinawans also used scythes, which occasionally severed enemies' limbs. The hairpins worn by well-groomed women were sometimes stuck into male flesh, even by other males. But in George Kerr's words, the Japanese "had been nurtured for centuries in traditions of war, which exalted skill in close combat and glorified the mystique of self-sacrifice. Not so the Okinawans."

land, and the dreaded typhoons that destroyed hundreds of fishing craft and thousands of houses year after year. No famine moved Satsuma to reduce its demands. A document written twenty-six years after imposition of the taxes suggested that the kingdom's income had fallen by some 60 percent.

Satsuma also seized total control of Okinawa's foreign trade, which became more profitable when Japan was closed in 1636. Not subject to the Japanese prohibitions, Okinawans continued trading abroad. That was a large loophole for the Shimazus, whose profits waxed, since other provinces had no such access to foreign goods. The artful lords ordered the Shuri court to maintain a fictitious independence so that the China trade would proceed undisturbed. Okinawans were thus forced to fish, as a native scholar described the arrangement, but forbidden to eat the catch. Unable to rebel, they could only accommodate, stall and temporize — but, in the end, pay their duty to remorseless Satsuma, which watched everything through the sharp eyes of its concealed overseers and watchdogs.

Outside Satsuma, vast changes followed Perry's visit. Reformers argued that the only way to overcome the enormous crisis of foreign competition was to sweep away the old order. The Meiji Restoration, named after the Emperor whose reign began in 1867, is taken as the turning point between feudal and modern Japan. Four years later, Tokyo, which had assumed responsibility for the Ryukyus from the Shimazus, informed China that Okinawans were Japanese.* Peking also claimed them in a kind of defensive reflex. Okinawans played no part in the competition for Okinawa.

The Chinese would have won a landslide victory in a referendum asking which court Okinawans least disliked. But Japan mounted an expedition, and weak China eventually recognized the sovereignty of expansionist Japan.

Dismayed Okinawans watched new teams of overseers arrive from Tokyo to impose its will and cultural truncheons on the island. "Loochoo" was changed to "Ryukyu" in 1875. Four years later, troops occupied Shuri Castle. The monarchy was abolished, the islands were annexed. The King's exile to Tokyo ended seven centuries of recorded history as an independent kingdom or kingdoms. The effect on national life and the national spirit was catastrophic.

Okinawa's subsequent history was essentially one of Japanization,

* Tokyo's real prize was control of Korea, for which it used its claim on the Ryukyus as a lever on China. Five years later, Japan opened Korea more painfully than she herself had been opened, threatening use of military force and finally applying brutal oppression. Meanwhile, she accomplished her first annexation in the Kurile Islands.

for which it paid heavily in cash. Three years after annexation, the tax burden was twice that of the mainland prefecture closest in size and population. Forty-three years later, in 1925, the disparity between revenues paid to Tokyo and appropriations for island expenditures had tripled. Tens of thousands of farming families gasped and wept. There was scant pity for them on the mainland, where student digs posted prohibitions against Koreans, Okinawans and dogs. The worst racism was openly scandalous. A pavilion outside a 1903 industrial exhibition featured women from a local brothel smoking long-handled pipes in a thatched-roof house. A guide — whip in hand, as if dealing with animals — passed them off as members of the Okinawan nobility. Protests from Peking and Seoul put an end to similar displays of Chinese and Korean women, but the Okinawan show went on, despite imploring objections to this degradation of supposed fellow citizens. With their greater racial "deviance" than Koreans, Okinawans were made to suffer even more grievously for their failure to be pure Japanese, that most valued national quality.

Tokyo solemnly explained that the gap between Okinawan and mainland living standards could be closed only gradually — while it continued to widen. Textbooks treated Okinawa as a foreign country but, disingenuously, claimed the Ryukyus had been Japanese since near prehistoric times; Okinawans and Japanese were declared to be of a single race, culture and language. Even after Okinawa and the Ryukyus farther south were designated Okinawa Prefecture, they continued to be treated like a colony. Most prefectural governors felt insulted by their "exile" to the backwater and despised the natives. Tokyo was wont to replace the few who tried to take their plight seriously. Even during the best "reigns," most Japanese on the island considered native farmers laughable yokels and all Okinawans racially inferior, as proved by their lack of dedication to *bushido*, "the way of the warrior."

Some modernization was launched. Slowly, often reluctantly, Tokyo expanded the school system, school being where the fullest effort was made to convert easygoing Okinawans to devoted, disciplined citizens of the Empire. The Japanese language was mandatory in schools and government offices, part of a campaign to suppress Okinawan dress, customs and names along with the language. Okinawans were not permitted to vote in national elections for twenty-two years after the residents of other prefectures. It was more than forty years before their legislative representation was put on an equal basis with that of other Japanese subjects. They remained second- and third-class citizens, regularly excluded from their own island's specks of luxury. In the mid-1930s, some of Naha's best hotels and most fashionable streets remained reserved for Japanese officials and businessmen who arrived from the mainland to govern and control the commerce.

After their annexation, many Okinawans were as opposed to having their youth serve in the Japanese Army as the Army was opposed to recruiting from that "inferior" material. They warned that maintaining an armed force on the island would invite invasion by foreigners with whom they had no quarrel. Many Okinawan boys didn't have to serve anyway, since far more than on the mainland were below the minimum height and weight. Poor, nonindustrialized Okinawa, which lagged behind in almost every such way, would contribute less to the war effort than any other prefecture.

By 1939, the high school curriculum included obligatory military training and the Army stopped rejecting most Ryukyuan boys. Okinawans were further trapped in the mainland's mutually exclusive policies of cultural assimilation because they had to be made Japanese and continued colonial treatment because they could never make the grade. Genuine assimilation was almost impossible even for the rare native who intermarried across the wide general gulf.

When the war began, a sharp intensification of the old campaign to impose Japanese order on loose native ways succeeded chiefly on the surface of public life, largely in the cities. With their rounder features and more relaxed movements, the islanders' very appearance belied the claim of some Japanese — when it suited them, usually in demands for more sacrifice — that Okinawans were as Japanese as they. The residents of the former kingdom differed from the mainlanders in a hundred cultural ways, from their gentle humor to their lack of concern for racial purity and Imperial divinity. The "yokels" continued producing their beautiful textiles — which irritated Prime Minister Tojo when he stopped in Okinawa on his way home from a 1943 visit to the Asian continent. "What do *they* have to do with the war effort?" he snapped.

The young and the elite, still struggling through the Japanese-regulated schools and Japanese-dominated institutions in order to achieve their ambitions in everything from medicine to business, provided most of the exceptions. Some thought the island as a whole could advance only through the mother country that controlled the economy and the influence. "To put it as clearly as possible," Okinawa's first newspaper had preached in devotion to total assimilation, "even our manner of sneezing should be the same as that of Japanese main-islanders." Many educated, influential Okinawans joined the crusade to expunge Okinawa's "peculiar" cultural diversity, its very identity. Some of the brightest tried, like Masahide Ota, to prove their loyalty by becoming more Japanese than the Japanese. But the great mass of farming families remained almost entirely in their old world of tiny fields and ancestral tombs.

Perhaps the most salient contrast with the Japanese was in the attitude toward life and death. Okinawans revered their ancestors but not as warriors. The most noticeable man-made feature of the landscape was the great number of tombs. The earliest had been in caves that honeycombed the island. Later, when aboveground structures were constructed, most families spent as much money and effort as possible on the dwelling place for all eternal spirits. One of the two most prominent designs was shaped like a little house, often built into a hill unsuited for cultivation. The other, probably imported later from China, looked like a turtle's back, the turtle being a symbol of long life — or, as many had it, a vagina opening into a womb, the idea being that all return to their source after their earthly passage. The Okinawan versions had a oddly gentle beauty. A visiting artist was surprised by the "extraordinary fine shape" of even poor farmers' efforts.

The family tomb was the site for picnics and holidays. Three years after death, the bones of the decomposed body were washed, then placed in a beautifully colorful ceramic urn inside the tomb for thirty-three years, when a memorial service was held and the now floating spirits were venerated — but with no glorification of death, let alone hunger to serve or sacrifice for a nationalist cause. Like Tadashi Kojo, many Japanese men who wanted to give their lives for the Emperor seemed less interested in a good life than in a stylish death, signifying superior moral commitment and the unconquerable Japanese fighting spirit. Even the minority of Okinawans who tried hardest to copy the Japanese ethic spoke of Okinawa as distinct from Japan, largely because her Emperor cult and world mission were artificial interests. The Normal School boys wanted nothing more than to cultivate a romance with a brave, honorable death, but the idea was foreign to the vast majority of Okinawans.

Stunning Japanese victories from 1931 to 1941 did convince many Okinawans that Japan, not Okinawa, was indeed divine and destined to rule the world. Until then, they had long been skeptical of nationalist ambitions and military methods, and had felt much good will toward the United States in particular. Many of the sixty thousand Ryukyuans who emigrated by 1930 were in Argentina, the Japanese mainland and Brazil, with Ota's father. But many went to Hawaii and

California. The savings sent back from their chiefly laboring wages there represented riches to their families.

Pearl Harbor wasn't enough to squelch those good feelings. In the Normal School, where Ota's best friend had a passion for English, there was little notion that large numbers of Americans had to be killed. But propaganda about Americans' polluting lust and racism was much intensified, especially in the schools, when Japan began losing the war. Japanese cartoons of sweating, apelike Americans hung in classrooms and filled magazines. Endless articles and broadcasts warned that the enemy's deepest desire was to rule the world and to torture, rape, murder or enslave all Asians; that even American children had been utterly brainwashed to "Kill Japs!" The magazines urged their readers to "annihilate your hateful foe!" In light of the triumph of equally outrageous propaganda in better-educated Europe in the 1930s and 1940s, it is not so surprising that the message got through.

Now, in 1944, most Okinawans felt torn. They were proud to see their island transformed into a center of Japanese activity, happy to play this crucial role for the Empire after their long relegation to the most menial ones. However, some resented the black market, shortage of goods and lowered living standards, since money could no longer be sent in by émigrés abroad — as well as the inevitable rapes and the Army's commandeering of so many of the slim civilian resources.* Still others, or the same proud people at different moments, felt themselves colonials trampled by Japanese combat boots and secretly hoped the potentially catastrophic battle would continue to be fought in the patriotic imagination.

Japanese officers were quartered in the homes of the rich and educated, and it was they and the schoolchildren, even those less elevated than Ota, who were most likely to link their fate to Japan, believing that the greater the sacrifices, the more honor would be won from Tokyo. Families lucky enough to be assigned non-arrogant officers were honored to drink sake with their guests. Here was a chance to prove that Okinawa wasn't the backwater for which she had always been taken. After the war, many of the elite — if they survived — who had felt a greater association with the mainland than ever would prefer to forget how much they had wanted Japan to win: how as teachers they had exhorted their charges to compete for frugality by bringing to school the scantiest lunch (a rice ball with a pickled

---

*Very few rapes were reported because Okinawan women tended to be caught up in the general patriotism or as intimidated by the mood of national crisis as by the offending soldiers themselves. And not all natives were victims. In some cases, young Okinawan women sold themselves to soldiers, or their parents sold them.

plum); how they feverishly praised Japanese ways as writers and editors. Anguished men and women would wonder how they could have abandoned Okinawa's culture for Japan's.

But nothing could have been further from the yearning minds of Masahide Ota and his fellows. When the 32nd Army began arriving in 1944 and its highest-ranking officers clustered in Shuri's administrative and cultural centers, the students were thrilled to be so near their Japanese heroes. The headquarters of the newly activated 32nd Army were on the hill just above the Normal School. It was beyond the boys' faintest doubt that the immensely impressive men who came and went from there would easily deal with the enemy if he was foolish enough to attempt an invasion. What could have been more certain than those splendid officers' promise to smash the American devils to smithereens?

"Ordinary" Okinawans were less exhilarated. Long defenseless against natural disasters and powerful visitors, they had an old saying about smallpox — a terrible disease that, however, had to be treated with courtesy and care if the wind brought it to the island, and with prayers that it would leave as soon as possible. Now those farmers and workers had no chance to resist the hostilities into which Japan was pushing and dragging them, even to talk resistance except with trusted friends in secluded places. The only escape, for which most of the people quietly prayed, was for their little homeland not to be invaded. Yet it was clear that a white enemy craving to torture their families to death had to be defeated if he did invade. "Drive them off quickly," they thought, "before they can kill us or damage the island." There was no alternative.

That is why the first months of the military build-up worried them. Soon after the commander of the 32nd Army arrived on March 29, 367 days before the start of the battle, a story spread that he had interrupted a speech to dash, wincing, to a window. General Masao Watanabe had heard an airplane approaching! Though he was relieved to recognize a friendly silhouette in the sky, the gloomy general told his audience that roars up there would no longer necessarily be Japanese. Watanabe warned that the enemy would almost certainly land, in which case all Okinawans would share the Army's fate. "Be resolute and go down in *gyokusai*," he urged, repeating an insistent new Imperial slogan. *Gyokusai* — literally a gem shattered into myriad pieces — meant dying an honorable death for the Emperor. The mainland's cry for a hundred million *gyokusai* could be translated as "Better we all die."

Watanabe's indignation over his inadequate supplies was predictably contagious. "An enemy landing here means just three things," he was said to have informed civic leaders. "Death for you, death for me, death for all of us. Have you seen the tanks and antiaircraft guns we've got on this rock pile? Just so much junk." He was in bad health — suffering a nervous breakdown, some civilians believed — when he was rotated after four months. He might have been replaced in any case: after Saipan's fall in July 1944, Imperial General Headquarters at last saw Okinawa not as a rear base but as a possible enemy target, where a top commander with a proper force was needed. In August, eight months before the start of the battle, troopships and freighters crowded Naha harbor while formations of silver-winged warplanes flew overhead. Okinawans watched wide-eyed as a parade of tanks, trucks and artillery pieces clanked by, cracking their asphalt streets. "Our island was turning into the mightiest fortress in all the Pacific — a fact that filled us with pride and apprehension," a native novelist recorded. "Many secretly prayed for deliverance from the horrible war which, some of us felt, Japan was imposing on us."

The 32nd Army was becoming Japan's hope for the new Tennozan.

5 · From Manchuria to Okinawa

We now knew that only Okinawa lay between the home islands of Japan and their invasion; so did our captors.
— An Australian dying in a Japanese POW camp

We were very confident we would beat the Russians. We knew almost nothing about American weapons, tactics or industrial power, but felt we could beat them too. Our training had blinded us to all reality.
— Tadashi Kojo, 1985

No, thank you, no more war. We were fooled and betrayed by a segment of professional soldiers. War kills victors and losers alike.
— A survivor of the *Toyama maru*

I still remember some Okinawan phrases I learned at that time. For some reason, all of them have to do with hospitality.
— Ikuo Ogiso, a Japanese soldier

CAPTAIN KOJO was troubled. Except for attending service schools, he had served in Manchuria throughout his four years as an officer, but now his division was pulling out. Had the years of fervent training to smash the Russians been for nothing? Was the Pacific War going so badly that the jewel of the Empire had to be exposed to those predators? Kojo didn't know that the fall of Saipan — breeching an Absolute National Defense Zone established less than a year earlier — had prompted Imperial General Headquarters hurriedly to shift forces, especially to Formosa. Still, the order to withdraw was disturbing.

His fifteen-thousand-man 24th Division would be the largest and best-equipped component of the Japanese force on Okinawa, but it traveled there light: much transport and service personnel had to be left behind. Kojo's 22nd Regiment, less the battalion that had been shipped to the atoll in the Carolines and some eight hundred men sent to China, boarded trains in July 1944, just as Dick Whitaker was traveling to boot camp and frail General Watanabe was spending his last days in command of the new 32nd Army on Okinawa. A thousand miles overland to Pusan in southern Korea, then only two hundred, most in relatively safe coastal waters, to the Kyushu port of

Hakata, eighty miles north of Kagoshima and home. Kojo had seen his family only three times since graduation but did not call them now: troop movements were top secret. His younger brother hadn't told him he was headed for Saipan before he died there.

Kyushu rumors about the fighting on the Empire's various fronts were discouraging. When Kojo's men learned of their destination, most were relieved that it wasn't a South Pacific island or the presumably doomed Philippines. Okinawa was Japan, however non-Japanese in culture. Still, many assumed they'd spend their last days in that outland — and soon, since it or Formosa was the enemy's logical next target. Noncoms distributed envelopes to each man for nail clippings and a lock of hair, the traditional mementoes for families of the dead.

Kojo didn't use his envelope. To be among the great number certain to perish on Okinawa would be an honor for him and his family. But he believed he would see Japan again. When his officers asked about their chances on Okinawa, his carefree "I don't know and don't care" was intended to boost their morale with a display of the supreme confidence required of Japanese command. It was also the truth.

His men were less poised. Not that they doubted eventual victory. If necessary, a miracle would ensure this, such as the one that had saved thirteenth-century Japan from Mongol invasion — and to which Okinawans are believed not to have contributed. The Mongols under Kublai Khan were far superior in military technique and experience, but sudden typhoons destroyed two invading fleets, the second of which, in 1281, may have been the largest naval force until then, five times larger than the Spanish Armada three centuries later. Japanese priests took the Divine Wind — *kamikaze* — as proof of the power of their prayers. Their flocks took it as evidence that theirs was indeed a sacred nation, inviolable and unconquerable, a belief that would sustain the fervent people through many hardships foreigners considered impossible and pointless. The troops waiting for transport to Okinawa were convinced the heavenly favor that had seen the country through grave crises before would do so again — but that didn't make their own lives sacred. Scratchy records broadcast the vaunting "Sinking Song," an earlier Tokyo hit and still the rage there in Kyushu's lagging south. "Instant sinking, instant sinking / That's the triumphant shout." But everyone knew the droves of ships going down were no longer the enemy's. America's "Hit Parade" waters now included the Ryukyu steppingstones straight to the homeland. Locals whispered about bodies washing up on nearby shores, for whose cremation little wood remained, and about fishermen reluctant to put to sea because the cursed submarines prowled even Kagoshima Bay.

A stunning two thousand Japanese bottoms had already been sent down, most of them by submarines tearing the network of Imperial sea routes to ribbons. Only 5 percent of the production of conquered Asian oil fields reached Japan in 1944, down from 15 percent in 1943. After the Okinawan fighting began eight months later, not a single ship arrived with supplies or reinforcements. But that too counted for nothing, despite all talk among noncombatants at home — repeated with greater passion and almost equal irrelevance after the use of the atomic bomb — about why it had to count.

Now even *Yamato* was pressed into service as a troopship, but most troops went to Okinawa in a grab bag of inferior vessels. The 450-mile journey dragged on for four scorching days, passengers retching with nausea and foreboding although one or more of the Ryukyus was always in sight. The worst rumor about previous convoys was true. Six weeks earlier, a converted merchantman named *Toyama maru* had sailed from Kojo's native city of Kagoshima with the entire 44th Independent Mixed Brigade. The torture began even before the lines were cast off: Japanese troopships were furiously overcrowded. At the much happier beginning of the war, a poet wrote of hellish suffocation alongside explosives in the "infernolike heat" of his ship's "dungeonlike" hold. Now the "agony of transport ship life," as an Okinawa-bound soldier put it, was greater. "We were worse than caged animals . . . [we were] like criminals, ready to be tortured." He noticed yellowish streaks in a lead ship's wake.

> A ship transporting one to two thousand soldiers means that much waste. There was nowhere on an overloaded freighter to provide for that necessary function, so toilets were hung like birdcages on the side of the ship. I couldn't believe this at first. Rows and rows of boxes with a hole in the middle swayed like swings in the wind. We had no choice. There was no other place to do it. We held on to the swing's rope and did it directly into the ocean. In the Army, nothing is discussed — and you can get used to anything, thank you . . . To be on the swing and perform the necessary function exposed to all the world — the pity is that I got used to it too.

Toyama maru's wake was a deeper yellow, for she was transporting six thousand men. One of her two engines was out of commission. Half a dozen smaller ships adjusted their speed to hers. Japanese soldiers were heroes of endurance, but the summer heat that stewed their vomit in the ovenlike compartments was as bad as anything this obedient group remembered. The ship used to serve the China trade. Squashed in three levels of what they called "silkworm shelves," the eleven soldiers in each six-by-twelve-foot area had no room to sit up and so little air that they feared suffocation. June sea winds blew some of the men's "birdcage" waste back on deck, where they had to step in it, then carry their soiled shoes into their berths to prevent theft. Such conditions caused illness and death — of two men from just one artillery battery on one typical voyage from nearby Kagoshima. It was a life for beasts, one private observed — to himself, of course. Such "subversive" thoughts were never expressed aloud.

On *Toyama maru,* a former health service clerk named Yoshizumi Waku went up on deck from the stinking inferno below but couldn't stomach breakfast even in the fresh air. Until a draft call that reached deep among grandfathers, feeble specimens and other deferred categories, Waku believed he was safe from further fighting because he'd already served three turns in Manchuria and China. But there he was, hearing the dreaded, frenzied shout from the port side.

"*Torpedoes!*"

U.S.S. *Sturgeon,* a battle-tested American submarine, had fired four.* Most Japanese troops were below during the moment of stupefying flash, pain, thunder and terror when all of them hit, tearing vast holes in the ship's sides. Thousands of drums of gasoline in the cargo turned the holds into crematoria. Most who survived the explosions drowned when the hulk went under almost immediately, but screams continued as more drums detonated among the living struggling for wreckage in the water. Fighting to stay afloat and free of the flames, twenty-seven-year-old Shigeo Yamaguchi, formerly an agricultural consultant to a district farming association, also fought the thought that he was about to join the seaweed forever. His father had died when he was four years old — the very age of his own eldest son. On the morning Yamaguchi had left his tiny home to answer his draft call, that eldest grabbed him by the neck, shrieking, "Don't go, Papa! Don't go!" Yamaguchi regretted not having held the boy tight for a second. He had suppressed his urge so that visiting friends

---

*The far cleaner submarine, which had tracked the convoy's smoke for hours, was also painfully cramped with men whose sweat coursed down their rash-blistered skin, mixed with moisture dripping from the boat's interior. And Captain Charlton Murphy's periscope revealed the menace of a dozen antisubmarine escorts and at least two planes. The torpedo wakes brought a relentless, four-hour hunt by at least four escorts, which made run after deliberate run, dropping some 70 depth charges that exploded near enough to pop the boat's sea valves open and smash her lights. The bow planes developed such a loud knock that their use had to be stopped lest the noise give away the boat's position; maneuverability was further impaired when the master gyro was damaged and the magnetic compasses spun like tops. Any one of the depth charges — or bombs, for airplanes joined the hunt and pursued it until dark, dropping bombs steadily — might have easily crushed *Sturgeon's* hull, delivering her 72 crew members to a frantic death. They held their breath and trusted, rightly, in their skipper's cunning.

wouldn't see him commit such an unpatriotic act. To have comforted his child would have betrayed spiritual weakness, much disapproved in the Japanese dedication to war and the satisfactions of its sacrifices.

Yamaguchi and Waku would be among the 10 percent of survivors. Some fifty-six hundred men, over a quarter as many as those who would die on hellish Iwo Jima and almost twice as many as those who would go down with *Yamato*, were already dead but would not figure in Okinawa's grand tally since the battle was still nine months away.*

The 22nd Regiment's turn for voyage to Okinawa came in mid-August 1944. The convoy hugged shallow water and zigzagged its short runs in the open. The ships delivered the twenty-eight hundred troops, groggy but intact.

Captain Kojo's unexpected pleasure at his first sight of Okinawa was heightened by the contrast with stark Manchuria. Even as Naha harbor struggled to accommodate the rush of ships, he could see exotic fish darting through translucent water. Vivid coral fringed a tranquil island beckoning with many hues of green.

Ashore, he was further taken by stands of pine trees bordering roads and the luxurious vegetation. Even Naha's red-light district (Tsuji Machi), when he was invited for dinner there, seemed another example of Okinawa's "beautiful culture." He also saw that "unspoiled beauty" meant much greater poverty than even his poor Satsuma's. But Okinawans were more easygoing, happier and more hospitable than any people he'd seen. Few over forty-five spoke enough Japanese to give him directions. However, all were so gracious in their rustic way, smiling and bowing to the "Yamato soldiers," that even his gruffer men were touched.

Although Okinawans were officially Japanese, the 32nd Army was concerned about friction where so many troops crowded an already overcrowded island. The soldiers were ordered to build their own barracks of bamboo and straw and not to fraternize with civilians without authorization. (Some disobeyed.) Only battalion commanders and those above could mix and choose their own quarters. Smartly uniformed Kojo rented a room in the house of a prosperous farmer with a sixteen-year-old daughter, Yasu, in middle school. The captain noticed that Okinawan girls were far less straitlaced than Japanese, perhaps because the subtropical heat brought early sexual maturation. Yasu knocked on the handsome visitor's door at night.

---

*While the 44th Independent Mixed Brigade had waited for transport in Kagoshima, military postcards were distributed and all were ordered to inform their families of their safe arrival on Okinawa. Clutching these postcards, many families would struggle to understand how their men had been lost at sea.

She was beautiful and charming and he liked her very much but succumbed only twice. The other times, he reminded himself that pleasure would weaken the concentration of an Imperial Army officer preparing for combat.

The farmer's house bordered Kadena Airfield, south of Okinawa's neck. Kadena was the field to which Masahide Ota and other boys of the Normal School had walked from Shuri in order to help with the early stages of construction. Kojo's 1st Battalion had been assigned to defend the two miles between the dirt runways and the long, open beach where the American landing was expected but where almost nothing had been prepared. No antitank or antipersonnel mines were available, not even barbed wire. And Kojo sorely missed the regiment's horses. All but four had been left behind when the officers were told at Nishi-Toan there would be no feed for them at their destination. As a battalion commander, Kojo had one of those four, but the regiment lacked even carts for transportation, and only a portion of the division's support units had been shipped from Manchuria. That meant the remaining men would have to be worked harder than ever.

Okinawa was alive with feverish digging. Kojo's battalion joined to gouge out bunkers in rises that dominated the beach near the airfield. Through his company officers, he kept the pace furious during round-the-clock shifts. An ordnance shop fashioned picks and shovels from wagon rails previously used in the transport of sugar cane to refineries. Those without tools used their hands. Without transportation from supply depots, there wasn't quite enough food. The men's fare was chiefly rice and miso soup with sweet potato greens.*

In two months, American planes and surface ships would join submarines in totally severing Japan's sea route to Okinawa. It was a measure of the supply problems as early as the autumn of 1944 that the soldiers received almost no mail. Ships that managed to arrive until October were too packed with essential gear and too busy to bother with letters. When American troops landed, their mail, the importance of which the brass understood, was delivered in canvas bags almost as regularly as ammunition and water. Units would receive their "wonderful," "tremendous," "terrific" boost to morale

---

*Forty years later, Kojo remembered eating more or less what his men ate — never even a piece of fish — but his men recalled as wide a difference between officers and enlisted men in rations as in everything else, at least until the unit went into combat. An orderly of another officer in Kojo's battalion would break off a speck of his tofu before serving it and savor the treat. It was when they were in against-all-odds combat that the considerable distance between officers and men closed, much as in English units under great stress. Certainly few men had the luxury of geishas from the red-light district, whom a few battalion commanders less single-minded than Kojo continued to enjoy, in some cases until the fighting — and destruction — approached their positions.

when they were pulled back from the line, sometimes only a few hundred yards. (One 6th Division Marine got eight letters on a single day in early June. He wrote back that they made him "beam with joy" even amid the horrors of combat, which he didn't describe.) Letters sustained Dick Whitaker and most other American front-line fighters when they might otherwise have found it impossible to continue. Those from Whitaker's mother, who wrote every single day he was away, came in bunches of three to half a dozen — from Saugerties, ten thousand miles away. But Japanese soldiers were almost isolated in one of their own prefectures, 350 miles from the mainland. Infantrymen who served until the end of the campaign got one or two letters, or none, during the interminable ten months.

Officers also treasured every word from home. During breaks from inspecting his fortifications, Kojo sometimes retired to a patch of shade to read a letter from his wife for the *n*th time. They had been married ten weeks before he left Manchuria — a culmination of what had begun as a kind of duty for the twenty-four-year-old captain who knew no women, let alone marriageable women, apart from occasional tea house courtesans and prostitutes. That was not unusual for Academy officers, with their disdain for civilian life. But an elder brother disliked the thought of Tadashi going through life without a family.

His brother, who worked for a Tokyo publisher, showed Kojo's photograph to the assistant of a friend who taught at Meiji University. The assistant, the daughter of an engineer high in the Ministry of Communications, whispered that she'd be glad to marry the handsome captain. For Kojo, almost any outwardly suitable woman would have done, since he had no thought of taking any time from his military duties for marriage.

Then his brother sent Kojo a photograph of the young assistant, a large print especially prepared for arranging marriages. He was enchanted, and even more so by the delicacy and refinement of her letters. With arranged marriages the norm, neither felt awkward. But despite embarrassment over his own unpracticed writing style, their ease with each other in their correspondence delighted Kojo further.

He arrived for the marriage at Tokyo Station in April 1944, dashing in his cape and proud of his position in the unconquerable elite of regular Army officers. He pretended not to notice his future in-laws searching among the officers on the platform, the better to observe and sustain his pose of nonchalance. But he was smitten even before his fiancée's mother spied *Kojo* on his trunk. Young Emiko was even more attractive than her artful photograph.

Kojo's first glance also discerned the quality of her upbringing. The combination of a modern, citified face and traditional kimono, coiffure and modesty made Emiko a rare blend of contemporary chic and old Japanese virtues. Her large eyes expressed both subtlety and wholly unexpected femininity. He thanked his luck when she raised them to his.

Although Tokyo's saturation bombing was a year away, the city had much changed since his last trip there, when he was a candidate for a course for spotter officers, just a year earlier. All lights were blacked out, few nonbasic foods were available and Kojo couldn't find a tailor to make a new uniform for the marriage. None of this grazed his soldierly certainty of Japan's victory — about which he actually forgot for moments. In the days before the marriage, Emiko's mother suggested the betrothed take walks in the family's wealthy suburb, still interspersed with farms. Although much more articulate than most regular officers, Kojo spoke with the reserve and in the dialect of his Satsuma, where real men used few words, while Emiko's voice shimmered with the sophistication of generations of Tokyo residence. It chimed in his ears like exciting music.

On the couple's trip to Nishi-Toan, the bride's beauty showed in everything from her kimonos to her cultivated but unaffected smiles. A major on the same train would tell the transfixed bridegroom that he wondered whether the captain's companion was his bride or sister: the two seemed as intense as first lovers and as comfortable with each other as old friends. Such pleasure and intimacy were new even to Kojo's imagination. The five days on the train and few weeks in a house just outside his desolate camp were by far his happiest.

Now Emiko's loving letters to her husband on Okinawa confided how much she missed him. She promised a visit, hinting that her influential father could arrange it. Kojo smiled at her naïveté, returned the letters to his pocket and again assumed his Academy-bred rigidity. Vast amounts of work lay ahead before he could mangle the American landing.

Much of the digging was completed by mid-December. Pride enlivened the soldiers' songs, which echoed from the hills in the evening, slightly relieving their exhaustion after five grinding months. Kojo, still a quick-tempered stickler, was relatively pleased with his nearly finished fortifications, further protected by coral growth overhead. He shifted his men to more training.

He would not engage the enemy on the beach. The immense power of American pre-invasion bombardments on other islands had shown that to be too costly. This time the defenders would stay burrowed in until the enemy bombardment stopped for his landing operations. The 24th Division's artillery — organized in its own units, separate from the three infantry regiments — would also remain in protected emplacements, opening fire only when the landing craft approached. The artillery and antitank guns had been intended for destroying the mechanized, heavily armed Soviets. Its concentrated firepower on top of the regiment's own guns would maul the enemy during his approach and prevent him from digging in on the beach. As at Iwo Jima, it would tear the Americans to bits — and then the poised infantry would appear from the safety of the refuges now being constructed for a massive counterattack.

Kojo relentlessly practiced his battalion's thrusts and feints for that great slaughter. He knew his old-fashioned bolt-action rifles were no match for the enemy's great firepower. (His men preferred an even older rifle than that 1939 model, designed to use the same ammunition as the standard heavy machine gun.) But Americans were amateurs. Japanese professionalism, training and spiritual strength would win the day as so often in China, where furious bayonet charges had often panicked the enemy. Never mind that there it was the Japanese who were better equipped. His own troops excelled in the hand-to-hand death struggle that would nullify American material advantages. Happy for the luck that had placed him there to shatter them, Kojo relished his first chance for real combat.

Operational plans were reviewed at regimental headquarters, on a hill overlooking Kadena Airfield. Battalion commanders sat in the first row, in front of their company commanders. At one such meeting, the regimental ordnance officer demonstrated a charge with a delayed-action fuse that would demolish enemy tanks when men sneaked up and shoved it beneath the vehicles' bellies. The ordnance officer showed a wooden box that housed the makeshift new weapon.

He opened it and disappeared except for the portion of his legs inside his boots. The accidental explosion wounded a dozen fellow officers. Everyone in the first row, including the regimental commander, was rushed to a hospital. Only Kojo shook off his daze, refused treatment and told his orderly to fetch his horse. It was his solemn duty to remain composed in the face of the worst possible shock. Personal pride and a desire to be worthy of his ancestry combined with his intense training to reveal no weakness.

He rode back to his battalion and held out nearly a month. His headaches were unbearable, his fever was extreme and pus from his ear stuck his head to his pillow. When he was taken to a hospital, his doctors hoped it wasn't too late to save his life.

6 · Early Damage

I hope to God we won't have to go on any more of those screwy islands.
— One of the 19,000 Marines wounded on Iwo Jima

The Japanese Empire's strategic need to hold Okinawa was absolute.
— Thomas Huber, military historian

*[Okinawa was] the most important operation of all, the logical conclusion
to the historical Central Pacific campaign . . . the last important bastion
guarding the homeland . . . a foot in the door for the final poke at the Japanese Empire.*
— John Toland, *The Gods of War*

*In the midst of [the] final military preparations, the bewildered ordinary
citizens were left to make ready for the crisis as best they could. Families
hurried to the countryside to conceal books and clothes and other goods
in the family tombs or in pits dug in the ravines beyond the suburban
settlements.*
— George Kerr, *Okinawa*

NEARLY seven thousand Ameri-
cans and twenty-one thousand Japanese died on Iwo Jima, in a sense
unnecessarily, for although B-29s would use its eight square miles
for emergency landings after bombing Japan, it would never become
the major base planned by American strategists. That dose of war's
boundless bad luck wasn't shared by civilians because there were
none on the garrison island. But Okinawa would surely never be op-
erationally unnecessary. Just 350 miles from mainland Japan and 500
from China, the "piece of offshore rope," as the name meant, was
well positioned to cut off Japan from her occupied territories on the
Asian continent while serving as an "unsinkable aircraft carrier" for
attacks on the home islands.

It was also a fine staging area for the American invasion, planned
for late 1945. Large enough for assembling the necessary armies,
Okinawa offered excellent anchorages in sheltered bays within easy
striking distance of the mainland. Its flat land was well suited for air
bases for continual operations against targets in easy aerial range. No
one suspected that the first B-29 raid on the mainland would take off

from the island on the war's very last evening because a new kind of bomb would obviate the need for more raids. For ten times as many people as on "screwy" Iwo Jima, Okinawa would be another unlucky draw, especially since a different "aircraft carrier" might have been chosen.

Admiral Ernest King, Chief of Naval Operations, preferred Formosa, 380 miles southwest of Okinawa, as a base for simultaneously linking up with the weakening Chinese allies. But King was persuaded that too few troops were available to capture Formosa's large territory until the war in Europe was won. Okinawa was doomed on October 3, 1944, when senior Pacific admirals meeting in San Francisco decided to take one or more of the Ryukyu islands instead. Although Japanese strategists continued to guess the enemy's choice would be Formosa, they kept reinforcing Okinawa too, where Tadashi Kojo's battalion was digging its bunkers above the beach near Kadena Airfield.

Task Force 58, as it would be designated, struck Okinawa just a week after the admirals' decision in San Francisco. The Fifth Fleet's awesome Fast Carrier Force that would dispose of *Yamato* seven months later comprised no less than ten carriers, six fast battleships, eight escort carriers, five light cruisers and, on an average day, over sixty destroyers. It launched its heaviest single-day raid on October 10, 1944. Nearly fourteen hundred strikes dropped six hundred tons of bombs and fired thousands of rockets on that opening shot against Okinawa. On recently opened Yomitan Airfield — two miles north of the Kadena field, for whose defense Captain Kojo was responsible — Japanese maintenance and service crews had just helped dispatch planes to Formosa and were breakfasting on the flightline. Although a high degree of air-raid readiness had been in force for a week, enemy planes were so unexpected, rather as at Pearl Harbor, that the men assumed their own were returning for some reason. Antiaircraft guns fired belatedly at the vapor trails of the attacking craft, all much too fast for them. Five Japanese fighters managed to take off; none returned. Among the debris on the ground — of warehouses, an engine plant, a component factory, field headquarters and operations shacks — a headless corpse bubbled blood. Then the fuel depot blew, as if to guide in another enemy wave.

Four more waves crippled additional airfields with fresh bombs and rockets from their carriers, then with strafing runs. The raiders also sank over sixty-five vessels, including twenty cargo ships and a destroyer overwhelmed by a swarm of Grummans as it zigzagged frantically out of Naha. Thousands of rounds of artillery shells were destroyed, as well as five million machine gun and rifle rounds and a month's supply of food for the entire 32nd Army. Naval planners were particularly pleased that eighty-eight Japanese aircraft, a serious threat to a landing fleet, were demolished, three quarters of them on the ground. The skipper of an air group from the carrier *Enterprise* circled in the late afternoon and found nothing profitable for more dives. The raid was so successful and the photographic intelligence so useful for the invasion's preliminary planning that two months would pass before it was repeated — in January, with greater duration and force.

Japanese troops unknowingly glimpsed the future. When three fighters from another field were shot down almost immediately after taking off, soldiers lost their "naïve hope" that "all would be well if only our planes would get up into the sky." At a military ball the previous evening for command officers, the leaders (overwhelmingly Japanese) of the prefectural government and the cream of Okinawan society, General Isamu Cho, the 32nd Army's Chief of Staff, promised that the enemy would meet "complete destruction" if he dared attack. The grand affair in the best Naha hotel lasted until early morning. When the enemy did attack hours later, the main radar malfunctioned, the first American wave began its descent before it was recognized and antiaircraft performance was dismal.

"The enemy planes' nimble movements eluded our old-fashioned three-step shooting method and we couldn't sight at all," lamented an antiaircraft gunner who felt American pilots held his battery in contempt. "But the real blow was the poor quality of our detection equipment, which kept us from knowing about the approach of such a huge enemy force until the very last minute. Reconnaissance, communication, coordination — all were defective, [telling us] that we on the ground would now be at the mercy of the enemy's excellent airpower. Yet we all still firmly believed in *our* airpower, which would retaliate for the enemy's treacherous attack. Our only hope hung on new planes arriving quickly, before the enemy task force could sail away." *

This first encounter with Americans — which was also the first combat experience for many Japanese — shocked large numbers in

*The arrival of formations of planes from the mainland three days later, on October 13, enthralled Japanese soldiers and many civilians, deep in foreboding after the American raid. "Riveted on the beautiful machines with the emblem of the rising sun," a soldier remembered, "our eyes became hot with tears." After furious preparations and throaty songs, a huge force took off the next day to avenge the raid. The antiaircraft gunner watched them circle over Naha's smoking ruins before heading toward an aerial battle on the Formosan Sea. Of the 300 planes meant to return to the field where he waited, not one appeared. "All night, the lighted beacon swiveled in vain." Imperial General Headquarters announced that a "highly successful" attack had destroyed TF 58 — which was now on its way, totally unscathed, to support the Leyte landings. The lie was believed.

the Naha area. But civilians were more deeply stunned, for their losses far exceeded the military's. Until now, Okinawans had known only air-raid scares. The first serious one, four months earlier, just before *Sturgeon* sank the *Toyama maru,* sent them huddling in backyard foxholes as American bombers flew past toward the mainland, an hour's flight north. Such false alarms were of little help to those preparing for the real thing.

Despite the war emergency's air-raid drills, training with bamboo spears and the digging of shelters under Japanese direction, Naha remained a late-rising city. When the first wave of Grummans and Curtises awakened residents that October 10, it was their sound — "tinny" after the deeper pitch of less advanced Japanese engines — that warned them. No siren sounded before the first bombs landed on the outskirts.

Explosions literally shook the city. The brunt of the attack hit the port, where ammunition stacked amid supplies on the piers blew up, augmenting the damage of American incendiary bombs. An October wind spread the conflagration through houses of paper and wood. New waves of planes broke off the feverish efforts of volunteers to control a hundred fires. Some detachments took refuge and prayed. Many were singed by racing flames on roads clogged by residents trying to flee the city. Naha's population of sixty-five thousand made it by far Okinawa's largest city. At least 80 percent was destroyed; most witnesses thought 90 percent. Roughly a thousand civilians, twice as many as military personnel, were killed.*

The old capital of Shuri on high ground above Naha took few hits. The hill complex containing the headquarters of the Japanese 32nd Army as well as several divisional and artillery command headquarters was completely undamaged; so was the Normal School, where the patriotic resolution and the anti-Americanism of Masahide Ota and his classmates was further strengthened. But Naha lay in shock. The attacks that had begun in early morning lasted until evening. When the alarm was finally lifted, Okinawans left the shelter of trenches, caves and family tombs, some to climb surrounding hills.

* Tokyo protested to Washington through Madrid that the "deliberate" bombing of the civilian population and nonmilitary targets violated international law and the principles of humanity. In light of Japan's instigation of the war and its even less discriminate bombing of Asian cities, that gesture was pathetic or outrageous, depending on one's humor. Japan was first to use terror bombing of a civilian population, in the Chinese city of Chapei in 1932.

Okinawan civilians also suffered heavily from more kills by American submarines. On the very night of October 10, one sank a ship returning to Naha with some 500 laborers who had been conscripted to build a military airfield on Yaeyami Island, one of the Ryukyu group about 300 miles southwest, almost at Formosa. Their deaths too usually go uncounted in the campaign's casualty toll.

One described "Okinawa's capital, the entire city of Naha," as "reduced to glowing embers. The setting sun blazed behind the writhing remains of the city, producing an illusion that the sun itself had set Naha on fire. Looking at the smoldering ruins, we realized that real air raids leave no time for wet straw mats, buckets of water and ladders."

Ten days later, a Japanese medical corpsman disembarked from "the living hell" of a ship's hold. His voyage had taken a month because his wretched ship arrived as Naha blazed on October 10, and turned back to Kagoshima. Screams from torpedoed sister ships made a worse nightmare of the second trip but the corpsman's joy at returning to terra firma lasted only until he saw Naha. "It was still smoldering. A black sticky liquid oozed from a destroyed sugar warehouse and stuck to the soldiers' marching shoes."

Many evacuees returned to Naha when the ruins cooled, some to rebuild what they could of their houses or erect crude shacks in the undamaged outskirts. Classes resumed in the open or in still-standing houses, children again singing "Thank you, dear soldiers." With warehouses, offices, factories, and shops destroyed, there was a rush for new jobs, some with the 32nd Army. A kind of military harem went up in the burned-down red-light district, some of the ladies impressed into service by the Army and paid almost nothing. But most of Naha, including schools, hospitals, and libraries, could not be rebuilt. Six months before most American civilians had heard the name "Okinawa," "October tenth" — or simply 10/10 — entered the Okinawan vocabulary as shorthand for tragedy.

Evacuations from the island had begun before 10/10. Mainland Japanese, some 5 percent of the population, were first to leave for home. Many officials of the prefectural government that had been girding the natives for war were gone before it arrived. On July 19, the prefectural government ordered native young and aged to join the evacuees. Parents hesitated. Send their precious children away? To Japan with its anti-Okinawan prejudice? But schoolteachers were among those who quickly complied.

As a senior teacher, thirty-seven-year-old Seitoku Shinzato was both more Japanized and more concerned with upholding authority than were most Okinawans. Shinzato knew that, should the enemy really invade, children would hinder military operations. And if, as some Okinawans whispered, the child-bayoneting American beasts killed everyone on the island, Okinawan blood *had* to survive somewhere. Nothing was more important to Okinawans than perpetuation of the family line — which is why Shinzato himself had been adopted as a boy by a rich, childless uncle. Besides, food was already scarce. The 32nd Army had ordered cows and pigs slaughtered for general consumption, so the native population would have to rely almost fully on the sweet potatoes formerly used for animal feed. Apart from the government order, which had to be obeyed, Shinzato felt it was right to evacuate his family. He took his mother and his wife, together with his three young children, to the necessary pier. A schoolteacher too, his wife would be responsible for forty children during their evacuation in Kyushu.

Three ships bearing some six thousand evacuees departed from Naha on August 21, almost two months after the sinking of the *Toyama maru* with the loss of nearly the entire 44th Mixed Independent Brigade. Shinzato was left alone with his ambivalent feelings. Days without word from his family made him more and more anxious. There was no guarantee they would survive — and what would happen to them in Japan if they reached there safely? Like the majority of the elite, who strongly identified with the mother country, Shinzato nevertheless thought of her as "alien."

The family had left on the *Tsushima maru,* a freighter that had sailed from Shanghai with a cargo of silkworm cocoons for the home islands and stopped in Naha to pick up the evacuees — and to discharge soldiers transferred from China.* The dockside partings had been full of tears. "Papa, papa, will we ever be able to see each other again?" Two weeks later, rumors circulated that one of three crammed ships that sailed together from Naha had failed to reach Kagoshima. Full of foreboding now, Shinzato traveled north to his native city of Nago to ask his terrible question of a police captain who worked with the 32nd Army. The senior teacher reckoned that the policeman might tell him the truth because he was a former pupil.

No, nothing unusual had happened, the policeman stated with a face that betrayed him. Shinzato bit his lip. When he was alone, he sagged with angry grief. He tried to comfort himself with the thought that his wife and mother were both brave women who would have managed to die together without becoming frantic. But he could not comprehend why he was alive and the children he had sent away to save were dead.

The unmarked freighter had been torpedoed at 2 A.M. by U.S.S. *Bowfin* near Aku-ishi Jima (Bad Stone Island), roughly midway be-

---

*Those soldiers had hoped they were heading home. Kenjiro Matsuki, a former first baseman for Japan's first professional baseball team, woke up to find, with great disappointment, that he was about to be unloaded at Naha rather than Kagoshima. The star athlete described his horrific war in *Matsuki Ittohei no Okinawa Horyoki* (The Story of PFC Matsuki, a Prisoner on Okinawa). Matsuki's book and other accounts by Japanese survivors were translated for me by Tamako M. Yorichika.

tween Naha and Kagoshima. Shinzato's children were asleep, together with their mother, grandmother and seven members of Shinzato's brother's family. One thousand, four hundred and eighty-four women and children were lost, ten times the toll of New York's Triangle Shirtwaist Company fire, which had horrified America in 1911.* The number almost equaled the killed-in-action of some American divisions about to fight the costliest battle in their history on Okinawa.

*Ten-year-old Taeko Uehara was saved by a sailor who pulled her onto a raft sturdy enough to weather a storm before a small ship arrived for rescue. At Kagoshima, the 177 survivors were instructed not to talk about the sinking and to send postcards back to Okinawa saying all was well. Police had already warned the passengers of the two unharmed ships never to mention the fate of *Tsushima maru*.

7 · Japanese Leadership

Erect, lean-featured and composed, Ushijima exemplified the best in samurai virtues. Even without noticing his insignia of rank, one would have been aware of his exalted position in Japan's military hierarchy.
— James and William Belote, *Typhoon of Steel*

He was a true Japanese officer, a hero of the bravest sort, yet kindly. I wanted nothing more in life than to be a little like him.
— Tadashi Kojo

THE MAN who replaced Masao Watanabe as commander of the 32nd Army was Mitsuru Ushijima, one of Japan's most respected and liked general officers. After generations of inferior prefectural governors sent from Tokyo, Okinawans were relieved and flattered by the choice. It did not occur to them that a strengthened losing side in war only prolongs the struggle, in the end causing more damage to both sides. They had no way of knowing that they themselves, the civilians, would bear the heaviest damage as a result of the 32nd Army's great improvement under its excellent new commander.

The universal admiration for General Ushijima was reinforced by his evocation of Takamori Saigo, a soldier, statesman and poet who greatly contributed to Japan's modernization following Commodore Perry's arrival. Saigo the Great went on to disembowel himself in a sea of his followers' blood after a catastrophic rebellion, precipitated by dissent over the question of invading Korea. But the whole political spectrum, from extreme militarists to liberal democrats, cherished the "peculiarly Japanese combination of qualities" that earned Saigo the reputation as the last true samurai. The frugal man, almost alone among his contemporaries to care nothing for medals and honors, became the Meiji Restoration's only truly popular hero. Having helped begin the commercial and industrial transformation, he died defending the national honor and faith against corrupting Western ways in the name of uniquely Japanese virtues.

A Japanese who somehow did not know Saigo's origins might easily have guessed: such stately mien and so few, often stumbling, words was the Satsuma ideal. Dedicated samurai families like Saigo's poor one raised their boys to cherish simplicity and modesty as well as bravery and service. Young Tadashi Kojo's uncles often recounted episodes of sacrifice from the life of Saigo of Satsuma, as he was otherwise known. "You must be a real man," they told him. "Like Saigo."

Ushijima now gave Kojo a living model of a true Satsuma samurai — and a special model, for he and his commanding officer were almost neighbors, from the same Kagoshima stock, caste and reverent memory of Saigo. Ushijima's association with Saigo was so strong that many thought he resembled the legendary hero physically. Ushijima was actually smaller, but still tall for a Japanese and a figure of commanding presence: so much the picture of a winning leader that his appearance alone inspired his soldiers. His officers revered him. One of the 32nd Army staff first met Ushijima in 1928, when he visited a club for junior officers. The already distinguished major seemed more an elder brother than a field officer, no common thing in an Army with piercing attention to rank and its trappings.

Ushijima was then the military training officer at his alma mater, Kagoshima's First Middle School. He had requested that post, which would have shamed many majors, because he liked teaching and disliked promoting his career. One evening, a tipsy passerby mistook his residence for a restaurant* and entered, clapping his hands. "Quick, bring sake and something to eat. I'm hungry and thirsty." Mistaking him, in turn, for a friend of her husband's, Ushijima's wife hurried in with the family dinner and sake. The visitor meanwhile had noticed samurai swords in a rack with calligraphy that belonged in no public eatery. But as he made to slink away, an imposing man in a kimono entered and bowed. "You're welcome. I'm glad you came."

Now very embarrassed, the uninvited guest did his best to apologize and leave, but Ushijima insisted that fate had brought them together and the stranger was his guest. They drank and talked far into the night.

Ushijima remained known for that kind of charm even after distinguishing himself with infantry units in the field, when talk spread of his victories and bravery. Some liked him also because he remained inarticulate in public and kept his speeches short. Like Saigo, he

---

Ushi means "cow" to a farmer, "beef" to a cook. *Jima* (pronounced *shima*, "island," when it stands alone) looks somewhat like a character for a bird or a chicken for cooking. A jaunty hand had painted both characters on a lamp at the gate of the imposing, samurai-style house Ushijima had rented, a kind favored by fashionable restaurants where geishas were sometimes invited to join the guests. Even sober eyes might have mistaken them for (deliciously broiled) "chicken and beef."

seemed incapable of promoting his self-interest in the often fierce competition for advancement.*

Japanese commanders were valued more as symbols than as hands-on leaders, more as embodiments of strength than strategists or policymakers. One of their primary functions was to radiate some of their Emperor's sublimity and benevolence, together with a resolve so strong that nothing on earth could shake it. Ushijima's field officers perceived the charismatic general as a kind of Mount Fuji, an immovable, unflappable guarantor of their victory — who probably stood above daily decisions and left all but the broadest strokes to his staff.† In Kagoshima, where other strong but silent generals had grown up within a stone's throw of him, it was almost a motto that real men didn't bother with details. Even in high staff jobs, such as senior deputy to the Ministry of the Army, Ushijima seemed little interested in the give-and-take of intensely debated matters. Ambitious officers chastized subordinates and carped at their reports; silent Ushijima often signed blindly. Yet superiors were struck by his section's marked improvement, achieved largely because his subordinates admired his inability to quibble or nag.

His reputation continued to grow during his command of an infantry division in Manchuria. In 1942, he was honored by appointment to command the Imperial Academy, of which he was of course a graduate, as it strained to produce for a war racing to its zenith. Four years earlier, a fire in the cadet barracks had resulted in severe demotions. When another blaze destroyed some administrative offices, officers braced for more wrath — but Ushijima's smile remained serene. Instead of scolding or reporting the damage to the military police for further investigation, he thanked the officers for their work containing the fire. Hideki Tojo, reviled by Americans as Prime Minister and Minister of the Army, ordered severe punishment, including the dispatch of the "offending" officers to the front, if appropriate. Ushijima held firm against his fury. Arguing that the full responsibility was his as commandant, he said he would never send an officer to fight as punishment — and he prevailed. Such incidents heightened the fervent loyalty of his staffs. General Korechika Anami, then Minister of War, was among many high officers eager to be ap-

---

*When chosen for the staff of the Minister of War in 1932, Ushijima at first declined the coveted appointment, explaining that he didn't feel up to the job, having served only in out-of-the-way places. He had never set foot in the War Department building.

†This practice became traditional after General Iwao Ohyama left almost all particulars to his chief of staff, Gentaro Kodama, in the Russo-Japanese War. But not every later chief of staff, including Ushijima's on Okinawa, could match Kodama, an outstanding strategist who had studied under a disciple of Germany's superb Helmuth von Moltke.

pointed commander of the 32nd Army. Few grumbled when Ushijima was selected.

Most Okinawans were as cheered as the garrison itself by the "magnificent" Ushijima's arrival in August 1944. When they caught sight of him, they saw an effortlessly friendly hero who stopped to chat with young soldiers and — amazing for a Japanese bigwig — to thank startled student volunteers who were helping dig fortifications. Field officers like Captain Kojo found him the commander under whom they had dreamed of serving, an accomplished professional with a record of great bravery under fire, yet also kind and broad-minded. His personal qualities were much more than a secondary matter for them, since the "Japanese fighting spirit" with which he infused the 32nd Army counted more than its armament or equipment.

When civilians saw Ushijima's chief of staff, by contrast, they often saw a fierce countenance excoriating a quivering subordinate. It was fiery Isamu Cho who, the night before the devastating October 10 air raid, boasted the enemy would meet "complete destruction" if he dared attack Okinawa. Cho's reputation as a firebrand and intimidator was as deserved as Ushijima's as a father figure.

Fifty-one-year-old Cho was also a lieutenant general, although of course junior to Ushijima. His notebook was universally dreaded. He brushed a record of his orders into it, including each project's completion date. Officers who failed to meet their deadline had the pages shoved in their faces as they were roasted.

Cho's officers considered him very brave, which was where his temperamental likeness to Ushijima ended. Many who saw nothing of Ushijima except a confident smile from an imposing presence endured outburst after thunderous outburst from his burly chief of staff. "You fool, can't you do *anything?*"

The "fools" included bright young officers whom Imperial General Headquarters had sent from of its own complement to the staff of the 32nd Army. The best came to feel that Cho's bark was worse than his bite; their explosive mentor was simply unable to talk softly, especially now, when driven by fierce desire to complete his tasks before the possible invasion. The regulars knew of his political activities and admired him for them, as well as for his charisma and rhetoric, which boosted the 32nd Army's morale. Personally, Cho was outgoing and likable. Besides, if he demanded the dotting of every *i* in reports to him, that was his job as chief of staff, just as Commanding Officer Ushijima was supposed to hold himself above such details.

Still, the contrast between the two lieutenant generals went far deeper than billet or personality. In the best traditions of military officers everywhere, laconic, mild-mannered Ushijima was totally apolitical. In the worst tradition of Japanese militarism, eloquent Cho was immersed in strident jingoism. Without his kind, the Battle of Okinawa would never have taken place.

Japan's conquests in the 1930s were remarkable for being initiated not by the governing authorities or even a hot-headed faction of them but by field officers who acted on their own. Radical majors and colonels fabricated pretexts, mounted attacks and presented Tokyo with *faits accomplis* it was unable to reverse, partly because civilian leaders felt intimidated by the Army's fervent expansionist cliques, partly because the battlefield triumphs, glorified by the press, produced wild cheers from much of the public. Those middle-level officers counted on moderates being too weak to restrain the expansionist sentiment or stop their unauthorized operations. With the blessings of some important politicians and generals, it was they who dragged Japan, not quite kicking and screaming, into her greedy war by compelling support of their unprovoked aggression.

Cho was among the most passionate of the insubordinates. He joined the notorious Cherry Blossom Society (Sakurakai) at its founding, in 1930. The evanescent cherry blossom's disappearance after its brief life was an ancient symbol of the samurai's readiness to die for his sovereign at a moment's notice. An old saying had it that the warrior among men was as the cherry among flowers. But together with self-sacrifice, the Sakurakai pledged to cleanse Japan of liberal democrats and other "decadent" Western influences that were polluting her traditional virtues. Military dictatorship was the salvation.

Isamu Cho stood out even from ultranationalists who were utterly convinced that poor, virtuous Japan had been grievously wronged by hypocritical evildoers and that right would be done only when the Army, sole repository of the national honor, wielded its sword to eliminate foreign enemies and domestic weaklings. Although the society's members (who would number just over a hundred at its peak) were to be majors or above, an exception was made for florid Captain Cho, prime mover of its most militant faction.

Cho was one of eleven members who prepared a coup d'état in January 1931. Their plan to murder the Prime Minister and install a general as dictator was abandoned at the last moment, but nine months later they carried out the celebrated Manchurian Incident. Field-grade officers blew up a section of the Japanese-owned South Manchurian Railway, claimed that Chinese had done the insulting damage, and invaded. The carefully prepared Kwantung Army tramped through the whole of Manchuria in months.

Most of the great business and financial trusts (*zaibatsu*) initially opposed the adventure. So did the court aristocracy surrounding the Emperor and the elected government the Army supposedly served. All succumbed. But fearing that "weak-kneed" diplomacy would sacrifice the Army's glorious gains, Cho and a second ringleader led another attempt to replace the government with a military dictator — who was to appoint Cho himself to the crucial post of chief of the metropolitan police. This plan called for the assassination of the Prime Minister; a conspirator later testified that Cho insisted on threatening the Emperor "with a drawn dagger" if he proved reluctant to sanction the new cabinet. Higher officers thwarted this plot too, perhaps because such incredibly blasphemous talk exceeded the bounds of even the superpatriots. Cho was arrested in a Tokyo geisha house where he had passionately argued his case for violence during the planning sessions.*

But civilian judicial authorities were powerless to punish Cho amid the patriotic euphoria induced by the Kwantung Army's easy devouring of Manchuria. Nor would the Army discipline anyone with "pure motives," as approving higher officers characterized the conspirators'. For those episodes of blatant high treason, Cho wasn't shot or imprisoned, not even court-martialed and cashiered. The stormy petrel was merely given a pro forma lecture by the Inspector General of Military Education — who was going to be the conspirators' new Prime Minister — and transferred to a pleasant post in the Kwantung Army: evidence of how well the most violent, disloyal "patriots" had already intimidated the Army and governmental leadership. It had become dangerous to question even the most extreme acts proclaimed to have been taken for the national glory.

From Manchuria, Cho helped pressure the Army high command to support making it the puppet state of Manchukuo by circulating a rumor that the Kwantung Army might otherwise declare its independence. As a regimental commander in 1938, he was one of two ringleaders of more "direct action," this time an attack on a Russian position on the Manchukuo-Soviet border. The Army was about to be drawn into another border skirmish, but Emperor Hirohito broke with the accepted practice of ordering whatever his General Staff "advised." To the fury of many General Staff officers, His Majesty refused to sanction a major new conflict.

---

*The lover of strong drink and pretty women also liked the Golden Dragon tea house in the red-light district, where he would perform a dance with his sword when alcohol fueled his naturally high spirits. His co-conspirators at the Golden Dragon included Lieutenant Colonel Kingoro Hashimoto, the intelligence officer implicated in the deliberate 1937 sinking of the U.S. gunboat *Panay* in the Yangtze River.

Ardent Cho persisted. During another desperate battle with Soviet border troops, he and a fellow officer urged their men to make suicide attacks against the enemy's tanks. Cho himself was said to have slept soundly under severe enemy fire during an earlier engagement. Now he and his companion demonstrated Japanese coolness under fire by pulling down their breeches and standing exposed on a sandbag parapet. As chief of staff of the Japanese Army that later overran Thailand, he took it upon himself to press Vichy France to cede certain territory to her — which Japanese troops quickly occupied. In all these actions, he exhibited contempt for anything not useful to Japan, an attitude that underlay the Army's often appalling treatment of non-Japanese soldiers and civilians. As a leading staff officer at Nanking in 1937, he gave a secret order, which he later claimed to have faked, for the disposal of thousands of Chinese prisoners. His commanding officer's directions were apparently to let the captives go. Lieutenant Colonel Cho changed that to "Finish them off!" before passing them on. The subsequent brutalization of the Chinese capital was perhaps the greatest single act of willful cruelty until then: six weeks of maiming, rape and murder during which up to seventy-five thousand Chinese were shot, slashed, and burned to death, including many thousands of adult, aged, and infant civilians.*

Cho and the scrupulously neat Ushijima differed sharply even in dress; the chief of staff was wont to put his feet on his desk, unbutton his tunic and enjoy a smoke. He also remained fond of good drink. Near the slaughterous end of the battle, fine sake and Scotch were still in supply in his quarters, which were regularly visited by attractive women. At a crucial turning point, when 32nd Army headquarters abandoned its underground sanctuary, he sent a soldier back to fetch something he'd left behind: a life-sized photograph of a celebrated actress named Isuzu Yamada. The soldier complied at great risk to his life, under a cascade of American shells.

*The Tokyo War Crimes Commission would sentence Cho's commanding officer to hang for his part in the Nanking atrocities. Major General Ushijima's 36th Brigade was first to storm the walls and enter the capital. A distinguished professor of Chinese history in Beijing answered a 1989 query by observing that "most scholars believe, when discussing the Nanking Massacre, that Mitsuru Ushijima, as the former commander of the Japanese Army, must be responsible for the offense of his troops." However, Chinese sources are otherwise silent about his role at Nanking, and Japanese officers who knew him before and after believe it "unimaginable" that he participated in atrocities — of which I have been able to find no other evidence, including in detailed Chinese accounts. Japanese comments about Ushijima's record in China stress that, as hard and bravely as he fought, he was uncommonly considerate to his defeated enemy. If true, these stories support the Satsuma ideal of the bravest and most resolute soldiers who, however, show mercy and even tenderness to vanquished enemies. This standard was held in contrast to those of warriors elsewhere in Japan who extirpated their enemies to the last man lest they rise again.

In addition to Ushijima and Cho, younger staff officers of the 32nd Army had also been in Nanking.

But no difference in personality and temperament, not even their opposite positions in political involvement, came between the two or their model working relationship, the equanimous commanding officer acting as final arbiter for all that his excitable chief assistant prepared. Cho always shouted a smart "Yes, *sir!*" to his commanding officer's instructions and never contradicted him. And Ushijima, who had never attempted to stop the Imperial Way radicals, knew that his zealous right hand, even more than the rest of his staff, shared his desire to achieve an impossible task — and a belief in Japan's singular virtue. He had chosen Cho as his chief of staff for that reason. Their team excellence promised the worst for Okinawans, Americans and Japanese together.

8 · Final Japanese Preparations

The Americans still don't seem to admit defeat. Their bombers are attacking the homeland. There are rumors . . . that Okinawa is about to be attacked.
— A nineteen-year-old gunner on *Yamato*, days before the American landing on Okinawa

Of course the tide must turn. The glorious spirit of our nation will overcome the enemy. Our brave young kamikaze pilots are sinking their ships and striking terror into their hearts. We shall fight on if a hundred million perish.
— The reply of the gunner's father

I never realized the battle was hopeless or we were finished until I was taken to my detention camp and saw the stocks of American supplies and equipment. It was all new to me. It was overwhelming.
— A Japanese POW from a regiment devastated five weeks before the end of the campaign

We don't have to fear Americans; they consider war a sport. With that mentality, they're certain to lose to the Japanese fighting spirit. Answer: *Yeah, a sports team against a suicide squad.*
— Two members of the Okinawan Home Guard on the eve of the American landing

WHAT CHIEF OF STAFF CHO whipped the 32nd Army to complete was an unprecedentedly effective complex of fortifications. Much of Okinawa's terrain of sharp rises overlooking flat plains was ideal for defense. Tens of thousands of Japanese soldiers and Korean laborers gasped all day in the sun — and through the night — to improve it with a network of strong points featuring integrated systems of observation, firepower and reinforcement. The number and scope of those works far exceeded those on Iwo Jima and other islands.

For 32nd Army headquarters, an ancient cave complex beneath Shuri Castle — atop the hill above the Normal School — was much enlarged and improved. The main tunnel was fifty feet below ground at its shallowest point. Thirty-two chambers and designated areas along its thirteen-hundred-yard length and side shafts accommodated a thousand men, the equivalent of a fighting battalion. They included a dispensary, a kitchen and pantry, a telephone switchboard chamber, weather and typists' sections . . . everything from General Ushijima's quarters to intelligence and operations rooms, and all ventilated by ducts with blower fans. (The well-stocked pantry was overseen by a chef whom General Cho had brought over from the mainland, together with a supply of fine Scotch whiskey.) American intelligence would locate this installation shortly after the start of the fighting, but even the heaviest air and naval bombardments would cause little damage except near one of its concreted entrances. The working spaces were virtually impervious to conventional explosives.

From the agony of the battle, Japanese soldiers would remember their months of preparation with nostalgia. But now their life was only sweat and tears. New recruits who had been disgusted by civilian profiteering while soldiers were dying for Japan saw little of the compensatory honesty and justice they'd hoped to find in Army life. Bullying veterans monopolized water, food and every perk. The Imperial Rescript still had to be recited from memory. The beatings for slip-ups or a "bad attitude" were even more severe than before because digging put the roughneck senior soldiers in a foul mood. When those "vicious, gangster-type" noncoms, as a junior private called them, were out of earshot, some victims comforted themselves with thoughts of retaliation if the Americans landed. A few actually looked forward to battle in the hope that anything had to be better than their present condition.

Spring brought merciless heat. A large army prodigiously sweating while mixing vast amounts of concrete made water scarcer than ever on the island. Severe restrictions on showers and laundry were a harsh privation to men fondly devoted to bathing's rituals and pleasures. "We couldn't wash our dishes, our clothes, even our hands after relieving ourselves," a soldier later lamented. The rapid spread of skin infections brought itchy torture even to the few who were not performing heavy labor. (No one thought of how Okinawans were coping without the huge portion of their scarce water commandeered by the Army.)

The rations were so meager that men found picking, chopping, and eating radish leaves "an indescribably happy occasion." "I can't bear just a cup of rice for a meal with no side dishes at all," one complained. Some cooks ordered soldiers to gather mulberry leaves for mixing into the rice, but the tough greens were hard to swallow and stuck in the mens' throats. A thin soup, oily with pork fat and dressed with a few pieces of squash, completed the main meal. Still, ordure accumulated so fast that one artilleryman's turn to shovel it into a bean paste keg and lug it to a swamp of sewage came every ten days. "Why so much waste? Because soldiers couldn't bear their hunger and secretly bought tapioca buns and steamed sweet potatoes from civilians" — although one little bun cost a private his daily pay.

During a regular "first-year soldier training" session, a senior private ordered a waste disposal team to fall in with their boots in their hands. The bully scrutinized them, then pointed to Norio Watanabe's. "What's this?" he thundered. Watanabe, a former free-lance photographer from Osaka, had cleaned and polished his boots with his usual frightened care, but a speck of excrement remained on a heel. "Tell me," screamed the senior private, "from whom did you receive this item to keep and maintain?" As required, diminutive Watanabe replied that he kept and maintained his boots for the Emperor. "What? You know that and still put shit on it? Lick it off! Eat it!" For all his knowledge of Army ways, Watanabe could not bring himself to obey. His hesitation increased his superior's rage. The senior private lashed out with his fists until Watanabe finally endured his new humiliation. "No matter what, we must blindly obey everyone of higher rank."

The troops were kept at their digging day and night. Caves and more caves were needed for "barracks" and command posts, for supply and ammunition depots, for a whole strategy and existence based on counterattack from underground. The simplest fortifications were made by enlarging the natural grottoes and burrows in which the subtropical landscape abounded. A thousand men worked around the clock for nearly a year, gouging the most elaborate holes, which had up to four stories carved from their hills and escarpments. Many were supported by timbers and, when there was time, provided with cross-ventilation. A selection of the tens of thousands of stone and concrete tombs that dotted the countryside were fitted out with guns and supplies, and thus converted into makeshift pillboxes.

Okinawans dug too, some hired, some as conscripts. Thirty-nine thousand men — every fit male between sixteen and forty — were drafted, of whom about a third were used as laborers and twenty-four thousand were issued rudimentary uniforms in the Home Guard, or Boeitai. Teenage students assigned to units with no nearby living accommodations had to walk up to twelve miles every day, which took four hours or more, both to and from home. In the fortified areas, most notable public and private buildings had been taken over by the Army. Almost all schools were barracks. Awed children watched growing numbers of soldiers drill on their dusty school grounds while their parents wondered whether civilian life would disappear entirely. But there was no alternative to helping prevent Americans from bayoneting their children. Many Okinawans volunteered, or were volunteered through their civic institutions, and worked harder than ever in their lives. They had only hand tools and a handful of trucks; the 32nd Army's full array of heavy construction equipment consisted of two bulldozers and one earth roller. A million tons of dirt were removed from caves in straw baskets balanced on heads and shoulders. New airfields — of the twenty-two planned for the island — were leveled with pickaxes and hoes. The laboring at Yomitan and Kadena Airfields, to which Masahide Ota and other Normal School students had been assigned for years, was a minor preliminary to this massive effort.

Where not enough tools could be commandeered from farmers, Army officers in charge of the projects told civilians to use their bare hands. Many did, including children. The limestone of many hills was easy to dig, but the coral, which in many places had a depth of twenty to sixty feet, was harder than concrete. Little dynamite was available. There was no iron for reinforcing concrete and too little concrete itself. The October 10 air raid had destroyed most of the gasoline allocated for the 32nd Army's trucks. Therefore millions of timbers for shoring up the caves, tunnels and entry shafts had to be brought down largely by hand from the mountains of the north, then loaded onto little native boats for transporting south. Civilians shared the extra work with the troops.

With too little protein and fresh vegetables, many grew weak on the relentless labor. Cynics joked that they were being trained for grave digging, which would be next. Recent conscripts in the Home Guard joined those who feigned illness. (Students who thought to leave the digging to others were told they would not be graduated without putting in their time.) Many more developed chronic colds and diarrhea, causing those previously exempted from physical work to be enlisted for the "slave labor," as an Okinawan later put it.* Like real slave labor, this variety could kill. After months of grueling work in dank caves or under a burning sun with no rain, men began collapsing. "The Corpse Guard" took them away.

Isamu Cho oversaw the digging, but its mastermind was Ushijima's chief operations officer, the only senior holdover from Masao Watanabe's staff. Colonel Hiromichi Yahara, a talented tactician with a pragmatic bent, looked his part as a realist who relied more on his intellect than on a heart stiffened with "Japanese spirit." His broad range of planning experience included a year as an exchange officer

---

*"Those back from digging sleep in the shelter," another Okinawan reported. "I could say 'like pigs,' but pigs in a pigsty sleep stretched out in comfort. . . . But when you're truly exhausted, the body will find it possible to sleep in any place and position."

in America. In this sense, the forty-two-year-old graduate of the Military Academy was the least "Japanese" of the leading triumvirate, more Western in outlook than the samurai traditionalist Mitsuru Ushijima or the mystically inclined Cho. Yahara's contribution helped make the 32nd Army's leadership Japan's acknowledged best in the Pacific, but there had been debate about keeping him on Okinawa. Knowing his dry personality and bent for facts and figures, Imperial General Headquarters feared he might clash with the romantically aggressive, optimistic Cho, who had become his superior.

The two would indeed clash at critical moments in the fighting, but they were allies in a larger sense; for the overall strategy of digging deep and counterattacking from their underground shelters — moreover, counterattacking only selectively and only as a defensive tactic — was the 32nd Army's largely self-made response to what it knew would be overwhelmingly superior enemy firepower. And as the military historian Thomas Huber pointed out, this cautious, self-preserving response ignored both Japanese military tradition and Ushijima's insistent superiors in Formosa and Tokyo. The brass wasn't pleased when General Cho flew to the capital to report on the preparations. Why, they pressed, was the 32nd Army so committed to caution? Why was so little of the beach defended?

Ushijima stood his ground, and Yahara continued to plan the defense in keeping with his view of war as above all a science. During the 10/10 air raid, he had three divisions at his disposal, supplemented by some smaller armored, artillery and service forces and the 44th Independent Mixed Brigade, partly "restocked" by local conscripts after most of its men were lost on *Toyama maru*. The strongest of those units was the crack 9th Division, whose high morale and long history of combat experience more than made up for its relative lack of heavy armor. Colonel Yahara positioned this backbone of the 32nd Army in the backbone of the defensive position, behind a natural line of high ground protecting Shuri and Naha. This left the 24th Division above the beaches where Yahara correctly foresaw the Americans would land, and where a heavy concentration of practiced artillery would devastate them when they were most vulnerable, discharging their troops and equipment. Then infantry regiments, including Captain Kojo's, would emerge from their deep bunkers to hit fast and hard in the close combat where Japanese superiority would prevail.

Staff officers were supremely optimistic in public and fitfully so in private. No defenders on previous islands had thrown a landing force back into the sea, but none had been nearly so well prepared, and the present ones longed to succeed just this once. Some understood that such a feat would make no difference in the long run. The enemy would make a second or third landing, eventually certain to succeed, since the defense had so few reserves and no way to replenish supplies that were short to begin with. Others hoped a bloody mauling of a major landing would compel America to seek tolerable peace terms instead of courting worse with an invasion of the mainland.

But such illusions soon vanished, together with the pleasurable anticipation of obliterating the landing force. The reason was an unlucky guess, or grave miscalculation, by Imperial General Headquarters, which removed the 9th Division to bolster the defense of the Philippines. The division's twenty-five thousand men were shipped there via Formosa in December, but the Philippine cause seemed lost before they had completed their trip. (The last pockets of Japanese resistance on the Philippines actually held out until early March 1945, five weeks after the landing on Iwo Jima and four before the one on Okinawa.) Not sent on, they weren't sent back either, partly in fear of more sea travel, partly because Formosa — which still seemed more likely to Japanese strategists than Okinawa as the next American target — had already been drained in vain support of the Philippine garrison. Ushijima's best division remained on Formosa during the rest of the war.*

Through his operations officer, Ushijima had tried to persuade Imperial General Headquarters not to act on their devastating decision. Yahara argued with logic and passion that no effective defense of Okinawa could be guaranteed without the 9th — and if it had to be withdrawn because the Philippines was to be the decisive battle, General Ushijima preferred to accompany it and die in that battle. He had a clear idea of what to expect from IGHQ. During his own Tokyo tours, he had helped draft encouraging telegrams with empty promises of heavy reinforcements to commanders on other islands invaded by the enemy. But with a chance for at least a stalemate if the 9th Division anchored his defense on Okinawa, there was a hope that this case might be different. Tokyo, however, held firm and twice faltered on promises to send replacement divisions for the 9th. Eager as the government was to bolster civilian morale by maul-

*This prompted a laugh of frustrated rage from Premier Kuniaki Koiso — who had replaced Hideki Tojo in 1944 — when the Okinawa landing was reported to him. Koiso remembered a lunatic's prophecy that the target would not be Formosa, the guess of most military experts, but Okinawa. Still, the threat of American submarines that kept the 9th Division useless on Formosa provided some compensation for Ushijima: significant quantities of arms originally destined for the Philippines remained on Okinawa. Partly as a result, the 32nd Army, although it remained hopelessly undersupplied compared with the invaders, had more weaponry, especially artillery, than the defenders of any previous Pacific island.

ing the enemy on Okinawa — and perhaps even prompt the Americans to agree to cease hostilities — Japan's de facto rulers at Imperial General Headquarters, who could not imagine surrendering on any American terms, were already girding for a decisive battle on the mainland. Orders for the dispatch of the replacement divisions were therefore countermanded; better they defend the home islands.

Although field commanders like Tadashi Kojo did not allow the transfer to affect their morale, higher staff officers calculated that the 9th Division represented almost half the 32nd Army's fighting power and knew its loss was a "shattering blow" to the defensive plan. Some would later speculate that it was also a personal blow to Ushijima: when the 9th sailed, he began to have thoughts about atoning for the "failure" of his inevitable defeat. It was almost an unwritten rule that generals' adjutants were polished young officers from the elite of Academy graduates. When a Naha gentleman asked Ushijima why he'd flouted this tradition by appointing a roughhewn man up from the ranks, Ushijima's answer was a knowing smile. The questioner knew the unconventional adjutant was a master swordsman who would ensure a swift, sure beheading as soon as the general plunged his saber into himself.

In any case, Ushijima was now utterly without illusion about his future. He remained the model commanding officer radiating unshakable spiritual strength, without the slightest outward sign of disappointment or doubt about the future. But the withdrawal of the 9th Division and the refusal to replace it were unmistakable evidence that Tokyo had already conceded Okinawa and saw the coming battle as a mere delaying action.

Yahara had no illusions either. Estimating that American divisions had five to six times the firepower of the Japanese, he calculated that the attacking force as a whole would have twelve or more times the 32nd Army's, not including their air and naval support. His elaborate preparations for the decisive counterattack were scrapped for a new strategy based on his sharply reduced resources. One of his options was to concentrate almost all his remaining forces on level ground opposite the landing beaches, but he rejected it for what he called his underground "sleeping tactics." Instead of the cherished "decisive battle," where winner takes all, Yahara prepared for a war of attrition, otherwise called containment by a "strategic delaying action."

Much reorganizing of service, administrative, and engineering units into infantry battalions had to be undertaken for the diminished defense. As units moved to new sites during their massive repositioning in December, a gigantic explosion destroyed nearly half the 32nd Army's supply of munitions. Although small quantities of supplies were still arriving by air, Japanese shipping had nearly ceased after the 10/10 air raid. Chief of Staff Cho considered the loss of so much irreplaceable ammunition a heavier military blow than Naha's virtual destruction those two months earlier.

Now Yahara prepared a completely defensive campaign. Some Japanese officers calculated that a single battleship's firepower exceeded that of a full division. Knowing the enemy's control of the sea and air would give him an immeasurable advantage in firepower beyond its 12-to-1 superiority on the ground, Yahara saw the sole solution in withdrawing from the bunkers above the beaches, burrowing even deeper into better fortifications inland, and waiting to engage the Americans seriously only from there.*

The Yahara-Ushijima strategy was not only defensive but also defeatist in the sense that it allowed for no more than brief counterattacks with no hope of eventual victory. But although the great majority of Japanese lived on that hope, Yahara preferred pragmatic results to the comfort of a fantasy. He had to plead his case — especially to calm the fervently aggressive Cho — against the grain of the Japanese upbringing on attack and more attack. But knowing there was no way to save Okinawa or prevent the total destruction of the 32nd Army, the realistic colonel reckoned his only goal could be to make the outcome as costly as possible, for which protection from the enemy's supreme firepower was crucial.

Thus the pace of the digging increased even more, especially since the redeployment of the remaining Japanese forces — which would continue until hours before the landing — required units to abandon their laboriously constructed fortifications and begin again. Perhaps no digger in the world could keep at it longer and more intensely, with fewer tools and less nourishment, than the Japanese soldier. Nothing he had dug anywhere exceeded his achievement here: enough underground refuge for the entire 32nd Army, with all its ammunition, weapons and other supplies. This was no supplementary effort to provide cover during battle but a fundamental approach, following the single most important Japanese military decision, that would result in the construction of over sixty miles of tunnels on an island whose surface roads were much lesser engineering achievements.

The diggers were more or less comforted by the ultimate reward

---

*American tacticians later suggested that this was Ushijima's single serious mistake: even without the 9th Division, he should have redistributed his remaining forces to defend his original positions above the beaches. That would have allowed him to delay defeat even longer and kill more Americans, his only attainable military goals. Otherwise, those American students pronounced Ushijima's tactical decisions after the start of the battle to be sound and sometimes brilliant.

spelled out in a slogan composed for them: "Confidence in victory will be born from strong fortifications." Knowledge that their safety would depend on their effort — since each unit built its own works — also bolstered them and encouraged diligence. Some service units had occasional hours off to fish, drink in the beauty of Okinawa and her women and take pleasure in the natives' kindness. (A few medics learned New Year's greetings in Okinawan and went about "uttering the strange phrases," as one put it, in a confident mood, buoyed by holiday rations of sake and sweets.) The luckiest combat units had a few visits to Naha's famous red-light district, rebuilt after the 10/10 raid and staffed, or closely supervised, by the Army.* Others had no time off whatever apart from a brief visit or two to houses of native volunteers. One man remembered only digging the ground and sleeping on it during the nine months since his arrival. "We slept on rocks and gouged rocks . . . We endured every conceivable suffering in a soldier's life while building our position."

More months of feverish work produced new shelters, the best of which were like railroad repair tunnels, well ventilated, equipped with drainage for the sour wetness underground and protected by a hundred feet or more of earth above. Tracks were laid for mounting heavy artillery and entrances were camouflaged: Iwo Jima had bitterly demonstrated the Americans' skill in detecting the source of incoming fire, then destroying the guns with savage shelling from their ships, planes and artillery. Japanese gunners were forbidden to fire until the last minute, after which they would quickly roll their guns back out of sight.

All this was preparation for exacting the highest price for surrendered territory. A military historian recently described the 32nd Army's final operational plans as amounting to "nothing more nor less than denying the enemy the ground, foot by foot." But Yahara wrote and distributed a pamphlet entitled "The Road to Certain Victory," and Japanese soldiers remained ignorant of the underlying pessimism of his strategy. Civilians suspected even less, although they too were disturbed by the loss of the 9th Division. They watched their ancestral tombs turned into bunkers and saw "roadsides and hillsides that had been their private world turned into foxholes and machine gun positions with black, hollow openings." Realizing the battle was

*Okinawan courtesans and geishas were generally reserved for officers; Korean women, some brought from Korea and the Japanese mainland as comfort girls, serviced the men in the ranks — at extremely low charges, in keeping with their minute pay. Up to a dozen women were attached directly to some of the larger units. The Army had seized many of the Korean girls, some as young as twelve and thirteen years old, by force.

imminent, they "shivered with their image of the enemy" — who, however, would never be allowed to ravage their land.

Only a handful of civilians guessed there was no hope whatever of anything beyond prolonging the forthcoming battle in order to give the mainland more time to prepare for *its* Tennozan. Very few stopped to think that what was to come later in the year on those Japanese home islands would be even worse than the ordeal about to begin on Okinawa: more like Ushijima's resistance if the 9th Division still anchored it.

9 · The Boys in the Pacific

Think not of death as you push through with every ounce of your effort, fulfilling your duties . . . Fear not to die for the cause of everlasting justice. Do not stay alive in dishonor. Do not die in a way that will leave a bad name behind you.

— From *Battle Ethics*, a pamphlet distributed to all Japanese on active service a month after Pearl Harbor

An endless stream of evidence ranging from atrocities to suicidal tactics could be cited . . . to substantiate the belief that the Japanese were a uniquely contemptible and formidable foe who deserved no mercy and virtually demanded extermination.

— John W. Dower, American historian of the war

Probably in all our history no foe has been so detested as were the Japanese.

— Allan Nevins, American historian

Goodbye, Mama, I'm off to Yokohama . . . I'm going to slap a dirty little Jap.

— From a popular wartime song

There have been just and unjust wars throughout history but there is very little difference in the manner in which people have been propagandized to believe in them.

— Andy Rooney of CBS

DICK WHITAKER had a week's leave after boot camp, then two months of infantry training — through November 1944 — at North Carolina's Camp Lejeune. He was shipped to the West Coast on December 1, a few weeks before General Ushijima lost the 9th Division. Still hoping to be a hero, the wiry lad was almost guaranteed to remain unsung even if he swung it. War's meager proportion of glory to misery was much lower for Americans fighting in the Pacific than in Europe.

Location alone ensured them the worst fighting and least recognition. Europe was not only geographically and culturally closer to home but also far more pleasant. Rare Pacific liberties afforded little to take liberty with; sand and sun were not much fun when the only change was monsoonlike rain. Even rear areas afforded only a tent for home, insect plagues attacking dirty skin and much disease. So much was nastier on the scorching or humid atolls and islands that a law of military life might have decreed the paradox: worse treatment for those who already have it worse — and more of it, since Pacific fighters' average tour lasted much longer.

Actually, a strategic decision was largely responsible for the imbalance. Eight months before Pearl Harbor, the Joint Chiefs of Staff, as the heads of the American services would shortly become, secretly agreed with their British counterparts to focus America's primary effort on Europe if and when she entered the war. Roosevelt and Churchill's first post–Pearl Harbor meetings confirmed that "only the minimum of force necessary for the safeguarding of vital interests" elsewhere should be diverted from the "decisive" Atlantic-European theater. However Churchill's eloquence influenced Roosevelt, the menace of the Third Reich in occupied Europe justified that decision. Given time, her U-boats might cut communications between America and Britain. With more time, her scientists might produce devastating secret weapons — as they did, only slightly too late. The "Germany First" strategy was sound.

But it dedicated less support for the "boys" in the Pacific, who were facing rougher conditions. It wasn't true, as many of them believed at the time, that their fight was merely a "side show."* But those in Europe did get more supplies, headlines and applause for fighting their tamer war.

Superb as he could be, the German fighting man was an easier enemy than the Japanese, for he fought — the ordinary Wehrmacht soldier as opposed to members of the SS and other special units — more or less according to the same dictates as the Allied soldier, with more or less the same purpose and limits. With rare exceptions, his goal was to kill others, not to die gloriously. Therefore he surrendered when the odds became hopeless — when there was no sense, in the European understanding, to continued resistance. Or his commander surrendered for him. Whole divisions, entire armies of Germans surrendered; but no Japanese.

Before Okinawa, only a statistically negligible scattering of Japanese soldiers had been taken prisoner, even after stupefying bombardment and even when there was no point in fighting on except death — which *was* the point. Just over a thousand dazed defenders of Iwo Jima's more than twenty-two thousand were eventually captured, but only at the very end of that campaign, roughly a month

*William Manchester, a veteran of Okinawa turned writer and historian, fumes inexactly but understandably about storming Japanese-held islands with decrepit weapons because all modern ones were sent to Europe.

before the start on Okinawa. Men fought to the death in the most literal sense, often ending with a suicide charge in pursuance of the remotest chance of killing an American before falling. Few veterans of the European theater could comprehend the implications without personal experience of it.

One year before, when Imperial General Headquarters had decided it could no longer supply its Rabaul garrison, 100,000 Japanese soldiers were left to fight or starve to death. The few captured unconscious, a former Australian war prisoner wrote not long ago, "constantly attempted suicide when they revived in an American or Australian hospital — by pulling out IVs, tearing open newly stitched wounds, and even (when their hands were tied) by trying to bite off their tongues."* When symbol-conscious General MacArthur ordered the recapture of Corregidor, some two thousand of its three thousand Japanese defenders died by blowing themselves up in an underground arsenal.

Like his fellows and superiors unknowingly bound for Okinawa, Dick Whitaker would have had great trouble crediting Japanese culture's very different attitude toward "the last debt." In the West in general and America in particular, death was an irreversible end to a brief earthly appearance, a verdict feared because its sentence was unknown. Tears, repentence, sackcloth and ashes naturally followed — whereas Japanese death was much more tolerable. In both major religions, Buddhism and Shinto, it was more a part of life than its end. It involved much less judgment, let alone final judgment to possible eternal damnation.

Few Marines suspected that boot training gave them a better chance than most to grasp Japanese attachment to the community. While Western religion, philosophy and culture nourished a unique individuality, a sense of self separate from all others, Japanese upbringing forged far more identity with the group. The cherished goal of *wa*, "harmony," could never be achieved by indulgence in individual needs and rarely except through sacrificial pain. Especially in military affairs, Japanese men were prepared to believe that "death is lighter than a feather but duty heavier than a mountain."

---

*Russell Braddon cites an Australian POW camp where 1104 Japanese tried to kill themselves as atonement for having surrendered. "None had surrendered as we had surrendered, with hands held high and an irrational optimism, and all had been treated with immense consideration by their Australian guards ... Loathing the stigma of captivity, almost every Japanese had assumed a false name. They never even asked one another about their family ... and they positively dreaded meeting anyone who had known them in less painful days. All of them had been nursed back from unconsciousness (had they not been unconscious, they would have blown themselves up; had they not blown themselves up, a comrade would have shot them) but none doubted that he had become a nonperson for whom there was no longer any family, homeland, honour or future."

Thousands of years on their cramped home islands made the almost racially homogeneous Japanese members of one large family in certain ways. This did not preclude savage warring among factions and feudal lords any more than in an actual family. The work patterns of their agricultural society also conditioned its people to see themselves as members of a team. Farming, especially of the all-important rice crop, put a premium on cooperation, not on individuality. Japanese tended to see themselves as seedlings of a crop sprouting indivisibly. To be different was to court instant notice and fearful isolation. "If a nail sticks out," went one of the most repeated sayings about upbringing, "hammer it in." A close observer suggested almost half a century after the war that to understand Japan's morality one must imagine "a situation in which good behaviour is constantly determined by individuals' views of how others expect them to behave; in which they can never think 'To hell with them'; and in which conformity to social expectations is not an unfortunate compromise but the only possible way to live."

Most Japanese were therefore snug in their own society, extremely uncertain and uncomfortable with outsiders and wont from their earliest years to think of what was defined for them as the common good rather than of self-assertion.

This was the soil in which *bushido* grew. "The Way of the Warrior" was originally established as rules of conduct for samurai,* retainers who wielded their swords for feudal lords. Elevating courage, valor and loyalty, it corresponded in some ways to the chivalric codes for European knights. *Bushido* stressed self-discipline, reverence for nature, magnanimity, simplicity, modesty and unquestioned obedience. It was pervaded with gratitude for the blessing of being Japanese. Luxury, display and boastfulness were very much not the way of the Japanese warrior.

To deter all samurai from changing sides, which they had done with some ease in medieval Japan, the notion was introduced that this brought loss of honor — strong discouragement in a society where shame stung painfully. Surrender was also deeply shameful. Suicide was preferable, especially since Japanese culture included no prohibition against it. *Harakiri*† came to be regarded as a highly honorable act, reserved primarily for samurai, at the top of the commoners' social scale.

---

*"Samurai," probably from a verb meaning "to serve," originally referred to a member of the sovereign's guard and later extended to high-ranking warriors privileged to ride a horse.

† *Seppuku* is ritual suicide, the rite of *harakiri* performed as remonstrance with prayer and pain, by cutting open one's abdomen. *Seppuku* has remained a solemn word; *harakiri* has become somewhat vulgar.

True samurai were never cowardly enough to court or hasten death. *Harakiri* was appropriate only when every resource had been exhausted and no hope remained to pass yet another test. Since most samurai who actually fought were practical as well as fierce — and the code, like most of them that prescribed knightly virtue in other societies, was constantly ignored — suicide was relatively rare.

It was even rarer in the seventeenth to nineteenth centuries, when central control became strong enough to stop almost all feudal fighting and samurai became more bureaucrats than warriors, the committee more powerful than the sword. Still, the practice was celebrated and idealized, chiefly by fervent noncombatants. When the act could be extolled in comfort rather than performed, legends, epics and plays spread its thrilling virtues among armchair admirers, as American Westerns celebrate manly violence. Nonfighting myth makers — dandies pining for the samurai past, as Ian Buruma recently described them — became more samurai than actual working samurai had been. *Bushido* was propagated far less by men who had to fight to the death or kill themselves than by comfortable fans of the drama. Although its roots went deep, its modern glorification arose after three centuries of peace, when the valorous "had little else to do but worry about rules, appearances [and] style . . . warriorhood without wars was soon reduced to a set of stylish postures."

A strong undercurrent of radical militarism ran close to the surface of Japan's relatively democratic 1910s and 1920s. When it broke through and pushed the country into her imperialist wars, ultranationalists menaced political, social and cultural life — and held up *bushido* as a code of national behavior. Never mind that it had been devised for an elite in individual combat or that it mandated benevolence toward the weak and conquered. Never mind that the feudal code could have rare application in modern combat. "The code of *bushido* says that a warrior lives so that he is always prepared to die," the outspoken, nonmystical captain of the light cruiser in *Yamato's* screen told his crew as they got under way. "Nothing has been so abused and misinterpreted as this adage. It does not mean that a warrior must commit suicide for some slight reason. It means that we live so that we shall have no regrets when we must die. Death may come to a man at any moment, no matter how he lives. We must not forfeit our lives meaninglessly." But few Japanese knew the origins or understood the concept. From the 1930s onward, it was exploited in the service of the tyrannous twentieth-century obscurantism that overwhelmed the nation and prosecuted the war.

With this distortion, death was elevated from a slim possibility to a civic, or at least a military, duty. For half a century, every Japanese schoolchild dedicated himself to his Emperor every morning, "worshiping at a distance" with bows to His Imperial Majesty's photograph or in the direction of the Imperial Palace. Assembled classes recited the Imperial Rescript on Education and were asked to name their dearest ambition. The daily reply thundered forth in unison: "To die for the Emperor."

A manual given each Army recruit spoke of "living and dying" with his fellow soldiers. "READ THIS ALONE — AND THE WAR CAN BE WON" lauded noble death — "Corpses drifting swollen in the depths of the sea / Corpses rotting in the mountain grass" — and described its rewards. All military life resounded with the need to die honorably and the patriotic and spiritual reasons for welcoming it. "Do not be afraid of combat and do not come home alive" was endlessly repeated. "Whether I float as a corpse under the waters or sink beneath the grasses of the mountainside," went a fighting man's hymn, "I will willingly die for the Emperor." Johnny, as Russell Spurr put it recently, never came marching home. The martial songs "left him rotting on some foreign field or dying hopelessly in a futile suicide charge."

By now, dying for the country was official policy rather than an expression of volunteer patriotism. Troops were unceasingly reminded that *victory of honor* or *death of honor* were their only alternatives; that self-sacrifice was sublime; that willingness to die was essential to "the Japanese fighting spirit," which would protect the righteous Empire from its evil enemies. "Do not disgrace yourself by being captured alive, but die," exhorted the Imperial Rescript for Soldiers and Sailors.

Of course there were degrees of belief in this. It was iron among the Army's backbone of Academy graduates, men like Mitsuru Ushijima and Tadashi Kojo. One such junior officer was wounded during the China war. A young Chinese officer who had studied under him when posted to Japan for instruction recognized him lying in a trench. He saw to it that his still unconscious former instructor was delivered to a hospital. The rescued man killed himself after his release to atone for the shame of his capture. Cadet Kojo was moved by the wholly understandable defense of his honor.

The belief was weaker among reserve officers; still weaker among the drafted rank-and-file; weakest among unmotivated nonconformists, softies and recent conscripts who had hoped to escape the draft. A soldier on Okinawa who was among the handful of his battalion's survivors would remember the Japanese people as wearing two faces during the war's final years. "The one turned to others around them said, 'Fight and die for the country.' The other, turned inward and shared by the family, said, 'Don't die; survive at all costs and come home!'" Those who did return home to find tear-soaked telegrams mistakenly informing family of their death realized that their parents were not the uncompromising patriots they had pretended to be.

Norio Watanabe, the draftee from Osaka ordered to lick the spot of excrement from his boot on Okinawa, bought no part of *bushido* at all. Nothing in Army life or philosophy appealed to the former photojournalist, who had fervently hoped his bottom-of-the-barrel draft category would keep him a civilian. Just before Pearl Harbor, a fellow journalist risked a treason charge to urge him not to die in the likely imminent war with America, but Watanabe already knew how silly that would be. Photographing for Osaka's General Motors division three years earlier, he had viewed a company film. Images of GM's mighty Detroit plants was enough for the "misfit" to see immediately what the Army brass could never grasp: taking on America would be madness.

Watanabe's slight size protected him from call-ups into early 1944, but everything he saw of the war as a civilian further convinced him of that madness. He was summoned to a police station one day to explain a young nephew's behavior: the boy had been caught strolling in a park without his gaiters. "This is a time of national emergency!" lashed the outraged police. "Our soldiers are dying at the front!" The incident took place in traditionally liberal Osaka, whose merchants used to disparage the military. Watanabe had to apologize abjectly.

He was thirty years old when his despised draft notice finally came, a year before the start of the fighting on Okinawa. Clenching his teeth during basic training — to keep them from being broken — he quickly realized that the real reason for his beatings was the Army's conviction that fear was the best teacher of obedience. "The beaten lose their minds," he observed, concluding that loss of mind had got Japan into the war in the first place.

Kenjiro Matsuki was another exception. When Kenjiro was a boy, a kindly uncle had supplied him with baseballs fished from a stream that ran from an athletic field to the uncle's little farm in Honshu's impoverished north, across the Sea of Japan from Vladivostok. Later, Matsuki's strapping size (by Japanese standards) and his love of baseball — introduced to Japan in the 1870s, two decades after Commodore Perry's visit — won him a scholarship to Tokyo's Meiji University: free room and board and a few yen in pocket money. The team was invited to play a series against American universities in 1929, an exciting experience for the big first baseman. He later played on an All-Nippon team that hosted a series against Lou Gehrig and other stars and spent part of the summer of 1931 in Hawaii, where he danced with a young woman, something he might never have done in Japan outside dance halls with paid hostesses.*

Matsuki played for Japan's first professional baseball team when it was formed in 1935. He went from the Hanshin Tigers' captain to assistant manager and finally to manager in 1940 and 1941. Happy memories of America deepened his sadness at the news of Pearl Harbor. What foolishness to extend the war, already far into China, to mighty America! (Of course he never voiced his opinion: a report to the military police would have put him in serious trouble.) But Matsuki's firsthand knowledge of America was very rare among Japanese soldiers, and uncommonly individualist Watanabe would demonstrate on Okinawa that he was an even more rare exception. Although few ordinary Japanese soldiers believed the whole of their military indoctrination, most preferred death to the intolerable shame of surrender. The sullen, broken sprinkling who did surrender in Pacific battles preceding Okinawa were convinced they could never return "disgracefully alive" to face the humiliation awaiting them in Japan, where their names would have been stricken from their villages' lists, their manhood forever effaced. Those who had died in a suicide attack or clutching a grenade to their chests, however, were generously rewarded. Their spirits went to Tokyo's celebrated Yasukuni Shrine — The Patriots' Shrine or Shrine of the Righteous Souls — where they began a better life mingling with the spirits of other heroes and achieved a closeness to the Emperor beyond their aspirations while alive.

Americans took this for fanaticism, but it may have been closer to a poetic passion that welled up beneath the reserved Japanese countenance. It was a triumph of emotion over logic, like Japan's very decision to attack America. But whatever its source, the heightened willingness to die was among the factors that made the Pacific War supremely brutal. Soldiers everywhere continued killing until they were beaten; the Japanese soldier was not beaten until he was killed.

Willingness to die also helped explain the atrocities against Allied prisoners of war. Another Japanese trait also played a part: the tendency to sense no restraints when dealing with foreigners — the not quite human *gazhin* — who fell outside their own community's highly structured restraints. Japanese children were raised to develop keen

---

*His feats of the field did not win the hearts of Japanese girls. Very few watched baseball in the 1920s and 1930s, and young members of the opposite sex did not lift their eyes, let alone speak, when they passed one another in the street.

sensitivity to the complex webbing of duties, debts and obligations that governed their society, all involving nuances and subtleties and rules that varied with time and place. It is almost essential, as Ian Buruma observed, to be brought up as a Japanese in order to acquire this sensitivity — "to have one's brains plugged into the social computer bank, as it were. The code is internalized in the same way that Christian morality is internalized in most Westerners. But when a Japanese is unplugged, by going abroad for instance, the computer can go berserk, for unlike Christian morality the Japanese code is not thought to be universal — it applies only to Japanese."

On top of this, many Japanese soldiers despised prisoners for allowing themselves to be taken. Some believed beheading was an act of compassion that ended their intolerable disgrace. How much better to give a prisoner a manly death than to prolong his "final degradation of the male spirit!"

It was easy for Americans in 1944 to see Japanese as inherently savage. The handful who knew something about their culture could cite the glorified barbarities — steel swords slashing human bone — that ran through Japanese history. But the country hadn't always mistreated prisoners of war. Defeated enemies sometimes received true *bushido*'s consideration and courtesy, as in the Russo-Japanese War of 1905, when treatment of Russian prisoners was often exemplary.*

In this war, however, Japan was far more brutal than Germany to American POWs. However savage the Nazi occupation was to civilian populations, however Soviet and East European prisoners suffered, Germany treated many Western POWs tolerably, no doubt in part because the thousands of Wehrmacht soldiers in Allied hands were an incentive to observe her obligations as a Geneva Convention signatory. But Japan lost few prisoners to the Allies and cared little for those despicable cowards.

The Empire held far fewer American than other Allied prisoners, principally English and Dutch soldiers and colonial administrators captured during her lightning seizures of European colonies in the months following Pearl Harbor. Over a million had died or were painfully dying in their gruesome camps. Disease and starvation claimed most of them. Others were beaten, beheaded and bayoneted,

---

*Russians received fine treatment at a model camp at Matsuyama and even extraordinary freedom of movement outside the walls. Prisoners, some of whom had surrendered quite easily, roamed the entire island of Shikoku, wandering into towns and homes. One explanation of Japan's scrupulous adherence to international laws was her current effort to win a revision of the unequal treaties imposed on her by the Western powers. But some Japanese now attribute the shocking decline in humanity from 1905 to 1945 to the same narrowness that would cause so much military grief. Early Japanese generals were of broad outlook and Confucian training. Later ones became far more specialized and less in touch with nonmilitary interests of any kind.

sometimes when tied between posts. There was also a range of un-speakable tortures. At Milner Bay, the penises of Australian prison-ers were cut off and the foreskins sewn to their lips. Then they were bayoneted, and a sign was left for when their comrades retook the territory: "It took them a long time to die."

Tokugawa Japan [in 1853], poor, proud and afraid, was about as differ-ent as a human society can be from plebeian, acquisitive, overconfident America.
— Murray Sayle

We pray God that our present attempt to bring a singular and isolated people into the family of civilized nations may succeed without resort to bloodshed.
— Commodore Matthew C. Perry's journal entry of July 9, 1853, the day after he arrived off Edo Bay

What caused that barbarity? Few Americans had any notion of the ripe hatreds in the Japanese memory. Raw pride imagined some ra-cial slurs, but others were real. There was good reason to be galled by American demonstrations of superiority, including opposition to Japan's wish for a racial equality clause in the Treaty of Versailles in 1919. In the States, Orientals were made ineligible for citizenship. California and other states segregated their schoolchildren and de-nied their parents the right to own land. The 1924 Exclusion Act was directed specifically against immigration from Japan, even though a gentleman's agreement sixteen years earlier had virtually ended it. Such gratuitous insults demonstrated that the Yellow Peril was at least as much in the American mind as in geopolitical reality.

The humiliations had begun earlier, at an episode hailed in Ameri-can history and reviled in Japanese. When Matthew Calbraith Perry arrived in Japan in July 1853, eighty-eight years before Pearl Har-bor, the country had been closed almost hermetically for over two centuries. Sealed borders kept foreigners from entering and natives from leaving — or returning, if they had been resident abroad. The crime of building anything larger than a fishing boat was punishable by death. The entrenched isolation magnified the terrifying specter of Perry's warships in Tokyo Bay.

A letter from Millard Fillmore, the commodore's well-meaning President, assured the Japanese Emperor of Americans' good inten-tions. His tolerant, democratic, peace-loving Republic recognized Ja-pan's right to govern herself without the slightest interference. But Japan's closure had led her occasionally to fire on foreign ships in distress — including an unarmed American merchantman sixteen years earlier — and to mistreat seamen shipwrecked on rocky coasts:

aliens who had violated the prohibition against entry. Although few were now killed, many were beaten. Perry had come to end that inhumanity and, incidentally, to secure coaling facilities for American ships and opportunities for her traders. His demands included nothing for the Japanese to resent, providing Christianity was presumed the highest good, for the Secretary of the Navy had confided that the mission's motive was to awaken the Japanese to their "Christian obligation to join the family of Christendom." Nothing to resent — presuming that good was served by opening a sovereign nation to America's economic, religious and national interests.

Washington's ideals were as enlightened as any of the time. It believed no nation had a right, for her own sake as well as for the common good, to exclude herself from progress, international trade, the rewards of science. But those good Christians did not rely on moral suasion to convince the heathen. They brought big guns.

Blinking at them, the Japanese could not fully appreciate their visitors' benevolence. They knew Westerners had forced their way into China just fourteen years earlier and that the British, annoyed by attempts to restrict the importation of opium, instigated the Opium War and easily triumphed with their modern weapons. The Chinese Empire's virtual disintegration quickly followed, foreigners extracting concession after concession from the rump. That recent history hardly helped Japanese recognize Perry's arrival as a gift of enlightenment rather than a threat. It was a devastating blow to national honor in a country where avoiding slights, not to mention blows of that force, was almost as important as food.

Perry's demands were moderate, at least in comparison with those the British, Dutch, French and Russians would make in his wake. Japan would surely have been compelled to bow more deeply if a Russian force, dispatched by Nicholas I, one of Christendom's great despots, had arrived first — which it failed to do by a mere six weeks.* Since *someone* was going to pry the country open very soon, better the young Republic than the cynical European powers that negotiated more arrogantly and mined concessions more greedily. But it was Americans who arrived first and began the process. An old Japanese folk song had warned of a "Black Ship . . . an alien thing of evil mien." Two of Perry's black-hulled ships also belched black smoke, the color by which the vessels instantly became known and remained known by every schoolchild of succeeding generations. The Japanese

---

*Russian expeditions had been planned for at least ten years. This one did not fulfill the Tsar's order to beat Perry to the punch because the voyage from the Kronstadt naval base in the Baltic Sea, and all the way around the Cape of Good Hope and up through the Indian Ocean, took ten full months.

had never seen steamships. The shore batteries had no hope against Perry's cannon. The country was submerged in panic and dismay.

It would not figure much in Japanese memory that Perry's squadron played a crucial part in the country's liberation from an often cruel feudalism whose borders were closed to tighten the rulers' domination. What most Japanese would remember is that the trespassers got their way through superior might. The "invasion force" of black ships became a national metaphor for menacing, humiliating foreign trespass on sacred Japan; a constant reminder, as Japanese saw it, that others wished her ill.* Their first sight of Western civilizers — down the barrel of American guns — fed their sense of themselves as being under pressure from the rest of the world, led by the United States.

Japan would undergo huge, often convulsive, changes before she began slashing and conquering in 1931. Roots deep in her own history and national psyche fed her glorification of militarism and urge to subjugate others. Quite enough Japanese believed the sword of the samurai was the soul of the nation well before the commodore arrived, and when gunpowder was introduced, they took to it like the Hebrews to manna.† Still, Perry's presumption and amazing cannon spurred Japanese impatience to build their own. The remarkable lesson learners mastered this one splendidly. They had good reason to believe that unless they could copy the barbarians' military technology, they would suffer more such humiliations, maybe even be carved up into economic colonies, as Western powers were about to do to much of the rest of Asia. The black ships were never forgotten. Their memory helped feed an appetite for conquest that would end in the Pacific War, when the emotional people, overwhelmed by their rages and fears, perceived Americans as "provocative symbols of a detested past" rather than as human beings. A cartoon celebrating Pearl Harbor depicted a dismayed Uncle Sam uncorking a giant samurai from a bottle: revenge for Japan's forced opening.

From a barbarous prisoner of war camp, Laurens van der Post perceived Japan's response as "a kind of accumulated revenge of his-

---

*The moral considerations may be clearer now, but some saw them even then. "The Japanese did not seek — they abjured our company; they did their utmost to keep us from their shores," warned a contemporary British writer. "It was only the terror of our fleets which thrust our society upon them against their will." Thirty years earlier, Americans were delighted by President Monroe's declaration that any attempt by a European power to intrude into *their* hemisphere would be considered a hostile act. Now Perry's demands were made with an assumption of superiority that mortified the Japanese, who had long and diligently convinced themselves of their own supremacy.

†Portuguese visitors introduced guns into Japan in 1543. Another early visitor described the Japanese as "naturally addicted to wars, wherein they take more delight than any other people we know." They loved the newfangled weapons.

tory on the European for his invasion of the ancient worlds of the East and his arrogant assumptions of superiority which had made him use his power . . . to bend the lives and spirits of the people of Asia to [the European's] inflexible will." Many Japanese temporarily forgot that Europe, meanwhile, had brought her much good. All that mattered was that since Perry's arrival, the proud people had been forced to live "a kind of tranced life" in the presence of the European, who prevented them from being their own special selves, with their greatness and illusions. "But now the spell was broken" van der Post observed, "and the built-up flood of resentment had broken through all restraints. Out in full spate, in the open at last, it swept the Japanese, normally so disciplined, but now drunk on what . . . appeared to be invincible military power, into a chaotic mood of revenge."*

Worst of all, it was self-righteous revenge. But it could not fully explain the barbarity because more was directed toward impoverished fellow Asians than toward high-handed Westerners. Japan's behavior on the Asian continent in the 1930s and 1940s was far more savage than the worst Western colonialism had been. The Greater East Asia Co-Prosperity Sphere, its hoaxing title for the conquered lands where it sloshed blood and sucked sustenance, spilled over with atrocities. "Japanization" of "inferior" Asians included slapping faces in public and massacring citizens; some ten million (mostly civilian) Chinese alone were murdered. The conquerors provided "an almost spellbinding spectacle of brutality and death," as a historian recently put it. In 1937, respected Tokyo newspapers duly — or falsely — reported a "friendly competition" by two officers to be quickest in beheading 150 Chinese with their samurai swords.

As for Americans, Japanese hatred waxed as the war situation worsened. By 1944, magazines were telling their readers that the more American beasts and demons who were sent to hell, "the cleaner the world will be." Classroom posters exhorted pupils to "kill the American devils!" Kill they did: a prisoner of the Japanese was seven times as likely to perish as a prisoner in the European camps of the Axis, and the statistics were worse for Americans alone. One percent of American POWs of the Germans died; 40 percent of the

---

*"It is remarkable how hostile one can feel toward people whose eyes and hair are of a different color," a Japanese novelist named Osamu Dazai wrote in his diary on hearing the news of Pearl Harbor. "I want to beat them to death . . . those insensitive American savages . . . Oh, beautiful Japanese soldiers, please go ahead and smash them!" As Ian Buruma pointed out, Dazai "was not some third-rate nationalist hack, but one of the great writers of modern Japan."

Japanese. One of the living, who happened to be a knowledgeable admirer of Japanese culture, was made to watch soldiers taking bayonet practice on live prisoners tied between bamboo posts and to witness executions "for obscure reasons like 'showing a spirit of willfulness' or not bowing with sufficient alacrity in the direction of the rising sun . . . I would never have thought it possible that in our time there could still have been so many different ways of killing people — from cutting off their heads with swords, bayoneting them in [various] ways, to strangling them and burying them alive; but most significantly, never by just shooting them."

The Imperial Army's Wake Island garrison shot over a hundred American construction workers who had been building airstrips when the Japanese landed in 1941, then claimed that the workers had died during American bombardments. Japanese pilots shot American rivals dangling in parachutes after bailing out. Their submarines sank a fraction of the tonnage sent under by American submarines, but Allied merchant sailors struggling in the water faced much greater danger. After a Japanese ship transporting American prisoners of war to the mainland was torpedoed, guards struggling to stay afloat machine-gunned prisoners nearby in the water. (Many of the prisoners would have died anyway in airless holds that drove them literally crazy with thirst.) Within days of the October 10 raid on Naha, a Japanese submarine's crew laughingly fired pistols and machine guns into the lifeboats of a Liberty ship it had just sunk.

The historian John Toland has argued that the Japanese-American war would not have been fought if not for the mutual misunderstanding and distrust, language difficulties — and racial prejudice, irrationality, honor, pride and fear among both peoples. Toland produced much evidence to show that "both sides feared things they need not have feared . . . we were damn fools like they were damn fools, it's enough to make you sick." But even the disastrous mistranslations of diplomatic communications he tellingly cites cannot expunge what *did* have to be feared. Americans were indeed damn fools, full of rigidity and self-righteous ignorance of the Orient; full of stupid, swaggering insults. But that was the principal cause neither of the Pacific War nor of its most awful excesses.

Whitaker's two months of infantry training in Camp Lejeune had far less hazing than boot camp; the trainees were now Marines, not "a bunch of fucking clowns." His transfer to the West Coast in early December 1944 — just as the 32nd Army on Okinawa was redeploying after the loss of the 9th Division — was a week-long train ride that featured twenty-four-hour pinochle games. The impatient young men believed that no humans had ever been packed together so tightly — while outside stretched the West's awesome vastness, a new spectacle to almost all of the little-traveled youth. The great expanse confirmed their country as the world's most beautiful, blessed and deserving. Underlying their attitude was a conviction that Americans were the most industrious, virtuous people, better than all others, immeasurably better than the dirty little buck-toothed Japs. There was also an assumption, as the journalist Murray Sayle recently expressed it, "that the whole human race is actually made up of Americans, or at least potential Americans, who need only liberation or enlightenment to behave like Americans" — a counterpart to the Japanese conviction that Japan was unique and superior. More than ever in love with their Land of the Free, the young warriors en route to California bitched about their conditions but wouldn't have traded places for anything with the soft civilians who were going to miss the great fight.

Righteous vengeance beckoned. The eighteen-year-olds knew little of the long nightmare of Japanese treatment of POWs, but what Whitaker had learned was enough to make him wonder whether Hitler was the worst enemy after all.

Several months after the Philippines had fallen to Japan in April 1942, the U.S. Army learned the fate of prisoners taken there from three escaped officers who managed to make their way to Australia. Officials kept the information secret for fear that surviving prisoners would suffer reprisals.* Only in January 1944 did the American public learn that men dying of thirst were stopped alongside wells and forbidden to drink, that others barely able to stand were booted and beaten, that an officer's finger was hacked off when he refused to surrender his wedding ring, that prisoners were forced to bury their comrades alive . . . and that over six hundred Americans and at least ten times as many Filipinos too exhausted to keep pace on a march from Bataan to a prison compound were clubbed, shot, buried and bayoneted to death. Almost four hundred Filipinos were hacked to pieces one day for no apparent reason at all.

There were some slight extenuating circumstances. Despite the admirable treatment of Russian prisoners in 1905, Japan's history was full of clan wars that ended in the gruesome slaughter of the last man of the losing side, sometimes women and children too. Now, with

---

*The execution of some of the downed Doolittle fliers — participants in an April 1942 raid on Tokyo by carrier-based bombers — was also kept from the American public for eight months.

beatings so important in the modern Japanese Army, it seemed natural to beat the enemy as well, especially those miserable cowards who had surrendered their dignity and manhood by allowing themselves to be taken alive. It is possible that the guards were unaware that many prisoners couldn't continue marching because they were close to starvation and racked with malaria, dysentery and other debilitating diseases. It is now clear that at least some of the killing was unintentional. Preoccupied with their attack plans and hard pressed to supply their own weary, hungry units, Japanese staffs had failed to prepare for the surprising — to them — number who surrendered.

Still, deliberate cruelty abounded, and Japanese soldiers delighted in it. Flies feasted on countless headless corpses in ditches. One American lieutenant was lashed to a telephone pole for his decapitation; his body was left dangling in the sun. American newspapers, in turn, blistered with disgust, outrage and confirmation that the "inhuman," "barbarous," "depraved" enemy was a bestial force from some headquarters of evil. The vicious cycle of kill or be killed widened the emotional gap between the Pacific and European wars. Everyone knew *some* Germans were good, but Japs were a racial menace as well as a dangerous enemy. Cartoons depicted them as mad dogs and hairy tarantulas rightly squashed by a combat boot. A magazine for Marines called *Leatherneck* specified who the good ones were in a caption under a large photograph of Japanese corpses: "Good Japs. Keep 'em Dying."

Whitaker read about the Bataan Death March when it was almost two years past. But the details gripped him like nothing in Europe and remained fresh in his mind as the train neared San Diego. He knew he'd be facing a "devious, cruel, bloodthirsty" enemy, maybe worse than the Germans. But he didn't yet know how they fought. He nurtured an assumption that the bowlegged runts in the sloppy uniforms — baggy trousers, wrinkled coats, ridiculous puttees — couldn't possibly be a match for his spit-and-polish, rough and very ready Marines.

Many Marines would sustain such bravado-laced illusions — part of what kept them "damn fools" about the Orient — all the way to front lines on Okinawa. Replacements for badly shot-up companies would be rushed in during lulls; and with no time to acquire "combat smarts," a shocking number of those green troops would themselves become casualties within hours. Their new platoon leaders tried hard to save them. One hurriedly lectured a new group of bewildered replacements as they huddled together against murderous Japanese fire from the hill nicknamed Sugar Loaf. Aching with exhaustion and shock from that day's loss of friends, the young platoon leader, up from the ranks after all his officers had been shot, concluded by pointing his pistol at the greenhorns. "And if I hear any bullshit about the Japs being lousy fighters, I'll shoot you," he said. "If one of you motherfuckers says they can't shoot straight, I'll put a bullet between your fuckin' eyes before they do."

Book II

---

10 · The Landing

Something of the wide, vaudeville range of European warfare was seen in the Pacific Theatre for the first time when American Army and Marine troops . . . invaded Okinawa . . . Most of the items of this particular variety show had been seen singly on the Pacific stage before . . . But Okinawa had them all and in most respects had them bigger.

  — John Lardner in *The New Yorker*

There were rumors of a landing up the coast. An occasional glimmer of signal lights at sea warned of a great fleet assembled on the horizon. Civilian interests were no longer of consequence. Families were fleeing into the hills, seeking refuge in old tombs and rocky caves.

  — George Kerr, *Okinawa*

When I saw . . . the American fleet, I doubted my eyes . . . The nearest ships seemed small, probably destroyers. Then middle-sized cruisers. Finally, way back in the mist, must have been the battleships. They looked like sumo wrestlers, squatting and waiting without the slightest movement for their turn in a match on some stage. Just thinking of what would happen if all those warships started firing sent shivers down my spine. This tiny island of Okinawa would be completely plowed under. Once it was such an unlikely event, this American landing here. Now it's a fact, right in front of my eyes.

  — An Okinawan father two days before the landing

You cannot regard the enemy as on a par with you. You must realize that material power usually overcomes spiritual power in this war. The enemy is clearly our superior in machines. Do not depend on your spirits overcoming this enemy. Devise combat methods with mathematical precision, then think about displaying your spiritual power.

  — General Ushijima to the 32nd Army

With our gun hidden deep inside the hill and camouflaged with branches, we waited for the enemy to land. We were full of apprehension, but it was mixed with eager expectation that swelled our chests.

  — A Japanese antiaircraft gunner whose battalion would soon switch to nocturnal suicide charges

The bombardment's gunsmoke and dust cloud changed the sky to yellow . . . The "massive iron" talked about since the failure at Guadalcanal has now descended upon Okinawa. The shells shot from hundreds of battleship, cruiser and destroyer batteries numbered thousands and tens of thousands a minute . . . The Japanese army, on the other hand, kept silent and did not fire a single shot.

  — An unwilling Okinawan conscript

To DISTINGUISH it from earlier
D-days, L — "Love," in American military parlance — was chosen to
denote the April 1 landing on Okinawa. Nothing as grim and breath-
taking had been unleashed in the history of the Pacific. Nothing similar is likely to be seen again.

This landing was even more impressive than the much documented Normandy operation the previous June, most of whose
ships, although marginally more in number, had to travel only the
width of the English Channel. Operation Iceberg, an undertaking of
the same immense scale, took place sixty-two hundred miles from
San Francisco, four thousand miles from Pearl Harbor, many days'
sailing from supply depots and anchorages the Navy had established
closer to the target.* "So vast was the operation," a military historian
summed up, "that the forces were staged and assembled across the
breadth of the Pacific, from the West Coast to Hawaii, the Marianas,
Leyte, Espíritu Santo, and Guadalcanal."

The movement of mountains of goods and equipment, from aircraft engines to drinking water to millions of candy bars, was an extraordinary feat in itself, and no secondary one, since the American
way of war relied on colossal quantities of supplies. (A Marine unit
crammed on an LST was dismayed to discover that the supplies included stacks of white crosses in the cargo spaces.) Twenty-two thousand tons of supplies had been delivered daily to Iwo Jima during
the fighting just ended there — only 15 percent of the daily total that
would be arriving on Okinawa. Twenty-five ships carried jeeps alone.
In two days, supply ships managed to transfer more cargo to fighting
ships at sea than a port the size of Boston handled in a week. It took
prodigious staff work to organize and coordinate the supplying,
loading and sailing of the vast array of vessels, with all their specialized personnel and equipment, so that they would arrive on time for
their ocean rendezvous. Love-day was the consummation of a stunning exercise in military logistics.

---

* Dick Whitaker made the acquaintance of such a depot a few days before Christmas.
His troopship's first stop after sailing from San Diego was tiny Banika Island in the Russells,
40 miles from Guadalcanal. After sundown — the days were too hot and humid for heavy
labor — work parties were ferried to a smaller atoll, where countless 55-gallon drums of
aviation fuel were stored under palm trees at the edge of the jungle. Throughout the
night, Marines loaded them onto trucks and reloaded them into barges at the water's edge,
helping pass a huge quantity of fuel through this one small depot among hundreds. Whitaker also witnessed his first death of the campaign on "Gas Island," when an accident
killed a member of his labor detail. An operation so massive and dangerous inevitably
brought thousands more.

If the purpose had been show, the operation would have entered history's hit parade of man-made spectacles. No fewer than 1457 ships and over half a million men participated in what a British observer called "the most audacious and complex enterprise yet undertaken by the American amphibious forces." Whitaker got his first inkling of its magnitude after his convoy joined a larger one — but still a fraction of the whole — at night. He went topside in the morning and blinked. "There were ships to the horizon, a truly awesome number. I couldn't have imagined that many ships existed in the world."

Four hundred and thirty of them were troopships. Their union with the largest armada ever assembled in the Pacific awed every man aboard. Some of those ships had long service records; others came straight from their shakedown cruises. They had sailed from eleven ports, from Seattle to Pearl Harbor to Ulithi, an atoll thirty-seven hundred miles west of Hawaii that provided a fine anchorage and base for forward operations.* Their number covered thirty square miles of ocean. Although no man could see more than a fraction of the whole, what he did see brought relief that "someone somewhere knew what he was doing. Getting all those ships with their specialized equipment and personnel to arrive all at one time at a dot in the Pacific gave us confidence. Maybe we'd be all right."

"There were battleships, cruisers, more cruisers — you wouldn't believe it," another said. "We were in the middle of a phenomenal amount of floating iron."

And: "Just for the hell of it — or to convince myself I wasn't dreaming — I started counting the ships. It was impossible. Too many of them, just too unbelievably many."

And: "I felt myself smiling inside. Maybe I'd be hit on this Okinawa where we were going, but there was no way we could lose with that incredible number of ships."

The submarine fleet alone, Task Force 17, contributed over fifty vessels, some of which had landed advance parties to prepare the beaches.† The 21st Bomber Command contributed over three hun-

---

*Ulithi also provided a kind of resort on the sandy island of Mogmog, where sailors could enjoy an afternoon of swimming, baseball and even two cans of beer inside a large coral reef. Whitaker and his fellow passengers felt this was luxury when their troopship stopped there on her two-week passage from Guadalcanal.

†Three days before the landing, a thousand frogmen smeared on silver body paint and swam to shore from landing craft some 500 yards out. While naval shelling and a strike by carrier-based planes forced Japanese beach patrols to take cover, these "half-fish and half-nuts" explored the coral reef, nourished by the warm waters of the Japan current, that fringed the landing beaches. Although no swimmer was hit, all were vulnerable to snipers on shore. This exceedingly hazardous work did not prevent some landing craft from being caught in coral on April 1, but the teams did manage to remove almost 3000 wooden stakes

dred B-29s; the aircraft carriers of Task Force 58 — which engaged *Yamato* one week later — supplied more than fifteen hundred additional planes, many of which had bombed targets on Okinawa for ten days before L-day. The fighting ships made up the largest assembly in naval history: over forty carriers, eighteen battleships, scores of cruisers, and almost 150 destroyers and destroyer escorts. These 318 combat vessels were roughly thrice the number the Imperial Japanese Navy had committed to the crucial Battle of Midway in June 1942, risking most of its fighting strength.

The American ships had poured fire onto Okinawa, especially on and around the landing sites, for six full days and much of their nights. The pre-invasion bombardment by ships and planes set a pattern for most Japanese on the island that they would follow until each man's death. As Colonel Yahara had planned, they hid underground during the day and sneaked out to do errands — later, to fight — at night. "Our activities begin in the evening, when the worst of the air raids are over," a surviving soldier recorded.

> Cooking, drawing water, washing and, more important, receiving more ammunition and moving our weapons. Transferring the sick and injured to medical facilities — all this must be done when naval bombardments keep cutting into everything, making us break into a cold sweat when the shells hit. Still, it's the Garden of Eden itself when no planes are overhead.
>
> "Let's go! The demon's gone!"
>
> Out we jump from our cave, run the tiny path to the foot of the mountain to find the small trench where our ammunition is hidden. It's dark on the return trip. We trace our way back to the cave, heavy ammunition cases on our backs, frantic to make it back inside *quickly*. Naval shells burst all around us.
>
> "Look out!" I say to myself, but the burden on my back would keep me from hitting the ground even if I tried. I flatten myself against the side of the rocky hill and wait for the shelling to stop, feeling the whole time as if my soul is wearing out. It's totally unsafe outside the cave even when the demons aren't flying above.

Japanese soldiers who had believed nothing could be worse than the first air raid of the previous October realized they were mistaken

---

that Tadashi Kojo's men and others had planted in the shallows. The teams risked their lives again the following morning by attaching charges to the stakes, setting fuses and swimming seaward before a huge chain explosion disposed of the obstacles.

Four months before the landing, a submarine had performed the arduous, dangerous task of taking a survey, at a range of only two miles, with a new kind of sonar that also detected mines. This was followed by minesweeping for the fleet, which required less courage from each officer and sailor involved, but was arguably as dangerous. It was certainly as essential, as the slogan "No sweep, no invasion!" suggested.

when a series of equally powerful raids hit them day after day in January 1945. Again they believed nothing could be worse — until the pre-invasion bombardment. They were mistaken yet again; worse came on L-day itself. In the small hours of April 1, the support ships and 564 carrier-based aircraft began raking eight miles of Okinawan beaches with the greatest bombardment by far in the history of the long Pacific campaign. Ten great battleships pounded the shore with their main batteries of 14- and 16-inch guns. Smaller broadsides from their secondary batteries and from nine cruisers, twenty-three destroyers, and almost two hundred gunships added to the enormous weight of metal: almost forty-five thousand 16-, 14-, 12-, 8-, 6-, and 5-inch shells, plus thirty-three thousand rockets and twenty-two thousand, five hundred mortar shells. Statistics are of course meaningless except to suggest that both sides felt the world was exploding with the "biggest thing yet attempted in the Pacific," this "mightiest naval force the world had ever seen," this "heaviest concentration of naval gunfire ever to support a landing of American troops," as described by the battle's historians.* The ten battleships alone could send 120 tons of high explosive onto Okinawa every minute, and all ten sustained their ferocity for three hours, flattening large circles of water with their shock waves, racking ears with their roar. For half a mile inland from the beach, about twenty-five rounds landed on every hundred square yards, which were also hit by planes, some using napalm. The air itself seemed to pulsate. The smell, smoke and head-splitting noise of previous amphibious landings had been stupendous. This was more; the most.

Then it stopped, still in predawn darkness. At 0406, the commander of the amphibious operation gave the traditional order to "land the landing force."

"We've all seen amphibious landings in the movies," a young naval officer wrote home, ". . . but the real thing is more spectacular than anything I ever dreamed of." The officer's vantage point was his Landing Ship Medium, which was launching Sherman tanks in huge flotation collars for their trip to shore. "The precision bombing of the beachhead by scores of planes, the monotonous shelling of the shoreline by the huge 'wagons,' the wave after wave of LVTs, small boats, etc., heading into the island constituted a display so formidable and awe-inspiring, I shall never forget it. It seemed so much like a tremendous dream, one couldn't feel fear. I'm thankful I had the opportunity to see it all from my grandstand seat in the pilot house."

---

*After observing the cannonade personally, the naval historian Samuel Eliot Morison wrote that "there was no want of bullets; only targets were missing, and much ammunition was wasted on cratering the fields of the Okinawan peasantry."

The spectacle impressed the enemy too. A Japanese soldier reported from an observation post commanding a view of the landing that "you can't make out the ocean color because of the enemy ships." A moment later, he made a conscientious correction. "I take that back. It's 70 percent ships, 30 percent ocean." When the morning mist lifted, a member of an antiaircraft unit saw a "magnificent" battle pageant under the sun. The start of the "ferocious" bombardment seemed like thousands of industrial plants all switching on their machinery together. Soon the landing area from the water to a mile inland was too covered by smoke as heavy as a volcanic eruption to make out the shore.

John Lardner reported the natives as "somewhat bemused" by all this — nonsense that could only have been prompted by ignorance of Okinawans and of real war, despite Lardner's reputation as a *New Yorker* war correspondent. The natives were actually full of foreboding. Since heavy American aerial reconnaissance revealed almost nothing about the Japanese positions underground, most of the pre-landing bombardment had no specific targets. Therefore, the majority of shells landed at random or slammed into civilian buildings. One Okinawan saw the torrent as "a bulldozer able to wipe out everything on earth . . . It felt as if the whole island of Okinawa would be pulverized and blown away." The giant fleet's week of bombarding was so much more menacing than the Okinawans had expected that all but the excitedly pro-Japanese kept themselves from thinking about it as they sheltered in caves during the day and tried to repair, provision or evacuate after dark. For civilians too, a routine that would last until the end of the campaign was already established: hiding and sleeping by day and trying to find provisions or new hiding places by night.

Shui Ikemiyagi, a Naha librarian conscripted into the Home Guard and later proclaimed a private second class (the lowest grade) in the Imperial Army, summed up the temper of the civilian majority, who hoped for the promised Japanese victory and tried to believe it would not cost them everything. The mood in his cave tended to be "gloomy and miserable." Some recently conscripted fellow Okinawans cried themselves to sleep, worrying about their families. Others chattered aimlessly; still others remained stone silent. Most wondered whether the imminent landing would bring their death.

> We spent the last week of March like criminals on death row. The instrument of execution was there . . . all ready for us. The only difference was that it was the American fleet instead of an ax or noose — and no time was set for the execution. But it was only a matter of time; it had to come sooner or later. That's what we felt

somewhere in our minds . . . We tried to suppress it and started to chatter a lot of nonsense. When no actual fear of death lurks nearby, we humans talk of it with composure, even laugh at it. But we stop mentioning death when it lies right in front of us.

Most Japanese soldiers were distinctly tougher. It was a tribute to their training, bravery and supreme commitment that the sight of the enemy armada, while impressing them with its size and "impudence" for steaming so "nonchalantly" into Japanese waters, neither seized them with fear nor informed them of the battle's inevitable end. That training, implemented amid the national hypnosis, was also what blinded ninety-nine in a hundred to how Japan's war had been ravaging others and why it couldn't possibly be won — blinded them even to evidence before their eyes, for many gazed with satisfaction at the immensely powerful fleet. They were pleased to see so many enemy vessels gathered for convenient destruction by Imperial planes and warships.

Much of the "pageant" was so massively more violent than anything the Americans had seen that most had moments of intense exhilaration. The smoke, smell and thunder of naval salvo after ear-splitting salvo were not merely stupendous but stupefying, overpowering. The din of some brass shell cases clattering on one ship's steel deck deafened "like a thousand cymbals falling down stone steps," remembered one man who waited for the order to enter his landing boat. But the troops readying themselves to climb down the nets to the boats would have been happy to tolerate ten times that noise. The first twenty-four hours on Iwo Jima six weeks earlier had cost fifty-five hundred American casualties.* More were expected on Okinawa, whose strategically more valuable territory was one-third closer to the mainland and also a Japanese prefecture rather than merely a possession. Rumor correctly had it that intelligence predicted L-day casualties of 80 to 85 percent, for which extra medical teams were going in with the first waves. Those troops were therefore grateful for every bomb, bullet and rocket of this heaviest bombardment ever to support an amphibious landing.

The infantrymen shouldered their weapons and backpacks and pulled themselves over the side, many carrying a hundred pounds of supplies and equipment. Sailors watched with a combination of camaraderie and relief that they didn't have to face the morning's carnage. Although shared suffering and hatred of Japan did not end

---

*Casualty rates in all Pacific landings were over three times greater than casualty rates in Europe.

interservice brawling in less tense moments,* the ships' crews now felt their hearts pull toward the men climbing down the nets. On U.S.S. *Baxter,* a twenty-year-old carpenter's mate, whose job would be to repair hit landing craft, watched with compassion. "You bet I felt sorry for them. You bet I wouldn't have wanted to join them. They didn't *show* fear, but how could they not have had it?"

As the huge roar of amphibious craft engines joined the gunfire thunder, sweat broke out on drawn faces. Even veterans of previous landings fought terror — or especially such veterans. This was John McMullin's fifth, "so I figured this had to be my time to get it; I'd been too lucky so far." "I don't know the words to explain how it is to be in combat," another veteran later apologized. "I was afraid, frightened and scared each time we jumped off the landing boats." And another: "Frankly, one of my nightmare moments was always related to the landing on the beach or being shot out of the water." A third: "For myself, I must confess that from chow at three A.M. till I climbed into the landing craft, it seemed I would explode from severe nervous tension." April 1 was Ed Jones's birthday. "I knew about Iwo. I thought I might have a very short nineteenth year."

Still, fear was only one of the emotions gripping the men as they squeezed into the bobbing landing boats breathing their oily exhaust. Another was relief to be off the mother ships. Whitaker's crossing from the States to his Russell Islands staging area, then to Guadalcanal and Okinawa, was typical. In San Diego he had been packed into a Liberty troopship for a voyage whose first leg alone took a month. Steel decks turned scorching under the equatorial sun. The hastily built or converted tubs with their troughs for latrines were torture for men squeezed together in the reek of sweat, urine and vomit. A deck officer reckoned, "You wouldn't treat sardines that way." The final four or five days had been one endless line for chow tasting like C-rations tossed into greasy caldrons. (Some Army troopships fed their passengers once a day, causing near rebellion among Marines who happened to have been crammed aboard among Army

---

*En route to Okinawa, Quartermaster Fred Poppe's converted LST, now a rocket launcher, had stopped at Pearl Harbor, where a tour of the ships destroyed by the infamous attack, with thousands of victims still entombed in the sunken hulls, swelled his patriotism and anti-Japanese passion to near bursting. Later Poppe was in line to have his photograph taken in a King Street joint when a tough gob behind him pinched one of the scantily clad hula girls who added zing to the photos. Her scream brought a larger, tougher Marine to the rescue. "You fucking swab jockey, do that again and I'll smash you."

The two fought until the Marine cracked a billy on the sailor's head so hard that it slipped from his hand. On the floor and bleeding badly, the sailor for some reason returned the instrument to the Marine, who hit him again before he was jumped by all other sailors in sight. Within minutes, blood coursed freely as hundreds stomped each other with everything they had, as in some free-for-all bar fight gone crazy. The little release of all-American madness was of course never mentioned in print.

units.) Many troops truly preferred landing and fighting the Devil himself, and surely the devilish Japanese, to spending another twenty-four hours in buckets whose gagging conditions grew worse on the final leg to Okinawa, when the fringe of a typhoon badly tossed hundreds of them, making a fetid mess of their lower decks. Most L-day breakfasts had been the traditional prelanding feast of steak and eggs — all they wanted! — but many men could manage only a few mouthfuls. At three or four o'clock in the morning, with the thunder of the naval guns reminding the men that many would be dead in the next few hours, it was too much like a convict's last meal.

The general who stated that Liberty ship transport "serves well in preparation for the hardships ahead" might have added that it also helped reduce reluctance to leave it for beaches on which machine gun nests, pillbox guns and dreaded artillery were zeroed in. Even without the torment of the voyage, some aggressive teenagers without wives and childen to consider would have been impatient. As Paul Fussell recently pointed out, combat's compensations — "the thrill of comradeship, the excitements of the chase, the exhilarations of surprise, deception and the *ruse de guerre,* the exaltations of success, the sheer fun of prankish irresponsibility" — console young men more than older ones.

"Sheer fun" would be rare on Okinawa, but older men shared with teenagers confidence in their training and certainty of victory. Deep pride in belonging to their units and an almost bodily satisfaction of righteous unity fed eagerness for the battle that was simultaneously feared. A mess sergeant in a tank battalion had paid $50 to his first sergeant in order not to be stuck in his rear echelon unit on Guam and left out of the fighting. A more impoverished buddy of his stowed away in order to be with his unit (and was later court-martialed for his initiative). After training endlessly for combat and absorbing all the indoctrination that went with the physical part of it, not to participate would have been a terrible letdown as well as a lucky break. To stay behind for some reason while buddies faced the test brought self-contempt.

In the hour before the battle, fear that one's own arms and legs might be among those soon to be blown off was exceeded by fear of failing in the eyes of the others — and that others would see the fear. As much as anything, that had been the purpose of their training: to make them perceive the danger as less fearsome than alternatives. An infantryman preparing to land in the first wave later spoke for almost everyone alongside him. "I think my biggest fear wasn't of getting hurt because like everybody else — until he's been in the line for weeks and knows this is pure bullshit — I was certain getting hurt is what happens to the other guys. This is crazy, but my biggest fear was whether the guy alongside me could tell what was happening in my stomach and whether I'd do something shameful when we hit the beach."

"I joined up to fight Japs and be a hero, but will I have what it takes?" a friend added. "Somewhere, I was scared out of my mind — but also scared that the guys next to me would see that."

In short, fear and apprehension were private emotions, shared but also covered up. "I wasn't just tense, I was scared half dizzy," a young infantryman remembered. "But even more than that, I was determined that nobody would see I was worried about anything. I think the main thing was not to show your buddy how frightened you were."

"You were more afraid of how you'd hold up under fire than of the fire itself," said another. "You prayed you wouldn't panic. You hoped like hell your landing craft would somehow never reach the beach, yet also hoped it was already there so you could get it over with."

And: "It was like a wide receiver going out for a pass. He wants the ball to come to him and at the same time is scared that he'll drop it, or get hit hard and fumble."

And most important: "You'd been trained never to let your buddies down. You knew how terrible that would be. So your fear of getting killed wasn't as bad as having to spend the rest of your life with your tail between your legs if you did let them down — a failure, a coward."

Buck Private Thomas Hannaher felt "dumb, dumb, dumb" for having voluntarily surrendered his asthma-caused 4F draft classification with the neat lie at his second medical examination in North Dakota — and choosing the Marines on top of that. "Dumb, dumb, dumb — one of the stupidest things I've done in my life." Everyone had seen films of the landings at Tarawa and other islands. Someone in his artillery battery had a radio and was listening to news about Iwo Jima. "That was when you decided God was worth knowing and it was a good idea to write some last letters. Because you knew this would probably be even worse than Iwo. You knew you'd be a casualty soon, that was just the law of averages." (The lucky ones had missed Tokyo Rose three days earlier, broadcasting "for you men standing off the shores of Okinawa, because many of you will never hear another program. Here's some music to remind you of darlings, jazz, home and mother.")

Hannaher realized this day might well be his last, though another part of him "knew" that wasn't possible. Resolution grappled with self-pity. Why did *he* have to be there that day? If he'd had an option, he "certainly" would have chosen to return to Guam. But without that option, he wanted to do his job. He still had to prove himself, and what better way? "I both hated the thought of being killed and wanted to be in combat. I was scared as hell but also proud to be with those going in now. I desperately hoped I wouldn't let anyone down. I was going to do this thing, and if I got through it, which I doubted, maybe life would be different when I got home."

Love of country was a given as night gave way to morning. All felt uplifted by belonging to their blessed, righteous homeland. But flag and country became abstract as the new day broke. What held mind and body together at H-hour was their sense of duty to their buddies, those squeezed in right beside them, and the unwillingness to lose face in their eyes.

(Needless to say, however, not even the intense tribal closeness cemented by the shared danger eclipsed all human nastiness. When Hannaher returned to his LST compartment after a few bites of the steak-and-eggs breakfast, he found that his Browning automatic rifle ammunition had been swiped from his bunk, leaving him to face his first combat landing with no bullets. He was lucky to steal parts of others' bandoliers before landing.)

> *As April 1 dawned, the bombing began with the magnitude of a hundred thunders striking at once. The smoke over the ocean was so thick we could see nothing there . . . A soldier from the small unit assigned to defend the beach came to tell us about the landing, amazing everyone that those men down there had survived the ten days of relentless bombing. How tenaciously they clung to life! He returned immediately to guard his position to the death — and, indeed, everyone at the landing site died fighting. Not one of them returned.*
>
> — A Japanese soldier positioned in an elementary school three kilometers from the landing

> *The cannonade reached its climax, compressing the hearts of Japanese soldiers with an elaborate cacophony such as a skilled drummer might beat out. Having thus assured the silence of the Japanese army on the land, the large transport ships offshore spewed forth small boats whose splendid formations traced white wakes in their arrowlike flight to the beach.*
>
> — The unwilling Okinawan conscript

> *Combat had offered no similar spectacle since the mass charges of the French knights in the Hundred Years' War. Here was the finest moment in the history of amphibious operations: an almost unbroken line of landing craft eight miles long simultaneously approaching one beach.*
>
> — James and William Belote, American military historians

You don't think that much when you're going into the beach. One thing is, you want to get out of that amtrac, because you're bunched in there with all those men, a great target. So you want to get out and you don't want to get out. You're sitting there with all that energy and you're psyching yourself up. I mean, football players don't just sleep all day, they get ready and psych themselves up. And that's what this was if you want to be honest about it: a football game where you kill or get killed.

— Al Franks, an American Marine who was wounded five minutes after running ashore

Perhaps fear accounts for the discrepancy in memories of the weather that morning. Some would remember an overcast sky and choppy waves, others a "glorious sunrise" with a "great red ball" of sun appearing above the hills toward which they were headed and casting a glow over a tranquil East China Sea. One man saw a change from one to the other, reading into it the divine intervention for which all but the determinedly atheist were praying — just as Japanese were simultaneously praying for the same intervention on their side, remembering the Divine Wind that helped them defeat the seemingly all-powerful Mongols. American believers were comforted by the knowledge that April 1 happened to be Easter Sunday, "a gloriously beautiful day," as one gratefully observed. "Even the sea changed from a raging turbulence to a peaceful, lapping water. It was as though God came on Easter Sunday to lay everything in readiness before us."*

Amid the tension, few remembered the small gunboats that led the way in for the thousand-odd landing craft, continuing to blanket the beach to the last moment with shells, rockets and mortars. Claustrophobia and extreme vulnerability increased the pressure on the infantrymen in their own boats. Trained to dig in for protection, they felt helpless in the water.

But the memory of the landing itself would be universally joyous. American intelligence hadn't even guessed that the landings would be virtually unopposed — even by artillery, for Japanese gunners had been ordered not to fire on the ships or landing craft for fear of revealing their positions and exposing them to devastating return fire. The Yahara-Ushijima strategy was still to delay all serious resistance for a better time and place.

Aerial photographs had pinpointed some of the menacing fortifications constructed above the landing beaches by Captain Kojo's battalion and others. But they did not reveal that almost all those posi-

---

*Actually, it was a cool, bright 75 degrees later that morning, fairly typical of Okinawan spring before the start of the rainy season, which is followed by an intensely hot, humid summer.

tions were abandoned: the captain's men had been withdrawn more than three months earlier, shortly after Ushijima lost the 9th Division. Nor did they disclose the quality of the troops that had replaced the highly trained 24th Division. The single regiment now protecting the beaches was no more than hastily organized service troops, chiefly airfield construction crews, reinforced by ill-trained, half-armed Okinawan Home Guard units, including high school students who had never fired a shot. The relief of the American brass was expressed in a radio message from Admiral Richmond Turner, commander of the landing operation, to his boss, Admiral Chester W. Nimitz, commander-in-chief of the Pacific Fleet: "Practically no fire against [landing] boats, none against ships . . . Troops advancing standing up." The even greater relief of those making the swift advance turned from an immense sense of deliverance to bafflement, which Taylor Kennerly, the leader of a machine gun platoon, recorded in a battle diary:

> As our boats raced toward the rising sun there was no firing, all was quiet except for the roar of the boat's motor and the slapping of the waves against the open boat which drenched all of us with water and spray. About 50 yards from shore, the dancing craft slammed into shallow water, the ramp splashed down and I ran out into knee-deep water, followed by a boatload of Marines. Still there was no shooting. As I splashed toward the steep bank 50 yards away, [I thought] "They must be waiting to see the whites of our eyes . . ." Scampering up the steep bank . . . I paused for a moment at the top . . . then plunged through a narrow row of bushes. There were the Japanese gun emplacements — empty. Yes, empty! What kind of trick was this? The whole situation was eerie . . . A white Easter bunny hopped out of the brush and disappeared behind one of the gun emplacements. Yes, it was Easter Sunday on Okinawa too. We regrouped and moved quickly inland.

Japanese soldiers were no less baffled. Believing their Combined Fleet to be intact and their planes lying in wait on the mainland and Formosa, they thought it "simply incredible," as one exclaimed, that the American fleet appeared in broad daylight, right before their noses. "Looking at the fascinatingly beautiful battleships spitting fire, we still couldn't quite understand that they had come to kill us."

Through the dense clouds of dust, debris and smoke left by the naval bombardment, they watched the landing in confusion and disbelief.

> From the transport ships that filled the ocean to the horizon, countless landing craft tracing white wakes set out, to disappear in the smoke. They kept coming relentlessly, in tens and hundreds, like arrows being shot in rapid succession and disappearing in the

smoke. The vanguard reached the beach; tanks, other vehicles and infantry ran up into Okinawan soil unharmed! . . . What a great opportunity! Why didn't our Air Force come and attack them? Maybe they were waiting for all the transport ships to come and line up for us. But that's just what they did — and still our planes didn't appear. Finally, the enemy began landing in a leisurely manner, so to speak, and made our airfields into *their* unsinkable aircraft carriers.

Thus the landing became more like a vast exercise than the real thing. Dashing from his landing craft, anxious and ready to fire, one Marine saw an earlier arrival sunning himself and flipping through a comic book. American fear shifted to amazement and euphoria. Remembering his wounding on Guam, a young company commander named Owen Stebbins felt an inner joy that he was still in one piece. Other veterans of previous landings wondered where and when the Japanese would spring their trap: April 1 was April Fool's Day as well as Easter Sunday. Still others grinned and yelped at their barely believable luck. Relief spread from jubilant infantrymen on the beaches to skeptical communications and intelligence personnel still on the ships. "I've already lived longer than I thought I would," exulted an Army infantryman after he ran up the beach and made it to the top of a little hill. The opposition wasn't worse than at Iwo Jima, as expected; it was limited to occasional mortar shells and snipers' bullets, relatively no resistance at all.

Forty miles to the south, the 2nd Marine Division was making a fake landing to deter Ushijima from rushing reinforcements to the real landing beaches. In that real operation, four divisions, two Army and two Marine, were landed at an eight-mile stretch of beach on the western (East China Sea) shore. Okinawa's width at that point, just south of her narrowest neck, is some seven miles to the Pacific shore. On their way across, cutting the island in two, American units encountered two airfields, including Kadena, Captain Kojo's responsibility until the accidental explosion that drove him to a hospital. Both fields were less than half a mile from the landing beach, but American planners, knowing that half a mile was a considerable advance against Japanese island defenses, had scheduled their capture for the third day. Defended only by a recently formed regiment of support troops, with little combat training and orders to retreat northward after delaying the enemy, they fell easily the first morning. One Marine noticed that nothing was alive — "not a goddam grasshopper or snake or fly" — on the way to the fields. Only a scattering of Japanese sheltering underground survived the tumultuous American bombardment.

The defenders of the slightly more northern Yomitan Airfield included Okinawan conscripts who had been issued uniforms but no arms. Shortly after it was secured, a neat green Japanese Zero appeared directly overhead, almost transfixing the Marines below with its red Rising Sun. The pilot made a graceful landing, apparently with important papers from the mainland, then taxied across the field, climbed from his cockpit and walked toward an airport building before realizing that the men gathered there were the enemy. They shot him as he tried to run back to his plane; looking down at the body, a Marine noted, "There's always some poor bastard who doesn't get the word." The expected counterattack by a full division using parachute forces — for the Japanese were known to favor the German doctrine of mobility and double envelopment — didn't materialize. A correspondent who had covered previous landings wrote, "This is hard to believe." Colleagues still aboard flagships concurred: "There must be some mistake." Bulldozers immediately began clearing the runways of wrecked Japanese planes and clever dummies of sticks, straw and cloth. By nightfall, Marine strike planes began landing, the first to operate from official Japanese soil since the war began.

That evening, a Marine artillery battery was fully ashore and ready to fire from a position near the beach. The men began digging in for the night, but found they were on solid coral that couldn't be dug. "We had to hope for no incoming fire, and luckily there wasn't any." Americans who reconnoitered the empty Japanese fortifications — those excellently positioned caves, gun emplacements, and pillboxes dug over the course of six months by Captain Kojo's 24th Division — realized they were even luckier than they'd thought. Despite the courageous feats of the Navy's underwater demolition teams, many landing craft were stranded for hours on coral reefs about a thousand yards out: target-practice range for enemy field artillery and heavy machine guns. The men had to transfer from the bouncing boats to amtracs (amphibious tractors) that rode out like sitting ducks. And despite all the weight of metal and explosive for softening up the invasion targets, despite that heaviest bombardment in the long Pacific campaign, only civilian buildings had been demolished; the defense works at the airfields and beaches were virtually intact. Their generally excellent condition testified to the unrealistic American value placed on mass fire of bomb and shell as well as to Japanese skill in choosing and fortifying sites.

If Ushijima hadn't lost the 9th Division, they would not have been abandoned; Tadashi Kojo would have led a charge with professional ruthlessness and a poised, unharmed battalion from his original position above the beach. The landing boats caught on the coral reefs would have become tombs; once ashore, the invaders would have been the prey that Captain Kojo had envisioned. "The hardest part of all was trudging in," an American remembered, using understatement to make his point. "The water was waist-deep. If we'd had to fight our way in, it would have been a job instead of a cinch."

The American Army, designated the 10th, had 541,866 men at its disposal: more than the Okinawan civilian population at this time; almost five times more than the defending force. The smaller American assault force also represented a considerable numerical advantage over the Japanese, even beefed up by Okinawan conscripts. By nightfall, some 60,000 of the 10th Army's 183,000 assault troops (of which 154,000 were in the actual combat divisions) were ashore, together with much armor, artillery, and supplies, and 15,000 service troops. "The U.S. Navy's most successful amphibious operation of the entire war was nearly complete," a historian recently summed up. American casualties were twenty-eight killed — most victims of two kamikaze crashes on land — twenty-seven missing, a hundred and four wounded, a fraction of what had been expected.* L-day had indeed been near to Love.

Marine losses in particular were trifling compared with previous landings: nine men killed, among them a nineteen-year-old medical corpsman named Truex, who, when the unit was forming up at Guadalcanal, had attached himself to a thirty-year-old New Yorker named Peter Milo. Milo never knew the boy's first name but admired his sunny personality. "Whoever wrote the story of Frank Merriwell must have imagined a man like Truex. Broad of shoulder, handsome face with a real square jaw and the temperament of a saint."

After rushing forward to take Yomitan Airfield, Milo and Truex were ordered to dig in and prepare for the expected counterattack. But like the Japanese soldiers who had dug the massive fortifications, Milo discovered the hardness of coral when his entrenching tool bounced right off it. He thought better of searching for the Engineering Battalion to ask for a pickax because even the textbook American landing had units scattered in the wrong places. "You can't imagine what 'fouled up' means until you make a landing on an enemy beach." Still, the former New York policeman was lucky enough to borrow a shovel.

As he was using it, he heard a familiar voice claim next rights.

---

*The force of some kamikaze crashes on the sea squeezed the legs of some men in landing craft so hard that they crushed their testicles, which had to be surgically removed.

Truex waited for the shovel near his jeep, with its large red cross. Hurrying there when he'd finished his foxhole, Milo bantered with his young friend about whose head was harder than the coral, then started back, laughing. He heard the roar of a motor and looked up to see his first Japanese plane, coming in low. He ran for all he was worth and was shocked to see two Army soldiers crouching in his new foxhole just as he was about to leap in. The GIs had been driving up with supplies and took the nearest cover. Milo could only "hit the deck and pray."

Twenty minutes later, someone told him Truex had driven over a land mine, probably while rushing to a casualty. What was left of his body had to be brought down in bloody parts from the roof of what was left of a native building. Okinawa's multitude of deaths soon put Milo into a kind of trance. "It was as if I'd left my body and was looking at myself like in a movie. I just didn't feel anything." But he could not forget Truex. When a day was set aside for the troops to "say so long" to fallen comrades after the end of the campaign, he searched in cemeteries. He believed there may have been no grave because the body could not be identified. In any case, he left for Guam without having found it; at veterans' reunions forty-five years later, Milo was still asking whether anyone remembered Truex's given name.

One of the 104 men wounded was Alexander Franks, whose platoon had left its troopship for landing in a roaring amphibious tractor, with its heavy smoke of exhaust.

> What are you thinking while you're waiting for your turn to land? During instruction, they tell you to relax then — but when you're in something like that, everybody's going to think his own thing, whatever most helps him cope with the stress.
>
> So what am I thinking? I'm thinking that I want to get out of the amtrac. You're cooped up with everyone there — and with your tension. You've psyched yourself up because you've got to psych yourself up — and you want to get out and relieve the tension. Besides, you can get seasick. Or a mortar can hit the amtrac and you're all gone.
>
> I'm also thinking, am I going to come out of this one alive? Is my buddy, sitting right there next to me, going to get killed — or am I? Yes, you actually think those thoughts while you sit there, trying to joke with your buddies. Trying to do a lot of talking, although you don't remember what you've said the minute it leaves your mouth. That's what's on your mind: am I going to get killed in the next few minutes, get crippled? This was my second landing; I'd also hit Guam. And I was just as scared. Maybe more so, because on your first landing, you don't really understand . . .

It seems like an eternity, circling and circling out there beyond the range of the shore batteries, waiting for your turn to land. *Am I going to come out of this alive?* I prayed. Believe me, lots of guys did. You ask the Lord to help you and your friends come out whole. Yes, your friends too — because you depend on that man next to you. If you can't depend on him and he can't depend on you, you're both gone, you're nothing.

When his amtrac at last headed in, Franks was much relieved to see no incoming shells. He was even more relieved to see no one falling around him when the vehicle finally stopped (although a few men were killed elsewhere during their first minute ashore) and he ran up the pebbly beach. He dashed up a little rise and dived to his stomach on top. When he got up to press on, a shell exploded just to his left. It killed the man next to him, a recent replacement in his squad, and knocked Franks back down. He realized he was hit when he couldn't get up again. His left arm and knee felt like a finger that's been banged with a hammer.

"It's an awful thing to say, but I think it was one of our own — a shortfall — because there were still no shells coming from the Japs; that was the only one I saw.* My first thought is, am I going to lose my leg? And then: *I'm alive and I'll be going home.* I'm deeply sorry to leave my buddies, I'm deeply sorry for them, but there's nothing I can do for them anymore. That new guy right next to me, two feet away, is dead, and I'm still alive. Still alive! And after the shot of morphine from the corpsman, I realize my arm and leg are still on me, so I probably won't be a cripple."

L-day was almost unbearingly exciting for Masahide Ota, the twenty-year-old native of Kume Island who had been appointed one of the three adjutants to the principal of the Normal School below Shuri Castle. Perhaps because it was assumed that the Normal School, so close to 32nd Army's headquarters in the tunnel under the castle, must have been mobilized earlier, this was actually carried out only the day before the landing, March 31. By that time, more than twenty thousand mostly teenage Okinawans had been taken into service with the Home Guard. Although not all the boys of the island's many middle schools were among the conscripted, the Normal School's teachers and entire enrollment of 360 students were taken into the fifteen-hundred-boy corps called Blood and Iron Scouts for the Emperor. The top twenty-two students — in the obligatory judo, kendo

---

*The majority of the assault troops experienced nothing heavier than sporadic mortar and sniper fire. Many who saw no Japanese fire whatever shared the impression that American fire — so-called own fire — caused many of the landing casualties.

and karate as well as scholarship — were formed into a subunit bearing the immensely proud name of a historical figure who had sacrificed his own life and his family's for the Emperor's protection. Those enviable ones, including the bright, diligent Ota, were assigned to staff intelligence at 32nd Army headquarters. A rudimentary shortpants uniform was distributed, but there was no time for any kind of real preparation. Despite the years of military training, the students hadn't even practiced firing small arms.

But now, on the morning of the landing, the second-class privates were heady with the thrill of being near the highest-ranking Army officers on an observation platform above a wall of Shuri Castle. Looking down at the huge enemy operation, the boys delighted in the idiotic massing of so many ships marked for the bottom. Ota's unqualified expectation of quick, total victory was further heightened when he saw the kindly, masterful General Ushijima calmly surveying the epic scene.* The boys believed exactly what they'd been told: that Imperial General Headquarters had been clever enough to lure the large enemy force to this place in order to destroy it in one go. As one of Ota's teachers put it, the whole American fleet, with all its men and equipment, had been drawn into a noose that would now be deftly closed. Ota felt a surge of exhilaration as he observed the stirring spectacle of war below. What an honor it was to participate in the glorious task of rapidly liquidating the sinister foe! He itched for his first assignment for staff intelligence.

Dick Whitaker was among the rich beneficiaries of the nearly unopposed landing. Had the Japanese met the assault force with the furious counterattack originally planned, he would have been rushed in to replace one of the profusion of casualties, with a good chance of being killed or badly wounded then and there. As it was, the first wave of American troops penetrated so fast and deep that by the time he arrived, in the third wave an hour later (although the waves often overlapped), the greatest need ashore was not more bodies but more matériel for the twenty thousand already there.† Their advance so far ahead of schedule caused an instant crisis in supplies. Whitaker's replacement draft was among five thousand Marines formed into work details.

---

*Knowing his Army's annihilation was only a matter of time, the general was merely playing his role as a Japanese commander. As the fighting progressed, he would maintain his tranquil mien and continue with his kendo exercises.

†As his amtrac circled during the formation of the third wave, he fell asleep. Years later, in a college psychology course, he learned that an overload of stress and apprehension can shut down mind and body that way.

Still untried in combat, he was an old hand at lifting and lugging. Floodlights were rigged on the long beachhead so that unloading from landing craft could continue throughout the night, except for relatively rare interruptions when the men took cover from Japanese scouting planes. Whitaker's detail also helped fashion an assortment of strewn metal, canvas and cardboard into a little "shack city" for some protection from the rain and sun between loads. However, nothing could help against an army of relentless fleas, much more formidable so far than the Japanese Army. The men bitched in good old military language. Fuck it, they didn't come to Okinawa to unload ships! They all knew the Marine Corps was invincible; Whitaker believed he was invincible too. Some of the older, married men would have been happy to stay where they were, but younger ones wanted *off* that goddam beach. They wanted combat — to pull their triggers, become heroes, grab some good Jap souvenirs.

On the fourth day, half a dozen of them took advantage of slack time to improvise a little scouting party. This was against regulations: no one in command would know where they were if they happened to be killed. But the ease with which the little Nips were being pushed back kept death an abstraction. The patch of woods farther inland had been secured days before: cleaned up enough of the enemy for combat units to push on. But one of the party pointed to a small rise a few hundred yards from the beach. "Hey, get that!" Whitaker's first sight of a live Japanese soldier — any living Japanese — brought a rush of excitement. *There* was the object of all his training, the whole massive effort on the island. He joined the firing until the enemy's sloppy helmet disappeared over the ridge, then continued to see its image in his mind's eye like a titillating target, charging him up even further.

The beach parties were broken up a few days later and their men were trucked to front-line units as replacements, but Whitaker saw few more real targets even there. Most of his group was assigned to the 6th Division's 29th Regiment Battalion; he himself to 2nd Battalion F (Fox) Company, which had advanced far north by the time he joined it. The company's fighting up there was almost over; American bullets now caused its worst wounds.

An air strike was requested one day when Whitaker's new platoon encountered a pocket of resistance on a mop-up patrol. The men were told to mark their own positions by making ground panels of ration boxes, ponchos, anything easily seen from above. Several F-4Us soon appeared: the celebrated Corsairs that had already demonstrated their enormous value in the north, where Japanese artillery pieces fired once and pulled back into concealed emplacements on steep hillsides, making them almost unhittable by naval gunfire. The Corsair, which carried more armament than a B-29, may have been the best close ground-support aircraft ever designed. The gull-winged beaut could circle for hours, then come in low and slow — not fast, high and inaccurate, like later jets — to bomb or strafe as close as two hundred yards to delighted friendly troops. Excellent coordination with ground forces, where observers operating down to the company level spotted for their strikes, made Marine Corsairs even more effective.

But one splendid Corsair on this raid missed or misread the ground panels, and strafed the wrong side. One Marine was killed; others wounded. Whitaker was too new to the company to know their names.* It was also a new — and an anguishing — experience to be the target of one's own magnificent weapons; hugging the ground in terror with the rest of his platoon, Whitaker viewed the great Corsair as a savage monster spitting murderous fire. He would soon learn to add such agonizing mistakes to combat's other costs.

No list has been compiled of men killed and wounded on Okinawa by own fire, but it would surely run to hundreds, perhaps thousands — many more than the number torn and blown apart by bulldozers, cranes, steam winches and aviation fuel handled by young men in a necessary hurry: the "industrial" accidents of a huge, extremely hazardous enterprise run under extreme stress with what otherwise would be called inordinate recklessness. No satisfactory trade-off was ever made between safety precautions and preparedness. The proportion of deaths grew as armies acquired heavier machinery, more volatile fuel, more deadly armament and powerful explosives.

In the field, it was impossible to have so many youths — and enemy troops — with so many weapons without constant accidents and mistakes. On Sugar Loaf Hill, where Whitaker would face his worst days in about three weeks, a second lieutenant would lose "a beautiful kid, a real fine, decent Marine" when a tank shell aimed at a Japanese target bounced off a tree stump and tore open the eighteen-year-old's chest. On little Iheya Island, fifty miles north of Okinawa, Marines were killed by rocket fire from ships that didn't know they were on the beach. And a variety of American bullets, grenades, mortar shells, artillery shells and even flamethrowers cut down American boys all over Okinawa — horrible mistakes without which a war can't be fought and whose number can't be fixed, be-

---

*On April 2, the second day of fighting, misdirected Navy planes hit the command post of an Army infantry company making its way south. Four Americans were killed and seventeen wounded.

cause, as one veteran put it, combat is "just too confusing for any kind of count of who killed whom . . . It could easily happen without anyone knowing."

A peacetime terrorist action that takes a single precious life is rightly emblazoned on headlines and abhorred. Infinitely worse losses on Okinawa were never described in print, even to the families concerned, because few officers were willing to write that their men had fallen to own fire. Lieutenant David Curtin's summary is as accurate as any: "We had more men killed by accidental fire than will ever be known."

11 · The North

You know from your map we're nearly equidistant from Kyushu, Taiwan and China at Okinawa — all these Jap strongholds close to 300 nautical miles, yet such pathetic resistance . . . We've surely got them where we want them now.
— An American naval officer, days after the landing

Having blinded us with countless airplanes and mortar shells, the enemy were marching — no, walking leisurely ahead as if on a picnic, their automatic weapons under their arms . . . Those soldiers functioned as feelers. One shot from us and they immediately used their portable radios to contact their artillery. Our small position would be blown up, hill and all, in two minutes.
— A Japanese soldier at about the same time

That night, my detachment was sent to Miwashi Elementary School for lumber to support our cave. That meant demolishing the school building . . . and making off with its beams and joists.
— An Okinawan conscript at about the same time

A VETERAN DIPLOMAT once advised a novice how to cope when dining with a dignitary from a country about which he knew nothing. "Ask the question that almost always makes you appear knowledgeable," he counseled. "Ask, 'And how are things going these days in the south of your country?'"

The assumption that life is more difficult in the south was never more justified than in the battle for Okinawa. The first days went so well everywhere for the Americans that staff officers wondered whether Ushijima was a genius or a fool, and a seasoned correspondent predicted the campaign would cost fewer casualties than any in the Pacific, even if the Japanese now tried to "turn and make a stand." Everyone asked everyone else where "the Japs" were. Intelligence could not answer. Cloud cover had interfered with prelanding reconnaissance flights, masking the fortress of Japanese power in positions still hidden by fresh nets and branches.

In fact, the heart of Ushijima's 32nd Army was just where Colonel Yahara's last plan had put it: waiting for the enemy in its fortifications in the southern eighth of the island. The first strong line lay less than eight miles below the southernmost landing beach and only about a dozen miles above the island's southern tip. The two Army divisions that fought south from the landing encountered its outer edge toward the end of the first week in the form of pockets of stubborn resistance, including valleys and draws protected by minefields and covered by well-camouflaged field guns. Fortified hills dominating the lines of advance were harder to take, but the sharp skirmishes for them fell into the category of the "normal" and the expected. The honeymoon would be truly over only when the main body of the defense was reached and the commander of the American Army divisions realized he could go no farther without a full-scale battle.

Meanwhile, the two Marine divisions were still enjoying a relative holiday. The 1st was encountering much less resistance than expected as it took a large portion of the island's center; the 6th hurried north. The campaign looked like a cakewalk, especially with Yomitan and Kadena airfields already launching close-support strikes to aid the Marines' advance. Yahara and Ushijima had expected those fields to fall, but not so quickly. When startling numbers of American planes began operating from them almost immediately, Tokyo ordered "utmost" measures to stop them. The 32nd Army had rueful second thoughts and wondered whether it should counterattack.

Japanese regret at having given up those fields so easily — a consequence of the questionable decision not to defend the beaches after the loss of the 9th Division — was deepened by recognition that the enemy's quick capture of Kerama Retto, a cluster of nine mountainous islands about fifteen miles west of Naha, would bring more trouble. The Americans had planned to ignore the jagged little archipelago until later, but Admiral Turner saw its deep-water anchorages as good places for transferring supplies, and pressed, originally against universal disapproval, for taking them as part of the invasion preparations. They were indeed taken during the last week of March. Their few hundred surprised defenders were easily defeated, Ushijima having transferred most of his force from there to Okinawa proper in the belief that Kerama Retto would not interest the enemy.

The Americans put them to immediate use as bases for patrol planes that would sink tens of thousands of tons of commercial shipping and as anchorages for repair ships and for fleet supply; they became the final depots in the vast logistical routes stretching from California. A bonus was the disarming of a potentially serious threat to the same auxiliary fleet. The Keramas were a base for Japanese sea-raiding units composed of 250 eighteen-foot speedboats armed with heavy depth charges that were to have severed the enemy's sea-based supply line with suicide charges at the larger ships. The little trap now failed: the tiny one-man boats were found in well-camouflaged coves, some being readied for surprise attacks that would never be made, others destroyed by their maintenance crews. (Another surprise for the Americans was the bodies of some fifteen native women and children strangled by grieving husbands and fathers to save them from a worse fate at the hands of the invaders. Some consideration of that event by the staff of the American 10th Army might have helped reduce later Okinawan casualties. Over five hundred civilians died on the Keramas, including many who were sent to meet the invaders when the Japanese force melted away.) Thus, the arsenal of suicide boats was much reduced, and Marines soon disabled others waiting in the rough coasts of Okinawa's north.* The 6th Division had already begun its rapid advance to occupy the whole of that remote, rugged north where the Japanese had once thought to organize the bulk of their defense.

The approximately fifty-by-eight-mile strip of rocky terrain above the line of the landing contained two thirds of Okinawa's territory but less than a quarter of its population. Apart from the large Motobu Peninsula, which juts like a large spur into the East China Sea, it is essentially an uninhabited and inaccessible mountain spine running northwest to the tip. Most of it was distinctly poorer than the south in 1945, even on the coastal roads, where almost everyone lived. Much was barren.

On the evening after the landing, a Marine detachment camped in a cabbage patch just inland from the East China Sea. Having advanced a spectacular four miles from their landing site along the west coast road — a dirt track, like most of the island's arteries — they were some five days ahead of schedule. There had been only occasional opposition from snipers in what seemed like toy villages of thatch-roofed "huts," as the men called the Okinawan farmhouses. Veterans of earlier campaigns exchanged nervously joyful expressions of disbelief. Where were the Japs? Would their trap be really diabolical? Or was it possible that all Okinawa was going to be a picnic? Men felt let down — and cherished the most pleasant letdown of their lives. Some initiates to combat began to wonder about the

*In all, about 700 suicide craft were hidden in the Ryukyus, about half on Okinawa. Some boats and swimmers based there did try to strike, the swimmers by leaving their craft for individual forays to blow up targeted ships. The dawn of a morning soon after the invasion caught 15 such swimmers approaching a destroyer in a canoe and on a raft. All instantly blew themselves up with hand grenades.

veterans' talk and war films. "Holy shit," a medical corpsman happily asked himself, "is all that hell and heroism stuff just more myth?"

The columns advanced up the coastal roads with the sea on one side, terraced hills on the other — and no sign of snakes. Very much worse had been expected of the island as well as its defenders. The prelanding briefings had warned insistently about the water. A microbe that produced "liver fluke" (schistosomiasis) was specified as having "all sorts of horrible results." Ominous descriptions had men visualizing woods teeming with three kinds of poisonous adders, more frightening to some than the enemy. Habu snakes in particular did have a history and a reputation on the island, but few were left* — mongooses had been imported in the 1930s — and most men had already begun throwing away the puttees they'd been admonished to wear, together with their gas masks and their helmets ("too heavy and not effective against bullets anyway"), anything to lighten the loads on their backs. So far Okinawa "belied the preinvasion intelligence that had depicted [it] as a sinister place," as the military historians James and William Belote put it, its air "laden with pestilence and the ground crawling with venomous snakes."

The East China Sea turned chilly when the sun went down on that April 2, but the spring day remained clear and pleasant. Marines in other units had taken photographs of the scenery that afternoon, including gently curving white sand beaches below the coast road. All were extremely tired after marching very hard on very little sleep since the eve of the invasion. The unit in the cabbage patch was so tired and so relaxed that the men took their time digging their foxholes for the night — and were stunned by sudden fire from Japanese howitzers in a hill above them. Of course they had been lectured and lectured to take cover *fast* whenever shelling started — before it started. But newcomers to combat saw the whole of their boot camp and infantry training as nothing compared with this terrible reality. The first rounds whistled over their heads and landed in the sea, but unseen Japanese gunners instantly adjusted their range to hit jeeps, inflict casualties, cause every American to dig furiously while he was almost prone.† Although a patrol sent into the hill managed to silence the howitzers before midnight, shock and fear kept most of the men awake during the night while corpsmen tended the wounded.

---

*And very few Americans would encounter one, now or later. Those who did were likely to make a meal of its broiled meat after days or weeks on cold K-rations.

† "I never repeated that mistake again," one of the targets remembered. "On every one of my 80 evenings after that, I first dug my foxhole, then took a crap or had something to eat."

The same group was more heavily shelled three nights later, when a nearby radioman was shot while his microphone switch was open. The group heard him and other wounded calling for help for hours. "Come and get us!" "We're pinned down!" "Help us out of here!" Volunteers were trucked to a field from which they could outflank the Japanese from behind. They climbed a hill, each with a hand on the belt of the man in front to keep from getting lost in the dark and the difficult terrain. (Those who saw their first Japanese corpses alongside the trail would not forget the sight.) Digging in at the top, they were told not to leave their foxholes because anyone who did might be taken for a Japanese infiltrator. No one slept during the rest of that night. Everyone fired at every movement. In the morning, two Americans were dead of own fire even before the others set out to neutralize the enemy artillery.

Each night as they pushed north, American artillery battalions settled in, whenever possible, on high ground, where they employed an updated version of the wagon circle, setting up machine guns and BAR men on the position's outer ring. As an extra precaution, thin wires were strung some fifty to seventy yards out from the perimeter, across the many footpaths leading down from the hills. Trip flares were rigged to go off when those wires were touched.

In such a position a few nights later, a radio operator's heart skipped a beat when a voice with a Japanese accent suddenly whispered into his earphones, "Americans die!" Then the line went dead. To be cut off from regimental headquarters for an entire night was considered an unacceptable danger; the operations officer had no alternative but to send out a communications sergeant to lay a new line. One observer "never felt sorrier for anyone before or since" than he did for that man. "Regiment was about a mile away and the night was black. Not only were there Japanese in between us, but he really didn't know where other trigger-happy Marine outposts were located . . . I think I'd have asked for a company of infantry to surround me." But the self-possessed sergeant took just two riflemen and two of his communications specialists into the terrifying blackness, where each sound would be a fatal giveaway of their position — and where, they were certain, the same Japanese who had cut the line were waiting behind some rocks, rifles poised, for the squeak of a roll reeling out a telephone wire to tell them when to shoot.*

---

*Although this group returned without casualties after several hours of hair-raising work, maintenance of telephone lines continued to be a severe test of nerves. Old lines were never repaired, previous islands having revealed the Japanese tactic of putting a pin in a line and waiting to ambush any repair party sent out to shoot trouble on it. But the

Those slight episodes among thousands suggest that the push north was easy only in comparison with what would come next. The luckiest units raced up the coastal roads of the Ishikawa Isthmus with the speed of a motorized unit — sometimes actually in vehicles — still elated over the scantiness of the enemy fire or, as with the most battle-hungry, affected with an acute sense of anticlimax. Some men found it "like a walk in the country, a picnic," as a young rifleman exulted, or, in a correspondent's neater image, like a house that was expected to contain vicious gunmen but turned out to be only haunted. The luckier companies were accompanied by a destroyer escort or smaller ship that steamed north at their pace to provide extra firepower from close offshore. A few men rode bareback on shaggy native ponies. They whooped in the fine spring weather. Some hooted at anyone who tried to warn them that Japs were savage fighters. Even when advance units entered Nago at the neck of the Motobu Peninsula — the largest town above the landing beaches, with a population of ten thousand — the chief danger came from nothing larger than organized rifle fire. Iwo Jima's first six days had claimed ten times more casualties than expected, a ratio almost reversed in Okinawa's north.

Other companies took only very scattered rifle, machine gun and mortar fire as they tramped ahead in single file, scouting the pine-covered hills and the terraces where the natives struggled to feed themselves. More harassment than serious opposition, the fire came from the hills or from behind sharp bends in the narrow, twisting roads. Heavy rain fell during the second week. "Patrols were nerve-racking," a young officer explained, "because you couldn't see the enemy until one of your scouts was killed." Tired, frustrated Marines peered everywhere as they searched houses along the way — or burned them to eliminate hiding places for the defenders — easing their anxiety about the counterattack that would surely soon begin by complaining about their blistered feet and cursing the sneaky enemy who wouldn't stand and fight in this "walking campaign."

But unlucky units that happened to encounter defensive positions had to work and fight as hard as anywhere. A veteran of island campaigns assured a medical corpsman that the Japs were hopeless shots

---

places for laying a new line in the same general direction were very limited. During the day, "we'd run like hell," as a survivor who would go on to work for a Connecticut telephone company remembered, "while the wire reeled out and the Japs watched from their hills and caves." During the night, it was as scary as combat.

The danger of being shot by one's trigger-happy fellows hardly decreased. Some Marines who ignored their solemn instructions not to leave their foxholes at night, usually to relieve themselves, were quickly cut down by other Marines, nervous in the sinister darkness and apt to fire at every threatening sound, which often meant any sound at all.

except at long range. During the first five days, the corpsman saw five Marines go down from distant single shots in the heart or head. Eight men in the platoon of a machine gunner named Melvin Heckt were killed and nine wounded on April 14 and 15; Heckt wrote in his diary that he had "never never had so many close shaves in all my life and I only have God to thank for being alive." Six men and the commander of an infantry company crossing a ravine not far away were cut down when small-arms fire suddenly opened up on them from dozens of well-camouflaged caves. A sergeant of another unit asked for volunteers to cross a difficult ridge. Four men offered themselves, and defenders picked them off one by one as they made the attempt. Two were killed, one crippled for life and the lucky one took shrapnel in every part of his body, including his testicles. That was the kind of incident that prompted the commander of one Marine regiment to call the northern operation "as difficult as I can conceive . . . I wonder how it was accomplished." Norris Buchter, a young communications man in that regiment, summed up the spotty resistance with better perspective. "There were lots of very serious moments up there in the north. There were units shot to shreds. The whole thing seemed easy only later, looking back after what we went through in the south."

> When I had a chance to look around, I was awe-struck by the beauty of the scene that stretched before me. I was on a fairly level plateau [on a high ridge overlooking the countryside], covered with green grass and pine trees. At one end was an old, partly decayed ruin of a Buddhist temple made from large rocks. A stone stairway led up to it. I followed the roadway, almost in a trance, through several flights of stairs until I stood on the highest point . . . The thick verdure seemed almost impenetrable from the distance. On the other side a sheer precipice dropped off . . . and gave the appearance of a medieval castle built on a peak and surrounded by a moat, complete with drawbridge and thick walls encircling the castle grounds. The cliff leveled off and stretched out toward the inlet to the east and stopped at the seashore . . . Below me about 200 meters away, a fire was rapidly licking up the fragile buildings in a town I think was Yami.
> — Major Sam Reid, April 12

Colonel Takehido Udo commanded the defense. Unlike General Ushijima, his classmate at the Imperial Military Academy, Udo was considered bullying and ineffectual. The local population quietly despised him.

Udo's twenty-five hundred men assigned to defend 436 square miles revealed the slight importance Ushijima placed on holding this two thirds of Okinawa's territory. Moreover, the "Udo force" consisted of bits and pieces of various groupings, including sixty survi-

vors of *Toyama maru* delivered back to him in pitiful shape a week
after the sinking.* Its core was two battalions of trained infantrymen,
but the others — at least half — were reservists, local conscripts, and
volunteers, together with members of disbanded naval units. What
Udo did have was an intimate knowledge of the tough terrain, including a mountain retreat that towered, on the Okinawan scale, to
fifteen hundred feet. It was protected by well-placed outposts with
good communications to his headquarters and a large supply of mortars and machine guns in addition to well-hidden field guns and converted naval cannon.

Some of his works confounded Americans for days. Artillery emplacements dug into mountainsides were equipped with tracks used
for rolling out the guns for a few quick rounds, then withdrawing
them immediately into the camouflage of surrounding vegetation.
"When we finally took the territory," one Marine remembered, "we'd
find tremendous devastation all around but the gun inside, still intact." Udo's own redoubt was high on Yae-dake Mountain, which
commanded the entire Motobu Peninsula, the only area he had
chosen to defend in earnest. Thickly covered by pine trees, vines,
brambles and an undergrowth of primitive palms, Yae-dake also concealed deep valleys that had to be crossed on the way to the top. Its
defenders numbered roughly two thousand — most of the entire
force — supported to a greater or lesser degree by four times as
many civilians in the area. The most menacing to the Americans were
several hundred soldiers manning a battery of heavy guns in a position cut into a steep face of the mountain. Distant, demanding Udo
supervised his operations from a mat on the floor of his headquarters, where three local women waited on him. Native accounts pictured fear in his eyes as he complained about the impossibility of
waging modern war without air support.

Marines attacked the sprawling mountain from two sides during
the second week of the campaign while American ships and planes
pounded the heights. This was the start of four fierce days of fighting, during which the commander of the Japanese heavy-gun detachment grew convinced the time was ripe to fire and frequently telephoned Udo for permission, but received no clear answer. After
their Herculean labor of dragging the guns through the jagged ter-

---

*The colonel himself had been the senior officer on the ship when *Sturgeon* sank it.
Northern Okinawans saw those survivors arriving "in very strange garb" — uniforms
blackened with oil, heads bandaged, skin swollen black and blue — and trying to attract
no attention so that the islanders would not know what had happened to the troopships
and nine tenths of the 44th Independent Mixed Brigade. "Their eyes held little life and
overwhelming fatigue. They had become stragglers even without fighting a battle."

rain up to their high position, the gunners now suffered frustration.* Americans discovered the position and attacked it heavily before it could do its full damage, while elsewhere on the mountain, violent clashes were taking place that required Marines to climb sheer cliffs under fire and engage in hand-to-hand combat on heavily forested ridges. One Japanese 75mm gun had much more success than the heavier ones, emerging from its cave to fire with great accuracy, then withdrawing quickly enough to escape destruction by heavy American naval gunfire, artillery, bombs and napalm. One Marine infantry company took sixty-eight casualties from this gun and other fire.

Udo sent his own infantry out to counterattack only toward evening, when the Americans felt it too near to dark to mount expeditions into the dangerous foothills. The going was made even tougher by uncharacteristically wavering Marine leadership. The commander of the 29th Regiment, a rigid colonel who clung to ways learned in the First World War, had trained his men so severely on Guadalcanal that many felt worn out, and although he was relieved on April 10, the results of his poor planning showed on Yae-dake. But the full mountain was more or less taken on April 16, after bitter hand-to-hand fighting for the peak, and this left no more objectives remotely as difficult anywhere in the north. By that time, other Marine units, taking "dollops" of ground daily, as one put it while still apprehensive about the easy progress, had already reached rocky Cape Hedo at Okinawa's northern tip.

Hiding somewhere on the Motobu Peninsula, Udo became an object of contempt to other Japanese, who didn't know his whereabouts or why he hadn't died honorably at his headquarters. Some of the other survivors formed small guerrilla groups that hid in the mountainous forests of Motobu and the rest of the barely inhabited north, eluding American patrols on Yae-dake and along the coasts. Young Okinawan soldiers who had been conscripted on the eve of the battle served those groups both as scouts and as small supplementary units of their own.† Their operations were much more effectively commanded by a Captain Haruo Murakami than by the disliked Colonel

---

*A corporal's patience snapped on April 12. Stripped to the waist and fired with drink, he charged into Udo's kitchen, screaming that the colonel spent all his time with women in his headquarters shelter. "How can we fight a war like this? Shame on the Japanese Army!" He threw a hand grenade, which scattered the women in the kitchen but didn't explode.

†A high school student named Yasuharu Agarie was among the guerrillas. Shot through the chest by an American patrol that killed some of his fellow students, Agarie tried to keep fighting although he was gravely wounded. The sixteen-year-old surrendered months later, only after his brother, who had spent years in America and returned to Okinawa with the invading forces, coaxed him out of hiding. Agarie went on to become president of the University of the Ryukyus in Shuri.

Udo, who was discredited after his defeat. A graduate of the Imperial Military Academy one year after Tadashi Kojo, Murakami shared Kojo's severe bearing, total dedication to military interests and supreme confidence in ultimate victory. Those qualities were common to almost all the young regular officers, but Murakami was better liked — at least more respected — than many, partly because he had made himself an expert in guerrilla warfare. When Udo arrived one rainy night at a Murakami camp in civilian clothes and what was considered an unfitting manner, he found a sign posted at the captain's headquarters: "Udo's Defeated Little Remnant Gang Not Admitted."

On April 20, the commander of American operations in the north declared it secured. Flag-raising ceremonies were held at the northernmost Cape Hedo and at 6th Division headquarters in Nago, where the commandant of the U.S. Marine Corps attended, having arrived on Okinawa, the Corps's central focus now, during an inspection tour of Marine units in the Pacific. The flag raisers in Nago included a detachment from G (George) Company of the 2nd Battalion, 22nd Regiment, apparently because the company, having moved rapidly up the west coast road, made a final exploratory patrol down the east coast to ensure the collapse of enemy resistance. G–2–22, the company's designation in military shorthand, had suffered only two battle-fatigue casualties during the weeks of routing scattered groups of riflemen in their path. Their toughest "battle" had occurred when a hunter-killer squadron of American carrier-based planes mistook the men for Japanese and repeatedly bombed and strafed them. They were lucky enough to take no casualties even then, although some of their weapons were destroyed.

The 6th Division as a whole counted almost two thousand Japanese bodies, compared with their own casualties of 236 dead* and 1061 wounded, roughly the "kill ratio" that was to prevail during the en-

---

*Many who fought on Okinawa much dislike the use of such formulas because, they feel, numbers can reduce the dead to statistics — whereas each was treasured in a way not easily understood by noncombatants. Austin Aria, a former batboy for the Philadelphia Phillies and once a major league prospect himself, was a 6th Division radio operator. A medical corpsman asked him to hold a flashlight on a delirious teenager while he tried to keep him from becoming one of the 236 dead in the north. "Honey, you know I can't dance, so why do you keep asking me?" the gravely wounded boy asked, hallucinating an exchange with his wife. He stopped breathing before morning, and Aria would never forget him.

Although Americans on Okinawa would grow almost numb to appalling outrages to the human sensibility and nervous system, few would take the deaths of their fellows more easily than Aria took this one, the first for him. It is worth repeating often that each death was a trauma, again in a way that those who did not share the other traumas of war cannot easily understand. Citing numbers — body counts in any form — tends to widen the gulf between those who know and those who don't know combat.

tire campaign. In comparison with Marine experiences on other islands, as well as what had been expected here, the painful, deadly
three weeks had been a cinch. An artilleryman whose battalion had
rarely used its guns except to "register" them with daily test firings
wrote that "it had been a great war." One infantry battalion had
marched all the way up the western coast road to the northern tip
without suffering a single casualty.

With the official pronouncement on April 20 that organized resistance had ended in the north, the 6th Marine Division turned to
mopping-up patrols and to savoring military life's little pleasures in
the field: cleaning weapons, taking photographs, picking up tooth-
paste, razor blades and cigarettes at the Red Cross tent, sacking in
whenever possible during the days of heavy rain, and working on
tans during the sunny ones. Manly recreation also beckoned. Ball
games were organized, first of all football because "we were young,
trained and spoiling for a fight," as one man put it. The games were
finally called off when injuries soared; there were broken legs and
bad cuts from coral that threatened infection. A group from the
same battalion found a boat and decided to slake their thirst for adventure by exploring a small island, almost certainly Yagaki, several
hundred yards offshore. They hurried back after discovering that
the island quartered a leper colony, leprosy being another of Okinawa's chronic scourges.

Soon many adventurous young men were hurrying to certain
premises near the village of Unten. It was hardly a common practice
of the United States Marine Corps in that straitlaced time to establish
a brothel, but there were reasons for an exception there. Of all the
Pacific islands on which the Marines had fought, this was the first
with a large civilian population, including many attractive women
and girls. Measures to avoid venereal disease and get rid of camp
followers, a few of whom had begun trading themselves for food,
seemed sensible. It also seemed a good idea to keep the men from
wandering into the villages and to prevent rape, of which there had
already been some complaints.

Unten, a site of captured nests for PT boats and midget submarines, was on the Motobu Peninsula, fifteen miles north of 6th Division headquarters. The volunteer girls, whom medical corpsmen inspected daily, worked in a large, well-cleaned house, putting in long
hours and making very good money by local standards. The custom-
ers too had to put in considerable time, first standing in a long line
to buy three-yen (thirty-cent) chits — scrip already issued in anticipation of the occupation — and condoms from corpsmen at a table,
then in a shorter one at the entrance to the house. They waited again

inside, this time in little cubicles, while a madame assigned their part-
ners. (One "older" man — of twenty-six — waited on his cubicle's cot
until a girl entered who looked thirteen. He gestured for her to go
back out and send in an older colleague with more curves, but she
returned with the madame, who told him to take it or leave it. He
took.) The existence of the "cat house" was of course unannounced
and unacknowledged, but the regiment's Catholic and Protestant
chaplains got wind of the disgrace and protested. "If my men want to
fuck, that's what they're going to do," countered the regimental commander with modern broadmindedness. Both chaplains requested
transfers.

But the best recreation was fantasizing about getting the hell off
Okinawa. Having secured the north, the victorious Marines told
themselves that their job was done and that "our chances of being
alive on V-J Day looked a little more promising," an infantryman
wistfully remembered. On clear nights in late April, some men could
make out the flickering of muzzle blasts forty or fifty miles south,
from where a distant rumble sometimes reached them. Private First
Class Eugene B. Sledge, who would write the great American memoir of the battle, tried to convince himself this was thunder, although
he knew better. Even since the first week after the landing, all 6th
Division Marines had heard rumors about difficulties in the south.

But they had only a vague impression of what those difficulties
really were and no idea whatever that many Japanese soldiers were
still improving their fortifications there, digging so hard and so long
every day that large numbers became ill. It was never more true than
among the happy Marines contriving to make life more comfortable
for themselves in the sparsely inhabited north that men in the ranks
rarely thought beyond each day's possible perks and specific duties
in their immediate surroundings. Some eagerly spread the only half-
joking rumor that they were going back to Guam soon, then going
home for Christmas.

In fact, they would be going to the great Shuri defense line before
the end of April. Their fighting had hardly begun.

12 · Civilian Dislocation

[The preliminary] bombardment was completely one-sided . . . Planes and gunfire . . . wrecked most of the enemy aircraft on the island, which was all to the good. Apart from this, the principal results achieved . . . were the destruction of villages and isolated farmhouses that had no strategic value.
— Samuel Eliot Morison, after personal observation from an American ship

We did not come here to play Santa Claus for the inhabitants of these islands nor do we intend to raise the standard of their living higher than the prewar level.
— Brigadier General William Crist, 10th Army Deputy Commander for Military Government

In the matter of civilians, [Marine officers] showed commendable restraint, especially considering that every Marine regarded Okinawans as Japs and would split no Oriental hairs whatever except to concede that these "Japs" looked very harmless and beaten down. The Okinawans we saw at first, cowering in the thatched houses of the little village of China — an apt name, since Okinawans are more like Chinese peasants than anything else — or hiding in nearby caves, were all women, old men, and children, every male civilian between 16 and 40 having been herded south by the Jap Army for labor duty.
— John Lardner in *The New Yorker*, May 19, 1945

I thought I saw some bushes out there that weren't there that afternoon. So we called for flares and saw the bushes moving — but stop when the flare went up. Then we threw about a dozen hand grenades from our foxhole right there and heard moaning all the rest of the night. In the morning, we saw that they were all young women, nurses or something, maybe Japanese, maybe Okinawan. One was beautiful, really beautiful — with only one arm and both legs dangling by just a little thread. She was still hanging on after her awful wounds and that full night of moaning. We had to put her out of her terrible misery.
— An American medical corpsman

ALTHOUGH Okinawan civilians were hardly Washington's greatest concern, their fate wasn't ignored. Knowing this was the first time United States Pacific forces would encounter a large unfriendly but noncombatant population, the War Department sought to minimize Okinawans' inevitable casualties and lighten their inescapable distress while pursuing its main interests of keeping them from hindering American efforts or aiding the Japanese.

The forces themselves could not be informed of any concern for civilians until their destination was revealed, which happened only when they were almost there. Not that many hadn't guessed. A large map of the Pacific had been tacked to a 6th Marine Division bulletin board on Guadalcanal. Four months earlier — at Christmas 1944 — Okinawa's dot had a heavy smudge from countless fingers that had touched it while officers and men speculated about their next destination. But no fighting man knew officially until he was at sea in his troop transport or landing craft, when a brochure distributed during prelanding briefings made the first mention of the "simple, polite, law-abiding" natives. "Okinawans are not warlike," it informed, "and they resent the high and mighty ways of the Japanese from the big islands to the north."

> Under Japanese rule, it's kind of tough to be an Okinawa [sic], because as true Sons of Heaven they don't seem to make the grade. They are used as manual laborers by the Japanese and when they are drafted they usually go into labor battalions. There are practically no Okinawa officers in the Japanese army. Even the officials sent by Tokyo to run the islands have kept themselves aloof from the islanders.

Each of the four American divisions that landed on Easter Sunday was allocated seventy thousand pounds of rice and soy beans and instructed to protect as many civilians as feasible by handing them over to separate military government (milgovt) units. This was a corps of doctors, corpsmen, quartermasters, civil administrators and engineers for building detention camps. Small teams of them were attached to the fighting units and moved up behind the advance, with drinking water and rudimentary medical supplies for the sick and wounded.

All civilian milgovt personnel, including about a hundred officers, had had basic military and bivouac training. Their mission was to evacuate unarmed natives from firing areas to assembly points in the rear. From there, women, children and the elderly were taken to camps in villages with undestroyed houses, where attempts were made to supply them with farming tools and to provide for a semblance of normal life. Those forward teams included Nisei — first-generation Japanese-American — interpreters essential for this humanitarian enterprise in support of the military effort to reduce native aid to the Japanese 32nd Army.

Apart from the exceptions of fools and sadists, milgovt personnel worked in good faith to ameliorate the harsh conditions of displaced civilians; the operation was generally carried out in accordance with orders, which were as charitable as could be expected in wartime, especially against so uncharitable an enemy as the Japanese. The relatively few natives willing and able to work for the American 10th Army — chiefly as road laborers and mess and hospital attendants — were paid the going 1940 wage of one yen a day, roughly eighteen cents. (Able-bodied men unwilling to work, of which there were mere handfuls at the beginning, were confined to stockades.) Minimum supplies of food prevented starvation, and potentially destructive epidemic diseases were averted. Many tons of DDT were sprayed around the detention camps against the chronic scourges of mosquitoes, fleas and flies, while staffs grappled with what one account called the chief discipline problem: "getting the people — the elderly women in particular — to use latrines."

On a personal level, some Americans felt deep sympathy for the desperate "Okies" and tried to help in every possible way. "They were crying and praying," said a young Marine whose platoon shot and killed "a lot" of civilians the first night as they tried to pass through its lines. "They didn't know where our lines were and we didn't know who *they* were . . . I remembered the movies of Japs butchering civilians in China and wondered whether we'd started doing the same." Such men, of which there were many, sometimes hugged and wept over the bodies of civilians they had mistakenly killed. They often showed consideration and generosity well beyond the call: medical attention for the wounded, transportation for the aged, C-rations and candy for the children. A scene witnessed by a staff officer of "an old sergeant feeding a native woman with a spoon from a can of peaches" would be repeated a thousand times. Accustomed to worse from some Japanese and expecting infinitely worse from American "beasts," most Okinawans bowed deeply in gratitude — those who believed that the gifts weren't poisoned.

On the other hand, milgovt's primary goal was to control an enemy civilian population at minimum cost. "Protection" meant herding as many as possible into the extremely overcrowded detention camps — eventually over a quarter of a million civilians in sixteen camps — where Okinawans were grateful chiefly because their expectations were so low. For although the War Department recognized that Okinawans were not racially, culturally or temperamentally Japanese, it did not make the mistake of expecting them to welcome the landing forces as liberators. "But by and large, they are still loyal to Japan," the War Department's brochure continued. "All they know about

Americans is what they get from Tokyo propaganda, so you can expect them to look at you as though you were a combination of Dracula and the Sad Sack — at first, anyway."*

And for all its good intentions, the brochure's first sentence revealed a smug disregard of what awaited the pastoral island of neat villages and beautiful groves of pine interspersed with terraced fields. "There's no use giving you a sightseer's guide," it cheerfully began, "because after the navy and the air forces have blasted the way for a landing . . . [Okinawa] just won't look the same." This is not to blame the brochure's writers and much less the troops preparing to land, for whom the pep talk was intended. Anyone about to hit the beach against the expected Japanese resistance deserved all the encouragement he could get, together with every softening-up shell. The primary cause of the horrific damage to Okinawa was the island's geography and history.

But Americans were also badly prepared to deal with their Okie prisoners. "Strange but simple people," a man mused about a grandfather and two young children who burst into tears when they thought they were about to be killed. For most Americans in 1945, "strange" usually came down to being non-American. But even the few world travelers couldn't have predicted the power of the Okinawans' fear. Few people take alien ideology or indoctrination seriously, least of all when they seem patently absurd, as in the case of Japanese war propaganda. Americans knew they were the good guys who wished innocent natives no harm; but most Okinawans, like most people everywhere, believed what they had been told: the invaders were thirsting to torture, rape and kill. One of the first groups of prisoners taken on Easter Sunday emerged from a cave drawing trembling fingers across their throats to indicate they were ready to die.†

---

*Those who did not get the brochure or a shipboard briefing were likely to know even less about Okinawa. Samuel Hynes, a pilot in the first squadron of land-based planes on the island, remembered that "no one had heard of Okinawa. [Squadron] intelligence knew nothing about it except for two striking 'facts'" in a mimeographed handout distributed to the fliers on Ulithi: "one was that the natives were not Japanese but a more primitive people called Hairy Anus. (This was probably a confused reference to the Caucasoid Ainu, a people indigenous to Japan, some of whom were among Okinawa's early settlers.) The other was that the island was infected with poisonous snakes."

†Unable to hand that group over because milgovt units hadn't kept up with the rapid advance, Marines guarded them while digging in and shooting the breeze. "Boy, I'd like to fuck her," said one private, indirectly complimenting an extremely attractive woman in the group. "Please don't do that," she replied in perfect English. The beauty had been on her way back to Japan from studying at UCLA when the war broke out, stranding her on Okinawa. Only her insistence that Americans were not rapacious savages had persuaded the group to surrender.

Japan was making much of the fact that her sacred country had not lost a war in twenty-three hundred years; America, that her blessed country had never lost a war at all. But for Okinawans, this was the first time in three hundred years that war was being waged on their land, a war between forces that terrified them. An artillery-man correctly observed in April that "there are hardly any young men left, only old men, women, and little kids." It was chiefly those too feeble or immobile to hide or flee — scatterings of the old, in-firm, and very young — who allowed themselves to be rounded up into the devils' camps.

Fighting units began meeting such terrified groups within an hour of the landing — far more of them than anticipated, for the great speed of the advance had bisected the island, cutting off scores of thousands who had intended to evacuate to the wild north. The first natives E. B. Sledge saw were "pathetic. The most pitiful things about the Okinawan civilians were that they were totally bewildered by the shock of our invasion and they were scared to death of us. Countless times they passed us on the way to the rear with fear, dismay and confusion on their faces."

Aged grandmothers covered themselves head to foot with quilts and shrank deep inside caves. When Americans removed the quilts, the women would "kneel and bow their foreheads to the deck time after time," an officer observed. "Palms pressed prayerfully together before them, they beseeched their discoverers most piteously to spare their ancient lives." As it advanced a few days after the landing, the unit of Peter Milo, the New York policeman who had lost his friend Corpsman Truex on L-day, was strafing all holes large enough to be cave mouths, then lobbing grenades inside. Just as one of the platoon was about to blast another such opening, a shrill cry sounded inside. The grenade was held back just in time. Two cowering young women with children eventually emerged, together with an old man. Bent almost in half, his white beard nearly touching the ground, he sup-ported himself with a staff.

One of Milo's platoon took him by the arm to lead him to a roundup of civilians they had just passed, destined for a camp. The old man broke away and shouted in terror to the women. As if the movement had been rehearsed, the three dropped to their knees in a neat line, the man using a chopping gesture at the back of his neck to plead for their quick beheading.

The same Marine picked him up, kicking and screaming, while Milo and a buddy lifted the children and headed for the camp, know-ing the women would follow. Milo's memory of the little girl's fearful trembling in his arms continued to haunt him forty-five years later. He offered her a candy bar.

> She looked into my eyes but made no move to accept the candy. Trying to encourage her, I took a little bite and chewed it. She just kept looking into my eyes. Suddenly I felt as though she was looking into my very soul. I found it hard to breathe and my eyes had a stinging sensation.
>
> When we reached the compound and they saw the other Okinawans, who were eating and laughing by now, the old man and the women relaxed and joined their conversation. I sat down on the ground with the little girl on my lap, and bit by bit she ate the whole bar, all the time her eyes never leaving mine. [Then] it was time to catch up with the outfit. I stood up, reached for my last Hershey bar, which would have been my dinner, and put it in the little girl's hand. After a few steps, I turned back to see her still looking at me.

On L-day evening, a Connecticut recruit named Irving Ortel dug in near Yomitan Airfield. A sharp-eyed platoon mate spied a Japanese infiltrator, with a pack on his back, creeping down a path to their clearing, and killed him with a burst from his Browning automatic rifle — after which the man was discovered to be a woman, her pack a child. "That really shook us up. We felt terrible. Then we got used to an awful lot worse."

For three months from that first night, shooting Okies by mistake was commonplace. The civilians contributed heavily to their own destruction by moving outside American positions at night, although repeatedly warned by leaflet never to move then. But their fear of the daylight blanket of bombs and shells, and of the immensely powerful invaders themselves, caused most to move *only* at night, and American units, unable to understand why civilians didn't get the vital message, continued to fire blindly during that worst time for both. Once one began shooting into the dark, all joined to blast away at any noise in the terrifying dark.* In the morning, the perimeter of their night positions was strewn with as many dead goats, rabbits and civilians as Japanese soldiers.

Civilians also contributed by collaborating with the Japanese. Each American who found evidence of native help to the enemy became

---

* An artillery battery dug in for one of its nights in the north across a creek from a little village. When one Marine fired because he thought he'd heard noises from there, all joined — and fired even more furiously when return fire indicated they were being encircled. Daylight established that the "return fire" was ricochets of their bullets off a cement bridge across the creek. However, the sheepish men continued firing just as furiously at unknown noises during the following nights.

less concerned about discriminating between Japanese soldiers trying to sneak in and blow them up and local families trying to save themselves. A few nights later, Ortel's platoon, dug in near the beach, heard movement close by. They grabbed their weapons to defend against the dreaded nighttime banzai attack — until word came down to cease firing: the people out there were civilians trying to return to their "huts," which the Marines had passed before dark. "Needless to say, we didn't cease firing," remembered Platoon Sergeant Edmund De Mar, the prewar Marine who had wondered where Pearl Harbor was. "Because how the hell did we know this? How the hell could anyone be sure they wouldn't banzai* and kill us?" They stopped firing only when the movement stopped, and in the morning saw a cluster of female corpses mixed in with those of Japanese soldiers. Some of the women had hand grenades inside their kimonos. So the platoon had been right to shoot them — but Americans didn't know that the women's grenades may have been meant for themselves: out of some mixture of pitilessness and a wish to prevent their torture, Japanese soldiers had already provided natives with the means of suicide. Many did not know what they would do with the weapons, only hoped that a right decision would deliver them at the last moment.

But neither could the Americans know, and discoveries of weapons hidden in kimono sleeves helped many resign themselves to dead civilians, especially since they were never certain, again with ample reason, of Okie intentions. Their confusion was reflected in the first letter home of Thomas Hannaher, the young private whose Browning automatic ammunition had been stolen from his bunk on the morning of the landing. The natives, he wrote during an hour of rest from the push north, "don't like the Japs either because they have treated them poorly." But the same letter also reported that "the natives here are Japs and cannot be trusted." Not quite true, but true enough for Americans to shoot first and investigate later. Even farmers and fishermen with poles were perceived as threats.

The Doberman war dogs of a point squad pushing north along a coastal road on April 10 suddenly froze. Tense Marines heard rustling in the brush only fifty feet away. A glimpse of old-fashioned leggings through that brush told Lieutenant Taylor Kennerly that

---

*The banzai charge by outnumbered, desperate Japanese troops had become a dreadful reality for Americans on previous Pacific islands, especially Saipan, and an even more dreadful nighttime contemplation. Literally "May you live ten thousand years," the word expressed total group resolution. At that time, "banzai" was wished only for the Emperor.

this was another ambush. "Fire, fire!" he yelled; three rifles and one BAR poised for the order opened up instantly. But when Kennerly heard female and juvenile screams, he shouted for the fire to cease and ran in front of his men, knocking their weapons upward.

The men rushed toward the sea and found three dead enemy soldiers, a live one and several women and children huddling together. The survivors' eyes bulged with fear until chewing gum, chocolate and cigarettes were distributed. Kennerly was relieved when the natives sensed what he already knew: his "young, kind Marines were not murderers of women and children."

But a bullet had ripped the arm of an Okinawan boy almost from his body. The bones were in smithereens, the hand gone. Laying the child on a blanket, Kennerly fed him candy from his pack while desperately thinking of what to do. One look at the huddled women told him which was his mother. At Kennerly's motion, she sprang up, knelt beside her child and cradled his head in her lap. The surviving man — perhaps Japanese, perhaps Okinawan — also advanced and clasped the boy's remaining hand.

The medical corpsman with Kennerly's squad had had no training in amputation and wouldn't try on the shattered little arm. The only help in that deeply rural area would have been the company doctor, but he was treating casualties in the column's rear. Time pressed hard; the point squad was holding up the entire regiment and the child's wound would kill him very soon. Dismayed, Kennerly decided he himself had to amputate, but could find nothing sharp enough in anyone's pack. The child's only prospect was a lingering, agonizing death. Praying that a gracious God would forgive him, the grieving lieutenant administered an overdose of the corpsman's morphine, then faced the harrowing duty of telling the parents.

> Who says that the nature and emotions of the Okinawan peasants are any different from those of middle-class Americans? The Oriental man is not prone to show his emotions in public. But there on that lonely mountainside, the husband placed his arm around his wife's shoulder and they both wept silently but bitterly, their bodies trembling in their anguish. Yes, I can sense that human nature is the same all around the world. As I watched the pathetic parents, my thoughts turned to my wife at home and our six-month-old son that I had never seen, and I breathed a prayer of thanks that they were spared the ordeals of war.

Late that afternoon, the weary company doctor found Kennerly digging in farther up the coast and told him the child would survive! The doctor had come across the family an hour earlier and amputated the dangling arm. The morphine hadn't killed the lad because it was old and had lost some strength. In fact, it had probably kept him alive — by mitigating his shock — until the amputation. Kennerly's misery turned to joy.

Most civilian groups cringed with fear until the barrier was broken, as often with a canteen of water as with a medical dressing or candy bar. With the centuries-old collective experience of taking refuge from typhoons, they had saved themselves from the pre-invasion bombardment by sheltering in their tombs and caves. A Marine reported in a letter home that "most of the kids are the cutest things you ever laid eyes on." Their plight moved most Americans when they had time and energy to be moved, prompting plentiful acts of individual kindness. The happy endings were cherished, especially in the midst of so many horrific ones. What these good, enormously burdened Americans did not suspect — even they, who were right there — was the trifling proportion of happy endings.

They did not suspect this because they never saw the majority of civilians. For the most part, they encountered only the very young and very old, those captured in almost all photographs of the time: the barefoot, blind, and crippled who filled Americans with sympathy until they had to duck the next bullet or shell whizzing toward them; the shrunken grandparents and the children with the round faces and dark, hungry eyes who prompted fleeting thoughts about the oneness of the human family. The Okinawans the 10th Army rarely met were the more or less healthy adolescents and adults with the means and stamina to avoid the American camps that would have been their best hope for survival, but which they took for the least imaginable alternative. Those with enough strength ran and limped and crawled to flee everything American, which is why only 126,000 civilians, slightly more than a quarter of the population, were in milgovt's custody by the end of April instead of the expected 300,000.

Forty years later, Taylor Kennerly would think often of the Okinawan boy, even search for him on a moving visit to Okinawa in 1987. Kennerly had no doubt that the child was spared because his Maker saw to it. "My honest conviction is that a gracious God is the giver and taker of life. How dare man assume that he can usurp this power?" But in 1945, Kennerly's frightened men, like so many others, would continue firing at movements in the night.* One morning

*Kennerly himself was wounded just over a month later as his platoon approached Sugar Loaf Hill on May 13, Mother's Day. Two machine gun bullets tore holes in his jacket, inches from his heart. Another traversed his foot and a fourth so shattered his ankle that he would leave a naval hospital only on April 1, 1947, exactly two years after the landing.

not long after the child's miraculous survival, the platoon found an entire family dead, including the children. The brave, good lieutenant's conviction of heavenly intervention does not explain why tens of thousands of equally innocent Okinawan children suffered precisely the agonizing death he could not countenance for his lucky boy.

> *The real war was tragic and ironic beyond the power of any literary or philosophical analysis to suggest, but in unbombed America especially, the meaning of the war seemed inaccessible. Thus, as experience, the suffering was wasted.*
> — Paul Fussell

> *It is apparent that the Okinawan people as a whole have not the remotest conception of the issues of this war as we see them.*
> — From an American naval officer's study written soon after the battle

Many Okinawan civilians had resisted until the last moment the prefectural government's shouts for all "nonessentials" to evacuate, especially farming families unable to leave the only patches of land they knew. That last moment came with the arrival of the enemy fleet a week before L-day. When dusk stopped the shells on March 24, the first day of the naval bombardment, the roads choked with traffic. Scores of thousands felt that anything would be better than the unholy cascade of explosives — which, like the 10/10 air raid six months earlier, reinforced the image of the enemy as wild beasts.

Throughout that week of pre-invasion bombardment, the central part of the island at night was like a giant anthill just destroyed. Bewildered families abandoned their tiny houses, most with nowhere to go and no means of support away from their fields. Some eighty-five thousand — about the same number as the Japanese in the 32nd Army — headed toward the far emptier north. Others scattered this way and that, seeking refuge in remote villages. Some groups crossed two and three times as they changed directions for some new place that promised a last-minute vision of safety.

Ernie Pyle would see sprinklings of refugees two weeks later and register Okinawans as "dirty" and "pathetic" — true enough of those. Almost all the families were slowed by their aged and infirm. Ablebodied men had been conscripted. Doubly hard pressed without them, women lugged all they could — pots and pans, meager supplies of food — toward the unknown. Many had never seen the villages of their destination. The handful of healthy refugee men carried the aged and infirm. The women bore bundles on their heads and infants on their backs while pushing disabled parents in carts — those lucky enough to have carts. When they caught their breath, they tried to calm children bawling with hunger.

Okinawa had an "excellent network of poor roads," as an American historian called it. The best were gravel, the others dirt trails for horse-drawn carts. On the east coast, almost directly across the island from the landing beaches, Yoshi Kamata, the wife of a prosperous wholesaler of soy bean sauce, fled with her five-month infant on her back, pulling her three-year-old with one hand and encouraging her six-year-old to keep going on his own. Her destination was a village of relatives some fifty miles north, but she realized the utter futility of her effort within an hour. The six-year-old bravely ignored his painful feet and stumbled on in silence, but his baby brother sobbed uncontrollably with fatigue. When he finally sat down on the side of the road, incapable of another step, groups of mute fellow refugees continued passing in the dark, most staggering under the weight of their bundles.

Yoshi Kamata panicked until she remembered that a bus went north from a village four kilometers ahead. Four kilometers seemed an impossible distance, but it was her sole hope of saving her dazed children. She grabbed them and tried to run.

Belching smoke from its charcoal engine, the bus was pulling away from the village when Mrs. Kamata dragged herself and her children within sight of it. To her great good luck, people noticed that the family was about to pass out. Luck again: although the groaning bus was packed beyond imagination, the driver stopped and opened the door. The passengers squeezed themselves in even more tightly, and the family was on its way to its relatives. Mrs. Kamata soon realized that hers was "the kind of luck that separated those destined to perish from those who would survive."

The village of Gushikawa, some seven miles due east of the landing beaches, was ordered to evacuate well before the landings, but the Sonan family remained. Tosei Sonan had been lucky until now; a neat bit of acting following a bureaucratic lapse had allowed him to escape conscription. The name of his parents' infant son Tosei, who died four years before his namesake's birth, had never been removed from the family register. The surviving Tosei, taken for the dead one, was considered too small and poorly developed mentally when he was called, four years too early, for military service. The examining officer labeled him "stupid." He began to act stupid and was dismissed as a half-wit.

The "half-wit" was actually more educated than the average villager; his father, who had failed to correct the family register, was a municipal office worker. Tosei took a job in a mainland factory when he could find no work on the island. Since returning, he had kept the family in rice, vegetables and an occasional fish, in addition to the usual sweet potatoes, on his fireman's wages.

The oldest daughter, Shigeko, was terrified when the pre-invasion bombardment jolted the island: some shells and bombs fell on Gushikawa. The eleven-year-old had learned in school about subhuman Americans who drowned deformed infants and killed healthy but unwanted babies by bashing their heads against a wall. She knew about their racist yearning to destroy and depopulate Divine Japan, except for the few attractive women they planned to keep for their insatiable animal lust . . . Little Shigeko was even more terrified on L-day, when the invaders drove from the beaches on the opposite coast, past Yomitan and Kadena airfields, and straight toward the Pacific coast — and trembled even more violently when she caught sight of two mad killers in a jeep passing Gushikawa. Two days later, as she rounded a bend in the road on her way to draw water from a well, she saw an American plane. Diving into the bushes, she escaped the pilot's fire, directed, she was convinced, at her, and ran home when another jeep passed.

Although her mother was angry that Shigeko broke the water bottle when diving into the bushes, the girl was spared punishment by the return home of her father, announcing that it was time to escape. The family set out after dark with all they could pack into a cart hitched to their horse. With her mother pregnant, Shigeko was treated almost as an adult, but her three younger sisters, aged six, four and eighteen months, needed care. Her grandfather's former wife, divorced only because she could not bear a child to preserve the precious family line, also joined the party. The Sonans embraced a neighbor who was remaining in her house, then left the village that had been their world. Terrified to stay, yet unable to accompany them, the old, ill woman who stayed behind embodied the civilian predicament: flee, stay, fight the incomprehensibly powerful enemy, or surrender to his bestiality? She was the kind most likely to be saved by the American milgovt units — but when her son-in-law, a conscripted soldier, managed to leave his unit for a peek at the house several days later, he found her dead.

Weeping evacuees with similar burdens packed the roads leading north. Leaving their home and ancestral tomb, the Sonans hoped their food would sustain them until the Americans were thrown back into the sea. But a bombed-out bridge over a river at the first substantial village on their route forced them to unhitch their cart and leave it behind with the bulk of their provisions.

Hampered by the slowness of the grandfather's former wife, they followed the east coast road, hid from the bombs and shells at daybreak and moved out again at twilight — as quickly as they could, for Americans were advancing fast behind them. When Grandmother fell far behind again the second night, Shigeko was left to wait for her. The eleven-year-old waited and waited, then decided to go back to look for the elderly woman. Just as she moved, a bomb or shell exploded in the spot where she had been standing a second earlier. But Grandma was less lucky; Shigeko searched for hours but never found her.

She caught up with the others, but when they could not reach the far northern village assigned them, they hid on Mount Tano, one of the most rugged of the northern mountains, almost in the center of the island's least inhabited area. The mountain woods there were often too dense for the family to see the sky; someone had to climb a tree or a crag to determine direction. Such exposure was dangerous: Americans often bombed and strafed any movement, their mortar shells felling treetops — until 5 P.M., when they apparently finished for the day.

The family's food was almost entirely gone, but the teenage Okinawans of the Blood and Iron Scouts helped when they could. They killed the horse and dried its flesh for eating. Shigeko never cried, even when she was starving. Her parents said she mustn't, and she knew she had to do what she was told.

What she did do was help hunt for food, which was easier after five o'clock but still very dangerous. When the 6th Marine Division's commander declared the north secured on April 20, his troops controlled chiefly the cities, villages and coastal roads. From there, they sent patrols into the interior to mop up Japanese remnants, some still trying to fight. Looking for food and water from nearby streams, Shigeko and her cousins encountered several enemy groups. Fear subsided in reverse proportion to the children's hunger, but when they did accept chocolate and C-rations, their parents threw them away, convinced that anything Americans gave Okinawans was poisoned. The famished children at last risked tasting new gifts on their own, but although they didn't die and some Americans actually seemed kind, Shigeko couldn't forget what she had been taught about their lust to kill Asians.

The Sonans continued hiding in remote parts of the lonely mountain. They and other families built a "village" of six straw huts, then left in fear that the cluster would be spotted by American patrols. Besides, the nearby food supply, sometimes only boiled grasses and tree bark, was quickly exhausted. Some families prepared to kill themselves before Americans could torture them. Others gave up the grim struggle after ventures to villages below, where locals assured them that Americans didn't kill civilians who surrendered, only took them to detention camps. But Tosei Sonan, his fear and loathing of Americans intensified by his years in Japan, remained convinced that any American he approached would shoot him on the spot.

Some civilians had been shot, even though, or just because, they disguised themselves as women with babies strapped to their backs. Some women, in turn, cut their hair and dressed like men in hope of escaping rape, of which there were enough incidents to nourish the fear. One day, two patrolling Americans* dragged a young woman from a hut they discovered near the Sonans'. Hiding in a tree, Shigeko heard terrified weeping while the Americans' heads moved in jerky motion. She knew that some adolescent girls smeared soot on their faces and wore men's clothes when they left their shelters. Those precautions and her parents' constant warnings allowed her to guess what was happening to the woman.

Food was a greater problem. When nothing could be picked up in deserted villages, Tosei sometimes boiled the safe parts of the sotesu, a primitive palm that grew on mountain rocks and had kept farming families of earlier generations alive after typhoons destroyed their entire crops. On their scavenging forays at dawn and dusk, Shigeko and her mother sometimes found discarded C-rations or rotten sweet potatoes in fields near the villages. Days were spent high in the mountain, nights in makeshift huts regularly visited by Japanese stragglers, the remnants of Colonel Udo's force. Some threatened punishment for failure to supply food. The Sonans had heard that the worst of them shot such "unpatriotic" civilians.

At the same time, American patrols continued to burn the huts they managed to find. Shigeko and her mother returned from a food foray one morning to find their own hut burned. Picking some charred bits of flesh from the ashes, they wailed for Shigeko's father and sisters — until the "dead" emerged from the woods demanding quiet because the patrol that did the burning might still be near. Recovering from their hysterical laughter, the women helped prepare for yet another move.

The Sonans were always on the move — they built and abandoned thirteen huts in various forests — and never dry in that spring's unusually wet rainy season. A night here, two nights there — and a critical debate as they drifted south again in search of sustenance. From a mountain called Ona-dake, they saw American ships stretching to the horizon. Perhaps to save the child she was carrying, miraculously

---

* Most likely they were from the Army's 27th Division rather than the 6th Marine Division; the two units had probably changed places by this time.

not yet lost, Shigeko's mother argued that Japan could never defeat such a force: it was time to go down from the mountains and give themselves up.

Dismissing this "nonsense," Tosei Sonan insisted the Combined Fleet or Special Attack Forces would soon arrive to smash the cowardly Americans and liberate Okinawa. Famished little Shigeko took her father's side because he knew far more about the unconquerable Japanese spirit and because she would never forget her school-learned duty: "Beat the Americans to death!" Now the skeletal children could climb the hills only with a desperate effort, pulling themselves up by clutching roots and branches. A virulent rash with a tormenting itch covered their bodies.

They wandered for two months, staggering to another mountain somewhere in the south where hard fighting had taken place. Every tree was charred to a blackened stump — on which Japanese corpses sprawled, bits hanging on the few remaining branches. The exhausted Sonans buried as many as they could but lacked the strength to dig deep enough to keep the feet from sticking out. Although rows of mortally wounded Japanese soldiers rasped and moaned in the nearest clearing, the family had to sleep there because night had fallen. The children gathered leaves and crushed them in their noses to block the stench of the corpses.

When Shigeko's mother gave birth, the Sonans had no idea that the Battle of Okinawa had been officially over for two full weeks. The new baby somehow managed to live her first few days, but Shigeko's malnourished, malaria-ridden mother had no milk, and the infant couldn't swallow gruel made from a handful of rice Tosei succeeded in buying. Now Shigeko's mother finally persuaded her husband to surrender; the children were all bones and bloated bellies. Down from the mountains, they were loaded onto an American truck, driven to a camp, fed and sprayed with DDT. Ten months later, they were permitted to return to Gushikawa, which had been burned to the ground, together with their house and all their possessions. Still, the battle was kinder to the Sonans than to civilian Okinawans as a whole, including those in the detention camps. In fact, they were among the luckiest families: everyone survived except Grandma and Shigeko's four-year-old sister, who died days after the end of their flight, unable to swallow at all.

> *In Okinawan, we say* **Nichi do takara**: *Life is the treasure. Whatever the reasons to fight and kill, however profound the causes or pretexts for war, they can't justify the result. Human lives are too precious to sacrifice.*
> — Masahide Ota, forty-six years later

For Masahide Ota, the prize student of the Normal School, L-day's thrill lasted hours. Senior staff of the 32nd Army — and of the 62nd Division and 5th Artillery Command, coordinator of all heavy artillery — spent much of that long day observing the American armada from the observation post at Shuri Castle, appreciating the enemy's colossal strength and landing skills but showing no concern. General Ushijima's smiling composure reflected Japan's invincibility and the Emperor's inviolability. Ota continued to believe that clever Japanese tactics had lured the invasion fleet to Okinawa. He told himself to control his impatience for its sinking.

The confidence of the Normal School's complement, all enrolled in the Blood and Iron Scouts, could not have been higher as they took up their tasks. Ota was in the subunit assigned to staff intelligence at 32nd Army headquarters. Every morning, the students walked the two hundred yards from the mouth of their cave to the headquarters under Shuri Castle, where they were briefed on battle and other war news: how many American planes had been shot down and ships sunk; how wobbly the faint-hearted enemy's morale had become. Most of the items came by radio from Tokyo. The boys took notes. Then the commander of their little unit, who happened to be a mean-spirited Japanese intelligence officer, dispatched them in groups of two or three to disseminate the fictitious offerings to towns and villages everywhere south of the Shuri Line. The boys shouldered their rifles and made their way on foot to spread their messages — all with a subtext promising early expulsion of the Americans from Okinawa — to local military authorities and civilians as far away as the island's southern tip. The mostly female and elderly civilians welcomed them joyfully even before hearing the glad tidings. Mothers and grandparents took the communication soldiers as substitutes for their own boys, almost all of whom were fighting with Army or Home Guard units. They fed them rice, already gone from the student cave in Shuri, and even meat. The boys stayed over a night or two, depending on the distance from Shuri, then returned for their next assignment.

Before the first week was over, they traveled only at night: enemy reconnaissance planes and firepower made daylight movement too risky. Soon they were ordered not to leave their cave for any purpose whatever except after dark. But their confidence remained unshaken even when the fierce American bombardment leveled their beloved Normal School. The severe shortage of food did not cool their patriotic ardor, nor did the first serious casualty among their group. That happened on April 12 (the day of President Roosevelt's death), when Ota and a close friend disobeyed orders by rushing outside to relieve themselves there instead of in their cave. Dashing back, they stood at the mouth to watch Japanese tracer bullets reach for the enemy planes that buzzed Shuri like flies. A chunk of shrapnel knocked Ota's friend flat.

His wounds were grave. The others quickly carried him to a nearby hospital cave. It was packed with a number of patients they could scarcely believe — so full of severely wounded Japanese soldiers that the boys were refused entry until one remembered he knew a doctor inside. That visibly exhausted doctor was found and persuaded to treat the first student casualty. With the wards overflowing, the others could only take their classmate back to their own cave and maintain a vigil throughout the night. The wounded boy had no mother; he called for his sister until he died. That unexpected reality on top of the hospital cave's frightening scenes put the first chip in the unit's morale, but also fed the boys' patriotic resolve. Now they had a personal loss to avenge on top of a sacred duty to fulfill. Swearing their own lives to repay the cruel Americans, the classmates reminded themselves that Imperial General Headquarters and the 32nd Army command had attracted the stupid, arrogant enemy to the island as a tactical move. "Let your enemy cut your skin / You cut his flesh. / Let your enemy cut your flesh / You sever his bones." They repeated the famous ditty; it made sense of their friend's death.

They had been digging a separate little chamber in their cave for the Normal School's principal, who, unlike many Japanese civilians on Okinawa, had neither escaped to the mainland when invasion seemed imminent nor tried to curry favor with the 32nd Army. Students and teachers loved and trusted Principal Sadao Noda even more than before the emergency. As the grim days passed, Noda fashioned a separate memorial tablet to each of his students killed when delivering news of the supposed battlefield victories. By mid-May, the tablets covered an entire wall of his chamber, and his despondency worried the survivors more than their own precarious safety. Going outside their cave to bury fellow students who died at Shuri required great courage as well as dedication.

The towns and villages to which they traveled continued to greet them as family. The inhabitants, almost entirely cut off from other sources of information, thirsted for news, especially encouraging news. But they gradually turned skeptical of the regular reports of great victories, and the boys came to feel guilty about conveying them. The trips took ever longer under the bombardments — especially for Kume-raised Ota, easily lost on the unmarked Okinawan roads — and became ever more dangerous. Several boys who walked south with Ota one night were killed just after they had dispersed for their assigned villages. Things also seemed worse at each return to Shuri. From one rice ball a day in early April, their food ration dwindled to nearly nothing. The lice-infested lads learned to feed themselves by scavenging in fields, chiefly for sweet potatoes, during their missions. All were brave, but the tension of constant danger on those assignments, followed by relentless bombardment and confinement in their cave, sometimes snapped young nerves. So many deaths! So little hope of escaping it, of even getting something to eat! The music teacher composed a song for them, based on a poem full of longing for the old days of peace under the shade of Shuri's ancient trees. Some boys had to fight tears when they sang it, seemingly in acceptance of their own deaths. A few screamed about the enemy in their sleep and slowly became useless. (Curiously, those who had led their class in military training were more likely to break than the quiet and meek, who tended to be better at keeping their wits under the enormous pressure.) But all remained proud to sacrifice for the highest ideals. It would have been treason to imagine that Okinawans could stop doing their duty for Japan.

13 · Ruriko Morishita, Nurses' Aide

What really gets me angry is . . . that [friends] want a Jap flag and I had chances plenty of them to get one. These Nips aren't carrying them anymore and Mom are they fanatical. They'd rather kill themselves than surrender. The women are just as bad as the soldiers and when I first hit this rock [Okinawa] it hurt me to see them killed. You know anyone with a mother, wife and sisters and aunts that I have naturally thinks of women as a little bit better than men and more or less puts them on a pedestal. But these Keisha girls are like dogs I guess and do all the dirty work. The Japs seem to have plenty of women with them in their caves. After seeing some of the work of the women though it don't bother me at all anymore to see them killed.

— From a letter home of a Marine who would later devote much effort to reconciliation with Japanese and Okinawan survivors

I can't describe the worst. The worst was indescribable.

— Ruriko Morishita, forty-three years later

O KINAWANS' commitment to Japanese goals remained uneven, the young generally more enthusiastic than their parents and grandparents. Although many Okinawan soldiers conscripted to serve with fighting units longed to drop everything and return to their families, boys as young as fourteen happily polished their new arms, and native girls served with equal pride, many as nurse's aides. Six high schools supplied 219 students for that work, which all saw as an honor and a sacred trust. Among them were 155 girls from the elite Himeyuri Girls High School and Himeyuri Teachers College in Shuri, the female equivalent of the Normal School. They became the counterparts to boys like Masahide Ota, selected for the most responsible student assignments.

The Student Medical Corps would later enter the literature of martyrdom as the Himeyuri (Princess Lily) Girls. Although their lot was no harder and their casualties hardly greater than among Okinawan women as a whole, the young daughters of the island's privileged families would make captivating characters for romantic literature and prettified Japanese films, cast in the glow of their pre-invasion purity. Many would end the war in what would become known as the Cave of the Virgins — with little exaggeration; those young "princesses" of the best schools were more protected from the opposite sex than the boys. Since the Confucian teaching to separate the sexes after the age of seven had arrived on Okinawa only with the Japanese school system in the 1880s, much of the island outside its few cities observed it less than rigorously until the general tightening of discipline during the war emergency after Pearl Harbor. The strictest adherence had always been in the Himeyuri schools, where such lapses as exchanging a spoken or written word with a boy earned quick expulsion.

The most enviable place to serve was the Haebaru Army Hospital. Although many Japanese fighting units down to regimental level had their own field hospitals and lesser medical installations, Haebaru boasted the largest and soundest installation. Directly subordinate to 32nd Army command, it was the best of the military medical establishment, which now far surpassed the civilian.

It was also a new facility. When the October 10 air raid demolished an earlier building in Naha, staff officers took the point about enemy airpower and decided to rebuild in a safer place, behind the Shuri Line. They chose a country site some five miles southeast of Naha, three miles due south of Shuri. The Okinawa Military Hospital, as it was officially called, was a series of man-made caves dug into the sides of a large, grassy ridge bordering the tiny farming village of Haebaru.

Hospital staff, including drafted Okinawan civilian doctors, lived in the village while military engineers supervised the digging, which was unfinished when the fighting began. Failure to complete the main tunnel left most of the twenty-one caves isolated instead of forming wings of the planned integrated system. When Himeyuri dormitories were also destroyed in an air raid two months after 10/10 — four months before L-day — many girls were moved to shacks thrown up just outside the construction site. Seventeen-year-old Ruriko Morishita, whose parents owned a small company that traded chiefly in molasses and lumber, remained at Shuri in order to finish her studies at the prestigious Teachers College. Her graduation day was hastily celebrated a week before the American landing, when preparations at the hospital became frenzied but remained hugely inadequate. Still hoping to become a teacher when the crisis ended, Ruriko moved in with the others at Haebaru, helping speed the hospital's preparation.

Ruriko was among the most patriotic as well as one of the oldest girls. All were assigned more or less at random, she to one of Ward Three's half-dozen caves for infectious diseases. (Ward One was for general medicine; Two for surgery.) Ward Three had quite enough to deal with even without further casualties. Japan's tuberculosis rate was very high, partly because girls who had caught it while working in textile factories spread the disease in their villages when they were sent home with it. Attempts earlier in the war to send carriers among the troops — recruited largely from those same villages — back to Japan from the conquered territories ended when American submarines ripped Japanese shipping lanes to shreds. Many soldiers were then returned to the front in the knowledge that no cure was possible. Now Okinawa's dank caves served as hatcheries for the bacillus.

When Ward Three's caves were declared ready, Ruriko and fellow aides began working light eight-hour shifts. Besides tuberculosis, the principal infectious diseases were amoebic dysentery, typhoid and malaria, but some patients were still recovering from the 10/10 air raid. Within days of the landing, however, Ruriko's cave was filled beyond capacity with newly wounded, and the shelling and bombing were so intense that the girls were forbidden to go outside except to fetch food from the mess cave, water from the well at the northern end of the ridge and medical supplies from stacks deposited near the cave mouths. But conditions inside became so foul that some started breaking the rule, especially during the regular early-evening lull in the bombing, assumed to be the American savages' dinner break. Some girls were killed on those ventures outside. The survivors had been living in a kind of dormitory cave, but now took to sleeping in the same caves as the patients. Surrounded by bodies ripped apart by bombs and shells, some prayed for instant death if they themselves were hit.

By mid-April, the medical staff stopped cheering the news of "victories" delivered by messengers. The wounded were brought in on trucks, stretchers and comrades' backs. Many were finished off by bombing, shelling and strafing as they waited in lines outside. Desperate screams sounded at daybreak when planes and shells attacked: "Please let us in!" Soldiers who had braved the heaviest American fire to carry battlefield mates to the hospital wept to see the lives of those wounded ebb away. But there was simply nowhere to fit them inside.

The girls were forced to sleep in a tangle of arms and legs, with hardly enough room to draw breath. Every square yard of floor space was packed with grievously wounded soldiers, an average of sixty or seventy to a cave, a total of perhaps twice the hospital's planned capacity of a thousand patients. Thick in grime and blackened blood, more wounded were carried in and laid on the floor. Relatively few had been hit by bullets. Shell fragments had caused most of the damage: bones crushed, flesh gouged out, hands and legs blown off. Space was found for the luckier ones on rock shelves cut into the walls. They were squeezed in there even more tightly than on the troopships that had brought them to Okinawa. Without the cross-ventilation from the unmade connection to the central tunnel, the only air was from the caves' narrow mouths; it penetrated no more than a few yards.

Otherwise, the caves were fit only for bats. The walls and ceiling oozed condensation; some were covered with tent cloth to prevent the water from dripping on doctors, nurses and patients. Most stalactites had been removed, but a few remained, "hanging down like huge, grotesque icicles." Sour smells of mildew and wet earth were joined by a stench of blood, pus, urine, feces and rancid sweat from combat-broken bodies. So many deaths at such a relentless pace made Ruriko sense that her own would surely come soon; that was the nature of things. Japanese personnel in nearby caves distributed hand grenades for personal use and showed the nurses' aides how to use them. Ruriko longed for two tastes before her time came: fresh air and clean water.

She learned to snatch minutes of sleep by leaning against a wall or standing up, even for seconds, as she groped in the clammy, stinking dark toward patients moaning for help or when holding candles during surgery. Apart from such stolen rest and the sleep of the drugged during their three hours off duty in every twenty-four, Ruriko and her schoolmates worked around the clock. Ward Three dropped infectious diseases almost entirely in favor of surgery. (Its doctor, an Okinawan pediatrician, had begun to train himself in surgery after the 10/10 raid, which convinced him that his island would not escape more devastation.) Except in the niches used for surgery, the lighting came from bottles of kerosene with wicks of twisted rag. Their flickering flames, half-starved for oxygen, barely penetrated the murkiness. Patients were faceless shadows — in some cases, literally faceless because theirs had been blown or burned away. Day and night were indistinguishable; weeks became one long nightmare.

Lice from the men with whom they were squeezed in infested the filthy cream of Okinawan maidenhood. There was no hot water for the patients, let alone the staff. Only the surgical areas were supplied with enough to sterilize the instruments. The untrained aides tried to shut out the cries of men operated on without anesthetic, then cleaned up as assigned. Inexplicably heavy amputated limbs had to be carried outside to holes or bomb craters. Numbing themselves, Ruriko and a friend lugged the heavier and more terrifying corpses outside, one by one.

Inside, relentless screams sounded from men going crazy with thirst. The girls were happy not to be able to understand some of their babbling and filthy curses. During lulls in the bombing, however, they did hear maggots wriggling into the wounded — like silkworms crunching mulberry leaves, they imagined. Although the little white worms supposedly prevented tetanus by consuming pus from the wounds, even the bravest soldiers moaned and screamed when their flesh was munched. The girls pictured the vermin eating the wounded alive. One soldier's jawbones had been crushed to pulp; his face so teemed with maggots that dozens fell onto Ruriko's hand when she tried to trickle rice gruel down his throat. Then she tried to see through the semidarkness in order to pick the wriggling creatures from his oozing wounds with crude wooden chopsticks — and could never finish because more and more soldiers cried out and she had to grope to them. The men for whom the aides performed this service were profoundly grateful. One watched the hand of a girl quietly work to free his wound — "open like a ripe pomegranate" — of its maggots. Then he looked at her face and saw "an angel in the midst of hell."

The teenagers also had to deal with every function of men, from whom they had been protected so assiduously before April. Ruriko had touched the hand of no man or boy apart from her father and brother since she was seven. Now she had to help strangers defecate and hold the penises of double amputees so they could urinate. She watched the regular nurses do this and resolved to imitate them. To control her trembling, she tried to deepen her numbing even more. "This must be done," she ordered herself. "I'm doing it for my country."

In despair over the ghoulish overcrowding, Ward Three's former pediatrician hardly worried any longer about cleanliness or his primitive supplies. Patients in urgent need of recuperation after surgery had to be sent from the cave because there was simply no room. Soon the self-taught surgeon was able to treat only the very worst patients — if they could be saved. The less critically wounded were ordered straight back to the front. Those with no hope were not admitted at all.*

But despite this, despite her own horror, Ruriko remained certain that "the good side" must win in the end. She was so convinced that

---

*Doctors told one of many soldiers who developed lockjaw soon after admission to the Haebaru hospital that it was fatal in nine cases of ten. "They just looked at me coldly and didn't give me any medicine or help me in any way because they thought I was going to die." Soon he was too weak to wriggle away from the corpse of a comrade "who was becoming a white skeleton before my eyes." The staff had neither the time nor strength to dispose of the body while the bombardments were especially heavy.

the enemy was the bad side that only the sight — months later, when she was a captive — of American medics treating other filthy, wretched Japanese prisoners made her understand she had been a dupe of Japanese militarism. And not even that marvel could cause an immediate change of mind; her first instinct was to take the American care for a trick. Now, in the cave, there was nothing to suggest that Japan did not deserve to win, as fated. The sacred country that had not lost a war in thousands of years could not lose this one. The Divine Wind would come again.

While many patients were eager to return to their units, the most gravely wounded were sometimes resigned. A few whispered to the student aides — although never to the aides' bosses, the military nurses — that they knew Japan couldn't win because they'd seen the enemy's overwhelming power and supplies. Exhausted Ruriko was surprised and disappointed. "You're just talking like that because you've been hurt a little," she scolded men lacking arms and legs. "You'll be better soon and come to your senses." Sometimes she warned Japanese medics about a patient with suspect patriotism. "We'd better watch that one. It's his mind."

Worsening conditions in the caves served only to strengthen the girls' resolve. Winning by surviving became a source of unchallengeable pride, which no one could take from them. They were the ones, they told themselves, who must save Okinawa. "Anyway, once we're dead," Ruriko reminded the others, "we'll go to Yasukuni Shrine." Wounded soldiers still able to smile coined a nickname for her: Miss Victory Day.

14 · Kojo Returns

Where on earth are our planes? Escaped somewhere? They didn't show up during the October raid and now either — no sign of even a single plane with the Rising Sun.
— A conscripted Okinawan laborer

There is talk that the Combined Fleet will come and destroy the enemy by Navy Memorial Day.
— From a diary found on a Japanese corpse

THE FIELD HOSPITAL to which Captain Tadashi Kojo was taken after the accidental explosion of the sample antitank charge was a converted schoolhouse. It hadn't been quite too late to save his life, but he hovered near death during the December week following his operation. Then his head throbbed and his hearing was severely reduced — but even a completely deaf person would have had no trouble registering the Americans' pre-invasion bombardment three months later, during the last week of March 1945. Bombs and shells shook the earth throughout the center of the island, including the fields where the patients lay. They had been led out of the little schoolhouse because any such relatively prominent building presented a likely target.

Kojo's recuperation was approaching a hundred days when that thunder announced the imminence of the enemy landing. He got out of bed, pulled on his clothes and set out to return to his cherished regiment.

A doctor stopped him. Lifting Kojo's heavy head bandages, he indicated the large, unhealed hole behind his left ear. "Captain, this goes straight to your brain. Infection here — and you're in great danger of it — means fairly certain death." When the doctor moved on, Kojo instructed his orderly to bring his horse to the hospital after dark. He slipped out and rode to regimental headquarters.

Regular transfers of higher officers to new duties was standard practice in the Japanese Army. Kojo thought this might have been suspended on the eve of the crucial battle, but a new commander of his 22nd Regiment had been flown in from a high staff job on Formosa just days before, the plane managing to land during a lull in the enemy's air attacks. Lieutenant Colonel Masaru Yoshida had hardly had time to meet his other senior officers by the time Kojo reported back for duty, let alone familiarize himself with his regiment's positions. But a new commanding officer was the least of the changes awaiting the captain. In the redeployments following the loss of the 9th Division, the 22nd Regiment had been shifted to a quite different position.

The men were digging new projects, having started from the beginning again. They were eleven miles south of their original fortifications protecting the beach near Kadena Airfield — and also well south of where the landing was expected, for the regiment was now in a kind of reserve. Its new area of responsibility covered from just below Naha Airfield on the Oroku Peninsula — itself about two miles southwest of the capital — to the city of Itoman, some four miles farther down the island's west coast.

When Kojo rode in from the hospital that night, a tunnel had been almost fully dug in a hill below Naha Airfield. That large new project already housed the 22nd's regimental headquarters, which had just been connected to a far larger bastion — headquarters of the Imperial Navy's Okinawa Island Command — deep beneath the same hill. This Naval Base Force, as it was known, was responsible for defending the six square miles of the Oroku Peninsula that reaches out toward China at Okinawa's widest point.

The Naval Base Force's deeply sunken headquarters were much more impressive than its potential as a ground fighting force.* A three-hundred-yard main tunnel cut entirely through the hill in a sweeping curve three stories high in some places. Power lines ran to a central station in Naha. With branches off the main tunnel, the complex had its own generator, its operations, cipher, signal, staff and medical rooms with hot and cold running water, even roosts for carrier pigeons, although the fine provisions for more modern communications included an equipment repair chamber. Officers' spaces had stuffed chairs and curtains; the quarters of the commander, Rear Admiral Minoru Ota, were proportionately more comfortable. The dank, concrete refuge, second only to 32nd Army headquarters below Shuri Castle, was packed almost solid with sailors completing

---

*The force was a conglomerate of all naval units on the island: construction, shipbuilding and engineering, naval air, service personnel for midget and suicide submarines, gunners for land-based naval guns and others. Only a third of its 10,000 men were Imperial Navy regulars; the others were Home Guards and Okinawans conscripted into other units. Some writers have associated the force with Marines, but although its overall commander, a rear admiral, was a specialist in land defense, most of his troops were poorly trained for land warfare. The several hundred who had taken basic training had no combat experience.

the installations, as later it would be packed with sailors manning the headquarters, well protected against bombardment.

Happy at Kojo's return, Colonel Yoshida appointed him the regimental operations officer, since a replacement had been put in command of the captain's old 1st Battalion. A highly capable second lieutenant already in charge of the operations department made Kojo's assignment nominal. He used the time for more recuperation, telling no one he still felt shaky. The enemy fleet was nearing the end of its pre-invasion bombardment. As the serene Ushijima gazed down at it from his observation tower at the castle, Kojo observed the same scene from six miles southwest, at the top of the hill above the two underground headquarters of the Naval Base Force and 22nd Regiment. The twenty-four-year-old captain felt almost honored by the immense parade of power the Americans had assembled to tackle them. At last the alien ships were there, far more numerous and mighty than he had imagined, but he remained utterly confident in General Ushijima's leadership and Japan's eventual victory. Abandoning the almost finished strongpoints above the landing beaches had depressed him after the furious work to complete them in time to crush the enemy there. Now he laughed at the Americans' even more furious bombardment of that same landing area — for it was empty! Let the big, fat enemy go on wasting effort while they, the military professionals, prepared for the kill.

Almost immediately after the landing, the 22nd Regiment's 2nd and 3rd Battalions were temporarily transferred from the 24th Division to the 62nd, Ushijima's only other full division, and ordered to join the main Japanese line on high ground protecting Shuri. This left the 22nd Regiment with only one battalion: the 1st, formerly Kojo's. It also left only two horses at regimental headquarters: Lieutenant Colonel Yoshida's and Kojo's.

Kojo allowed his to be ridden by a passionate horseman on the staff of the adjoining Naval Base Force headquarters. Although officers of different Japanese services tended to keep their distance from one another, the shared equestrian interest, and perhaps the approaching danger, drew these two uncommonly close in a matter of days. When Kojo, as his regiment's nominal operations officer, read a copy of the order from Imperial General Headquarters informing that the battleship *Yamato* was being readied to attack the American ships at Okinawa, he assumed it would be part of the great naval offensive anticipated by the entire 32nd Army. It was time to obliterate the American fleet, deal the invaders the decisive blow. But something puzzled him, and he inquired about it in a way that would have been inappropriate for a mere captain if the naval staff officer hadn't been a friend.

"Why just *Yamato* and her screen?" Kojo asked with uncustomary directness. "Why not the Combined Fleet?"

Kojo's generosity with his horse prompted the older man to reveal a momentous secret. "There *is* no Combined Fleet, the Americans have finished it. All we have left is *Yamato* and a few destroyers."

"I mean the rest of our ships," Kojo replied, thinking his new friend's jest about the Combined Fleet rather tasteless. "Why leave our carriers out of the attack?"

On that early April day in 1945, the disbelieving Kojo learned of the Battle of Midway in early June 1942, where the modern Imperial Navy suffered its first crushing defeat. Scores of Japan's best warships had steamed for the showdown at the western approach to the Hawaiian Islands, the men singing war songs at the top of their lungs, certain of annihilating America's Pacific Fleet. But that great gamble had ended in disaster; most of the highest and brightest Japanese admirals knew immediately that the loss of four heavy carriers and their air groups — hundreds of the country's best pilots — marked the beginning of the end. Midway was the Kursk of the Pacific: as the Russians would break the back of German armor there in July 1943, the Americans broke the wings of Japanese naval airpower here thirteen months earlier.* The Imperial Navy could no longer protect the Empire, let alone regain its supremacy. But now, almost three years later, many high-ranking Army officers in Tokyo still knew nothing of the war's sharpest turning point, for the Imperial Navy had taken great pains to conceal its fatal wounds and humiliation.†

Until that April day, Kojo knew nothing whatever either of the Midway disaster or of the Navy's subsequent decimation and the collapse of the Empire's lifelines. Tens of thousands of other high field officers, not to mention the civilian population, also knew noth-

*Isoroku Yamamoto, Japan's most respected admiral since he planned the masterly strike at Pearl Harbor, commanded the Japanese force at Midway from his flagship *Yamato*, which was participating in her first real engagement. After American carrier-based planes sank the cream of the Japanese carrier fleet, Yamamoto wept in his cabin.

Midway was further confirmation that carriers, not battleships, were the main armament of any modern fleet. *Yamato* herself remained several hundred miles away from the primary encounter and took almost no part in the decisive action. After this, Japanese naval forces won some brilliant minor victories with daring, almost exquisite skill. But the tide so turned at Midway that anything less than an overwhelming victory at every engagement was a strategic loss for the Empire.

†As would happen when *Tsushima maru* sank while evacuating women and children from Okinawa, survivors of the stricken warships were ordered to mention nothing about the losses. This was partly for the sake of Japanese morale in general but also to protect the Navy's pride. Admission of defeat, difficult for every military service in every country, was particularly difficult for the Japanese during this period when victory was essential to sustain the massive illusions with which the war was being pursued.

ing. As the Okinawan campaign progressed, the ignorance of 32nd Army officers of Kojo's rank and lower — most higher officers too — remained intact. Yet had they known, only the most perceptive would have understood the consequences, and that knowledge would not have diminished their commitment, partly because they expected victory on Okinawa itself. Even Norio Watanabe, the free-lance photographer from Osaka who had considered the war with America huge folly from the first, was now caught up in the spirit of the battle.

Watanabe's artillery unit was positioned just northwest of Naha, about five miles above where the two detached battalions of Kojo's regiment had been sent into the line, but part of the same defensive core centered at Shuri. From there, the hater of everything military watched enemy planes crash into the sea, and felt deep envy when American flying boats rescued their pilots from the water. His unit could easily have shot the downed pilots from its vantage point, but the company commander did not give that order, even knowing that rescued ones would be back to bomb and strafe them the next day. The commander's motive was more practical than humanitarian: no time could be spared from trying to destroy the enemy planes themselves. Besides, the battery was still trying to conceal its guns except during the actual moments of firing, and shooting pilots would have brought more swift, severe retaliation than shooting at planes. Headquarters announced that Watanabe's unit had accounted for fourteen enemy planes. He believed the real score was four or five, but despite his contempt for official lying and his conviction that Japan could not possibly win — which still made him almost an aberration — he found himself enjoying some professional satisfaction when American planes hurtled into the sea.

Weak as he still was, Kojo, with none of Watanabe's doubt or cynicism, looked forward eagerly to joining that game for which he'd trained his entire adult life. What did aircraft carriers really matter anyway — or the Imperial Navy as a whole? Kojo did not fully believe the naval staff officer's fantastic story of the Midway debacle; in any case, he remained convinced that the decisive struggle would take place on the ground. He watched the enemy landing, with massive quantities of equipment and supplies. He was more than ever aware that the struggle for Okinawa would be extremely hard and costly. But he also knew that the 32nd Army's main defenses hadn't yet been tested, because the new plan was to defeat the Americans well after they had landed.

General Ushijima was naturally less sanguine. He was in his headquarters deep below Shuri Castle when he was informed, days after the Easter Sunday L-day, that the Imperial Navy's last great ship was about to come to his aid. The secret signal included instructions for him to take advantage of *Yamato*'s sortie to counterattack on the ground the following morning, as the battleship approached. Ushijima disapproved of the idea and radioed advice to stop Operation Heaven Number One. He believed the first week of the ground war was still too early to counterattack; his Army's best hope of doing the greatest damage to the enemy lay in biding its time in its best fortifications. He also felt that his appreciation of the enemy's air domination and naval strength was better than that of the mainland strategists. Combined Fleet headquarters seemed to be living in a dream world, but he, Ushijima, needed only to go to his observation tower in order to see American warships stretching from Okinawa's bays to the horizon.

The general's impatient chief of staff, by contrast, was delighted and confident that the *Yamato* operation would help turn the tide on land by catching the enemy off balance. Isamu Cho knew in his bones that defense had never been the Japanese way. Attack and more attack was what had created the Empire and what would now save the day against the Americans by confusing and confounding them. These characteristic reactions of the commanding general and his chief of staff would manifest themselves in debates about the kind of war they should wage on Okinawa itself. When Ushijima heard about *Yamato*'s end on April 7, he snorted about the "infernal waste" and recalled that he had urged the Navy to cancel the adventure. "Banzai charges should be left to soldiers," he said — but he would use them sparingly in his own command because they were too wasteful, no matter how much they terrified the enemy. On the other hand, the chief of staff would continue to press for more operations in the spirit of Heaven Number One.

Ironically, the superpatriots like Cho, having provoked the war, were now helping to shorten it with gambles that squandered the remaining resources, while the nonpolitical warriors like Ushijima helped to protract the agony with their sober professionalism. *Yamato* was gone and Okinawa's north was falling with disturbing speed. But there were new ways to deal with America's extravagant material advantages. The turn of the kamikaze had just begun.

15 · Kamikazes

To blossom today, then scatter;
Life is so like a delicate flower.
How can one expect the fragrance to last forever?
— Admiral Takajiro Onishi

Living, to be overwhelmed with the immeasurable blessings of Imperial
goodness. Dead, to become one of the country's Guarding Deities and as
such to receive unique honors in the temple.
— A choice put to Japanese pilots

When I fly the skies / What a splendid place to be buried / The top of a
cloud would be.
— A kamikaze volunteer before setting out on his mission

The feeling of utter helplessness that wraps around you when you are
aboard a ship crippled by enemy action [hit us] . . . on Easter morning . . .
We had been warned to be ready for such a possibility but when it hap-
pened, it was startling, unbelievable and more than a little fearsome.
— Herbert Shultz, a combat correspondent

IN THE END, the primary official objective assigned to *Yamato* on her last mission was to scatter the defenses against an air assault on the American invasion fleet. The great battleship had been chosen both as the best decoy to lure the greatest number of enemy interceptors and as the stoutest target for withstanding their attacks for the longest possible time to give Japanese planes a turn against the American ships. Some nine hundred of them took part in that massive air offensive on April 6 and 7.

The attack was launched from a ring of airfields on the mainland, Formosa and occupied Shanghai in spurious coordination — since the Japanese High Command was weak in that way — with Operation Heaven Number One entrusted to the Surface Special Attack Forces. Innumerable waves of Japanese planes sank three destroyers, two ammunition ships, one LST and one minesweeper, and damaged a light carrier, eleven destroyers, two destroyer escorts and eight other craft off and near Okinawa. On the April 7 of *Yamato*'s sinking, more strikes hit a battleship, carrier, destroyer, destroyer escort and one other vessel of the fleet off Okinawa.

That use of Japanese aircraft defied explanation except in terms of a despairing passion for destruction at any cost. *Yamato*'s appeals for air cover even after she sailed went unanswered. Yet while American dive bombers were having their way with the Imperial Navy's unprotected prize battleship, the nine hundred Japanese planes were a mere two hundred miles away, swarming over the very ships that had launched the *Yamato*-hunting Hellcats, Helldivers and Avengers. Just after the veteran carrier *Hancock* launched her first strike on *Yamato*, a Zero slipped through the carrier's screen of battleships, cruisers and destroyers in one Task Force 58 battle group and headed straight for her starboard bow. It dropped a bomb on her flight deck, then put a twenty-foot hole there by crashing farther aft. Seventy-two men were killed and eighty-two wounded by explosions that set fire to *Hancock*'s hangar deck and twenty parked planes.

That Zero was suicidal, like more than a third of the planes dispatched on April 6 and 7 and roughly the same proportion throughout the Okinawan campaign. Altogether, the Japanese mounted just under nine hundred air raids on the island and the American fleet, a far greater effort than anything previous. Compared with five thousand to six thousand sorties by conventional dive bombers and torpedo planes — that is, by pilots who did not intend to crash on their floating targets — nineteen hundred were flown by kamikazes. (That is the American tally; official Japanese records document the loss of 2944 kamikaze planes.) But it was those "special" missions that prompted the greatest American consternation and fear, and not only because they caused some 80 percent of the damage to the fleet. Kamikazes greatly increased tension even from the extreme pitch of ordinary air attacks because every sailor on every ship was convinced they were aiming for *him*. A recent Japanese writer's hyperbole that "the sight of a single Japanese plane raised terror in the hearts of men on the enemy vessels" conveys an essential truth. A British historian saw an element of personal threat in suicide attacks that "had been absent from naval warfare since the days of boarding and hand-to-hand fighting."

The April 6 attack was the first massive one on American ships at Okinawa, but individual Japanese planes and small groups had been dogging them even before L-day. Kamikazes crashed into a battleship, two destroyers and a destroyer-minesweeper on March 27, when the fleet was preparing the landing, bombarding the island, and taking Kerama Retto, the cluster of little islands that the Americans had wisely seized before L-day. A landing craft was hit the next day. On March 31, carrier-based American fighters "splashed" two planes attacking the heavy cruiser *Indianapolis* — flagship of Admiral Spruance, commander of the Fifth Fleet and one of the original advocates of Okinawa over Formosa as the final steppingstone to Japan — and antiaircraft fire from the nearby *New Mexico* downed a third. But a fourth managed to scrape its wing against the cruiser's port side before careening into the sea. Its bomb crashed through several decks and exploded in an oil bunker, killing nine men and wounding twenty.

Half of the more than seven hundred planes that had attacked the fleet on L-day itself were kamikazes. Before dawn that morning, two explosions in quick succession awoke the Marines still fitfully sleeping below decks in a forward compartment of *Hinsdale*, flagship of Troop Transport Division 44, as it approached its transport area. *Hinsdale's* passengers had become so accustomed to the low hum of the ship's engines during their five days at sea from Saipan that the brief interval of silence following the disappearance of the throb seemed eerie. Frightened troops frantically dressed in pitch darkness, the ship having lost electrical power immediately.

As a hard list began, narrow passageways outside the troop compartments filled with men feeling their way toward ladders leading topside. A drily muttered "Looks like the Easter bunny sure brung us our egg this morning!" produced some nervous laughter. Shouts of "Corpsmen! Any corpsmen down there?" followed from above. One Marine managed to control his trembling hand enough to light a cigarette on the third try. At 6 A.M., after ten infinitely long minutes, an order was shouted down the hatches for all hands to proceed to their abandon-ship stations.

Not a shot had been fired at the plane until it was gunning full speed for the target and about to crash. The predawn grayness had hidden it from straining lookouts and its low altitude over the water had allowed it to evade radar, so no one aboard the ship, or the three dozen others in her transport squadron, saw the attacker visually or electronically until that last moment. The plane itself was also unusual. Most of those which crashed intentionally were flimsy, obsolete models — "like handmade paper planes," as one kamikaze ensign described them — that had been stripped of usable instruments, loaded with explosives and fueled for a one-way trip. The pilot of this advanced, first-line Tony fighter may have decided on his own not to return from his mission.*

---

*Americans gave Japanese fighters male names and bombers female names.

But in other respects, *Hinsdale*'s trial was much like that of scores of ships sunk or severely damaged by a kind of human bomb. The Tony crashed into her port side amidships at waterline. Two of its three bombs exploded with force violent enough to pop the cover of the plane's fuel tank a hundred feet into the air. Flames shot high enough to severely burn men on a wing of the bridge some fifty feet above. It seemed miraculous that few sailors and Marines at an early L-day breakfast were incinerated when the collision devastated the mess hall, shattering coffee cups and shooting scraps of food around like buckshot. More of the sixteen killed and thirty-nine wounded were in the engine room, into which the plane telescoped. The living passengers abandoned ship, "strung tight as violin strings." Dead in the water and with a gaping hole in her side, *Hinsdale* was towed to the Keramas for emergency repairs.

The worst of L-day had gone to ships hit roughly the same way. Twenty-four sailors and Marines on an LST participating in the false landing in the far south joined the list of the dead. Unlike the American infantrymen who were enjoying their seemingly miraculous good luck on land, sailors encountered fierce resistance from the first. The Japanese submarine force was too weakened to pose much threat; the surface fleet could muster only enough strength for the last effort by *Yamato* and her screen; the suicide submarines and suicide boats based in scattered shelters on Okinawa and neighboring islands would perform dismally, largely because many shelters would be captured before the craft could get under way. It was left to the kamikaze pilots to do almost all the sinking and killing, and they were to keep at it throughout the campaign; the Navy's ordeal was only beginning.

The attack of April 6–7, the days of *Yamato*'s sortie, hit twenty-two ships and sank eleven. This was particularly dismaying to Americans because carrier strikes on mainland airfields on the morning of the sixth were thought to have destroyed virtually all Japanese planes able to reach the fleet from there. Marc Mitscher, Task Force 58's commander, even assured his counterpart of this, the commander of the battleship and cruiser group carrying most of the big-gun naval bombardment of Okinawa. That would not be the campaign's last expression of American optimism stiffened with poor intelligence of Japanese camouflage, dispersal and digging — in this case, of vast systems of underground hangars, tunnels and barracks being completed at many mainland installations.

Crews of American ships also tried to convince themselves that the Japanese had "shot their bolt" with their kamikaze attacks; only isolated bases could still get any craft into the air. "Christ, we must have

knocked out every plane they had left on those home islands!" a lieutenant in a carrier's recreation room assured fellow players in a pinochle game. But late the same afternoon, the radar screen of the
destroyer *Leutze* revealed dozens of bogies some ninety miles west
and closing at two hundred knots. The pilots on that strike, although
worried about interception by squadrons of American planes that
stayed airborne for the purpose, took comfort in knowing that the
setting sun of twilight was the best time to attack. The first lookouts
spotted the formation thirteen minutes later; there were some dozen
planes too low over the water to have been seen by radar.

In minutes, pandemonium reigned on and above *Leutze* and *Newcomb,* a sister destroyer that joined the frantic antiaircraft firing with
her every gun but could not stop one plane from crashing into her
after stack and another from hitting her amidships with a large torpedo or bomb that demolished her vital parts with a stunning explosion. As *Newcomb*'s stores of munitions and oil products fed her fierce
blaze, a third plane hit her forward stack, spraying enough additional
aviation fuel over decks and sailors to send flames hundreds of feet
into the air. *Leutze* gallantly went to her aid and was crashed by a
fourth successful kamikaze among the dozens that were shot down
or that missed on their own.

Fire-control crews fought to save the searing wreckage of the two
destroyers. Smaller in scope than on *Yamato,* the agony was no less
intense in each devastated space. Men struggled to shore up bulkheads and plug rushing leaks. Healthy sailors tried to help the
gravely injured. Some were burned to death trying to fight flames
and reach trapped fellow crew members. *Newcomb*'s surgeon operated through the night in her wardroom, surrounded by destruction
and carnage.

Heroes fought to secure steam lines and extinguish fires in magazines. Crews of operable guns kept firing until they joined the total
of forty-seven killed and missing and fifty-eight wounded. But both
scorched wrecks were eventually towed to Kerama Retto and saved
— whereas even more intense attacks sank *Bush,* with a loss of thirty-
five killed and missing and twenty-one wounded. And casualties on
Colhoun, a fourth destroyer that had to be abandoned and sunk by
American guns, were seven of twenty-six officers killed and eighty-
seven of 307 men. No fewer than forty to fifty planes attacked *Bush*
that afternoon. One crashed between its stacks, allowing its bomb
to explode in an engine room; another hit her port side, starting a
fierce fire that killed all the wounded who had been taken to the
wardroom. *Colhoun* had fought off eleven raids before dawn that
morning, five in the space of fifteen minutes. Two previous kamikaze

crashes that afternoon damaged her so severely that the last one, by a pilot who persisted although his plane was ablaze, made little difference.

Of the nine more destroyers hit that day, one was sunk, two had to be scrapped and three went unrepaired until after the war. The Japanese strategy was to cut off American supplies and naval support with these air attacks so that they could more effectively deal with the enemy ashore. That was wishful thinking: even if supplied with sufficient planes and aviation fuel, the hot kamikaze — Divine Wind — would not have melted Operation Iceberg, as the Americans had code-named the Okinawan invasion. But it did cause the American Navy by far its greatest terror and torment of the war. Nothing of the kind had ever been mounted by any offensive force or endured by any defensive one.

The knowledge that pilots were intent on killing themselves in order to kill others was terrifying in itself, even in lulls between the attacks. It was also fascinating, because, as many American participants felt, the act was "incomprehensible" and "inhuman." American sailors wondered whether the Japanese who were resolved to blow themselves to bits were religious fanatics or simply drunk or drugged. Since no human, they believed, would willingly perform such madness, perhaps they were cleverly made robots. To the men who had to fight that macabre force, nothing did more to confirm the singularly sinister nature of their enemy. "The whole idea is eerie," said a lieutenant to a fellow officer on the carrier *Belleau Woods*. "I just can't figure out how anybody can just commit suicide without feeling anything. It's against human nature. It's against the instinct of self-preservation, if you ask me."

"It doesn't matter to those Nips," the other lieutenant answered. "They don't think the same way we do." An American admiral who observed kamikazes plunging at Okinawa put it more philosophically: "I doubt if there is anyone who can depict with complete clarity our mixed emotions as we watched a man about to die in order that he might destroy us in the process. There was a hypnotic fascination to a sight so alien to our Western philosophy."

In fact, the kamikaze phenomenon wasn't quite so alien to Western practice, if not philosophy. Occasional German pilots had used suicide attacks against Allied planes, although their superiors had never organized a special force of them. American and British leaders, Winston Churchill and Douglas MacArthur among them, ordered some of their commanding officers never to surrender in certain circumstances. In addition, Britain as well as Italy and Germany had very small units manning "special attack" weapons, chiefly small boats and planes, that made some nearly suicidal missions. (An Italian naval officer attached to such a unit pledged to win "the highest of all honors, that of giving my life for the King and the honor of the Flag.") Carrier-based American pilots of obsolete torpedo planes in the Battle of Midway knew they were taking off to probable injury or death, and reprieves were few in some instances: eight of eight from *Hornet* were downed attacking the Japanese carriers, ten of fourteen from *Enterprise,* and ten of twelve from *Yorktown.* The brave squadrons that lost every one of their planes came close to being kamikazes in some ways.

Every nation cherishes its tales of wounded heroes who, knowing they will die, charge the enemy, determined to do their utmost to stop him. "Give me liberty or give me death" might be seen as the philosophical and emotional underpinnings of the American Navy's experiments with near suicidal submersibles during the War of Independence and the Confederate Navy's similar interest during the Civil War. And a kind of suicidal desperation prompted Pickett's Charge. The Alamo, so elevated in the folklore celebrating American bravery, had something in common with Japanese resolution. Perhaps because everything Japanese seemed sinister or demented, it occurred to few Americans — even those who had loved *They Died with Their Boots On,* one of Hollywood's most popular offerings on the eve of Pearl Harbor — that their own myths sanctified warriors' sacrificial deaths. It is entirely possible that many more Americans would have been willing and even eager to die for honor and country, or at least applaud those who did, if their nation had ever faced the kind of total, supremely shocking national defeat that confronted the Japanese during the Pacific War's final years. For the kamikaze movement cannot be understood without taking into account Japan's unwillingness to accept the enormity of the defeat that loomed before her in 1945. In a similar situation, self-sacrificing pilots might have been American heroes if their lives had been given for their own side.

The American public was first informed of the practice, kept a strict military secret until then, during that very first week of April 1945, a month after Tokyo's horrific destruction in the March "fire raid." But the institution had been founded — as much as any single event can qualify for this in a country where the ultimate self-sacrifice had a long, honorable tradition — six months earlier, when a rear admiral commanding an air flotilla in the Philippines deliberately crashed a dive bomber on an American carrier. That fine officer, who had been raised in England and had begun his naval training with the Royal Navy after a public school education, was known for his Western attitudes. However, he despaired over the Imperial Navy's defeats and the decimation of his squadrons by skillful American carrier pilots in their fast, rugged Grummans. His own pilots, replacements for a great corps of aces who had been shot down or lost in sunk Japanese carriers, were so ill-trained that a third of them flying out from Japan to join him never reached the Philippines. And American raids were likely to destroy the others' planes even before they could take off to fight.

The admiral believed two dozen lucky Japanese pilots could stem the whole American advance by sinking its big carriers — not an absurd idea, especially after the whole Japanese advance had been stopped largely by the loss of the Imperial Navy's carriers at Midway. It would be simplistic to call him the usual "Japanese fanatic" for his dive onto U.S.S. *Franklin* in mid-October of 1944. In any case, he won a gifted ally, if posthumously. His deliberate crash horrified most Japanese staff officers almost as much as it did *Franklin*'s crew — but not Takajiro Onishi, a high-ranking admiral who arrived from Tokyo days later to assume command of the First Naval Air Fleet, including all land-based naval aircraft in the Philippines. Onishi had earlier encouraged pilots to perform just such crashes as a last resort. He would become known as "the father of the kamikaze," the name he was about to give his Special Attack Forces.*

Some of Vice Admiral Onishi's seniors considered him arrogant. His suicide notion shocked many in the Imperial Navy and elsewhere in the defense establishment. Onishi had the bluntness of warriors utterly dedicated to purpose and principle and unsuited to the ways of compromising politicians. Naval brass was much better represented by the man he relieved in Manila, a skilled professional who would fight to the death in suitable equipment but saw no value in needless sacrifice of his precious pilots. "When you can show me how to bring the men back from special attacks, I'll listen," Onishi's predecessor had said to the English-raised rear admiral who, in violation of his orders, would soon crash on *Franklin*. Then the imaginative, resourceful, fearless Onishi arrived to replace that more prudent commander and quickly organized a volunteer force, originally comprising thirteen pilots, resolved to put the major enemy carriers out of action for a week. That was the first organized use of suicide mis-

---

*Although "kamikaze" quickly became notorious in the West and is now used even in Japan, the proper name was *shimpu,* a different reading of the same characters with a more dignified, solemn ring, more fitting for the pilots' heroic undertaking. Like *harakiri,* kamikaze became vulgar. As Ivan Morris has pointed out, it is now a moniker for assorted daredevils, from taxi drivers to breakneck skiers.

sions in the Pacific War, although there had been isolated attacks before, some by damaged planes, a few premeditated.

Even though Onishi's initial mission hit two carriers and later ones also achieved some striking successes, the Imperial High Command did not approve the Special Attack philosophy until the enemy fleet was massing for L-day. (Air attacks had sunk only one ship and damaged a dozen-odd others off Iwo Jima.) But now Onishi had the satisfaction of seeing his once highly controversial approach incorporated into the defense plan, then elevated to an essential plank, as the highest Army as well as Navy officers convinced themselves that this last resort would change the course of the entire war. In that view, what happened on Okinawa itself would be of slight importance. In fact, many of the High Command now saw Ushijima's task as no more than delaying the enemy so that as many enemy warships and supply vessels as possible could be finished offshore.

> *As aircraft and fuel dwindled, the scale of kamikaze operations had to be reduced; but suicide attacks, which during Japan's death throes had become the principal manifestation of the country's will to resist, were never abandoned . . . the Battle of Okinawa more and more assumed the character of a culminating suicidal explosion.*
> — Ivan Morris, *The Nobility of Failure*

> *The special attack operations were truly impossible to bear in terms of our natural human feelings but Japan having been put in an impossible position, those unreasonable measures were all that was left to us.*
> — Emperor Hirohito, a year after the end of the war

As deputy chief of the naval staff after the fall of the Philippines, Onishi was in overall charge of mass kamikaze attacks against the fleet at Okinawa. The dashing but kindly looking man is correctly thought to have represented certain profoundly Japanese qualities, but these included some of which all peoples would have been proud. It was no accident that this dynamic maverick, who despised talk as a substitute for action, was Japan's leading naval aviator and chosen collaborator of the best naval brains — or that he had helped Admiral Isoroku Yamamoto, the "Japanese Nelson," plan his attack on Pearl Harbor. Onishi remained Yamamoto's close ally until the latter's death, in 1943. The model of personal courage was an impressive combination of traditional selfless virtues and mastery of technological advances. Many of his most idealistic junior officers adored him.

If Onishi was no heathen obscurantist, the kamikaze pilots were even less so. Most of the "treasures of the nation," as he called them, would have been treasures of any nation. A majority were in their early twenties — university students until their recent call-up. More of them had studied the humanities than engineering or the natural sciences. They tended to be interested in literature, including Western literature, more than in anything military. Even now they remained gripped by poetry. Symbols of Japanese beauty such as the rising sun dominated their last thoughts. One volunteer saw his commitment in the images of an eighteenth-century nationalist writer's verse: "What is the spirit of Yamato's ancient land? / It is like wild cherry blossoms, / Radiant in the rising sun." Just as those blossoms scattered without regret after spreading their short-lived radiance, the young hero explained, "so must we be prepared to die for Yamato without regret — such is the meaning of this verse."

Ivan Morris pointed out that far from the "fierce, superstitious, jingoistic fanatics that foreigners have usually imagined," most kamikaze pilots were in the upper ranks of university students in intelligence, culture, sophistication and sensitivity. As the Okinawan garrison was bludgeoned toward its inevitable defeat, driven superiors "requested" and otherwise pressed a small but growing number of young pilots and trainees to join suicide units, although the earliest had been volunteers. Now some were ordered to make the missions or were "volunteered" as a group by their leaders. Nevertheless, superior officers who actually selected pilots for the flights were likely to have too many genuine volunteers to accommodate. Straight to the end of the war, many units had twice as many eager candidates than available planes. Most were probably driven less by a desire to kill than to perform a lofty deed that would win admiration at their bases and a place among the country's heroes at the Yasukuni Shrine. Most of all, they wanted to sacrifice themselves for a more noble cause than personal advancement. Part of that cause was protecting their families and sacred Japan from foreign intrusion, especially since most truly believed their cherished nation and people would be forever destroyed unless they contributed their utmost, including the utmost in self-denial. But that sentiment rarely led to fear or loathing of the West and its soldiers. Their motives were truly higher: simply to give their lives for their country.

Written evidence seems to support such generalizations about the majority. On top of the great debt almost all Japanese youth feel to their parents for having conceived and raised them, many of the young heroes' final poems, diary entries and letters to their families so abounded in love and desire for virtue — if also in ignorance of their beloved country's Asian and Pacific atrocities — as to seem nearer the limit of human goodness than evil.

Dearest Parents,

Please excuse my dictating these last words to my friend [who is resting the paper on the fuselage of the writer's plane as it prepares to take off on the suicide mission] . . . Words cannot express my gratitude to you. It is my hope that this last act of striking a blow at the enemy will serve to repay in small measure the wonderful things you have done for me . . . I shall be satisfied if my final effort serves as recompense for the heritage bequeathed by our ancestors . . .

Words cannot express my gratitude to the loving parents who reared and tended me to manhood that I might in some small manner reciprocate the grace which His Imperial Majesty has bestowed upon us.

Mother . . . I do not want you to grieve over my death. I do not mind if you weep. Go ahead and weep. But please realize that my death is for the best and do not feel bitter about it.

. . . My greatest regret in this life is the failure to call you *"chichiue"* ("revered father"). I regret not having given any demonstration of the true respect which I have always had for you. During my final plunge, although you will not hear it, you may be sure I will be saying *"chichiue"* to you and thinking of all you have done for me.

The world in which I lived was too full of discord. As a community of rational human beings it should have been better composed. Lacking a single great conductor, everyone let loose with his own sound, creating dissonance where there should have been melody and harmony.

We are going to die. I will never fight for the Navy; I will fight for my country or for my personal honor, but never for the Navy, which I hate! . . . It is dominated exclusively by a clique of Naval Academy officers. [Another pilot called the Japanese Navy a "beast!" — but still willingly died for his honor and Japan.]

This is my last day. The destiny of our homeland hinges on the decisive battle in the seas to the south, where I shall fall like a blossom from a radiant cherry tree . . . I am grateful from the depths of my heart to the parents who reared me with their constant prayers and tender love. And I am grateful as well to my squadron leader and superior officers, who have looked after me as if I were their own son and given me such careful training.

Thank you, my parents, for the twenty-three years during which you have cared for me and inspired me. I hope that my present deed will in some small way repay what you have done for me.

More letters:

> My dear parents ... I shall be leaving this earth [tomorrow morning]
> forever. Your immense love for me fills my entire being down to my
> last hair. And that is what makes this so hard to accept: the idea
> that with the disappearance of my body, this tenderness will also
> vanish. But I am impelled by my duty. I sincerely beg you to forgive
> me for not having been able to fulfill all my family obligations ...

> The Japanese way of life is indeed beautiful and I am proud of it,
> as I am of Japanese history and mythology, which reflect the purity
> of our ancestors and their belief in the past ... And the living em-
> bodiment of all wonderful things from our past is the Imperial
> Family, which is also the crystallization of the splendor and beauty
> of Japan and its people. It is an honor to be able to give my life in
> defense of these beautiful and lofty things.

Letter after letter expressed gratitude for the chance to perform
the highest sacrifice for Japan's unique beauty and virtue. The volunteers' behavior during their final days further validates the sincerity and intensity of their desire to repay parents and nation "in
some small way." They did not become human robots or stop valuing
their lives. Air raids on their bases, where some lived in miserable
conditions despite their honored status, multiplied throughout the
Okinawan campaign, terrifying even some of the pilots scheduled to
die the following day. Yet many were indeed radiant that following
day when they made their sacrifice; high or serene without drugs,
despite American speculation about their use.

Of course there were exceptions. It goes without saying that not all
the thousands of kamikaze pilots were the studious, considerate, idealistic souls their parents would remember as their best, kindest sons.
Scores spent their final hours drunk on sake rather than on lofty
thoughts. Others made the gesture less from heroism than calculation: since everyone was going to die in the war anyway, better to
die a pilot, with its rewards — perhaps including a warship to one's
credit. Amidst the laughter and song, some wept with fear, regret or
frustration for having to sacrifice themselves to a hopeless cause
when they had only begun to live. A few refused to fly at the last
moment; at least one expressed his anger by strafing his command
post before flying off toward the enemy fleet. A larger number
masked their resentment — but they were a small minority. Most
young men experienced joy and elation when chosen for the honor —
and impatience, bitterness or self-hatred when not chosen. Some
burst into tears and cried unashamedly when not permitted to join
comrades on their final missions. Onishi spoke of the Divine Wind
being ushered in by the "purity" of the youth he loved, and here it

Okinawa as seen from the south *(Courtesy of the Keystone Portrait Studio)*

Shuri Castle, main building. *(Courtesy of Naha Publishing Co.)*

The Shurei Gate, or Gate of Peace, at the grounds of Shuri Castle. The sign requests visitors to observe the code of courtesy. *(Courtesy of Naha Publishing Co.)*

April 1945. Typical Okinawan landscape in arable plateau, with tombs built into slopes. *(W. Eugene Smith/Life Magazine © Time Warner Inc.)*

A rare photograph of *Yamato,* which the Japanese kept
only less secret after her construction than during. This
one was taken in early April 1945, days before the ship's
destruction. *(Courtesy of the National Archives)*

Yamato attempting to evade bombs and torpedoes on April 7, 1945.
(Courtesy of the National Archives)

Masahide Ota, on right, in the uniform of a Normal School student. The other young man is unidentified. *(Courtesy of Masahide Ota)*

Captain Tadashi Kojo in April 1944, three months before the 22nd Regiment was shipped from Manchuria to Okinawa. Kojo, age 23, had just been appointed commanding officer of the regiment's gun battalion. *(Courtesy of Tadashi Kojo)*

Dick Whitaker in Saugerties, New York, September 1944. Whitaker was home after graduation from boot camp, his only furlough in 22 months of service. *(Courtesy of Richard Whitaker)*

Army units unloading equipment soon after L-day. Dick Whitaker worked with a "beach party" nearby until he was assigned to the company. *(Courtesy of the National Archives)*

Marine convoy moves north on the Motobu Peninsula, in this section unopposed.

A Japanese 150mm gun in its reinforced cave on Motobu Peninsula. It was rolled out on tracks to fire, then quickly rolled back.

Abandoned fortifications above the landing beaches like those dug by Captain Kojo's battalion before it was repositioned.

A northern village with more than half of its houses undamaged.
(W. Eugene Smith/Life Magazine © Time Warner Inc.)

On May 11, 1945, two kamikazes crashed onto the
American carrier *Bunker Hill* at its most vulnerable
moment, when planes loaded with munitions and fuel
were waiting to take off from the flight deck. The
casualties numbered nearly 700: 353 dead, 43 missing,
264 wounded. The ship survived but was out of action
for the rest of the war. The destroyer *The Sullivans* is
in the foreground. *(Courtesy of the National Archives)*

A kamikaze Zero attacks the battleship *Missouri*—on which the surrender
ceremony would be held in Tokyo Bay five months later—on April 11, 1945.
(Courtesy of the National Archives)

American antiaircraft fire from Yomitan Airfield during a Japanese raid in April 1945. *(Courtesy of the National Archives)*

Sugar Loaf (right), after the battle.

Marines at the remains of the walls of Shuri Castle. *(Courtesy of the National Archives)*

Shuri Castle grounds during the final days of May 1945. *(Courtesy of the National Archives)*

Disabled American gun—its barrel protected by a helmet—during the
heavy rains of May 1945, when the digging of foxholes was often
impossible. *(Courtesy of the National Archives)*

July 6 issue of Whitaker's local newspaper. The photograph, typical
of those sent to the home front, had been taken 6 weeks earlier, when
Whitaker's company was off the line for a rest, and a combat photographer went from foxhole to foxhole looking for men who shared
the same hometown. In a neighboring company, Whitaker found
Thomas J. McCarthy, also a graduate of Saugerties High School,
and they posed. McCarthy was later wounded, but survived.
(*Courtesy of the* Saugerties Post Star)

A Japanese leaflet intended to undermine
American morale.

Captain Owen Stebbins, commander of Company G–2–22
of the 6th Marine Division,
during a break from training
on Guadalcanal, a few weeks
before sailing for Okinawa.
(Courtesy of Owen Stebbins)

Ernie Pyle (center) chatting with Marines, still wearing their leggings to protect against snakes, on L-day afternoon. *(Courtesy of the National Archives)*

This photograph was captioned "Good Nips" when published by the Marines. *(Courtesy of the National Archives)*

Marines evacuate a wounded comrade. *(Courtesy of the National Archives)*

A young Marine with buddies killed at the Shuri Line. *(Courtesy of the National Archives)*

Americans encounter Okinawans. In the photograph on the lower right, a Navy pharmacist's mate with the 1st Marine Division comforts a child found in a cave where Japanese soldiers were killed.

(Courtesy of the National Archives)

(Courtesy of the National Archives)

was, not in the fantasy of script writers or right-wing propagandists, but in the real hearts of highly educated, lovingly raised young men, trembling with desire to attain the highest of patriotic virtue.

Such details may blur a common Western image of the kamikaze movement as Japanese bizarreness and the conviction of many Americans at Okinawa that the suicide seekers were moronic or retarded. In fact, most kamikaze pilots were distinctly better educated and more refined than the bluejackets who degraded them on the strained, fearful ships. Still, the stark American ignorance of the culture from which the kamikaze movement grew and of the motives of its participants does not invalidate the sailors' and infantrymen's gut reaction that their enemy was in some way "nuts." A former kamikaze pilot — the sole survivor of his group of twenty-one officers — argued in 1989 that "this so-called suicide mentality" was hardly specific to the Japanese. "The spirit of self-sacrifice exists in all countries among all peoples, particularly among the young who are innocent and free of cynicism when they are in a wartime, life-or-death situation. World history, in fact, is filled with similar examples."

But despite such revisionist efforts by writers on both sides, the truth is that the kamikaze phenomenon as practiced by Japan in 1945 could not have taken place elsewhere.

The American infantrymen who threw themselves on Japanese hand grenades in order to save their buddies were expressing an impulsive, unthinking surge of camaraderie, not an intentional desire to kill themselves. The Alamo's defenders did not intend to die, except, perhaps, when it was too late for another choice. Jimmy Doolittle's pilots knew it would take luck to land in China after bombing Tokyo from the carrier *Hornet* in April 1942, but they had at least a hope and a chance. Those rare exceptions were no more the counterparts of kamikaze pilots than the swashbuckling Onishi was a naval officer like heroic naval officers elsewhere.* An uneducated American footslogger on Okinawa summed up the difference as tellingly as any historian or sociologist, revisionist or otherwise: "Our infantrymen landed on Pacific islands knowing they might die but hoping they wouldn't. Kamikaze men knew the outcome in advance."

*Commanding ever fiercer loyalty for his courage and boldness, Onishi would become the object of an intense cult by passionate junior officers until — and after — Japan's surrender prompted his suicide. It took him eighteen agonizing hours to die. He is reported to have said that "there will probably not be anyone, even in a hundred years, to justify what I have done," but his remorse came only after the inconceivable Japanese surrender. His every action having been based on that "impossibility," it now could seem that he had sent thousands of young men to a useless death — but not a meaningless one, as they had had the joy of dying beautifully for a just cause in which they believed.

Perhaps defeat was more shameful to Japanese, for whom loss of face could come so easily and bring such disgrace. Perhaps Japan's long tradition of fighting to the death against impossible odds explained the existence of an organized, mass force for such military unsoundness. The country's equally long veneration of mythical young heroes whose destruction, as Ivan Morris put it, guarantees society's survival and stability also surely played a role. (It was almost a prerequisite of Japanese tales that the young hero died achieving — or failing in — his lofty, spiritual aim.) In any case, whatever the practice's origin and however realistic its initial purpose of stopping the enemy's onslaught by sinking his carriers, it swelled into a largely monomaniacal escape to mystical salvation, in which sense it was characteristically Japanese. The mainland slogan about a hundred million *gyokusai*, a jewel shattered into myriad pieces, was now far more widespread and insistent than when General Ushijima's glum predecessor on Okinawa had cited it a year earlier. A rough translation was "Better we all die."

By that time, young Japanese were dying in a panoply of "special attack" weapons, including *shinto* (crash boats), *koryu* and *kairyu* (midget submarines), *fukuryu* (human mines), and *kaiten* (human or piloted torpedoes, also called Green Frogs). *Kaitens* — simplified midget submarines designed in 1943 by three very young naval officers — failed to achieve significant results at Okinawa. It was chiefly their hidden pens, carved out of cliffs, that had been captured in Kerama Retto and the Okinawan north, where Americans gaped at the little boats, each loaded with explosives and an impact detonator, in which men were prepared to head out on a one-way trip toward a selected ship. A few suicide boats of unknown type did manage to score off Okinawa, their targets never knowing what hit them — in one case with so much force that scraps of the dynamite were found on a neighboring ship's bridge the next morning. Sailors on ships loaded with munitions, dynamite and aviation fuel did not need a second order from their tense captains to "shoot at anything larger than a cigarette butt" that moved in the water at night.

The most important of Japan's other suicide weapons was the *ohka* (exploding cherry bomb), an aerial cousin of the *kaiten* conceived in disappointment that even the very small percentage of kamikaze planes that hit home often failed to sink American ships because their impact speed was too slow. The 1944 *ohka* promised much better results from crashing half a ton of high explosives at six hundred miles an hour. This secret weapon, which Radio Tokyo touted as a guarantee of American defeat, was essentially a rocket-powered bomb released near its target by a converted bomber. It had just enough fuel for a short, sharp dive, just enough wing area for slight maneuvering on the way down and just enough cockpit space for a man to squeeze into — for it too was manned, like a German VI rocket with a pilot.

Americans called this weapon *baka* (idiot bomb or screwball), as if in search of comic relief from the apprehension it generated. Pilots and antiaircraft gunners found the speedy rockets almost impossible to hit once they were launched. But before they were launched, their weight so slowed their mother planes and reduced their maneuverability as to make them sitting ducks for American interceptors. In their raids, too, *ohka* pilots maintained their sang-froid and gratitude for the chance to die honorably. The crew of one mother plane that released its guided bomb on April 12 reported that the *ohka* pilot, a twenty-two-year-old lieutenant, slept peacefully on some sacks in the rear of the bomber before being wakened as they approached the target, along with eighty kamikaze planes and a hundred escort fighters. But that was the only mother plane in a squadron of eight that managed to return to its base.

One hundred and eighteen of the 185 planes used in *ohka* attacks would be destroyed at a cost of 438 airmen, most among the Betty bombers' crews of eight. On one occasion, sixteen of sixteen Betty mother planes dispatched toward American carriers were shot down in ten minutes, despite a fighter escort of fifty-five planes (many of which developed mechanical trouble before the force approached its target). Although the invention failed to live up to expectations for this reason, improved versions, including a final one with an engine adapted from a German jet, were designed and produced right up to the end of the war for use against the fleet that would take part in the invasion of the mainland.

None of these other inventions was militarily significant, unlike the kamikaze planes, whose pilots embodied the peculiarly Japanese attitudes of the time even more than did the engineers who designed so many "special attack" weapons. Many pilots prized their death — even craved it — for its own rewards, almost as if it were more important than its purpose. Although the call was for "death simultaneously with a mortal blow to the enemy," the former was often the chief objective; the goal seems to have shifted from a desire to disable the enemy fleet to dying for its own sake. Standard military measures suggest that this was actually true in crucial ways, since the net results of the raids were pitifully disproportionate to their enormous expenditure in equipment and first-rate men. The human waste was the greater military folly: months or years of pilot training were squandered on this single, usually futile charge in the flying coffins. Yet

Imperial General Headquarters became so convinced of salvation by suicide attacks that it issued "an outrageous and unprecedented order," in the later words of the commander of an air flotilla that dispatched them from the mainland, "to the effect that *all* armed forces should resort" to this "lunacy."

> This proved that the High Command, utterly confused by a succession of defeats, had lost all wisdom . . . and degenerated to the point of indulging in wild gambling. The order was nothing less than a national death sentence. Like every military order, it was issued in the name of the Emperor and therefore not open to question or criticism, no matter how outrageous. Obedience was imperative; there was no alternative.

No doubt the young heroes had been prepared by a long history of Japanese mythology and literature, which elevates death as "the only pure and thus fitting end to the perfection of youth," as Ian Buruma summarized. Perhaps their longing was less for death than for what Buruma called "a supremely sensual state of unconsciousness" remembered from early childhood. Living in the center of their adoring mothers' universe, young Japanese children, especially male children, enjoy — and, Buruma argued, may be emotionally hamstrung by — extreme indulgence and pampering. Desire to return to their "dimly white dreamworld" of suckling and cavorting may help explain the general Japanese romance with death. In any case, the greater the likelihood of defeat, "the more certain it was that the Japanese would fight to the death in battle or kill themselves following defeat," as a former kamikaze pilot put it in 1989. The impossible odds at Okinawa enhanced rather than diminished the lure of an exquisite death, for the more obvious the futility, the greater the glory and seductiveness of the sacrificial feat.

This would be far from universally true among the 32nd Army's officers on land, especially among the more sensitive, educated, "liberal" reserve officers responsible for their men's lives as well as their own. Many of them would be caught between the military code's absolute requirement to be ready to die and humanistic feelings much intensified by their men's suffering. Besides, being sent out on suicide missions on Okinawa was usually not an honor but a punishment, meted out to men in bad favor — often just such liberal officers. But there were far fewer complications for the idealistic young pilots. "If I go away to sea, I shall return a brine-soaked corpse," pledged the old anthem that often ended the ceremony preceding the dispatch of kamikaze flights.

Self-destruction beckoned as invitingly as destruction of the enemy when the youth gunned their engines. Although the assurance was also repeated that *Yamato damashii* would triumph in the end — specifically that everything depended on Japanese spirit rather than the skill of the pilots — the pilots themselves, by this time often barely trained, appeared to believe this no more than that their sacrifice would effect the promised change in the course of the war. Although many hoped for this, many others were too bright and skeptical to swallow the promise or to respond to military fanfares. Still, they had pleaded for their opportunity to die because their object, like their leaders', was as much gesture as military tactic. It was just as important, perhaps more important, to express in this clearest way utter sincerity in a just cause, no matter how hopeless — or precisely because it was hopeless — as to damage the enemy's gargantuan navy. Tale after folktale depicted young Japanese heroes disregarding mundane considerations to follow blind sentiment and die for doomed noble causes. They had shown that life's meaning could no more be attained by the calculations of military advantage than by any other form of reason, let alone by pursuing individual self-interest.

In addition to expressing gratitude, the pilots' last letters also confirmed this supreme dedication to surmounting petty earthly interests. Attaining the longed-for spiritual victory over material comforts probably accounts for much of the young men's joy on the eve of the final flights. Such victory often required a "Zen-like suppression of reason and personal feelings, a blind devotion to direct action and an infinite capacity for hardship and pain." Takajiro Onishi called the lucky men "already gods without earthly desires." They had achieved their higher state by overcoming the paltry concerns of ordinary human existence. Many penned their letters in eager anticipation for their imminent beautiful or "splendid" death, "as sudden and clean as the shattering of crystal." With "no remorse whatever," they truly "never felt better." Conviction that they were headed for life's greatest glory contributed to their exaltation as they took off.

> We were bubbling with eagerness . . . I thought of my age, nineteen, and of the saying "To die while people still lament your death; to die while you are pure and fresh; this is truly *bushido*." Yes, I was following the way of the samurai. My eyes were shining as I stepped on board [my plane] once more. I remembered with pleasure [a fellow officer] quoting from a poem and telling me I would "fall as purely as the cherry blossom" I now held.

> Defeated but unconquered, men of the 65th Fighter Squadron were born separately but die together.

> Warmest greetings [to a brother]. I hope you are all well. As for me, duty calls more and more. What a fine reward determination

is. It gives one peace of mind. After all, the body is only an attachment of the spirit . . . Tell my friend Matsu to hurry up and become a flier.

I know that no purpose can any longer be served by my death but I remain proud of piloting a suicide plane and it is in this state of mind that I die . . . Tomorrow a man in love with liberty will leave this world. I may have given you the impression of being disillusioned but at the bottom of my heart I am happy to die.

Dear Parents:
   Please congratulate me. I have been given a splendid opportunity to die . . . How I appreciate this chance to die like a man!

Many Americans who would consider the use of the atomic bombs a cruel, racist mistake took no account of this yearning to die magnificently. Many would argue that the military facts proved Japan was defeated without the appalling slaughter at Hiroshima and Nagasaki — the same facts, to the extent that the Japanese knew them, which increased the appeal of a death that demonstrated denial of self-interest and even community benefit. Belief counted more than reason, the purity of the motive more than the result or the righteousness of the cause. The ability to defy rationality and logic was itself a triumph, which was surely why many young pilots felt only disgust and disgrace when they crashed without dying — and why others were plunged into depression when their missions were canceled or had to be aborted before they could make their sacrifice. Their feelings went beyond shame; in their own words, they felt deprived of death. The disappointment of one group that returned to its base alive because bad weather near Okinawa had concealed the targeted ships became acute when it learned that another group had nevertheless pursued the attack that day. Falling uselessly into the sea, those pilots accomplished nothing apart from their sublimely noble death.

But this merits surprise only if one forgets that rational measurement also made little difference in larger war issues. Japan was defeated not only before Hiroshima but well before L-day on Okinawa, yet the carnage there was only beginning.

If in doubt whether to live or die, it is always better to die.
   — A saying repeated to kamikaze pilots and other Japanese warriors

Once a Japanese man decides to do something, he carries it out to the bitter end, and at all costs.
   — A father and mentor to his son in a contemporary comic book for boys called *I Am a Kamikaze*

Many kamikaze pilots, even knowing they could not seriously damage the American fleet, hoped their demonstration of sublime dedication might shock the spiritually inferior enemy into defeat. Actually, however, they prompted the reverse reaction: the "diving madmen" reinforced Americans' conviction that only utter prostration was good enough for the demented Japanese.* Even if the men of the 10th Army and 5th Fleet had known that what attracted many kamikazes was less killing others than dying well themselves, precious few would have been interested. So much stark evidence of "degenerate" thirst for blood at such "inhuman" cost nipped any desire — slight to begin with among most Americans — to probe deeper into the unfathomable Oriental mentality. The cost ineffectiveness of kamikaze operations also comforted few Americans at Okinawa. After the lifting of the censorship of casualty and damage figures in July, following the campaign's official end, the Navy revealed that thirty-three ships had been sunk, chiefly by kamikazes, and 368 ships and craft damaged, more than fifty seriously.† Carriers also lost 539 planes, but the Japanese cost remained staggering, as on the first mass attack of April 6–7, when almost half the planes were lost. Of 182 "bogeys" to penetrate within shooting distance of Task Force 54, the big-gun bombardment force, on the afternoon of April 6, 108 were claimed shot down. TF 58 recorded a further 249 splashes, 65 by a single carrier (according to *Essex*'s own tally) on that day alone. On some days, up to 90 percent of the planes delivering mass attacks, conventional and kamikaze together, were destroyed — a total of 7830 for the three months of the Okinawan campaign. The kill ratio of the latter alone was naturally far higher, and most of the tiny percentage that managed to crash on ships instead of into the sea did so on superstructures, where they caused relatively superficial damage. Huge as the attack of April 6–7 was, the fleet comprised more ships than the nine hundred Japanese planes — and none larger than a destroyer was sunk that day or later. Some four thousand treasures of the nation died for this strategically minor wounding off Okinawa, most of them less than twenty-one years old.

---

*This was more than a case of mutual cultural ignorance hatching reciprocally misjudged attitudes. The supreme self-sacrifice of the suicide missions was in another way an expression of supreme selfishness. As a long line of Japanese protagonists in folklore and history had achieved their self-denying feats by heroically suppressing their own feelings, kamikaze pilots also ignored or discounted the feelings of others. The heroes did what was necessary to prove their utter purity and blind loyalty — and to hell with the larger consequences, in this case their enemies' frightened loathing of Japan.

†As with calculations of the bombing damage to Japanese cities, various reports give slightly different casualty and damage figures. These are probably accurate within a ship or two, although a recent Japanese study states that 15 ships, not including smaller craft, were sunk during the campaign and a further 225 damaged, 192 by kamikazes.

But what mattered to American crews there was their own hell, not the enemy's rabidness. When their ships were not under attack, their life was tolerable by Pacific War standards. There was often far too much rain and too little usable water: tense watches at General Quarters under deluges in April and May were followed by days and nights of blistering heat that turned ships into furnaces. Severe water rationing was the rule; shipboard evaporators could not make enough fresh water from the sea. The sun was so strong by mid-May that a careless touch of a plane parked on a flight deck could cause a burn, and the stifling heat intensified the rashes, diarrhea and outbreaks of boils in the overcrowded quarters. Still, most crews had dry clothes, relatively clean beds and three squares on most days — unimaginable luxuries to combat infantrymen.*

During the moments and hours of air attacks, however, supreme terror reigned on the ships. The destroyer *Murray* had already been hit by a torpedo that passed straight through her, from starboard to port. The converted landing craft of Fred Poppe stayed lucky, but nerves were just as strained there when General Quarters sounded. Poppe was in the shower one day when the gongs clanged; he looked through a porthole and saw a neighboring ship explode. "The whole thing simply blew apart. That got to me. It must have been a kamikaze, there were so many around." There was also fear of suicide boats and rumors of Japanese swimmers attaching charges to ships' bottoms, which prompted the posting of guards with submachine guns around the deck and men packing carbines or .45s when they went topside. "At night, anything that moved got riddled. Any sound, any sight including whitecaps — we were plain scared. And when one guy opened up, *everybody* fired at everything. So there were lots of near misses, ricochets, accidents." Poppe's fear further inten-

---

*Naval officers enjoyed themselves in some style. Lieutenant William Speck watched scrambling little figures being shot on Okinawa's ravaged landscape — and was "eating all the while with silver on white tablecloths" in the wardroom of the destroyer *Murray*. Actionless days provided hours of relative freedom from battle's misery. The rocket-launching converted landing craft of Fred Poppe, the Long Island sailing enthusiast whose flat feet had kept him from becoming an officer candidate, patrolled the Pacific coast for Japanese boats or unusual activities on her stretch of beach. Then Poppe was summoned back to Princeton, New Jersey, for a V-12 officer training program. His "priority" orders directed him to report immediately, but his captain kept him aboard until some vital business was settled. "We hadn't been paid for months but we'd been playing a lot of poker — so somebody owed me, I owed the captain, and the captain owed somebody else. It was all woven together and no man could leave without a calculator. We had to find out where the pay ship was and go there at the first opportunity. We all got paid, settled our debts, and *then* I took off."

Although Poppe loved his ship after "steering that little thing halfway around the world," he was "absolutely delighted, exhilarated" at the prospect of becoming an officer at last and very relieved to leave Okinawa alive and whole. But he had no doubt he would return as a ninety-day wonder to a much worse war off the Japanese mainland.

sified when he transferred to a much larger LST on the opposite coast, near Naha. "Kamikazes just poured at us, again and again, attack after attack. The sky filled with theirs, ours, dogfights, flak. It scared the shit out of us, far more than on L-day. We'd get warnings of about half an hour before they appeared, and the waiting was scary too, the knowing what was coming when those pilots' one wish in the world was to kill you."

The Japanese called their April 6–7 attack Kikusui (Floating Chrysanthemum) Number One. In addition to almost daily missions of one to twenty planes, they would stage nine more such mass raids at average intervals of a week, each lasting from two to five days and mounted from a variety of airfields that sent in their waves from several directions. The last Floating Chrysanthemum, number ten, would come on June 21–22, when organized resistance on Okinawa itself had collapsed and the 32nd Army's High Command was preparing to uphold their personal honor with the necessary act.

Those larger attacks provided "shows" awe-inspiring enough momentarily to divert combat troops on the island from their anxieties. The spectacle of an armada firing ten thousand guns faster than seemed possible to fight off swarms of attackers was mesmerizing. Norris Buchter spent L-day night on a slope several hundred yards from the beach where he had come ashore. The sky above the invasion fleet riding in the darkness offshore was so full of tracer shells from the thousand-odd ships' antiaircraft fire that it glowed like coals. "It was like a hundred July Fourths together. What a terribly magnificent carnival!" Others on high ground had a "stadiumlike" view of the macabre but magnificent action. William Marshall ran to the top of a coral hill one April night to see two sections of a destroyer giving off an eerie glow as they drifted apart, burning fiercely. When both sections sank, Marshall felt paralyzed by a "gigantic" explosion that sent shock waves up through the hill and a blinding light that flashed "as though several suns had detonated" into the night. When a kamikaze hit an ammunition ship on an earlier evening, John Grove blinked at "a huge multicolored fan of fire and shells" on the horizon. It was "the ultimate in Fourth of July shows — a magnificent sight, except that I knew it had to mean the death of maybe hundreds of Americans."

Medical Corpsman Joseph Bangert, the wise-guy son of John D. Rockefeller's personal driver, was "on the throne" — over a hole in the Okinawan ground — one evening just before the start of the battle for Sugar Loaf Hill when he saw two kamikazes attack *New Mexico*. One of the battleship's 5-inch shells exploded directly under the first plane, lifting it just clear of her mastheads, but the plane's bomb detonated in a stack, turning it into a giant blowtorch. The second plane was also hit several times but held on and crashed into the gun deck. The ship's reaction amazed Bangert. "That wagon took off like a shot, I guess to avoid other strikes. I'd seen a lot of those incredible gunfire shows by then, but I just couldn't believe a big ship could move that fast." (With fifty-four killed or missing and 119 wounded, *New Mexico* was not, however, listed among the badly damaged ships, because she was able to continue fighting.)

Dick Whitaker watched "the daily and nightly spectacle" when his company was pulled back for rest and replenishment on high ground, from which both the Pacific Ocean and East China Sea, where ships still extended to the horizon, were sometimes visible. "During the day, the ships threw up so much ack-ack that daylight almost disappeared in a million black puffs." (Sailors were surprised to find hundreds of hot pieces from those black puffs land on their decks and start some serious fires. That hadn't happened in training, but training had been incomparably less intense and close-quartered to other ships also firing with life-and-death desperation.) "During night attacks, the concentration of fire made a kind of twilight — incredible. A sea almost solid with tracers and gun flashes. So much fire would have seemed truly impossible if you didn't see it."

When Navy construction units nicknamed the Seabees landed soon after the combat troops to begin bulldozing for roads for American traffic, they erected a large movie screen on top of a hill from which the alternate show of suicide pilots diving on frantic ships could also be seen. Betty Grable vehicles were favorites, some repeated so often that the audience said the lines along with the actors. The movies stopped only when the film broke.

Although American troops would best remember night attacks that floodlit the sky, the Japanese usually timed their flights to arrive at twilight, when their planes were most difficult to see even if they'd been detected by radar. Whitaker noticed independently that twilight, when the planes appeared in a sky solid with smoke from anti-aircraft bursts, began to be the hour of the most awesome shows. It seemed to him inconceivable that a single attacking plane could penetrate such fire long enough to reach its target, but he watched in amazement as some managed this feat, then crashed into an oily fireball of their bombs, their fuel and themselves.

Ordinarily, he felt little sympathy for swab jockeys. At least they had good chow — incredibly good, he would discover on an involuntary visit to a ship. And they could take a shower at night (Whitaker did not know how rare showers were with water rationing) and jump into a clean sack — in contrast to his platoon, who slept, or couldn't sleep, in a hole in the ground "soaked to the skin, freezing our asses off and without the protection of a ship or anything else." But when kamikazes struck, Whitaker felt pity for those aboard. Most ships weren't hit but those which were could be even worse than foxholes: sailors couldn't dig in like Marines during their moments of terror. Infantrymen near the shore who could see the wreckage of ships blown to bits — sometimes with the bodies of sailors, sometimes by the dozens — were even more aware of the price being paid at sea.

Thirty-second Army spectators saw something quite different in the same extravaganza. The prelude was a chorus of sirens (activated by warning signals from American radar-picket destroyers far out to sea, although Japanese soldiers didn't know this) that also signaled a brief suspension of the bombardment of their land positions while the enemy's attention turned skyward. Many of the Japanese who profited from that blessed break felt guilty toward the young Special Attack Forces heroes. "But the enemy stopped shelling and bombing us during their attacks," remembered Kenjiro Matsuki, the first baseman of Japan's first professional baseball team, "so we could relax and enjoy some brief moments watching the Ryogoku."*

The sirens were like a master switch turning on the searchlights of the American ships and pointing them skyward, "a brilliant show in itself." Then the Japanese planes approached with their metallic roar. Picked up by the searchlights, they became the targets of "millions of antiaircraft bullets and shells . . . a panorama of incomparably gorgeous display." Another Japanese soldier remembered the nonessential lights of the American fleet going out "in a blink" when the kamikazes approached, "and the blazing stream of antiaircraft fire gushing upward with a terrifying explosion. Then we'd catch a glimpse of [a plane] hurtling down from the sky like a pebble lit up in the beam of a searchlight as it cut across the nearer sky, or sometimes wrapped in its own flame."

The ships' rapid-fire pompoms awed Japanese soldiers. They threw up tens of thousands of rounds to crisscross the lower sky "like some cosmic fireworks display" beneath explosions of higher caliber automatic shells, beneath, in turn, bursts of flak that blanketed the upper

---

*Tokyo's Ryogoku district was well known for its annual fireworks display over the Sumida River. Hearing the sirens one day, Matsuki reckoned he would be safe for half an hour and went to wash his face for the first time in over a month at a well near his cave. But for some reason, perhaps because that particular kamikaze attack didn't materialize, the ships quickly turned their searchlights off and resumed their bombardment, landing a shell so close to Matsuki that fragments hissed like hot pokers when they splashed into the well — into which he also jumped for protection. Rushing back to his shelter, he swore never again to take such a risk.

sky. The soldiers on shore prayed the planes would stay up until they could crash into the targets at which they were aiming with such stunning bravery. When they succeeded, they sent the additional spectacle of "pillars of fire hundreds of meters into the sky" together with a surge of joy through the beleaguered defenders on land. "He did it!" they shouted before dashing back to cover, often in tears of gratitude.

Soon the quick ventures from the caves to watch the spectacle acquired a more formal description: "To go worshiping the Special Attack Forces."

> Come evening, the mountain rumbles. A thunderous sound can be heard in the cave — from which we leap out, shouting, "Yeah! Our Tokkoki [Special Attack] planes have come!" We go up the mountain and see . . . that the clouds over the sea are red. The enemy fleet is firing its antiaircraft guns, all of them. Tens of thousands of tracers crisscross like a fountain, turning the sky above the ships fiery . . . Shining like a single grain of rice, our Tokko braves this barrage. The minute we catch sight of it, it hurtles toward the water in flames . . . or goes straight for an enemy ship, releasing a gigantic pillar of fire. Then the tracers . . . become sporadic. The sound of the firing, like the beating of a colossal drum, suddenly stops. And the eerie silence that follows really gets you. Some of us go down on our knees and worship toward the sea, worship the Tokko. "Well done! Thank you!" Everyone follows . . . that was some spectacle, that.

Inside the caves, maniacally exaggerated reports of the success of the air attacks provided more moments of exaltation. Masahide Ota and other young Okinawan messengers from 32nd Army headquarters at Shuri brought uplifting news about the kamikazes and other victories. An Okinawan newspaper printed there was a main source of news. On April 7, the paper reported, "our brave eagles" sank twenty-one enemy ships. On April 9, thirty were supposedly sunk and eighteen crippled; on April 13, nineteen sunk. "Our Air Force continues to attack the enemy fleet and task force with fierce intensity," the paper added. "Since April 12, our results include, as far as we could determine:

> Sunk: Carriers — 1, Cruisers — 2, Cruiser or Transport ship — 1,
>   Destroyer — 1, Transport ship — 1
> Damaged: Battleships — 1.

The arrival of such misinformation filled the caves with loud cheers. The tiny newspapers went from hand to hand, the proud possessors surrounded by soldiers who bent over them to read the great tidings for themselves. Few doubted that their (virtually nonexistent) submarine fleet was in the process of strangling the land enemy by destroying his overextended supply lines. They had no trouble calculating that the additional destruction of twenty to thirty enemy ships by air on good days would soon bring his control of the sea to an end — after which their brilliantly successful Air Force would turn to helping them on land. (By the end of the campaign, Japanese sources would claim that forty-nine carriers, battleships and cruisers had been sunk by kamikazes. The actual total in these categories was zero; a typhoon on June 5 did more damage to the heavy ships than any air attack.) That simple logic lifted the dejection caused by their retreats and the wretchedness of their underground existence. Hope and optimism so swelled every heart that cheeks seemed actually to shine in the darkness of the caves. Shigemi Furukawa, a former high school teacher, later saw this as part of "a curious battlefield psychology [in which] we took whatever 'information' fed our wishful thinking for certain fact, no matter how often we were disappointed."

The powerfully wishful thinking extended far beyond the battlefield to some of the highest commanders. Staff officers of Vice Admiral Matome Ugaki, Commander of the Fifth Air Fleet based on the home island of Kyushu, spoke of huge enemy losses after each Floating Chrysanthemum. The admiral himself, who also commanded the Special Attack Forces as a whole there, thought it "almost certain" that the first one, on April 6–7, destroyed four American carriers. "The sea around Okinawa . . . turned out to be a scene of carnage and a reconnaissance plane's report stated that as many as 150 columns of black smoke were observed." Ugaki told his diary on April 11 that "in the light of so many reports of crashes on enemy carriers, there can't be many undamaged ones still operating." Evidently the admiral — who would himself take off in a plane and disappear, an almost certain suicide, after the Emperor's call for surrender in August — was genuinely convinced that the enemy would soon be "finished off"; the American Navy's "extremely heavy" losses, he predicted, would culminate in its "tragic end" within two weeks.

Crashes on the carriers did force a few to suspend operations. The damage and losses were terrible in comparison with what the American Navy had suffered anywhere previously in World War II. But none of those carriers was put permanently out of action, let alone sunk, during the entire Okinawan campaign. On the second day of the Sixth Floating Chrysanthemum, a kamikaze suddenly dived from some low clouds toward *Bunker Hill*, one of the carriers whose planes had disposed of *Yamato* five weeks earlier. The Zeke hit the flight deck, setting parked planes alight in a huge conflagration. Just as its bomb penetrated the deck, a Judy dived almost vertically and did the same, its bomb, released before the crash, also exploding below. In moments, three decks were ablaze almost the full length of the ship, the inferno fed by more parked planes and aviation fuel in hangar and working spaces. The heat of the skyward-shooting flames melted metal and seared firefighting parties. Three hundred and ninety-three of her crew were killed and missing — many suffocated by the smoke — and another 264 were wounded, but *Bunker Hill* survived.

Three days later, in the interval between the Sixth and Seventh Floating Chrysanthemums, twenty-five of the twenty-six planes that attacked *Enterprise* were shot down by interceptors and antiaircraft fire, but the approach of the twenty-sixth made throats go dry on the carrier. The pilot knew his job. It became clear he would attain his goal in less than a minute.

> All the batteries were firing: the 5-inch guns, the 40mm and the 20mm, even the rifles. The Japanese aircraft dived through a rain of steel. It had been hit in several places and seemed to be trailing a banner of flame and smoke but it came on, clearly visible, hardly moving, the line of its wings as straight as a sword.
>
> The deck was deserted; every man, with the exception of the gunners, was lying flat on his face. Flaming and roaring, the fire-ball passed in front of the "island" superstructure and crashed with a terrible impact just behind the forward lift. The entire vessel was shaken, some forty yards of the flight deck folded up like a banana skin: an enormous piece of the lift . . . was thrown over 300 feet into the air.

A bomb exploding deep in a lower deck caused the worst damage. Fourteen men were killed, sixty-eight wounded. The last earthly picture of those about to die on deck was of the kamikaze "trailing his banner of flame and increasing in size with lightning rapidity." "The Big *E*" had been hit twice before, most recently by two planes within an hour. This time she had to retire for major repairs in a Navy yard, not to return to sea — like *Bunker Hill* — until after the war.

Royal Navy carriers consistently suffered less damage when hit. Five of them formed the core of a British fleet supported by two new battleships, five cruisers and fifteen new destroyers — twenty-seven warships that were designated Task Force 57, although it was no larger than the average of Task Force 58's many subdivided Task Groups, even with its motley collection of supply and service vessels.

TF 57's addition to Iceberg a fortnight before L-day had been less than the ballyhooed example of heartwarming Anglo-American co-operation. In England itself, GIs awaiting the invasion of France sometimes brawled with British soldiers, comrades in arms but rivals for pub space and women. In the Pacific, it was the high commands that wrangled over political and diplomatic issues. After catastrophic losses early in the war, senior British naval officers were keen to return to the Indian Ocean, where their former possessions in Burma, Malaya and Indonesia awaited recovery from the Japanese. Suspicious of this colonial interest, their American counterparts thought it a good idea to relegate the Royal Navy to a Pacific sideshow, as distant as possible from the main one — those Americans, that is, not opposed to British participation of any kind west of Hawaii. Admiral Ernest King, Commander-in-Chief of the U.S. Fleet and Chief of Naval Operations, and General Douglas MacArthur, Commander of the Southwest Pacific Area Forces, were among the brass who would have preferred to keep the Pacific an all-American theater by shutting Britain out. They and their followers wanted John Bull to share the glory of Japan's final defeat even less than they wanted American resources drained to supply British ships, which they swore to prevent.

In the end, the political leaders surmounted the military-strategic rivalries. Churchill offered Roosevelt the British fleet for Pacific island campaigns rather than for any Indian Ocean operation, and the President quickly accepted. But although American staffs were then characteristically generous with supplies, some high-ranking officers continued to nudge the Royal Navy as far aside as possible in order to "forestall any possible postwar British claim that they had delivered even the least part of the final blows which demolished the remains of Japanese seapower," as an English historian recently put it.

Nevertheless, British staffs worked unsparingly to make Task Force 57 a balanced, self-supporting force. Its main assignment was to neutralize Sakishima Shota, a small archipelago of islands between Formosa and Okinawa. They repeatedly bombed and shelled those islands, some of which had important military airfields that were repaired by sedulous Japanese soldiers and native workers after every strike. The fleet's location on that periphery, some three hundred miles southwest of Okinawa, guaranteed it would have little chance for publicity or glory and every chance of being attacked from enemy airfields on the Chinese mainland as well as nearby Formosa, where many Japanese pilots were more experienced and skillful than the young graduates of crash courses on the mainland.

The British ships were attacked hard and hit often. Beginning on L-day, when they acted as a decoy to divert attention from the vastly larger American force off the landing beaches, they served as a shield or "flying buffer" across the approaches to the battle site from Formosa and China. Occasionally they were the principal targets of a

given day's raids, kamikaze and conventional. But naval design rooted
in national attitudes kept their damage relatively minor and casualties relatively few. In Anglo-American clashes over strategy in the
European war, the British generally favored striking at Hitler's periphery in Africa, the Mediterranean and the Middle East rather
than crossing the English Channel to take on his main armies until
blockade and bombing had greatly weakened them. Determination
to avoid World War I's catastrophic casualties contributed to this
preference — and also influenced British naval architects. The largest difference between their carriers and American ones was a flight
deck of three inches of armor plating rather than of teakwood.

American designers disliked armored flight decks because their
weight reduced stability and striking power. TF 57's five carriers together provided only 244 planes, slightly more than half the number
on American carriers of equivalent size. (And their steel decks made
the crews' quarters even more like infernos after weeks under the
fierce sun.) They were also slower, less maneuverable and less protected by antiaircraft armament than their American counterparts,
deepening American doubt that they could look after themselves. In
fact, however, they looked after themselves very well because damage
control proved crucial for withstanding kamikaze attacks. All five of
TF 57's carriers were hit at least once, often with damage that would
have seemed grave before the advent of kamikazes. Against British
steel, the same aircraft that often penetrated "soft top" wooden decks
and exploded into havoc below usually "crumpled up like a scram-
bled egg," in an American observer's simile. "When a kamikaze hits a
U.S. carrier, it's six months' repair in Pearl [Harbor]," observed another American, the liaison officer with TF 57. "In a Limey carrier,
it's 'Sweepers, man your brooms.'"

It was not quite that easy for the Limeys; virtuoso pilots who
crashed with high impact occasionally pierced even their flight decks.
Still, Americans were repeatedly amazed when hits so severe that
they might have put one of their carriers out of action merely slowed
the British quarry for several hours or reduced their rate of launching and recovering planes. When a Zeke with a five-hundred-pound
bomb crashed on *Indefatigable*'s flight deck from an almost vertical
dive, the blast killed eight ratings but left only a three-inch dent in
the heavy steel, which was quickly patched enough to handle landings and take-offs. Even some multiple fires caused by several near
simultaneous crashes were extinguished within a quarter of an hour.
The chunks of the smashed Japanese planes — and of their pilots,
evidence of whom were found in skull splinters or a single finger
stuck to a bulkhead — were pushed across the steel and over the side,

together with the incinerated British ones, mostly American-made Avengers, Hellcats and Corsairs, that had been parked on the flight deck. The carriers were fully operational again.

At one point between provisionings, TF 57 set a Royal Navy record since Nelson and the era of sail: thirty-two continuous days at sea. Throughout them, they diverted a share of the Japanese planes from the vastly larger American fleet, and each kamikaze less was a blessing to TF 58. When senior American officers saw the scope and intensity of the Floating Chrysanthemums and counted their own casualties, their coolness toward the "Forgotten Fleet," as a chronicler later dubbed her, inched toward respect and even a little affection.

Of the stunning number of seventy-eight hundred Japanese planes lost, thousands were piloted by youths with barely enough training to get their craft into the air and attempt the quick dive they prayed would crown their deaths with the additional glory of a hit. Thousands crashed into the sea without even coming close to their targets. But as so much in war, that was a matter of chance. Men on unluckier ships became deeply impressed with the patience and cunning of other kamikaze attacks — and with reason: some volunteers were experienced, skillful pilots. The experts dived "with the velocity of a comet" for their targets' vulnerable parts, such as carrier elevators, and chose the most vulnerable moments, during plane launching and recovery. Those operations made quick maneuvering — the best defense apart from accurate, relentless fire from antiaircraft guns and airborne interceptors — extremely difficult. Captains had learned, as one put it, that it was "fatal" to hold a steady course during an attack. Artful Japanese timing also delivered carrier pilots waiting to take off in their own planes into a special chamber of hell: strapped into their cockpit seats, they saw kamikazes approaching and every sailor, except gun crews, racing for cover. (This is partly why so many hundreds of Allied planes were lost — not destroyed in the air but blown apart and burned when parked on flight and hangar decks.) Ships could rarely tell whether approaching aircraft were conventional or kamikaze until almost the last moment, when the dives began; kamikazes usually started theirs a moment earlier. When two or more dived in a coordinated attack from varying points at varying angles, they much increased the chances of a successful crash no matter how brilliant the maneuvers on the bridges of the targets.

Apprehension on the ships increased even further because the crews could rarely tell until this last moment whether the planes coming in were piloted by experts or novices. Looking up at five-hundred-pound bombs strapped to bellies or extra fuel tanks under each wing, they tried to guess. An almost empty plane could be lethal — or any part of it: in one case a wheel bounced off a kamikaze and decapitated a gunner, who had been firing furiously until the moment of the crash he was desperately hoping to prevent. Even near misses could cause significant damage, as with near misses of large bombs. One kamikaze totally disabled its target ship by hitting the water hard and close enough to flood both boiler and engine compartments.

> *Get the destroyers. Without their radar warning of our approach, we will enjoy great success.*
> — Admiral Matome Ugaki, Commander of the 5th Air Fleet

> *Although your historian himself has been under kamikaze attack and witnessed the hideous forms of death and torture inflicted by that weapon, words fail him to do justice to the sailors on the radar picket stations. We need a poet to do it, as John Masefield did . . . for old-time sailors in their freezing grind of rounding Cape Horn.*
> — Samuel Eliot Morison, the dean of American naval historians

Attacks against the capital ships naturally attracted most attention, but the tin cans and other attendant vessels suffered proportionately more. Human resources are almost always more strained on smaller naval ships, and many of those small ships in particular were intentionally stationed directly in harm's way: "sitting ducks off Okinawa," as one observer called them.*

To protect the main body of the fleet, the Americans established a ring of sixteen early-warning radar picket stations in the most probable approaches of the attacking planes, ranging out to about seventy-five miles from Okinawa's coasts and spaced so that contacts could be passed from one station to another. (This was in addition to Task Force 58's own picket group and to some seventy-five American planes always orbiting in concentric circles above the island and picket ships during daylight hours. Those carrier-based combat air patrols shot down hundreds of easy pickings but also risked flak from their own side's ships with daredevil courage during the thick of the Floating Chrysanthemums.) Destroyers and destroyer escorts did most of this dangerous picketing in slow-speed circles, although minelayers, smaller gunboats and landing craft were soon added in the effort to increase antiaircraft firepower against the swarms of attackers.

---

*Merchant ships manned by civilian crews were also fat targets. One Liberty ship struggling to offload at Okinawa was attacked by 72 kamikazes. The hospital ship *Comfort* was also hit, although probably in error, by a plane diving in flames and out of control. Six nurses were among the 28 killed.

The military irrationality of the kamikaze effort as a whole was aggravated by wasting far too much of it on the picket ships. It was almost inevitable that those unarmored little craft took a disproportionate share of the dives; many shaky pilots were unable to keep their rickety planes aloft long enough to reach the choicer targets of the carriers and transports. *Leutze, Newcomb, Bush* and *Colhoun* were among the destroyers and destroyer escorts that footed most of the crash bill. Kamikazes badly damaged thirteen American carriers, ten battleships and five cruisers off Okinawa, but only smaller ships, with their skimpier antiaircraft armament, went down: a dozen between late March and the end of June, in addition to three sunk by conventional air attacks.

Just before the final Floating Chrysanthemum, the commander of the radar picket destroyers wrote an action report praising his ships' "superb" performance throughout the campaign. He spoke of "acts of heroism and unselfishness, fighting spirit, coolness under fire, unswerving determination, endurance and qualities of leadership and loyalty exceed[ing] all previous conceptions . . . Radar picket duty in this operation might well be a symbol of supreme achievement in our naval traditions."

After witnessing kamikaze attacks personally, the distinguished naval historian Samuel Eliot Morison concluded that destroyer crews living in daily and nightly terror of them were probably under greater tension and stress for a longer period than had previously been experienced by any seamen serving in a surface fleet.

> Men on radar picket station, to survive, not only had to strike
> down the flaming terror of the kamikaze, roaring out of the blue
> like the thunderbolts that Zeus hurled at bad actors in days of old;
> they were under constant strain and unusual discomfort. In order
> to supply 650-pound steam pressure to build up full speed rapidly
> in a destroyer, its superheaters, built only for intermittent use, had
> to be lighted for three and four days' running. For days and even
> nights on end, the crew had to stand general quarters and the ship
> kept "buttoned up." Men had to keep in condition for the instant
> reaction and split-second timing necessary to riddle a plane bent
> on a crashing death. Sleep became the rarest commodity and
> choicest luxury, like water to a shipwrecked mariner.

This drew a greater distinction between kamikaze and conventional attacks than most Japanese themselves would have made. Many veteran pilots considered too valuable for the former flew strikes that were suicidal in all but name; they wore no parachutes and did not expect to return. By the sixth week of fighting on Okinawa, the demarcation between suicide missions and ordinary ones was increasingly blurred. "They were all human bullets," Denis and Peggy Warner pointed out, "whether they chose to die in kamikaze aerial attacks, in banzai charges, in *ohkas*, or on small boats loaded with explosives or aboard *kaitens*." And although most of the less publicized Japanese infantry was not specifically suicidal, its night attacks, especially when units had been reduced to near inoperative, were almost the same — sometimes precisely the same. Very few of Ushijima's eighty thousand regular troops expected to return to Japan, nor did the twenty thousand to thirty thousand Okinawans conscripted in the Home Guard expect to live, though a far larger percentage of them wanted to.

Besides, chroniclers understandably overwhelmed by what shipboard heroes faced during air attacks had little notion of the suffering on Okinawa itself. It is probably true that "never in the annals of our glorious naval history have naval forces done so much with so little against such odds for so long a period," as the commander of the radar pickets added. But the land battle was harder, and many Japanese units did a lot more with a lot less against incomparably greater odds for a longer period. Americans on ships hit by kamikazes had only a brief taste of the experience of Japanese soldiers on the island, who for months faced an almost constant rain of bullets, shells, and bombs.*

Still, the ordeal of the radar picket vessels was indeed unprecedented in many ways, and the strain could be even greater than on the valiant convoys to Murmansk, where the men of ships sunk by intense German submarine and air attacks found themselves in arctic waters. Here the kamikaze attacks went on and on, bringing dread to sailors who simply couldn't believe that the "crazy Japs" had more planes left after so many had been shot down. But the Japanese had thousands of planes left — never mind their sad condition — and the grim drama with the spectacular sights and unequaled intensity played again and again: the pilots' half-hypnotic last minutes in their planes, the tension on the ships below, the guns with the glowing barrels and hundreds of red balls almost constantly at their muzzles, the sky also red with tracers and "almost literally black" with bursts of antiaircraft shells, the sea churned up by spray from the shorts, the crew members' rush to toilets to cool feet seared by their decks,

---

*Some American infantrymen preparing to land on L-day also had a brief taste of Japanese life in Okinawa's caves. Ordered below on ships under air attack that morning, many felt so suffocated that they tried to force their way back on deck, willing to risk bombing and strafing for the sake of fresh air. But most Japanese lived months in caves that were at least the equal of the ships' holds in stink and lack of oxygen.

the absence of relief at shooting down any part of an attacking force because it was always the last plane that scored,* the hope that no crash would come amidships to make the ship go dead in the water and become a sitting duck, the gun crews' unflinching fire as planes did hit and engulfed them in flames, the jettisoning of anchors, torpedoes, guns and all other possible weight to try to save settling vessels, damage-control crews operating as bucket brigades when all power was lost and the fire hoses were useless, burned survivors struggling to stay afloat in a sludge of sea, oil and blood around crippled and sinking hulks — into which new bombs sometimes fell, knots of sailors using their last energy for an excited burst of swimming toward rescue vessels and dying of exhaustion, other knots drowned by big seas, crushed by the hulls of sister ships come to help or wriggling from their life jackets and letting themselves slide under although possible rescue was near because they could stand no more agony . . .

The destroyer *Laffey's* picket station during the Third Floating Chrysanthemum was on a straight line between Kyushu and Okinawa. Enemy planes filled her radar screen — up to fifty closing bogeys at one point — from first light of April 16. During one eighty-minute period, at least twenty-two planes dived at her from all points of the compass. Her decks were frequently strafed. One bomb scored a near miss; four others hit. One kamikaze splashed almost alongside; six others crashed home. (Eight hit another tin can on another day.) Ton for gross ton, it was perhaps a more intense attack than even *Yamato* had experienced, and *Laffey's* trial, until being taken in tow to Kerama Retto by a sister ship, lasted almost as long. Despite the explosions, flames and casualties — thirty-one missing and killed, seventy-two wounded — no gun was abandoned, although only 4 of her 20mms were operable when the Japanese broke off.

Those small-caliber guns proved little use in stopping a deter-

---

*That is to say, it seemed the last plane because it was the one that usually ended the game. For example, U.S.S. *Ditter* managed to shoot down seven of eight attacking planes, a hodgepodge of new and very old fighters and bombers, on June 6, the third day of the four-day Ninth Floating Chrysanthemum — but the eighth attacker flipped over and hit her port side. *Ditter*, a high-speed new minesweeper commissioned in October 1944 (just as Naha was hit by the 10/10 air raid), was sent straight to Okinawa from her shakedown cruise, then transferred to radar picket duty after a fortnight of assisting minesweepers. The ship's picket station was some 25 miles southeast of Okinawa when the kamikaze bomb opened a hole in her hull and exploded in the after fireroom, killing ten. Pieces of the plane were eventually found but nothing whatever of the pilot. (A bomb that landed in the fuel tanks of a sister ship the day before mercifully failed to go off.)

High-speed minelayers had been built to mine the coast of the Japanese mainland, a job already being tackled by B-29s. *Ditter* was towed to the Keramas for emergency repairs, then made her own way back, via Pearl Harbor, to the Staten Island yard that built her. She was decommissioned there exactly eleven months after her commissioning.

mined pilot. Even direct hits by the larger ones often failed to do that. (The destroyers' 5-inch mounts chiefly fired shells fitted with fuses set off by the planes' magnetic field.) One of the most remarkable scenes of the whole remarkable nautical tableau was of Japanese planes lurching forward on their collision courses even when repeatedly hit and in flames — even when their pilots were riddled and parts of the planes had broken off and spun into the sea. No amount of fire from a ship under attack ensured her safety until the attacker, or all the attackers, fell into the sea. That variety of enemy bravery added further to the anxiety. The hyperbole of a recent Japanese writer that "the sight of a single Japanese plane raised terror in the hearts of men on the enemy vessels" conveyed some truth.

It goes without saying that nearly all combatants in real battles are desperate to hit each other, but there was an added edge of desperation here, where nothing but shooting down the suicide planes *in time* and *far enough away* could save the targeted ships from fierce damage and brutal crashes.* When a ship's power was knocked out, as often happened, gun crews operated their guns manually — work so arduous that healthy young men with adrenaline pumping could keep it up for only two minutes. Nothing better illustrated the old Oriental proverb about dying twice when one knows one is about to die.

Permanent General Quarters would have exhausted the crews past the point where they could function. With hundreds of extra duties to keep the ships as ready and as free of inflammable materials as possible, steaming day and night under the usual normal high-condition watches was depleting enough. On top of that, nerves were "exposed and quivering like wires stripped of insulation," in the im-

---

*Such furious firing of course led to even more mistakes than usual when masses of young men operated an immense assemblage of guns. During the First Floating Chrysanthemum of April 6, a young officer on a landing ship medium saw four Japanese planes shot down. The ship's guns were still smoking when another plane approached in the late afternoon — a Hellcat, which was easily identifiable from everywhere but head on. When an LST opened fire, every other ship in sight joined instantaneously. (This was precisely the reaction of supremely strained Marines in foxholes after sundown, who all fired furiously into the night the moment one started.) The mistake was recognized just as the plane began plummeting.

Dazed gunners later talked about the tragedy, some insisting they had thought all along it was a friendly and fired only because everyone else did, others trying to comfort themselves with the thought that 4-to-1 was a respectable average. All agreed a terrible lesson had been learned, and when the dreaded General Quarters buzzer sounded again two hours later, the gunners quickly picked out another Hellcat from among the Japanese planes in the air — easily, because it wasn't flying head on at them. But nearby ships were less observant. As a column of black smoke still rose high in the air from the crash of the first Grumman, they opened their hail of fire on the second. The pilot desperately wagged his wings. The guns kept pumping out their thousands of rounds before the pilot cut his engine and landed some 200 yards away. Unlike his comrade, he was merely wounded, but this did not comfort the officer on the LSM. "I saw something today which made my blood run cold, something I shan't soon forget!"

age of one sober chronicler. And despite fire-control and damage-control skills honed in repeated encounters, the new repair berths in the Kerama islands swelled with what seemed to Americans a disastrous number of gutted ships and hulks. The final toll of naval casualties over the course of the campaign would be 4907 killed or missing and 4824 wounded, far more than in any previous battle of the war, including one-sided Pearl Harbor, where less than half that number died. Nearly 20 percent of the Navy's total casualties in the Pacific, Atlantic and all smaller seas throughout the war were inflicted off Okinawa. And the number of deaths would exceed the wounded, which was extremely rare in combat.

The Tenth Floating Chrysanthemum on June 21–22 would muster only forty-five kamikazes, down from the 355 of the First, of April 6–7. On average, the eight in between (on April 12–13, 15–16, 27–28; May 3–4, 10–11, 23–25, 27–29; and June 3–7) involved progressively fewer planes but without proportionate relief of strain on the targeted ships. And those Japanese numbers decreased partly because officers on the home islands had already begun husbanding for the struggle there, for which they would be able to muster ten thousand or more planes for kamikaze use. When B-29s joined TF 58's carrier strikers bombing mainland fields in mid-April, many Japanese planes were transferred from the Navy to Operation Ketsu (Last Resort) under overall command of the Imperial Army, whose honor required, unconditionally, a final battle on the mainland, whatever the odds, even if — or precisely because — there was no hope of winning. The specter of ultimate defeat increased rather than diminished the commitment to "special attacks." "I see the war situation becoming more desperate," a squadron leader wrote in his cockpit above Okinawa moments before following five of his pilots in their final dives. "All Japanese must become soldiers and die for the Emperor."

16 · The Shuri Line

We can never tell what a fatal blow the unyielding fighting spirit of Japanese soldiers on Iwo Jima and Okinawa have given the enemy mentally. When we compare the magnitude of this shock to the enemy with what we've lost on those islands, we can conclude that we are not losing the war.
— Prime Minister Baron Kantaro Suzuki, April 1945

The Japanese [in Okinawa's south] were in extremely well-thought-out, well-prepared positions, in terrain superbly suited for defense units. They were determined to . . . [make] American infantry and its support units pay dearly for every advance, and advances would usually be measured in yards rather than miles.
— Ian Gow, *Okinawa 1945*

It's going to be really tough, there are 65,000–70,000 fighting Japanese holed up in the south end of the island. I see no way to get them out except to blast them out yard by yard.
— Major General John Hodge, Commander of the American Army's Southern Landing Force

When we were up north, we knew the Army was getting the shit kicked out of them and we said it was because they just wouldn't get up out of their holes and move. We used to joke that one Jap machine gun was holding up a whole damn Army division. That was before we knew how bad it was down there.
— Joseph Bangert, medical corpsman with the 22nd Marines

O N THE MORNING of May 9, thirty-nine days after L-day and nineteen after the north was officially secured, Platoon Leader Paul Dunfrey huddled with forty-five men on the northern bank of a small river twenty miles south of the landing beaches. The brackish Asakawa (Asa River) runs almost due west from Shuri heights, oozing its way into the East China Sea a few miles above Naha. Lieutenant Dunfrey's platoon had been delivered there from relatively easy antiguerrilla patrols in the north only the day before. Beefed up by seventeen additional men from Weapons Company, they had been ordered to scout across the river.

The party made their last-minute weapons' check roughly midway between the river's broadened outlet to the sea and a burned-out bridge some five hundred yards inland. Then they waded across at low tide and pushed several hundred yards south to two low hills, making note of the defensive preparations — copious notes, for caves and gun emplacements dotted both hills. Many caves had entrances on both slopes; others housed artillery pieces covered by branches or canvas. Dunfrey supposed a third small hill a little farther south was even worse. "It wasn't very high but it had perfect firing positions down on everything approaching it, and I had to assume it was very well fortified — sheer hell to take."

As his scouts ran and crawled to him to report the findings in their sectors, Dunfrey was impressed by the enemy's fire discipline. The men had seen Japanese soldiers ducking back into caves and observing them from machine gun nests in well-placed vantage points; but all held their fire. The scope and ingenuity of their positions impressed him even more. Dunfrey had been promoted to lieutenant after his platoon leader was killed on Guadalcanal. On Okinawa, he had acquired more combat experience in the north, but had never seen the magnitude of defensive skill and strength that he did here. His unhappy job completed, he tried to hurry his men back to relative safety. The enemy opened fire when the unit was most vulnerable, back at the Asakawa. Many Japanese kept their positions concealed by firing only when his mens' backs were turned.

A little like the Japanese Army, Marines were much more practiced at advance than withdrawal. Crossing in chest-high water with rifles over their heads, the men made fine targets, especially Dunfrey himself, at whom much of the fire was concentrated. The loss of his young runner inches beside him caused an additional problem. A buddy of the dead man began carrying the body back, despite the additional risk to himself and Dunfrey's shouts to him to take cover. The lieutenant had to "kick ass" on the weeping corporal — one of his best men — and order his platoon sergeant to get him the hell back across the river *now*. A second man was killed in the group's ninety-minute struggle to recross the slim band of water.

Later that day, Dunfrey was summoned from attending to his wounded to 6th Division headquarters in a former Japanese command post captured by Army troops before the Marines' arrival from the north. About forty officers were in the spacious underground bunker, including Major General Lemuel Shepherd, commander of Dunfrey's 6th Division, and Shepherd's boss, Lieutenant General Simon Buckner, commander of the entire 10th Army. Dunfrey answered staff officers' questions and was dismissed. He started to leave, then turned back to ask permission to add something. He wanted to say that the questions hadn't allowed him to paint the full grim picture of the enemy positions he'd observed. When their artillery at last opened up on his men, there were not merely very many more guns than he'd expected but guns positioned to give the Japanese meshed lines of fire down on all lines of advance and excellent protection from American counterfire.

"Dis-*missed!*" roared a staff officer before Dunfrey could add his comment. But a second officer called him back. He was permitted to wonder aloud whether a frontal assault could take such Japanese positions.

At three o'clock the following morning, Dunfrey's weakened platoon was the second to cross a rope bridge strung across the Asakawa by engineers earlier that night. So much for the lieutenant's misgivings! The men had orders to hold their fire, light no cigarettes, move soundlessly. They hoped a dense fog blanketing the little valley would conceal an attack planned for dawn, three hours hence. But Japanese flares kept lighting the night, and when the leader of the first platoon to cross the bridge reached its far side, just ahead of Dunfrey, two enemy rifles were pointed at him from close enough to be seen through the fog. They didn't fire but did shoot down the American hope for surprise on this operation.

Still, the Marines moved out on time, at 6 A.M., almost blindly in the fog — whereas the defenders had pinpointed the necessary lines of advance in terrain they evidently knew perfectly. It was no surprise to Dunfrey that extremely heavy fire pinned down his men in minutes. Half an hour later, he felt a great thud in his stomach. Machine gun bullets and fragments of his belt buckle had severed his bowel; he could barely breathe. Much later, when the wonder of his recovery was under way, his surviving men would joke that his gasping probably woke all Okinawa. It continued into the afternoon. Although a corpsman risked his own life to reach the exposed lieutenant with morphine and sulfa, it was almost seven hours before he could be evacuated. The Japanese who had so scrupulously held their fire the day before were now delivering much too much of it to allow a stretcher to be brought out.

Paul Dunfrey didn't know he had a bit part in the campaign's feature attraction, in the sense that his action occurred at the outskirts of the main Japanese defensive line. If he had survived that morning without serious injury, his chances for the same during the rest of May would have been slight. Much worse was waiting for the Americans several miles farther south.

In the heart of the line a mile south of Dunfrey's wounding, the terrain of terraces, steep escarpments and rugged ravines approached perfection for defense. The Japanese had carved the limestone and coral of each commanding hill there into a kind of land battleship. Outdoing themselves in excavation and construction, the 32nd Army had fashioned "defensive masterpieces" largely impervious to the fire of the real American battleships offshore as well as of the land artillery and bombers. Many were contiguous or provided with protected access from one to another. Where possible, they had been tunneled with bends just inside the entrances to limit the fire entering the interiors. A single sector of well less than half a square mile would be found to contain sixteen hidden light mortars, eighty-three light machine guns, forty-one heavy machine guns, seven antitank guns, six field guns, two mortars and two howitzers.

The most extensive works were in the high ground protecting Shuri, which would have been difficult to take even with less shrewd and elaborate fortifications. Centuries of Okinawan kings had built forts on those best defensive sites in the south-central area. "The Japanese," a semi-official history tried to sum up about the huge enterprise, "took full advantage of the terrain to organize defensive areas and strongpoints that were mutually supporting, and they fortified the reverse as well as the forward slopes of hills. Artillery and mortars were emplaced in the caves and thoroughly integrated into the general scheme of defensive fire."

Shuri Castle was the keystone of Ushijima's strategy of a war of attrition. Even 16-inch naval shells could not disturb the deep, vast tunnel beneath it — almost thirteen hundred feet long, with blower-assisted ventilation shafts — that served as 32nd Army headquarters. The castle stood on a high knob near the city's southern edge. East and west from there, the line was carved and constructed across the island's full twelve-mile width. Anchored by the Asakawa on the west coast, the Shuri heights in the center and a hill mass at Yonabaru on the east (Pacific) coast, this mighty system of artfully placed fortifications was like a Corregidor for the bulk — perhaps seventy thousand troops — of the 32nd Army. For all the late start, logistical difficulties, interference by American air raids, loss of the 9th Division and other setbacks, the defenders had built their most formidable positions of the Pacific War on terrain best suited for them.

Americans who inspected the works after the battle — young men who in 1945 knew little of the Japanese capacity for toil — could hardly credit that they had been completed in under a year. "I couldn't believe those underground forts," one Marine said, speaking for thousands. "Two-tiered quarters, running water, everything beautifully engineered — it was like ships inside the hills. That's why you never saw a Jap most of the time: they'd be bombed, bombarded, napalmed — and safe inside those thousands of caves. And caves with mouths so small you wouldn't see them until you were almost right on them and they started shooting. Bingo!"

In and out of the caves, hidden positions were placed for the best flat-trajectory fire directly on areas where attackers would have no cover or concealment, and for the best protection, often in compartments radiating from the tips of trenches. Major and minor strongpoints were integrated to provide intersecting, interlocking fields of fire for artillery, mortar, machine gun and small-arms fire, and the vantage points from the heights facilitated their coordination for rare accuracy, economy and effect. Mounted on tracks, artillery pieces could be rolled to the mouth of their camouflaged cave or emplacement, fired once or twice and rolled back out of sight, some around a bend, before their positions could be fixed — as in the north, but with thirty times more guns. Little zeroing in was required because everything had been pinpointed on a tight grid. In short, every boulder, depression and clump of trees was covered. The attackers would have to advance fully exposed; the defenders were relatively safe so long as they stayed hidden.

A network of trenches, galleries, caves and tunnels — some complexes almost two miles long — featured the added advantage of exits at both ends and sometimes on the flanks of the hills. Careful "engineering" of unit deployment allowed limited resources to be shifted and concentrated through that network to meet battle needs as they developed. All this, in addition to improved living quarters in the larger fortifications, was the best that Colonel Yahara, the brilliant operations officer, and General Cho, the fiercely goading chief of staff, had been able to devise and demand from their troops, the indefatigable diggers and movers of earth, during the year of preparation. Fine brains managing prodigious labor had produced a defensive tour de force.*

---

*A Marine intelligence report summarized the advantage of what it called Okinawa's cave-defense system: "1. It affords all-around protection for infantry from naval gunfire, air strikes, and artillery fire. 2. It affords fire positions for small arms, automatic weapons, and even artillery. 3. It affords space for headquarters, storage, and barracks and makes them relatively safe. 4. It is a system of mutually supporting strongpoints. 5. It is a defense in depth and offers opportunities for withdrawal actions involving relatively small casualties by utilizing reverse slope or flank exits. 6. It offers good cover and concealment for individual riflemen and automatic weapons." And so on. Once again, American reconnaissance had failed, as it would continue to fail even with its much improved technology in the Vietnam War, to uncover the nature and magnitude of the defenses as well as the number of defenders, which it underestimated by almost 40 percent. (Intelligence failures in the Persian Gulf War, both on the battlefield and in the assessment and destruction of Iraq's nuclear facilities, differed in specifics but were in some ways similar.) The same summary confirmed that the full significance of caves with more than one exit would become clear only later. "When a firefight [i.e., shooting] occurred and it was necessary [for

Military histories rightly dwell on Ushijima's "maze of caves, interconnecting tunnels well stocked with grenades, [with] approaches well mined and covered by barbed wire [and] supported by fierce mortar, artillery and machine gun fire," but it may be enough to say that Americans began speaking of "the Little Siegfried Line" and learning that it was manned by an enemy as formidable as the Germans. By early May, the general nature of the Japanese resistance on the island's southern third had become clear, and it was the worst possible kind for an offensive campaign, fought entirely from skillful underground complexes under commanders whose ultimate purpose was to die in combat. The American optimism of early April was replaced by an acceptance that Okinawa would be no exception to the Japanese rule of savage fighting for every rise, hill, tomb and cave. On the contrary, it promised to be the war's harshest confirmation of the rule until the even bloodier fighting that would have to follow on the mainland.

Against such opposition, it seemed sensible to take one's time, blasting and blasting again with every available shell before advancing with bodies — which is what the forty thousand troops of the Army's 7th and 96th Divisions had been doing almost since L-day. While the 6th Marines were racing for Okinawa's north, the Army was bearing the brunt of the warfare on a hard grind south. The first serious barrier, the northernmost from Shuri, stood only a few miles below the landing beaches. Five days after L-day, strongpoints there slowed the advance of many Army units to less than a crawl. They were forced to attack Cactus Ridge and the Pinnacle again and again before taking them, with heavy casualties. (Although hills and rises were identified by numbers on the map, the customary American nicknaming began immediately.) The Pinnacle, atop which Commodore Perry's party may have planted an American flag ninety-two years earlier, was only some forty feet high. It served as an introduction to rises that seemed piddling until the attackers' approach prompted fire from concealed caves, bunkers and a collection of stone and concrete tombs converted to pillboxes. The tactical mean-

---

the defenders] to reinforce the units on the forward slope, reinforcements were never sent out of the exits on the forward slope. Instead, they were sent out of exits on the right and left flanks and rear of the hill to deliver flanking fire. Also, this enabled them to assume more advantageous positions. By using side exits, reinforcements could also be sent from the units on one hill to a hard-pressed garrison on an adjacent hill position." Many attackers did not fully grasp this strength-sustaining mechanism or understand why Japanese fire remained so intense after all the American fire into their positions. But all saw the gory results.

ing of interlocking fire from adjacent rises and hills became clear to everyone. It left no weak point to attack.

Those small fortresses and even smaller ones in between had given just a taste of what lay ahead. On April 9, two battalions of the 96th Division's 383rd Infantry Regiment launched a major attack on seemingly unimpressive Kakazu Ridge, which actually anchored a major defensive line some four miles north of the main Shuri Line. Its defenders repulsed powerful thrusts. Soon both Army divisions were engaged. It took one seven days and over eleven hundred casualties to advance six thousand yards. It took the other three days of intense attack to capture a single small hill in a line studded with them. Kakazu Ridge remained untaken.

After a week's delay, Army units tried again, on April 19, as part of a general offensive against the whole line, the Japanese side of which was softened up with the biggest bang of the entire Pacific War so far. Three hundred and twenty-four American artillery pieces fired nineteen thousand shells at enemy positions. Eighteen warships joined the immense bombardment; 650 planes dropped bombs and napalm and fired rockets and machine guns. This was the "industrial" aspect of the American way of warfare: before the end of the campaign, Army and Marine field guns alone would fire 1,766,352 rounds.

But they were far less effective than ordnance statistics implied against the Japanese way of fighting there, which was to stay underground, ignore casualties and rush out to fight when the bombardment let up. However restricted and weakened by the bombardment, Japanese soldiers retained the power to fire rifles, machine guns, mortars and artillery pieces at chosen moments. Some perfectly positioned antitank guns wreaked havoc until American infantrymen could knock them out. In one small action below Kakazu Ridge, those guns and squads armed with satchel charges — the kind that had wounded Tadashi Kojo when it accidentally exploded — swiftly destroyed or immobilized twenty-two of thirty American tanks. The situation was so favorable for a counterattack that Ushijima ignored his own prohibition of them and ordered a small one. Soon nearly sixty American tanks were blown up or captured.

When Americans managed to gouge openings in the line, the defenders rushed to seal them, using their network of tunnels and hidden trenches. Hole after hole was plugged, day after day. "You can't bypass a Jap," an Army officer lamented, "because a Jap doesn't know when he's bypassed." Kakazu Ridge wasn't taken until April 24, when Army commanders discovered that its defenders had withdrawn, hidden by a fog and an artillery barrage the previous night, to the next series of more formidable hills about a mile farther south.

Still, the Americans *were* advancing, however slowly and painfully. Prudent minds still considered it safest and surest to tread ahead cautiously against the unusually difficult opposition, relying on sheer weight of metal to efface it. That was the conviction of most of the 10th Army's staff, including General Buckner, commander of the 155,000 American troops on the ground, who had been present in the bunker when Paul Dunfrey reported the findings of his reconnaissance probe.

Simon Bolivar Buckner, Jr., was a stolid man who liked to take as few risks as possible. If it had been up to him alone, Okinawa might have been less costly in American infantry casualties — but only at the expense of greater naval losses over a longer period, among other strategic considerations. (Those considerations did not include the welfare of the native population, whose suffering was bound to increase with the length of the campaign.)

Buck Buckner had soldiered for thirty-seven years since graduating from West Point, in 1908. Exemplary service before, after and during World War I lifted him to the rank of brigadier general in 1940, over a year before Pearl Harbor, and to lieutenant general two years before L-day. As much as a parallel was possible in two countries of such contrasting culture and traditions, Lieutenant General Simon Buckner was an American version of Lieutenant General Mitsuru Ushijima. Like Ushijima's, his upbringing and training seem to have pointed him toward his command on Okinawa almost from birth. In Buckner's case, birth was in Kentucky. His father, a Confederate Civil War general and hero who escaped from a Union prison and later surrendered Fort Donelson to General Grant, attained the rank of lieutenant general, and later had a distinguished civilian career that included the governorship of Kentucky.

Big, physically tough Buckner may have been less extolled and a shade less prominent in the American military establishment than Ushijima in the Japanese. But he was equally devoted to soldiering and only soldiering, and his combination of attributes made him one of the most respected and popular of the Army's top brass. As Ushijima had commanded the Imperial Military Academy, Buckner had had the same honor as commandant of West Point in the late 1930s, where he was straightforward, fair and very demanding, especially of the cadets' physical conditioning. A punctilious cadet himself, he liked his charges to be the same. He was also the picture of a general, down to rugged good looks topped by thick white hair. At fifty-eight, a year older than Ushijima, he kept himself in probably even better shape. To one of his soldiers he seemed "big, handsome, ruddy, strong-bodied."

More to the point, the leading Army schoolmaster, as he was known for his long experience as a student and teacher in the highest staff schools, had a firm command of battle strategy and tactics acquired in study and in demanding field assignments. He led the American campaign in the Aleutian Islands in 1943, and his decoration for "exceptionally distinguished and meritorious service" was more than the standard Army boilerplate. Although a commanding officer's personal example was generally less important to American troops than to Japanese, GIs generally admired Buckner. He trained his men hard but his commanding presence was free of arrogance. As much as any infantryman could have positive feelings about anyone at headquarters, most of the men on Okinawa felt that the commander and his staff were a skilled, veteran collection of officers.

Buckner had assumed command of the 10th Army in August 1944, the month when Ushijima took command of the much smaller 32nd Army. If the campaign against Formosa hadn't been canceled, he would have led it with the same force. On Okinawa, he was commanding three Marine divisions as well as four Army ones. But to the considerable extent that he went by the book, it was the Army book. His instinct was to defeat the enemy by applying the Army's standard relentless use of superior force. Moreover, he naturally leaned toward the conservative side of the generally conservative Army; except for a brief tour in aviation, he was an infantryman with special skills in tanks. "We will take our time and kill the Japanese gradually," he had told correspondents about his intentions for May. And now, during May: "You will see many Japanese killed. You will see them gradually rolled back . . . but you won't see spectacular advances because this isn't that kind of fighting."

But the Old Man of the Mountain, as he was called, was under pressure to fight something more imaginative than the step-by-solid-step kind of war he had planned before L-day. The pressure was applied by, among others, his superior, Fleet Admiral Chester W. Nimitz. Nimitz was the most prominent admiral to have urged Okinawa over Formosa as the next target after Iwo Jima. This gave an extra measure to his concern about the progress of the campaign, about which he had not shared the early optimism. After the first week's relative ease, other brass contemplated quick victory. Vice Admiral Richmond Turner, Iceberg's overall commander, who had issued the "land the landing force" order, sent him a jocular radio signal on April 8, the day after the sinking of *Yamato:* I MAY BE CRAZY, BUT IT LOOKS LIKE THE JAPS HAVE QUIT THE WAR, AT LEAST IN THIS SECTION. Nimitz's succinct reply reflected his character: DELETE ALL AFTER "CRAZY." It was the following day that Army units first encountered the Little Siegfried Line in the lumbering shape of Kakazu Ridge. Soon Admiral Turner's overconfidence would switch to hot-tempered criticism of General Buckner.

Buckner could not have pleased everyone. All overall commanders everywhere had to reckon with a fundamental difference between the Army's and Marine Corps's fighting styles, the Army generally attacking much more deliberately with heavier weapons than the leaner Marines, who moved out faster with less equipment and more initial risk. Army forces usually had the wherewithal for campaigns of attrition and tended to fight them as long as the defense remained organized and powerful. Marine leadership, always in a hurry, thanks to limitations of time and supply, believed that fewer men would be lost in the end by constant advance, if possible with flanking movements, than by burrowing into foxholes while softening them up — and allowing the enemy's artillery and mortars to work them over at the same time.

The Marine credo had been developed chiefly in smaller campaigns than this one, and against less entrenched opposition, where the men did what they were best trained for: storm beachheads, win quick victories in small areas, ship out to the next destination. And it was not a logical certainty that units moving forward rapidly suffered fewer casualties than those which waited in position until weather, support and other factors were favorable. But rapid advance did boost morale, on which the Corps heavily depended.

Not having read a word about strategy or tactics, Dick Whitaker was full of talk about "assault," "take," "capture." He'd been a Marine long enough to know that "our philosophy was advance, advance, advance. It became a battle only when the advance was stopped for some reason." Every teenage private knew he wasn't winning if he wasn't advancing. When the strongpoints on Okinawa stopped the Marines now, in early May, it was almost inevitable that some of their staff and higher field officers proposed outflanking them with another amphibious operation well south of the Shuri Line. This wasn't entirely an Army-Marine conflict. A few high Army officers had already pressed Buckner to land a force farther south. One was Major General John Hodge, commander of the XXIV Corps that comprised the 7th and 96th Divisions. The commander of the 77th Army

Division — which would be badly bloodied by Tadashi Kojo's 22nd Regiment when it joined the line in the south after taking Kerama Retto and Ie Shima — agreed. But the more overt pressure to move Buckner from his slug-it-out strategy came from the Marine commanders, perhaps unaware of their scattering of allies among the Army generals.

Unhappy with what they saw as Buckner's lack of appreciation for maneuver, the dissidents, who included Major General Lemuel Shepherd, the commander of the 6th Marine Division which had taken the north, wanted to shorten the campaign with a daring, disorienting end run.* They specified that it should be made by the 2nd Marine Division, which had gone into reserve status after feinting the landing in the south on L-day in order to deter Ushijima from moving reinforcements to the real landing beaches. (Pretending to have been driven off on April 1, the division repeated the ruse the following day before withdrawing to Saipan.) That division, a veteran of amphibious assaults, was now to return to the place of its feint, the southeast beaches of Minatogawa on the Pacific coast, which was promising enough to have been an alternative site for the real landings. Supported by these arguments and by General Alexander Van-

---

*Douglas MacArthur's use of a Marine division for a more daring amphibious strike behind the enemy lines at Korea five years later led to the quick retreat of the powerful North Korean forces, although that is no proof General Shepherd and the others were right on Okinawa. Coming from the Army school, MacArthur was cautious, but the same General Shepherd worked closely with him in planning and executing the bold Inchon landing. Shepherd was assisted by an exceptionally resourceful staff officer named Victor Krulak, his Chief of Operations on Okinawa.

The strategic issues in Vietnam 20 years later were not precisely parallel because there it was the allegiance of the peasantry that needed to be won more than territory. Still, some elements of the Army-Marine conflict remained the same, especially the determination of the commanding officer, a man much in Buckner's educational and professional mold, to win with pulverizing firepower. The Marine generals, including Victor Krulak, tried to convince General William Westmoreland that the standard Army approach couldn't work in Vietnam. But "for Westmoreland to have conceded they were right," Neil Sheehan observed, "would have been to deny himself the war he wanted to wage of mass troop movements, artillery barrages, skies filled with helicopters and fighter-bombers, and the thunder of B-52s."

On Okinawa, over 14 million tons of bombs alone were dropped on Japanese positions by mid-May — without significantly denting the heart of the defense. Stubbornly hoping to hit the enemy so hard that infantry would eventually be able to advance easily, most Pacific Area planners overestimated the value of massed artillery fire and naval bombardment, assisted by air strikes. They also consistently underestimated the enemy's acuity, resourcefulness and thoroughness of preparations, together with his bravery and endurance — an error perhaps furthered, as in Vietnam, by assumptions of racial superiority. Buckner's intelligence reports in particular consistently overstated the damage to Japanese installations. For all the terror the bombardments struck in the Japanese and misery they caused by keeping them underground, enemy soldiers were relatively safe if they remained in their caves and fortifications until American infantrymen were in shooting range.

degrift, the Marine Corps commandant who visited Okinawa and attended the flag-raising ceremony in the north, the Marine strategists pressed their case.* They were convinced that Buckner's predictable frontal assault took more time and cost more lives in the end than quick, hard strikes that would keep the enemy from making his skillful retreats to the next prepared barriers — as at Kakazu and elsewhere. Such withdrawals at the last nocturnal moment before the besieged barriers were overwhelmed were allowing the Japanese to sustain their defenses just as they had planned them.

Buckner's rejection of these proposals was grounded in soldierly resolve — he had made up his mind — and in the very caution of which he was accused. Kamikazes had cost the Tenth Army two ammunition supply ships. The commander and his staff insisted that another front would break down his supply system (although the 2nd Marine Division, which was on alert status on Saipan, insisted it had enough supplies and logistical support to sustain itself for at least a month of fighting on Okinawa). Buckner also wanted to keep the 2nd Marine Division fresh for the July landings planned for a tiny Ryukyu island halfway from Okinawa to the Japanese mainland. Besides, the general argued, the 32nd Army's tactics and artillery strength and the steep cliffs dominating Minatogawa and other possible landing sites, from which Japanese guns had a direct line of fire to the coral-strewn beaches below, would have made a new amphibious operation "another Anzio but worse." A few high naval officers also doubted proper cover could be mounted for another landing there, although high-ranking Japanese officers believed Minatogawa would have made a good landing beach for the Americans, and Colonel Yahara was convinced that they would take advantage of it soon because it would be their most damaging move.

Buckner surely wouldn't have changed his mind if he had known that a landing below Shuri would have largely averted a catastrophe in store for Okinawan civilians. He might have reconsidered if his intelligence had suggested what else the Little Siegfried Line had in store for the 10th Army itself. But it didn't; his confident prediction of hard but not overly hard victory was based on the optimism of ignorance. With reporters, he emanated his usual firm competence without rigidity. He took the bull by the horns at one press conference now, opening it by comparing a secondary plan of attack to a

---

*Vandegrift actually joined a few others who preferred a site farther north, but still behind the Shuri Line, in Nakagusuku Bay, which would be renamed Buckner Bay, with no irony intended.

general's navel: "You'd look totally stupid without one, but it serves no purpose." This disarmed most of the reporters but not all the best ones, including Homer Bigart of the *New York Herald Tribune,* one of the few whose articles had dealt with Okinawa's larger strategic and logistic problems. Bigart's criticism of Buckner for not staging a second landing to catch the Japanese in a pincer movement sparked a heated controversy back on the home front six weeks after the event. Although politicians and journalists knew but a fraction of the hardship caused by the Shuri Line, that was enough for recrimination. In late May and early June, American newspapers would publically criticize Buckner's conduct of the campaign. By that time, the Marine Corps commandant had returned to Washington and its resident press corps — surely not coincidental timing.*

Newspapers predictably gave more prominence to accusation than defense of Buckner. Some complained about his devotion to wooden frontal tactics; others went much further, suggesting the "ultraconservative" campaign was a "fiasco" and "a worse example of military incompetence than Pearl Harbor." Admiral Nimitz joined those who deplored the criticism, especially at a press conference of his own on Guam, where he, a team player by nature, applauded Buckner and praised the Army's "magnificent performance." But that admirable exercise in tribute was intended to mask interservice friction, and it too came in June, after the fact. Perhaps the admiral didn't want another major landing by then, but now, when it mattered, his reaction to Buckner's leadership was quite different. When the advance was stalled and the four hundred planes of the Third Floating Chrysanthemum swarmed over the fleet and the debate became most heated and relevant — when interservice wrangling, in fact, threatened to break out into the open — Nimitz flew from Guam to Okinawa for some straight talk with Buckner.

Like the Marines, the modest admiral wanted faster results in order to reduce the kamikazes' unprecedented damage to his fleet. He may also have been having second thoughts about the whole cam-

---

*MacArthur also joined the controversy, but only after the end of the campaign. The general accused the commanders on Okinawa of unnecessarily "sacrificing thousands of American soldiers." Capping yet another strategic argument, he specified that there had been no need to drive the Japanese off the island: having pushed them into the southern third, there was no need to push farther, since the territory already taken well served the purpose of providing airfields, anchorages and land for mobilizing troops for the invasion of the mainland. The remnants of the 32nd Army holed up in the southern enclave could not threaten that use, whatever little forays they made at night. MacArthur claimed the casualties those forays cost would have been far fewer than in the straight-ahead assault on the best fortifications. In time, the Japanese would have died on the vine without the need for such sacrifice.

paign — the "ill-considered decision to take Okinawa by storm," as one historian described it, that left "no other way for Buckner but straight ahead into the sausage machine." In any case, the huge toll in American ships and crews deeply disturbed Nimitz, and he was uncharacteristically sharp in a meeting with Buckner on April 23. Was the general adding to the shocking toll of sailors' lives by being too slow and timid, as many naval officers believed? Nimitz told Buckner to speed things up. Buckner countered that the ground campaign was an Army operation, *his* business. Conceding this, the ordinarily soft-spoken Nimitz restated his point without mincing words. "I'm losing a ship and a half a day. So if this line isn't moving in five days, we'll get someone up here to move it so we can all get out from under these damn kamikaze attacks." (Although this of course went unreported to 10th Army troops, the magic of scuttlebut quickly informed them of the substance of the commanders' conversation. A lowly Marine's diary entry a few days later speculated that "Perhaps Nimetz [*sic*] put a spark up Buckner's but [*sic*].")

Whatever the merits of the conflicting strategies, however many tens of thousands of lives might or might not have been saved by dropping characteristic Army caution, it must be said that lack of information and imagination played a large part in the ultimate decision, together with the tendency to underestimate the Japanese that had been present from the start. In retrospect, the lack of imagination seems to approach lack of concern. Some of the bloodiest weeks in American history were coming, and when the results are compared with the planning, the latter appears hugely inadequate. As so often in war, the larger possibilities and potential consequences, which ought to have been clear from previous wars, were set aside or not raised at all. Buckner had already chosen his tactical objectives, and his intent to reach them with firepower and more firepower remained unchanged. He would never make the end run behind the Shuri bastions, but he did try to get the line moving again, partly by exchanging one of his Army divisions for the 6th Marine Division. His order for that exchange came on the fifth day of the five Nimitz had given him. It is what delivered Paul Dunfrey's platoon down from the north to the defensive fury at the Asakawa on May 9 and 10, ten days after all of Okinawa was supposed to be in American hands, according to the plans.

The Army got the best food, best equipment, best weapons, best artillery. The Marines got all the crap left behind. Sometimes the only way to get replacements and ammunition was to go into Army supply dumps and scrounge — practically steal the stuff. They tried to fight by relying on all

their supplies because they weren't going to use their own lives — and when that failed, the Marines had to go in and clean out the enemy. This is why there were those bitter feelings about the Army, and they were justified.
    — Norris Buchter, 22nd Marines

We believed, probably correctly, that we were put in the field to do more at less cost than other servicemen. But maybe Marines took a perverse pleasure in being so spartan.
    — Clyde McAvoy, 4th Marines

We passed the 27th Army Division as we went in to relieve them. Every one of us felt the only reason we were going south and they were going north was that they had fucked up again.
    — Dick Whitaker, 29th Marines

We were really disgusted with the Army in this operation. Every time a shell went off, they dug in deeper. You'd think they were holed in instead of the Japs.
    — Buzzy Fox, 22nd Marines, letter home

The Army division exchanged for the 6th Marines was a National Guard unit from New York that had been sent into overseas combat — a rare exception in American practice — with little reorganization. No one who hasn't fought in the "killing zone" within rifle range of the enemy has a right to criticize those who have. But the record shows that the 27th Division, having gone to combat with less than the usual preparation, had a higher than average percentage of inexperienced officers. (A few of the Division's wounded were heard to remark that some of their brass were better politicians than warriors, since National Guard promotions often owe more to political than to military skill.) On Saipan, where it fought the year before, its failure to match the achievements of other units in the bloody line had led to controversy.*

The 27th's sixteen thousand troops were roughly the same human stuff as in other divisions: "kids who came from the same places we did," as a heroic Marine named Daniel Dereschuk put it. Even most Marine leaders acknowledge that the man-to-man difference between Marine and Army troops in action is insignificant. If anything, therefore, this proves only the importance of training — especially, in this case, for senior officers. On Okinawa, where the 27th was sent

---

*Controversy was a staple of the few joint Army-Marine operations in the Pacific, swaggering Marines almost always jeering GIs for their alleged inferiority in everything. It went much further and higher on Saipan, where Marine General Holland (Howlin' Mad) Smith, a corps commander, was so displeased by the 27th's performance that he relieved its commander, sent it back into reserve and swore never to use it again.

into the line on April 9, when the going in the south got rough for the other Army divisions, it saw heavy action during the rest of the month, principally at Kakazu Ridge and two deadly strongpoints — Item Pocket and the Urasoe Mura Escarpment — of the next major Japanese barrier south of Kakazu. It lost many men but made slow headway, perhaps necessarily slow against the superbly prepared positions,* and eventually achieved a vital penetration of the enemy line. Many of its companies distinguished themselves, but two fled in disarray from intense fire, one of the rare such instances during the entire Okinawan campaign.

Few Marines knew anything specific about the record of the 27th on Saipan or Okinawa — or on Makin or Eniwetok, where it also fought. Even fewer knew that it had originally been in "floating reserve" status at Okinawa, earmarked for garrison duty after the island would be taken. Or that, despite slowdowns and setbacks at the deadly positions against which it was hurriedly committed, it often fought hard and well, sometimes splendidly, by normal infantry measures. Sixth Marines in particular had no idea that Ushijima's real defense had been prepared in that southernmost eighth of the island from which they were most distant. But the facts would have made little difference to most Marines, almost all of whom disliked and distrusted all Army units as such. They had an "underlying contempt," as a critically admiring corpsman who tended their wounded put it, for all non-Marines apart from chaplains and corpsmen. "If you weren't a Marine, you weren't much of anything."

Special contempt for the Army in particular was built into their elite training, one of the prods that charged them to do more and better, advance faster against more seemingly unassailable positions, than miserable soldiers. William Manchester has told of some Marines sending two souvenir-hunting Army officers to their almost certain deaths on Okinawa by pointing them in the direction of Japanese snipers. If this was true, it was an "awesome example," as Dick Whitaker called it, of the bad feelings between the 6th Marine Division and 27th Army Division in particular — but not an unbelievable example. Every Marine considered every soldier a "doggie," and barked at him, Manchester added. Most Marines more or less despised dog-

*Item Pocket, a large rise located in the I or Item grid square on the American battle map, was one of Okinawa's best natural defensive positions and most cleverly prepared, a particularly lethal citadel of skillfully mounted armament with no way to approach it except by exposure to its many bands of interlocking fire. The cluster of hills included a series of coral and limestone ridges, all extensively tunneled for movement of men and supplies, some by a narrow-gauge railroad. All also protected the others with perfectly positioned machine gun and mortar emplacements. Taking the interlocking ridges required repeated feats of arms and bravery from one of the 27th Division's infantry regiments.

gies all the way up to their top dog in the Pacific, General of the Army Douglas MacArthur.*

Although Marines had taken higher casualties on many islands, at this point it was the reverse on Okinawa. When the 6th Marines were sent south in late April and early May, Army casualties were seven times greater than theirs. The many dangerously weakened Army units included the 383rd Regiment, which, although badly mauled during its attacks on Kakazu Ridge, had to relieve the 382nd Regiment because the latter was down to half strength, double that of a third regiment, the 305th. (The Army's 383rd Infantry Regiment continued to perform superbly.) The 27th Division had also been severely shot up during its hardest two weeks in April, which cost almost as many casualties as both Marine divisions suffered during the whole of the month, more than either would take during their hardest weeks just ahead. The 27th's losses at Item Pocket three miles north of the Shuri Line were proportionately the highest of the entire campaign.

If Marines knew none of this, they fumed with the knowledge that they were indeed less well supplied than their larger sister service. Some lads on Okinawa with no previous contact of any kind with the Army and great curiosity about it gaped at their first sight of just a small Army unit's "whole great fleet" of trucks. The grudge Marines nursed for their poverty, a combination of self-pity and defiance, served as another prod to show up the fat, dumb doggies by striking harder and faster with less. They also felt entitled to appropriate Army treasures. One June evening, Dick Whitaker would come upon an Army tank unit setting up its mess tent — itself a startling extravagance for Marines in combat, who lived entirely in holes and ate rations. Whitaker and a company mate named Jack Crary entered the tent to find a mess sergeant inside, together with a stack of canned hams. Ham was a great luxury after months of fighting on Marine subsistence. Crary asked for a can, and the sergeant told him to fuck off, whereupon Crary unslung and pointed his rifle. "Too bad you feel that way, but we're taking that fucking ham anyway!" Judging that this rabid animal, a typical Marine, was serious, the sergeant handed him the can and the two interlopers backed out of the tent

---

*Marines were convinced the supreme commander and national hero not only gave them the hardest, most dangerous assignments but made them do without proper equipment and supplies. They sang bawdy songs about the master of self-publicity and the theatrical gesture. Manchester also told of coaching Okinawan children to beg for cigarettes from passing Army units — except that the children weren't saying "Give me a cigarette" as they thought but "General MacArthur eats shit." Another chant taught that the 27th Division ate the same.

like Hollywood bank robbers — until Whitaker saw his favorite weapon, a Thompson submachine gun, hanging on the tent's center-pole. "Well, as long as Jack's taking the ham," he reasoned with impeccable Marine logic, "I'm taking that." He grabbed the second prize as the two made a stealthy escape into the Okinawan night.*

Even Marines of the lowest rank and interest in military theory had a practical sense of the differences in fighting styles. They knew they were not only trained but also organized and supplied, or undersupplied, for fast assaults as opposed to the "ponderous" Army's "plodding" advances, attempted only when an overwhelming numerical advantage had been assembled, together with supplies "that would stagger any Marine officer," as a veteran put it. Or, as jaundiced Marines sneered, Army advances were not made at all. "Those lumps just stayed in their foxholes — and what foxholes! like houses! — and hoped artillery would do their jobs for them." (The scorn would intensify when the Marines, caught in the enemy's deadly fire in the south, heard that one of the 27th Division's first actions when it replaced them on mopping-up and occupation duties in the north was to close their brothel. "And after all the trouble we went to setting it up, those doggies couldn't even run a cat house!" a private would wail.) Although there were many stirring exceptions to the rule in the huge Okinawan campaign, it remained generally true that Marines' determination to advance with relatively small forces against all opposition was usually fiercer than the Army's. Recognizing this difference, most soldiers thought of Marines as gung-ho savages or idiots who craved glory at any cost.

Marine "push" had been amply illustrated during the race to take the north. On April 10, after one of the 6th Division's two regiments had cleaned out some heavy enemy artillery and secured much of the large Motobu Peninsula, its colonel asked his boss, the division commander, for a twenty-four-hour break to give his tired men a rest

---

*Although Whitaker happily used the tommy gun during the rest of the campaign, Marine thefts occasionally produced unwanted side effects. An artillery battalion driver on his way to pick up supplies on the beach one day spied an unguarded Army supply depot and loaded his truck with whatever he could grab quickest. Back with his own unit, he found the entire load to be canned pineapple. Forty-five years later, some of the "boys" who had gorged themselves on too much of that fabulous fruit treat still wouldn't touch it. In one of thousands of equivalent situations among the Japanese, a private in Captain Kojo's starving battalion was permitted a go at a supply cave whose rice sacks had gone rotten. He grabbed a tin of what seemed like wheat flour instead, imagining delicious boiled dumplings as he courageously lugged the tin through a shower of American bombs and shells to his own unit's cave. "We're having dumplings! In just a few minutes — dumplings!" The famished men held their breath as the can was opened. Forty-five years later, Kojo's former soldier still remembered that episode whenever he saw ground pepper, the contents of *his* prize.

and a chance to change their socks. The heavily decorated veteran of many hard battles was relieved of his command the following day — and although angered by this, his men were also proud of the relentlessness with which they were driven.*

Finally, the Marines up north had heard many rumors about the performance of the "useless" 27th Division, and the nearness of mortal danger gave rumor the advantage over truth — even if the truth had been available. The stories ranged from the division's being pinned down and unable to move, which was partially true, to its having left a Marine division exposed when it broke and ran on Saipan, which was the kind of exaggeration on which Marine scuttlebut thrived. The 27th had supposedly let its attacks go to "disaster" because it had lost control of its units, had "lost its colors" when officers "couldn't get their men to move," was so low on morale and integrity that it couldn't even recover its dead — the most unforgivable failure to Marines, since honoring their dead fused Marines' half-mystical comradeship. "So the 27th's behavior was inexcusable — and that's not just rumor because I was one of the Marines who recovered some of their dead for them under enemy fire. Simply notorious!"

But other rumors were silly, and Marines, ignorant of what the Army had been facing in the south for almost a month, exulted in spreading them. Admiral William Halsey, who alternated commanding the 5th Fleet, had supposedly "told Buckner that he was going to pull his Navy and Marines out of Okinawa if he couldn't get the Army to move its fat ass." What most bothered 6th Division Marines with access to real news from the south were reports that Japanese firepower, especially artillery, was devastating, and that their own brothers in the 1st Marine Division were being killed unnecessarily because the 27th Division was leaving them exposed on the flanks (as they heard it had done to Marines on Saipan) by not advancing on schedule to silence that artillery. And naturally the 6th Division also feared that this would mean the end of that other, "good" rumor — that they would soon be out of Okinawa and back on Guam.

The transfer itself could have provided a war movie's comic relief. When an Army jeep drove into Marine territory in the north during the last week in April, the Headquarters Company of Peter Milo, the

---

*General Lemuel Shepherd, the division commander who dispatched the battle-tested but compassionate colonel, would go on to become the Marine Corps commandant. His operations officer on Okinawa, Lieutenant Colonel Victor Krulak, was the officer who 20 years later would try to dissuade the Army in Vietnam from attempting to blast its way to victory with sheer weight of metal and explosive.

former New York policeman, were building showers and otherwise making life comfortable for themselves. They exchanged no words with the doggies in the vehicle, who drove to a small native building, nailed a board to its door and drove off. Milo was first to reach the door. "This Building Reserved for the 27th Division Chaplain," he read. You must be kidding — for who? Everybody knew the 27th Army Division was fooling around down south, so what would its chaplain be doing up here?

Confirmation of the dreaded answer came at assembly the same morning, when a major announced that their division was about to replace the 27th. General Buckner had ordered the switch, and the Marine commanding officer had promised to make up for the 27th's lost time.

By the time the two units actually changed places days later, Marine wags had posted road signs reading "Marines and Men" pointing south, and "Army" or "27th Division" pointing north, together with "USO" and "Rest Area." Almost all Marines shouted cocky abuse at the "retreating" doggies, whose trucks sometimes passed within inches of theirs. Some friendly GIs tossed candy bars at Marines, who flung them back with additional insults and barks. A few soldiers pretended to film Marines, mocking their supposed hunger for glory and publicity. "Go ahead and bark," some shouted back to the Leathernecks. "You bastards live like dogs anyway." The greenest Marines were likely to fling the sharpest digs; combat veterans tended to be less antagonistic. But all cast an envious eye at Army riches. When a 27th Division truck tipped over the soft shoulder of a meager road, a group of 4th Marines ran to help, saw that the doggies' carbines were better and stole them, running off while the others were reloading the truck.

Forty years later, 6th Division veterans would dwell on the exchange, that fleeting interval in their weeks or months on Okinawa, a demonstration of their greater ease in talking about the peripheral aspects of military life rather than combat. For what really made the memory durable was that it marked the trauma of returning to battle from the relative comfort and safety of antiguerrilla patrols and occupation duty up north. "I'd never been in combat before, so our fighting in the north surprised me," one Marine remembered. "I mean, the pretty weak opposition and few casualties. We thought we were done with Okinawa and would be leaving soon, so going back into the slog down south — that was a shock." A much mellowed veteran ventured in retrospect that the taunting of GIs was "all bravado" to mask anxiety: instead of the fantasy of going home for Christmas, they were going in to take over from the fucking 27th, which couldn't keep up its end. Another remembered that the resentment of the Army really took root only after the Marines arrived in the south "and began to get the crap kicked out of them." For it wasn't merely more combat they were returning to but hardship that surpassed almost all they had experienced.

17 · Sugar Loaf Hill

The 6th Division was up against the Sugar Loaf, main western anchorage of Shuri line, where there took place a combat not exceeded for closeness and desperation by that at the Conical or Shuri Castle itself or Iwo Jima or any other.
— Fletcher Pratt, military historian

The biggest and fiercest battle in the post V-E world was in progress last week in Okinawa. U.S. troops were advancing in the old-fashioned, inescapable way, one foot at a time against the kind of savage, rat-in-a-hole defense that only the Japanese can offer.
— *Time*, May 21, 1945

[Sugar Loaf is] the most critical local battle of the war . . . the bloodiest battlefield in the world.
— *Newsweek*, May 21 and 28

The terrain is just right for the Nips and many American boys are falling. I thank the Lord that I am in artillery. We have it bad, but not as bad as the Marine infantry.
— Thomas Hannaher, in a letter home, May 21

THREE MAIN DEFENSIVE LINES crossed Okinawa's south. The first, anchored by Kakazu Ridge and a collection of contiguous rises including Item Pocket, had been broken, chiefly by Army units, but at a cost that had started the wrangling among the American services and prompted the challenges to Buckner's judgment. The Okinawan campaign was already longer than those for Saipan and Iwo Jima, and although its eighteen thousand casualties, forty-five hundred in the week beginning May 5 alone, were still about a quarter less than Iwo Jima's, the brass knew the greatest blood-letting lay ahead. It was time to shorten it by breaking the back of the defense. The ventures of Paul Dunfrey's platoon across the muddy Asakawa on May 9 and 10 were feelers for a general offensive the following day, General Buckner's response to demands that he get moving again. The full-scale attack on May 11 was intended to penetrate the second and best line guarding Shuri.

It would take place across the full width of the island where the

10th Army was stalled, about twenty miles south of the landing beaches. The 7th Army Division was enjoying a brief rest after a brutal month taking the Pinnacle and another defensive system at a group of hills near Kochi, where Captain Kojo's battalion helped mangle it. Each of the other four divisions faced extremely formidable barriers at their places in the line. A large hill mass called Conical Hill confronted the 96th Army Division on the Pacific coast. The heights of Shuri itself awaited the 77th Army Division. On the other flank of those heights, the 1st Marine Division faced Wana Ridge and Wana Draw, a giant moat that might have been created for the slaughter of anyone mad enough to enter it. By comparison, the obstacles in the path of General Shepherd's (and Paul Dunfrey's) 6th Marine Division, just down from the north, seemed less difficult. The 6th remained on the west coast facing the East China Sea, where the Asakawa and the Asato, another river farther south, rimmed some three miles of relatively flat land.

Most of the 6th began the May 11 offensive on May 10 because the Asakawa had to be crossed and then some fairly open ground covered before the main fortifications were reached. For G (George) Company of the 2nd Battalion, 22nd Regiment, that May 10 started in the predawn darkness, but not on a pontoon bridge; in its zone, on the 6th Division's left flank, the Asakawa was shallow enough for the men to wade across. G–2–22 was a typical Marine company typically convinced it was far better than typical. Like most of the nine rifle companies in the 22nd Marines, it was made up of green new men and savvy veterans of combat elsewhere in the Pacific. The company's young commander, Captain Owen Stebbins, had fought on the Marshall Islands and Guam after graduating from Officer Candidate School. Having been wounded on Guam, he was as relieved as anyone at the ease of the company's landing on L-day and relatively painless April in Okinawa's north.

Stebbins's grandfather had owned a large ranch in Northern California. Raised on his mother's secretarial wages during the Depression, Stebbins played football for Fresno State College. The good-natured sportsman seemed to take everything in stride, giving his men, who much admired him for his combat experience and fairness, confidence that "nothing ever fazed him." But after crossing the Asakawa in that morning's dense fog, he was no less amazed by the scope and skill of the Japanese preparations than Paul Dunfrey had been in the same lake of fire. "Their camouflage was so superb even in fairly open territory that some of my men were hit by machine gun fire from five yards away. And they had the terrific discipline to hold their fire until our patrols passed and they shot them in the back. Or until our men came almost right up on top of them — so near they couldn't use mortars or grenades to knock out the machine guns or get back the wounded, who were just too close."

When two of Stebbins's three infantry platoons were pinned down almost immediately, he was faced with one of the agonizing decisions that torment company commanders in the field. A scout who had come within yards of a hidden Japanese machine gun was cut down and lay where he fell. Was he dead or feigning? Stebbins felt he couldn't attack the emplacement with grenades, mortars or heavy automatic fire if his man was alive. He risked using his binoculars, whose glint in the sun now rising over the Japanese position would make him a special target by marking him as an officer. From two hundred yards away, Stebbins saw the body wasn't moving — but hesitated to use heavy armament until he was sure. Then the element of chance took over that forever determined life and death on the line. A medical corpsman who had already saved several men by braving pinpointed hostile fire went out to try to rescue the scout while the machine gun still chattered. The wounded man was alive because he happened to have fallen into a crease in the ground, where further bullets whizzed over him. That fortuity and the corpsman saved his life, but the corpsman himself was hit and killed. When Stebbins had time to think beyond the demands of the field, he saw that twist of fate as yet another confirmation that combat was a constant roll of dice. "The element of luck is enormous. One guy's miracle is the next guy's death."

Two very long days later, Stebbins's platoons were again pinned down by heavy, accurate fire from a hill in their path. Lieutenant Colonel Horatio Woodhouse, the commander of the 2nd Battalion, had earlier assigned a platoon of tanks to attack with Stebbins's company; having crossed the Asakawa under artillery fire the previous night, the tanks stopped some eighty yards back because of increased antitank fire as the force neared that hill in Target Area 7672 G. Stebbins was in a foxhole designated an observation post, some three hundred yards forward of the company command post, where First Lieutenant Dale Bair, the company executive officer, or second in command, was positioned with the machine gun officer. The 1st Platoon was on Stebbins's right, the 2nd Platoon on his left, and the 3rd Platoon in a reserve position, just behind the company command post. Second Lieutenant Edward Ruess, leader of the 1st Platoon, dashed to consult with Stebbins in his observation post. He said that some of his men had moved onto the hill, but that he needed help because heavy fire was pinning down the rest of the platoon and inflicting casualties. "What happened to the tanks?" he asked.

Stebbins knew his first job was to plan how those tanks should move up to join the attack. Standing up for a better look at the terrain, the captain was quickly hit by three machine gun bullets. Stebbins would recuperate for several months in a hospital and then go home, whereas the same burst that raked the observation post, no doubt aimed at him, the officer, killed his runner — by that time, the single surviving rifleman in his forward observation post. Stebbins's other runners had all been hit earlier by mortar fire.

Meanwhile, Ruess had run back to his men, dodging, ducking, hitting the ground every ten yards, then jumping up and sprinting again. Platoon leaders were the officers who stood or crawled beside, or ahead of, their men in battle. Stebbins and other G Company officers knew Ruess to be among the best of many battlefield prodigies, a Marines' Marine, virtually idolized by his men for his combat leadership. He was the very picture of a rugged warrior and a model of tender concern for his platoon. Early in the morning of May 12, on the arduous way to Sugar Loaf, Stebbins had noticed a dirty bandage Ruess tried to conceal. Shot through the hand the day before, shortly after crossing the Asakawa, the lieutenant hadn't reported it and went without treatment in a battalion aid station because he would not leave his men when things were getting difficult. Stebbins also knew that Ruess would never let his platoon stay pinned down long, which is why the captain had chosen 1st Platoon to lead the way onto the "prominent hill." "Absolutely fearless" under fire, the "tiger-quick" Ruess would show himself to draw fire from — and fix the positions of — machine guns that had pinned down or hit his men. When he returned to his position below Sugar Loaf now, he tried this daring move again in an effort to locate the fire engulfing his forty-odd men. But this time there were too many concealed machine guns firing too great a volume of fire. He was killed.

The runner killed beside Stebbins in the observation post had a walkie-talkie radio that had kept Stebbins in contact with his command post farther back. Unable to locate the radio — which would be found the following day on the body, which had tumbled into some bush on a decline — Stebbins crawled to the rear until he was spotted by one of the tanks. It radioed to the command post, and stretcher bearers were dispatched from there to bring the captain back. While he was being bandaged, he told Lieutenant Colonel Woodhouse, who had run to the company command post from his battalion forward observation post, that the tanks were needed without delay.

Woodhouse took First Lieutenant Bair — who replaced Stebbins as company commander, as he himself would be replaced within a few hours — to where they could coordinate another attack on the hill. Runners were sent to the three platoons to say that Dale Bair had taken command of the company because Stebbins had been hit, and to tell the platoon leaders to ready their men for a tank-supported attack that Bair would lead. The leaders were to consult with Bair about the plan of attack. The hill had to be taken quickly because fire from there was holding up the entire advance in the area.

The battle casualties among the lieutenants serving as platoon leaders had been especially heavy in the two days following the crossing of the Asakawa. Stebbins had also lost the leader of his 3rd Platoon on that same advance — to mortar fire in the morning fog of May 10. His place was taken by Platoon Sergeant Edmund De Mar, the Brooklyn boy who had wondered where Pearl Harbor was when cursing the Japanese on Pearl Harbor Sunday. Now twenty-five years old, De Mar wasn't called Pops, like so many men over twenty, but Mommy, thanks to his regular admonitions to his teenage charges during their training on Guadalcanal. "Do I have to be a mother and father to you?"

When the runner arrived with the messages from Bair, Mommy was in a protected little position near the company command post, several minutes' run behind where Captain Stebbins had been hit. Despite the delay during the previous hours and the casualties to the company's two other platoons, the new obstacle gave no indication that it would be uglier than others in the two miles of bloodshed since the Asakawa. The "prominent hill," as the Americans referred to it, stood at the end of a slight draw that formed a corridor leading up to it. A similar rise called Charlie Hill had fallen the day before to the 1st Battalion, after a day and a half of tank and infantry assault supported by naval gunfire. To the wounded Stebbins, this new hill, stark and barren except for a few scrubby trees, looked no more ominous than "previous hills and other steep inclines; we had absolutely no reason to expect it would be any different from the day before." To De Mar, studying it again from a few hundred yards north, it seemed "just another lump, a brownish incline with a little knoll on top."

G Company's return to combat had been hard. After suffering only two casualties — both from battle fatigue — during its weeks in the north, it had lost nine men to exceptionally heavy artillery, mortar and small-arms fire in just two days in the south, including five killed on the first day alone. The 3rd Platoon had fully shared in these casualties on the way from the Asakawa, escaping from one action only with the aid of a smoke screen. But the company would look back to those two days pushing south to TA 7672 G as almost easy going. At least everyone could still keep track of the killed and wounded. Soon replacements coming up would get cut down before the men learned their names.

Actually, De Mar was reassigning the functions of the missing men in his weakened platoon when the runner arrived with the order to meet with Lieutenant Bair. De Mar had twenty-eight men left of a full complement of forty. According to the plan, they would be joined by nineteen men still fit for action from dead Ed Ruess's 1st Platoon and be supported by the tank platoon. They would take the hill immediately because its machine guns and mortars were badly chewing up everything in sight, including other companies.

The tanks were waiting in a depression not visible from the hill. When Lieutenant Bair gave Platoon Sergeant De Mar and the replacement for Ed Ruess the plan of attack and those men reviewed it with the lieutenant commanding the tank platoon, they took the usual precaution of squatting far enough apart so that one mortar round could not hit them all. They were eager to learn one another's names to avoid calling out "Lieutenant!" or "Sergeant!" — another way of making themselves a priority target to snipers who shot first at anyone in command. The plan was straightforward: De Mar and his men on the left, Bair and the reduced 1st Platoon on the right, and the tanks moving out at the same time. A machine gun section also would give fire support as they went up.

The tank commander wanted assurance that he wouldn't be left "high and dry." Tanks were a great advantage to the infantry they supported, and the American 10th Army had vastly more of them than the Japanese 32nd Army. But in that kind of combat, with such accurate enemy fire, even the best American Shermans also represented a danger: they were bait for concentrated fire. Veterans learned to control their first instinct to crouch behind them for protection and to mistrust the false sense of security they provided. Especially when antitank guns and other armament zeroed in on their whistling and clanking, the instinct of troops at their sides was to scramble as far from them as quickly as possible, leaving them vulnerable to dreaded Japanese infantrymen with satchel charges. Against powerful defenses, therefore, tanks needed the protection of infantrymen as much as infantrymen needed the extra punch from tanks; communications between the two was maintained through little telephones behind a hatch in the rear, through which infantrymen spoke to the tankers inside.

De Mar urged the lieutenant in command of those four Shermans not to worry; "We'll stick to you like flies on shit." They synchronized watches. Jump-off time would be 1600 on a signal from Lieutenant Bair.

De Mar returned to his platoon and gave the word to its squad leaders. Final preparations were made for the attack. Waiting was a miniature prelanding limbo, the men hoping the moment would come soon and that it never would. De Mar worried about his men, about the steady Japanese fire from both flanks, about communications because his radio had been knocked out. He looked at his watch. It was just before 1600. It would be nice, he mused, to be somewhere else. The lead Sherman's hatch cover closed and it started off with the 3rd Platoon.

It was only minutes to the hill. Starting the climb, De Mar and the others suddenly saw that it was thick with guns. Tank fire ripped down camouflage, exposing dozens, maybe hundreds, of emplacements now sporting gun barrels and muzzle flashes. They didn't yet know that some of the most damaging fire pouring down on them — incredibly fierce fire, unlike what any of them had ever experienced — was from *other* hills. De Mar had no time to look at anything other than his men, some of whom were already down. The tanks were being hit just as fast by expertly placed and concealed mines and antitank guns. Two were put out of action almost immediately.

The crest was only a few hundred yards away. Hoping audacity would compensate for their lack of deception and maneuver, the two platoons charged straight up and reached it, but with a much reduced complement. Bair spread his remaining dozen or so men into shell holes, but the fire was so intense and the Americans' firepower already so diminished that the lieutenant, his radio communications also out, sent a man back to report that G Company would need help to hold the summit. Racing and dodging back with his message, that man could see little movement among De Mar's group on the left. All he could think was that they were getting the hell beaten out of them.

Nothing De Mar had seen in combat, let alone in films, had prepared him for such concentration of incoming fire. It had very quickly killed many of his men, including one he had known when stationed in Panama in 1942, and stunned many survivors, most now unable to function as fire teams. Soon only a handful remained unhit, most prominently Bair. The big, burly first lieutenant was a man of few words who, like Ed Ruess, had been among the noncommissioned officers selected for officer training in the Marines' need for more officers to replace casualties. A veteran of the Marshall Islands and Guam campaigns, he presented a fine target — but served as an inspiration to the men — as he tried to see to the wounded and rally the others. He motioned to De Mar: something about one of the disabled tanks. Then he was violently spun around; De Mar saw that a large chunk had been ripped from his upper leg. But powerful Bair picked up a .30-caliber light machine gun from alongside its two dead operators, threw a belt of ammunition over his shoulder and, like a John Wayne character, laid out lead in the direction — one of the directions — of the enemy. With so much more fire coming in, it wasn't long before he took a second hit, this time in one of the arms in which he cradled the machine gun. The fearless lieutenant continued firing covering fire so that some men could crawl to help others who had been hit going up the hill. His third hit, directly in the buttocks, sent him spinning down and out of sight.

De Mar threw some of his supply of grenades — the action was too fast and instinctive for him to remember how many — and started on his way to answer Bair's motion to him. Then he felt as if someone had taken a log from a fire and slammed it with all his might into his leg. He went down and couldn't get up. Still down, he saw one of his 3rd Platoon men spring up and bang on a disabled tank with his rifle, after which the crew fired furiously for a moment — against what looked like "thousands of Japanese coming at us," as a crew member would later put it — until they ran out of ammunition and escaped through the tank's emergency hatch. Other crews continued firing although their tanks were burning, then leaped out to help wounded riflemen.

There was no place to make a stand anywhere. Much later, in the sweet luxury of being alive to cherish the memory, De Mar would quip that that was a situation from which General Custer would have cut and run. Dirt had jammed his rifle. He had no cover or protection. Knowing that a sniper was poised somewhere on his left, maybe the same one who had already hit him, all he could do was hug the ground for all he was worth. Pushing and willing his body down, he heard cries — from about ten yards away, he guessed — from a private named James Davis, whose size had earned him the nickname Little Bit. Strong and tough despite that size, Davis was only eighteen years old and his wounds were obviously very bad; he was now crying for his parents to come get him. De Mar grunted for him to shut up: any noise there would probably be a fatal noise. When Davis eventually did fall silent, De Mar hoped it was because he had heard him.

Disabled in that precarious position on the crest, De Mar realized that his situation was extremely serious. He thought of his own parents and of his sister and brother-in-law's new baby. He looked at his watch. It was 1645. It seemed to him that forty-five days, not minutes, had passed. Now no American, including Bair, seemed to be firing any longer, and he could see none except dead and wounded. He tried to stay calm. "Where *is* everybody, what am I going to do?" he asked himself again. He decided to wait, head as flat on the ground as he could push it. It would soon be dark. His leg was numb and he had lost a lot of blood, but he knew he could crawl. A figure slithering down the hill in the dark would most likely be finished off by his own troops, who would take him for a Jap, especially at night when Japs were the only ones to move. He didn't even have that night's password. But those were problems for later; now he could only lie where he was, still surprised and dismayed by the dense, accurate Japanese fire from big guns, small arms, hand grenades, mortars.

Some time later, he heard a whisper. "De Mar, you hit bad? We asked for smoke [a smoke screen] up here to get you guys out. Can you crawl?" De Mar didn't recognize the voice of the man risking his own life for his, but the sense of comradeship gave him an incredible lift.* "Can I crawl?" he whispered back, his head still half-buried in the mud. "I can crawl back to the States. Lemme know when the smoke is down; I'm not moving until then."

De Mar later discovered that the screen, when it was laid down, came from 140 smoke shells fired by the surviving tanks. He started down. Someone joined him from behind and cut off his pack to make his crawling easier. Finding a little ditch, he squeezed into it for cover and kept crawling until his hand touched the body of a rifleman from his platoon — with a bullet hole between the eyes. De Mar tried to pull the body with him, but the helper behind him urged him just to get down off the hill for now. Although it would have been a five-minute stroll from summit to bottom, the incomprehensibly intense enemy fire made their progress painfully slow. Soon De Mar came on Lieutenant Bair, badly bleeding from his wounds but trying to get his machine gun operating. De Mar tossed him his pistol because he believed he had some hand grenades left for any Japanese who might try to hurl satchel charges against the tank he hoped would take him back.

Reaching a tank, he saw Davis's body lying under its cannon, where it had been pulled by Jim Chaisson, the man who had run to the command post for reinforcements, then run back up the murderous hill to help his buddies. A tank man quickly dressed De Mar's wound,

---

*That was so common among Marines that it barely deserves mention, except to emphasize yet again that the most important product of their training was a sacred sense of comradeship. Medical corpsmen who tended the Marines developed the same sense of obligation and almost never failed to respond to calls of "Corpsman! Corpsman!" from the wounded except when ordered not to because the fire was too intense. In many such instances, the officers and noncommissioned officers who issued those orders themselves went into killing zone to reach the wounded. In this case, the man who came to De Mar's aid was not from G Company; he was the driver of one of the tanks, hit by a mine.

but Mommy refused to move until all known wounded had been brought down from the hill. Then he was hoisted up onto the turret, where another man was soon lifted beside him. De Mar recognized the voice of the driver who had rescued him from the hill and could tell he too had been hit, although the "tanker" wouldn't let that depress him. "I did you a favor, you can do the same for me," he bantered in a request for medication for his wound. Taking out his battle dressing, De Mar leaned toward the young man and asked where he'd been hit when five fast rounds cracked out. Four hit the "expeditionary can," five gallons of spare water or oil on the turret inches from De Mar's head. It all took a second. The fifth round hit his savior behind the ear, splattering blood and brains all over De Mar. Holding on to the now grievously wounded boy as the tank roared off, he reached for his grenades and found he had none; his pouch had been shot off.*

When the tank made it back safely to Fox Company's command post, men reached for De Mar, but he told them to see first to the tank driver, who had been badly hit. No, they told him, the other man was dead. A Fox Company sergeant whom De Mar knew asked how things were going. "Pretty rough on that goddam hill," he answered, not suspecting how much rougher it would become. The full strength of the defenses was still beyond his imagination — or that of any American, including General Buckner.

Those were the first assaults on Sugar Loaf Hill, as it was christened two days later.† No further attempt was made that day, for the battalion commander, now aware that the objective was far more difficult than originally believed, withdrew G Company and called for air strikes. Starting the next day, the sequence of attacks became so confused, with so many Americans cut off from their units, that it was impossible to keep track of who reached the summit before he fell.

---

*De Mar didn't see and couldn't yet know that all the tank crews were helping save G Company's wounded. Healthy Marines — among them Private Jim Chaisson, the man who had run down the hill to report to Colonel Woodhouse that G Company needed help, then run back to the fighting — clung to the rear of the two operative tanks while they dragged them, sliding painfully on their stomachs, to wounded comrades unable to move. Still under fire, they carried the wounded back. In cases where the wounded lay in open areas blanketed by enemy shells and grenades, the tanks rode out and straddled them while the crew pulled them up through the escape hatch underneath. Everyone took the same deadly fire throughout the improvised rescues.

†During a conference with his acting company commanders on May 14, Lieutenant Colonel Woodhouse called the hill Sugar Loaf, a name he had used for objectives during training exercises on Guadalcanal. The Japanese continued to designate it 51.2 hill or "heights."

Besides, holes from both sides' shelling — the Japanese chiefly from Shuri — were so large that men who crouched in them couldn't see members of other units yards away. What was known for certain was that five of De Mar's 3rd Platoon were killed and ten wounded on May 12, a casualty rate of 50 percent. Other platoons lost even more men — so many that by May 14 all three of G Company's rifle platoons and the three attached machine gun sections were consolidated into one platoon under a second lieutenant who would be killed that night on Sugar Loaf. If such losses continued, they would quickly prostrate the 6th Division.

The "prominent hill" looked to most Americans less like anything involving sugar than a rectangular loaf of coral and volcanic rock. Stebbins and De Mar were not alone in wondering how such an object, seemingly less significant than the Kakazu Ridge finally taken by the Army, could cause such slaughter. To the 6th Division staff, it was not even a major objective, merely a midway station wanted as a platform for fire support against a higher hill called Kokuba about a mile farther south, beyond the Asato River and slightly behind Shuri. Sugar Loaf's three hundred yards or so of frontage rose abruptly to a height of sixty feet from an area of plain before it, an unhappy feature to those who had to cross that open country. But the hill itself was low enough, especially in relation to the others in view of it, including the Shuri heights, to appear almost negligible — a "pimple of a hill," as one Marine called it forty years later, still trying to fathom how it could have been so evil. A young man in good shape — that is, every combat infantryman — could run to its crest in three or four minutes. Yet Sugar Loaf Hill would cost more killed and wounded than any other single Pacific battle, on Iwo Jima or elsewhere.

The next assaults were prompted not only by the continued need to take the hill for the sake of the advance but also to stop its defenders from rolling down hand grenades on American wounded lying at the base. But G Company was losing its power to attack on its own. Of the 215 men with which it had started on May 12 — down from the full complement of about 250 — only seventy-five, including just three officers, were fit to fight by nightfall. It became known as "the shot-to-shit company," one of many.

The summit was reached again the next day, but rapid counterattacks drove the attackers off and away. On May 14, Sugar Loaf became the focus of an entire division that was largely stalled. The 22nd Regiment was ordered to take the hill before nightfall at any cost, but more Japanese artillery from Shuri and more deadly fire from unapproachable antitank guns repulsed all their attacks, starting in early morning.*

In the late afternoon, the commander of the 2nd Battalion, still hoping to achieve his objective by the end of the day, ordered the remnants of G Company to advance again, this time together with F Company. When the force of 150 reached the base of the hill two bloody hours later, 106 had been disabled, together with three of their four supporting tanks. Amazingly, the intensity of the mortar and machine gun fire seemed to have increased, making the evacuation of casualties more difficult than it had been for Dale Blair, Edmund De Mar and their groups two days earlier. The will of the survivors seemed in danger of fading as fast as the daylight and the ammunition.

Although riflemen normally carried almost two hundred rounds in their rifles, belts and bandoliers, the counterattacks from the reverse slope and flanks depleted their supply in minutes at the top of the hill. But twenty-six men from a supply echelon now arrived with much needed replenishment, and Major Harry A. Courtney, Jr., the battalion executive officer (or assistant commander) had an idea. Courtney had spent the day and previous night with the forward units to bolster their morale after the loss of so many of their senior officers, especially G Company, which, after the wounding of Stebbins and Bair, was under its third commander, a lieutenant formerly in charge of a machine gun platoon. Now Courtney formed up the new arrivals with the survivors of F and G Companies. Pressed against the base under mortar, grenade and small-arms fire, the twenty-eight-year-old major told the group that he wanted volunteers for a banzai of their own: unless they took the hill that night, the Japanese would be down with a counterattack in the morning. "When we go up there, some of us are never going to come down again, but that hill's got to be taken and we're going to do it. What do you say?"

All said yes, but the hill wasn't taken for long. By evening, the killing field in front of it was littered with the hulks of smoking tanks, shell holes and casings, and wounded men who could not be recovered during daylight: snipers were everywhere, and all approaches to the hill that gave the slightest protection of defilade were covered by intense mortar fire. While Courtney and his men stormed up after

---

*The tanks had become genuine sitting ducks for defenders waiting where they had to advance. One man would count 33 hulks after Sugar Loaf was finally taken. A battalion farther east that had approached the Shuri Line with 60 tanks ended with six operables. Mechanical problems disabled a few of the lost 54, but Japanese fire accounted for far more, some where tanks moved out to straddle wounded riflemen in exposed areas.

dark, Americans near the base braved continuing fire to collect the dead and wounded from the earlier attacks. At the same time, the exchange of grenades near the crest was at such close range that members of Courtney's group could hear Japanese grunting as they tossed theirs uphill. When Marines answered, their grenades raised so much dust that the hill slope was obscured. The dust turned to mud when a drenching rain resumed a few hours later. Then the rain of Japanese grenades grew more accurate and was supplemented by equally accurate mortar barrages. Courtney was killed by a hand grenade or mortar shell shortly after he reached the crest and leading a charge against an imminent counterattack. (He was one of four 6th Division Marines later awarded the Medal of Honor, three of them posthumously; Dale Bair received the Navy Cross.) The leadership on the hills passed to Ed Pesely, another first lieutenant up from the ranks, who had taken over F Company earlier in the day when its commander was shot in the hip. The thinning force dug in and kept throwing their grenades to try to avert the counterattack. As American ships fired illumination shells across the front, Pesely and his men saw Japanese gathering. One grenade in a steady barrage shot fragments into Pesely. Bleeding from the chest, he radioed to Colonel Woodhouse that he could see the faces of Japanese on the slopes below, some clinging to bushes. Woodhouse told him to try to hang on; he would get as much fire as he could from every possible artillery battery, Marine and Army. The lieutenant colonel stayed on the radio with him all night, calling in coordinates for that artillery fire to save the remainder of his battalion. Shortly after dawn, what was officially described as "only a handful" of survivors — probably fifteen of the sixty men who had stormed the crest with Courtney — withdrew, slightly protected from the severe Japanese fire by a morning mist and by reinforcements taking their turn to charge the hill.

One of the lucky fifteen was Wendell Majors, a G Company rifleman who realized sometime after midnight that he was the only man left alive on the hill's left flank. Private Majors began inching closer toward what he hoped would be friends in the center when a Navy star shell burst into light overhead. He dashed for the cover of a shell hole, jumped in and felt a searing jolt. A bayonet fixed to a rifle, one of many weapons abandoned in previous seesaw charges by both sides, had entered the back of his right thigh and was protruding from the front. Majors fought fierce pain until the predawn light, when he managed to crawl and roll to help at the bottom of the hill.

Another of the lucky fifteen was Irving Ortel, who was helping with the administration of De Mar's 3rd Platoon until he was given a machine gun platoon of his own in the emergency of the soaring casualties. "The shells kept raining down and our tanks were smoking from hits. Guys were all over the place, wounded, bleeding, dead — and the living could hardly move because you simply couldn't without getting hit. I stopped below the crest to bandage some of the wounded and load them onto amtracs that took them back. Then it got dark and I stayed there all night because the air was still really thick with Japanese fire. Tanks came up with smoke just before dawn and I got out. The platoon was down to a few men. We just didn't have any guys left."

Those who were in fact left had reached the limit of endurance. Major Courtney had assigned Corporal Dan Dereschuk to protect his right flank with two machine guns and eight G Company Marines — all sunken-eyed with exhaustion after five days with almost no sleep since crossing the Asakawa. The corporal had actually fallen asleep, his entrenching tool in his hand, in the act of digging his foxhole the previous night. He was even more spent now, but there could be no sleep. Dereschuk's face ached from shrapnel wounds suffered the previous day. Mortar fire knocked out one machine gun and steady firing burned out the barrel of the other. The corporal's eight men dwindled to three, one alternately crying out and moaning from a stomach wound. This brought more grenades on Dereschuk and the other survivor; when they could do nothing to quiet the delirious Marine, Dereschuk knocked him out with a punch to the jaw by the light of a star shell. He managed to evacuate the wounded man on an amtrac when relief came at dawn.

So far, the attempts to take Sugar Loaf had been disastrous. After the seesawing of May 14, the 2nd Battalion was a skeleton and the entire 22nd Regiment was down to 62 percent of combat efficiency. May 15th was no better. The pitch of that day's fighting probably exceeded any in the division's history. Bad weather and the proximity of the attackers to the defenders had much reduced naval and air bombardments. They resumed early in the morning of the fifteenth, but when the ships and planes let up and the Marines moved out in new attacks, they were met by a furious counterbarrage of artillery and mortar shells. One killed the commanding officer of a battalion and his orderly, together with a tank company's executive officer. The same shell, which landed before 7:30 in the morning, wounded the tank company commander and all three of the same infantry battalion's company commanders. The Japanese counterattack that drove the last of Major Courtney's group from the hill pushed forward until early afternoon, retaking some precious ground in front of Sugar Loaf. By the end of the day, no progress had been made elsewhere. The 2nd Battalion, including Owen Stebbins's G Company, had to be withdrawn because it had taken over four hundred casualties, almost half its normal complement.* Further reduced by sickness and exhaustion, the battalion was down to 282 effectives out of its normal complement of roughly a thousand men.

The night was spent under particularly heavy artillery and mortar fire. Two boys had returned to combat that afternoon, their wounds from up north patched on a hospital ship and in Hawaii. Not finding their unit before dark, they had to wait out the night. The caves were too packed with other Marines sheltering from the fire to squeeze in, so they lay down just outside one of them, under a tepee formed by two huge rocks. A shell found its way even into what seemed that perfect cover and killed them before they could rejoin their buddies.

Only the Shuri Line in general has been more studied by military analysts than the segment of it at Sugar Loaf — attention well deserved, for this was a particularly fine example of the design and engineering achievements everywhere on that awesome barrier. All the skill and sweat of Japanese groundworks were in full evidence here.

The terrain favored them almost by the nature of things; defenders almost always fortified the high ground, toward which attackers had to fight from below along predictable routes. In this case, the Japanese had a better view of the attackers than usual, especially from the Shuri heights, dominating the whole area. Their cave exits on the rear slopes and the flanks as well as the forward slope allowed defenders protected from American shells to rush out to counterattack Marines who had reached the summit — and rush out in force, because an unusually elaborate network of tunnels provided safe access for reinforcements. In addition, their machine gun emplacements, hidden mortars and other defensive arrangements had been sited with particular care, probably under General Cho's personal direction.

It was equally important that Hill 51.2, as the Japanese continued to call it, did not stand alone in the defensive scheme, although the Marines began by attacking it alone. Much to the contrary, it was one component of a triangular system, whose two other components were hills on both sides, Horseshoe on the right and Half Moon, or Crescent, on the left. They formed a funnel for pouring dense fire down on Sugar Loaf, especially on every square yard of the summit whenever Americans approached it, as Sergeant De Mar and those who followed him discovered. Chances of surviving without a hit were

---

*G–2–22 was down to one officer, a lieutenant who had become the company commander, and an uncounted scattering of enlisted men.

measured in minutes rather than hours. Additional heavy artillery from the Shuri heights, northeast of Half Moon, was less accurate on individuals but more devastating to groups. More voluminous and more accurate than that yet encountered on the island or in the Pacific, the combined fire also ravaged troops attempting to flank Sugar Loaf from either side. And since many of the mortars were on the reverse slopes of Horseshoe and Half Moon — aimed or adjusted with the help of spotters — they were largely protected from American artillery and mortar fire until Sugar Loaf was taken.

Few Americans there, as elsewhere in the best Japanese positions, saw the defenders at all. "We were fighting an underground enemy the whole time," one of them realized after catching on to their strategy. But the Americans could advance only by exposing themselves. "Hell's half-acre," the bare ground beneath Sugar Loaf and the other hills, provided almost no defilade or cover. It exposed the attackers to simultaneous crossfire from the several interlocking sources within the complex. Students of the battle later estimated that weapons zeroed in from unseen and unreachable positions caused from 50 to 75 percent of American casualties.

"At first we were totally unaware of the power of the whole defensive line and of Sugar Loaf's part in it," Captain Stebbins put it with restrained regret. "We felt our company would take it alone on that first assault. The whole idea of Marine training was that you *will* take your objective. It would take several days to begin realizing how little we understood, to begin grasping the extent to which this hill was fortified with pillboxes, a maze of tunnels, interlocking automatic weapons, and its approaches covered with high-velocity antitank guns. It would be another day before the triangular defense system, all mutually supporting, would become apparent. And it would be understood only later that the triangle was the key to the defense of that whole side of the island."

From the air, the full line bore a resemblance to a series of spokes radiating down and out from the hub at Shuri. Sugar Loaf was at the end of the one that reached farthest toward the western coast and Naha. That made it the key of the barrier protecting both Shuri and Naha, and explained Cho's personal interest in the preparations there and the special reinforcements ordered by Ushijima. The American planning was less skillful. No brilliance could have spared the infantrymen severe casualties. "No matter how heavy the supporting fire," a historian of Pacific combat has put it, "a moment arrived when men had to stand up and run across naked ground into a level stream of bullets." But that moment might have been better chosen on Sugar Loaf. Its fortifications were further argument for devising something more imaginative than the Tenth Army's bludgeon. New evidence of the cost of that strategy would have strengthened the case for outflanking by the landing in the far south advocated by General Buckner's critics. But the Commander evidently gave no further thought to the matter. No infantrymen in the fighting units are known to have joined those critics aloud, but a few began to wonder, when off the line for breaks after their mauling at Sugar Loaf, why they seemed to be fighting a Japanese fight, almost hand-to-hand, despite their huge advantage in equipment and firepower. Some sensed there had been poor planning and leadership at the highest level. Of course their notions about the strategy in general were speculative, but it is fair to state now that the much-vaunted, perhaps congenitally overoptimistic American intelligence had again failed, in this case to give unit commanders like even Captain Stebbins and Sergeant De Mar any idea of the deadliness of the Japanese preparations. Surely this helped swell the casualties.

A final factor favoring the Japanese was their months of artillery training during preparations for the invasion, for which forward observers happened to use Hill 51.2 for spotting. This gave them such knowledge of the terrain that "they often didn't have to adjust their artillery because they fired on the right spot the first time . . . We couldn't have done them a better favor than attacking here," according to General James Day, who fought on Sugar Loaf and later studied the battle on many returns to Okinawa. "We were beautifully zeroed in." Sergeant De Mar knew that without the later study. "It was like target practice for them from all those damn hills. They had every foot covered with grids." Above all, it was the pounding from big 150mm guns at Shuri — hardly seen before in the Pacific — that made the battle stunningly new and horrendous for the Marines.

As the crow flies, Sugar Loaf Hill was about a mile from the 32nd Army headquarters in the tunnel deep beneath Shuri Castle. The battles being waged simultaneously along the rest of the ten miles of the main Shuri Line — separate pitched battles into which Buckner's general offensive had broken down almost immediately — were equally ferocious, if not all as much a seesaw between attack and counterattack.* This was a classic of static defense. The Shuri Line

---

*Unit commanders on Sugar Loaf, not to mention the men, had very little notion of what was happening elsewhere on the Shuri Line. The exception was the battle for Wana Ridge and Wana Draw, on the 6th Division's left flank. The 1st Marine Division's inability to take those objectives for another week further hampered the 6th Division because it allowed the defenders to keep firing heavy artillery at them from the west side of the Shuri heights. Thus 6th Division unit commanders were much concerned about the progress of the 1st Division at Wana.

was accomplishing for the Japanese much of what the French had hoped from the Maginot Line, and that was far more a local than a national feat, since Imperial General Headquarters' support of Ushijima had been minimal for a campaign of that importance. This was a result of Tokyo's early optimism in seeing Okinawa as principally a forward air base — a notion eventually abandoned because there were too few planes and supplies to pursue the strategy of destroying the enemy at sea — and IGHQ's later resistance to the Ushijima-Yahara strategy of a war of attrition fought from underground because it clung to its fundamental belief in attack. Finally, there was the general shortage of arms and equipment that worsened for Ushijima once IGHQ had decided that the Tennozan of Tennozans, for which everything possible had to be husbanded, would take place on the mainland itself. Thus the Shuri Line, with all its arrangements, was chiefly the "private" creation of the 32nd Army.

Almost a quarter of a million men faced each other on both sides of that line: "two great armies," in William Manchester's telling image, "squatting opposite one another in mud and smoke . . . locked together in unimaginable agony." World War I was one of the consuming interests of Manchester, whose Marine father had died in the carnage at the Argonne. "In the deepest combat [there] . . . battalion frontage [the length occupied by the battalion's thousand-odd men] had been approximately eight hundred yards. Here it was less than six hundred yards . . . about eighteen inches per man . . . on a battleground that was about as wide [actually a few miles wider] than the distance between Capitol Hill in Washington and the Arlington National Cemetery." The military analyst Thomas Huber agreed that "The fighting on Okinawa had features that were all its own, but even so its dynamics bore a startling resemblance to the fierce no-man's-land fighting of World War I."

Mommy De Mar's "adventure" at Sugar Loaf's summit was extraordinary only in that his platoon was the second — after Ed Ruess's earlier that day — to experience the combination of fire directed there. Almost without exception, the Japanese had constructed a fortified position on every hill and ridge line, with other positions heavily covering its approach. In the worst cases, each little knob and crease in the land was a link in the defense; taking those next knobs and creases, just ten yards away, were operations in themselves. A rear-echelon Army colonel who visited one of the easier sectors of the line during a relative lull in the fighting was almost as overwhelmed by the sight of the hardships as a civilian might have been.

There is nothing colorful about such an engagement. The rapid staccato of machine gun fire continued along with the crack of .30-caliber rifles and carbines. The plop of mortar shells as they left their muzzles punctuated the incessant hail of other hardware. The whole valley was covered with a thick pall of smoke that completely obscured the sky overhead. The sun was rarely visible and only appeared as an aureola from our position. On the road, several hundred meters away, stood one of our disabled tanks that could not be recovered due to the enemy artillery and mortar rounds falling in the vicinity. The burst of our own artillery shells was clearly discernible as they landed on the hill in billows of flame and smoke and the whistle that accompanied them and then the boom of the guns in the rear. Our ears were filled with the din of battle and the smell of gunpowder penetrated our nostrils with a burning sensation. This, however, was almost overcome by the stench of rotting flesh while the sting and stickiness of the flies became almost unbearable. The . . . dirty, slimy troops around us seemed somewhat oblivious to most of these happenings, only concentrating on their particular job. Some drivers and messengers even attempted to catch a few minutes' sleep under their ponchos during their respite.

It was no miracle that two such congregations of men could cause each other so much torment; just the best that both could do at their level of technological development. By this time in the island war, both sides had learned lessons that could only make the fighting harder — the Americans, among other things, that massive general bombardment did far less good than imagined when the enemy was protected underground (a lesson largely unlearned by the time of Vietnam); the Japanese, that the banzai attacks to which they had resorted in defense of other islands was far less effective than the methodical warfare they were waging here.

Despite the Marines' conviction that they were being used for "target practice," the Japanese agony was greater than theirs. Sugar Loaf's defenders were remnants of the 62nd Division, which had opposed the American attacks in most of the south, reinforced by the 15th Independent Regiment, airlifted to Okinawa the previous July to supplement the 44th Independent Mixed Brigade, most of whose regular troops had just been lost on *Toyama maru*. Led by a highly skilled colonel named Seiko Mita, the 15th Independent Regiment had also suffered heavy losses. But the Sugar Loaf complex had to be held as long as possible, and Ushijima committed some of his last reserves of well-trained infantry troops to reinforce the defense. Mita was sent three additional battalions during the night of May 15.

One of the reinforcements was a former farmer named Masatsugu Shinohara.

When the Americans had landed, Shinohara was stationed about fifteen miles east on Tsuken Island in the Pacific, or Philippine Sea — on the opposite side, that is, to Kerama Retto. Tiny Tsuken controlled the entrance to large Nakagusuku Bay, which the invaders needed for anchorage and landing supplies. Some 250 Americans set out in ten yellow rubber boats to take the little dot on the morning of April 6, the day *Yamato* got under way for Okinawa. The little Japanese garrison on Tsuken had a field gun, two heavy machine guns and four mortars. As the boats approached, Shinohara, leader of a mortar section, hurried up the island's largest hill and chased them off with some deadly rounds. American bombs shook the island on the following days before amphibious tanks led a second landing. Of the Japanese force of sixty, twelve lived to follow their orders to find a way to rejoin the rest of the regiment on Okinawa. Their way turned out to be rowing tiny fishing boats the fifteen miles and sneaking through the American force already controlling the Okinawan coast where they landed.

On Sugar Loaf's rear, southern slope, Shinohara and other Tsuken survivors crept through trenches to carry mortar shells to their positions. To avoid the enemy observation planes that constantly hovered over them — although Americans perceived their planes as often grounded by bad weather — they did this at night and tried not to move in daylight except when firing their deadly mortars. They ate only dried biscuits and did not sleep during their seventy-two hours on or beside the hill.

As the prodigious defensive works and their firepower dismayed the Americans, the Japanese thought, to the extent that they had strength to think about anything beyond the next minutes, that they were like children fighting giants. But although the battle seemed hopeless, it was essential to hold Hill 51.2, the strategic anchor for nearby Shuri. Some remembered the feats of arms, courage and endurance on the 203 Heights, a key hill in the high ground around Port Arthur that the Japanese had had to take in order to destroy the remnants of the Russian fleet in 1905 — and which they did take at terrible cost. Few hated the Americans now; they had no energy for that. But all knew that the enemy, as obsessed with Sugar Loaf as they themselves, must be killed because failure would lead directly to the loss of Okinawa and the same kind of vicious assault on the homeland. Therefore they took comfort in the Japanese firepower, although it always seemed too feeble to them — and although the heavy artillery from Shuri, American consternation at its accuracy notwithstanding, killed many Japanese too. When Shinohara and the others from Tsuken were at last withdrawn from Sugar Loaf, only five of the original sixty were alive. The commander of their little force was among the majority killed on the hill.

The Americans, even those who had landed on Okinawa loathing everything Japanese, retained no more energy than their enemy for the luxury of hatred. "We were past hatred, past bitterness. This was simply the ultimate athletic contest that you had to win. A contest with literal sudden death and no overtime."

The same machine gun that got Captain Stebbins got me too . . . Someone pulled me behind a knocked-out tank but they hit it again. I don't know what happened to the other guys because the concussion busted my right ear drum and I couldn't see or hear for a couple of hours.
  — Marvin Zimmerman

When you got to the top, the Japs were just waiting for you and cut loose; all hell was being kicked out of our units. I was very, very lucky, one of the few to come down — by crawling over bodies.
  — Joseph Bangert

A buddy and I were told to man a machine gun about 30 yards away . . . A mortar and hand grenade barrage interrupted us about halfway there and pinned us down. I was in a foxhole I don't know how long. During that time a grenade went off in front of my face and blew my helmet to the back of my head. I didn't get a scratch and I grabbed the helmet and reset it. I don't know if I'd been unconscious for any length of time. I looked over at the machine gun we were headed for and saw two dead Marines by it and thought it's a good thing we can't get there — it's well exposed and if we do get there, we'll be two more dead Marines . . . Suddenly I heard a "poof" behind me. I turned around and saw that [my platoon leader, a first lieu-tenant] was killed instantly by a direct mortar hit and the body was a black hulk. A little later, a Marine ahead of me began calling for a corpsman. (I found out later the corpsmen were all dead or wounded.) The Marine finally gave up calling and crawled [out] . . . As he passed, I saw that his right foot up to the middle of the calf had been blown off.
  — Declan Klingenhagen about some thirty minutes of the morning of
  May 15

After ninety-six hours at Sugar Loaf, many Americans were too exhausted to remember what happened with much clarity, although "exhaustion" is too ordinary a word to describe their condition after several straight days of fighting between fear-filled nights with little or no sleep. Company commanders knew that numbness was likely to take over at this point; some of their men could hardly tell in which direction they were looking or whether their rifles pointed up or down. Mental exhaustion of this kind led to many extra casualties because not enough adrenaline continued pumping to prevent stupid mistakes through loss of concentration.

Most of the 22nd Regiment was approaching this state on May 16, which many considered the 6th Division's hardest day of the campaign and the war. Several companies of the 29th, including Dick Whitaker's, had recently joined the battle. Units of both regiments launched a general assault on the hill from the front and both flanks, and were met by crippling defensive fire. The crest was reached again, but fierce barrages of mortar shells and artillery fire from Shuri fell on the attackers. All advance units had to be withdrawn by nightfall. Replacements had replaced replacements, and reformed units were again so badly shot up that some survivors had to take their organization into their own hands. Although the defenders had finally betrayed signs of being worn down, the day's huge losses had again produced no gain in territory.

Before dark on that May 16, Anthony Cortese of Company I–3–22 ran to the top of a little hill called Chocolate Drop. He looked at Sugar Loaf through his lieutenant's binoculars and "couldn't believe what I saw; it was covered with dead Marines. A few enemy too, but mostly our guys, maybe a few hundred in my view alone, not counting where I couldn't see." Cortese also saw some Japanese rebuilding their positions and ran back to tell his lieutenant that Sugar Loaf had to be softened up with more artillery before they went in. "But the next day, up we go up into the slaughter, just like the others."

That next day, three battleships moved in close to blast Sugar Loaf, Horseshoe and Half Moon with their heavy guns while aircraft carriers launched waves of bombing strikes. Then all three hills were attacked, the 29th Regiment assuming the brunt of the fighting while the exhausted 22nd, down to 40 percent of combat efficiency, held its positions. One of the exceptions was Cortese's company 245 men, who were thrown into the battle and ended with three fit to fight. Two of those three, including Cortese, quickly set up a machine gun to stop a counterattack until yet more reinforcements could be rushed in.

Dick Whitaker was told that his go at Sugar Loaf was the eleventh. His stint unloading invasion supplies on the landing beaches had ended six weeks earlier. When assigned to F Company, Private Whitaker had been made a helper in a machine gun squad, charged with lugging ammunition to the gun and protecting it with his rifle. Now he was still one of the sloggers who bore supplies and stayed ready to take over if the gunner and assistant gunners were hit. Each of his two cans of .30-caliber ammunition, carried in addition to his pack and his own M1 ammunition, weighed about twenty pounds. But the hill itself seemed to him, as to all the others in the previous ten charges, almost insignificant in size, especially in its present condition, blackened and denuded. Unloaded, he could have run to the top in a few minutes.

His platoon began running shortly after seven o'clock on the morning of the seventeenth, single file, Whitaker third in line. Mortar fire cascaded on the little column as if the Japanese had been preparing for it alone throughout the night. Running, panting, sweating, thinking of nothing, not even of what his body was doing, Whitaker pushed forward and upward as if the absurdity were happening to someone else. Three squads with three water-cooled machine guns followed a replacement lieutenant whose name Whitaker could not remember; the young graduate had appeared only hours before to take over the platoon.

The attack plan to move right at the crest of the hill never had a chance. Whitaker couldn't tell where the fire was coming from, only that it was enormous. Having heard the expression "withering fire," he understood that this was it, compared with which nothing before, except certain artillery bombardments, came close in terms of pure danger. By the time the men neared the crest, stunningly accurate fire from mortars, machine guns and rifles deluged them; the Japanese had zeroed in on every inch around the top of the hill. Shells and bullets rent the air with swishes and whistles; hot metal shook the ground. And when they reached the crest, the Japanese lobbed a shower of hand grenades on them from their unseen positions on the reverse slope.

For the lucky, the next minutes seemed years. At the crest, Whitaker's platoon couldn't unlimber their guns to fight. Even if the right targets could have been found, it was impossible to set up the machine guns because each move out of a shell hole or scar in the ground brought another burst of fire. Whitaker's gunner was hit. The new lieutenant was killed four steps in front of him. The platoon finally managed to set up despite the appalling casualties, but the men were so outgunned that they hardly knew where to shoot. Desperate nonstop firing burned out the barrels of all three machine guns. Whitaker realized that even if they managed to hold the crest, the Japanese on the reverse slope would continue to pin them down indefinitely. Only now did he fully appreciate how securely dug in the enemy was, with so much armament. He was frightened out of his mind yet impervious to fright because the scene was beyond his ability to grasp. Besides, there was no time for fright.

And now there was no hope of holding the crest without perhaps total casualties. Down the line from him, more men kept getting hit as they sought cover until someone, Whitaker thought a sergeant, yelled, "Let's get the hell out of here!" But getting out proved harder than getting up. Whitaker and John Senterfitt, another private, picked up their gunner, groaning from a bad stomach wound, and tried to take him down to safety. Their every move was watched: fierce mortar fire resumed the moment they started down. Panting from the strain and from exhaustion, they took a measure of refuge in a shell hole to catch their breath and get a better grip on the gunner. Other men passed them, carrying and supporting other wounded. "Corpsman!" they yelled. "CORPSMAN!"

By the time Whitaker and Senterfitt crawled to the bottom and across a portion of the open "killing area" to the marginal protection of the back of a small elevation north of the hill, a Corpsman was waiting for their gunner. Without glancing back to smoking Sugar Loaf, Whitaker carried the noise of its ferocious fire in his ears. It was not yet 8 A.M. He had no idea of the tactical, strategic or historical significance of the battle, now in its fifth day; he knew only that his fifteen minutes going up, taking fire, and coming down had been a nightmare without equal.

It would strike him later that "War is hell" was a silly metaphor because "no one has been to hell with the possible exception of Dante." He would prefer "Hell is war"* — but such conceptual notions did not come to him in the filth, fear and stretched nerves of the fighting itself. Nothing mattered then that wasn't real, immediate, instant. Ernie Pyle's intimation was accurate in this, if in little else about combat. One of Pyle's last observations on Okinawa was that "life up there [at the front] is very simple, very uncomplicated, devoid of all the jealousy and meanness that float around a headquarters city." Men still worried about themselves and their buddies after coming down from Sugar Loaf. *Did we get everyone off? Did we leave anyone up there in that hell?* Whitaker slowly felt immense relief that his duty on Sugar Loaf was temporarily over, together with a vague hope that he wouldn't have to go up again. It was up to his officers to think and to order that the hill must be taken. Whitaker only thought — or felt, since there was also too little energy for proper thinking — that he was profoundly glad to have made it down and that maybe he wouldn't have to face that particular challenge again.†

---

*A Marine gag has a man hit on Okinawa going to hell and finding out only two weeks later he'd been killed. "That's how horrible life was."

†Later in the campaign, Whitaker joined those who wondered for a moment whether someone might have made a mistake deciding to assault Sugar Loaf. Wasn't something wrong that they had had to charge the inferno so many times at such cost only to keep

Attack, counterattack, attack, counterattack . . . each time American units were pushed back, it was with many or most of their men killed or missing. The wounded were pulled into caves and craters until corpsmen or fellow fighters chose a time to risk slipping out to them. Scatterings of unhit men left behind in holes fell asleep from exhaustion that conquered even fear of their hopeless situation out there all alone. Part of F Company would go up again, but without Whitaker's decimated platoon. Later on May 17, E Company of the same 29th Regiment was driven off three times by the same heavy fire capped by bayonet charges. Although a fourth attempt might have succeeded, their ammunition was exhausted and too few men were left to spare help for the wounded. Ordered to withdraw, the company discovered it had suffered 160 casualties.

The Japanese did not know that the attackers could not persist much longer because no more replacements were available. But Japanese casualties had also been extremely heavy, and the general in command of the defending force doubted whether he could hold on another day. Assembling the last of his reserves from the caves of Horseshoe and Half Moon, he told them that fresh troops would arrive to help them in three days; meanwhile, they must defend Sugar Loaf to the death. After dusk, he sent them to reinforce the shredded units there.

But the Americans had taken enough of the little rises to detect their movement. No fewer than twelve battalions of Marine artillery fired violently on the intended reinforcements, probably killing and otherwise disabling all but a dozen. (In all, 6th Division artillery fired 92,560 shells in the Sugar Loaf engagement.) This helped quicken the end for the Japanese the following morning, May 18, when the commander of D-2-29 Company conceived of a winning strategy. He sent half his men around the right side of the hill with tanks, then the other half, also with close tank support, around the left flank as soon as the defenders' attention was engaged on the right.

This turned out to be the final charge. The 1st Marine Division's taking of Wana Draw and Wana Ridge at last — its Shuri Line objective, two miles northeast — had silenced some of the artillery fire from there. Here, enough ground had been taken and enough damage done to the Japanese guns on the triangle's other two hills to enable the tanks to work their way ahead while eighty men from D

---

being beaten back? What was wrong was that no one had suspected how strongly and skillfully that hill complex was defended. Had his regimental commander known, he might have tried to bypass it by advancing farther to his right, closer to the beach, but that would have left too much area under Japanese guns. The hindsight of even those few days strengthened the case for another major landing to outflank the whole of the Shuri Line.

Company ran up the forward slope to the summit. Although six tanks were quickly knocked out, others encircled the hill from both sides and fired into the Japanese positions on the reverse slope while the infantrymen showered them with grenades. An hour of savage fighting followed, desperately brave Japanese squads charging with satchel charges. The defenders were weakened enough by then for the Marines to dig in. The caves still housed scattered groups of Japanese survivors, but the superbly organized system of defense was at last cracked by nightfall. Gaining control of the "pimple of a hill" had taken a savage week of attack, capture, repulse, and further attack, by some measures the hardest single battle in the Pacific War and hardest for Americans anywhere in World War II.

The next day, General Shepherd, commander of the 6th Marine Division, received a dispatch from his immediate boss, a subordinate of Buckner's. RESISTANCE AND DETERMINATION WITH WHICH ELEMENTS OF YOUR DIVISION ATTACKED AND FINALLY CAPTURED SUGAR LOAF IS INDICATIVE OF THE FIGHTING SPIRIT OF YOUR MEN X MY HEARTY CONGRATULATIONS TO THE OFFICERS AND MEN CONCERNED. But the battle still wasn't over. On the morning of May 19, Shepherd replaced the 29th Marine Regiment with the 4th, the division's last reserve, units of which felt that *they* had finally secured Sugar Loaf, since resistance continued, together with fire from other hills.* That night, a 4th Regiment Marine sat in "one of the deepest foxholes I'd ever seen," on the very top of Sugar Loaf. His squad, assigned to protect a mortar section that was firing over the hill, was down to four men. Naha's smoking ruins, only two miles southwest, could be seen from the crest now that there was time to look. Flares from nearby warships "kept the area as light as day, all night long. We lost many men that night and the next day. So did the Nips. There were piles of Japanese bodies. They had been collecting for as many days as the battle lasted . . . I noticed we too had bodies that had been lying dead for several days. The stench was indescribable."

Sister companies D and E of Whitaker's F Company took heavy casualties on May 19 and 20 from Japanese on Sugar Loaf's rear slope. "Taking a hill was a very loose term there," Whitaker's company commander explained, "because our men hadn't gone *within* it, where many Japs were still fighting from all those caves. My own

---

*Substantial resistance continued at least until May 20, when a machine gun squad was included in reinforcements sent out at 10 P.M. — one of the few American advances at night — to support an infantry company that had suffered heavy casualties repelling a counterattack. The squad's sergeant had just managed to find cover in a trench when "all hell broke loose between Sugar Loaf and Horseshoe Ridge."

company advanced closer to the sea and used standing Jap foxholes for cover, but the Japs knew those positions perfectly, of course, so we had a night of terrible casualties after Sugar Loaf was officially secured. There seemed no end to it."

The ubiquity of casualties had given Sugar Loaf an aura of fatality. When James Day, wounded on the hill as a young corporal, returned forty years later as the general in command of all U.S. forces on the island, he understandably made a study of his old fighting days. Day concluded that more men were killed per square foot on Sugar Loaf — mostly in "the killing area," an open plain about the size of six football fields — than anywhere else, including the larger and longer battles. The profusion of casualties stunned even the toughest veterans. Nearly three thousand were killed and seriously wounded;* roughly the same as on all of Tarawa and more than at Casino, and up to 50 percent more than the worst battle for a single position on Iwo Jima. But the numbers cannot convey their effect to people outside the survivors of the shattered combat units. The dismayed Marine who lamented that "battalions melted away, companies vanished" was not resorting to hyperbole. Parts of four battalions were mangled. Several rifle companies ended with a dozen men out of the normal complement of more than 240. In two of them, not a single officer or staff noncommissioned officer survived; in many others, privates ended in command of their shattered platoons as they withdrew. In Marine Evacuation Hospital Number 2, four or five men receiving transfusions in shock positions on litters, feet higher than their heads, learned that they were the only survivors known at that time of an entire rifle company. Medical personnel observed that their dismay on discovering this was exceeded only by that of the green troops who had still been in boot camp at L-day, seven weeks earlier, and were introduced to combat at Sugar Loaf.

So many tanks had been knocked out that some tank companies alternated crews on the remaining vehicles, but it was the other way around in the infantry. Eleven of eighteen company commanders, including Captain Stebbins, had been killed or wounded. Scarcely any of the original platoon leaders escaped. In Company G–2–22, Mommy De Mar was the only one — by the skin of his teeth — and he himself was a substitute. "For the men who had been pushed into this fierce cockpit for eight days," a survivor remembered, "it seemed like an eternity."

* An additional 1289 men were lost to sickness and combat exhaustion.

18 · Close Combat

Okinawa had a thousand Sugar Loafs. Everyone in combat had his Sugar Loaf.
— Dick Whitaker

Boot camp was designed to see if you could take it, then to make you take much more, far beyond your normal limit, so nothing would faze you in combat. It was amazingly grueling, which is why no Marine ever forgets his drill instructor. But it was also nothing compared to the real thing. There it was physical and mental endurance; on Okinawa it was death.
— Norris Buchter

Every day you lived for one day more. That was where your horizon ended, the limit of your plans.
— Edward (Buzzy) Fox, machine gunner

SUGAR LOAF'S seizure opened the way to other strongpoints, none of which would cost so much in casualties. Something snapped for the Japanese, as they knew it would, when the pivotal hill finally fell. Now the campaign would move more swiftly toward the American victory that was never in doubt.

But that is the historical view, reached in retrospective examinations like this one, which are as distant from the war as the three thousand daring new swimsuit advertisements installed in New York subway cars during the weeks when the Shuri Line was mangling twelve thousand American bodies. No American who pulled himself out of a foxhole at dawn knew that a climax had been reached around May 20. The fighting remained equally desperate, if smaller in scope, at hundreds of untaken fortifications. Each day was still another day of "maybe" for every man. Together, the two Army divisions east of Shuri took almost as many casualties as the 6th Marine Division suffered on Sugar Loaf to the west. Measured by numbers of casualties, the 1st Marine Division had it worse during the first two weeks of May than the 6th Division during the two weeks that included Sugar Loaf.

Okinawa's southern landscape was studded with hill turrets that repelled like the posts of a pinball machine. There was the Chocolate

Drop–Wart Hill–Flattop Hill complex, the Tiger–Charlie–Oboe Hill complex; there were Hen, Hector, Conical, Oboe, Red, Nan, Mabel, William, How and Dick Hills, Rocky Crags, Kakazu West, Hill 60, Hill 178, Skyline Ridge, Ryan's Ridge, Gaja Ridge; hundreds of ridges and rises festooned with hidden gun emplacements, scores of escarpments where the Japanese positions, although less effective in their aggregate, were just as murderous to those hit by a howitzer shell or machine gun bullet. The stories of the fights for those places differed chiefly in their duration. The colonel commanding the Army's 383rd Infantry Regiment, which took Sugar Hill — eight miles east of Sugar Loaf, near the opposite end of the Shuri Line — saw "the greatest display of courage of any group of men I have ever seen."

Radio Tokyo caught the incongruity of the lethal obstacles' colorful nicknames. "Sugar Loaf Hill . . . Chocolate Drop . . . Strawberry Hill . . . Gee, those places sound wonderful! You can just see the candy houses with the white picket fences around them and the candy canes hanging from the trees, their red and white stripes glistening in the sun. But the only thing red about those places is the blood of Americans. Yes sir, those are the names of hills . . . where the fighting is so close that you get down to bayonets and sometimes your bare fists . . . I guess it's natural to idealize the worst places with pretty names to make them seem less awful . . . Sugar Loaf Hill . . . Chocolate Drop . . . Strawberry Hill — they sound good, don't they? Only those who've been there know what they're really like."

Perhaps that broadcast intentionally omitted such names as Hand Grenade, Hacksaw, Bloody and Tombstone Ridges. There was also the ironically named Easy Hill on the Oroku Peninsula, where units attempting an encircling movement took fire from unseen fellow units, and Lenly Cotten, the boy who had schemed himself into combat by going AWOL, couldn't fire for fear of helping Japanese troops cut down Americans. Cotten's platoon leader shouted for binoculars so that he could "see something," and someone handed him a pair. That exposure of a tool of command brought instant death. A bullet shattered his head before he could focus.

There was Charlie Hill, just before Sugar Loaf, where a squad of sixteen flamethrower operators was cut to five. Two of those five were advancing again when a stunning barrage of mortar fire landed a shell between them, killing one of the pair and picking up the other and tossing him through the air, the flamethrower ripped from his back. The next day, the survivor was resting below the hill, nibbling on a C-ration's can of hash. A shell from a smaller mortar hit the boy next to him in the back of his neck, blowing off his head and shooting his bloody brains all over the survivor and his meal. The rugged volunteer for the dangerous flamethrowing duty vomited uncontrollably.

The fiercest artillery fire to hit Melvin Heckt's machine gun section came at 7 A.M. on May 21. It missed Heckt's trench by yards. Then he joined an attack on a ridge slightly south of Sugar Loaf, which had been more or less secured three days earlier.

> *Donvito* was first to be hit. Shrapnel in the hip. *Dunham* was next.
> He received a concussion and possible broken collarbone . . . Next
> *Ward Bowers* was killed by Nip artillery . . . We were in a couple of
> bomb craters. *Cullen* was passing by with a piece of shrapnel in his
> back. *Andriola* was helping him walk back when a Nambu [machine
> gun] opened up and wounded Andriola in buttocks and Cullen in
> leg. *Hassell* . . . ran out to drag them in out of the fire land and was
> hit in nose, mouth and arm. McGee and Congdon ran out and
> drug Cullen, Hassell and Andriola to safe positions. The artillery
> and mortar fire became heavier and more intense so I took my sec-
> tion and ran across the open field to *Baumhard*'s 3rd platoon. It is
> lucky we moved out for Congdon was killed in the location from
> which we came and probably more of us would have been killed
> had we not moved. *Maritato* was hit in buttocks and testicle. *Acuna*
> was hit. We tried to set up lines and contact A Company. I placed
> machine guns in and had the men get in a ditch . . . Supposedly
> this was the safest position anywhere. But the Nips lobbed a mor-
> tar right in the ditch and killed instantly 3 of my men, *Jennings,*
> *Ablett* and *McGee. Simmons* was sitting with the other three and re-
> ceived shrapnel in the leg, arms and side . . . that makes 6 men
> killed out of my squad. Too damn many boys to lose for any damn
> land. Poor Red McGee was blown all over the side of the hill. Only
> his red hair and scalp remained where he had been sitting.

May 23, when the unit pushed toward the outskirts of Naha, was similar, except that several survivors "cracked up" under the strain and one of the KIAs was a sergeant: "Good old Al, a staff sergeant who carried ammo when he could have been in rear echelon — a boy who volunteered for everything." One of that day's wounded had a leg blown off. "They carried him into [a] wrecked hut and amputated with a kabar and pocket knife. *Davis* took it like a man and only screamed once. *Tex Durisoe* sharpened the knife and off came the stub." Now five were left in Heckt's machine gun section, eight having been killed, nine wounded and one more or less permanently deranged. So it went for many fighting units. While it was strategically downhill from the breaking of the Shuri Line's cornerstones, and historically inevitable, very few on Okinawa at the time had any notion of that — or much notion of anything beyond the demands of the hour.

*You were always wondering what the next five minutes would be like.
Words like "tomorrow" and "next week" had little meaning. Life was all
about* now.

— Dick Whitaker

Most men in the lines on Okinawa knew, and were reduced to caring
about, little more than what was happening in their line of sight:
what threatened from the next cave or rise or tree stump. Those who
lived a week or more became marvelously expert in this. As death
powerfully concentrates the mind, constant proximity and fear of it
honed animal instincts and senses into a new nature. By the time Dick
Whitaker's Company F–2–29 reached Sugar Loaf, on May 17, he
knew that "the difference between life and death often depended on
what we saw, smelled and heard."

Officers and noncommissioned officers learned to take special precautions because they were special targets. When Captain Owen Stebbins was hit on May 12, it was almost certainly after Japanese machine
gunners spotted Ed Ruess running to his little forward observation
post for a quick parlay. They followed that runner and aimed for the
captain, the top man. Perhaps Japanese determination to eliminate
leaders derived from the heightened importance of leadership to
their own units. In any case, their expertise at it made privates compassionate for their officers. Day after day, single shots took down
sergeants and second lieutenants crouched with their men, communications specialists carrying radios, everyone involved with command. Over the din of artillery, mortar and machine gun fire, the
lone crack of a sniper's rifle would be heard, then the thudding
impact into flesh — and men would see a chosen target go down.
Night after night, infiltrators found their way to the foxholes of those
marked Americans, having watched their units all day to select them.
"I can't tell you how many lieutenants we went through," a Company
G–2–22 private said, summing up the Japanese success.

That is why distinguishing armament such as .45-caliber pistols
were tucked out of sight, why Captain Stebbins and all other officers
rarely risked using their carefully concealed binoculars, and why
"you never, ever mentioned rank in the field," as Ed De Mar put
it, "because any Nip in earshot would immediately know where to
aim." Japanese snipers seemed uncannily skilled at selecting anyone whose loss was likely to hurt more than that of an ordinary
infantryman. Their units waited patiently for such target opportunities — in one case, staying hidden for hours until a major who
commanded a Marine battalion could be shot as he crouched between two staff officers. "It was amazing how they could pick out

anyone in command, sometimes just from the way they talked to others. That's why everyone tried to look as dumb and dirty as everyone else."

Americans also learned to hide everything — maps, binoculars, stripes or bars of rank — that would distinguish them from privates. A Marine tradition of close integration of officers and men in the field helped them assimilate quickly. Men learned to talk to officers without postures that might disclose subordination. Salutes were anathema. "Any rifleman who saluted an officer on the line, targeting him for an enemy sniper, would have been in deep trouble," William Manchester noted.*

Manchester had much Marine company in his contempt for Army leaders who put themselves in peril by maintaining rank's rituals and rigamarole on the line. (In fact, this revealed as much about Marine snobbery as reality, for despite the Army's generally greater distance between fighting officers and men, most Army combat units quickly learned the same lessons as the Marines.) De Mar remembers laughing at Army officers who wore their insignia in combat. "The day before *we* went in, everything came off, everything and anything that could single you out. If you didn't know a captain or a major by sight and he came up to you, you wouldn't know who he was — and if you guessed, you didn't show it to those Japs out there watching to see who gave the orders. This became second nature." Similarly, medical corpsmen tried to be known personally by the units they attended so that wounded men would call "Jones!" or "Bangert!" instead of "Corpsman!" or "Doc!" — which Japanese soldiers sometimes shouted in order to pick off the men who ran out to help.

New replacements rarely had time to learn their corpsmen's names before they were in line. Their failure to know and sense a great deal more accounted for the high proportion killed or wounded on their first days and even hours through such mistakes as peeking out of their foxholes to investigate a sound — perhaps a lure — that veterans knew wasn't worth the risk. Thousands of replacements came up to the front full of expectation and anxiety, saw the unimaginable truth of combat, for which none was prepared, did something with-

---

*Almost all other manifestations of "chicken shit" also disappeared among forward fighting units. "And they didn't dog you to do the things you knew you had to do," a Marine private said of his several officers, unless you were a green replacement and hadn't had time to learn." When things were going well, the relation between officers and men was closer to that of coaches and players than anything learned in basic training — and those particular coaches, who risked their lives with their charges, were more often loved than resented. Even then, Dick Whitaker sympathized with those who had to exercise command, "an incredible burden when just taking care of your own ass was a twenty-four-hour-a-day job."

out the necessary artfulness, and — all in their first day — were delivered to a rear medical facility with grievous wounds and eyes still dumb with shock and disbelief. Graves Registration units picked up perhaps a thousand first-day corpses.

A cool Southerner named James Burden had been a boot camp drill instructor, yet "couldn't imagine how awful combat was; it was just unbelievable." No matter how rigorous Marine infantry training tried to be, only combat itself could teach genuine combat smarts. The training made much of never bunching up so that no single mortar shell could hit more than one or two men, but green men kept being killed in bunches formed of fright. It wasn't until they saw this happen that an instinct to stay apart developed — yet not too far apart, since riflemen needed each other's protection on every flank. Then that instinct was further refined, and they kept the proper distance in varying terrains of plains, hills, woods and escarpment.

American infantrymen who survived a month in the line became as professionally skilled and personally cauterized as infantrymen anywhere. From the positioning of canteens to the placement of an extra knife or .45 pistol under their shirts, everything they wore and carried was readied for the quickest use, the best chance to kill before being killed. Experience had taught that all the skill in the world counted less than good luck in this, especially during an assault against a fortified position, when no one had any control over what ground a hidden Nambu light machine gun would spray or where a mortar shell would fall. Everyone knew that some of the most reckless men went miraculously unscathed and some of the most prudent and expert were blown to bits; that practice of every measure of protection couldn't prevent his own number from coming up. Still, expertise offered slightly better odds of surviving. Men had seen the slack of rifle slings spell the difference between life and death.*

---

*Needless to say, experts argued about such fine points as whether or not to tape down hand grenades. Many hung them on the handiest place, the straps of their packs; some feared they might explode there, or one would fall off. The trade-off of added safety for a second's delay in using the weapon was disputed, but not by those whose experience brought them firmly down on one side or the other. Norris Buchter, whose unit had been caught by Japanese artillery in the north before they were properly dug in, was on watch one night in a small ravine just below a trail the Japanese used for nighttime reinforcement of Sugar Loaf. Ordered there precisely to stop this, Buchter heard stealthy noises advancing on him — not from Americans, he knew, because Americans almost never moved at night. He woke the several Marines with him before his sharpened eyesight made out the faintest of moving shadows in the ravine. He pulled the pin of a hand grenade, tossed it well and heard it drop without exploding: his sergeant was among those who hated grenades, perhaps because he had seen some of the terrible accidents they inevitably caused, and had ordered his men to tape them — tape that Buchter had forgotten to remove from the handle. "From then on, I taped nothing, *nothing*, no matter what anyone said. Those

As in all modern wars, ears became acutely sensitive to menaces broadcast by sounds, especially of the varieties of incoming fire. Each whoosh, whine and whizz identified a bullet or shell type, with its individual trajectory and proximity. One low-velocity shell could actually be seen approaching, tumbling end over end. This was the new Japanese "screaming meemie" or "box car" or "garbage can," an 8-inch mortar detonated by a propellant charge struck with a mallet. The 32nd Army had twenty-four of those weapons. Their launching shriek — "like a locomotive from hell" — and earthshaking thunder when the 650-pound shells hit shred the stretched nerves of even the veterans who knew they were extremely inaccurate, unlike the little Japanese knee-mortar, a simple, deadly weapon that gave almost no warning.

Many veterans were also convinced they could smell the Oriental enemy, just as the enemy could surely smell them, the consumers of so much animal fat. "Nip smell" was said to be "sweetish," a little like that of talcum powder. One man described it as "a kind of perfume — unmistakable once you smelled it. If you did in your foxhole at night, then every nerve quivered until dawn — and sure enough, you'd find evidence that your perimeter line had been penetrated. But you didn't need evidence; you had your senses."

Combat also developed a kind of medical wisdom. A wounded man able to walk with help or talk clearly prompted smiles: those were signs that he wasn't in serious shock. "Even at the tender age of eighteen," an infantryman remembered, "you learned a lot from war about the different aspects of wounds and what reaction to expect. Many men about to die, for instance, instinctively called for their mothers. The plaintive cry 'Mama!' was one of the worst sounds on the battlefield. People who called Mama didn't survive."

But combat smarts pertained mostly to movement. The sharpened senses and new powers of observation and analysis instantly assessed the relative dangers of new strongpoints and terrain. A silent counter recorded the number of Japanese rounds expended, since the dreaded Nambu light machine gun, for example, almost always fired bursts of six to eight rounds. Eyes registered possible evidence of mines and booby traps almost automatically. Bodies were purged of superfluous movement.

At every moment, a new, semiconscious process considered each

---

particular Japs ran off even though my grenade didn't explode, but now they knew our position and the rest of that night was terrifying . . . A grenade not going off in the dark sounds funny when you tell the story later, but nobody laughed at the time, believe me. Usually you didn't have a chance to learn from your mistakes because they got you killed."

movement before it was made. Should the window of that half-standing house be peeked through from the left or right? Should the next grenade be held an extra two or three seconds to prevent the Japanese targets from throwing it back? Should it be thrown with the right hand or left, which would allow quicker operation of the trigger finger? Should the delay be three seconds or five following another man's dash from a bomb crater — and that rock ahead be jumped over in one bound or two? Perhaps a previously little-used area of the brain made these constant life-or-death decisions, calculating how long it was safe to remain in a position during a firefight. Is it time to move *now*? Is a sniper or machine gunner zeroing in on me?

No rushed movements, except in extremis; never noisy movements. Communication in a new language of gestures and motions of the head. Motor skills improved. Bodies attuned for supreme silence and stealth.

Silence meant reducing the unavoidable burden of combat gear to a minimum. "Every day you learned more," as one Marine put it, "and the more you learned, the more you chucked from your kit. You lived by your wits, which meant traveling light." Gas masks had been discarded on the landing beaches, and the bulkiest nonessential equipment, such as supply packs with the extra pair of boots, quickly followed. A Confidential Army report entitled "Principal Lessons Learned in the Okinawa Operation" would confirm that "experience has shown that a soldier will not carry equipment for which he has no apparent need." Every unneeded item — apart from Japanese souvenirs — was jettisoned and every essential was fixed on the body or in the pack so that it wouldn't shift; metal was especially well wrapped in sound-absorbing paper and rags. "If you had to move quickly, even with full gear, the only sound would be your muffled footsteps," Whitaker remembered. "If a crane picked up a combat Marine and shook him fiercely, you'd hear nothing."

With some of their self-inflation also discarded, the Marines came closer to their notion of themselves as the best fighters in the world, although the more worldly would later doubt whether they had been better than the best Japanese. In any case, veteran infantrymen would realize how much combat had changed them — almost into a new species with vastly developed physical senses, and almost everything else, including ethical considerations, shed like hazardous baggage. Although that was nothing new in war, this largest land campaign in the Pacific was long and intense enough to reduce more participants to this primitive state. Infantrymen on Okinawa came to feel that their changed bodies and nervous systems — muscles, senses, instincts, *everything* — had been designed for war and war alone.

Very few thought about this then, partly because almost all powers of observation and analysis were engaged in the animal survival, partly because the adjustment to the new environment had been complete enough to make it seem almost natural. Survivors merely recognized that they had begun to fit their savage world. Norris Buchter's first view of combat veterans on Guadalcanal, where the 6th Marine Division was being formed, had frightened him. Their savage look showed an indifference to, or contempt for, normal social interests. "They were jungle animals, nothing we could relate to, nothing to fool around with — dirty and really tough and probably on the verge of going wacky from battle fatigue, and you could feel that: they belonged to another world." After six weeks on Okinawa, he heard a replacement speak of his group in the same way — "Hey, you're not fit to be with; you don't even look like Marines!" — and realized he had become the same creature; had *had* to become the same. "It's from living on the edge too long, living in the ground all the time, using your wits each minute to survive. It's watching, listening, thinking of what to expect next — not like just an animal but a hunted animal. You do what you have to but you've seen so much awfulness and horror, it's just a different life, indescribable."

> *Time had no meaning. Life had no meaning . . . I had resigned from the human race. I just wanted to kill.*
> — An anonymous American veteran

> *The only glory was in surviving, in staying alive.*
> — Robert Sherer, Dick Whitaker's company commander

But beyond their heightened animal instincts, most men in the lines had a more limited perspective than almost anyone farther removed, perhaps because ignorance of events outside the immediate environment was necessary to free minds for the concerns of survival. In any case, Owen Stebbins felt his men's real life was generally twenty yards on either side of their foxholes, and Manchester agrees: "No Marine in the middle of a firefight, however clever he may have been, knew any more about the foe than the rifleman in the next foxhole." Many on Okinawa literally didn't know where they were during the fighting. "I obviously knew when we got into Naha," said one. "Otherwise, I had almost no idea; I was a private. We weren't told and maybe we didn't want to know or couldn't know; our minds were full of other things."

Dick Whitaker had never heard Napoleon's saying about the combat soldier seeing only the pack of the soldier in front of him but knew exactly what it meant. "Maybe the Japanese soldiers knew more than we did. At least they might have recognized some landmarks: this was the hill they used to watch the stars from; that was the road they used to take to the beach, or to Yoko's hut. We didn't even know where we were or what lay beyond the nearest trees. We certainly didn't know our direction unless the sun was shining. All we had was a grunt of 'Follow me' from somebody in front — and a hope that he knew where the hell he was going, which he often didn't."

Hundreds of men died on Sugar Loaf never knowing its nickname, let alone official designation. Many of the survivors had finished their fighting there before they learned details that would roll from the tongue of war buffs. Superiors didn't necessarily keep those details from the participants out of calculation; it was just as likely to be a sharing of ignorance. "I think one of the reasons we were never told anything was that nobody knew anything," concluded Stuart Upchurch, who turned eighteen five days after L-day.

"I followed orders, not knowing what they meant," said a Sugar Loaf survivor from another company. "When my platoon sergeant or lieutenant said we were taking Hill 63 tomorrow morning, that meant nothing to me. Hill 63 was just another ugly mound with blackened tree stumps that you and your guys had to crawl up, hoping it wouldn't be your last, and that your platoon, your world, would be there that evening so you'd have a few hours together before spending another nightmare of a night."

Thomas Hannaher from Minnesota would become one of the campaign's more thoughtful veterans, remembering with horror what it had cost his friends and Okinawans. But during the fighting itself, Hannaher was almost wholly unaware, as he had to be, of most concerns larger than keeping his head down and his weapon oiled.

> I was one of many know-nothings on Okinawa. I was a private, no stripes . . . almost anyone could order me to do something. I knew absolutely nothing about the overall battle plan, much less the plans for my battalion and battery and gun section. I was in my own very tiny world. Eat, sleep, work and wonder — what am I doing here? Will I be killed? Why me? And even if I do live through it, what next, the great battle of the Japanese mainland? How long could my luck hold? And there was nothing, absolutely nothing, I could do about it. I had to just take it as it came.

Hannaher's private world was hard enough. His battery of 75mm pack howitzers — the last of the pack guns, so named in World War I because they could be disassembled, packed on mules and reassembled farther on — operated closer to the infantry than other artillery apart from 37mms and heavy mortars. Still, that was a precious few hundred yards from the front lines, where life, as he was among the first to admit, was far harder. One ridge made a huge difference. "It was no lark for us," another artilleryman remembered. "We lived with quite enough danger even when we weren't shelled — a man on the gun next to mine was killed by muzzle blast, for example. But we didn't have that constant feeling of imminent death, of counting your days because they're numbered. When we saw those ragged, groggy infantrymen trudging a road somewhere, we felt real admiration for them. *They* were on the fighting edge, the real war — and we felt proud to support them, but from a different world."

American infantry got phenomenal support from those close-range howitzers in addition to long-range artillery like the powerful Long Toms, the vast naval flotilla's massive guns and the swarms of Army, Marine and naval aircraft. But as the writer Bill Ross said about Iwo Jima, the ultimate weapon on Okinawa two months later remained a young man with a bayoneted rifle. Everyone in the real war knew that, which is why infantry officers, those most perishable creatures, looked slightly down on all others, even those in tank units. "Speaking very simply, land had to be seized and held," said Owen Stebbins of G–2–22. "That was the only way the war could be won — on the ground."

The proximity to the Japanese on the ground depended on place and time: whether they had fortified an area and when they decided to make a charge. But at the moments of contact, it was the closest men came to the enemy in that war, often close enough for Whitaker to hear Japanese songs, whispers, the clatter of utensils — and, once, a shout of "Babe Ruth eat shit!" "If you left your foxhole and advanced, sooner or later you'd meet a Jap who was out there with a single purpose, to kill you. That's how close, the twenty or thirty paces you could lob a grenade. Or when you got in a firefight, you didn't have time to raise your weapon and aim, you just fired and fired and fired from any possible position and hoped your buddies kept pouring it on while you reloaded. But close was what it was all about, wasn't it? That's how you took ground."

The infantrymen on whom everything rested in the end usually hugged the ground as tightly as they could. Very occasionally, something drove a sprinkling of them to the kind of feat dramatized in war movies: an unmanageable surge of adrenaline or exhaustion even beyond the ordinary or a man's fear that his nerves were snapping because he truly couldn't stand the terror of being pinned down any longer. Sometimes it was a saintly calculation that all would die unless one took an otherwise lunatic risk. The spurs of battlefield gallantry are harder to understand than those of battlefield breakdown; even Okinawa's certified heroes disagree about why they performed their wild, momentous acts. Some say devotion to their unit; others, that an evil enemy trying to kill their beloved friends is explanation enough. One former sergeant who heroically charged Sugar Loaf in dazed exhaustion swears it was all a mistake because he had intended to run away from the fire instead of toward it. Then, when all Americans near him were shot, he "just lay at the crest, absolutely quivering with terror, until first light, when friendly company came racing up. Luckily, neither side knew which one held the crest that night, so neither side shelled it."

Mistakes and lack of imagination — or stupidity — were indeed among the explanations of supreme courage. Some men couldn't imagine themselves dead. Those who made conscious decisions to risk everything were perhaps the most brave of all, but others "just became too utterly disgusted with battlefield's unspeakable existence," as one modestly rationalized his own motivation. "They became so full of revulsion against that hideous life that anything was preferable."

Some heroes appeared "unnatural" to average infantrymen — as a man who would be awarded the Navy Cross seemed to a machine gunner who watched in wonder as the future medal winner "stood up like a bear with his BAR, shouting, 'Come on out, you sons of bitches!' A man who stood up on the front line day after day almost looked like he *wanted* to get killed. He must have had a screw loose. No sensible man would do those things." Some of that species of hero would become problems in civilian life. A few were psychopaths.

Whatever the reasons, it is the handful forced up from their cover on those few occasions, who plunged into a wild leap of shouting, charging and firing against an enemy position, that make up a substantial part of American accounts of the battle, such as a lore-filled homage by James and William Belote entitled *Typhoon of Steel.*

Captain Nelson C. Dale, Jr.'s Company L caught it — and dished it out — in a ravine cut by a small stream. Its second platoon had barely cleared the neck of the ravine when small-arms fire burst from scores of well-camouflaged caves dug horizontally into the side of the ravine. Captain Dale fell badly wounded with six other Marines. His executive officer, Lieutenant Marvin D. Perskie, took over as the men recoiled and took cover.

There could be no thought of abandoning the attack. As Perskie recalled later, "We had to get those men out of there." After various outflanking maneuvers had failed, Perskie yelled, "Let's go, men," leaped to his feet, and ran down the ravine followed by the company. This time the attack burst right through, with the flame-thrower men dousing the caves with liquid fire as they passed. Emerging Japanese toppled to the riflemen. One cried weakly, "Banzai." "Banzai, hell," a Marine retorted, knocking him sprawling with a burst from his Browning automatic rifle.

When superiors heard of such exploits, a medal was likely, even the Congressional Medal of Honor, of which twenty-three, the largest number of any campaign in the war, were awarded for conspicuous gallantry on Okinawa.

Less than 25 [of an infantry company of some 250] now remained effective amid signs that the Japanese below and on Horseshoe had been organizing for another attack. Enemy fire intensified. But Colonel Mita's infantry were not having it entirely their own way, for one of the surviving Americans was Corporal Donald (Rusty) Golar, a self-styled "storybook" Marine. Golar, a light machine gunner, used to tell his sometimes unbelieving buddies who thought him a blowhard, "I'm looking for Japs." After Guam many began taking him at his word. "You watch that Rusty," they would say. "Just watch that redhead!" Now that redhead was behind a Browning light machine gun, a camouflaged helmet atop it bobbing with each burst as its owner squeezed the trigger. When the Japanese would begin shooting at him from another direction, Golar would boom, "Yeah!" wheel his gun about, and take them on. Finally, Golar had no more ammunition. "Gotta use what I've got left," he yelled to a buddy, Private Donald Kelly of Chicago. He drew his .45 caliber pistol, emptied it, then stood up and pitched the empty weapon toward the spurts of enemy fire. Dashing about, Golar collected hand grenades from the fallen, then hurled them down Sugar Loaf's reverse slope. When he ran out of grenades, Golar found a BAR and fired until it jammed.

"Nothing more to give them," he yelled to Kelly. "Let's get some of these wounded guys down." He bent over a Marine with a chest wound. "I'll have you in sick bay in no time." But as he walked with the Marine toward the northern rim of the hill a bullet struck him. He staggered, Kelly recalled, "but he put the wounded man down. Then he went over to the ditch with a surprised look on his face . . . I saw him sit down and push his helmet over his forehead like he was going to sleep. Then he died."

June 19 brought a final Medal of Honor feat. Technical Sergeant John Meagher of the 305th Infantry, 77th Division, mounted a tank to direct gunfire in the Medeera pocket area, jumped from the vehicle to bayonet a Japanese running at the tank with a satchel charge. Then he ran back to the tank, grabbed a machine gun, and firing from the hip rushed a pair of enemy machine guns, finishing off the last of the second gun's crew by wielding his empty weapon from the barrel like a club.

And from a history of the 6th Marine Division:

> Private James L. Lore was advancing with a flamethrower against a cave [on Sugar Loaf] where seven Japs were manning a machine gun. Four of them ran to one side of the cave's entrance, three to the other. He killed the four in one searing blast, then turned on the others. He was able to set their clothing ablaze, but his flamethrower suddenly went out and they started for him. With no weapons, weighted down by the hose and tanks on his back, he turned to run but tripped over a communications wire. As the burning Japs closed in on him, it occurred to him to spray them with the incendiary fluid. Lore grinned as he told how he "stopped them with a blaze of glory."

But every combat infantryman knew decorations were no true record of battlefield conduct. (The cynical would say they were designed by noncombatants as encouragement to keep them at the filthy job.) A topheavy percentage went to officers sheltering in battalion command posts two hundred yards behind the line while their units took some deadly objective. Many heroic acts went unrewarded because no one survived to witness them. "I saw men do braver things than those who got the highest decorations but were never cited," says an Okinawa veteran who doesn't wear his own medal because, he insists, celebrity earned or unearned only further distorts combat's awful reality. "Honor belongs to the dead, and I don't want to do anything, wear anything or say anything that romanticizes the hellish misery called war."

Although that attitude is extreme, all participants in combat learned that luck largely determined who won medals, which was as unfair as who survived and who got killed. Few infantrymen lack stories of real heroes who were never decorated. Some of the bravest men walked away after their heroic acts, wanting and getting no reward other than that of saving their comrades. On the evening Major Courtney led his band up Sugar Loaf, he assigned Corporal Dan Dereschuk to protect his right flank with two machine guns and eight men from Company G-2-22. As the eight dwindled to three, one with a bad stomach wound, the two utterly exhausted and partially wounded "fit" heroes kept the Japanese at bay with rifles and hand grenades. When they were evacuated at dawn, Dereschuk was patched up and went back to combat without rest or a citation.

And whatever the merits and demerits of awards, the rare courage of the standouts represented a tiny fraction of the total man-hours on the line. A military historian's study concluded that only a quarter of men under fire in World War II and the Korean War fired back. The majority were too frightened to put into practice their intense training focused on precisely this. Although American infantrymen, especially Marine, surely performed far better than average on Okinawa, they spent much more time taking cover than leaping up from it. The Whitakers dug into the ground, vision restricted to the patch of charred, pockmarked terrain they could see from the lips of their foxholes, had a severely limited, personalized perspective of the campaign. The luckiest would endure six more weeks of more or less blindly following men in front and hoping to stay alive. They would enjoy no glimpse of the larger picture, that luxury available to survivors. In that sense, this account is as misleading as all others about the reality of war in the killing zone. Books about combat are a kind of reverse of combat itself, and to the degree that the Battle of Okinawa was harder than its predecessors, that is more than ordinarily true about this one.

News of Nazi Germany's collapse and of V-E Day reached Okinawa the day before Paul Dunfrey scouted the south bank of the Asakawa, four days before Sugar Loaf. Many of the ships in the bays held services of thanksgiving, and the big fire-support wagons and cruisers joined field artillery in a huge noontime salvo at enemy positions. The Japanese targets had no idea what had brought about the earth-shaking thunder until several days later — but neither did many Americans on the ground.* And even those who did know didn't care much. To men soaked with rain, covered with mud and peering

---

*The Japanese learned from American leaflets, which in this case, unlike the news of *Yamato* and other great Japanese reversals, they tended to credit. Educated soldiers had much feared the loss of the European ally but said little now beyond some praise for Germany for having held out as long as she had against enemies on two fronts. And even the educated continued to wait for the arrival of the Combined Fleet to turn the tide there on Okinawa.

Some nonmilitary items in the 8 million American leaflets dropped on Japanese positions during the campaign — "Night Baseball Revived in America," "Shirley Temple Engaged" — brightened otherwise wretched cave life for a few. But the majority continued to dismiss the war news as attempts to weaken their morale, even while appreciating the fine quality of the paper. Far cruder Japanese leaflets composed for the Americans stressed the uselessness of their endeavors and the death it would bring them, together with suffering for their families. Some items also stressed what a pity it was that American fighters were allowing their women to be ravished by men back in the States. "Don't you know what this operation to Okinawa is destroying your glorious mother land?" read a handwritten scrawl on a V-mail form that had evidently been taken from an American body. "Your useless battle will fat the dogs in Okinawa by yourselve's corpse. Imaginate your wife crying at the sad news."

Meanwhile, Tokyo Rose kept broadcasting. Whitaker heard one of her lines as "I got mine last night, your best girl got hers. Did you get yours?"

ahead for a glimpse of a rifle pointed at them as they ducked from mortar rounds, Europe meant little more than a place that was draining off the best supplies. "To hell with that war" was the typical reaction to the news in foxholes isolated in strain and fear. "This is the one I'm worried about."

Dick Whitaker felt the defeat of the enemy whose panzers and Stukas had been the baddies of his boyhood games "was happening on another planet. We didn't think much about what was going on over on the next hill, not to mention Germany." Eugene Sledge and his fellow Marines were "resigned only to the fact that the Japanese would fight to total extinction on Okinawa . . . and Japan would have to be invaded with the same gruesome prospects." "They told us it was all over in Europe but it sure as hell wasn't all over for us," another Sugar Loaf survivor remembered. "Your perspective in combat is the next ditch, the next minute. The thing we really cared about was how soon some troops would be here from Europe to help us out."

The death of Franklin Roosevelt on April 12, almost a month earlier, had greater significance for many fighters, most of whom had known only one President in their lives and took the loss personally. But it was on the ships anchored near or patrolling around the coasts that the greatest shock and grief were felt, as well as in the supply forces and combat units not in the line at the moment. Replacement troops on their way, unknowing, to Okinawa from the States also had more room for such feelings and time to express them. Many wept. But those actually fighting felt only some pangs of sadness. They were too busy trying to catch their breath, catch some sleep and stay alive. Their chief worry was whether the President's death might prolong the war.*

In America, Roosevelt's death and V-E Day were among the larger, closer events that helped keep the desperate hardships on remote Okinawa from reaching the public consciousness. Roosevelt's funeral, daily evidence of the collapse of German defenses, and Truman's early weeks in the White House seemed more important, relevant news. Throughout the first month on Okinawa, editors allotted far more space to the dramatic assault on Berlin and the German surrender, which came on top of the greater prominence they gave the

---

*There was no break on the battle front while civilians were grieving on the home front. On the night of the President's death, an Army staff sergeant named Beaufort Anderson tried to stop a Japanese counterattack on Kakazu Ridge with a single-handed countercounterattack. When his supply of grenades ran out, he grabbed some mortar shells, but there was no mortar to fire them. Anderson banged the shells against a rock to release their pins and threw fourteen by hand against the advancing party.

European War to begin with. Mussolini Dead! Americans Meet Red Army on the Elbe! Berlin Falls! Hitler Suicide in His Bunker! Compared to this, the Okinawan campaign was just another slog on a distant island; the greatest land, sea, air battle in history was usually reported on inside pages. By the time of the worst fighting on Okinawa, attention was already shifting to new stories, again more dramatic, of the death camps and other Nazi secrets, the future of Europe and the imminent invasion of the Japanese mainland. After Germany's collapse, Okinawa became what one historian called "the vortex of the war," but that recognition would never enter the public consciousness.

Few dispatches from the island offered clues to the nature of the fighting; instead, they conveyed an optimistic summary of its overall progress and provided color about men interviewed behind the lines. Reporters weren't exactly prevaricating in this. It is worth repeating that "serving" in 1945 was in most cases quite different from actually fighting. In many historical periods, authentic combat, the real thing, had been a relatively small part of military life, involving far fewer soldiers for far fewer days than the planning of it. Armies prepared by drilling, conferring and cleaning latrines; only the men on their outer edges fell to bludgeons, swords, scimitars and arrows. Technological development further reduced the proportion on the front lines, more sophisticated weapons requiring more personnel to service them. The greater the distance from the fighters' homes at which the battle was fought, the greater the numbers needed for transport, supply and bookkeeping. "The worst of war is hell, but there isn't much of the worst . . . and not many soldiers experience even that much," a journalist-veteran recently summarized. Or, as a student of military affairs put it, "Battle is no more characteristic of war than copulation is of marriage."*

Thus the Americans who fought their way past the deadly Okinawan caves represented a tiny fraction even of those serving in the Pacific at the time. Each man at the front was supported by nineteen others, usually from a considerable distance. Most of those nineteen endured varying degrees of discomfort but were as spared from the real horror as civilians. It was only within rifle range of the enemy where the world went mad, where life was so unlike anything previously known, that those just a quarter of a mile behind could not easily imagine it. Most reporters ventured no closer than five hundred yards behind this point.

*Edward N. Luttwak argued that this opens the way to understanding why "armed conflict can still survive the human experience of combat, instead of being swept away by the outrage of those who have been in its hell and have come back to tell the tale."

It is largely as a result of the misinformation supplied by reporters that Americans have been led to think of themselves as the great saviors of the world . . . The public is forced to swallow whole the idiotic stories of utterly uninformed men on so vital a matter as the enemy we have been fighting.

— Lieutenant j. g. Donald Keene, a Japanese language specialist who served on Okinawa

Most men didn't talk about it. It was not that they did not want to talk about it, it was that when they did, nobody understood it. It was such a different way of living, and of looking at life even, that there was no common ground for communication in it.

— James Jones, a former combat soldier

Ernie Pyle went farther than most. World War II's most celebrated American correspondent landed on Okinawa on L-day afternoon and quickly began filing stories with his flair for the intimate. The tough-but-gentle humanist had compelled Congress virtually single-handedly to award mud-slogging doughboys and Leathernecks the Combat Infantryman's Badge and extra pay. (The Marine establishment declined both, asserting with some justice that all Marines were combat troops.) As in the European theater, where he had won his name and affection by writing from ground level rather than from command heights, Pyle appeared to tell it like it was.

"Infantry's Friend" even toured a sideshow on the little island of Ie Shima, just four miles from the Motobu Peninsula, where Colonel Udo's mountain artillery slowed the 6th Marine Division's race to the north. Ie Shima, one of several offshore islands close enough to be almost extensions of Okinawa, accommodated the critical asset of Asia's largest airfield on its eleven square miles. But photographic evidence indicated that it was undefended, and absence of fire on attacking American planes seemed to confirm that, as did information from a Japanese officer, rescued from a sunk motor boat, that all installations there had been evacuated. However, that was bad reconnaissance supported by *dis*information. The airfield lay beneath a strongly fortified mountain.

Pyle visited Ie Shima on April 17. The next morning, a machine gun fired on the jeep taking him toward the fighting through territory already captured by the 77th Army Division. The riders leaped into a roadside ditch, where a bullet in the temple killed "the most famous and beloved civilian of all the United States services." A good military history asserts that the shock brought the Okinawan campaign to the attention of millions back home. Not really. The loss of that single life simply became news; but battles that took thousands, not to mention the conditions that locked tens of thousands in daily agony, remained nearly unknown.

The fighters themselves were not immune to awe of the famous. They quickly erected a sign in memory of the fallen celebrity: "At This Spot, the 77th Infantry Division Lost a Buddy, ERNIE PYLE, 18 April 1945." A quarter of a century later, a concrete monument with the same inscription would be one of just three memorials to the Okinawan campaign's appalling number of American dead — 240 on Ie Shima alone before the six days of fighting there ended.*

The irony is that Pyle's dispatches from Okinawa, as elsewhere, were far too pretty to convey any sense of the fighting's filth and pain. His stories came closer to honest reporting than almost all others but still missed by a mile — as they had to. "It's humiliating to look back at what we wrote during the war," a Canadian reporter later said. "It was crap — and I don't exclude the Ernie Pyles . . . We were a propaganda arm of our governments . . . We were cheerleaders. I suppose there wasn't an alternative at the time. It was total war. But for God's sake let's not glorify our role. It wasn't good journalism. It wasn't journalism at all."†

Pacific War reporting outdid itself in masking rather than conveying the hardships, partly because they were so extreme. Most dispatches from Okinawa revealed less about the real war than about how the powers pumped up morale with half-truths. Many took their readers farther than no information at all from a sense of what was actually happening there: although they contained some facts, their tone, underlying assumptions and overall effect fed the usual misconceptions and standard prevarications about combat. A few officers who visited battle sites and took the trouble to jot down their impressions got much closer to the truth — as in a nonprofessional's report on the "battle-scarred, demolished" village of Gusukuma.

> I was surprised to feel that the ground was soft and soggy under my feet. I looked down to see the knee of a dead Japanese soldier

---

*A thousand men were also wounded. Yet John Lardner informed *New Yorker* readers that this was a "quick and otherwise [except for Pyle's death] unnoteworthy little special campaign."

†Quoted in *The First Casualty*, Phillip Knightley's telling exposé of war reporting. Lloyd George had put the reality in a nutshell: "The correspondents don't write and the censorship would not pass the truth." Although Pyle, "the common soldier's spokesman," did come a half-step closer to some aspects of the real thing than most, Paul Fussell had grounds to recently liken his copy to "emissions from the Office of War Information."

Pyle's outlook also helped explain why Europe's less grueling and cruel fighting got more recognition. Sent to the Pacific in late 1944 under heavy official pressure, he continued to feel the important war was in Europe. And his treatment of Okinawan civilians helps explain why that aspect of the campaign, the major story, was never told at all to the good folks back home. His little vignettes had Okinawans going their Oriental-inscrutable ways while they were actually suffering horrendously.

protruding from the dirt. As I stood, somewhat horrified, maggots oozed from the remains. The stench was terrible . . . green flies were everywhere, blowing the bloated bodies. I stepped into the entrance of a large cave and saw . . . the half-clothed body of a Japanese soldier. A rat scurried away to hide beneath a pile of rubbish. I noticed the body had a ghastly hole in the stomach where the rat had burrowed, feeding on the dead flesh. The soldier had been dead for several days and had swollen to an abnormal size. His legs burst his wrap leggings and a bulge protruded over his shoe tops where the shoe would not permit it to swell further . . . his eyes were bulging from his head and his close-cropped black hair seemed ready to pop from his head.

But the scores of accredited correspondents omitted almost all such details, especially when they pertained to the home team. Most of their "human interest" stories and "Hi, Mom!" features about hometown boys could only mislead readers about life in the field; some of them ludicrously distorted Japanese behavior. And there was no mention of all-night retching with disease and fear, no moans or screams or mental disintegration, let alone shot-off faces and testicles. Pyle's accounts of the misery ventured all the way to the infernal buzzing and biting of Okinawan fleas and mosquitoes, as if that was what distinguished infantrymen's ordeal from normality. While skirting the truth of life in the field, such "reporting" conned readers into believing that was just what they were reading. Eugene Sledge, the tough, pious eighteen-year-old Marine, later revealed the truth in his memoir; it would have almost nothing in common with the dispatches of the professional journalists. "I felt sickened to the depths of my soul," he wrote of his first taste of combat. "I asked God, 'Why, why, why?' I turned my face away and wished that I were imagining it all. I had tasted the bitterest essence of the war . . . and it filled me with disgust."

If not the *why* of war itself, then the why of ignoring its bitterest essence is plain. No one could be an independent observer. Reporters played on the same team as the fighters or didn't get to the game at all. Having provided exclusive access to the material, the military exercised tight control on how it was written up. A reporter with a conviction that the truth was more important and with the courage to defy all convention of supporting the American line would neither last long nor achieve anything in print. The great war correspondent John Steinbeck knew that "the foolish reporter who broke the rules would not be printed at home and in addition would be put out of the theater by the command . . . We were all part of the War Effort. We went along with it and not only that, we abetted it."

Battle hardships were couched in images of a hard-fought but essentially sane sporting event. "Leathernecks and doughboys of the 10th Army held the Japanese key fortress of Shuri in a giant cup-shaped pincers today as they turned both ends of the Okinawa battle line." Even the best journalism in the most authoritative pages now reads like slick fluff.

Whitaker's cheery letters to his parents left the bitter essence unmentioned for the same reasons: to reassure them, to avert superiors' obligatory censorship and to mask his inability to convey the awful reality of his life to outsiders.* Others' letters tried to hint that there was much to tell, but their writers despaired of getting to the immensity of it. "So far I have been very lucky," went a typical passage on American Red Cross stationery, "and I know it is because of all your prayers and . . . mine. I have a lot to tell you when I am in a position to and that isn't right now." But this man, like so many survivors when they returned, was never able to tell his family, to which he was very close. "There was no way to describe or convey it because it was beyond every imaginable aspect of life."

> You could always tell whether men were moving up or coming off the line. Usually those coming off had samurai swords jutting from their packs. And they had a different look — dull, sightless eyes showing the strain, misery, shock, sleeplessness, and in veteran fighters, the supreme indifference of young men who have lost their youth and will never forget it.
> — William Manchester

> I arrived as a replacement in the middle of May and boy, was I happy to get off that miserable troopship and rocking landing craft! But I was already ducking by the time the ramp came down. Okinawa didn't have a landscape, it had a glimpse of hell on earth . . . I spent my first night in the replacement area, awaiting assignment. There were screaming dogfights above, kamikazes crashing into ships and artillery fire I couldn't tell whether was ten miles or ten yards away. I was scared. And just miserable. In a few hours, the rain water was up to my waist.
>   I could see why replacement bodies were needed so badly. The casualties were tremendous. Near us was a huge mound of personal belongings — of the dead. I was never a thief, but this was survival: my boots were all mush inside and I had to get some dry socks. And that gave me another fright because a big Marine at the mound, maybe who'd just lost a buddy, almost shot me for reaching into it for a pair. And I hadn't even seen the fighting yet.

---

*Like many only children, Whitaker worried about the great blow his death would deliver to his anxious parents. His letters did manage to inform them at least where he was when this was still secret. The private code in his "I had a letter from *G*eorge *U*nderhill yesterday, he's fine, he said *A*unt *M*arie had seen him last week" revealed he was on Guam. (Italics added.)

Then I was rushed to Sugar Loaf and couldn't believe the look of the guys coming down from there. I don't mean the wounded or the dead but the living who didn't look alive either. Young kids who were old. I was assigned to a machine gun squad under a 30-year-old, I thought. I just couldn't believe he was 19.
— Buzzy Fox

Most human life, and not only human, is spent avoiding pain and discomfort of one kind or another. Beneath the social reasons, one wears clothing to avoid the pain of exposure and eats to avoid the pain of hunger; mothers nurse infants because, among other reasons, not to do so causes pain. Similarly with the avoidance of emotional pain. What men endured on Okinawa was so frightening and painful that many try to make light of it, even joke about it. Just in terms of eating, sleeping, staying dry and evacuating, it was as tough a 24 hours as anyone could imagine.
— Dr. Edmund Shimberg, who served as a 19-year-old corpsman

It was almost like a dream because in the midst of the brutality and horror you just went about your business, sometimes without even time *to be afraid.*
— Edward Jones

It's really very hard to describe what it was like on Okinawa. I'm not sure even Marines who weren't in combat would believe the horror.
— Dick Whitaker

Here I am now twenty years old and I don't feel a day over forty.
— Melvin Heckt, during his fighting on Okinawa

The mud was knee-deep in some places, probably deeper in others if one dared venture there. For several feet around every corpse, maggots crawled about in the mud and then were washed away by the runoff of the rain. There wasn't a tree or a bush left. All was open country. Shells had torn up the turf so completely that ground cover was nonexistent. The rain poured down on us as evening approached. The scene was nothing but mud; shell fire; flooded craters with their silent, pathetic, rotting occupants; knocked-out tanks and amtracs; and discarded equipment — utter desolation . . .

I existed from moment to moment, sometimes thinking death would have been preferable. We were in the depths of the abyss, the ultimate horror of war . . . I believed we had been flung into hell's own cesspool.
— Eugene B. Sledge on the ten days of fighting at Wana Draw, two miles northeast of Sugar Loaf

All this gave the home front, less equipped to picture Pacific conditions to begin with, a much vaguer notion of the fighting on Okinawa than it had of the more familiar "old countries" of Europe. The American public was further disadvantaged because generations had been protected from the bombing, shelling, shooting, gassing and mutilation Europeans had endured. Apart from the minority who fought, Americans were uncommonly ignorant of war and its costs, unusually conditioned to assume the victims to be among the enemy who had brought things on themselves. (By 1945, Japanese civilians, who had also taken it as natural that bombs and shells fell on others, were acquiring the experience of being the target.) But even if reporters had lived on the killing edge and could have reported honestly, the battle's ways differed too greatly from anything most readers could imagine to convey in newspaper or radio copy. Life at the Shuri Line was absurd even without the bullets. Almost all infantrymen had moments and hours of feeling the experience wasn't happening because it couldn't happen, it was too unnatural.

Most of Okinawa's heavy annual rainfall came during the rainy season, four weeks or so that usually began in May and could amount to ten inches a day. The spring of 1945 happened to be much wetter than usual. Clouds rolled in early from the East China Sea and lay low over the island, delivering heavy, ceaseless rain day after day — greater deluges than most Americans had imagined possible. Typhoons dumped extra water in the island. One writer claimed that all previous rainfall seen by Americans was "reduced to the status of Scotch mist." Even without a sharp wind lashing their faces with drops, they were often too dense for men to make out their fellows in neighboring foxholes.

Fires for coffee and hot food were impossible. Ration tins overflowed with rainwater in minutes. Ponds of ochre floodwater on the lowlands became lakes that swallowed eight-wheel trucks. Replacement troops dug their first foxholes, took cover in them and were in water to their waists within an hour. Or couldn't do even that well: the souplike mud was too thin to scoop out for a proper foxhole, and so slippery that some men used their precious rifles as walking sticks.

No one on the line had a moment's escape from the mud that submerged people and equipment. "You were knee-deep in it" Joseph McConville remembered. "Sometimes you slept standing up in it." Wet for days on end, the men shivered in their puckered skin. The outbreak of typhoid occurred during those downpours. "Jungle rot" spread from feet to the crotch. Ringworm in the belt area was sometimes so painful that combat troops could not wear their packs or cartridge belts.

When the mud dried in June, the dust became furious — but in May that would have seemed positively inviting. In World War I, a painful condition caused by prolonged exposure to wet and mud was called trench foot. Now it was "immersion foot," and as in Europe thirty years earlier, dry feet became a longed-for luxury. Dick Whitaker's reeked of mud and the sweat of exertion and fear. He wore the same socks, like the same underwear, for weeks. In normal life, his stinking platoon mates would have had trouble standing each other or themselves. Men who found streams for washing on their breaks from fighting had to cut off their socks. When a jeep towed up a large tank of water one day to where Whitaker's platoon had been pulled back from the line, he decided it was time to use a clean pair he'd been saving in his pack. Each man in the platoon was allotted a helmetful of water instead of the usual canteen. Whitaker had a bath with his and felt gloriously clean. Then he dressed, saving his treasured clean socks, which were also brand-new, for last. Standing on the island of a big rock, he lost his balance pulling on the second sock and fell into a pond of muck.

It was more tragic than funny at the time — too much like the rifles that fell into the same stuff when a bullet or shell knocked their users flat, then wouldn't fire because the bolt became too clogged to seat. When enemy soldiers on Sugar Loaf approached one man whose rifle was useless with mud, he frantically kicked the bolt home with his foot, then had to hope it wouldn't explode in his face when he fired. He was lucky. He kept kicking and firing.

The battles for Sugar Loaf and all the other strongpoints of the Shuri Line took place during the most torrential deluges, which were adversity enough by themselves. Pilots would wake at night, hear the rain beating on their tent roofs and wonder whether it would ever stop. Mornings would be "dark, gray and the rain still falling." They lived "in a world of water and mud," their feet stuck in the gluey bog of the "company street" of tents, their clothing and bedding never dry "so that night and day our bodies were always in contact with something damp and unpleasant." But those were the lucky pilots in the rear who *had* tents and bedding to get wet, unlike the infantrymen. After charges at strongpoints in the Shuri Line, the clusters of survivors huddled not only in mourning for their dead and fear for themselves but also in the misery of the cold rain that soaked them all day. Manchester remembered wondering "in a idiotic moment — no man in combat is really sane — whether the battle could be called off, or at least postponed," because of the appalling weather.

Battlefield mud's "misery beyond description" intensified the infantrymen's labor by many times. Okinawa had few paved roads. Before the war, vehicles using them during the dry months produced a blinding cloud of dust from the dirt tracks. Now that thick red dust turned to sludge that clung to tires and boots, retarding all movement. Men without a suction-breaking covering of burlap bags on their boots needed help to pull themselves out. Jeeps got mired.

Trucks, tractors and bulldozers came to the rescue and were swallowed. Tanks disappeared in lakes of ooze. Some transportation of supplies by parachute drops and small boats was improvised, but many of the drops fell too near enemy snipers to be recovered and others broke apart because the sodden parachutes failed to open in the rain. (A few killed and wounded Americans by landing on them.) In the end, infantrymen, often near exhaustion from combat's physical demands and mental tension, had to take on the extra supply work of carrying as much as they could on their shoulders and backs, wading through quagmires impassable by motorized transport and left to human legs driven by the insatiable need for ammunition and other supplies.

Much of war's literary and cinematic dramatization blithely ignores this "grueling facet of the infantrymen's war," as Private Sledge later called it. It implies that ammunition happens to be at hand whenever needed for giving the enemy hell. Every time veteran Whitaker saw a movie hero who never ran out of ammunition, he remembered the constant worry on Okinawa, where a few minutes of intense firing could exhaust the precious supply and leave him defenseless. (Thanks to the lugging, Whitaker's company in fact rarely ran out of anything except grenades, which they expended very quickly when caught in ambushes.)

The average infantryman — even those not lugging extra weapons like machine guns, BARs, flamethrowers and satchel charges — was a small walking arsenal. He heaved his way through the mud with his rifle, backpack and a cartridge belt containing eight to ten clips of eighteen rounds each, a considerable burden in itself. Two to four hand grenades dangled from his belt, together with a white phosphorous grenade or two when they were available.* The combined load made very heavy exercise of combat's running, dashing and crawling under deadly fire.

Many infantrymen hauled much more even when motorized transport still functioned. As an ammunition carrier for his machine gun platoon, Whitaker was saddled with two steel boxes of .30-caliber ammunition in addition to the other burdens. He and other carriers improvised cushions and shoulder straps from empty ammunition belts to relieve the pain of the handles cutting into their fingers. Still, their arms felt "as if they were coming out of our sockets" after twenty minutes of lugging — and it sometimes went on for hours.

---

*That supply could be used up in minutes during emergencies; only the weight kept most men from carrying more. Dick Whitaker had a constant fear that an enemy bullet would hit one of the grenades he clipped to his cartridge belt or pack strap. He often envisioned the result: "Messy!"

They struggled with the weight and pain, weakened by lack of food, sleeplessness and at least a touch of dysentery. Bringing up rifle ammo, machine gun belts and hand grenades when much of the front was a morass — and when Japanese artillery, skillfully zeroed in on every road near the Shuri Line, forced men into rice paddies — took a predictable toll. Carrying the wounded was even harder and more nerve-racking. Slogging them through the deep, sticky mud in boots that weighed several extra pounds because they dripped with it was brutal labor. Strong young men became so exhausted that they hesitated to put down their loads for fear they wouldn't be able to pick them up again. The advance was more rapid after the Shuri Line was broken, but this often meant lugging more supplies over greater distances. An ammunition carrier in another machine gun platoon bore his load across one large rice paddy farther south, then fell to the ground. "If a Jap had come around a tree and aimed at me, I truly wouldn't have been able to move. That wasn't exhaustion but stupefaction."

In keeping with Murphy's Law of war mandating that those who have it worst should also be worst sustained, fighting men on Okinawa ate wretchedly. Combat so strained the nervous system that many did not want to eat despite their enormous expenditure of energy. All had almost constant thirst, and worried about supplies of water only less than of ammunition. Brought up in five-gallon tanks, the water always tasted of oil, although this may have been the power of suggestion. The grateful recipients dropped a purification pill — not always effective against dysentery — inside the "slimy green shit" and drank as if in the desert. But many had to force themselves to eat.

Basic nourishment was almost always available in the form of a K-ration in one's pack. The little box contained a sardine-size can of "ungodly" hash and cheese or ham and eggs, soluble coffee or lemonade, and some hard biscuits. The larger C-ration offered a slightly more tempting can of pork and beans but was heavier to carry, an important consideration to men weighed down by so much else, especially since there was often little time or desire to eat. Like athletes in a tough competition, fighting men lack energy for hunger. Constant fear and revulsion of the battlefield's loathsome sights and smells further depressed the appetite; the stomach's steady shrinking tightened the cycle. Almost everyone lost fifteen to twenty-five pounds. Starting thin, Whitaker could hardly afford his loss of twenty pounds (which was average). He lived for days on cigarettes, included in the K- and C-rations and otherwise distributed free, and "dog turds," fortified fruit-and-chocolate bars that provided quick energy and did not melt in heat. "You carried them in your pack until you thought you were starving. You took one bite and felt stuffed."

Whitaker ate his single hot meal during his fighting in the south about a week after Sugar Loaf, when word was passed down that everyone should assemble with his mess kit because a truck was expected with some mess hall chow. No one in the platoon had a mess kit by then. The metal was likely to rattle dangerously, and combat Marines had learned not to tote around anything so nonessential. Whitaker did have his canteen cup, into which a scoop of raw hamburger meat was plunked when he reached the truck. A second mess attendant pushed an orange at him to cap his feast.*

Another man remembered his single hot meal arriving by parachute. But some had no hot food at all in two months of savage fighting. Kitchens were closed when the going got tough. Mess staffs were the first to be shifted to combat duties as riflemen and stretcher bearers.

Near the end of the campaign, a mobile kitchen was opened for a Marine unit that had had no hot food in nearly two months. A radio operator salivated as he speared a piece of hotcake, but he couldn't eat it, this time not for lack of appetite. Fearless flies twice the size of any he had seen in America flew into his mouth before he could rush his first bite in. He ate nothing despite his hunger.

Lice and fleas were separate scourges for the combat troops. The fleas, which usually resided in native goats, infested many of the beaches, houses and villages. Men who never slept a night on a beach, a native straw mat, or in a cave could not avoid picking them up as they pushed through. Foxholes were quickly infested; few infantrymen were spared — American or Japanese. "I borrowed Shimazu's razor and shaved," read the May 3 entry of a diary found on a dead Japanese soldier. "There was no night work" — a lucky break for him — "but it was hot and there were so many fleas and lice that I couldn't sleep a wink." But all insects that made Japanese cave life unceasing torment played second fiddle to flies, black or blue-and-green monsters that feasted on the garbage, excrement and rotting corpses strewn over the battle sites.

Japanese soldiers had been harried by tenacious, seemingly angry flies even before the fighting began. "They were as big as horseflies," one remembered, "with red heads and fierce, glaring eyes. They swarmed all over our faces whenever we came close to the piles of garbage." Flies had previously fed on native night soil and other de-

---

*He had a second hot meal when he was evacuated to a hospital ship in early June. He heaped his tray high on his way through the chow line, but his shrunken stomach would accept only a few mouthfuls.

cay — but not extravagantly, since little was thrown out in prewar Okinawa. The piles of garbage that grew while those soldiers dug the fortifications did nothing to diminish their number. Now the Japanese Thirty-second Army's untreated wastes were insect heaven, exceeded only by the unaccustomed treats of combat's rot that littered the landscape.

By mid-May, the swarms were larger and more relentless. When Americans were lucky enough to be pulled off the front line for rest and regrouping — only a few hundred yards back, but with less likelihood of being hit — hot coffee often waited. Flies would attack it even as it was being poured and gulped, the hand not holding the cup fighting them off with maddened waves. Whitaker was one who craved coffee — anything liquid — despite his dead appetite. "But if you put down a cup for one second, you could hardly see it when you looked again. The surface of the coffee was covered solid by huge black insects. Or green ones."*

Americans believed the flies' trips from the corpses to their coffee helped spread the dysentery that plagued nearly everyone to some degree. (There was also a mild outbreak of typhoid, caused by bacilli that fed in the native and military night soil.) Virtually universal weakness and loose bowels prompted some Marines on the line to leave their precious cover to run to a corpsman for paregoric. Many who would not take that risk had to mess their pants. Whitaker was among the majority who had at least a touch of dysentery much of the time. On bad days, he would vomit when he lay on his stomach and lose control of his bowels when he lay on his back. He "tried to do neither — to *live* — by finding a position on my side. Not always easy in a foxhole filled with mud and water."

One product of the endemic dysentery lay in front of everyone's eyes and noses. Combat fronts were without sanitation facilities. When there was time and the risk was acceptable, a hole was dug several inches into the ground — a luxury during action on the line. Normally, the surface of the ground had to do for the hurried func-

---

*The 6th Marine Division's most extraordinary encounter of all with flies was in late May, when units passed the ruins of a sugar refinery near Naha — which was also remembered as a landmark in a plain of otherwise utter ruin, the only structure in sight still partly standing. Vats opened by Japanese or punctured by American bullets left a pond of molasses around it. The thick, dark ooze stuck to the boots of the advancing units and attracted flies even larger — some remember many times larger — than the grotesque specimens previously seen. Fearing an epidemic, officers called in planes to spray the area with disinfectant. The Japanese, probably suspecting that the spray marked the start of chemical warfare by the racist American beasts, began shelling furiously with the remains of their artillery. The Americans who had left their gas masks on the beach on L-day were just as frightened that the Japanese beasts would use this as a pretext to start using their own chemical weapons.

tions, the rain, shelling, garbage, dysentery and rotting corpses in their various colors making the land on which infantrymen lived all day and night worse than open cesspools.* The pus and puke and slime and shit of a quarter million harrowed men mixed into the battlefields' seas of mud.

John Keegan pointed out that battle, always unpleasant for a minority of its participants, "has increasingly become an intolerable experience for the majority"; modern warfare has transformed "the very environment of the battlefield into one almost wholly — and indiscriminately — hostile to man." Veterans of combat on Okinawa make the same point by suggesting (after Bill Mauldin, the famous war cartoonist) that anyone truly interested in war's degradation can glimpse it in peacetime. This requires only living in a hole in the ground filled with water, mud, excrement and gore, and listening to a recording of ceaseless artillery thunder. Without the touch of dysentery to drain the researcher's strength and the swarms of flies feasting on the product of feverishly running bowels, without the maggots and stink of decaying corpses and the near impossibility of proper sleep, without even the shells, bullets, exhaustion and fear, a week or two there, in a drenching rain and filthy wet clothes and without proper food, will begin to provide an inkling of an existence not conveyable by words or film.†

Eugene Sledge, whose searing memoir about Peleliu and Okinawa comes closest to the impossible, fought with the 1st Marines at Wana Draw, two miles northeast of Sugar Loaf. The stink of a "half-flooded garbage pit" in one area in front of Shuri Castle was worse than usual, but Sledge's life depended on spading into it for cover. At eight inches, he encountered "a mass of wriggling maggots that came welling up as though those beneath were pushing them out." He had to keep digging. Minutes later, his spade hit a rotting Japanese corpse — "dirty, whitish bone and cartilage with ribs attached" — and an overwhelmingly nauseating odor. "How I managed not to vomit . . . I don't know. Perhaps my senses and nerves had been so dulled by constant foulness for so long that nothing could evoke any other response but to cry out and move back . . . Having to wallow in

---

*When a man was sent on a mission alone, to scout a ridge, secure a building or check a radio wire, his buddies often sent him off with a reminder to "keep a tight ass." Unconsciously or otherwise, that good luck wish and admonition to come back alive derived from the prevalence of messing one's pants in such situations when bullets and shell fragments hit. Forty-five years later, one perfectly sane veteran packs toilet paper even when traveling to a luxury hotel. "I just can't leave my house without it. I can't forget how we lived."

† Recent films that have begun to show young men gripped in combat's pandemonium of shocking noise, confusion and terror necessarily leave out the smells, together with such nuances as trying to keep from skidding at critical moments in mud streaked with blood.

war's putrefaction was almost more than the toughest of us could bear."

When those who volunteered to retrieve Sugar Loaf's dead found the body of Major Courtney on May 15, they had to break the legs of the future winner of the Medal of Honor and stuff them underneath for the smaller "package" that lessened the danger of the dash back down through the Japanese fire. That afternoon, the weary, revolted litter bearers from the 29th Marines' Headquarters Company hitched a ride to their command post in a raucous amtrac with about twenty corpses and eight inches of sloshing water in its well. Three men squeezed into the cab and the fourth rode above the well, supporting himself on a handle. When the vehicle climbed the first knoll, all the water, now full of maggots and body pieces, rushed back at that fourth. He lost his grip and fell into some three feet of this stew. The amtrac's roar drowned out his hysterical screams. When it reached the top of the knoll and started down, he was thrown to the other side of the well, still struggling to pull himself out and involuntarily swallowing gulps of the putrid liquid. Up and down the hills, the eighteen-year-old's swallows and wrestles with the corpses continued until he blacked out. "What I was thinking then and all through these years [until the 1980s] was 'Enough, *enough!* We have been abused enough!'" But he was unable to talk about what he thought — to mention such episodes at all — for forty-one years, until he fought to a breakthrough with the help of an enlightened veterans' hospital.

Sledge knew why men didn't talk about such things at the time. "They were too horrible and obscene even for hardened veterans. The conditions taxed the toughest I knew almost to the point of screaming . . . it is too preposterous to think that men could actually live and fight for days and nights on end under such terrible conditions and not be driven insane. But I saw much of it there on Okinawa and to me the war was insanity."

Perhaps combat's largest dirty secret is the pervasiveness of filth and human decay. When replacements made their way toward the front lines, they heard a rumbling like a distant thunderstorm. This grew louder and more ominous as they approached the heavy guns and the clamor of battle itself: the roar of tanks, whump of mortars, shriek of rockets, whoosh of shells streaming through the curtains of flame and dense dust of cordite. Sometimes men in amtracs couldn't hear their roaring engines over this din, which was heightened by shouts and explosions. But the smell hit before the noise level rose to maximum. Manchester called it "a stench of piss and shit and rotting human flesh . . . You are with men, all of whom, like yourself, have some shit in their pants and otherwise stink of battle. It was not an animal life but worse." Sledge found it an "overpowering" stench of death . . . "The only way I could bear the monstrous horror of it all was to look upward away from the earthly reality surrounding us, watch the leaden gray clouds go scudding over and repeat over and over to myself that the situation was unreal — just a nightmare — that I would soon awake and find myself somewhere else. But the ever present smell of death saturated my nostrils. It was there with every breath I took."

> *It was always "one more hill." You were always told it was the critical one till you took it, then there was one more.*
> — Mitchell Zampikos, 22nd Marines

> *Everybody expected to be hit sooner or later. Almost everybody had been hit already, we ended with over 100 percent casualties in our platoon and company . . . For some reason, known only to God, I wasn't wounded at Okinawa . . . Why I was one of the chosen few I'll never know.*
> — Stuart Upchurch, 22nd Marines

Death was so common that infantrymen felt an odd dichotomy. They had come to treasure the lives of their fellows, who shared their nightmare and could be lost at any moment, more than they had treasured any other. Yet all their lives together seemed of little consequence to the forces that made war and had delivered them to this one. Coming from a culture that valued individual life, they took time to comprehend a world where it was scorned, except by those who were menaced, where the purpose was to extinguish it. For Lenly Cotten, the major lesson learned on Okinawa was that "we were the expendable ones. Someone had to be expendable."

Especially heavy casualties among front-line units' young officers meant the men couldn't remember their platoon leaders' names or even faces, as when Dick Whitaker went up Sugar Loaf. Those officers came and went too fast; replacements were hit before anything about them could sink in during the jumble of battle and the necessary concentration on more urgent matters. Only two of Company I–3–22's twenty-one officers who landed on L-day were not killed or wounded. Several companies replaced some of their officers three and four times.

Second lieutenants in rifle companies seemed to Sledge a special species made obsolete by modern warfare. "They were wounded or killed with such regularity that we rarely knew anything about them other than a code name and saw them on their feet only once or twice." The platoon tended by Corpsman Joe Bangert, the former wise guy, went up Sugar Loaf twice, and he "couldn't tell you my own lieutenant's name because we lost him so fast — and so many others."

Stuart Upchurch's platoon kept shrinking as it pushed southward after Sugar Loaf and the Shuri Line. "We'd gone through so many lieutenants by this time that we started to just ignore the new ones. They really couldn't tell us anything we didn't know. The smart new lieutenants did well to listen and learn from us."

One second lieutenant in command of the platoon of James Day, the corporal who would become a major general, was killed; his replacement died of wounds in a hospital. Most other officers in Day's company fell, together with many of their superiors. His battalion commander and the battalion executive officer died in action. His regimental commander, a replacement for one seriously wounded on Sugar Loaf, was killed days later. Nearly the entire regimental command structure was lost — and most of the troops. Day's battalion started with 1145 men on April 1. When its fighting finished in June, some three thousand past and present men were listed as having belonged — which meant each man had been replaced twice: about two thousand casualties had come and gone.

On the day before Christmas of 1944, a furious football game had been played in the Mosquito Bowl, a field pounded out of Guadalcanal's coral. Kick-off time was 0830 in deference to the great heat and humidity. Thanks to the Corps's appetite for recruiting athletes, the teams, representing the 4th and 29th Marines, were studded with former college and professional stars, some of whom considered that Mosquito Bowl game, played without shoulder pads or helmets, the roughest of their careers. Fourteen weeks later, at least twelve of the sixty players had been killed on Okinawa, including a tackle on Wisconsin's 1942 team (ranked number three in the country) who had returned to combat after being wounded, a former captain of Notre Dame,* and an All-American end for Wisconsin — spoken of as a future U.S. senator — who fell leading an assault against the last defensive stronghold on the last day of organized resistance. The remaining players were wounded or injured almost to a man; thirty-one received the Purple Heart. The game's spectators fared better only by comparison: casualties among the nine infantry battalions that watched the game reached 75 percent: four hundred officers and 7822 enlisted men killed and wounded.

After a few weeks on Okinawa, a college graduate who had been

---

*"Irish George" Murphy was captain of the 1942 team. The first lieutenant's platoon was one of the first sent up Sugar Loaf, where the men pitched grenades over the crest but were answered with terrible fire from the reverse slope. Murphy ordered a withdrawal and helped evacuate the wounded. After carrying a machine gunner to an aid station on his second trip, he sat down to relieve his panting and was hit by a mortar shell. He staggered to his feet and fired his pistol toward the enemy before dying — without having seen a daughter born after he'd been shipped out from the States.

haunted by not making officer realized how lucky that failure was for him. Remaining lucky, he would be the sole member of his eleven-man machine gun section not killed or wounded seriously enough for evacuation. He had started as an ammunition carrier like Whitaker, but all ten men in front of him were shot "like ducks in a row — I was the last duck, but the campaign ended just in time." This was common: Melvin Heckt's machine gun section ended with two lucky men; six out of the sixty-two in the platoon. Some Marine rifle companies lost over 100 percent of their personnel. It was 153 percent in Sledge's company, which finished with 11 percent — twenty-six out of 235 officers and men — of those who had made the landing. Of course that included replacements, although many were hit so quickly they were never added to their units' rolls. The same number was left of Owen Stebbins's G–2–22 Company, two platoons of which ended with only three men from L-day, one of whom was seriously wounded twice. Army infantry units suffered similarly, prompting efficiency experts who later analyzed the campaign to recommend attaching a Graves Registration platoon to each regiment because the number of personnel who dealt with the bodies "proved insufficient . . . and necessitated the employment of front-line troops to evacuate the dead."

> *Heads were bandaged with bloody gauze and faces were hardly recognizable. Almost every type of wound imaginable was evident. Everything I saw brought home the grim reality of the terrible effects of the war. What do those men have to gain amid all this misery while others sit back and reap huge benefits or perhaps complain because of the lack of some pleasure or convenience?*
>
> — Kenneth Cecil observing the treatment of American Army casualties on May 21

> *The absence of screw-ups [in his field hospital] wasn't as remarkable as the absence of cowardice among the fighting men, but maybe both came from the same source.*
>
> — Hospital Apprentice First Class Edmund Shimberg

Only quick, skillful treatment kept the number of KIAs from doubling and tripling. American medicine was as good as anything in all of Operation Iceberg, distinctly better than American intelligence and strategy.

Paul Dunfrey, the first lieutenant who scouted south of the Asakawa for the major assault of the Shuri Line, could not be evacuated for many hours because Japanese fire was too fierce. A bullet had severed his bowel and a probable second drove fragments of his belt buckle into his intestines. He was saved when doctors on a hospital ship used a new technique, later described in a collection called *Miracles of Surgery,* to fuse his bowel.*

Young Forest Townsend, a self-described "country green kid" hit by a Nambu machine gun as he dashed across an open field outside Naha, eventually lost consciousness in his water-filled shell hole. He briefly came to in a battalion aid station. The next time, he was lying in what he took for a field hospital tent. Desperately thirsty, he was given a wet rag to suck. "What the hell's wrong with this island?" he shouted in his delirious craze for water. "Aren't there any wells on it?"

His wound seemed unimportant until he had trouble breathing when he awoke a third time on a hospital ship. His distinguished-looking surgeon came from near Philadelphia's Main Line — not Townsend's territory. The eighteen-year-old would remember his savior's hands the rest of his life. "They were the most gentle hands I ever knew, with real healing power, honest." The surgeon told Townsend that the bullet should have killed him but his heart must have moved a fraction of an inch when it struck. "Amazing. Miraculous. With that kind of hit, I'd say you were one in ninety-thousand to live."

But of course Townsend's recovery was as much the result of surgical skill and the general quality of care as any miracle. Much would later be made of how earlier island fighting served to heighten the ferocity and deadliness on Okinawa. Analysts attributed the enormous mutual cost to both sides' application of lessons learned along the way. That was only partly true, for much learned earlier had no application; actual combat required as much improvisation on Okinawa as elsewhere. In medicine, however, lessons *had* been learned and great progress made in lifesaving techniques. Special landing craft equipped for surgery delivered the wounded to hospital ships. Penicillin and the new sulfa powder worked wonders, like the sterling collection of specialists in burn treatment, internal medicine, and brain, chest, and every other relevant branch of surgery. Better knowledge and practice of transfusions saved hundreds. Refrigerated whole blood, much better than plasma for reviving bodies in grave shock from loss of almost all their own blood, had first become available to Pacific fighters on Iwo Jima two months earlier. Over fifteen thousand gallons were flown from the States to Okinawa in a

---

*But its long-term effect wasn't known at the time. After Dunfrey spent ten months in hospitals, a doctor told his wife to take him home and have a good time because he had about five years to live. He was vigorously alive forty years later.

matter of days. The new methods and techniques helped reduce the mortality rate of the wounded to half that of previous Pacific battles, approaching the achievement in Europe.

The exceptions came during the most dire emergencies, when doctors could not get to hopeless cases — a terrible moment for their friends. John Townsend (no relation to Forest) delivered a Marine badly wounded by machine gun fire to a battalion aid station and was told to place him with a dozen others under a tree. Townsend had never heard of triage. "Sir," he protested mildly, "if you leave him there, he'll be dead in thirty minutes." A doctor explained that since there was no hope whatever of saving the Marine, he had to work on other men carried into the tents because they did have hope. Not all infantrymen five minutes away from the strain of battle took this explanation with such understanding as young Townsend, especially when the wounded men were close buddies. Some would not accept "man playing God" with their beloved mates. A few exploded and threatened to shoot the offending doctors. But such episodes were rare because the majority of cases met the opposite response from medical personnel, who spared nothing to save everyone possible — and so often succeeded.

Some wounded were frighteningly disfigured. Okinawa produced World War II's first American "basket case": a master sergeant shorn of all four limbs. The sergeant was walking ahead of his men to spot mines when he stepped on one that blew off both legs above the knee, one arm above the elbow, and mangled the other hand so badly that it had to be amputated. But even he survived because his vital signs were still functioning when he was carried to a hospital. (Still slightly deaf and suffering from shock when he was returned to the States a month later, he thought he'd make "an excellent propaganda photo to end all wars.") Unless the wounds were nearly fatal to begin with or corpsmen or fire-team buddies were pinned down by impossible enemy fire and prevented from starting the usual speedy delivery to a hospital, men who were hit had an excellent chance to live, another American compensation for the misery of combat.

Since front-line troops had little chance of ending their fighting except in death or temporary disability, the quality of medical care assumed even greater importance. A nonfatal wound was a man's best hope of coming out alive. What was nonfatal naturally depended largely on what was done to keep it so.

The sequence of care began right on the line. Medical corpsmen, one in each platoon, applied first aid on the spot. They carried bandages and gauze, packets of infection-inhibiting sulfa, vials of morphine in self-contained hypodermic needles, and little bottles of brandy and blood plasma. The next step back from the front line was the battalion aid station, often only two or three hundred yards back but out of small-arms range. This was usually a tent with better-supplied corpsmen or occasionally doctors who patched minor wounds, after which many men went straight back to their units. But aid stations overflowed with pain during intense fighting, especially after artillery and mortar barrages. Chests rent with deep gashes, limbs torn off, stomachs shot open, intestines spilling out, testicles severed, eyes numb with shock and wide with agony, eyes gouged out, youthful faces blackened by burns and etched with tears, teeth gritted to stop moans, death cries, death rattles, final gasps, hardened medical personnel fighting to save lives and fighting tears when they lost . . . A short sequence of such scenes on film would have educated the home front about the real nature of war.

Quick delivery of the seriously wounded to a better facility was crucial. The average time was indeed very short in battlefield terms, rarely more than a few hours from the moment of wounding. The men were carried or transported to their division's collecting and clearing company, and from there to a field or portable surgical hospital, or to a splendidly equipped white ship with a comforting name such as *Hope, Relief,* or *Solace.* Many were still in shock, eyes glazed or dulled from morphine, bodies slumped and faces twisted with the tension of battle. But conscious patients saw the floating hospitals as vessels of great beauty even when their hundreds of beds were full. That was the case throughout the hardest days on the Shuri Line, when transports converted for medical use and even unconverted transports were pressed into evacuation service. The ships commuted to Guam and Saipan, from which men were air-lifted to base hospitals in Hawaii or the States. The other way out was aboard a veritable bridge of transport planes that took hundreds of patients daily to Guam. In June, roads in the far south were quickly converted to airstrips for faster evacuation by hospital planes.

The outward journey of Gunnery Sergeant Emil Rucinski, of Company B–1–22, was as typical as any. His platoon leader was hit on the morning of the same May 10, two days before the start on Sugar Loaf. The lieutenant was evacuated with a shattered arm, followed by the platoon sergeant when he too was hit that afternoon. When the platoon dug in for a long night of heavy mortar fire from the Shuri Line's forward positions, Rucinski was the new leader. The platoon resumed its advance in the morning but artillery fire from the enemy's high ground produced many cries of "Corpsman!" The men dug in again while the sergeant made his way some ten yards to his company commander for instructions; as Rucinski crawled, a sniper waiting for a shot at someone important claimed the third platoon leader in fifteen hours. Rucinski felt as if a baseball bat had whacked him to the ground. Remembering his training, he stayed calm and called for a corpsman.

The bullet had entered the left side of his chest, shattered a rib, ripped his diaphragm and badly mangled his kidneys and lungs. A corpsman gave him plasma and morphine, then stretcher bearers brought him back to his battalion aid station, from which a jeep soon took him to a landing craft. He and other casualties were hoisted onto a converted transport ship that fought off kamikaze attacks while waiting a day or two offshore. Treating Rucinski on the way, the ship's medical services delivered him, after stops at Guam and Honolulu, to a medical receiving station in San Francisco. Later he was sent to a hospital in Virginia — the nearest suitable one to his West Springfield, Massachusetts, home — until his discharge in January 1946, seven months after his wounding. By the end of the campaign, almost thirty-one thousand men, 80 percent of all battle casualties, would be evacuated similarly, half by ship, half by air.*

Before their initiation to combat, cocky, green Marines tended to belittle corpsmen. Their underlying contempt for all lesser beings who were not Marines was often sharper for those "not like us," which implied more than an organizational difference. (Corpsmen belonged to the Navy rather than directly to the Marines.) Sometimes they scoffed at "those fairies" — but when the time came, the cheap deprecations gave way to battle's fierce male tenderness topped by deep respect and gratitude. Dick Whitaker's PLEASE DON'T FORGET THE CORPSMEN! would be a common plea.†

---

* William Manchester was delivered to a naval hospital in Hawaii that treated the gravely wounded. The wards were packed. Litter-bound patients were shown some of the films that gave the majority of the American public their images of the war — as entertainment. From as far from combat as possible, actors like Ronald Reagan helped fashion Hollywood's mythology, which was exceeded only by that of the Japanese, with their crude, ugly fairy tales of Japanese good and American bestiality.

The films included *The Sands of Iwo Jima*. Later, Manchester's ward was treated to a visit by its star. John Wayne wore a fancy cowboy outfit, down to spurs and pistols, and greeted the wounded with a self-satisfied, "Hi ya, guys!" Manchester had the pleasure of seeing the Hollywood warrior humiliated by stony silence. "Then somebody booed. Suddenly everyone was booing." A documentary minute of this episode under the credits of some phony war film might go far to showing the difference between combat and its show-business exploitation.

† Army medics won equal gratitude from the wounded. Desmond Dossa, a Seventh-day Adventist who refused to carry a weapon, remained the only unwounded man in extremely hard fighting for a position on Kakazu Ridge.

Dossa carried fifty wounded men, one by one, to the edge of a ten-yard drop and lowered them to safety by rope, all under heavy fire. Japanese infantrymen learned to love *their* medical orderlies in the field with no less reason — orderlies from their own units, that is. One went up Sugar Loaf no less than eight times, heroism that was probably commonplace but hard to document because so few survived.

When Joseph Bangert was rushed in to replace a corpsman just killed on Sugar Loaf, his platoon had to shout the dangerous "Corpsman!" instead of "Bangert!" because no one knew the new man's name. Bangert also knew no names and had trouble learning them during his baptism under fire because his platoon kept getting replacements for "guys shot bad, guys shot worse, guys killed. There were bodies everywhere and I can't tell you how many lieutenants we ran through." Bangert saw men with chests, bellies and faces ripped open. One was alive with half a head. Some tried to joke about getting their "lucky ticket home"; just a few asked to be shot. "Don't let me go out like this, Mac. Put me out of my misery." But even some of those cases survived, to their own surprise.*

Field hospitals were clusters of tents serving as a combined evacuation center and early-day *M*A*S*H*. Hospital Apprentice First Class Edmund Shimberg, one of the dog's bodies in Corps Evacuation Hospital Number 2, had arrived on Okinawa with some skepticism. "Before we set up and started functioning as a hospital, we were a running joke for ourselves: 'This screw-up outfit will never be worth a dime.' But everything came together when it had to." The neurosurgeon of that single facility was world class, the urologist widely published; the surgical group as a whole, apart from a hidebound executive officer, provided the highest current standard of care — with no concern for the cost that Shimberg could detect; expense was "simply never considered."

Shimberg stopped swabbing floors and changing dressings to assist with surgery when it was performed throughout the night. Numerous trauma teams working with extreme urgency gave the tents the look of a large city hospital's emergency ward after a natural disaster. The nineteen-year-old volunteer from the Bronx (who would become a respected physical therapist after the war) noticed that the surgeons, especially during the worst at the Shuri Line, never looked at the calendar, let alone the clock. "It was just ceaseless, excellent work . . . We lost patients, but very few. If they were brought back to us alive, their chances were very good because the medical practice was superb."

In the end, ninety-seven of every hundred wounded Americans lived — including Dale Bair, hit three times in the first assault on Sugar Loaf. But even with that admirable record, total casualties for

---

*Postwar reunions would give many men the happiest shock of their lives when they saw the "return" of what had seemed certain corpses in Okinawan mud. One man saw Emil Rucinski after his hit: prostrate, blood-soaked and seemingly without the slightest chance to live. At a Marine reunion decades later, he turned white when a grinning apparition who looked like Rucinski — and was — entered the room.

the campaign would be 35 percent of the troops engaged, stunning by American standards. Of the 24,511 Marines killed in World War II, 3440 — 14 percent — died on Okinawa. A further 15,487 were wounded there. More than 1 percent of all American World War II casualties were suffered taking the island's 875 square miles, which constituted about 0.6 percent of the territory of Japan.*

It is not quite true, as Marines like to remember, that they were stalwart to a man. One of the failures was a young private who shot himself in the toe as his company advanced toward the Shuri Line. A junior officer of the same company — not Whitaker's, but among the Pacific War's most experienced and best — "mysteriously disappeared," in his company commander's words, after four of his six fellow officers had been hit on the first day at Sugar Loaf. The company had only two officers for the next day's critical fighting. The missing one was found to have turned himself in "sick" to his battalion aid station. Another officer of a company whose casualties exceeded its complement, thanks to replacements, stayed behind to cover his men's retreat one day until volunteers ran back with a poncho to drag him out from where he lay wounded. A corpsman later noticed his leg wound bore signs of powder burns.

A thousand men were pinned down by machine gun fire on the way to Sugar Loaf. Waiting for the order to push on again despite the fire, one of them burst out crying, threw away his rifle and started crawling to the rear. The rest of his squad followed the book by retrieving his rifle, stripping it down and tossing the parts in all directions so that they could be of no use to the enemy. There was also a little-known case of a fine field officer, a colonel, losing his command because of failure. This too happened during the assault on the Shuri Line, during which units temporarily resting near the western coast

---

*Accidents caused an increasing percentage of those totals amidst combat's chaos and fear. "So many guns, so many accidents," an infantryman put it whose rifle went off when slung on his back, killing the man behind him. The last round usually left in machine guns killed many others; at least one man blew off his own head when he tripped installing flares for use that night. And American planes continued to be shot down by American guns, despite wings wagged desperately by doomed pilots.

A Marine platoon was on a small hill in early June when five magnificent Corsairs appeared to strafe and fire their rockets at Japanese positions ahead. Then a sixth Corsair made the kind of error that happened almost daily in one form or another. The pilot fired on the wrong side of the line. The platoon lost 11 men.

Melvin Heckt's diary entry of May 25 records one man in his platoon killed and two wounded by Japanese mortar fire as they moved up a ridge in pouring rain. The rain continued throughout the night. The men got very little sleep as they lay in water and were attacked by sporadic enemy grenades. On his way to bring up more grenades, a man saw someone running and challenged him several times. "No answer. He fired and the man fell. We ran up there and there was Ed Lamberson dying and in two minutes dead. If Ed had only answered!"

Being shot at by one's own caused special anguish. Shooting one's own caused more.

could still see kamikaze attacks dealing the American fleet its un-precedented damage. After the admirals' pressure on the generals to advance more rapidly, Major General Lemuel Shepherd ordered Sugar Loaf taken "at any cost." When the cost became horrendous, one regimental commander — a tough, fully battle-tested Marine colonel, but surely under great stress himself — told the general that he could not order his decimated regiment to carry out another at-tack on the lethal hill. As with the colonel previously in the north, he was relieved, and his replacement did give the order.*

His men obeyed. Incidents of refusal — of officers' orders or cor-porals' — were astonishingly few. Whitaker was among the over-whelming majority of Marines who never saw or heard of one, or of cowardice. Not to advance when ordered was inconceivable for all but a statistically negligible minority, no matter how difficult and dangerous the objective, how strong the probability of being badly wounded or killed. This is not to say that most men *wanted* to charge the Japanese guns and caves. Naturally, most did not volunteer for such madness but waited to learn whether they'd been picked, usu-ally hoping they wouldn't be. A fine Marine named Declan Klingen-hagen was lucky enough to be skipped by his sergeant for what may have been the twelfth assault on Sugar Loaf.

> I was sitting in a trench dug out of the bottom of a small hill and I was apprehensive . . . I wasn't hiding because there were other Ma-rines around but I hoped no one would see me. I guess I was feel-ing fear . . . At one point, a longer-time member of my squad saw me and asked why I wasn't going with the assault. The sergeant was nearby and told the member to leave me alone; it was all right.

But Klingenhagen had been on Sugar Loaf three days earlier, when a mortar barrage killed his lieutenant and so ravaged the rest of his squad that only four men were left to withdraw. One of those four was badly wounded, another lasted only until he reached the bottom of the hill, when he fell dead at Klingenhagen's feet with a bullet hole in the center of his chest. Yet although the eighteen-year-old private "sure hoped" it wouldn't happen, he also knew "I would join the assault if told to."†

---

*A battalion commander ordered to take a fiercely fortified hill in the 1st Marine Divi-sion's territory just east of Sugar Loaf asserted that his men were "all used up . . . half of them belong in sick bay." The assistant divisional commander replied that the battalion commander, a lieutenant colonel, had his orders and that heads would roll if they weren't obeyed. The latter saluted with a "Yes, sir" and left, eyes tearing. "We'll take the fucking hill," he told an intelligence officer, "but I don't care if I come off it or not." The hill was taken and the battalion commander wasn't wounded until later.

† Klingenhagen never asked why his sergeant protected him but guessed it might have been because his earlier trauma on Sugar Loaf occurred during his very first action as a

A widely accepted military maxim has it that a combat unit that has taken casualties of 30 percent or more cannot sustain its fighting spirit. Many front-line units on Okinawa went far above that, Whitaker's 29th Regiment to 82 percent. So however true it was, as many Japanese survivors later saw it, that the Americans' assured victory was largely a matter of applying their greatly superior resources in a chiefly logistical-industrial operation, it is also true that both managers and proletariat at the killing edge of the job behaved exceptionally. Even if true, the old adage that war is 90 percent logistics in no way diminished their record of courage and concern for fellow targets. The scattered exceptions who couldn't fulfill the supreme demands made of them proved the rule of surpassing esprit de corps.

Dick Whitaker was among those to whom it never occurred not to obey every order, and so far his hits had been trifling. Shortly after his charge up Sugar Loaf on May 14, he and the other survivors of his platoon were on the back slope of a little rise a hundred yards north. Filthy, exhausted and numb, they had lost all their machine guns on the hill. Whitaker still didn't know the name of the lieutenant who had been assigned to them the day before and died yards from him on the crest. He did know that his wasted platoon would be ordered up again soon — but maybe not now, maybe not until tomorrow. That was all the future the men wanted to think about as they rested in the partial protection of the little rise.

Whitaker dug his foxhole deeper and stuck his shovel in the mud. He put a cigarette in his mouth and leaned down toward a buddy's match, his left hand remaining on the handle of the shovel, directly in front of him. A sniper's bullet caught him in the hand, exactly where his heart had been a second earlier.

He made his own way to his battalion aid station, about half a mile to the rear. Cleaned and dressed, his wound seemed less serious than when the bullet struck. Three days later, a doctor pronounced him fit for duty, and he returned to his unit, which was even smaller because it had charged Sugar Loaf again in his absence.*

Two weeks later, the 4th and 29th Marine Regiments attacked the

---

new replacement. He probably remained in a kind of shock when the assault in question was being organized.

* A month to the day after Whitaker was hit, Marine Corps headquarters in Washington wrote his parents that he had been wounded in action against the enemy on May 18. (It was actually May 16.) "Your anxiety is realized and you may be sure that any additional details or information received will be forwarded to you at the earliest possible moment." That moment came more than a month later, when the campaign was over and Whitaker back on Guam. "With further reference to the notification from this office regarding your son . . . additional information has been received that he returned to duty on 20 May 1945."

Oroku Peninsula, site of Naha Airfield and of the tunnels of the Naval Base Force and Captain Kojo's regimental headquarters. The day after their amphibious landing there, on June 4, Whitaker's platoon dodged small-arms fire from below as they advanced along the top of a ridge. Then they came upon a forward artillery spotter peering through his binoculars. Whitaker asked what his objective was. The lieutenant handed him his glasses, through which he made out three Japanese soldiers studying a map on the next ridge. "Watch this!" said the spotter, calling in some coordinates by radio. Moments later, the platoon heard American shells whizzing past. The three Japanese disappeared, together with the entire top of the ridge.

Whitaker woke up in an amtrac about half an hour later with no memory of how he had arrived there. Blood flowed from his nose and he couldn't hear. His helmet and rifle were gone. He supposed he was in the hands of a Graves Registration team, since the vehicle was also transporting poncho-wrapped bodies. In fact, he was being evacuated to a hospital ship (where he had his second hot meal). His head hurt badly. He would never find out what had caused his concussion.

He told his shipboard examiners that he didn't feel "too bad" and was returned to a regimental hospital ashore. After a night there, he was checked again at his battalion aid station, which turned him loose to return to his outfit. Part of him "knew" he would come through alive and without a disabling or disfiguring wound. Another part accepted how unlikely this was. "All those people around you were getting hit. Your turn just had to come too."

This second contradiction pulled at all sound infantrymen. They hoped their turn wouldn't be *now*. As in other battles and wars, each man secretly believed he was the exception. Somehow, in some way, his turn would never come — but, at the same time, reason accepted the heavy odds against this.

"You do get letters from home and you keep reading them," reflected Norris Buchter, who grew up in relative comfort in Connecticut. "But you've lost the feeling that you'll ever be back in that other world. You've even lost the habit of visualizing tomorrow; *today's* the day you're still living and all you can think about. It's a funny thing not to really expect to make it any longer. But you get to a time when you've seen so much death that you're resigned to your own coming sooner or later. With so many guys dying, you'll join them — that only makes sense."

Evan Regal, a lad from a struggling farm in upstate New York, felt certain that "it was a question of time. You might survive this battle or that, but sooner or later they'd get you; that was unavoidable. I tried not to think about it. I knew guys who had premonitions they were going to get it the next day — and often enough that's when they actually did get killed." Regal was the classic combat schizophrenic operating on reason, which told him the odds were small that he would make it without being killed or seriously wounded, and faith, which assured him that that's precisely what he would do, although he had volunteered for especially hazardous assignments. "Myself, I always had the feeling I was going to make it through, despite all I was in."

But Mommy De Mar, the solicitous platoon sergeant, observed his men gradually tilting toward pessimism. "After a while, a lot of the guys who'd been out there didn't expect to make it. You've seen so much death. It's a funny feeling, but you expect your own death has got to come sooner or later. You do think of home, but you sense you're never going to see it again. The rest of the world, the rest of *you*, is just cut off. You're there for just one thing: to kill until you get killed."

"Until you get killed" wasn't merely fanciful, since Americans in the Pacific (like Soviets in World War II) did not go home after serving a year or two but stayed "for the duration" — which usually ended in their death or serious wounds. Or in breakdown, for although their spirits very rarely refused to obey an order, their nervous systems failed more often.

> The normal strain of combat, the constant threat of death from enemy artillery, was too much for many of the soldiers and Marines; they "cracked up" and had to be evacuated. They were not cowards; some were veterans of Leyte and earlier Pacific campaigns. Okinawa was simply too much for their nervous systems.
>
> — James and William Belote, *Typhoon of Steel*

> There is no such thing as "getting used to combat" . . . Each moment of combat imposes a strain so great that men will break down in direct relation to the intensity and duration of their exposure . . . psychiatric casualties are as inevitable as gunshot and shrapnel wounds.
>
> — From *Combat Exhaustion*, an official American report

> Psychiatric hospitals proved invaluable during the assault. Plans have been made for their continued use in future actions.
>
> — From "Principal Lessons Learned in the Okinawa Operation," a confidential Army report

> Things happen so fast in combat you often don't realize what you're doing. I wasn't really scared until after I was hit and evacuated to a field hospital. Then I wanted to hide, to duck every time a plane went overhead — I was terrified.
>
> — Gilbert Kanter, 22nd Marines

Some wore wild-eyed expressions of shock and fear. Others whom I knew well, though could barely recognize, wore expressions of idiots or simpletons knocked too witless to be afraid anymore. The blast of a shell had literally jolted them into a different state of awareness from the rest of us. Some of those who didn't return probably never recovered but were doomed to remain in mental limbo and spent their futures in a veterans' hospital as "living dead."
— E. B. Sledge, With the Old Breed at Peleliu and Okinawa

I was scared shitless most of the time and probably had some form of battle fatigue from April 1 till the day we quit and went to Guam.
— Dick Whitaker

When one goes into combat, he can adjust or go crazy. Only one or two percent crack up. I think that figure is remarkable.
— John Townsend, 29th Marines

It's a good thing the Lord helps block out unpleasant memories. I don't think one could vividly remember those feelings and still have his sanity.
— Robert H. Jones, 4th Marines

If it occurred to few Americans how demoralizing their resources and firepower were to the Japanese, fewer Japanese questioned the assumption that the Americans' material superiority gave them an easy time. The truth is that the relentless defense of a well-fortified enemy determined or resigned to fight to the death strained Americans to their limit and beyond. The horrendous weather alone would have been enough to cause some battle fatigue. Living wet and rough day after day with too little food and never enough sleep led to sheer physical exhaustion and its inevitable effect on the nervous system. Tough young bodies that could have coped for six or seven days with the extremely abnormal demands, even with the deprivation of sleep, succumbed after weeks — in some cases months — of cumulative exertion, adding nervous breakdown to fever, pneumonia, malaria and a range of respiratory infections from the exposure. Combat's additional demands hugely augmented the strain: the bursts of savage close fighting against heavy concentrations of mortars and machine guns whose tension could not be dissipated because those who pulled back the usual hundred yards remained under artillery fire.

A handful of Americans broke down after their first taste of that chaos and dread. Even L-day had been too much for a scattering, including a few in the boats who remembered the blood of earlier landings. A larger number feared they couldn't survive more such experiences — but did until incapacitated by a single gut-wrenching sight such as a buddy disintegrated by a mortar shell. But most came apart after cumulative debilitation, the result of the long exposure to so much bitter fighting where death was "as fantastically near" as a man inches away.

Well after the war, the American Army conceded that as many as one of its soldiers in ten suffered battle fatigue. The Army even commissioned the distinguished filmmaker John Houston to produce a documentary about the subject — which it kept from public viewing for forty years: Houston's film would not have enhanced the image of the infantryman as Rambo or lured viewers to recruiting offices. Psychologists learned that the number of shell-shock or battle-fatigue casualties increased in geometric proportion to the intensity of incoming fire and the length of exposure to it — which, again, is what distinguished Okinawa from previous campaigns. A confidential Army report entitled "Principal Lessons Learned in the Okinawa Operation" would stipulate that "troops should not remain in the front lines for more than two weeks. Constant alertness, coupled with the strain of continuous shell fire, causes a physical and mental fatigue which greatly decreases the soldier's effectiveness." That warning was felt necessary after the longer stints in the line on Okinawa because high casualties left too few replacements for Americans' usual rest rotations.*

The first great concentration of enemy firepower at Kakazu Ridge produced the first surge of "walking dead," for which the 10th Army soon had to assign an entire field hospital. The evacuation of battle-hardened veterans of earlier island campaigns confirmed that longer pounding from Okinawa's more elaborate fortifications caused higher levels of strain. Sugar Loaf claimed no fewer than 1289 shell-shocked Marines, almost half as many as the killed and wounded. The 10th Army as a whole suffered almost twenty-six thousand "nonbattle" casualties, most psychiatric, during the campaign. An extraordinary fourteen thousand occurred at the Shuri Line, that heaviest concentration of incoming fire predictably producing the highest rate.†

Some sufferers babbled incoherently or suddenly leaped up and tried to charge a machine gun nest of "dirty yellow bastard Japs" who had been decimating their units. Others trembled, sobbed or

---

*Marines had less chance than usual to rotate their units in the field because the Marine contingent on Okinawa, the III Amphibious Corps, had only two divisions, the 1st and 6th, instead of the customary three to a corps. The XXIV Army Corps had the 7th, 77th and 96th Divisions.

†The youth of the troops, especially among the Marines (since the Corps always took them younger for their harder punishment), no doubt kept these numbers from being even higher. Roughly 80 percent of the Marine divisions were under twenty-one. "I myself was only eighteen," remembered Joe Bangert, "but I kept on saying 'those goddam stupid kids' to green replacements, as if I was ten years older."

wet their trousers. A few shouted that they had to get away from the front or hallucinated about Japanese demons or their families at home. Still others screamed weirdly, fought wildly — with the strength of their dementia — and had to be restrained by their fellows, sometimes with fists. This happened to the most hardened, admired veteran officers and to some of the bravest men who had performed the most valorous of feats. Their buddies recognized that they had simply reached the breaking point.

But most battle-fatigue cases did nothing crazy. They simply stopped functioning as soldiers or Marines — a condition the others also recognized, and led them to help in a battalion aid station. Their ghostly pallor and dazed faces went beyond the "normal" signs of shock. Their eyes were glazed, their movements slowed, and their "witless" expressions announced — sometimes as clearly as among those who "went crazy" — that their nervous systems could absorb no more; they didn't care any longer, maybe didn't want to live in such conditions. Over twenty-five hundred would be discharged, to remain more or less detached from reality in civilian life.

Sometimes doctors and corpsmen, recognizing signs in exhausted men before others saw full symptoms, designated them "blast concussion" cases to get them off the line for rest before they cracked. But professional eyes were fallible. Breakdowns also came later. One ammunition carrier in a machine gun squad became its leader when all others were killed and wounded, mostly one by one. In the end, he was the only man in the squad to last the entire campaign. Despite the tremendous pressure of his full eighty-two days on Okinawa, at Sugar Loaf and other pitched battles, he remained cool, full of combat wisdom, and very helpful to replacements — many of whom took him for twenty-five years old, not his actual nineteen — straight through to the end. One replacement watched him choose the direction for the machine gun to point at night, where to set up the trip wires, what crucial last thing to tell everyone in the squad. "His toughness and savvy saved me. His skill and leadership held us all together" — until he was back on Guam, where he cracked during preparations for the invasion of the Japanese mainland. "The last thing I remember about him was carrying him out of his tent on all fours."

Being under fire was indescribably terrifying. I tried to force my whole body up into my helmet. But even a young kid brought up in a liberal tradition didn't spend his time philosophizing on the horrors of war. It was only do your job, survive, *and what's for chow tonight.*

— Edmund Shimberg, corpsman in a hospital on Okinawa

I now duck at every shell, whereas I used to laugh as they went over . . . We who remain have God and only God to thank for our being alive.
— Melvin D. Heckt during his fighting

There was no glory. The only thing you could feel good about was surviving. You felt good for that day by day, hour by hour, which is how you lived.
— Buzzy Fox, machine gunner on Okinawa

Cowardice and heroism are the same emotion — fear — expressed differently.
— Oliver Stone

Fear produced the sharpest exacerbation of battle fatigue. It was so pervasive and its causes so obvious that mention of it would be unnecessary if not for the volume of combat literature and dramatization — the kind on which most Marines like Whitaker had been raised — in which it escapes all notice. But one of the central memories of veterans looking back from the perspective of forty-plus years, and with the candor prompted by the approach of their natural deaths, is the terror that squeezed their throats and stomachs.

Fear gripped even when the most gallant deeds were being done; that was inevitable, since there could be no gallantry without it, as Captain Stebbins observed in the field. "We were all out there afraid, and the fear bound us together," a company commander observed. With or without memorable deeds, no minute of any day was free of some degree of fear. "You get scared, you remain scared," Whitaker remembered. "Anyone who isn't scared is lying or a fool. It's terrifying. And you learn to live with it." Whitaker's company commander never retired even to battalion headquarters during his months of fighting — and remained scared. "There's no way a man can prepare for the horror of advancing into an area where an enemy he can't see may end his life any second. The bark of his machine guns, snap of his mortars, whistle of his artillery tear at him. No one grows up expecting to face that stark terror. It's beyond description."

Every normal infantryman quivered and dripped with sweat. No notice was taken of messed pants, especially under artillery bombardments, when men lost control of their bodies.

On the first night after Whitaker was delivered from the north in relief of the 27th Army Division, his platoon began taking artillery fire before they could dig in well. Whitaker later guessed that the Japanese had learned of the Marines' arrival in the line and wanted to rattle them. He imagined they were using every heavy gun they had. The barrage became accurate and furious in minutes.

Unless stymied by coral, Marines liked to dig their holes about eighteen inches deep and just wide enough for two bodies. (When there was time, they would dig deeper pockets at the four corners into which enemy hand grenades could be kicked before they exploded.) That first night in the south, Whitaker and others had to use Army foxholes, which they found so wide as to leave them miserably exposed. Protection was further reduced by the low-trajectory Japanese fire, which had some shells apparently bouncing off the ground and detonating in the air. Two men in Whitaker's company were blown to bits. The others huddled for much of the night in dismay and terror.

Prolonged shelling is the hardest trial for most men in combat. For the Americans on Okinawa, the strength of Ushijima's Shuri Line again made that trial harder than on other islands. That the Japanese endured far more and were more courageous (although measuring courage in the sharply contrasting contexts is difficult, the Japanese having their different attitude toward death and expectations of behavior) in no way diminishes the American ordeal. The 32nd Army had a greater concentration of heavy guns in greater variety than was available to the Japanese in any earlier Pacific campaign: 317 guns, howitzers and heavy mortars of 70mm or larger, in addition to a relatively large number of smaller mortars and 333 heavy machine guns, 1200 light machine guns and a large supply of grenades. The heavy artillery had only a thousand rounds of ammunition per barrel to expend, and their operation was further restricted by what the Americans would have considered woeful communications and coordination. But they were under the command of another lieutenant general, Kosuke Wada, one of Japan's most respected artillerists. Despite all the limitations, the volume of their fire, and their unusual accuracy, shook the 10th Army.

Americans from field officers to new replacements were awed and horrified by the skill of the Japanese artillery in zeroing in on them. During major bombardments, shells landed forty yards away, then thirty, then closer, until — as an Army doctor described it — they found a neighboring foxhole and spilled the brains of a man's buddy all over him. Sledge found the "whistle and scream of the big steel package of destruction" almost unendurable. Bombardment was "an invention of hell . . . the pinnacle of violent fury and the embodiment of pent-up evil . . . the essence of man's inhumanity to man . . . I often had to restrain myself and fight back a wild, inexorable urge to scream, to sob and to cry [with] terror and desperation." To Private Gilbert Kanter, the pounding on the way to Sugar Loaf was "beyond the imagination of anyone who hasn't experienced it. I was still in a supposedly safe place, but my body was shaking by itself. I had only four days of fighting, but that was enough; it was too terrible. I looked up and saw some birds, miraculously alive in that insanity and even chirping. I wondered which of us was really the intelligent species."

In his tent at Yomitan Airfield, the pilot Samuel Hynes identified two kinds of fear of shelling. The first, constant and inescapable even for personnel in the relatively secure rear, was of not knowing the moment when a shell with your name on it would land. That never left: "the steady subliminal fear that . . . soon now — right now — as you crossed the road, exposed and helpless, the shriek would sound and the shell would fall, carrying your death . . . *Now!*, walking down the hill to the head. No, *now!*, sitting at dinner. No, *now!*" But it was mild compared with the fear during the actual shelling, when the bravest men couldn't stop trembling. Far as he was from the concentrated Japanese barrages at the front, Hynes nevertheless felt pure terror.

The pandemonium of the bombardments — pitiless, inexorable, ear-splitting — was unbearable. All saw that the shells making the unholy noise caused much uglier wounds than bullets. The approach of heavy shells that could be heard from a far distance prolonged the macabre suspense; battle-hardened men came to feel that the whistle alone could achieve the enemy's goal. Anyone not in a hole at that time dived frenziedly into anything available. The inability to do anything to save oneself from the monster was probably the most intolerable feature. A Navajo Indian named Mike Kiyaani was in a foxhole near Sugar Loaf one night when heavy artillery started at his company from near Shuri. He had seen the results before. This time, screams sounded as the shells advanced toward him. Then a friend was blown out of his foxhole, ten feet away. Kiyaani didn't realize that he too was hit, only that his friend was dying — and did die in the morning. But what dismayed him most was his fatal impotence as the murderous shells approached. "If you'd get up and run, you'd be shot up even quicker — so you wait there and go crazy."

Fear built to such a pitch during those cowering hours that men stopped trying to hide it from one another. The last seconds of the flight of the shells were agony. Even those which missed shook the ground, shocked the ears and brain, and sent hot fragments through the air, sometimes with body pieces. The young Marine who shot himself in the foot — blowing off several toes — did so after a dazzlingly accurate barrage of 150mm guns landed a hit on a nearby foxhole, blowing its two occupants into little red chunks. Together with the feeling of utter helplessness, such pounding and suspense drove some of the men, including a few who had performed the bravest exploits during firefights when they could shoot back, over the edge of sanity.

During its eight weeks in the south, Whitaker's company was pulled back half a dozen times to several hundred yards from the front, where it was much safer. Since Japanese snipers could be accurate at five hundred yards and more, constant checking of the surroundings became second nature. Still, life at that distance from the edge was tolerable by comparison — except when Fox Company took fire from artillery or from the screaming meemie, whose shells approached slowly enough to be seen. Their fear soared to another peak.

It all happens so fast in combat that you don't have time to be scared; you just run from one casualty to the next, do what you have to without thinking. When you get scared is in your foxhole at night, remembering what happened to guys you knew, thinking of what's going to happen to you. It was so bad that some men couldn't sleep and others couldn't do anything but sleep. Lots of men hated nighttime long after the war.
— Joseph Bangert, medical corpsman

It's pitch black and you smell that unmistakable smell of a Jap. You don't say anything to the man in the hole with you, just make a sniffing motion with your nose and maybe reach out and try to touch someone in the next hole if it's near enough or throw a pebble there. For the rest of the night, your senses are like springs and your heart feels like it might run out of control.
— Dick Whitaker

Night was the worst. They might launch a banzai attack and even if we killed one with every round, we couldn't kill them all. Knowing that when you're in that foxhole with only one other man was a terrific psychological strain.
— Major General James Day, USMC

All combat troops should receive extensive training in night operations. Troops, in general, lacked confidence in their ability to accomplish night missions efficiently.
— From a (U.S. Army) 17th Infantry Regiment Operations Report

The day was never long enough because the night was the longest, loneliest time of your life. From sunset to daybreak nobody moved. Your heart pounded. You prayed for daylight. You were just SCARED all the way through.
— Buzzy Fox

All [chosen for night attacks] were resigned, yet almost all remained terrified. No matter how accustomed the men grew to the incessant shelling, they turned petrified when death approached close enough to mutilate their friends and announce their own time had finally come.
— Kenjiro Matsuki

A final trial for the Americans surpassed the others. For all its repetition, darkness never became easier to endure. The infantryman who said that "every night was a night of horrors" spoke for everyone. "I mean *every* night. You never got used to it."

The 10th Army would declare the island secured on June 21. The average American infantryman who managed to stay unhit and unevacuated the full eighty-two days dug some seventy foxholes as he advanced. He occasionally stayed two nights in the same hole or spent one — to say "sleep" with the noise of artillery duels, small-arms fire and mosquitoes is misleading — in a tomb or the ruins of an Okinawan house. Otherwise, no one had to order him to dig. No sane man chose to spend a night on the surface.

Marine infantry tried to set up by late afternoon. If no high ground could be won for this, any small rise had to do. Each company's three infantry platoons spread out, giving the machine gun squad the favored position and a bit more protection on the highest ground with the best field of fire, and leaving the mortar squad a few yards behind, where it took a fix on everyone else for when those others would request flares. The "poor sonofabitch" who operated the backpack radio was often a Navajo, like Mike Kiyaani, who communicated with tribesmen in his native language, unintelligible to anyone who did not grow up in Navajo culture. This was to foil the significant number of Japanese who understood messages in English; Navajo was as secure from eavesdroppers as any code.* The operator burrowed in at the company command point, another hole. He could curl his antenna under his arm when moving during daylight but had to extend it at night: a magnet for sniper fire.

Read This Alone — And the War Can Be Won, the manual issued to each Japanese recruit, jeered that "Westerners, being very superior people, very cowardly and effeminate, have an intense dislike of fighting in rain, mist or darkness. Although fine for dancing, they can't conceive of night as a proper time for war. IN THIS, if we seize upon it, lies our great opportunity." The Japanese Army did make excellent use of night attacks throughout the war. On Okinawa, many 32nd Army units observed Americans fighting more according

---

*Each Marine division had eight to ten Navajos, most so tough that they had taken boot camp in stride. They worked in teams, switching from stations at a command post and farther in the field. Other Marines were much impressed by their bravery.

to the clock — like office workers or factory hands, as they saw it — than soldiers. They speculated that the enemy's great advantages in numbers and equipment made him overconfident. And noticing less discipline than their own in such duties as standing watch, they sought to take advantage of the lapses when the "office workers" closed up shop in the evening.

But night excursions became more a necessity than an opportunity after the early weeks. To leave their caves for close combat — the only kind in which they stood a chance — was suicidal during daylight. Therefore Japanese soldiers were forced to fight in the dark.

They still heard pep talks about how effective *kirikomi* — penetrating the enemy for hand-to-hand combat — had been in previous battles, but current observation told them the contrary. They knew they would be likely to set off "torrential" firing on themselves by touching the trip wire Americans rigged around the perimeter of their night positions. Still, they attacked as ordered — sometimes with enthusiasm, feeling they had to try *something*, after hiding in their caves all day, to counter the enemy's relentless advance; more often with resignation because "night attacks became synonymous with suicide attacks," as a spared man noted. "I'm sorry," an officer told him on the eve of an outing, "but go and resign yourself to being slain." When the time came, the selected men crept from their caves with as many grenades as they could tie around their waists and sometimes ten-kilogram explosive charges on their backs. Another soldier who watched such parties leave night after night saw them begin to take their deaths for granted. "They accepted the fate of summer bugs that fly into the fire and burn themselves."

The Japanese kept a finger raised as they crawled toward American positions. When able to detect the protective wire this way without setting off the trip flares, they straddled the wire, got in closer and used their grenades and satchel charges — or bayonets and knives. Those who managed to avoid the wire again and make it back to their caves were enormously excited and proud. "Nothing pleased them more," remembered a soldier about the small percentage who returned alive and unwounded.

Few members of the 10th Army stopped to think that the enemy's preference for night came chiefly from a need to avoid the devastating American firepower. Most thought operating in the dark, where men were certain to make mistakes and kill themselves, was a stupid way of fighting, one that confirmed the low-life Japanese as bloodthirsty fanatics. "If they're going to be killed anyway," Whitaker speculated about Japanese motives, "I suppose they don't give a shit about how or when as long as they take some of us with them." But

why mattered as little to American infantrymen as the ideals of kamikaze pilots mattered to American sailors. All they had to know was
that the sneaks liked to do their slaying at night, when penetration
was often lethal. You stayed in your hole, waiting and hoping. *They*
crawled around out there in the dark, in control of everything outside the position. It could be the end of you if you made a mistake.
You had a better chance if you didn't, but the sharpest eyes often
couldn't see the killers coming.*

Each foxhole was almost a sovereign unit for the night. Each
seemed to its pair of occupants the only sanctuary in a demented
universe. That other body pressed up against yours contained the
only living soul that could help you keep your sanity in that whole
mad world. If it is good to have a friend alongside when walking in
dark woods or entering a dark house, it was infinitely better there.
The foxhole mate didn't have to be a buddy in the sense of a man
with whom you spent free time. That he was a Marine and had come
this far was enough; the Corps forged transferable trust. He was a
link — the only one — to normality, a reason for hope.

The norm for standing watch was four hours on, four off. The
general practice was to stay awake as long as you could, then wake
your buddy, who stayed awake as long as *he* could before waking you
again. Those standing watch strained to interpret every sound in the
tyrannically menacing dark, strained to see — often through heavy
rain — the killers before they struck. It was like a game of hide-and-
seek, one Marine remembered, "except with the ultimate stakes."
The Japanese knew the terrain better. Especially at night, they knew
where you were, but you could only guess about them. What you did
know was that they camouflaged themselves cunningly and would
spend hours inching up to you with infinite patience.† Some crawled
to within yards or feet without being heard. Sometimes inches. Sometimes all the way, despite your precaution.

In those cases, the percentage of deaths was high and the wounds

---

* A *Life* magazine photographer who spent time at the front with the 7th Army Division
in May confirmed that "the full horror of war comes at night. The artillery is worse, the
rain is worse, the flares undress you. You lie in a hole dug out of mud and see shadows
and hear sounds not there in the daytime. When dawn comes, your body still aches . . .
and that's when somebody mumbles, 'They'll stand me up before a firing squad before I
make another invasion.'"

† Night tended to prompt the most respect, albeit grudging and backhanded, for the
Japanese ability to take pains. Ed De Mar greatly worried about their skill at camouflage,
which had been demonstrated in training films. "You'd see a small bush, perfectly ordinary — and after a while, it'd start to move! A Jap soldier! Then you'd see a Marine with
his stuff: a twig in his ear and another up his ass. Those Japs were *really* taught camouflage — and jungle fighting, everything. Anyway, they had the edge because they'd been
doing it for years." The implied contradiction of the conviction that the Marine Corps was
the "greatest fighting unit in the world" went unnoticed.

grievous because many were inflicted from directly above the foxhole or actually in it.* On the second night after the landing, an infiltrator's grenade exploded between two of Melvin Heckt's platoon mates in a hole six feet away and killed both instantly. Several nights later, a Japanese team sneaked up on a foxhole of Captain Stebbins's G–2–22 Company. The pair in another hole mere yards away heard nothing until one of the attackers had crawled almost on top of their target with a satchel charge that failed to detonate, to the Americans' great good luck. "That was up north, when things were easy. But that waiting for them to do the same went on every night. Hearing the noises, feeling the tension in your throat. Every night!"

An infiltrator crept up unheard to the hole of a Marine from Chicago named Ray Eustace during the night of May 12–13. His bayonet entered the back of Eustace's neck, pierced his throat, sliced down through his chest and one lung, and exited at the armpit. Few infantrymen who served more than two weeks failed to see such casualties with their own eyes, within ten or twenty yards. All at least heard of hundreds of successful attacks, and the near misses heightened their fear almost as much. Paul Gibson set a trip flare in the bottom of a drainage ditch into which Japanese had crawled on previous nights to lob grenades into his platoon's foxholes. Gibson heard his trap go off in the middle of the night but no flare went up. In the morning, he found it lodged in a Japanese throat.

So the watch standers had reason to sense hideous death in the thousand countryside sounds they heard or imagined they heard. "When I was on watch, I listened and *watched*," said a laconic man. "I wanted to survive." The darkness seemed darker than any previously experienced, even to American fliers. A pilot reported that "lights glared if not blazed" on the Okinawan territory already taken. "The fleet for miles from both sides of the island was also lit. But from the line of combat and below [south], pitch black." Drenched with cold rain, those off watch shivered in their puddles of water and mud — and not only mud, for if sanitation was bad during the day, it was worse at night, when few were crazy enough to leave their holes for anything. Most tried to use an ammunition carton or a grenade canister and throw their waste into the slime outside their holes, but much of it stayed inside.

Dysentery's effects didn't lessen after dark. And on any given night, a number of the men were vomiting from stress and ordinary

---

*The difficulty of wielding a rifle in a foxhole at night led to a great demand for Colt .45 pistols. When Whitaker managed to get one, he slept with it in his hand or tucked into his belt. Despite a fear of "shooting my balls off while half asleep," he always kept a round in the chamber, the hammer half-cocked and the thumb safety off.

sickness. "Poor kid," ran a diary entry about a man whose symptoms were commonplace in every unit. "Regurgitating and emitting his bowels all night. He is twenty-six and has twenty-five holes in his body; all twenty-five were shrapnel wounds." Many were reluctant to bail any slop from their holes at night for fear of the noise. Even with a good poncho, even after the hardest day's fighting, most men found sound sleep almost impossible until their exhaustion approached infirmity. The buddies of eighteen-year-old Declan Klingenhagen thought him dead because he slept through a fierce mortar barrage much of one night without moving a muscle.

Merely maintaining mental equilibrium in the mire was an ordeal. Whitaker "never found a comfortable position . . . Always wrapped in a poncho, always with a weapon at hand or *in* hand — for weeks on end." If nothing else, men worried about deadly snakes slithering into their foxholes. Besides, although each Marine knew he could count on his foxhole mate, some watch standers did doze off. However great their exhaustion, the off-watchers rarely got more than snatches of sleep. An uninterrupted hour was rare.*

On many nights, neighboring foxholes more than an arm's length away might as well not have existed. Whitaker often felt the next hole "was almost on the next planet. You can't be absolutely certain they're not asleep over there. You can't communicate with them anyway because a whisper can get you shot — and Japs often slipped in, knifed the pair in the hole next to yours, and kept going for others." This was why men frequently got no answer when they sensed a penetration and called to a neighboring hole, even though they were certain the neighbors were awake. There was always a special fear of being cut off from one's fellows and left exposed alone to Japanese brutality; but even greater fear prevailed when the danger was within yards. No one wanted to give away his position, everyone knew that a whisper traveled like a bugle at night.

Platoon leaders had wider communication. Fine black wires were strung from their radios to the company command point, which was just another foxhole. Every half hour or so throughout the night, an operator at the command point checked the other positions. He blew into the transmitter as softly as he could, a mere hint of exhalation, and murmured, "First Platoon." The acknowledgment was even

---

*On one occasion, Dick Whitaker thought he would finally get more. After several straight nights of "sheer misery" in holes filled with cold water, the deluge became so heavy that he and his mate calculated the Japanese couldn't attack through it. Even then, they would not use a tomb for shelter because no matter how unlikely a penetration, a single grenade might blow up everyone inside. But the two crawled to a relatively dry cave some 20 yards away. After about an hour, Whitaker woke with a start and reached for his trousers, up which a large rat was crawling.

fainter, the barest trace of a whisper. "First Platoon." Then another exhalation and "Second Platoon." Answer: "Second Platoon." The sound — or sound of an impulse sent through the wires by a little wheel, cranked as gently as the operator could manage — was sometimes enough to attract a bullet in the hand or face of the communicator at either end. One night after Whitaker had become a company runner, a man he called answered slightly too loudly. Whitaker heard the instant high-pitched chatter of a Nambu machine gun; then, over the wires, the operator's muffled moan.

The equipment was simple and reliable. An unanswered call might mean the man on the other end had heard something and was afraid to give away his position, but it was usually treated as evidence that the enemy had penetrated and killed. In that case, the company commander sent a man out to inch toward the silent platoon, using the wire as a lead. That man knew Japanese soldiers might have the same wire in their hands while crawling the opposite way — toward him — from out there in the blackness. When Whitaker was dispatched on the terrifying mission one night, he was only yards out of his hole in the direction of the mute platoon when heavy fire suddenly broke out there. Whitaker realized the man hadn't answered because the infiltrators had crept so close that a whisper would have "sealed his doom."

Radio operators at higher headquarters faced an additional dilemma nightly. Their little switchboards had visual taps that dropped when someone came on the line — but to keep their eyes free to look for infiltrators instead of monitoring the switchboards, most did not disable the mechanism, which also produced a ring when someone cranked. The tiny tinkle sounded like thunder in the darkness and "scared us out of our skins each time we got a call," recalled the operator of a switchboard code-named Buckshot. "Break it down" was jargon for "end of transmission." He was so frightened that instead of saying, "Break it down, Buckshot" he sometimes stuttered, "Buck it down, Breakshot."

Whitaker now had all the psychological defenses necessary to live as a combat animal, but they did not ease the dark hours for him. "The *quiet* out there. So much more terrifying than any horror-movie score. You're so lonely, so isolated. The world consists of you and your foxhole buddy. Your lives are in each other's hands on your turns trying to sleep. But that's not all you need each other for. He's the only other human being in the world, the only thing you have to keep you sane."

One evening, two of Whitaker's hardened buddies gouged out

their hole a few yards forward of the line — perhaps because they were under fire and had to dig in a hurry — in a kind of point position. One was killed during the night and the other had to spend the rest of it alone, deprived of a companion to share the madness and fear. At dawn, he was confirmation of the general rule that "to feel alone in combat is to cease to function; it is the terrifying prelude to the final loneliness of death." Whitaker helped take the incoherent man with the petrified eyes back to an aid station.

"You can't understand what night was like. It was the most awful time in the world. To be in a foxhole and hear something in the pitch-black void was the most terrifying of all possible experiences. It tore your heart out. Nobody cared what they shot at out there as long as it stopped those terrifying noises. You got up in the morning and saw a collection of dead things where the noises were, from goats to rats to Japs to civilian children. That too was terrible, but there was no way to tell what was coming at you hours before."

Seasoned men knew not to be trigger happy. Infiltrators often used a noisy movement or quick burst of their own as a lure to locate enemy positions, which was why Americans were instructed to fire at night only when absolutely necessary. "But terrified of everything that moved," as one put it, "we fired at everything." "Somebody fires at a rattle of leaves," another explained. "And when one person fires, everybody fires."

The fusilade would continue for several minutes and stop at no particular time. Americans would try to determine who among them had been hit, if anyone, and get help for the casualties. Evacuating the wounded, like getting more ammunition when supplies were spent, was doubly difficult in the re-established silence. American bullets swelled the number of those casualties: the jittery blasting away "at everything" intensified the danger of "own fire" hits in the dark. "The idea," said one, "was to shoot anybody on his feet first and then inquire. You just couldn't distinguish in the split seconds you had, so nobody dared get out of his hole for fear of being shot by his buddies." Kenny Geiman's closest call came when a clank of metal against a helmet woke him — enemy grenades had to be armed with a tap after their pins were pulled — and he saw Japanese eyes staring at him. Screaming, he rolled out of his hole into some brush. The screams set off a volley from neighboring holes and Geiman was saved, but he had forgotten that night's password and had to spend the remaining hours in the brush, motionless except for his quivering. In the morning, sixteen bullets were counted in the Japanese corpse. Geiman knew he too would have been shot to pieces at the first sound he made. Most men had similar or worse experiences when own fire actually hit them or their buddies.

Protective measures were perfected. When they had time, Americans rigged their wires around the perimeter of their group of holes — the wires Japanese tried to detect by crawling with a raised finger — then strung them with trip flares and pebble-stocked tin cans. A machine gun set up to fire in a wide arc at chest level would blast everything at the first sound of pebbles dancing in the can, indicating the wire had been touched. The trip flare — "a thing of beauty" because "it was like having someone else on watch in addition to just your foxhole buddy" — was slight reassurance against the dreaded surprise of a bayonet or grenade. It would freeze the infiltrator for a few seconds, "all the time you needed to get off a shot" that often "spelled curtains for the Nip."

Trip wires brought results with or without the machine guns and flares. A Marine typically remembered "not one single night when we didn't catch at least one crawler out there. The average was maybe half a dozen — lots female. We didn't know who they were, maybe just natives who got caught trying to survive, maybe girl friends of the Jap soldiers doing reconnaissance for them — some were armed. But there was always *somebody* trying to sneak in and kill us; at least that's what we had to assume they were doing."*

Americans could also call for larger flares, a startling sight, and relatively less dangerous when one's foxhole had been dug well — shallow, without telltale mounds of earth around the rim to reveal its position. The call for flares came in whispers over walkie-talkies. "Mortars. Mortars. This is Second Platoon. Gimme a flare up front. Right now." Soon an amazing luminescence was in the air, lighting everything as if for a film about ghouls. "Everything" included oneself: Whitaker felt flares were like "a thousand searchlights thrown on you." It also lit up sheets of slanting rain and scatterings of corpses — usually Japanese, but also American when there had been no opportunity to retrieve them. The phosphorous light — stark but greenish, garish yet ghostly — was a final eerie touch. Hallucinations were frequent in the macabre setting witnessed by men dumbfounded by fatigue and deprived of sleep. Sledge saw dead Marines rise from waterlogged craters and wander aimlessly, trying to tell him

---

*Platoon Leader Mitchell Zampikos spotted a tiny mound near his hole one daybreak after a night during which he kept hearing faint noises but could see nothing. Soon he saw movement inside and was certain a small animal was about to emerge. Zampikos ordered his men to hold their fire, then saw an elderly Okinawan woman pull herself out. "What a sight! She really did live like an animal all night in that tiny hole and in that rain."

something or ask for help — but he couldn't be sure those weren't nightmares because his exhaustion may have left him more asleep than awake.

The freakish light floated down in its parachute, yet seemed to stay up forever, an eternity. Among the things it lit was filthy water in the moonscape's craters, disabled field guns, upside-down amtracs with ragged holes in their bottoms where mines had demolished them, burned-out tank carcasses. Together with the absence of all vegetation except for blackened stumps, the wreckage seemed to confirm that some great natural calamity had recently destroyed the area. The dreaded infiltrators were also usually there. Sober veterans remembered them running, dodging and ducking for cover at almost every flare — "*always* out there," Whitaker specified, "always on their way to penetrate or charge us."

Japanese flares seemed to hang in the air terrifying minutes longer. In either case, Marines froze, their helmets just high enough above their holes so that they could see. They froze if they were caught in a higher pose: the slightest movement in the light would make the man a target. Of course Japanese soldiers also knew to freeze and often passed for corpses. Flares could work as well for the other side: light was light, after all, and although it was "really nice to catch a dozen Japs out there," the advantage was reversed when the enemy was better prepared. A common backfire was catching sight of but failing to shoot infiltrators before they had time to see where to toss their grenades. The need to use flares judiciously explained the practice of requesting them through the company commander, who tried to keep control of the situation at night. While all hated the darkness, they hated that unearthly light too.

And although the nights grew shorter in May and June, each additional ordeal, flare-lit or otherwise, seemed to last longer than the one before. Men bolted up from their semisleep, saw their buddies peering out for the menaces, and closed their eyes again but couldn't shake their fear. This had nothing to do with the advances associated with victorious campaigns. Each man went on to remember his nights in an individual way that is also communal:

"I lived through some days nobody would believe. The blood, the filth, the deaths — but the nights were worse. You always think about a banzai attack, but you try to hold your fire until you actually see one of them because otherwise you give away your position. You can't see what's out there and you don't know anything except that you can die any minute. The suspense is fantastic."

"Tropical sunsets are beautiful, right? But when you knew what was coming, you hated them, *hated* them."

"From sunset to daybreak, nobody moved. You just waited for dawn, couldn't wait for it, your heart pounding, your finger on the trigger. You never got used to it. Know what I mean by *looking forward* to the kinds of days we were having? But at least you could see during the day; it didn't have that constant terror."

Whitaker's worst night after his first artillery bombardment in the south took place on the Oruku Peninsula, which his regiment helped invade by amphibious landing two weeks after Sugar Loaf. Again, the company had no time to dig in well because they were taking heavy sniper fire as evening approached. Whitaker and his mate — John Senterfitt, with whom he had come down from Sugar Loaf — had to scrape their hole right next to the shoulder of a dirt road at the bottom of a hill, nearer than anyone else in the platoon. It was a moonless, pitch-black night. They had no communication with anyone else. Other foxholes were only yards away, but that was too far — and the other men probably couldn't hear the careful sounds on the narrow road. But Whitaker and Senterfitt heard them: whisperings and tiny noises of concealed movement that suggested the enemy was massing for a banzai attack. They were convinced they themselves would get shot if they called for mortars or a flare. "We were dead ducks if we moved an inch. So we froze for four hours, the Japs yards away. 'A night of horrors' isn't just a saying; there *is* such a thing. Every night."

> *In closing this diary, I would like to say this much about my service in the Corps. I wouldn't take a million for the experiences or give a penny to do it again.*
> — Melvin Heckt, 4th Marines, after the Okinawan campaign

> *War is a brutal, deadly game, but a game, the best there is. And men love games. You can come back from war broken in mind or body, or not come back at all. But if you come back whole, you bring with you the knowledge that you have explored regions of your soul that in most men will always remain uncharted.*
> — William Broyles, Jr., a veteran of Vietnam

Profound satisfactions and even joys partially compensated for this torment. For all but the handful who enjoyed killing, the first came from the exhilaration of having survived a trip to the far edge of human experience. Years later, when Dick Whitaker thought of Sugar Loaf, he felt great pride, mixed with some well-deserved conceit, in having been among the few who fought on the cursed hill. One trip up, the charge from his fifteen minutes of terrified bedlam there, was enough to last a lifetime — and has. "Just to say [forty-four years later] that I went up Sugar Loaf is enough. Just to *know* it, because there aren't many people I want to tell, maybe because not many can understand." Okinawa's hundred other battles, only quantitatively less harrowing than Sugar Loaf, endowed almost all survivors, apart from those who never recovered from battle fatigue, with a similar reserve of self-esteem. "The best thing that ever happened to me." "Nothing can ever dim what we did there." "The proudest moments of my life." It is not too much to say that everyone who saw actual combat cherishes a lifelong memory, terrible but sublime.

Understandably, this pertains far more to American participants than to Japanese, most of whom — including those who later became grateful to be alive — were ashamed of having survived. And even without the Imperial soldier's obligation to die rather than surrender, surviving on the losing side was, of course, emotionally very different. "There is no comfort like that of going into battle with the certainty of winning," said the future Confederate General Joseph E. Johnson when he spoke of the Mexican War to the future Union General George B. McClellan. Very few Japanese survivors share the feeling of the American infantrymen, most of whom feel grateful to have known those months, which killed almost a quarter of a million people in an area about the size of Long Island.

The other joys came from living in the nether world of combat, paradoxically an escape from the dullness and dreary constraints of ordinary life. Living on the edge was anything but release from its own iron laws, but it did provide heady freedom from many of civilization's restraints, an intoxicating sensation for most young men. It made them high while it drove them low with fear and misery.

The supreme intensity of combat dominates everything else, cutting away all other problems. In this respect, its power and appeal are greater even than lust's.* It delivers its participants to hell on

---

* Although most of the boys were virgins, there was an immediate resurgence of sexual interest after the war, especially among the 29th Marines sent to Tsingtao to handle the surrender of Japanese forces there and "screw ourselves silly," as a pleased veteran put it, with Chinese women. Even on Okinawa, nonfighting units managed some activity, as in the 6th Division's short-lived bordello in the north and in rapes. One replacement even claims to have witnessed a regular practice of homosexual acts in trucks taking off-the-line troops to the movies and, after the end of the campaign, to known meeting places behind boulders just off the East China Sea coast. "The water out to the three rocks . . . was shallow. It looked as if you could walk to China without getting your shins wet . . . I saw a steady march of men to and from the rocks. Some stopped at the first rock, others went on to the second and third. Men waded back at leisurely intervals. Then I noticed the men wading out there were stiff; the men coming back were limp . . . According to [a veteran], it had been that way in the outfit since Saipan."

Young men also told stories of other young men masturbating during breaks in the shelling — a release of nervous tension rather than an expression of recognizable sexual drive. Edmund Shimberg, the corpsman who went on to become a physical therapist, is not surprised to have seen little evidence of anything sexual. "Libido, a force usually mis-

earth, but simultaneously to utopia, which largely explains why "thoughtful, loving men can love war even while knowing and hating it," as William Broyles recently wrote. In World War II as never later, the complex, often contradictory impulses feeding this love embraced righteousness. Most Americans on Okinawa drew great satisfaction and strength from fighting for God, democracy, justice — a blessed cause, they felt, that lifted them toward ultimate goodness. When Paul Dunfrey, the platoon leader who scouted the Japanese defenses south of the Asakawa, was severely wounded on May 10, he was concerned for his exalted goals as much as for himself. "Even though I was scared like hell, I wanted to keep fighting. I'd joined the Corps to fight and win and I was sorry I wouldn't be able to continue." Utterly secure in their conviction that fighting and winning were vital to civilization, Americans were sustained by a moral reward even amidst the unspeakable filth and torment. The basest features of the front didn't tarnish the sainted mission they had visualized before their fighting.

When Emil Rucinski, the gunnery sergeant turned platoon leader, was gravely wounded on May 11, he asked for and was given absolution. Evacuated on a stretcher, he supposed he wouldn't make it, but the thought didn't depress him. "Of course I had some morphine in me by then, but I think I was at peace with the idea anyway. Because I had a patriotic conviction, remember that? I was doing something important for my country, so I took it as an honor if I was going to die."

Replacement Forest Townsend was uneasy, like almost all replacements, because he hardly knew anyone in his new squad. And he was "scared to death" by the intensifying artillery fire as the company he had just joined pushed south. "Any man who said he wasn't scared — replacement or veteran — had to have something wrong with him. You just can't live through those shells raining down on you without fear." Still, Townsend knew he'd been well trained and was doing what had to be done, surrounded by the best fighting men in the world.

On a late May morning, Townsend's squad had to cross an open field on its way to leveled Naha. Two men made it to cover on the far side but an enemy soldier popped up from a hole in the ground when Townsend was halfway across with his heavy BAR. The Japa-

---

construed to be entirely sexual drive, was directed elsewhere, to the acute needs of the moment. I have a hunch there weren't many horny combat Marines; they were too busy trying to stay alive. I guess you might say, 'When fear of death comes in the door, sexual drive goes out the window.'"

nese whipped his light Nambu gun around and fired it at its high-pitched clip, *tat-a-tat-a-tat*, even before aiming. Townsend's BAR fell from his hands as the bullets spun him around and down. An inner voice had time to comment that this was the way it was when you were hit, even as training and instinct shouted commands. Find cover fast, *any* cover; don't let him finish you off. He saw a shell hole only feet away, slid into it and was shocked again by rain water from the recent deluges rising to his waist, his bleeding chest, his armpits. When it stopped at his chin, he reckoned he wouldn't drown if he could keep his head up. But the eighteen-year-old had already seen stacks of American bodies and knew he'd been hit very badly.

"*Am I going to die here?* Well, if I have to," he thought. "Mother wouldn't want it, but she and Dad will be proud of me. Very sad, but also very proud, the whole family — so it's really okay."

Tens of thousands hurt as badly as Townsend, Dunfrey and Rucinski took similar comfort. Their composure helped medical personnel straining to save them despite their massive wounds and mutilations. A corpsman in a surgical tent tended a parade of casualties who seemed unfazed despite fierce pain. When the temperature of a young Marine with a head wound exceeded 107 degrees, he became one of the earliest cases to be packed in ice from a hospital's ice maker. "His fever was raging, he was dehydrating and his pain was excruciating, but he lay there without a word of complaint. Those men — and boys — were absolutely remarkable."

The pride and sense of reward that sustained this stoicism didn't surprise that corpsman. "Whatever their individual resources, all of them had a fantastic support system. They had constant nurturing — at least rhetorical — not only from their comrades but also their families, communities, government, the whole society. America had only one face, and that face told them they were on God's side, fighting the good fight — which was just what they felt as they lay there, suffering but proud. No one questioned the rights and wrongs because all knew they were right. Therefore no one really questioned the need for the suffering. That idealism helped a lot with the whole nightmare."

> *At the critical moments, you do what's in your heart, not what you've been trained. But your heart feels what it's been trained to: that you can't let your buddies down. Because you're nothing without them, you've learned that's not just pep talk. You depend on that man next to you absolutely and he depends on you, which is why you're more than family. You pray as much for him to come out alive as you pray for yourself.*
> —Al Franks, 22nd Marines

*When we reached the bottom [of Sugar Loaf], one of the Marines headed
. . . [out] about ten yards to help a wounded Marine lying on the ground. I
followed to help out. The Marine squatted to help the wounded Marine and,
as I came up behind him, fell back dead at my feet with a bullet hole in the
center of his chest . . . I took off, heading for the cover of a disabled tank.
As I left, one of the other Marines yelled, asking me to leave my rifle with
him. Instinct and boot camp training told me not to give up my rifle . . . but
he needed it and I couldn't refuse.*

— Declan Klingenhagen, 29th Marines

*The only other glory besides surviving was seeing people stripped bare of
all their artificiality and developing feelings for them unknown anywhere
else. Respect, affection, loyalty, love — everything came out of need,
as in all human relations, except that here it was far greater than in
normal life.*

— Robert Sherer, Dick Whitaker's company commander

Would you do it again?
Sure.
*Even knowing the horrors and misery — and that you'd have a good
chance of not making it if you did it again?*
Sure.
Can you explain why?
*For the right country and the right cause. I think every one of us would
have.*
Despite everything?
*Sure. And for what we shared. Nobody worried about who you were and
how much money you were making or weren't making. You had* real
friendship, real *closeness for maybe the first and last time. You weren't
making an impression by telling everybody you were a millionaire because
that, or being a floor sweeper, didn't make a damn bit of difference. Nobody
cared about those things. All you knew was you depended on that guy next
to you and you loved him. I never found that again.*

— Answers by Joseph Bangert, one of the flag raisers on Okinawa's
southern tip

For Marine infantry, their fellows were it, *the only family they had.*
— James Day, the corporal who became a general

But Americans' inspiriting uplift from fighting for the highest national cause usually remained in the background. In the foreground
was a handful of beloved comrades. Combat's second joy, sometimes
even its first, was a love as difficult for outsiders to know as the horrors that sired it.

The love fed on trust. Unlike that of ordinary friendship and romantic attachment, this one was total: everyone's life was constantly
in the hands of his platoon mates. This bond could not be broken

"by a word, by boredom or divorce or by anything other than death," as Philip Caputo wrote. Ordinary life's usual mean motives and jockeying for personal advantage vanished in the reliance on and concern for one's fellows. Those who endured the grime, gore and torment together felt themselves elevated toward absolute selflessness. In this way, all combat offered some of the kamikaze pilots' exhilaration at being liberated from petty considerations. It compelled men and also freed them to act more unselfishly, lovingly, nobly than they ever had or would. The intensity of this devotion was comparable only to the surge parents feel for their young children when they are endangered. But here the emotion was reciprocated, prompting an intoxicating spiritual gratification.

This exalted intimacy had never been imagined before and would rarely be achieved again, even with wives and family. Andy Rooney thought it paradoxical that "when man is closest to death, he is also closest to complete fulfillment and farthest from loneliness." Yet this condition is less paradoxical than causal, and Rooney himself can identify the cause: "He is dependent, dependable, loved and loving." Class position and social origins counted for nothing in the world of instant death and maggots feasting on severed limbs. Marines in particular were Marines, not members of other groups. "It was all the same who you were and where you came from because you *were* the same, struggling with higher forces."

Blacks remained the exception. Still not acknowledged as "the same" on Okinawa, they served in segregated Army units — some fighting, a majority in support services such as transportation and laundry — and nowhere at all in the Marines, apart from a scattering of orderlies.* But although some Jews had encountered coarse anti-Semitism during training and on their troopships — even, occasionally, in some rear areas on the island itself — ethnic and religious

---

*But Okinawa broke down even some of those barriers, as in a Marine medical unit that returned to Guam in July, after the campaign. The men were to be fed in a base mess hall until its own galley could be set up. When base personnel directed a handful of black stewards who had served in the officers' mess on Okinawa to a separate, segregated table, the Okinawa veterans protested. "They simply refused to eat there under those arrangements," one of the corpsmen remembered. "Because when the fighting got furious, those stewards also served as litter bearers and general helpers under fire. If they were good enough to be shot at with the rest of us, they were good enough to eat with us. That's what we'd learned, including our large sprinkling of Southern rednecks — and we prevailed in the end."

As for the Navajo Indians who served as communication specialists, there was little overt discrimination. Still, they tended to seek their own company when not on the line, living together in separate tents when their units were in training. Many years later, when Dick Whitaker learned about racial minorities' sensitivities to real or implied slurs, he would regret automatically calling them all "Chief." But this practice was grounded in innocent ignorance, not prejudice against the Indians, for whom, as combat buddies, there was much affection.

antagonism evaporated in the strain and compensatory love of combat itself. When pulled back into temporary reserve, men of all faiths almost indiscriminately attended services held by Catholic, Protestant and Jewish chaplains. "Even the atheists prayed," one man remembered with only marginal exaggeration.

Most men of the three major faiths never witnessed a single moment of religious hostility, only some teammate-like banter prompted by love. Infantryman Gilbert Kanter was shot in the throat near Sugar Loaf's crest. On L-day, six weeks earlier, he had thrown up on a landing craft and was surprised that the man on whom his vomit settled "never said a thing, not even 'You dirty Jew.' And from then on, there was never even a hint of anti-Semitism; we were like one." Jews were such a small percentage of the Marines on Okinawa that some companies had none, while in others nothing distinguished them. One Jewish platoon leader carried "a little black book" and asked some of his men to read a few paragraphs, evidently the Kaddish, over his body in case he was hit. When he was killed about an hour later, one man inched to the body and read the passage.

William Manchester pronounced men brothers who had been tested by battle. "They may have nothing else in common and that doesn't matter. They come to know each other and love each other as no one who hasn't experienced this can quite understand." For boys of unloving parents, their units, despite all the severity and bravado of Marine training, became their first real family, with all the meshing and devotion they somehow knew had been missing — and more. For those like Whitaker, whose home lives had lacked nothing in affection, the new family of total partnership and interdependence brought an emotional elevation more intense than anything in civilian life. The brothers would go their divergent ways after Okinawa, returning to peacetime's individual strivings. Over the course of forty years, those ways would diverge more and more widely from what had been the common interests of unformed teenagers in service. Many would find they had little in common, or held opposite views on fundamental political and social issues. Still, when Marine veterans of Okinawa met at reunions almost half a century later, their old love filled the vapid motel banquet rooms.* The "fierce male tenderness that men feel for flesh and blood in war," as Laurens van der Post called it, remained almost palpable. They were buddies for life.

---

*Even after many reunions the love embraced dead comrades. Dick Whitaker spoke for all the living, who always remembered that there were "many, many others who did more, endured more and suffered more than I. I came home whole. Many left body parts behind; many never left Okinawa at all."

Van der Post likened this bond of devotion to fire. It spread over Okinawa along with the devastation — no hotter than on other Pacific islands but igniting more souls in the war's largest, most difficult campaign. Each man fought to keep his inner group alive. If a buddy got hurt because he himself had been careless, let alone cowardly, he felt it would haunt him forever. Letting the others down was seen as worse than surviving at that cost.

This too was different from the Japanese. Their courage had to be greater than that of the superbly courageous Marines if only because they had so much less firepower in so many more deadly encounters — and little rest, no replacements. But that did not reward them with victory. They couldn't even hope to keep their buddies alive.

Brotherhood was harder to sustain in units that were disintegrating, as many Japanese units soon were — an especially demoralizing calamity to a people who view themselves primarily as members of a group. The ultimate loneliness Americans felt when cut off from their fellows was even more frightening for Japanese. Yet many units did hold together as they were being destroyed, engendering a multitude of kindnesses that would never be recorded because every man in those units died.

When one of Captain Kojo's companies faced what promised to be total annihilation, a group of friends dug a hole outside their cave to make sweet bean soup, a delicacy. Even protected by a tent, the fire under their pot had to be small — two or three slim sticks at a time — lest the approaching enemy see it and kill them all there and then. The very old beans remained stone hard after a long period of anxious boiling. American mortars were landing within yards of the tent by the time they were finally ready and the pot was rushed inside the cave. Each of some thirty men had one cup of the treat. "They didn't sip it, they actually licked slowly, savoring the sweet taste of the beans. No one said as much, but we all knew that this was our farewell party."

After dignified observance of such symbolic acts, Japanese soldiers expressed much of their fierce male tenderness in an attempt to respect the dead, a large number of whom, however, could not be buried. American fire made it impossible to recover most bodies, a more difficult task for the retreating side in any case because the dead often lay in enemy territory. Still, thousands of Japanese took huge risks to bury their friends. Battlefield camaraderie — sealed, perhaps, by a higher degree of love while there was little hope of anything but joining those bodies — was the only joy in many units apart from the satisfaction of not failing under the severest ordeals.

Kuni-ichi Izuchi, the artist whose grueling apprenticeship to the master artist had made basic training seem easy, almost missed the Okinawan ordeal. He was in an Army hospital in Peking, his leg gashed by a mortar, when he heard that his unit was being transferred. He begged to be certified fit, got his wish and accompanied his comrades to Okinawa.

The passionate patriot had been born Kuni-ichi Yamauchi; Izuchi was the name of the fellow soldier to whom he became closest on Okinawa. When Izuchi was killed soon after L-day, Yamauchi fought to find his body in a shelter, then severed the left hand and found some wood to cremate it. The mates had promised each other that whoever survived longer would bring some bones of the other to his family. But when Yamauchi too was very badly hit and dragged himself around for days without help or medical aid, he became so weak that Izuchi's few bones were nearly more than he could carry. Still, his promise remained sacred even when he fell into a stupor, a breath from death. When he returned to Japan in 1946, he presented the bones to his friend's family — and when he married Izuchi's sister the following year, he took her name, a not uncommon practice when the bride's family lacked a male heir.

Japanese soldiers performed a hundred thousand such acts of heroic devotion to their buddies and their memory. Still, the losers in the battles also lost some of the sense of compensation for their misery. The nature and mood of veterans' reunions was one measure of the difference. They were much longer in starting in postwar Japan, because of the shame of being captured as well as the paucity of survivors. Decades later, gatherings of the defeated were substantially more somber and spiritual than gatherings of the victors, although the defeated have written more books about their experience and seem to reflect more deeply on it.

Dodging enemy shells and bullets, we carry the stretchers south, weak from our long unnatural life underground, gasping from the weight. On one stretcher, Takai tosses and babbles . . .

We finally reach Asato village but can't find the hospital cave. Takai complains his hip is stiff and Takagi, a close friend, stoops to massage it. Looking comfortable now, Takai closes his eyes. He was so restless on the stretcher coming here but now he's too quiet. I touch his forehead. It's very cold . . . Each time it gets colder. No pulse. Can't hear his breathing.

"Ah, his life is ebbing away!" No matter how you try to fend it off, life mercilessly dwindles, second by second. We grasp his hands, put our faces on his chest, tremble as time passes relentlessly . . .

Takai's face has death written on it. His unfocused eyes stare at a corner of the sky. The dirt and sand blown on his pale cheeks from the enemy's howitzer fire look like freckles.

"Takai, Takai!" An old buddy of his from Manchuria can't bear it any longer and cries out loud . . . We take clippings from his hair and nails. Always very neat, he has no extra growth of either. We bury him at the foot of the mountain and place a green branch in his canteen on the spot.

— Shigemi Furukawa

I remember the single road, narrow and rough, through the rice paddies . . . and the narrower path to the tree line rising beyond the paddies. This was a no man's land. He was on that path, lying face up with his throat cut, never going back to Detroit. Tony Marinelli, Marine private. 1945.

Day dreaming, 1981 . . . Easy time . . . a fat man is sitting by the pool, in shorts, looking at the water, puffing a big cigar. Tony smoked cigars, big cigars. With that name he should have played shortstop for the Tigers instead of smoking cigars on Okinawa and getting killed . . .

Harry is the man in charge [of the bar]. The maker of fine drinks in the sun. The opener of beer cans, the hot dog chef, the man who knows all about this Everglade town.

There's a blonde at the bar alone but talking to Harry, who is leaning back on a chair, squinting into the sun. A lady sips a Bud from the other side of the bar, looking across at the fat man by the pool.

Around the pool, three couples are sunbathing, stretched out, feeling that Florida sun.

A quiet afternoon . . .

The fat man at the pool flicks cigar ashes and bites down, looking at the pool.

Would Tony have been fat now? No, don't think so. He was lean and dark and short with coal-black hair and a tricky little smile that made you like him.

Hard to remember him alive. Too easy to remember him dead, with a cut across his throat, wet blood running like a river down the side of his neck.

No more cigar for Tony.

No chance to be fat, to sit in the Florida sun.

"Harry! Two beers."

One for Tony and one for me.

— Thomas Hannaher

Every Marine still loved the Corps, with its honorable bloodline and heroic ancestors, now his own. Each still believed he was part of "the best damn fighting outfit in the world," ready to bash any dissenting American head even in the exhaustion of battle with the enemy. Yet that extended family now also receded to the background. When the Okinawan going got toughest for the 6th Marine Division in mid-May, as it had been tough for Army units since early April, abstract goals mattered less and less. Most men in the line for more than forty-eight hours came to feel they were fighting not for the Corps, let alone for God or Democracy, but for the handful of fellows at their side. Edward (Buzzy) Fox's concerns were universal. "My world was the ten guys in my squad." (The squad was down to ten because no replacements for their casualties were available.) "Five to ten men, they were the only ones that counted. And maybe my Company to some extent. To tell the truth, I didn't really care about the other companies — or anything else. There just wasn't enough strength or imagination."

To some degree, this narrowness of focus was merely evidence of the limitations of human energy and concentration. Whitaker later reflected that generals perceived the world as masses of men and equipment, captains as deployments of companies, sergeants as movements of platoons. The ordinary Joes like himself had all they could do to cope with the welfare of their own fire teams of five or six men. Besides, those half dozen were in closer physical proximity — on top of one another day and night for months — than family members with separate beds and rooms. Stripped of their privacy and social skins, they fought, slept and performed all natural functions, as well as battle's unnatural duties, in total togetherness. Sharing everything, they savored what well might be their last human contact. Fire teams lived more like wolf litters than human brothers.

The cubs' age drew them further together, as eighteen-year-old Walter Kaminsky quickly discovered. "We were physically tough on Okinawa, really, truly tough — but inside, just teenagers who needed their families. And the guys in your unit were the only family you had and maybe the last you'd ever see."

Kaminsky, from a poor, close Chicago family, needed that support as much as anyone.

When we joined up, we thought the Marines would be all storming beaches, charging up hills, maybe blood running into the sand. But Okinawa was just as much about friendship and loyalty. It was about kinship, trust, getting to know other people and love them more than anyone before or maybe since. Love in combat is far easier to come by than in civilian life. You need your buddies because they're the only thing between you and that hell. It sounds corny but you're eager to give to them — totally. You fight among yourselves sometimes but like brothers fight. And when you see a brother killed, nothing's more terrible. Your eyes may be dry but everybody can see your tears.

Yes, you like some men in your platoon more than others, they're a mixture of good and bad like anywhere else. But when Joe Smith over there is taking fire, it doesn't matter if you don't have a great affinity for him. He's in trouble and you're all equal. He's your brother and that's a very precious thing. I knew there was nothing anyone could do for me if I was killed. But I also knew that if I was captured, my buddies would come get me out — the whole U.S. Marine Corps, if necessary. That was my feeling and it was very precious.

Gregarious young Kaminsky was wounded the day before the start on Sugar Loaf. He made his way back about a mile to the tent of a field hospital, where most of the other patients were recent young recruits just like him. But without his platoon brothers, he felt cut off from his country, the 10th Army, even his beloved Corps. Bereft of the intimacy of the cubs' litter, he was suddenly a vulnerable teenager alone in the alien world. His depression threatened to disable him longer than his wrist wound.

During his rounds to comfort patients, a priest named Eugene Kelly saw his blank eyes staring into space. "What's your name, son?" he asked.

"Kaminsky, Father."

"No, your first name."

"Walt."

"Hey, Walt, two guys were looking for you. Just before we started talking. They went out there."

Knowing the visitors must be his buddies, Kaminsky leaped up, ran in that direction and continued feeling better even after other patients assured him no "two guys" had been there. From then on, he lovingly called Kelly "the Lying Priest . . . But if there ever was a good lie, that was it — he snapped me out of my stupor. He knew what buddies mean to a combat rifleman, something different from anything else in the world."*

Human virtue fell short of perfection even here. A few braggarts, cowards and hoodlums were unregenerate; there were thieves who stripped bodies of their wristwatches because "the gravedigger will get this stuff otherwise and I know he'd rather it went to me." But those few rotten apples didn't spoil the barrel. Thousands of Kaminskys and Whitakers hurried back to the front as fast as they could instead of staying a deserved extra day or week in the hospital; they

---

*By that time, handsome, much-loved Father Kelly had become a master comforter with little physical comfort to give. One replacement who arrived from soft Stateside duty during the week of the heaviest casualties was sent directly to the Shuri Line and couldn't hide his shock at the human toll. The priest — "looking like Zapata" with his .45-caliber pistol and belts of ammunition — spied the newcomer's dismay and engaged him in conversation. Learning he'd been playing ball for his unit in New Jersey, he assured him he'd surely survive the battle because he had an athlete's extra advantages of quick reflexes and split vision. "Later I realized he probably told every green Marine the same thing in one form or another. It was all charmed malarkey, but when he gave it to me, I thought he was the greatest living American. It was the best possible bunk because it really made me feel I'd live."

lied to their doctors in order to be pronounced fit for combat. "The hulks with limbs shot off and stomachs blown apart were evacuated," remembered Corpsman Bangert. "Some considered themselves lucky because they had their 'ticket home' and would probably live. But lots of men with bad wounds begged to be patched up and sent back to their units. Unfortunately, we had some of the most patriotic boys in the world — but mainly they couldn't bear the thought of their buddies still in danger out there. That's what drew them back to combat even after they'd lived with its unbelievable awfulness."

Of course everyone wanted to go home. At the same time, many wanted to continue sharing their buddies' burden, even knowing — since most units served for the duration — that their service could end only in grave wounds or death. Manchester's horror of combat's degradation and carnage made him wonder why he checked out of a hospital early to hurry back to "almost certain death" on Okinawa. "It was an act of love. Those men on the line were my family, my home. They were closer to me than I can say, closer than any friends had been or ever would be. They had never let me down, and I couldn't do it to them. I had to be with them rather than let them die and me live with the knowledge that I might have saved them. Men, I now knew, do not fight for flag or country, for the Marine Corps or glory or any other abstraction. They fight for one another."

Such loyalty helps explain their obsession with recovering their dead — and scorn for men who didn't share it. It was driven by more than respect for the remains. Every Marine had an iron resolve to save and honor a slain buddy's precious memory and reputation. Therefore, an unrecovered body, deprived of its proper treatment, was the worst possible loss. "It was part of the bargain we all made, the reason we were to willing to die for one another," Michael Norman recently wrote of the same commitment in Vietnam. Men crawled into the killing zone not because they were ordered but because "each believed that if his had been the body . . . other Marines would have come for him." Death didn't end the fight for one another. A man who performed many recoveries on Okinawa specified that this was essential not for the corpses, which didn't know what happened to them, but for the living, "who could count on a decent burial just like he would count on his buddies never letting him down in any hell."

Some tried to sustain this union's emotional ecstasy even from the States. Their "weaker" part had dreamed of being back home with a "million-dollar wound" serious enough to make them unfit for combat but not civilian life. After Sugar Loaf, the mail began to include letters from men who were in U.S. hospitals with that lucky degree of damage — and who felt alienated from everyone who hadn't been in combat. On the line, they had seen their buddies volunteer to recover the wounded and the dead from the terrifying fire of no man's land. Although numb from fatigue and shock, they themselves had volunteered, seeing and performing acts of the purest selflessness in the grip of the tender manly love. Only the light of those bonds could lure anyone back to the madness.

> *My heart pounded inside whenever I saw a buddy get hit and even more so when they died. We were taught to carry on and we knew we could not stop and dwell on the tragedy around us.*
> — Robert Jones

Two weeks after the end on Sugar Loaf, Manchester was in the courtyard of a tomb on the safer back slope of a hill with a man named Rip Thorpe and a third buddy. They heard the shriek of a screaming meemie approaching from Japanese territory. Although the chances of the huge mortar shell clearing the top of the hill and landing on their side seemed remote, Manchester sought protection in the tomb's entryway. The shell landed in the courtyard, where Thorpe's body disintegrated, sending fragments of bone into Manchester, together with chunks of shrapnel. Thorpe's "flesh, blood, brains and intestines encompassed me."

Most infantrymen who fought for a week or two on Okinawa suffered the same supreme shock and horror of seeing a combat friend instantaneously destroyed inches away. Many wept openly when their buddies were killed out of their sight. Within their sight, and their hearing, the effect was predictably worse — the crunch and squish of fellow cubs in the litter being dismembered or atomized. Two days after Sugar Loaf, one platoon lost six men, most from a single squad. One died from a direct hit by an artillery shell while covering the three nearest men with his body. A buddy's grief increased even more when the dead man had to be listed as "missing in action" because the small piece of a leg and a hip that could be found wasn't enough to identify the body.

Two boys sheltered in a foxhole next to Eugene Sledge's on Half Moon Hill, one of the three in the Sugar Loaf complex. The next hole had three. A screeching shell passed no more than a foot over Sledge's head and exploded two holes down, where a man was sitting on his helmet drinking C-ration hot chocolate. Sledge saw him go straight up in the air and the others die. The two youngsters in the hole next to his were also killed instantly.

Evan Regal was on the back side of Charlie Hill two days after being wounded. A Japanese knee-mortar shell landed on the neck of a man a few feet away and blew off his head. A larger mortar shell had landed in a two-man foxhole of Owen Stebbins's Company G–2–22 the day before it crossed the Asakawa for its advance toward Hill 51.2. Those two survived — trembling fearfully — because the shell failed to explode. The day before that, two friends had disappeared when an artillery shell did go off in their hole.

Irving Ortel enjoyed a break in Naha's southern outskirts after fighting through its rubble. No one expected full security within a thousand yards of the front because nothing that close was reliably free of metal slicing the air. But in that area, believed to be "pretty secure," Ortel and a mortarman named Prince were sitting on their helmets, playing cards on an ammunition box. A single shot rang out. The bullet imploded Prince's head and he died before he could utter a sound. Although Ortel had seen a great deal of death, especially during his charge up Sugar Loaf weeks before, this was his time to temporarily lose his mind. "Usually when someone was hit, you shouted for the corpsman once or twice and tried to stop the bleeding until he came. But this one was too much; maybe it was combat fatigue. Although I didn't know it then, I kept screaming over and over for a corpsman — even though nothing could help my friend Prince."

Few infantrymen were spared splattering by their friends' blood and flesh. Brain matter seemed to horrify them most, with intestines and other organs not far behind. When a bullet grazed the teeth of Ed Jones — known as Teeth because he smiled so much — he waited for the bleeding to stop, then pushed on, also south of Naha. But he had to stop when he saw what a bullet did to a man who caught it full at the upper teeth. "His whole mouth was simply gone. It was just *terrible*. I wasn't so good at forgetting that."

Anthony Cortese, the man who had seen a sea of dead Marines on Sugar Loaf from Chocolate Drop Hill, survived that battle. A month later, he again took heavy fire while advancing up another hill in the deep south. His new platoon leader, a green lieutenant just arrived from the States, ordered him to scout the enemy positions with two other men. They started up the hill. A shell landed nearby, killing one of the two others and blowing off Cortese's jacket, showering him with shrapnel. It also blew off the legs of the young third scout. "How can I forget that? You could see his rear end *end* but he was alive. He tried to pick himself up and couldn't believe what he saw: he had no legs. He died right there. How can I ever forget?"

Anyone not hit after a week or two had "a horseshoe in his hip pocket," as Robert Sherer, Whitaker's company commander, put it, amazed by his own luck. Everyone remembered incidents of missing death by an instant, like Manchester in the tomb — of taking a step away and, before his foot came down, seeing a man killed in the spot he had just vacated. But what invested that experience with too much emotion for normal nerves to bear was that the other man was likely to be a combat friend, loved more deeply than all but the luckiest lovers. (Few of those teenagers had *had* lovers before they joined up.) Inches away, bullets and shells turned the dearest creatures on earth, the objects of their fierce male tenderness, into offal and ooze that stuck to their own helmets and faces.* The shock, disbelief, dismay were beyond noncombatants' imagination. The trauma and bereavement contributed heavily to the general loss, if only temporary in most cases, of much of what distinguishes human beings from lower forms of life.

> *I could not reconcile the romanticized view of war that runs like a red streak through our literature — and the glowing aura of selfless patriotism that had led us to put our lives at forfeit — with the wet, green hell from which I had barely escaped.*
>   — William Manchester

> *I was in a large cave with lots of tunnels branching off the main "hall." The whole thing was full of Jap corpses, but suddenly I saw one breathing, although his eyes were closed. "Hey, we've got a live poggie here," I shout as I release the safety on my submachine gun. Then I drill a pattern right into his chest — and* think nothing of it! *That's pretty gruesome. That's how it was.*
>   — Ed Jones

> *One of the things I learned [as a war correspondent] was that war makes no national or racial or ideological distinctions as it degrades human beings.*
>   — John Hersey

So much savage death numbed combat infantrymen, who became the killers they had to become. Ethical considerations had to be jettisoned for this, like the gas masks and other excess baggage from the heavy packs. But most men could not leave their moral sense entirely behind when they crossed into the battlefields' other world. Many

---

*When the dearest creatures were old friends, the hit did not have to be inches away to have the same effect. Peter Milo, who lost his buddy Corpsman Truex on L-day, had the joy of running into an old friend from the Bronx on May 12 as their units approached Sugar Loaf. The intense defensive fire limited them to a quick hug, but Milo, who was with the 22nd Marines' Headquarters and Supply Company, promised to find the other man the next day. Several days of the furious fighting had to pass before he could do this — and was told that a mortar shell had blown his face off.

were further scarred by knowledge of what the "bestial, monstrous and vile" things they had to perform, as Manchester saw them, did to their humanity.

The sight of mutilated bodies and body parts alone was enough to dehumanize. One eighteen-year-old saw a pair of "nonchalant" Japanese legs standing beside a low wall, and the torso, sliced off by an artillery shell, on the other side of the wall. He laughed. But another part of him kept asking why he himself was still alive; bullets surely intended for him had killed his buddies. He would continue asking "Why? Why? Why?" for forty-five years.

Sledge once saw a Japanese gunner sitting upright with his eyes wide open, although the top of his head had been shot off. The skull was full of water from a night of rain, and Sledge noticed a buddy flipping chunks of coral inside and watching the splashes. It reminded him of a child tossing pebbles into a puddle. "It was so unreal. There was nothing malicious in his action. This was just a mild-mannered kid who was now a twentieth-century savage."

When Dick Whitaker's company was dug in under heavy fire near Sugar Loaf one day, his platoon leader sent a runner back for help from a flamethrowing tank, one of America's most fearsome weapons, which had its first major use with the 10th Army on Okinawa. The tank moved up to shoot streams of napalm into a cave from which machine gun fire had been hitting Whitaker's platoon. Japanese soldiers who ran from the furnace were squirted with napalm — which, however, failed to ignite. One of the tankers saw to this with a tracer bullet, turning a man fleeing from the cave into a torch — which prompted a throaty cheer from the platoon. "That was our war," remembered Robert Sherer. "Yes, that Jap had been machine-gunning our people moments before — but he was a human being. And we cheered that incredibly horrible sight, the burning of another human being, because we'd been reduced to something non-human. Whatever the justification, we'd become savages too."

Buzzy Fox registered the spiritual metamorphosis the day before he joined the line as a "green and naïve" replacement.

I'm in a sorting area about a mile from the front — and a guy there tests his rifle on a cow. I think that's terrible. "Listen, Mac," he answers, "with all this rain and mud, I gotta make sure this thing [his M1] *works.*" I still think killing an animal unnecessarily is stupid — until *my* time in foxholes. Then I'd even borrow some officer's .45 in case I had to fire in a hurry at night, because an M1 never seemed enough to me. And I'd have been happy to test my rifle on a live animal if any more existed on the island. Because every tiny little advantage, every *anything* you can do to stay alive, is worth it. What do you care about animals anymore when you've seen stacks of dead buddies and you know you can join them in one second?

One day, I thought I'd try to get down some food, so I sat down on a log instead of the ground. Then I noticed it wasn't a log but a charred Jap corpse. And I didn't move; it didn't faze me a bit. A dead body, another human being, meant nothing to me — because it was Japanese and I myself had become something less than human.

The loss of human values may have been no worse than other aspects of the Okinawan fighting, but it might be called the ultimate degradation. "You can't ask a man who's been in combat how he feels about those things when he does them," John Townsend said later. "If you want to know that, go to a slaughterhouse and ask the men there what they feel about their jobs. You're dealing in meat, not lives. All you're concerned about is yourself and your buddies."

"I resigned from the human race . . . I just wanted to kill," another Marine put it. A very small percentage were sadists who enjoyed smashing and killing, but most were ordinary American boys, raised on the Ten Commandments. However they had relished the thought of killing Japs during training, the act of doing it, and of "living like an animal, reduced to the lowest possible level," degraded them. Sledge knew that no combat infantryman turned killer would ever be the same; something in all of them had changed forever. Perhaps it was their ability to be revolted by doing as well as suffering revolting acts. They were not just living in conditions that taxed "the toughest I knew almost to the point of screaming" but were contributing to depravity, an acceptance that human life was not at all sacred.

Book III

19 · Kojo at the Shuri Line

We fought hard on Okinawa, maybe harder and better than any Americans before. But would we have won without our enormous superiority in numbers, firepower and supplies, our control of the air, our ability to replace men and equipment? If the Japanese say that's what licked them, I think they're right. We didn't win because our fighting men were superior; the Japanese were as good or better.
  — Clyde McAvoy, 4th Marines; later a businessman in Tokyo

We had firepower of all types right down to Fox Company. We could deliver a withering, concentrated field of fire that would take out anything within 100 yards. As I look back, I realize it was mainly that superiority that allowed us to win.
  — Dick Whitaker

The American soldier fights largely to save his ass. When you corner him, he's tough, but when things go badly, he thinks of how to get the hell out of there. The Japanese soldier was very different.
  — John Toland, historian

The Japanese soldier was a remarkable man. To have fought so well with no air cover, no naval support and virtually no support whatever required enormous resilience and skill.
  — James Day, the Marine corporal who would become commander-in-chief of U.S. forces on Okinawa in 1985

While some of the [American planes] fly overhead and strafe, the big bastards fly over . . . and drop bombs. The ferocity of the bombing is terrific . . . What the hell kind of bastards are they? Bomb from six to six.
  — From the diary of a Japanese superior private

TADASHI KOJO's fighting began on April 26, while the 6th Marine Division was still in the north and the five other American divisions, one Marine and four Army, were making their unacceptably slow progress against the main fortifications. Kojo joined the battle on the Shuri Line, just northeast of Shuri itself. To the participants, the four miles to Sugar Loaf on the west might have been forty miles: the battles for the major strongpoints seemed like separate wars.

Kojo's division was still the 24th. The other Japanese division on Okinawa, the 62nd, had been formed to put down insurgencies and defeat infantry forces in China. Lightly armed to begin with, the 62nd had lost half its fighting strength bearing the brunt of the defense since L-day. In late April, General Ushijima felt he no longer had to fear a second major American landing in the deep south and ordered the 24th's 22nd Regiment out of reserve to face the American advance. Colonel Yoshida, the recently arrived regimental commander, established his field headquarters on a hill a mile behind his forward troops. Captain Kojo wasn't with him. Still recuperating as the regimental operations officer, he was sent to Shuri for briefings and preparations for when the 22nd Regiment would be reassembled. Without troops to command, apart from his small operations staff, Kojo nevertheless considered the tropical uniform insufficiently officerlike. He dressed like Ushijima, in his regular uniform with breeches and a pith helmet.

Actually, only the 1st Battalion of the 22nd Regiment was available to respond to Ushijima's order, the other two having been detached earlier and already severely mauled. On April 26, two days after that essentially hale 1st Battalion was committed, its commander was killed by a direct hit of a naval shell on his headquarters, also on a hilltop. Kojo was ordered to replace the dead major — that is, ordered back to the 1st Battalion, which had been his before the accidental explosion that almost killed him. Leaving his personal effects in the regimental tunnel south of Naha, he resumed command of the men he had trained in Manchuria and led during their first months on Okinawa. They were now defending a long ridge behind the village of Kochi, a critical highpoint guarding Shuri. As the crow flies, 32nd Army headquarters lay only some two miles behind them, almost due southwest.

That key position was attacked the next morning. After so much digging elsewhere, including the abandoned fortifications commanding the landing beaches, the men had had no time for anything more than foxholes: advance positions for their caves slightly to the rear. Kojo himself was in a small cave fifty yards behind the main ridge, on the rear slope of another small rise. After nearly eight singleminded years girding for combat in the Imperial Military Academy and Army, this would be his first engagement.

But not quite his first experience of enemy fire. During the 10/10 air raid seven months earlier, one of his orderlies — he had had one for himself and one for his horse — was killed by strafing while Kojo himself mounted to check his other men taking cover under trees. Then, on the eve of the American landing, his new regimental commander asked him to show where his regiment was deployed. Riding their horses along a beach below Naha after dark, they took unexpected fire from an American warship. While Colonel Yoshida, a combat veteran with much experience at Singapore and elsewhere, ignored the shells until some came very near, Kojo was startled enough to rush somewhat awkwardly to cover. Now, however, he felt no fear whatever because most of his adult life had been preparation for precisely this. If the fastidious captain knew anything at all, it was what to expect and do in battle. His confidence in General Ushijima and never-defeated Japan remained absolute.

He had the same confidence in his training, which is why it took him disastrously long, as he would learn when it was almost too late, to correct his mistakes. Among American misconceptions about Japanese soldiers was the conviction that they were born jungle fighters. Americans headed for Okinawa were no exception. Veterans of previous island campaigns and of atoll mustering places knew all too much about the "absolutely atrocious, murderous" climate in which "you actually sweated while you swam in the ocean, supposedly to cool off." Most men associated the vile heat and humidity with the "Jap jungle rats," assuming, as one put it, that "Nips lived from birth in that awful, miserable unhealthiness." Even the respected John Hersey wrote as a war correspondent that Japanese "take to the jungle as if they had been bred there." (This went along with Hersey's reference to them, later much regretted, as animals.) The truth was that most Japanese were trained for quite different conditions and had to learn as painfully as anyone to adapt to the jungle.

Another misconception was that they were "natural" defenders. In fact, Japanese knew far less about defending than attacking fast and hard. A sixteenth-century feudal edict required commanders to "choose the most opportune moment, then attack with all they have. In this manner, the troops are spared prolonged hardship and struggle. It is the only rational course."

Kojo's constant training for offensive moves had begun at the Military Academy, where cadets were assured that a single spirited Japanese division properly fired with dedication to all-out, decisive attack could defeat three better-equipped Soviet divisions. More relevant for him now was that the Army's professional and emotional devotion to offense had relegated defense to something almost unnecessary, if not actually unworthy. Officers imbued with the absolute need for a "victory of honor" or "death of honor" helped build morale but also tinged defensive tactics with shame. The 24th Division was a partial exception to the consuming Japanese passion for forward mobility because it had trained to face heavy Soviet armor, but that wasn't the same as training for defense. Kojo's occasional defensive exercises in Manchuria took place on paper, never in the field or with a belief that they would be needed. And as little as he knew about defense, the reserve officers who served as his company commanders knew even less.

Starting at Kochi with slightly less than his full complement of a thousand men, Kojo instructed the company commanders to position them on the forward slope of the ridge, from where they could observe the American advance and rush out to meet it at opportune moments. The position was in sight of a large collection of enemy warships anchored in a bay less than five miles away. That first day, naval gunfire joined American mortars and artillery in delivering what felt like a horizontal squall of shells. Kojo registered unhappily to himself that American firepower was "unbelievably" more powerful than anything he had expected; almost a new kind of warfare entirely. As on subsequent days, he saw little more because it kept him underground until it let up at twilight. Inspecting his force then, he found a startling number of men had died without having fired a shot. The American fire here was ten to twenty times heavier than the Japanese fire that would decimate the Marines at Sugar Loaf and the other strongpoints, and the Japanese, with no relief or any replacements, suffered proportionately more. With bloodshot eyes, Kojo's weary troops would sometimes fire their machine guns and small arms at advancing Americans, who often shouted and retreated. Minutes later, however, shells would burst above them, "red lights flickering in their black smoke," as a soldier defending a neighboring position remembered. "Then the fragments rain down on us and we can't lift our heads."

Needless to say, not all Japanese units were pounded all the time. But many soldiers at strong points like Kochi that were hit day after thunderous day came to feel their sector had been selected for special bombardment — and with the 10- or 12-to-1 American advantage in ground firepower alone, their conviction was based in reality. Massive concentrations of artillery, heavy mortars, naval fire — a battleship or cruiser provided gunfire support for each American Army regiment — and aerial bombs reduced even some American troops to "stupefaction or numbness," as one put it, before they advanced into the "wreckage of earth" where the explosives had landed. Like shelled Americans, the Japanese felt the frustration of being unable to do anything against the firing from long range. In Kojo's battalion, Yoshio Kobayashi perceived the enemy's firepower with typical dread. "There was no dead angle or safe place anywhere. Bombs and shells came from land, from the sea, from the sky — from every angle. If you were in a valley, trench mortars did the job. One step out of your cave and your fate was in the hands of God. Every inch ahead was a black unknown." A fellow target put it more directly: "It's sheer wonder that any foot soldiers managed to live."

The supremely professional Kojo was less concerned. "So this is real combat," he told himself. "Very costly." But he did not react to the cost and his noncommissioned officers would not have dreamed of complaining. Reckoning that the time must soon come for the bayonet charge for which the battalion had practiced so long and ardently, he anticipated his chance to make the Americans panic, as his predecessors had done to the Chinese in the Sino-Japanese War.* Meanwhile, Kojo kept his men on the forward slopes, where they could see — and be seen by — American observers.

Almost a week passed and nearly half his men were lost before he "woke up," in his own phrase. He ordered his company commanders to keep less than a tenth of their forces, one or two men from each platoon, in the forward slope's foxholes. All others were to remain under cover on the rear slope until the enemy's big guns let up and their infantry approached. Although Japanese forces had used reverse-slope deployment, against superior firepower on other islands, Kojo was so unpracticed in defense that he considered himself something of an originator when he at last put it into practice.

Days later, his force had been reduced from nine hundred to about three hundred. But although casualties continued — men's limbs and heads were blown off daily — they were much diminished; his new deployment was working well. His attackers were the 17th Infantry Regiment of the Army's veteran 7th (Hourglass) Division, which had performed admirably in the Aleutians under General Buckner and at Kwajalein before sharing the brunt of the bitter fighting in the south from the first week in April. They would move out every morning after their breakfast, sometimes supported by tanks, including the new flamethrowing model that shot its napalm far into caves with relative safety for the operators. Kojo's skeleton crew of spotters on the forward slope would alert those waiting on the rear one, relaying their coordinates. Mortar crews would fire at those coordinates until the Americans pulled back. The same sequence was usually repeated in the afternoon, after which the defenders would take cover for the enemy's late-afternoon artillery and naval bombardment.

*Full realization of the futility of his plans would come only after the war. What did bayonet practice have to do with the real war on Okinawa? Kojo would ask himself. What good were bayonets against flamethrowing tanks? For that matter, what good was most of what he had practiced in Manchuria? Firepower, in which deluded Japan was pathetically inferior, counted most in this very different war.

Kojo's best contribution to this surprisingly powerful defense was the novel use of the knee-mortar, as the simple little weapon came to be known from the height to which it reached when its base was held to the ground with the toe of a boot.* That smallness and simplicity provided some substantial advantages. Because it could fire its 5-centimeter, grenade-size projectile almost straight up and down, the knee-mortar could be used at extremely close range and almost any angle, and it was uncommonly mobile and accurate at those closest ranges. In addition to its grenade-size projectiles, it also fired grenades themselves, which packed more explosive power than the American version. The weapon was often deadly just where American mortars, of which the smallest was almost twice the size, had to stop firing for fear of hitting friendly troops.

American infantrymen on Okinawa had already developed a hatred for mortars. "They were the cruelest weapon of all. They could be carried anywhere by a single man, be fired from safe positions and quickly moved to avoid retaliation once someone spotted their location. They couldn't be heard by the target until too late. They caused very high casualties." Knee-mortars, the clever little version that could "drop their shells right on your head, that's how accurate they were," rated special loathing. "Whenever we evacuated wounded over open ground," an American remembered, "we ran like hell because they could almost pinpoint the stretcher." And they made so little *whump* that there was no warning to take cover.

Each Japanese infantry platoon had a squad of four knee-mortars, and there were three platoons in a company, three companies in a 22nd Regiment battalion. But instead of the usual deployment under the platoon leaders, Kojo concentrated the thirty-six weapons into one unit under his personal command. This produced what American military historians would call "an exceptionally effective system" of concentrating fire on attacking companies and platoons.

Although some 24th Division artillery was still operational, the gun crews faced the same difficulty as elsewhere on the island: each firing revealed their positions and provoked a far greater concentration of return fire from American ships, planes and field pieces. Rocket and other fire would eventually find the caves into which Japanese gunners pulled back after letting off their scant few rounds. And there was virtually no mobility. Japanese artillery was also restricted by the inability of supply troops, let alone trucks, to move anywhere during daylight. Kojo came to accept that the "almost constant" presence of

---

*Early in the war, Americans erroneously thought it was fired while being braced against the leg or knee, which may also account for the name.

American planes overhead made dashes by his squads to new positions extremely risky. By early May, the planes would "pounce on a single soldier who moved." This gave the knee-mortar even greater significance to him, as to all units whose firepower had to come almost entirely from their own armament.

Kojo's machine guns, easily concealed and fired from very low to the ground, were also highly effective. Day after day, ten- or fifteen-second bursts from his dozen skillfully deployed guns cut down lead Americans, after which the main body of the advance halted and retreated. Unless American tanks joined the push, the defenders sometimes briefly achieved equality in equipment in such encounters because the attackers had only the armament they could carry — and heavy artillery support had to cease for fear of causing "own fire" casualties. Americans had been told they were superior to the enemy in every way. "Each one of you is much better than the Japs," went their briefing in the troopships and LSTs en route to the landing beaches. "You're much better physically and much better mentally. You've got better weapons and supplies. So you'll be able to lick them hands down when it comes to the fighting." But it wasn't nearly so easy when it came closer to a fair fight in terms of equipment: man against almost equally armed man.

Kojo and his men learned to rush to the surface and prepare for those close encounters the instant bombardments let up. On May 3, the battalion helped shred a major assault on the ridge. The young captain reckoned he could check the advance of an entire battalion if just two or three machine guns remained operable, for those Americans seemed attached to daily schedule and fought with great caution and concern for their lives — more, he thought, as if they were working on some gigantic industrial operation than engaging in military action. Kojo believed this cost them heavily in the end: the step-by-step advance — instead of the quick victory that an all-out, go-for-broke attack would have won them — was a gift to his tactics.

Lower-ranking Japanese shared his puzzlement over American prudence. A thoughtful soldier at the eastern anchor of the same line, also under siege by an Army unit, observed that Americans never made surprise attacks. "First of all, they provide a protected zone, construct roads, put up a bridge if it's down, level a wide area for parking their vehicles, which are loaded with weapons and supplies. Once that solid base of operations is established, they start advancing one step at a time.* No fear of surprise attacks, but their

*An American military history compared such "creeping" advance to that of "the tireless inchworm." It was characteristic of Army — as opposed to Marine — tactics.

advance is like a mountain moving slowly at you. Against that, our resistance is like a child playing with a little firecracker, so we have to retreat." Kojo, however, was unimpressed with anything American apart from the logistics and lavish matériel. He speculated that any Japanese unit on the offensive there would have gone for the jugular, whatever the casualties.

His men thought the same. They were surprised at the Americans' apparent unwillingness to sacrifice a single life and less than impressed by what that said about their courage and resolve. Many Japanese elsewhere on Okinawa were taken by American bravery — of pilots who dived through antiaircraft barrages, for example — and noted to themselves the contradiction of their teaching about American softness and weakness. At Kochi, however, even Japanese privates considered their enemy too cautious. The Americans weren't opposed by any artillery to speak of, yet they continued to avoid risks. At the same time, Kojo's men were envious that the only time Americans did seem to take them was to recover their dead and wounded, whereas they themselves were so short of supplies that they were forced to look at corpses, their own as well as American, as sources of something useful.*

Apart from the few forward observers, the men lived in their unimproved caves during daylight. Larger, better shelters in the Okinawan south and in the Shuri Line itself were packed with civilians. Most tried hard to be cooperative and to compromise, but people cooking, eating and living their entire lives in the enormously overcrowded spaces inevitably got on one another's nerves. Some began to hear the endless refrains of favorite prewar songs as elegies, for which the bombardments outside served as drumrolls. Women stopped menstruating in those mole-hole conditions. Losing "the last particle of their female charms," as a native account put it, they became "physiologically identical with men." Ventures outside the shelters were made only for food, for which all searched "with the sensitive noses of hungry animals," and for excreting. That function was fraught with distress because it inevitably exposed the performers to exposure to shell fragments. Many latrine trenches began mere yards from caves exits; excrement overflowed their walls because the stress on top of a diet heavy with unhulled rice balls made by dirty hands kept stomachs sickly. But the desire to defecate was suppressed "with

---

*When Japanese soldiers found American corpses, they first hunted for tommy guns, which they envied most. K-rations came second, although they threw away the cheese, being too short of water to make soup, which they assumed it was for. Dumbstruck by the supplies of American Marines when they saw them, they would not have understood Marine resentment of the GIs for their riches.

the utmost effect" even when it filled bodies with yearning "from abdomen to breast."

The thousand occupants of the less crowded and much better equipped 32nd Army headquarters under Shuri Castle lived like slightly more developed underground animals. Night barely differed from day in the deep, dank tunnel, with its warren of companion-ways and smell of disinfectant leaking from the medical center. The lights were permanently on; disorientation was inevitable. Half-naked off-watch soldiers lay snoring in shared berths or on moldy bales of rice. Underground water soaked the lowest berths, but some who shared them liked the coolness. The stifling heat never dissipated. Staff officers found pretexts to linger in the passageways serviced by blower-assisted ventilators, where they could suck in precious fresh air. Even Colonel Yahara, Ushijima's gifted operations officer who had planned the defense from underground, began to feel that he was "being dragged to the bottom of hell," and the dauntless General Cho began mumbling to his mother in his sleep. But everyone derived some strength from the lantern-lit slogans on the walls: "Be a shield to your Emperor!" "Don't die until you annihilate your foes!" "Stick to your guns until you die!"

Kojo's troops two miles northeast were precisely those shields sticking to their guns. Their suffocating burrows made all caves behind the lines luxurious by comparison. The holes reeked of smoke, gunpowder and the human odors of men long unwashed and under supreme stress. When the commander of another battalion told one of his soldiers that Okinawa had to be held at least three years, the soldier was stunned. Had he heard correctly? How could that be possible? Three more years in their dungeon seemed worse than the mass slaughter they would face when sent on an all-out assault. The final physical and psychological touches to the purgatory at Kochi were scores of moaning, severely wounded men inside the caves and hundreds of corpses just outside.

But the living soldiered on with little surprise. The absence of alternatives helped steady them. Surrender was never considered. Even if they could somehow arrange to meet Americans for surrender, it would only bring a more hideous death. Most Japanese soldiers remained convinced that the enemy yearned to kill them in monstrous ways. Bestial Marines, whose real purpose in Asia was to rape and murder Asian women, were believed to have qualified for the Corps by murdering their parents. The "demons" and "beasts" got their laughs castrating prisoners and running them over with tanks and bulldozers.

And if Japan lost the war, ordinary American GIs would also torture, mutilate and drastically depopulate the homeland.* Even the one in a thousand who disapproved of Japanese militarism knew that "prisoner of war" was "an abominable phrase," as one such rare exception put it, that would make him afraid to face friends and relatives — if he ever had that chance, given that he might be taken to America for a life of hard labor.† In short, surrender would mean no longer being Japanese. And the dishonor would hasten the rape of everything sacred, from Japan's women to her heritage and beloved Imperial family, by barbarian occupiers who hated the beautiful land. Such a life could not be worth living.

That conviction reinforced the stoicism of Captain Kojo's battalion. The men had been conditioned, at least since their first years in school, to obey authority without question and to suffer any amount of hardship in dignified silence — and to believe that the display of will would overcome all obstacles in the end. On top of that, they knew that a quick death in combat was preferable to the disgrace of capture, followed by a lingering death at the hands of a hated enemy. Among Kojo's soldiers were a high proportion of natives of the northernmost main island, Hokkaido; they were known in the Army as slow to learn but extremely tenacious. Kojo supposed they were glad to be fulfilling their duty, even knowing it would end in death. Few supported their elite commander's belief in their happiness, but most were proud that their knee-mortars were exacting such a toll on the enemy. Even fewer cried "Long live the Emperor!" when hit, but some did assure their platoon mates they would see them again at the Yasukuni Shrine. Their promise was only partly in jest. More men tended to use "for the sake of our country" in conversation, and *Hissho no shin-nen!* ("Victory no matter what!"). The bravest possible stand on Okinawa, with the greatest damage to the Americans, might prevent an invasion of the mainland, where their families would be at the mercy of the evil enemy. And since Tokyo knew better than they that a loss of Okinawa would open the way to that nightmare, they continued to bolster themselves with talk of the massive rein-

---

*This notion was less farfetched than it may seem, since many winning sides in Japan's feudal wars had done unspeakable things to losing sides, sometimes torturing and murdering every survivor. The sixteenth-century feudal ruler who promulgated the edict requiring his commanders to relentlessly practice attack also declared that he would never "mar the hallowed rites of battle with acts of kindness" because "the only mercy in battle is to be merciless." This was believed to speed the way toward promised peace after the purge. Meanwhile, even fugitives of holy places were searched out "on every hill, in every valley," and besieged fortresses as well as battle sites became places of carnage where servants and children were butchered along with soldiers. "The whole mountainside," a contemporary writer reported of one such complex of fortified temples and shrines, "was a great slaughterhouse and the sight was one of unbearable horror."

†A few bold Japanese did speculate that the shame of surrender might be lessened if Japan lost the war, in which case the Emperor himself would become a prisoner.

forcements on the way to relieve them.* Very few soldiers suspected that Okinawa had already been written off as a sacrifice to gain time for the decisive battle on the homeland.

Those illusions went with a refusal to accept larger realities, not only of the destruction of mainland cities by bombing, about which they had little idea, but also of the course of the battle elsewhere on Okinawa itself. Reason suggested it could not be going well. But even more than when *Yamato* was sunk, no bad news was believed unless accompanied by direct proof, manifestation of the power of mythology and propaganda and of the survival instinct that helped sustain faith in Japan's divine invincibility.

Circumstances enhanced the Japanese capacity to believe. Raised on their isolated islands with deep mental barriers to the outside world, the great majority of civilians honestly and genuinely accepted their leaders' bizarre accounts, spread by the press and radio, of the progress of the war. With even less information and more urgent need to trust, the 32nd Army had reason to deny the evidence of their eyes. Those few who glimpsed the massive American fleet from high ground still did not appreciate its significance. To some degree, nearly all believed the Imperial Navy and Air Force were biding their time for the right moment to obliterate the enemy. Of course some of Ushijima's troops merely held to old habits and followed orders without much patriotism until their time came to die. Of course there were doubts at the bottom of many hearts. But to air them openly "would have invited certain trouble," a soldier of another unit remembered of this period, "so we all talked bravely. Looking back at that time now, it was as if we were on death row, talking about a possible reprieve."

The dismaying American advantage in numbers and equipment reinforced the sense of mission. Unfair odds swelled patriotism. (Hadn't Japan always been treated unfairly, after all? Always been threatened, since the arrival of Perry's black ships? Hadn't her need to expand been fired by abiding poverty and oppression by others?) They also stiffened the Japanese fighting spirit. The conviction that

---

*Rumors about the long-awaited counterattack had the 9th Division returning from Formosa and other forces landing in the far south. With full conviction, it was reported that the Combined Fleet was steaming north from Singapore, was taking on provisions at Formosa, was waiting to pounce from one of the Ryukyu islands farther north. New secret weapons were discussed, some of which, such as suicide motorboats, once actually existed but had already been destroyed in their pens. There was also talk of the Americans' overextended supply lines and supposed depletion of arms and men. Some grapevines put their casualties at 2000 a day. (The actual American average was about 4000 casualties a week in May and 3000 a week during the whole of the campaign.) Soldiers also told one another that Japan and America were poised to sign an armistice — on terms favorable to Japan, of course.

Yamato damashii would be decisive in the end was as deep as the 10th Army's conviction of the superiority of the American way of life. It was part of Japanese consciousness, a "fact" of life. This did not mean that 32nd Army soldiers did not have a quaking fear of death nor a constant hope that one's turn would come tomorrow rather than to-day. But much more than Americans, they were prepared never to return home from Okinawa.

The Japanese endurance at Kochi and elsewhere was partly bol-stered by a desire to serve a better cause than individual advance-ment. Virtually all saw the Emperor as the father of the nation and felt they should be willing to die for him without regret. Their emo-tions, though not easily expressed, ran deep. In fact, the soldiers' tendency to act on emotion rather than on reason helped condition them to accept the idea of extreme sacrifice. They were caught in the kind of self-hypnosis most strikingly manifested by the kamikaze pilots.

The group pressure to do one's duty came on top of this. Every American training officer knew that men were able to function in battle because they feared failure in their comrades' eyes more than they feared death. That was more true of Japanese, whose fear of ignominy had long played a greater role in society, and to whom subservience of individual interests to group discipline had long been accepted. While an American battalion might fight to its last man's death if its members felt their families' existence depended on it, alternatives would surely be discussed, perhaps even surrender in order to fight another day. But the least gung-ho among Kojo's men accepted that this life had to end before a better one could begin: the reward for a worthy death. A soldier who was amazed to survive summed up the mood: "I never thought I'd come home alive. It was clear to us all what would happen. [But] we could do nothing else."

To the Americans, the resistance by units such as Kojo's went beyond formidable to murderously unnatural. Those were the days when much of General Buckner's Army remained stalled and the pressure on him to get the line moving again — pressure by his boss, Fleet Admiral Nimitz, among others — was mounting to its peak. The American offensive of May 11 to crack the Shuri Line was still a week away, but plans for it were being made; 10th Army headquarters understood that a major undertaking was needed to break the back of the defense that was so much stronger than anticipated.

In particular, American appreciation of the "Jap fanatics'" fighting skills at Kochi Ridge increased. Kojo's concentration of accurate fire was too serious a menace to try to overcome in one attack; the policy of steady destruction with superior firepower would be maintained. But the Japanese showed no signs of being destroyed, despite pressure on the 7th Division from the Army Corps' headquarters. In the second week of May, the "utterly exhausted" 7th was replaced by the 96th, fresh from a ten-day rest and reinforced. The new attackers remained as cautious, probing mornings and afternoons but pulling back regularly when the mortars, which Kojo had learned to use only after the Americans were fully exposed, began cutting them down. Tank-supported American penetration proceeded on both flanks of Kochi Ridge, but Kojo's 1st Battalion held on, buoyed by their own endurance. They would have been buoyed even more if they had known that daily enemy casualties now exceeded their own.

This was the kind of defense by attrition that Colonel Yahara, Ushijima's operations officer, had dreamed of: Japanese tactics and tenacity were almost a match for American equipment and might. American firepower would pound the position much of the day, shaking the earth and threatening to collapse Kojo's little headquarters cave. But however miserable this made the inhabitants, most were protected and ready to move out the moment the bombardment stopped for the skirmishes between sub-units with small arms in which they stood a chance, because the Americans couldn't make use of their roughly 50-to-1 advantage — including naval and air support — in firepower. Kojo and his men were happy to be making the enemy's advance minuscule and expensive.

The 1st battalion was reinforced by an understrength rifle company commanded by a Captain Kiguchi, a friend of Kojo's one class below at the Imperial Academy, and of service in Manchuria. Kiguchi, a typical Academy graduate, appeared simple despite his intelligence because he had no civilian interests whatever. He was very cool, eager and brave. Despite his pleas to join the fighting, however, Kojo insisted that the junior officer was his guest and kept his 180-odd men in reserve — until, after about a week, further steady attrition of the battalion left him little choice. Exuberant Kiguchi ignored all dangers, dashing to his machine gun positions and occasionally to confer with Kojo. He seemed so impervious to enemy fire and his requests for permission to blow up American tanks with satchel charges were so insistent that Kojo reluctantly gave it, reminding him that a commander's loss is disastrous to his men's morale. Kiguchi succeeded in blowing up one tank, but a close escape on a second attempt prompted Kojo to withdraw permission.

As for Kojo's men, they were weakening because of massive fatigue as well as the reduced but regular daily casualties. After enemy shelling stopped in the evening, they dragged themselves to complete tasks that could be undertaken only in the relative safety of darkness: repairing their trenches, carrying their wounded to an underground first-aid station and supplying themselves. With rest breaks, the work details would last until dawn and the resumption of the shelling.

Water was the greatest personal need. This was no longer the chronic shortage that had kept them from washing during the months before they went into the line. Now there was so little that men had trouble swallowing the biscuit that supplemented their rations. Thirsts were so great and constant that some risked leaving their positions in daylight to sneak to wells below the ridge. Otherwise, they brought in water at night from supply caves in the Naha area, three or four kilometers south. They made that journey on foot.

It seemed to them that the Americans had limitless supplies of ammunition, while they were restricted to four or five rounds a day from each mortar. After one day of particular success, a warrant officer happily reported the good shooting to Kojo. "Yes, but you expended more rounds than necessary," the captain said reprovingly. The entire 32nd Army was in great need of supplies. A handful of Japanese ships had risked sailing to Okinawa after the 10/10 air raid, but none arrived with either replacement soldiers or matériel after L-day, and the trickle delivered by air all but stopped during the first week in April. However, Kojo's stinginess with ammunition was grounded in the local emergency rather than in the general shortage. He worried about running out during an attack on *his* position; each shell, like the drinking water, had to be brought in on the men's backs at night.

They also carried in their food from the supply caves, which were stocked for a week of full-scale fighting. After that, rations, apart from the hardtack, were reduced to a single daily rice ball, often rotten from the heat. The cooked ball, about the size of a fist, had a sour, salty pickle inside. Few were any hungrier than combat Americans, despite weeks of fighting all day and working much of the night under extreme duress and the constant threat of death. Still, they burned so much energy with so little replacement that all became severely weakened on top of their exhaustion. With no rest and — unlike the severely strained Americans — no replacements, the undernourished soldiers grew so tired that some began sleeping straight through the bombardments. Inexorably, they were being ground down.

*Command of the skies over Okinawa lay completely in the hands of the U.S.
Air Force; the Japanese Navy had already been rendered impotent. Thus
the fate of the 32nd Army was just a matter of time.*
— Saburo Hayashi, *Kogun: The Japanese Army in the Pacific War*

Dark, gloomy days went by and the Emperor's birthday drew near.
— Shigemi Furukawa, *The End of Okinawa*

*April 29: the Emperor's birthday. The worse it gets for us, the more hope
grows among the soldiers.*
— Ikuo Ogiso, *Ah, Okinawa!*

Back at 32nd Army Headquarters, senior officers' distress over the
erosion of their strength elsewhere on the front mixed with worry
that limiting the action to defense was undermining morale. Colonel
Yahara, still the consummate realist by Japanese standards, tried to
stiffen morale by pointing out how much strength had been pre-
served even after a month of severe fighting. No Japanese force on
any other island had held out so long or retained so much power for
further resistance. But few others found comfort in such logical but
uninspiring thinking. A powerful disillusionment in Yahara's "pas-
sive" or "negative" strategy set in. Staff officers grew increasingly impatient to *be Japanese* by striking back.

Many privates at the front also yearned for something, anything,
that promised relief from their wretched existence in caves where
"we were on the verge of losing our sanity from suffering inside," as
a typical dweller described it. Even caves that had communications
with others were constantly being isolated when American shells cut
their telephone lines. Many soldiers began to feel blindfolded. The
battle wasn't only between the poor and rich in equipment and supplies. It was also between those who were mobile and those imprisoned in a fetid refuge that would protect them only until they died
in it.*

The image of an offensive was better than the underground reality
of filth, suffocating stench and dizzyness from too little oxygen. One
sober soldier noticed that those "imprisoned" in his "miserable" cave

---

*The men's hatred of their constraints bore on the disadvantages of defense from un-
derground. The caves were a kind of counterpart to American tanks in offering protection
from enemy fire, even more protection than tanks themselves. But they also relegated the
occupants to nearly complete immobility. Planning officers could see little of the enemy's
moves. When reports were delivered to them after evening inspections — reports often
delivered on foot because so few lines of communication remained operable — it was too
late to react to changes on the battlefield, even if the available Japanese forces had been
mobile. Thus the soldier who complained that "we donned a new kind of armor and called
it a cave, which bound us hand and foot" unknowingly described a larger tactical truth.

began to "wish, agonizingly, for a decisive sortie." Another was "quite pleased" to leave his "stinking, soot-filled" cave for what would probably be his end.

If the fierce Japanese defense confounded Americans, Japanese infantrymen were the more confounded by the failure of their Air Force and Navy to appear.

> We look up at the sky every morning thinking, "It must be today!" But all we see overhead are enemy planes, like a swarm of bees.
>
> "They won't come," some soldiers say pessimistically. "No more planes are left in Japan, that's the only reason I can think of for their not coming."
>
> "No, they'll surely be here," others insist. "Planes always come just when everyone gives up."

The approach of the Emperor's birthday, the most important national holiday, swelled hope throughout the Army. Thousands of caves were now sustained by thoughts of the promised issue of sweet potato brandy (which most didn't get) and by the giant swarm of Japanese planes that would appear on April 29. That was when reinforcements would surely arrive to start the inevitable crushing of the brazen enemy, the moment of relief from the "merciless hurricane" of American fire, the day when everything would at last move forward. The time for revenge! A medical corpsman drew strength from the "unspoken expectation" that "a gigantic counterattack" would be mounted to "turn the tide of the war at one huge blow!"

> On that day, a mass of friendly airplanes and a landing force had to come to our aid. So we went to the opening of our shelter to watch the sky — but the day came and went like all others, raining enemy bombs and shells. We saw not a single set of silvery wings bearing the Rising Sun. Everyone's common dream faded into thin air. Our only comfort was in Imperial Headquarters' exaggerated announcement of the results of the [kamikaze] attacks.*

Kojo's surviving soldiers, accustomed to living by starlight, used that morning's early hours for their usual brief break for relaxation before the start of the American bombardment soon after dawn. They ate their cold, moldy rice balls and assured themselves that the Combined Fleet, for which all had been waiting since their fighting began, would arrive before the end of the sacred day. Although the decimated Imperial Navy was planning nothing of the kind, a tense staff meeting *was* taking place in the headquarters tunnel deep below Shuri Castle.

---

*Hope for salvation was then transferred to Navy Memorial Day, May 27, but much of the trust was gone by then.

The conservatives had prevailed until now, but advocates of switching to offense were growing bolder. Certain "fire-eaters," as Yahara called them, were said to be so bitterly disgusted that they openly threatened the colonel's life. Predictably, the most fervent deprecator of defense and spokesman for attack was Lieutenant General Isamu Cho, Ushijima's fiery chief of staff. Rumor had it that the ultranationalist planner of several assassinations of ministerial "weaklings" during the 1930s encountered Yahara in a corridor of the tunnel that morning, grasped his strategic adversary's hands, brought his burning eyes close to Yahara's, and pleaded with him to accept the need for an offensive. "You have your own ideas, of course, but I beg you — please die with me." Cho's hot tears were said to have wet Yahara's hands — and to melt his cool reasoning, for the colonel reportedly blurted out, "Yes, I understand!" in spite of himself.

If this exchange did take place, the two nevertheless clashed sharply at the staff meeting later on the Emperor's birthday. It was a culmination of the struggle embodied by Cho's passion for action — or romantic self-sacrifice — and Yahara's commitment to rational economy of force — or the dreary limits of harsh reality.

So far, Ushijima, the final arbiter, had continued to lean in Yahara's direction. Cho had urged a major counterattack four weeks earlier, two days after L-day. Now is the time to smash the still-unorganized enemy, he pleaded on April 3. But the commander, swayed by Yahara's command of the tactics of modern warfare, canceled Cho's plan for a massive charge against the newly landed Americans. The secret signal to Ushijima on April 5 informing him that *Yamato* was about to come to his aid included instructions to take advantage of the sortie to counterattack on the ground, starting the morning of April 7, when the great ship was scheduled to arrive off the coast. Cho was delighted and confident that the operation would catch the enemy off balance, helping turn the tide quickly on land. Attack and more attack was what had created the Empire and what would save the day against the confused Americans. However, Ushijima disapproved of the idea and telegraphed advice to stop the operation. He believed that this first week of the battle for Okinawa was still too early to counterattack; the best hope of doing the greatest damage to the enemy lay in biding time in the best fortifications. He felt, too, that his firsthand appreciation of the enemy's air domination and of the strength of his Navy was better than that of Combined Fleet headquarters, which seemed to be living in a dream world.

Cho again lobbied passionately for a counterattack on April 12, but Yahara's opposition helped limit it to a very modest operation. Since then, however, emotion, if not reason, swung steadily to Cho's side.

His instinct to strike grew as the 32nd Army's resources and optimism dwindled. Now, on April 29, he still believed Japanese resolve could negate the American material advantages, just as Yahara still believed that preoccupation with "honorable" death before it was necessary was self-indulgent. Cho's basic idea remained unchanged throughout April: to generate close-quarter chaos on the battlefields in order to engage the enemy in the hand-to-hand combat at which the Japanese excelled. Individual Japanese soldiers would defeat individual Americans. The spokesman for reckless offensive argued eloquently and persuasively — at least to the impatient staff officers who cheered him — that too much time had already been wasted. If things kept on, the Army would soon lose its offensive capacity, then its ability to resist at all. The only hope was to snatch life from the midst of death by mounting a massive counterattack while the means still existed. If the 32nd Army would not survive it, the enemy wouldn't either. Mutual annihilation was better than the steady attrition that could end only in certain defeat.

Yahara was almost alone in opposing this "do or die" scheme and entirely alone in challenging it openly. Annihilation was inevitable either way, he countered, but an ill-conceived counterattack would almost certainly hasten it. In modern battle, an attacking force usually needed a 3-to-1 advantage for success. Attacking a superior force with an inferior one was not merely risky but reckless. Until now, the ability to slow and hurt the enemy had rested on the excellence of the carefully situated fortifications. But the Americans had captured too much high ground for the Japanese to get adequate cover on reverse slopes if they left their present ones. The advantage would be reversed, guaranteeing even greater losses and failure to fulfill the 32nd Army's primary duty of prolonging the battle as much as possible to give the mainland more time to prepare for an invasion.

Yahara's brief for his defensive strategy was all but shouted down by a chorus of angry patriots who craved action at any cost. And when the staff took its decision to Ushijima for ratification, the commander approved, though reluctantly, and ordered his chief operations officer to stop arguing in a way that would undermine the Army's unity and morale. This was rare behavior for the ordinarily amiable commander. He scheduled a massive counterattack for May 4.

Five days of intense planning and preparations followed. The 24th Division — Kojo's — would be the main attacking force; the 62nd was too weak to participate. A tank regiment and the 26th Independent Infantry Battalion were moved up from reserve and committed for the first time. Artillery was readied for movement into prepared positions. The spearhead of the offensive would be in sight of Captain Kojo's position, although other 24th Division units would make the initial breakthrough. Then a wide collection of attacking forces would rush through the gaps. The final objectives were positions a full five miles north, halfway to the landing beaches, where the first main defensive line, including Kakazu Ridge, would be restored. By then, two American Army divisions would have been destroyed. The men of the 24th Division were ordered to "kill at least one American devil for every Japanese" — an extremely optimistic goal, since Japanese losses had been roughly 10 to 1 until now, even with their protection underground. But the mood was exhilarant. Attack at last! Victory! Honor!

The Fifth Floating Chrysanthemum was launched to coordinate with the counterattack. On May 3 and 4, 125 kamikazes dived at the American fleet, sinking a destroyer and putting seventeen other ships out of action. (Five crashes on another destroyer killed and wounded ninety-eight men, but frantic efforts by the living crew kept her afloat.) On land, the Japanese began their softening-up for the offensive during the night of May 3–4. The big guns began firing at 0450, while a small banquet, served by attractively dressed office girls, was still in progress in the headquarters tunnel. Steadily accelerating fire from the newly placed Japanese artillery and return volleys from American batteries and warships produced an almost unendurable din. As dawn approached, Japanese pieces delivered half an hour of full bombardment. This firing of the first full salvos in the thirty-four days of fighting — instead of the previous few rounds fired before the guns were pulled back into hiding — was a grim surprise to the Americans. The four thousand rounds into the 77th Division's zone, and twice that into the 7th Division's, was almost certainly the most powerful Japanese barrage in the Pacific War so far.

Captain Kojo could not know that it caused relatively few casualties, apart from cases of battle fatigue because most Americans were dug in "deep and dry." He did know that the flash and thunder of Japanese fire filled him and his men with glee, especially after having had no liaison with artillery units and having seen no attempt by artillery to support his position until then. "How powerful our artillery is!" he rejoiced to himself. "What a day this will be!" Cho's argument that attack would greatly boost morale seemed proved.

Kojo's 22nd Regiment was assigned to screen the advance of two attacking regiments with heavy fire and smoke, then join the advance in a leapfrogging action ahead of those vanguard units. Only what was left of young Captain Kiguchi's rifle company would join the initial strike. Kojo knew nothing of Yahara's opposition to the idea of the counterattack, but his regimental commander told him he would be in no hurry to join the advance, and he later learned that Yahara had confidentially advised some sympathetic officers that not all units need participate.* Visiting his underground chamber on April 30, the day after the crucial staff meeting, Cho pleaded so movingly for his cooperation that the coolheaded Yahara promised, through a flood of mutual tears, that whatever happened, the two would probably die together on the island. That response was testimony to the captivating passion that had made Cho so valuable to the ultra-nationalist cause before Pearl Harbor. But Yahara's sobriety and determination not to doom the 32nd Army to premature destruction returned during the following days, when the operations officer worked cautiously behind the scenes to try to save what he could from what he considered a suicidal enterprise.

In fact, the debacle was at least as bad as he predicted, despite initial American surprise. Almost a thousand valuable men were lost without purpose when Japanese amphibious units were spotted approaching both coasts. Those who survived destruction in the water by American artillery were slaughtered on the beaches, far from their targets. Navigational errors brought some boats directly into the sights of American batteries, where troops shouting "Banzai!" helped pinpoint the fire on themselves.

On land, Japanese detachments attacked while their own artillery fire burst around them, most with total failure. After the early hours, when battlefield positions were fluid and some small units of both sides moved toward annihilation by the other's guns, Japanese weakness in numbers and logistics rapidly became manifest. Delayed by faulty transportation, two battalions of the 89th Infantry Regiment, a sister regiment of Kojo's 22nd, were caught in the open by American artillery, which cut down almost another thousand men in minutes. Most of the others were finished before the morning was over, by which time the great offensive as a whole was also over in all but name.

Quickly recovering from their surprise, American units used their immense firepower, especially from mortars, with devastating effect. "The 'all-out' offensive evaporated like a brief dream," a Japanese survivor lamented. "When dawn arrived, our forces, which had taken advantage of darkness to penetrate enemy territory, were exposed on the surface [that is, not in a cave] and cut down by the typhoon of

---

*The 32nd Army's political infighting also manifested itself in the selection of units for participation in the attack. Some were chosen because superiors had scores to settle with their officers, indicating that, despite the rhetoric, a fate other than glory was expected for them.

enemy fire from ships, planes and howitzers."* Two nights later, a few bloody stragglers from an attacking platoon dragged themselves back to the cave of that survivor to report no gain whatever for the massive losses. All realized that the huge expenditure of irreplaceable ammunition had also been for nothing, and "miserable and gloomy days" returned to the cave after its forty-eight hours of hope.

Only one battalion managed to penetrate about a mile to the north. Part of a sister regiment of Kojo's 24th Division, it was commanded by Captain Koichi Ito, who was also twenty-four years old and involved in his first combat after taking command of his battalion in Manchuria. Ito had overcome a schoolboy bout with tuberculosis to win acceptance into the Imperial Military Academy, where he became perhaps an even brighter exemplar of regular Army officer resolve — that is, less connected to anything unmilitary — than his classmate Kojo. Since arriving on Okinawa, he had received a total of one letter and hadn't concerned himself about how many arrived or didn't arrive for his men. (Also like Kojo, Ito would later regret having been too engrossed in strictly military concerns to think of such matters.)

Although Ito hadn't heard of the sinking of *Yamato*, he was among the few who could have guessed. His one letter had been from his father, a former naval officer who happened to be friendly with a high-ranking strategist fired for refusing to help plan the war against America. "If you start a war without first equipping the Air Force to match other leading nations," the strategist warned, "Japan will be in ashes and you will hurtle to hell." This rare acquaintance with dissenting views gave Ito an unusual perspective on the war. He and an Academy friend once actually confided to one another, with great care, that Japan couldn't win. But no such thoughts weakened his commitment or drive. Before the American landing, he rode his battalion relentlessly and won the highest commendations for digging fortifications, then refused to allow a severe case of dysentery get him sent home on the eve of L-day. Now the implacable professional again distinguished himself.

Ito's battalion was situated a few hundred yards west and behind Kojo's on Kochi Ridge. Jumping off from there, he alone managed to advance as planned and survive the first day with most of his force

---

*Like most Japanese soldiers, this one had become so used to death that it provoked little reaction in him. But he took a moment to reflect when a fellow soldier who managed to escape the slaughter told him that a cave he'd left less than a week before was now packed with wounded, and a little brook in which they used to wash was so full of corpses that the water was red with blood. "If I closed my eyes, I could see the scene."

intact. The iron captain attacked again at midnight, still hoping to spearhead the planned general breakthrough. He fired a flare at a hill mass called Tanabaru escarpment, from which the Japanese had been driven almost two weeks before, to show he'd reached his first major objective, but he was so surrounded by enemy guns that he had to keep all heads below ground and communicate with his officers by tossing messages tied to rocks into their foxholes. Just over a third of his six hundred men — down from a thousand before May 4 — were alive when he extricated himself, with supreme bravery and skill against overwhelming firepower, on May 7.

Before then, Ito's haggard battalion destroyed twenty-two tanks and twenty-nine airplanes and inflicted heavy casualties. The success of his small force with its severely limited armament and support — no tanks, rocket launchers, flamethrowers — suggests what the Japanese might have achieved with greater supplies, not to mention even partial air support. But Ito's resourcefulness, tenacity and luck made him the exception that proved the rule; the counterattack was acknowledged as having collapsed even before he set out the second time that midnight. On the evening of May 5, the 32nd Army announced it would "temporarily" suspend the offensive, claiming it had inflicted sufficient damage. To spare Cho and the staff officers who supported him, Ushijima took that action on himself.

If it saved face for anyone at headquarters, it could not undo the sacrifices of this second major strategic mistake after letting Kerama Retto and the airfields at Yomitan and Kadena fall with almost no opposition. The loss of nearly seven thousand of Ushijima's best troops was catastrophic at this stage of the fighting. The 24th Division had been disastrously weakened, especially in the 22nd Regiment's two sister regiments. Japanese artillery was decimated. The exposure of the previously hidden ordnance enabled American forces to pinpoint and destroy nineteen heavy guns on the first day alone. The first offensive use of tanks resulted in their almost complete loss. The 27th Tank Regiment, with all its light tanks and half its medium destroyed, would never again fight as a mobile unit; the six that survived would be converted into earth-covered pillboxes on the Shuri Line. Tenth Army casualties, heavy as they were by American measures, barely exceeded those of hard days of storming Japanese defensive positions. Instead of the prescribed kill ratio of 1 to 1, the Japanese lost up to twenty for every American — and proved Yahara correct. He had erred only in not predicting that the inevitable would happen so quickly and decisively.

Even Cho now accepted that the 32nd Army could no longer think of offense. When they heard of the decision to abandon the counterattack, angry young members of the staff demanded an explanation. The discouraged Cho apologized and did what he could to stem their despairing tears; Ushijima is said to have summoned Yahara for his own tearful promise to be guided by his advice in the future. Soon some of the young women who handled clerical work in the underground tunnel were ordered out, over their protests, to rejoin the civilian population: a sign of the carnage the staff foresaw in the near future. Staff officers of course carried on, but "a pall of gloom" settled on them, as a scholar described the effect of the May 4 failure, "and it never lifted."

> *Genuine information came from the front in the person of blood-covered casualties. We were losing ground, slowly but steadily. The American advance wasn't rapid but had a frightening assurance. First, saturation bombing and shelling eliminated enemies from an area. Then the infantry advanced, led by tanks. It was no longer a glorious man-to-man fight but a grotesquely one-sided process in which a gigantic iron organism crushed and pulverized human flesh.*
> — A Japanese soldier

> *I sometimes wonder how we'd have done without our 10-to-1 superiority in combined manpower and maybe more in supplies — without that naval armada and our incredible firepower. I'd have wet my pants if I'd been a Japanese soldier.*
> — An American Marine

> *During this period [in early May] the chief obstacle to the 7th Division's advance was a network of Japanese positions around Kochi Ridge and Zebra Hill . . . Previous attacks had demonstrated that the defenses here could not be overrun in a single attack but required a tedious, methodical destruction of individual enemy soldiers and positions.*
> — From an account by U.S. Army historians

> *All our training paid off. Despite the enemy's overwhelmingly superior firepower, my men never panicked. I myself felt truly calm. But our training also included much that was totally irrelevant to modern warfare and blinded us to reality.*
> — Tadashi Kojo

> *Intelligence and diligence can stand against even the most extreme technological superiority. But not forever. Ultimately, brave men and overwhelming firepower will always defeat brave men alone.*
> — Thomas Huber, *Japan's Battle of Okinawa, April–June 1945*

The failed counteroffensive sapped strength from the Shuri Line. The expenditure of so many shells reduced each gun's daily allowance from fifty to fifteen. That restriction, and the loss of many pieces, lessened total Japanese artillery firepower by about half. The weakening of infantry forces required more service and support units to be thrown into the line. By American standards, Kojo's 24th Division, down to three fifths of its original strength, was no longer a proper fighting unit.

Casualties in Kojo's 1st Battalion hadn't grown during the two days of hopeless gesture, but now he had to face heavier enemy pressure without Kiguchi's help. The junior captain's company was among the units either destroyed to the last man or left with wounded who could not make their way back to their lines, some of whom would kill themselves to avoid capture. No survivor returned to Kochi Ridge. Kojo later learned that enemy tanks had massacred most of the unit hours after their advance down from the ridge.

The American units opposite the position regrouped and resupplied fast enough to resume their offensive on May 6, two days before V-E Day. They added gasoline and napalm to their ordnance, and tried to throw ten-gallon cans over the hill to burn out Kojo's men. But those same men mustered enough fire the following day to force the retreat of two American infantry platoons that had taken part of a small adjoining hill. The rain also helped the defense. Hard as the deluges were on Kojo's men, they caused more disruption to the attackers; as in other sectors, the heavy equipment on which most of the American units relied — especially Army units — became mired in impenetrable mud. But Kojo's casualties continued. "The man who reported the names of his friends who had been killed one day would be among the names reported the following day," a soldier from a similarly besieged unit recalled. One by one, two by two, five by five, Kojo's troops dwindled. He felt as if the unit he commanded was going from a battalion to a company to a platoon.

During the first week of fighting, there had been enough men to evacuate the gravely wounded to the regimental tunnel south of Naha, where the medical facility remained. (Dozens burned by flamethrowers could not be helped even there because supplies were inadequate. Most treatment was limited to stopping hemorrhages.) Then evacuation ceased and ambulatory wounded were given first aid and returned to their posts immediately. Able-bodied men were so few that the chief medical officer, a first lieutenant with whom Kojo was becoming friendly, was ordered to join the fighters with all wounded — about two hundred men — strong enough to hold a rifle.

The opposite traffic, back to the tunnel, was more pathetic. Some of the gravely wounded who could crawl tried to make their own way there — "like night worms," as one man saw them. Others did not make the effort, preferring to die where their fallen comrades lay. Many bled to death in as much cover as could be arranged for them. Kojo was saddened by his inability to help them but took their great bravery as normal and even envied the "lucky" who had departed. They had won honor and an end to suffering, whereas the living, their nerves worn to nothing from the lack of sleep and the ordeal, had to keep going until the only relief would come for them too.

Kojo's molding as a Satsuma boy and Academy cadet — his twenty-four years of training for sacrifice — enabled him to accept the losses with slight concern. The men from whom he continued to stand apart also accepted their lot without complaint. Accustomed to living with severe deprivation for protracted periods, they were also sustained by their regiment's long record of valor in combat. (Kojo would later speculate that their enormous endurance and sacrifice for the nation was almost a natural culmination of their hard lives.) Only one company commander suffered a kind of shell shock. When his casualties reached 90 percent, that lieutenant, a reserve officer, requested permission to return to the regimental tunnel to hunt for reinforcements — a very rare impertinence that prompted the necessary refusal from the regular Imperial Army captain. "NO!" Kojo's fierce shout interrupted his subordinate's plea. "You will stay where you are!"

Otherwise, he saw no cases of battle fatigue or mental breakdown, which he would not have understood anyway: such weakness wasn't permitted — which probably helped prevent it. But the men had normal feelings. Okinawan May is like southern Georgia's. When the rain let up, and sometimes even when it continued, temperatures soared in the airless, little caves. All-day confinement to those holes in the ground — with the extreme shortage of clean water — would have been torture enough, as Private Yoshio Kobayashi put it, without "the smell of blood and sweat [that] mixed with the putrid stench of the wounds to suffocate us."

Kobayashi was among the lucky few: his communications duties gave him more chance than most to leave his cave. But although that provided relief from the "inferno-like" confinement, it brought the more immediate danger of exposure in the open. Weeks before, a communications mission had taken him to a beach bare of all cover. His fervent prayers not to be spotted by American planes went unanswered. Kobayashi and a fellow communications soldier gripped a six-inch telephone pole for futile protection while a Grumman made four or five strafing runs at them. When the plane finally turned away, the targets ran so desperately that Kobayashi believed his heart would burst. The two men collapsed into a deserted cave and continued on their mission after sundown, laden with a heavy radio in addition to their rifles and packs. Hands numb, drenched in hot and cold sweat, crossing streams in total darkness because bridges were demolished, they kept taking cover because shells and bombs fell on them "as if by signal" whenever they set out on a main road. Breaking off at dawn because they were certain they'd be killed in the open during daylight, they set out again in the drizzle of dusk and met a master sergeant in the smoke of a recently leveled village. He told him that their destination was already being overrun by Americans. But to their delight — since Japanese units often took interest only in their own and had little knowledge or concern about others — he gave them directions to their company. They set out again for their Shuri fortification and soon reached the end of their odyssey.

> First we saw dead horses [from other, presumably artillery, units]. Decomposed, emitting the nauseating stench of death. Next came a large crater that must have been made by a 500-kilogram bomb. A soldier lay dead at its bottom, sprawled face up, his shoulder soaked in blood to the chest.
>
> We walked on . . . [to] where we met wounded soldiers retreating from the front. No one looked alive. Some dripped blood from the hip down, some were supported by buddies, their own heads covered in blood. I'd never seen anything like that and thought I was going mad. Corpses piled up on both sides of the road, some half-skeletons, others bloated with gas. The stench nearly suffocated me . . .
>
> Somehow we made it to company headquarters. Familiar faces met us outside our cave position. We shouted and embraced them, congratulated ourselves for being alive. But many of our comrades were already dead. Senior Private Homma joked that he was a self-appointed funeral director.

Some of Kojo's men kept up the black jokes at Kochi, but the captain himself never said anything faintly humorous. In Manchuria, he had relaxed for occasional moments of banter. Here, under fire, he was more strict and so remote that the lower ranks — whom he rarely comforted or even talked to — hardly thought of him as a fellow sufferer. His higher noncommissioned officers admired his sterling military qualities and bearing more than ever. Still a stickler for the rules, still following every possible letter of the book, young Captain Kojo kept his figure as straight and neat as possible in the circumstances. But he was so committed to fighting to the utmost that he seemed to have no personality. The men had called the major who took over for the injured Kojo "the Old Man," but they had no nickname for this ramrod, who looked and behaved like a model for instruction manuals.

And it was true that Kojo was glad for this opportunity to do his duty, shoulder his responsibility, defend his honor.

As the enemy's regular morning and afternoon attacks intensified, his men grew so weak that he was surprised not to be subjected to a major American attack. Kochi Ridge now represented a significant bulge on the map; all territory on both flanks had been taken. But Kojo's line was as thin as a thread. The loss of the 32nd Army's edge in the May 4 counteroffensive had put the men in a kind of shock, adding to the numbness caused by the relentless strain on their undernourished minds, bodies and nerves.

It in no way detracts from American triumphs over their horrendous hardships to acknowledge that Japanese soldiers endured far worse with more fortitude and many fewer breakdowns. They lived in the same mud, even thicker with blood, gore and mashed brains. They were more infested with vermin, more debilitated by disease, more overrun by maggots feasting on their beloved comrades' rotting corpses. Their rations were not to be compared. And the number of shells fired at them, shells that blew their comrades to bits just as effectively and could cause just as much terror, exceeded the number they fired at Americans by fifty or a hundred times. If American Army analysts of the Okinawa fighting concluded that troops should remain in the line no longer than two weeks because physical and mental fatigue from the need for constant alertness and "strain of continuous shell fire . . . greatly reduces the soldiers' efficiency," what of the Japanese soldiers in May? Kojo's men were truly unsung heroes. Brave to begin with, they were long past fear — except those who actually saw small arms about to fire at them — after their exposure to the worst for so many days. They kept to their duties despite daily killings and gruesome maimings by mortar barrages that seemed to approach machine gun fire in intensity. Yet their physical condition after the weeks of fighting on empty stomachs and with only cat naps worried Kojo more than the drastically inadequate supply of ammunition, which still had to be carried on foot from three or four kilometers south.

The American Navy took a break at five o'clock most afternoons, and the worst of the day's shelling and bombing finished at dusk. Before night obscured the terrain, Kojo left his cave with his orderly and several young officers to inspect his remaining forces. Twice mortar rounds killed all others in his little group. Miraculously unhit and unhurt, he now allowed the shared pressure of the day-and-night ordeal to narrow slightly his Academy-taught distance from his men. But discussion with Colonel Yoshida, his regimental commander, on a hill about a mile behind his was limited to two or three talks throughout this period. Even before the fighting, intrabattalion communication was good but not communication to higher regimental command. The Academy also heavily stressed the need for self-sufficiency among battalion commanders, who were supposed to be able to assume command of a regiment or division if necessary.

Therefore there was none of American command's give-and-take between superior and subordinate. Kojo reported his situation to Yoshida but never requested help; Japanese field officers assumed that their superiors knew who needed reinforcements and when. What he did do was maintain composure in the face of difficulty, the clearest mark of the Academy graduate. He did not have to remember his responsibility to present an image of unshakable confidence to his subordinates because he still felt calm, if no longer confident. This was war. Emotion had no place in it. His duty was to fight serenely to the end; his machine guns and mortars were still inflicting casualties — which is why the enemy hadn't yet taken the ridge. Kojo even reckoned that American casualties at this stage might be heavier than his own, although he had no idea that his resistance was among the most stubborn in the entire campaign.

Perhaps the highest tribute to the defense mounted by his and other units was the frustration of the American command. Much of the mighty 10th Army still remained stalled, despite the weakening of the Shuri Line by the failure of the May 4 counteroffensive. The general American offensive to break through the line would be launched on May 11, followed by the first assault on Sugar Loaf the following day. As a prelude to that, Lieutenant Paul Dunfrey led his scouting party across the Asakawa on May 9. He crossed the muddy little river roughly four miles west of the Kochi Ridge, on the other side of Shuri. Kojo's retreat began the following day.

On the evening of May 10, he was ordered to pull back about eight hundred yards to three small hills in sight of his previous position. The other two battalions of the 22nd Regiment had returned from their detached duty to the command of Colonel Yoshida, each with some hundred survivors. Together with Kojo's men, including a dozen from his Headquarters Company, the entire 22nd Regiment — whose starting complement had been about thirty-three hundred men — consisted of roughly three hundred combat troops nearing the extreme of fatigue. Kojo's were so spent that the regimental commander reinforced them with fresh men pared from the regimental color guard. Since the Emperor himself had presented the regiment's colors, and their capture by enemy troops would be the greatest disgrace, Yoshida's gesture spoke for itself about the battalion's condition. The sum of its three fighting companies was approximately two platoons.

Now Kojo deployed them on the rear slopes. With Shuri only a few thousand yards behind him, he did not have to be ordered, as he was, to hold his position to the last man. Among those men were some of his toughest noncoms, including a few veterans of the China War. They continued to repulse the advances of the enemy, who tried to forge ahead on May 11 — as part of Buckner's general offensive launched that day — then seemed to fall into apathy after their weeks of attacks. Kojo believed he could have held the new hills for weeks with rested men and adequate supplies, but both had dwindled to near nothing within days. Thirty men were too few to fire the mortars or to carry their shells. The 1st Company now consisted of only one man: the company commander, a replacement first lieutenant. The 2nd Company, commanded by a sergeant, had half a dozen "troops"; the 3rd Company ten. Morale did not crack, but everyone moved in a permanent stupor. At one point, enemy tanks started up to surround Kojo's position. He and the chief medical officer discussed suicide, but the rain turned so violent that the tanks pulled back and the two lived to fight another day.

The end came on May 16, two days before the Marines' final assault on Sugar Loaf, four miles southwest. A nearby hill defended by another unit fell, giving the Americans a clear, short line of fire on Kojo's positions. But the Japanese in observers' positions slept, exhausted to prostration. Many awoke minutes before they died. Having at last made a final charge, the Americans blew them apart with hand grenades at close range. Surprised by the overrunning of those positions, the men slightly to the rear felt panic for the first time.

Surprised too, Kojo ran through the smoke of the white phosphorous grenades into a cave in the largest of the hills. That shelter, originally for artillery spotters, had a second entrance in addition to its mouth: a ladder-rigged shaft leading to a hatch at the top. A handful of Kojo's men ran with him. The rest were dead.

Several dozen badly wounded men were already in the observation post. Kojo whispered an order to stop their moaning. He heard American shouting overhead but hoped that absolute silence inside might allow them to go undetected until they could sneak out at nightfall. He peered through the blackness to try to see how many men were capable of moving.

A first lieutenant who had run in with him — 1st Company's replacement commander — had no stomach for more. "This is hopeless," he whispered. "I'm going to die here." Kojo, who was as exhausted and depleted as his men, suddenly lost heart too. The American shouting overhead grew more excited. He knew there was no escape from the hand grenades or satchel charges they were readying to toss down the hatch. The game was up; the situation was indeed hopeless. Surrender never entered his thoughts. There was only one way out.

Kojo felt no pain or panic, not even disappointment or nervousness. He would have liked to see his wife and family once more, at least let them know how and where he died. Otherwise, his training or exhaustion kept him utterly calm.

"I've done my duty," he thought with satisfaction. "I fought with honor and fulfilled the purpose of my life. Now it's the end." He put his pistol to his temple, felt the barrel there and enjoyed his visions of beautiful Emiko during their happy trip to Manchuria.

He curled his finger around the trigger, ready to pull. Something hurtled down the hatch at that instant. The explosion of an American satchel charge, devastating in the confined space, tore the pistol from his hand.

Kojo did not think of resorting anew to suicide when he regained consciousness. After his last-instant reprieve, some counterforce made him prefer to live until someone killed him, which would be soon enough. He would resume fighting until then.

He was badly shaken but apparently otherwise unhurt. His death would come quickly if Americans entered the cave, and without resistance, since he couldn't find his pistol in the pitch dark. Their voices, still overhead, told him he could not try to leave until they did. He groped through the observation tunnel in search of other survivors. There were two: the despairing first lieutenant and a senior private, a courageous knee-mortar specialist who had fought the entire campaign. His Academy spirit reviving, Kojo gave the lieutenant a pep talk, but in vain: the reserve officer remained determined to die where he was. But the private was eager to fight again.

The explosion or subsequent shell fire had sealed the mouth of the cave. Hours after the American voices stopped, Kojo and the private began digging with their hands. Finally, the two known survivors of the 1st Battalion squeezed out and into the silence of night. They wriggled like worms into the shell holes that pockmarked the hill until an enemy sentry spied them about twenty meters from the cave. His shots missed. They huddled in their hole for a time, then began crawling again, down the slope of the hill, past American silhouettes, toward the new Japanese line.

They reached Benga-dake Hill and found Colonel Yoshida's head-quarters cave toward midnight. The regimental commander knew that Kojo's position had been overrun because his young operations officer had ignored the shelling to check from another observation post. Now Yoshida seemed happy to see Kojo alive, although he had known him less than two months. "I always put you in the most difficult positions," he said. "I had to — but I regret it nevertheless." He put out his hand. "You fought very well. You deserve our congratulations."

Kojo fought back tears. Of course he must show no emotion. But he knew — and was profoundly happy his regimental commander knew — that his position had held out longest on that front.

20 · Ushijima Abandons the Shuri Line

*Behold! What is a bell? A bell is that which sounds far, wide, and high . . .
It will echo far and wide like a peal of thunder but with utmost purity. And
evil men, hearing the bell, will be saved.*
  — From the inscription on a scarred, dented sixteenth-century bronze bell
  dug from the ruins of Shuri Castle

*Naha was a graveyard, its people vanished with its buildings . . . Nothing
lived in this desert of stone [and] carpet of rubble.*
  — From a Marine Corps film

A homeland was destroyed.
  — From a film of the American Armed Forces' Far East Network

OTHER SHURI LINE barriers fell
almost concurrently with Kochi Ridge and Sugar Loaf, whose finales
were two days apart. The 6th Marines pressed on to Horseshoe
Ridge behind Sugar Loaf, the 1st Marines pushed up through slaughterous Wana Draw below Shuri itself, and the American Army divisions took Conical and Sugar Hills as well as the Wart Hill–Flattop
Hill–Chocolate Drop triangle east of Shuri, where the defense network almost equaled that of the Sugar Loaf triangle to the west.

May 11 to 21 could hardly have been more savage at every muddy
knob and slope below those barriers. The 96th and 77th Army Divisions together reported 2271 wounded and 402 killed and missing.
The dead below Chocolate Drop struck one observer as a skirmish
line lying down to rest. Most of the sixty thousand Okinawans and
Japanese dead so far had been killed while manning the line.

Fewer than five hundred Japanese prisoners had been taken, many
unconscious or too badly wounded to resist or kill themselves. That
was an astonishingly small number in relation to the territory lost,
the 32nd Army's vast inferiority in firepower and the number of its
dead. There were even fewer American prisoners, partly because
Americans did not think to surrender, convinced — with good reason — that raising their hands would mean almost certain death.
Scores of wounded GIs and Marines played dead when enemy soldiers emerged after dark to check bodies and strip them of wristwatches and rations. Those who lived to tell the tale endured kicks

to their gaping wounds, fingers poked straight into their eyes and
booted jumps on their testicles. Almost all who failed such tests with
a gasp or moan were bayoneted or shot to death.*

There were very few American prisoners at the Shuri Line itself;
almost all the dead had died in combat. But 10th Army staff believed
they could see the end after those critical ten days which melted the
core of the defense. Gleanings from interrogations of the few Japanese prisoners supported the American assumption that Ushijima
was making his final stand where he had most hurt them. The Japanese also took it for granted that they would remain in the rump of
their Shuri bastion until the last man was killed by the enemy or by

*Survivors of the troopship that had been sunk with the entire 44th Independent
Mixed Brigade aboard witnessed more atrocities not far away. Although the *Toyama maru*
was traveling in close convoy, almost a full day passed before its 600-odd half-dead survivors were rescued from the water. Eventually, some were delivered to Ishigaki Island,
roughly halfway between Okinawa and Formosa, where they shared a scattering of rifles
and hand grenades to stand watch on the island's airfield, from which kamikaze units took
off to attack the American fleet at Okinawa.

Two weeks after L-day, three American airmen parachuted onto an Ishigaki beach after
their Grumman Avengers were shot down or ran into trouble. They were captured and
interrogated. The commander of the island's naval garrison, which had suffered casualties
in an American air raid the previous day, ordered holes dug near his headquarters.

Two prisoners were delivered there by truck the same evening of April 15. Twenty-
eight-year-old Lieutenant Tebo, a high school teacher before the war, and twenty-year-old
Sergeant Taggle had been so badly beaten they couldn't walk. Dragged toward the holes,
they were bound, blindfolded and gagged. A Captain Makuta, proud of his beheading
skill acquired in China, swung his sword the moment Tebo was pushed to his knees. His
body tumbled into the hole.

The second swordsman won the privilege of being executioner after losing three of his
men in the previous day's air raid, then spent hours proudly informing his men he'd been
chosen. He managed to cut through only half of Sergeant Taggle's neck, but sailors kicked
the body into his hole. Then a second truck arrived with Sergeant Lloyd, for whom a less
honorable end had been decreed because of his unwillingness to answer during his inter-
rogation.

Lloyd too was beaten, then tied to a stake. About thirty men of a howitzer platoon
watched, so large a number because their officer had ordered all to be there. Two sergeants
used sticks to beat the bound captive in the stomach. About a dozen more men followed
suit, until the order was given to switch to bayonets. Some 50 men practiced on Lloyd for
a half hour under the supervision of officers who demonstrated the proper technique.

Two other Americans were beheaded on Izena Island, some 15 miles north of Okinawa.
On Ie Island just off Okinawa's north, the stragglers — after the battle in which Ernie Pyle
had been killed — included Japanese fliers rescued after crash landings and officers
trained in guerrilla tactics. They captured an American pilot shot down during an anti-
kamikaze reconnaissance flight. Several days later, they led their captive to the beach
where he had rowed in on a little rubber raft after parachuting. The officers gave it back
to him, said he was free to leave, and shot him in the back as he was inflating the raft.

Ie's big airfield had been launching American planes for weeks, but the stragglers continued operating. Two more Americans who reached that part of the shore met the same
fate. In a way, those atrocities were a logical consequence of the execution of three American fliers who had participated in the celebrated Doolittle raid on Tokyo in 1942. A military court sentenced them on the basis of a law adopted a week earlier and applied retro-
actively. After years of merciless Japanese bombings of civilian targets on the Asian
continent and in the Pacific, that law made it a capital offense to bomb Japanese civilians
or nonmilitary targets.

himself; their commander had called on them to defend the line to the death. A plan to pull in all functioning units from farther south for a last-ditch effort near the 32nd Army headquarters tunnel circulated by rumor. However, on May 22, the general called a conference in the tunnel to discuss newer contingency plans with his senior staff and fighting units' highest officers.

With no more than a third of his combat strength to defend little more of the line than Shuri itself, Ushijima knew the full difficulty of his position. Imperial General Headquarters had abandoned the pretense of supporting a decisive battle on Okinawa. A week earlier, while his "land battleships" ringing Shuri were still repulsing their attackers, Ushijima had requested reinforcements, warning that the fall of the line would mean the end of his organized resistance. The laconic leader came as close to imploring as any Japanese general could — and won a promise of commando-type raids.

One was actually mounted two days later on Yomitan Airfield. That field, taken on L-day, now teemed with American planes refueling and loading armament for more strikes. The Japanese allocated twelve obsolete bombers for the raid, each to carry a dozen paratroops from an elite unit. After landing at Yomitan, the air crews planned to join the suicidal charge with grenades and explosive charges. But mechanical trouble kept four of the planes on the ground, and when radar detected the approach of the others, American antiaircraft batteries fired an "almost solid" crisscross, which knocked out seven of the remaining eight.

Riddled with shell fragments, the single surviving plane managed to belly-land at Yomitan, where the crew leaped out with the dozen commandos, demolition charges tied around their waists. They destroyed or damaged twenty-seven planes and much aviation fuel and munitions before they were killed to the last man. (American casualties were two killed and eighteen wounded.) Glad tidings went out to the soldiers of the 32nd Army: the field was retaken. In fact, the Americans cleared it of debris and had it back in operation early the following morning, and the Japanese made no further attempt to land airborne troops on Okinawa, so close to their airfields in China, on Formosa and on the mainland.

Only the kamikaze raids continued. Like them, this first attempt to put a force on land confirmed to Americans that their enemy was incorrigibly fanatic. Samuel Hynes, whose eyes stayed clear and honest throughout the campaign, concluded that the point of the May 24 raid was self-destruction rather than destruction. He was appalled by his own conclusion that "the true end of the war for the men I was fighting against was not victory but death. And spectacular death, fire and explosions, the body bursting in a terrible, self-destroying orgasm. One of the [raiders] had held a grenade in his belly and blown himself up."

The May 24 raid was coordinated with the Seventh Floating Chrysanthemum's 165 planes. But Tokyo's fulfillment of its promise of more suicidal attacks against the American fleet provided little reassurance for Ushijima: Imperial General Headquarters now almost certainly valued kamikaze operations more for delaying the inevitable invasion of the mainland than for trying to prevent the 32nd Army's certain defeat. Ushijima had had no illusions about winning since he lost the 9th Division. Now he had none about reinforcements of men or arms. He was more than ever on his own.

However, he did have options — which was why he called his key conference on the evening of May 22 to announce how he would forestall the end.

Two evenings later, American spotter planes flew over Shuri Castle to help direct gunfire from several ships led by U.S.S. *Mississippi*. Her gunners had no idea that this wasn't the first time a battleship of the same name had closed on the same target.

The first *Mississippi* was Commodore Perry's sometime flagship on his momentous voyage to Japan in 1853. Matthew Calbraith Perry was the elder brother of the naval hero Oliver Hazard Perry, whose Lake Erie victory forty years earlier opened the way West, and whose "We have met the enemy and they are ours" spurred America's conversion from underdog pacifism to expansionist power. The less famous brother served with equal distinction, pioneering the American Navy's conversion to steam and displaying the same vision of national interests when acting as a statesman. He was thorough, astute, devoted — and strict, pompous and vain. He mingled notions of the esteem due him as America's representative — to peoples he and his peers considered inferior almost by definition — and as a wearer of his prized golden epaulettes.

The sixty-year-old commodore — then America's highest naval rank — stopped in Okinawa en route to presenting his demands to Japan. There he behaved in his patriotic, autocratic manner, dictating terms to unwilling hosts, who were far more hapless than the Japanese and innocent of all offense. Of this first American-Okinawan encounter, appalled members of his party said, "Poor Okinawans!" A clerk on *Mississippi* (who would rise to admiral) called Okinawa "a mouse in the talons of the eagle."

The squadron arrived in May 1853. The magistrate of Naha sent gifts of animals, vegetables and other treasures for those who had been long at sea. Perry ordered them removed. The underage King — of a single dynasty that had ruled for almost seven centuries — was served by an elderly regent with a long white beard and what struck one of Perry's men as "the most dignified demeanor." Perry sent representatives ashore to invite him to call; the regent tacitly accepted him as his superior by agreeing. But Perry secluded himself during the courtly regent's tour of his ship, and finally received the alarmed man and his entourage to inform them that he intended to call on the castle.

One American thought the Okinawans looked grave enough to be "going to an execution." With great courtesy and tact, they implored Perry not to make his call, begging him also to know that their laws and customs did not permit unrestricted visits on shore. They insisted there was nothing to see in their poor little capital of Shuri; so eminent a person as the commodore surely wouldn't wish to enter its meager castle. Perry countered that he would "expect such a reception as became his rank and position as commander of the squadron and diplomatic representative of the United States." And as soon as the Okinawans left, he gave orders that his men could go ashore wherever they pleased. Ignoring repeated appeals not to persist with his self-invitation to the palace, the commodore pursued it on his chosen date.

He left the port in his most impressive full-dress uniform, borne in a sedan chair he had ordered made for himself. "As the procession moved through the winding road lined on both sides by trees and flowering shrub," he later wrote, "I cannot conceive of a more beautiful pageant." The beauty included a band from *Mississippi* and *Susquehanna,* two field guns decorated with American flags and two companies of Marines whose presence finally forced unarmed Okinawans to open the graceful, symbolically important Gate of Courtesy that led to Shuri Castle. The band played "Hail Columbia" as the "guest" entered. Before going ashore, Perry had informed the Secretary of the Navy that he was "conciliating [the Okinawans'] friendship." Now some members of his party watched his gun-toting overbearance in dismay. A lay missionary and Chinese linguist who served as his translator managed to escape the censorship Perry tried to impose on reports from Okinawa, lest any contradict his own. "It was a struggle between weakness and right, and power and wrong, for a more high-handed piece of aggression has not been committed by anyone," the missionary wrote. "I was ashamed at having been a party to such a procedure, and pitied these poor defenseless islanders."

So it went for the remainder of this visit, as well as during a second one, when Perry returned after putting his demands to Japan. Some of the American slights were unintentional. The regent honored Perry by sending him some sugar cane sweets, the island's best. Every Okinawan would have been overwhelmed by the delicious confection ordinarily reserved for the royal family. Perry complained in his diary that "all they gave us was some hard, tacky biscuit." Okinawans provided other unwanted landing parties with food but also surrounded them with "guides," who ran in advance of the visitors, ordering natives to hide from them. Perry's officers called them police, and displayed their irritation. On top of cultural misunderstandings, there were calculated American insults, a rape by an American sailor and an intentional break-in: officers sent ashore to secure housing forced open some locked gates and took possession of what turned out to be a schoolhouse. (Begging for the party to leave, one Okinawan official said that his people were "very small" but Americans were nothing of the kind. When all attempts at repossessing the schoolhouse failed, however, Okinawans brought fruits and vegetables for its squatters.) Other commandeered buildings included a temple, and threats to occupy Shuri Castle itself were supported by maneuvers on ship and shore to display the squadron's overwhelming power.

America's lordly representative could be thoughtful and gracious when it suited his purpose. In a charitable moment, Perry called the Ryukyu Islands "as pleasant . . . as any in the world" and Okinawans "industrious and inoffensive." But he quickly resorted to displays of force at Okinawans' every failure to show the deference he felt was due him and his country. His courtesy calls continued to be displays of discourtesy; his ability to find offense in imagined slights rivaled that of the Japanese — and he swelled with pride at those methods, which he called "interpos[ing] a little Yankee diplomacy" against his inferiors. From leaving in the middle of a royal banquet in his honor to dismissing legitimate explanations as "devious," Perry behaved as if it were his right to command Okinawans and their duty to obey. Setting out for Japan the second time, he left behind an armed party, proclaiming he would hold the Ryukyus under "limited authority" until he had secured his objectives in Tokyo.

It should be said in America's defense that Washington hoped the commodore would be kinder. Secretary of State Edward Everett, celebrated orator and former president of Harvard, had told him to establish himself in the Ryukyus "with the consent of the natives" and to pursue "the most friendly and conciliatory course." Everett wrote Perry that "the friendly and peaceful character of the natives encourages the hope that your visit will be welcomed . . . Forbid, and at all hazards prevent, plunder and acts of violence on the part of your men toward these simple and unwarlike people . . . Let them from the first see that your coming among them is a benefit, and not an evil to them."

And it should be said in Perry's defense that the same imperious resolve that abused the gentle islanders was necessary for his diplomatic assault on Japan. He knew that Commodore James Biddle, his predecessor in trying to negotiate with Japan seven years earlier, had been repulsed, scornful Japanese interpreting his conciliatory approach as weakness. A Japanese sailor flagrantly insulted Biddle in 1846, nine years after Japanese had fired on an unarmed American merchant ship. Perry's big stick on Okinawa was partly to warn Japan that America would not be trifled with again. Besides, he wasn't acting in a political vacuum but in a carve-'em-up time of seapower and self-assertion. Okinawa happened to be one of the prizes in a compelling competition among European powers for influence and empire. That was the spirit of the colonialist, expansionist age, which hailed the white man as teacher. Without America, things would have been worse for the Asian territories that would be seized anyway.

If the eagle held Okinawa as a mouse in its talons, the Russian bear was more dangerous. Patriotic Americans had good reason to mistrust the other colonial powers foraging in the Pacific. Never mind that America herself had been a collection of colonies not long ago; now they hated to see their virtuous young Republic left out. Perry's personal hauteur aside, he was only trying to protect against the old empires that were eager to claim all the rich prizes of trade, prestige and domination for themselves. He might simply have taken a slice of Okinawa, as the British had taken Hong Kong from China just eleven years earlier and the Portuguese took Goa from India.

But Okinawans felt little gratitude. Perry's instructions to the regent's aides for convincing him to sign an agreement laid power on the line.

> It will be wise, therefore, for the [Okinawans] to abrogate those laws and customs which are not suited to the present age, and which they have no power to enforce, and by a persistence in which they will surely involve themselves in trouble . . . Let the mayor clearly understand that this port [of Naha] is to be one of rendezvous, probably for years, and that the authorities had better come to an understanding at once.

The commodore used the same tone to the regent's representative, overcoming his resistance by a threat to land his Marines and occupy Shuri. "It is repugnant to the American character to submit to such a course of inhospitable discourtesy . . . though the citizens of the United States . . . are always regardful of, and obedient to, the laws of the countries in which they may happen to be." This self-righteous rot rested partly on implied racial superiority, as if Okinawans had not enough of that from Japan. Before his last departure, Perry demanded a treaty stipulating that Okinawans must in the future service American ships and citizens "with great courtesy and friendship." A preamble stated that the servants were signing voluntarily. When they refused, the Marines were again sent ashore to force them. Meanwhile, a party had planted the Stars and Stripes on a pinnacle they named Banner Rock, as if Okinawa were an American discovery.

Having done his homework, Perry knew why "the simple islanders" didn't invite him to Shuri Castle and pointedly asked that his sailors not stay ashore. An English ship had received the usual Okinawan hospitality only thirty years earlier, but in the meantime the Satsuma lords ordered Shuri to keep foreigners out. At sea, Perry wrote the Secretary of the Navy that Okinawans, "disarmed, as they long have been . . . have no means, even if they had the inclination, to rebel against the grinding oppression of their rulers." (Perry never saw the regent at all — Satsuma officials directed him to remain hidden — but only a stand-in, whose ordinary function was to manage foreign affairs.) Instead of feeling greater compassion for the semi-captives, the commodore pushed them harder. Instead of understanding their plight, he inflicted further punishment on them. And although Perry assured the Secretary of the Navy that any pressure he might have to apply on Shuri would ameliorate the Okinawans' conditions, it did nothing of the kind. Solely concerned with American national interests, in his own expansionist view of them, the commodore was convinced of his virtuousness. At the same time, he was not above passing off his high-handedness as cordiality the Okinawans much appreciated. That became the pattern of American-Okinawan relations: severely one-sided exchanges that would take place on the weak party's land, at his expense. The poverty of that land only tightened the seemingly paradoxical cycle, for that is the condition under which powerful and self-righteous often extract the most.

Perry rested his actions on "the laws of stern necessity" and "the strictest rules of moral law," America's goodness and wisdom making the justice of his demands "self-evident." Japan's consistently worse aggrandizement grew out of greed for Okinawa's trade and her sense of herself as supreme — without the Christian self-assurance, but with other myths of similar effect. The two powers that held themselves morally superior in their respective ways blithely violated a defenseless people who made no such claim. At one point before Satsuma's conquest, a Shimazu lord offered to settle a debt with possession of the Ryukyus, to which he had no claim whatever. And Perry proposed annexing Okinawa as a base for military operations against Japan if his mission there failed. Such were the attitudes of rapacious earlier centuries, as if the twentieth would be easier on the Okinawans.

Displays of force had been enough to give the commodore his way on the inoffensive, defenseless island. Now, ninety-two years hence, the later *Mississippi* took aim on the same Shuri Castle, her gunners making ready to put an end to the sixteenth-century monument and center of national life.

Little was left of the surrounding area. Except during bad weather, most places even hinting of defensive value on the island's southern third had been under fire from sea and air for almost sixty days. Shuri heights had been a prime target from the first. An expert has calculated that 200,000 rounds of artillery alone were fired into the little city of about five thousand houses and twenty-one thousand inhabitants. Hundreds of thousands of mortar rounds also fell there; hundreds of air strikes were made with up to thousand-pound bombs. Naval shells completed what a native account called the "laughter" of metal shrieking through the air.*

But the walls of Shuri Castle, built in Chinese style of coral block by ten thousand people three centuries earlier, had withstood the pounding. It was the mile of those walls, twenty feet thick at their base and towering to more than forty feet, on which *Mississippi* trained her 14-inch guns on May 25, 1945. American infantrymen with time to look could see naval shells cooling from white to red as they arced through the air toward the target. *Colorado* joined with her 16-inchers. But the massive ramparts showed little sign of damage after a full day's fury by both wagons. Cracks began to appear only after a second day of almost continuous salvos. *Mississippi* moved closer inshore for a third day of work. By the evening of May 27, the huge walls had crumbled and the ancient castle from which Okina-

---

*Okinawa took heavier naval bombardment for a longer period than any other battle site in history. Task Force 54, the invasion fleet's gunfire support unit, fired over a quarter of a million shells, to which *Mississippi* contributed 9000 over six weeks, a good share during her special assignment now.

Although the north generally fared better, American artillery very heavily damaged its only city of Nago even after the Japanese had evacuated. Scores of schools were leveled because they might have — and turned out not to have — served as barracks or for other military purposes.

wan kings had ruled, the epicenter of Okinawan culture for five centuries, was rubble.

Around it, the city was all shell craters and wreckage. A venerable Japanese artist had extolled its loveliness shortly before the war. He had visited almost all of Japan's castle towns and cities, "but if anyone was to ask me which was the most beautiful, I would answer without hesitation Shuri of Okinawa." Another Japanese admirer of Okinawan culture explained why. Other castles were grander and other beauty spots were more impressive, wrote Muneyoshi Yanagi in 1938. But Shuri Castle's site, structure and views — of the sea and gentle, undulating hills — formed a unique ensemble. "How can we find in Japan such a perfect combination of nature and culture? What city is surrounded by beautiful hills and water on all sides and contains a dream-filled castle inside, as well as well-maintained palaces, temples and houses of historic value?"

Now all was gone. The castle area was about three hundred acres, the size of a large college campus. An American reported it "completely demolished." Only stone fragments remained of the fairy-tale little roads that had wound to gardens and ponds. Magnificent ancient trees of green and red leaves that had provided gracious silence and shade were stumps, some still smoking. Around them, the city was cinders, dust and a stench of rotting flesh. Quaint paper-and-wood dwellings with stone walls and pretty little terraces had been blown to bits or burned to the ground, hardly leaving an ash. Occasional slivers of red roofing tile were still recognizable in heaps of debris.

The bombings accompanying L-day had begun the destruction. When Japanese soldiers occupied the grounds of the old royal residences a week later, they drove away Okinawan custodians who were trying to bury or otherwise protect priceless treasures, from rare antiques and other magnificent gifts of Chinese emperors to portraits and ceremonial artifacts of the Okinawan dynasty. Now, in late May, the loss was virtually total. The soot blew over the remains of the main artistic and spiritual treasures, starting with the celebrated Shurei Gate, through which Perry had triumphantly passed. The Confucian Shrine and national museum had disappeared. A Chronicle of the Okinawan People, from the fifteenth to sixteenth centuries, had been buried for safety and was almost certainly still there, but Okinawans would find it gone when they were permitted to return to the old capital.*

---

*The 22 volumes were snatched as souvenirs and smuggled to America. When they were located, a naval commander returned them after almost ten years of pressure and pleading.

Naha's devastation was also complete, although the Americans needed a few more days to mop up snipers and mortar platoons concealed in its ruins. On May 23, five days after the securing of Sugar Loaf, from whose crest the capital's smoking rubble could be seen, the first American troops crossed the normally sluggish Asato River, now swollen and muddy from the relentless rains. Those advance units of the 6th Marine Division fought their way into the capital's northern outskirts. Its commander had tried to give his men some training in the unfamiliar street-to-street fighting, but with no time to acquire combat smarts in it, they feared being shot by fellow Americans as well as by enemy snipers hiding behind the remains of garden walls.* The stench of rotting bodies was so strong that the troops felt the taste at the back of their throats. The pilot of an observation plane flying over the dead city a few mornings earlier had had to cover his face with his hands, even several hundred feet in the air and with fresh sea breezes blowing. Another pilot saw one wall standing — not a single entire building, but "just that one white wall . . . rising uselessly from the ruins."† From Naha, the destruction spread out everywhere. The same pilot, no more concerned with civilians than the average Marine, also noticed that "all the villages had been destroyed and the people who lived in them killed or driven into camps."

From the ground, a Marine infantryman saw the former city of sixty-five thousand — almost 15 percent of Okinawa's population — as debris. "Naha was a deserted, bomb-leveled pile of rubble without even a passable street, just total destruction." Dick Whitaker's imagination was richer, perhaps thanks to the contrast with Guadalcanal and other primitive or deserted islands he'd seen in the Pacific. In early June, when his company pushed through the largest city ever taken by Marines — also the first Japanese city taken by any Americans — fragments of theaters and other buildings suggested to Whitaker that it may once have been a fine liberty town. But other Marines saw only a blackened, smoldering wasteland where "practically not one stone remained on any other stone except for in an occasional piece of a building's façade." "Every ship in the harbor,

---

*Those troops naturally remember much more about their own difficulties in Naha than about the city itself. Throughout the grueling night of May 23–24, Marine engineers built footbridges and carried hundred-pound steel sections on their backs so that a larger Baily bridge could be built over the Asato — under fire from Japanese artillery — the next day. Then tanks rolled across, but Naha was too filled with rubble and debris for them to contribute much to the tense job of clearing out hidden defenders. The Japanese force was small but well equipped with mortars and machine guns. The unaccustomed work took a week.

†In fact, one building on the north side of town was intact and would house the first new Okinawan store when the American military government opened it two years later.

The young evacuated the even younger. *(W. Eugene Smith/Life Magazine © Time Warner Inc.)*

Evacuation from a village before it took fire. *(W. Eugene Smith/Life Magazine © Time Warner Inc.)*

Evacuation *(Courtesy of the National Archives)*

Marines clear out Japanese in June 1945, after the fall of the Shuri Line.
(Courtesy of the National Archives)

Marine riflemen wait for the explosion of a charge before closing in on a Japanese refuge. *(Courtesy of the National Archives)*

A section of the third and last natural defense line in the south, which was taken in late June 1945.

Lieutenant General Simon Bolivar Buckner, Jr., with General Joseph W. Stilwell on June 7, 1945, when Stilwell was on an inspection mission from Washington. When Buckner was killed 11 days later, Stilwell returned to Okinawa to replace him. *(Courtesy of the National Archives)*

Lieutenant General Mitsuru Ushijima in May 1943, as commandant of the Imperial Military Academy. *(Courtesy of Mainichi Shimbun Press)*

Colonel Isamu Cho in August 1938, when he was still involved in the Cherry Blossom Society's ultranationalist activities. *(Courtesy of Mainichi Shimbun Press)*

The civilian survivors of Ie Shima were deloused, then permitted to bathe. Shortly after this photograph was taken, during the third week of April 1945, all were deported so that Americans would have secure use of the airfield. *(Courtesy of the National Archives)*

Japanese prisoners in late June 1945. Some hid their faces in shame.
(Courtesy of the National Archives)

A lithograph by Samuel Jacobson in memory of the prisoner he shot at the urging of some Marines he encountered while taking the Japanese back from the front. *(Courtesy of Samuel Jacobson)*

Under American supervision, a captured member of an Okinawan student corps gives first aid to a girl roughly the same age as Ruriko Morishita, Miss Victory Day.

Japanese soldiers and Okinawan civilians surrender from one of the huge caves in the far southern end.

(Facing page) A Japanese soldier attempts to flee below the cliffs near the southern tip in late June 1945. The beach is strewn with bodies, clothing, helmets and discarded weapons. *(Courtesy of the National Archives)*

Japanese soldiers wade out to surrender to small craft just off shore.

John Senterfitt and Dick Whitaker at th 6th Marine Division reunion in San Antonio, Texas, September 1991. *(Courte of Richard Whitaker)*

Hiroshima in mid-October 1945, 10 weeks after its destruction by the first atomic bomb. *(Courtesy of the National Archives)*

every boat and every bridge, every street and building had felt the overwhelming power of our supporting arms," boasted the *History of the Sixth Marine Division* under a photograph of the ruins. The capital prompted little American sorrow, perhaps just because too little of it remained to suggest what had been lost.

The sorrow of most Okinawans also was focused elsewhere. The razing of the main port and by far largest city was a secondary blow to their morale, not only because it had been functioning as only half of itself since the 10/10 air raid. Although the Japanese had changed the capital to Naha soon after annexing the island, Okinawans continued to love and revere the seat of their ancient dynasty. For all its commercial importance, Naha had never replaced Shuri as the cultural heart and soul.

An American observer saw the ancient capital's destruction as so complete that "I doubt if the castle or the surrounding village shall ever really be rebuilt." "Nothing was left of the ancient city," an American historian with long residence on Okinawa summarized later. "The palace was gone, the temples, the great gates, and the ancient gardens of the Shuri gentry." Gone too were the ancient artifacts reposed in these places. Together with the monuments, manuscripts and historical records, they had been the national memory and register. Okinawan scholars spoke of "obliteration of the entire cultural heritage." The loss to world culture and civilization was incalculable and irreplaceable.

Weary, wary units of both the Army and the Marine Corps entered Shuri two days later. Droves of Japanese and Okinawan corpses and rotting trunks of Army horses lay amidst heaps of rubble containing shreds of civilian clothing, tropical helmets and pieces of gas masks. The hardiest architectural survivors were the bell tower and concrete walls of a small Methodist church built four years before Pearl Harbor and the concrete shell of the two-story Normal School where Masahide Ota, now delivering messages for the Blood and Iron Scouts for the Emperor, had studied to be a teacher.

Just two groups of unwanted foreigners had previously forced their way into Shuri during its long history as the capital: the ruthlessly expansionist Satsuma Japanese, who invaded in 1609 to end the island's independence, and Matthew Perry's landing party in 1853. With good intentions and bad, out of callous greed and perhaps unavoidable necessity, brave warriors of the same two nations had now managed to demolish completely what they had formerly penetrated. Proportionate to national wealth and heritage, the London blitz, the razing of Berlin and even the blockade of Leningrad

were slender by comparison to this loss of almost all the symbols of
Okinawa's independent past. By this measure, the imminent devastation of Hiroshima and Nagasaki would also be much less significant.

More than the desolation, what interested and surprised 10th Army
staffs was that the final push into the headquarters city encountered
less opposition than anticipated. The resistance in fact came not from
the Japanese 32nd Army making its last stand near the headquarters
tunnel but from skeleton rear-guard units assigned to delay and deceive.

For Ushijima had evacuated the bulk of his depleted forces during
the previous days. That was what he called his May 22 conference to
announce, although he had been planning the unexpected move
since May 18, the day Sugar Loaf finally fell. Some of his divisional
commanders disapproved. Although the south teemed with caves,
few had been converted to the kind of strongpoints used so effectively until now. It also seemed right to fight to the end in the main
fortifications where so much blood had been lost. Chief of Staff Cho
originally preferred that policy, as did the chief of staff of the 62nd
Division, which was too weak even for proper withdrawal. But Colonel Hiromichi Yahara, the chief operations officer, criticized their
desire to die an honorable death at Shuri as useless sentimentality,
and the unpredictable Cho suddenly gave in. Eventually Ushijima,
the more farsighted commander with a view of Japan's larger needs,
overruled all objections. That was why Shuri's capture, at last, would
be less significant than the Americans had expected. Instead of sig-
naling *the* end, it was *an* end — of the hardest fighting, but not the
greatest killing.

Militarily, the evacuation was a great success. Thirty-second Army
headquarters was installed in an excellent, if far less elaborate, position in the far south, just a few miles below Minatogawa on the east
coast, where the 2nd Marine Division had feinted a landing on L-day
and critics of General Buckner's frontal tactics proposed a real landing to outflank the Shuri Line. The staff quickly resumed operations
from there — but once again, the benefit to Japan, this one even
more temporary, was at Okinawa's expense. During the rest of the
campaign, and for decades afterward, civilians would pay the heaviest price for Ushijima's skill.

Okinawan well-being was little higher on the American scale of
priorities, but the missed opportunity to save precious American lives
would have saved tens of thousands of civilians. Had 10th Army com-

manders known of Ushijima's withdrawal, they probably could have shortened the campaign by weeks, bombing, shelling and outflanking it into a rout. But the critical, eleventh-hour operation was superbly accomplished because the Japanese had good luck on top of their astonishing ability to persevere despite tremendous hardship, loading and marching all night on empty stomachs. The rearguard force fought cleverly and skillfully enough from its remaining strongpoints, even making some light attacks on enemy positions, to allay American suspicions for several crucial days, the same days whose foul weather helped prevent reconnaissance and intelligence from making sense of the movements of men and equipment that *were* spied on the roads south of Shuri.

The pullout began almost immediately after the May 22 conference when the rain was still so heavy from low-hanging clouds that the aeronautical ceiling remained effectively at zero even in places not covered by ground-level fog. Fast, last-minute withdrawal was nothing new for Ushijima. He had used it all along — at Kakazu Ridge on April 24, for example, where he had fired artillery barrages and taken advantage of a foggy night to fall back from the fortifications there just before his troops were overwhelmed.* Instead, they pulled back to the Shuri Line farther south. Southern-moving columns spied during partial clearing on May 26 were bombed and strafed, with heavy casualties. But since other columns were reported moving north, the leaders assumed that Ushijima, far from withdrawing, was replacing his wounded and most exhausted troops with fresh ones from reserves in the south. More confusing was that some of the columns appeared to consist of civilians dressed in white.†

It made sense to the Americans — further misleading them about the clever withdrawal — that Okies were evacuating south from Shuri. American planes had dropped tens of thousands of leaflets on the city urging civilians to do just that and to wear white for protection from shooting. Those circumstances were largely responsible for American intelligence misinterpreting the heavy movements on the roads until the rains returned with a vengeance on May 29, 30, and 31, reducing visibility to near zero just when the last major unit of Captain Kojo's 24th Division pulled out.

Thus the massive withdrawal was accomplished with far better or-

---

*Americans were surprised when they finally took Kakazu and found it scarcely defended. But 10th Army headquarters hadn't learned the lesson or forgot it by now, a month later.

†Many such "civilians" sighted from the air were actually Japanese soldiers in civilian dress. This distressed even the most pro-Japanese Okinawans because they foresaw that Americans would naturally take less care not to shoot civilians after uncovering the subterfuge. But those anguished Okinawans could do nothing.

der than the Japanese could have expected in their dismal circumstances. As before, Ushijima hadn't waited to be encircled. Excellent planning under Yahara and stoic execution had extricated the 32nd Army to fight not just another day but almost another gory month. When the skies cleared and intense air reconnaissance resumed, American staff officers were amazed that so much of the garrison had managed to pull out. American appreciation would increase after the war, when the 32nd Army's hardships became better known. But even now there was grudging admiration of the operation's scope and execution, more easily given since Americans knew they were over the worst and many remained overconfident. Even at this stage, they underestimated the Japanese ability to endure hell in order to "die gloriously" killing the enemy.

But neither side knew that Okinawa would suffer most for the withdrawal's tactical success and stubborn purpose. And had they known, they could have done little about it. The civilian population was not their business after all, or only peripherally their business. It was all they could do to fight their unprecedentedly demanding war.

21 · South from the Shuri Line

The corpses were like yellow mud in the rain. When it cleared up, they became mummies in the heat. Adult faces shrunk to the size of a child's and turned black, except for the teeth, which shone white.
— Yoshio Kobayashi, one of Captain Kojo's men, about his retreat
  from Shuri

Tadashi Kojo left the Shuri Line critical days after the general withdrawal. His mental and physical condition reflected the 32nd Army's as a whole.

After clawing his way from the observation post where he had attempted suicide and crawling to regimental headquarters, the Captain was in no shape to exercise command even if his battalion had still existed. He spent the next twelve days in a kind of reserve in a signal center not more than a kilometer from doomed Shuri Castle. That was the first relief from the exhausting fighting that had begun for him on April 26, three weeks of continuous tension with almost no food. Now he rested in the protection of a large, well-built bunker on the rear slope of Shuri heights, watching radio and telegraph operators at work. He did not wonder why he no longer wanted to kill himself. He sensed only that that time had come and gone and that he now wanted to die in action. Without replacements, resupply or possible relief from the American onslaught, that would surely be soon.

His command consisted of 1st Battalion's dozen survivors. While he rested, Colonel Yoshida, the regimental commander, scratched together a few men who had been left behind around the regimental tunnel near Naha Airfield. More replacements arrived from airfield maintenance crews and other service troops pulled largely from hospitals, some recovered only enough from serious wounds to limp and hobble. Soon the once highly trained and spirited battalion of over a thousand men had a ragtag collection of some forty souls, about enough for a platoon, with one light machine gun and several knee-mortars. Their morale matched their combat readiness.

It sagged further when Colonel Yoshida passed on Ushijima's order for the general withdrawal. This dealt a greater psychological blow than any the enemy had delivered directly. For all the pain of defending the Shuri Line, the cost to Americans had heartened the battalion. All knew their jobs and did them well. Holding on to the fortifications had provided a feeling of accomplishment, a kind of victory. Now the resort to futile improvisation replaced that with anxiety and despair. (At least unconsciously, most Japanese soldiers sensed that their Army did not excel in improvisation.)

As long as the High Command were in their bunkers on Okinawa's high ground, the fighters had retained enough mental strength to cope with their staggering losses. The news that they were leaving strongholds previously considered militarily sacred was the straw that finally broke the morale of many, an admission of defeat from superiors whose confidence had held them together. Abandoning those positions destroyed their faith in eventual victory — a central pillar of morale in every army. The strain on Kojo's survivors drastically increased when the promise collapsed and they had to fight on without hope. "Americans are chasing us, encouraged and totally motivated," one said of the forthcoming retreat to hastily prepared or wholly unprepared positions. "Our ratio is one against more than twenty. In planes, our zero against their limitless number. This is not the way to run a war."

The rest of the 24th Division pulled out, using the last of its operable trucks for its remaining equipment and ammunition. Men who had learned their night driving in Manchuria were at the wheel. But the 22nd Regiment remained at Shuri because it was assigned as a rear guard for the withdrawal. The job fell to Kojo, since all that was left of the regiment was all that was left of his 1st Battalion.

They too left on June 6 for the south bank of the streamlike Noha River, some five miles south of Shuri. Some wounded were still too feeble to pick up the weapons of comrades killed beside them on the march. Kojo's rest had been much too short for him to recover from the effects of hunger and exhaustion on top of the wounds from the accidental explosion before L-day. His own weakness depressed him as much as the weakness of his force. He felt he had fulfilled his duty at Kochi, where he had clung to hope against hope. Although part of him had known that everything on expendable Okinawa was intended merely to delay the enemy's invasion of the mainland, from whose defense no precious resources or equipment could be diverted, another part knew that the plans of Imperial General Headquarters to counter the American advance kept changing. He fantasized that Okinawa was part of the final, inviolable circle that would be defended with all available national resources. After all, it was part of Japan. He told himself it was inconceivable that it would be left without support and reinforcements.

That fantasy now evaporated. Although Kojo continued to take some satisfaction in having done his best at Kochi, the fight had gone out of him. He could do little more than stumble on to the dismal end, trying to mask his pessimism with a Japanese officer's prescribed serenity. He silently agreed that it was a mistake to leave Shuri, where at least some supplies of food and ammunition remained and where there was a slight advantage of familiarity with the terrain and operational procedures. The 32nd Infantry Regiment, sister of Kojo's 22nd in the 24th Infantry Division, had been sent south weeks before and had surely used the time to prepare positions and lay in supplies. Kojo suspected murderous chaos awaited the units unable to do the same. Everything he had previously accomplished in the Army had been grounded in preparation and procedures. Now the officers did not know the terrain where they were headed, let alone have time to dig in on advantageous high ground. With no protection of any kind against the enemy's enormous, ceaseless firepower, they would be targets, not fighters.

His new adjutant reflected the change of mood. An artillery officer whose unit had been destroyed near Shuri, First Lieutenant Yatsugi had come up from the ranks with wide Army experience. He was assigned to Kojo shortly before Kochi, where he frequently buoyed up himself and others with reassurances of triumph when the Combined Fleet arrived. "When's it coming — today?" he would ask with a smile during the worst bombardments. He never missed a morning to wonder whether that would be the day for the battleships and carriers to appear; his trust was so infectious that even Kojo began doubting the naval officer's whisper that the Combined Fleet no longer existed. Now such cheery chatter was gone. Yatsugi and most of Kojo's men held their tongues in Kojo's presence, but they were deeply discouraged, especially, as Yoshio Kobayashi put it, because they had no idea where they were going or "what would happen when we got to the unknown destination."

> We moved in silence in the torrential rain, gunfire sounding near and far, through and over corpses whose eyes shone dully in the light of flares. We were ordered to stop to eat at a roadside cave but it was filled with water up to our knees, and floating corpses pervaded its interior with the peculiar stench of death. I managed to bring a rice ball to my mouth but threw up after a bite.

The enfeebled soldiers were ordered to carry as many weapons and as much equipment as possible. They could not also carry the wounded, whose number seemed endless. (The chief medical officer's rucksack served to transport the battalion's entire medical supplies, chiefly some bandaging.) One man with both legs smashed crawled on all fours, his knees wrapped in rags. Few had any more strength or inclination than Kojo to notice hordes of civilians even worse off who were trying to evacuate: grandmothers tugging at children of three and four who had seemingly forgotten how to cry; a baby screaming on the back of a mother dead long enough to begin to disintegrate.

Once the men had guarded their rifles with their lives. "Any little scratch on them," Kobayashi remembered, "would have got us sent to the stockade." Now the rusty things trailed in the mud. The young bearer of the regimental colors alone retained something of the old spirit, never faltering no matter how close enemy bullets and bombs approached. But only the tassels were intact of that 22nd Infantry Regiment flag that had led confident soldiers into battle as far back as the Russo-Japanese War.

Still, slivers of good luck were enough to dispel the exhaustion and demoralization. When the rain "miraculously" let up, the group enjoyed the "incredible" additional luxury of no rain of American bombs and shells; it had broken off for some unknown reason. The sky actually turned blue and the mood picked up enough for jokes — until the bombardment resumed hours later. A detachment from this group enjoyed another moment of relief when they were sent on to the temporary 1st Battalion headquarters and found it after midnight, dodging shells as they dragged themselves through the mud. The new cave, a former emplacement for destroyed 150mm cannon, with tunnels to accommodate supply trucks, was large and sturdy enough to give its inhabitants a sense of security despite the paucity of ammunition and almost total lack of food. Its solid protection was much needed during an intense enemy assault on the position the following day. The battle was small but fierce. Toward the end of the long, possibly last day, the soldiers caught sight of Americans advancing on them from the top of the hill opposite the cave. There was enough Japanese artillery to fire on them. One of Kojo's burned-out men who saw American bodies blown into the air wanted to dance at the sight.

His joy was brief. The Japanese guns resumed their silence and the enemy approached again in a blaze of automatic fire. Bullets hit the roof of the cave around the men's heads — and the heads themselves. Kobayashi loaded his muddy, rusted rifle, aimed at one of the Americans closing in to kill him, and pulled the trigger. To his despair, he heard a click. Throwing away his "soul of a soldier," he desperately gathered pebbles, rocks and rags for ammunition. ("Little good they would do, that I knew.") The soldier in front of him screamed, "I'm hit!" and tumbled. His chattering stopped and he became still.

Kobayashi accepted that his turn was next but dusk came before it did and the Americans broke off to make their night preparations. After dark, Kojo radioed an order to cease radio communications because he believed the enemy was locating the waves to pinpoint their shelling. He also ordered his communications section to evacuate their cave — a seemingly suicidal task, with the Americans encamped just outside. But a new miracle brought salvation for Kobayashi and others. They found a rear exit from the cave that opened onto a rocky slope. The wounded remained silent despite their fearful pain as they were dragged down the jagged incline. With no idea of where they were and only the outline of flare-lit hills to guide them, the communications unit wandered about in desperation, but finally found its way to its destination: the town of Makabe, about a mile short of Okinawa's southern tip.

The battalion's next destination was the same as that of the communications section: the crossroads town on which many units had already converged in confusion. Makabe was only four miles south of Shuri, but Kojo, unable to walk unaided, could not reach it in one night. After dusk on June 8, two of his men gripped him under his arms and the party set out. The night was dark, the downpour relentless. Except for the private who had survived with him at Kochi, his men were all new; hardly knowing them, he felt himself only their nominal commander. Kojo had lost some of his interest in fighting together with hope and faith. His only support was his duty to behave like an officer, an expression of pride to which he clung as his men half-dragged him through the mud to a midway stop.

Too weak to take in others' condition on the roads, he did recognize a new low of anguished desperation where he stopped to rest. It was at a field hospital in the village of Kochinda, halfway to Makabe. That outpost of mutilated bodies and corpses was disbanding in the face of the enemy advance. Two rice balls, potassium cyanide and hand grenades were being distributed to those unable to evacuate. Ashen nurses told Kojo that the most severely wounded had already been injected. Everyone who could walk or crawl was urged to find his unit in the field, though no one in authority had an idea of where those units were.

A voice cried out to Kojo as he took in that appalling scene. "Mister Instructor, sir. Please, Mister Instructor!" Japanese recruits undergoing their difficult adjustment to Army life remembered their training officers no less than American Marines remembered their drill instructors. Despite his strictness, Second Lieutenant Kojo had been a popular regimental training officer in 1940, when he first joined the 22nd Regiment in Manchuria — but the voice surely would have pleaded to anyone recognizable. Kojo turned toward it and made out a former trainee with one leg just amputated near the hip. The weeping soldier said he knew what was in store for him because the hospital was disbanding. Even if he knew how to walk on one leg, he could get nowhere through the deluge of rain and sea of mud. Like many in the hospital, he was lost, with no idea of his unit's location, and he knew that many despairing Japanese soldiers from other units would not help stragglers like him on the grim roads. But his old training officer's providential appearance gave the new amputee a surge of relief and hope against hope. Alternately smiling in happiness and grimacing in pain, he begged the captain to take him with him.

Kojo's composure had already been shaken. Perhaps the tears he felt beginning to form were for himself and his hopeless position as much as for the doomed supplicant. It took all his will power to keep himself from breaking down. "I'd like to help you but I can't," he said, regaining his self-control. "You know I'm responsible for my troops and I must catch up to them . . . But don't give up. There's no reason for pessimism just because things look difficult at the moment. Get back to your unit even if you have to creep." Dragging himself to a nearby hill, the captain used his sword to cut a makeshift crutch from a stand of bamboo. He would have to fight tears again much later when he learned that the amputee was miraculously among the 32nd Army's 10 percent of survivors.

Kojo left the following night for Makabe, again supported by soldiers. When he arrived at the 22nd Regiment's new headquarters, he found the full regiment — with its other battalions — beefed up to about three hundred troops, most of whom were like those he had seen leaving the hospital, gravely wounded men who preferred dragging themselves back to their units to killing themselves. Many had arrived without weapons and the regiment had none to distribute. The new headquarters was a slightly enlarged former emplacement for machine guns. There were no machine guns now, nor other supplies; not even a structure worthy of the name. The once proud regiment's only purpose was to delay the inevitable as long as possible.

The mess was catastrophic to morale, for as the Americans had shown in fighting on despite heavy casualties at Sugar Loaf — and the Japanese had demonstrated even more eloquently at the Shuri Line — morale's single most important ingredient, more important even than belief in eventual victory, is the commitment to comrades that overrides commitment to oneself. But with almost all the old comrades gone, loyalty and cohesiveness counted for little. Most men had joined their units only weeks or days before, when those units were already pulling apart.

The 32nd Army's disintegration acquired a momentum of its own. Although nearly all remaining units were being squeezed into the island's southern tip, organization and communications were so feeble that Kojo knew even less than before of the fate of the Army as a whole, except that it was collapsing. (Specifically, he didn't know that his 24th Division, with some eight thousand shaky men strung out on the west coast, was in far better shape than the once-proud 62nd Division, which was down to about three thousand troops.) A few units on southern mountains were fighting almost as at Shuri — but less as an integrated army than as additional testimony to the last reward of dying honorably at one's gun.

Knowing he could do nothing to make his own band into a fighting unit, Kojo felt his demoralization deepen. It was almost a relief when Colonel Yoshida ordered him to take twenty men, together with his new adjutant and one more officer, and defend a small ridge about half a mile away, at Maesato village. The new position was a few hundred yards from the western (East China Sea) coast and just over a mile south of Itoman, Okinawa's fourth largest city, which had been known for its beautiful women and was now a heap of debris. Kojo knew this would be his last position and he told his men so. "This will be our final stand. We will die here."

Then he deployed them. The twenty men had half a dozen rifles and many grenades as well as the knee-mortars and light machine guns. The immediate trouble was the composition of the naked rise. Americans had found it impossible to dig foxholes in coral even with tools; those phantoms of men with none could not scratch the surface. When the American advance reached them on June 20, they could only lie on the ground during the mortar barrage. Kojo himself had the protection of the only bush in sight. The violation of the first rule of infantry warfare — Take cover! — disturbed him more than anything before. He had put up with a great deal. Not to be able to give his men cover was crushing.

He could not communicate with them during the day without risking instant death. When he checked the first night, fifteen were alive. The next day, some signal troops among the survivors brought him a radio message from Colonel Yoshida, still in a cave on a hill less than a thousand yards away. "We are being attacked. If possible, return your battalion here." Kojo answered that he would try as soon as it was dark. He could see American planes, guns, tanks and flame-throwers attacking the general location of his regimental headquarters. That was the end of the 22nd Regiment. Yoshida's last message before he died was the traditional one, promising to fight to the end and wishing Kojo luck.

> *The fire from [American] ships was coordinating perfectly with [our] artillery. We were slowly reducing what was left of that damn Nip artillery and we were getting less and less shelling from the Japs.*
>
> — Joe Fater, 8th Marines

> *American flamethrowing tanks seared [Okinawa's] hillsides with gallons of liquid fuel, roasting hundreds of Japanese hiding in caves. As survivors ran out, waiting infantrymen fired clip after clip into them.*
>
> — William Craig, The Fall of Japan

> *The Japs and their screams meant utterly nothing to me. How can you expect anyone to understand that unless they were there themselves — actually in a foxhole getting bombarded and watching their buddies get killed? All these people who talk war and don't have the faintest idea of the hell it is! The only ones who know are the ones who were there.*
>
> — Evan Regal, Marine flamethrower

> *If anything moved in the mouth of a cave you were blowing, you fired away like you fired at any noise at night. I didn't think twice whether civilians or soldiers were inside . . . My remorse about human beings being shot in there disappeared pretty quick because this was survival. I wanted to live. I wanted to go home. And I wasn't going to take chances, no chance was worth it.*
>
> — Buzzy Fox, G–2–22

> *I saw a shriveled-up old Jap man [an Okinawan] being flushed out of a cave near the bottom of the hill by five Marines. The man stood there obviously scared to death. The five Marines surrounded the man in a circle and each had a .45 automatic pistol pointed at the Jap. It struck me that if he twitched or sneezed, the five Marines would have shot themselves up. However, nothing happened, and two Marines took the Jap to the rear.*
>
> — Declan Klingenhagen, D–2–29

General Buckner believed the Japanese evacuation of Shuri, no matter how lucky and skillful, had come too late to confront his 10th Army with more than isolated moments of stiff fighting farther south. Ushijima was fatally short of arms and ammunition. Roughly four fifths of his machine guns and nine tenths of his artillery pieces were destroyed or inoperable. One way or another, a quarter of his remaining troops, ten thousand to fifteen thousand men, had been lost during the withdrawal. Roughly a fifth of the combat forces in place on L-day were in fighting condition. A fifth of that fifth were seriously wounded; almost every survivor was exhausted. The thirty thousand men left on June 4 included many from construction and support units, some without proper weapons. Real strength was less than that of a proper division against the four and a half vastly stronger American divisions chasing him. "It's all over now but cleaning up pockets of resistance," Buckner assured correspondents on May 31.

But the big-gun advocate and his well-supplied staff greatly underestimated the misery waiting in the last eight square miles still in Japanese hands. Although no more Shuri Lines lay ahead, the third of the south's three east-west mountain spines rose six miles farther south. Japanese were retreating to almost anywhere they could find, but principally to strongpoints that had been well prepared by units of the 24th Division and the crack 9th before it was sent away. And many old and new dangers confronted the Americans on their way to that last high ground.

Every night still belonged to the enemy. When a replacement named Wilson made out Japanese faces behind four little bushes approaching his foxhole one night, he held his fire for fear of hitting his platoon's command post, another foxhole nearby. Instead, he made the startling decision to leap up to inform that command post. Even a larger man than smallish Wilson running in the dark without shouting the password or some other warning risked being taken for Japanese. After a few steps, a bullet grazed him above an eye. To his great good luck, that shot was from a carbine rather than a heavier American weapon. The carbine jammed before a second shot could be fired. When its owner clubbed Wilson with its butt, the replacement was lucky again because the weapon wasn't heavy enough to bludgeon him to death before he was recognized. Such incidents still happened because the more desperate Japanese now took greater risks at night and many Americans were correspondingly more trigger happy.

One such desperado slithered into the foxhole of Dan Maczko, a 4th Marines machine gunner, at about 3 A.M. on June 12. Maczko grabbed his arms as the Japanese tried to pull the pin of a grenade. Maczko fought the grenade away, then struggled to wrest away a big club — with which he beat the enemy before stabbing him with his own kabar knife. In the words of a chronicler of his platoon, he finally "threw the Nip out of the hole and shot the bastardly Nip."

Stuart Upchurch heard an unseen Nip slip in near his foxhole several nights earlier. A sharp-eyed platoon mate finally saw him and threw a grenade. Upchurch heard groans, then the blast of a second grenade — not American, he could tell — and felt bits of flesh blown all over him: the infiltrator had held the second grenade, his own, to his chest. Near midnight, another "little Nip" penetrated even closer than the first until caught by a 10-gauge shotgun from about four feet away. (Marines loved shotguns and filched all they could from supply depots.) The blast tore off some of the second infiltrator's face, severed a hand and blew apart his chest. Still later that night, a third Japanese ran back and forth just outside the platoon's line until he was killed by a cascade of grenades.

Japanese persistence puzzled and frightened the platoon. "They'd come to our lines, we'd kill them and that was that." But the generally diminished success of infiltration into night positions in June wasn't for lack of effort. Many Americans felt a greater threat just because the sorely pressed enemy appeared more reckless in the dreaded dark. "At every rise, you never knew," said a Marine whose company took more casualties after than before the Shuri Line — although that was rare. "Every night, you never knew."

Every daybreak was still greeted with relief before the advance resumed. During the first fortnight in June, Army divisions pushed south on the east coast and Marine on the west toward that last mountain spine in Japanese hands. A participant in this fighting on more level, open ground described it as "being in a one-acre park with someone you had to find behind some bush and kill before he killed you." Makeshift Japanese positions occasionally pinned down units until they were extricated by smoke screens or tanks. And groups of Japanese riflemen still found their targets. An American squad encountered a large rice paddy one day and knew they would be "clay pigeons" there because enemy snipers covered it. But the squad had to cross. They ran in single file, ten yards apart — as fast as they could through the watery, knee-deep mud. Sure enough, some were hit.

Still, the obstacles were less deadly than at the Shuri Line. Far less effective use of terrain by the Japanese made the going much easier through that bushy, scrubby land than under the superbly fortified hills. The strain of the daytime fighting was also reduced by the sharp drop in incoming artillery and mortar fire and many fewer machine gun emplacements.

And the weather improved. In June, the mud dried to make inordinate dust. A single car on prewar Okinawa's dirt roads raised a thick cloud of ochre particles. Now there were fleets of trucks, tanks and self-propelled guns, each of which "temporarily blinded you until the slight breeze could clear the air," an Army officer noted. "It was hot and sultry and the sweat caused the dust to stick to you in thick layers and then furrow by the streams of sweat pouring from face to chest." The dust choked and blinded so regularly near the main roads that one of the principal expert recommendations about equipment after the campaign would be for "goggles and dust respirators [to] be issued to all personnel." Still, all this was easier to take than the mud, as long as there was a steady supply of drinking water.

With less danger creeping, crawling and tiptoeing to Japanese-occupied caves, the Americans could devote relatively more attention to flushing them out. Some units liked to skirt as many caves as possible. More tried not to miss any in their path, since many surely housed the coming night's infiltrators. Dick Whitaker's second wounding, the one that earned him an examination on a hospital ship and a night on an actual cot in his regimental hospital, took place in early June. Feeling better for his rest and hot meal, he returned to his company and found his machine gun squad reorganized in his absence because it had been reduced to shreds on Sugar Loaf. Other survivors were reassigned; he was made a runner for his company commander.* But when the company was advancing in early June and its commander had no messages that had to be delivered at a given time, Whitaker advanced with the others.

> You're moving ahead fairly rapidly until you see a buddy's arm go
> up or you hear a "Get down!" or "Watch out!" Everyone takes
> cover instantly, and you find out the trouble's usually a cave ahead.
> You approach it extremely gingerly. You cover yourself and your
> every nerve strains for more information. You can't tell from the
> mouth how big it is. You don't know who's inside — how many ci-
> vilians, how many Japs, what they're armed with. It could be doz-
> ens getting ready to charge out or shoot from inside. Sometimes
> you hear somebody in there bellow an order as soon as they've
> heard you approach. Next you hear grenades being tapped on hel-

---

*The company commander chose likable Whitaker for this job after his previous runner had been shot through the head while standing beside him. The slain runner's twin served in the same company: two Iowa farmboys so identical that girls didn't know when they playfully switched in the middle of double-dates and so inseparable that they seemed parts of one whole. The nonrunner brother was lying in a hospital, shredded by shrapnel from a grenade at Sugar Loaf, when he heard that his twin had been killed. "It was too hard to understand. The grenade landed right on me and I was spared — but my brother died instantly. Why? That's what still bothers me."

Whitaker generally liked his new job, apart from having to carry a walkie-talkie for the company commander's communications. When it was not in use, he could sling it under his arm, more or less hidden. But he quaked when he had to use it, antenna extended to mark him even more clearly as a priority target. "I hated the thing." And although the new work had him frequently running from squad to squad to warn them to stand by to move out, he generally remained as ignorant of the larger picture as the ordinary footslogger. His announcements were often greeted with questions about where the hell the squads would be going. "In most cases, I didn't have the foggiest goddam notion."

mets to arm them. But all you can see is a black hole with signs of recent use — and that spells death because you're a perfect silhouette if somebody gets you in his sights from inside that blackness. Besides, there were often tunnels or passageways to other caves nearby. The whole thing was spooky. The whole thing spelled DANGER.

To drive the occupants from where they could deliver return fire, the attacking unit fired heavily into cave mouths and gun ports — with the help of tanks, when available (as at Kojo's final position). Then they usually shouted, *"De-te koi! De-te koi!"* — "Come out! Come out!" — loudly and repeatedly, often with bullhorns. A few linguists added *haba-haba* to their vocabulary. Word eventually spread among Japanese soldiers that this new phrase was intended to mean "quickly, quickly." Perhaps it was a contraction of the correct *hayaku, hayaku*, perhaps a confusion with *baka*, "stupid," for some Americans learned to say *De-te koi bab-bab!*, thinking they were adding insult to their command. Others added *shimpachina*, "we'll give you food and water."

Whatever the shout, the "blowing" party went to work if no one complied in a reasonable time. Thousands of caves were "neutralized" by a method so practiced that it would have been routine if not for everyone's knowledge that a second's lapse in concentration could easily be fatal. Part of a team kept the occupants from peeking outside by pouring heavy rifle and BAR fire into the mouth while another part "mounted" or "straddled" the cave and looked for cracks, crevices or an air hole — ventilating shafts in more elaborate installations — on top. From there, one of a variety of explosives was dropped inside, or several in combination.

When explosions sounded inside caves before any payloads were dropped, the suicides they signified were welcomed for easing the work and danger. In that case, valiant or foolhardy American volunteers sometimes entered caves from which no sounds had escaped for an appropriate time — and those men were often appalled.

At one dark opening in a limestone hill, an interpreter repeatedly shouted the "Come out!" call from fifty feet away. A woman in faded pantaloons and a ripped blouse eventually appeared at the mouth with a naked baby on her back and a child of about five at her side. The woman began walking out in response to assurances she wouldn't be harmed — until angry shouts from inside the cave drew her back. Americans had learned that cave occupants often came out only after talking things over with one who had peeked outside. But this was one of the times everyone remained inside. Three blasts soon shook the hill, and Marines found ten shattered bodies in the darkness inside. They included the woman, now headless, and the two children, their arms almost severed. Another baby lay near them. Pieces of infant and parental flesh adhered to the cave walls: a common sight. Many American teams entered caves to see families clustered together, their torsos ripped apart or brains blown out by a grenade exploded by a father or mother who was clutching the children.

But suicide explosions were not relied on for a full flushing because in many cases — including this one, where live civilians huddled at the far end — only some of the occupants killed themselves or others. The attackers had to do most of the work themselves.

Experienced cave blowers tried to save their dynamite satchel charges for the largest targets. A demolitions specialist would crawl to the hole, or sometimes the mouth, with the charge, light it and wait six or seven seconds to prevent the occupants from tossing it back out, which often happened to inexperienced teams. Then the specialist would run. In other cases, fragmentation and white phosphorous grenades were used, or gasoline or napalm that had been brought up in fifty-five-gallon drums ordinarily used for flamethrowers, then poured into the upper openings and ignited with a phosphorous grenade. Holes were occasionally drilled into cave roofs where none existed or were too small, or the ignition grenade or grenades were thrown hard into the mouth. A few Americans used homemade bombs of C-2, an explosive putty packed in a can with a grenade for a detonator, since unaccompanied grenades were rarely effective except in the smallest caves. General Buckner called all this the "blowtorch and corkscrew" method, something highly inflammable being the blowtorch and explosives the corkscrew.

White phosphorus, a marking round also used to make smoke, stuck to the skin and could not be removed by water or any solution available to the 32nd Army or civilians.* Marines liked it not for that but because its smoke provided cover for them when they decided to storm a cave, the most dangerous moment of all. Occasionally American grenades set off munitions stored inside. Although supplies of Japanese shells were scanty in the south, their petric acid sent up an acrid yellow smoke that was more lethal than hand grenades themselves in enclosed spaces. More died from inhaling it than from the explosions and flames.

Similarly, flamethrowers caused many more deaths by suffocation

---

*As fellow Japanese soldiers tried to remove the chemical, the afflicted man burned with a blue flame or, as some saw it, an eerie luminescence that reminded them of massed fireflies. They wiped and scraped in vain; it melted holes in the flesh, often down to the bones. By the time most men lost consciousness, the mud around them also glowed with the phosphorescence.

than by burns, the flames consuming all oxygen in many of the smaller caves. The weapon that most terrified Japanese soldiers was the new long-range flamethrower mounted on a Sherman tank. The 75mm gun had been adapted to shoot a mixture of gasoline and napalm. The range was extended by lengths of flexible hosing attached to the gun barrel to reach caves in unapproachable terrain. Although not the final answer to cave cleaning that American Army planners had hoped for, the tanks helped greatly.

Otherwise, ordinary, man-mounted flamethrowers were used, and it was a measure of the universality of fear even now that those who operated those symbols of World War II inhumanity themselves trembled every time they approached the mouth of a cave — with good reason. Each waddle to the cornered enemy by a man operating a flamethrower was an act of faith and courage. With ninety-five awkward pounds of equipment and volatile liquid strapped to their backs, the volunteers for that hazardous work could not carry a rifle or a carbine — terrifying in itself. (Napalm, which began to be supplied during the campaign, was a boon because it shot farther, allowing the flamethrower to stand back a precious few more yards from the mouth of a cave.) They had to be careful not to trip and fall, in which case they couldn't get up without help and might easily be incinerated by a bullet hitting their own tanks. They couldn't even walk properly, let alone crouch or lie flat; silhouetted against the sky from inside the dark caves, they were vulnerable targets prevented from obeying the infantryman's first instinct to find cover. "You couldn't see them in there, but they could see you — a perfect bull's eye without a rifle," Evan Regal recalled, still a little wide-eyed at the memory. Regal's mother had given him a parting gift when he left the States: a little Bible with covers of lightweight steel. "I kept it in my breast pocket, thinking any bullet that hit me at least wouldn't be in the heart. But it probably wouldn't have stopped a bullet from close up. And no matter how short of ammunition they might be in there, all it would take was just one. My heart pounded when I went out — *every* time. Every time for every man with a flamethrower."*

Sometimes it took a combat eternity of fifteen heart-stopping min-

---

* Regal belonged to the overwhelming majority who felt his opinion of boot camp had become valid only now. At Parris Island, he had hated his drill instructor so passionately that he swore to kill him — "I mean *kill* the sadistic bastard" — if he ever managed to see him in combat. The DI was corraled in a round-up of Stateside Marines to replace the unexpected casualties on Okinawa. "Believe it or not, I happened to meet him on Okinawa after I'd actually been in combat — and I thanked him for saving my life time after time by teaching me right. Because Okinawa was so much worse than the worst day of boot camp that there was no way even to guess until you were there. You won't believe either if I tell you. You have no way to understand, like I didn't."

utes to approach a cave and find the necessary stable footing, which is what made flamethrowing a gallant as well as a revolting activity. Infantrymen learned that casualties among flamethrowers were much higher than their own. ("I stepped over hit flamethrowers like logs," recalled one rifleman after a particularly bad day.) Knowing their vulnerability and value, the riflemen with whom they worked tried to give them as much cover as possible, but it was always too little. Evan Regal and three others were all of the sixteen flamethrowers who survived on Charlie Hill, that small strongpoint just north of Sugar Loaf. The tough farmboy had volunteered for several kinds of dangerous duty before ending with flamethrowers. ("They figured if you were stupid enough to step forward for that, you were also strong enough. And I was too young to know what I was getting into.") Fearless on the outside, he quaked within.

> Every time I had to walk up to a hole, I was scared out of my mind because I was a sitting duck. No matter how much fire your buddies laid down in the mouth of the cave, you had no protection at all, which was the opposite of everything you'd learned about combat. Sometimes you could see their helmets inside, sometimes their eyes staring right at you, or you could hear them talking — and you didn't know how many there were. So you were scared shitless because you never knew when you were going to be hit — but you had to do your job; there was no other way.
>
> You pulled the triggers — there were two — just as soon as you thought your flame could reach them. In it went, and all hell'd break loose. You heard the shuffling and the screaming and almost always some would come running out, their hair and clothes on fire, for the riflemen to pick them off. The heat was just too intense for them to stay inside or they suffocated from lack of oxygen. Gasoline could glance off sometimes, just searing them, but napalm stuck to their skin like jelly glue even when they ran out, and we used napalm most of the time on Okinawa.
>
> But it's hot for the flamethrower too, even when the flame doesn't bounce back from real small caves. And once you squeeze the triggers, you're helpless for those five to seven seconds while the flame shoots out. You're also helpless when your tanks are empty — so you're as good as dead if lots of them come rushing out and the riflemen miss one. That's why the only thing you think about is killing them as quickly as possible. "Oh God, let me get this job over with fast. And let me get them *all* before I get shot." You have utterly no compassion for their screams because you've seen so many of your own cut down and you know it can be *you* the next second; if you give them the slightest chance, they'll put a bullet between your eyes. You also know the Japs never took a single prisoner on Okinawa — they killed everybody if they over-

ran one of our positions. So no matter how many times you've done it, you're *scared*. And all you care about the Japs is that they fry fast.*

To observers ignorant of the occupants' obligations and intentions, cave flushing might have seemed an unfair slaughter of the trapped. To the attackers, it was arduous work fraught with risks, for which they'd have been happy to have an alternative. "This is all a bloody business," one Marine wrote home about those weeks. "But I'm here and digging my foxholes just a foot deeper than the next guy. I've said enough prayers to write a full-size book and thanked God twice as many times."

> *For the next two days we were engaged in blowing caves, pouring gas down the ventilating shafts and dropping hand grenades. Finally we called for flamethrowing tanks . . . We killed the little banks of Japanese that still rallied forth.*
>
> — From a Marine's personal history of the battle

> *When Americans called Japanese soldiers to come out of their caves, they would put hand grenades under their armpits. Outside, they'd get as close as possible to the Americans, throw the grenades and try to fly back into the caves. Not very noble, but there was simply nothing else they could do to resist. Anyway, such tactics only work once. The Americans learned to order us to raise our hands higher.*
>
> — Masao Murata, 15th Independent Mixed Regiment

After the explosions, the attackers readied to resume firing on the mouth unless the blasts had sealed it or bulldozers moved up for that task, as later in June. Nerves remained strained even after a cave had been bombed or scorched and riddled with bullets. Each man in sight of an entrance remained a potential target from within because no volume of fire or explosive could reach all recesses of the larger caves.

When occupants began emerging, natives were often first, sometimes pushed from behind. Almost all Americans tried not to shoot civilians; a large percentage inevitably failed because they had learned to fire at the slightest hint of unusual movement from anyone but children and the elderly. Blasting civilians was a devastating experience for most, especially when they hadn't known who was

---

*Only once did Regal feel remorse for burning humans, when he was sent to torch one of the tombs being used as pillboxes on the same Charlie Hill where he would soon be wounded. He told his officer he couldn't be sure whether an American lying right in the path where he would shoot his flames was dead or alive, but fire from the pillbox was causing so many casualties that the officer ordered him to proceed in any case. "That job tortured me for months, I mean having to shoot so near one of our own. But never shooting Japs."

inside the caves. Dismembered corpses of women and children deeply shocked teams that peeked inside — but they were among the costs of that war, just like gunned-down civilians who emerged. As they couldn't differentiate before the blast between caves sheltering Okies and Japanese and a mixture, they had no way to tell the categories apart as people stumbled out. A religious Marine found it "pretty hard at first" to accept that "our people were shooting human beings who weren't necessarily military. But after I saw what their people — including civilians — did with their hands up, I worried about us, not them. I wanted to leave Okinawa alive!"

What cave occupants did with their hands up was a variety of tricks, performed mostly by soldiers rather than civilians; but many were now wearing the others' clothes. Some feigned surrender just long enough for a thrust into a loin cloth for a final grenade. Although the percentage was small, their number was large enough to ingrain the lesson into the jittery Americans. "A Jap makes a move to give himself up but lifts his arms at the last minute and out tumble two hand grenades," said Evan Regal. "This wasn't talk; I *saw* it. You couldn't trust a single one of them."

That is why all civilians between the ages of roughly ten and sixty were regarded as potential booby traps and why the prime rule was "not to take your eye off the devious gooks for a second" until they could be searched. "If they had anything less than a terrified look on them, fingers tightened on triggers," a veteran remembered. "We were pretty terrified ourselves, and some of us were pretty eager to fire away." "If you didn't feel so goddam threatened yourself, you might have had tremendous pity for the human wreckage in those underground dungeons," a fellow added. "The specimens who came out were horrific. Everybody dizzy with hunger and thirst. Starving Okinawan boys in Japanese uniforms. Younger kids in just pitiful shape, and lots of wounded ones — mutilations — of all ages. The caves worked over by those awesome flamethrowers were simply terrible; I can't describe it. People burned to a crisp, giving off that ghastly smell! But you couldn't have real pity because you yourself were so wound up and concentrating on the danger facing *you*. So if those civilians didn't have that fear on their faces, they were dead."

During the night of June 11, a long line of civilians wrapped in dirty blankets headed toward an American unit from the south. They had nearly passed the forward positions when a vigilant sergeant noticed something wrong. He and his men raked the line with machine gun fire, then found that many of the group were Japanese soldiers with grenades and demolition charges under their blankets.

A few days later, Anthony Cortese, the Marine who had been

shocked to see Sugar Loaf strewn with American bodies, helped throw a heavy charge into a large cave from which no one had emerged in answer to the usual *De-te koi* calls. He might have held back had he known there were many women and children inside, but that wouldn't have solved his problem. "We had to assume Japs were in there too, and what about *them*? Besides, I'd already done a cave where civilians came out first, then a Jap soldier with hands up. Suddenly he throws himself on the ground and the man behind him, dressed as a woman, starts firing from a Nambu strapped to the first guy's back. We all started firing the minute he hit the ground and killed over a dozen civilians together with the two Japs — but what could you do? What you *couldn't* do was take a chance."

Soldiers emerging without civilians were watched as closely, even when they were dazed from the explosions. One barrel-chested Japanese with his hands held high aroused the suspicion of a lieutenant from Captain Owen Stebbins's G–2–22 Company. The lieutenant didn't know precisely why he shot him dead with his carbine from fifteen yards, but as he fired, he alerted his men with a great shout of "Fire in the hole!" This sent them instantly prone, saving their lives when the carbine round caused a large explosion. Barrel Chest had wired himself up to blow apart as many Americans as possible together with himself.

Much later, a handful of Japanese would express regret for such subterfuge in accounts heavy with sorrow, chiefly for themselves. Kenjiro Matsuki, the first baseman for Japan's first professional baseball team, watched fellow soldiers make a white flag in order to inch within grenade-tossing range of Americans. The veteran sportsman was "ashamed" to relate such things, "yet what else could we do at that point?" Perhaps this was a new expression of Japan's old tendency to believe her oppression by foreigners justified exemption from the rules.

Dick Whitaker approached caves with typical anxiety. "You'd see a stick peeking out with a white rag tied to it — but what was on the other end? Civilians? Japs? Japs trying to draw your fire so they could get in a last shot back? Let's say a woman comes out, then a woman with a baby, then a couple of kids — and then a man. Who the hell is he? If he's a soldier, is he armed? Years later, we learned the Japanese Army had a percentage of Okinawan Home Guard conscripts who took their families with them when they retreated. But we had no clear idea *then* of the relationship between civilians and soldiers."

> By mid-June, lots of the Japs were stripped. Maybe they hoped
> there was less chance we'd kill them if they were out of uniform.
> Most had blank faces that revealed nothing whatever, at least to us,

about what they were thinking or feeling. Their hands were usually up and some did a lot of jabbering. Maybe they were saying how sorry they were, how sincerely they wanted peace, how they'd have come out of their cave earlier if they hadn't been afraid their own fanatics would kill them. But maybe *they* were those fanatics, telling their buddies, "Okay, *now* give it to them," or "Two more steps and we'll finish those American devils." We just didn't know whether they were some sorry privates who had had it and truly wanted to surrender or hardcore sergeants who were going to pull another stunt and accomplish their last goal in life of killing you together with themselves. The one thing we did know was that this was totally unpredictable.

Infantrymen find some security in predictability, which on Okinawa further decreased when units pushed on from caves to comb more fields and patches of scrub. The day after Whitaker was made a runner, his new unit was held up atop a slight rise in an area that had been subjected to some preliminary clearing. Privates were rarely told and rarely asked the reason for such happy delays. Sometimes it was to wait for water or supplies or because something had bogged down a neighboring unit. More often, a line needed straightening to make it less vulnerable before the advance was resumed. After the weeks of deluge and mud, a welcome sun was shining. That sun would quickly grow stronger, replacing the hardship of perpetual wet and cold with tropical heat and giving Whitaker one of his indelible memories of that June: a Japanese body — actually hundreds merged into a single image — so bloated by gas and maggots that its skin was about to burst as, he thought, on a boiled knockwurst. But for the moment, no Japanese, dead or alive, was in sight, and one of the small party on the little rise walked down from it and some fifty yards away to relieve himself. Living together like the wolf litter and plagued by dysentery, the others took no notice of his activity — until a friend of Whitaker's named Gene Lewis detected a movement some twenty-five yards from the man squatting in the field. It was a Japanese soldier sneaking up on him with a bayonet tied to a bamboo pole.

Lewis was alongside Whitaker. He dropped to a prone position and whispered, "Watch this!" When his rifle was steady, he shouted to the man in danger, pointing to the advancing bayonet. "Hey Nick, what's *that?*" The sight of the approaching bayonet caused Nick to cut short his business, pull up his pants and grab his rifle, all in one triple-speed movement. When Lewis shot the intruder a second later, the others laughed until their sides ached.

A similar incident two months earlier might have ended tragically for the group instead of providing comic relief. If Lewis had shouted before getting set for a sure shot, the Japanese might have thrown a grenade at Nick. If one of the others had charged down the rise before Lewis fired and the soldier with the bayonet was the point man of a patrol behind him — or bait for an ambush — the charger might have got shot. But before opening the curtain on his little comic number, Lewis knew exactly what was needed to be certain of a kill and did it instinctively, while the others, also instinctively, made no move except to take aim too and survey every bush in sight before they laughed.

What bothered American infantrymen now was that the new, fast-moving advance devalued some of their dearly acquired combat wisdom. The enemy, formerly underground, was now visible — *became* visible from seemingly nowhere, requiring unpracticed split-second responses. Some popped up from what Marines called "spider holes" because, as one put it, "you couldn't believe a human being could fit into such a tiny space." Spider holes seemed to be everywhere. One American tank fired smoke shells into the mouth of a cave and saw wisps rise from thirty nearby holes in the ground — not all occupied but all potentially so. The openings covered with leaves or branches were often undetectable until an American was on top of them, when a "spider" might fire and disappear again.

Whitaker's company shot enemy soldier after enemy soldier on the advance in June without gaining much sense of security. "You're crossing a field of grass up to your waist, advancing in a good line, when somebody suddenly stands up thirty yards away. Is he armed? Is he bait? Does he want to surrender or commit suicide — or does he have a Nambu strapped to his back? Then another pair of hands goes up and another — and it's scary. It isn't what you've grown used to. It happens very fast, and you better react even faster. Even when just one Jap puts up his hands, that never happened before, when they were fighting from their fortifications. A lot of our earlier lessons went out of the window because now you never knew what they'd do, truly surrender, blow themselves up, blow *you* up. They were growing more and more maniacal. Some seemed to switch from one goal to another in a fraction of a second."

On watch at his machine gun as dawn approached on June 11, Melvin Heckt saw a gang of Japanese charge over the sandy ridge where the squad was dug in. Their shouts curdled blood. "Banzai! Marine, you die!" Heckt readied to mow them all down, but the machine gunner's dream turned to nightmare when sand jammed the gun — and his rifle too. One screaming "bastard" dived straight for Heckt, bayonet fixed. The seconds seemed an eternity. Heckt tried and failed to get the machine gun working. He was certain his time had come — until other men in the squad opened up and killed about twenty Japanese as close as five yards from the position. Heckt discovered the man who charged him had no rounds in his chamber. "Just a bayonet. That's enough. If he could have fired, I wouldn't be writing this today."

This mixture of courage and folly kept American nerves stretched. When some of Whitaker's company were hit one day and Whitaker's walkie-talkie was out, Lieutenant Sherer, his company commander, sent him to fetch stretcher bearers. Whitaker ran out and returned with them, by which time the line had advanced. He was alone with Sherer, who asked whether a nearby pile of rocks had been cleared. Whitaker thought it hadn't and approached it as ordered: a small pile, as if for making a wall, with a kind of porthole that could easily have been for a rifle. His entire body thumped to his heartbeat. When he was close enough to shoot from a good angle, his submachine gun jammed: the one he had stolen from the Army mess tent. Although nearly paralyzed with fear, he managed to inch still closer and was able to drop a grenade in the hole. He was saved, but shaken — a daily or hourly occurrence.

One of Whitaker's patrols brought him to a field hospital more hurriedly makeshift than the one where Tadashi Kojo rested during his withdrawal from Shuri. A pathetically emaciated Japanese lay prostrate on a bunk, waiting for an American corpsman's examination. The picture of defeat seemed too weak to move — until he pulled a grenade from his loin cloth, jerked out its pin, and hit it on his fist to detonate it. A member of Whitaker's team shot him before he could throw it — and confirmed one more time for one more patrol the detestable dictum that the only good Jap was a dead one. Whitaker would not take the slightest risk involving the slightest trust or "humanity" to find out when the maxim wasn't true.

On patrol another day, he approached a sparse pine forest bordering an open area. Venturing where no Marine had set foot before was reason enough for extreme caution — but just as he entered the woods, his weariness and hunger instantly disappeared and his senses were turned on like those of a deer that smells a bobcat: he had spied a little pile of fresh human excrement. The next twenty minutes, until he moved on without incident, strained his every nerve beyond measure. His much lessened fear of enemy firepower had been replaced by fear of the uncertainty. The Japanese had never fought in ordinary ways; now, pushed from their fortifications, they could be counted on only to do something crazy.

Medical, veterinary, supply and other personnel were brought in to make good the losses. As a result, the [Japanese] line units consisted of men with a variety of specialties, none of which was combat.
  — Thomas Huber, military historian

Our forces are without planes, warships or tanks. Because we are abandoned, we have no hope other than to die resisting. This is said to be the resolution of everyone from the army commander [Ushijima] down. Our medium artillery is destroyed and we have not even one piece left . . . We have come to our end in this despicable land. How I would like to return safely!
  — From a diary found on a Japanese soldier

Thirty to forty of our soldiers were lying on top of one another and I heard faint groans indicating that many were still alive. There was no way for me to save them. The three others in my group joined me and we conferred. There was nothing to do but retreat.
  — Kenjiro Matsuki on his retreat from a key defensive position a mile east of Kochi Ridge

Death was no longer for victory but only for the sake of dying.
  — Shigemi Furukawa about the same period

The 32nd Army's "crazy" behavior now was caused by its squeeze between the obligations of the national military ethic and the extremely unequal battle conditions. Over sixty thousand men had been killed in May, in ways much like those which wore down Tadashi Kojo's 1st Battalion. The reduction of Kojo's thousand men to the dozen survivors was similar to the losses among all units defending the Shuri Line. Although Iwo Jima, where less than 5 percent of the garrison survived, was slightly worse for the Japanese proportionately, its twenty-two thousand defenders were less than a third the number already dead on Okinawa.

Some Wehrmacht units defending Normandy the previous summer deeply impressed Allied commanders with their ability to hold out and even counterattack despite appalling casualties. But many German weapons, unlike Japanese, were better than the corresponding Allied ones. And the panzer divisions that fought with extraordinary skill and tenacity despite their dismal prospects did not nearly match the Japanese feat of endurance on Okinawa. By this time, most of bloodied troops — there was only a small number still uncommitted in the far south — were living with their own excrement, drinking muddy water from bomb craters, dying of gangrene. They had little to look forward to beyond being killed by enemy shelling, strapping explosives to themselves to become "human bullets" against tanks, or going on suicidal night raids. Perhaps only a Japanese Army could have endured that, and sustained its awesome seventy-two thousand casualties by the beginning of June, without mutinying — or coming to its senses, as most Japanese too would understand "sense" after the war. The wonder was not that organization and discipline were deteriorating but that they had remained intact so long.

But something essential had changed with Ushijima's decision to withdraw from the Shuri Line. The news shook even units less shattered than Kojo's. Gloom stalked the 32nd Army.

Koichi Ito, Kojo's classmate at the Military Academy, was among the regular field officers determined to continue inspiring his men with a display of the old composure and confidence. Ito, whose battalion had made the only successful advance in the ill-fated May 4 counteroffensive, remained resolute though he knew the prospects full well. His pride in being Japanese and self-respect as an Army officer kept his haughty captain's persona intact; his thoughts were concentrated on honor, duty and anything that might hurt the enemy. "When we lost comrades, we were certain we would follow them sooner or later. Of course we held our lives dear, but our deepest wish was not to be captured. The wounded were sometimes killed to prevent this when we withdrew. I myself couldn't kill mine, so I ordered them provided with means for suicide, accepting that some might choose not to use them. If those men therefore became prisoners of the enemy, that couldn't be helped. Some were weak, some dishonorable, as in any human group. But I was determined to give all I had for the sake of Japan and the Imperial Army."

Thanks to the importance the Japanese attached to their leaders, a large number of battalion commanders remained alive — but, as in many cases like Kojo's, too physically and mentally exhausted by their weeks in the line to radiate the prescribed confidence. And without similar shielding, a great proportion of company commanders — the lieutenants and junior captains — were *not* alive. This had a directly detrimental effect because a leaderless Japanese unit was not considered a unit at all. Contrary to the American practice of promoting the most senior subordinate, such Japanese units were often regrouped into others. Now the 32nd Army's great number of losses and last-minute reorganizations lowered morale even further.*

* The plummeting of morale was little slowed by new variants of rumors about impending salvation, some intentionally circulated. Japanese officers promised their men a counterlanding, aided by airborne troops, but only if the 32nd Army held on until June 20. Elaborations of this myth had the 9th Division returning in triumph from Formosa and, once again, the Combined Fleet and Air Force joining in the massive, decisive attack.

American rumors were less wild but also plentiful. Men of the Marine units that landed

Many Japanese were beyond being inspired in any case. Holding on to the main fortifications had given them some compensation for their enormous losses. As long as headquarters continued to function beneath Shuri Castle, fortitude, poetic belief and self-hypnosis sustained the sense of accomplishment essential for morale. No people were more moved by symbols than the Japanese — in this case, the Japanese pluck, resolve, strength and ability to prevail over richer Westerners that was symbolized by the Shuri Line. It was testimony to Japan's invincibility. And because military leaders' display of confidence was so important to the surpassing Japanese spirit that "guaranteed" victory, the decision to abandon the symbol signified despair. The shock and pain of evacuating broke the will of many, stripping them of their moral stamina just as exit from the last of the major fortifications stripped them of their best — as they saw it, their only — protection.

Study later established that the critical factor of combat stress is its duration, even more than its severity. American medical personnel on Okinawa — and the infantrymen themselves — needed no research for this, knowing the importance of their withdrawals from the line for rest periods. To contend unrelentingly with the inhuman emotional and physical stress would have been more than they could imagine — and rightly so because psychologists found that all men, including the best and bravest, eventually break. (A solid month of unrelieved combat produced some degree of battle fatigue in nearly 100 percent of American troops.) It was a shining credit to regular officers like Kojo, to Japanese notions of service and loyalty in general, and to the whole of Japanese society that so few of the defenders had cracked. Or it was a condemnation of that society, since far more would have lived if officers and senior soldiers had not been unthinkingly resolute and blindly loyal.

In any case, their resolution began snapping now. The loss of faith caused by leaving Shuri undermined inner resources. The rarity of friendly artillery's dulcet roar was another dark sign, as well as a tactical deprivation. A few of the 10 percent of Japanese big guns not destroyed or abandoned were broken down into pieces for futile transport farther south, where they would not fire again. An infantry unit on the dismal trek south came upon a single heavy gun still intact. With no mechanical help of any kind, its crew was struggling to tug it, centimeters at a time, through the deep mud of a devastated

---

on the Oroku Peninsula told themselves they would be pulled off Okinawa when the peninsula was cleared. "High Command predicts June 10 as end of the struggle," Melvin Heckt recorded in his diary a week earlier. "We will then board ship and sail to Guam."

road in a driving rain — a miserable spectacle repeated often during the withdrawal.

Although no people easily accept defeat, the proud Yamato men who had sacrificed so much for "inevitable" victory found it particularly incomprehensible. They had not necessarily believed that the brave would live and the cowardly would die. But they had expected at least to see some evidence that the *side* of the brave and virtuous would be rewarded. Now this hope, which had helped Captain Kojo's men die stoically at Kochi Ridge, was gone.

The decimation of the 12th Independent Infantry Battalion had begun earlier than for Kojo's unit — on L-day itself, near the landing beaches. Private Kenjiro Matsuki was dismayed by the American bombing that went on "all day long, relentlessly," followed by naval shelling "all night long," as if the purpose was to destroy "not only humans but the last ant." In ten days, 350 men remained of the battalion's proud, dedicated fifteen hundred. The remnants retreated, one unit eventually to a vital strongpoint at Maeda, two miles almost due north of Shuri and a mile west of Kojo's position at Kochi. Not long before the last of Kojo's force there was overrun, that unit withdrew. On the way, Private Matsuki heard a group of fellow soldiers making a night attack from a shelter. They left under cover of darkness and prepared to assault an enemy-held escarpment. After the booming order of "Attack!," Matsuki heard machine gun fire from the American position, then a howling of "Whooooah . . ." and "Ohweee" — "a tragically heroic" sound that lasted for several minutes at the escarpment while enemy machine guns continued firing. Experience had told Matsuki that most dying soldiers called for their mothers rather than shouting anything more glorious, as in Army hype. But now he actually heard a chorus of the celebrated "Emperor! Banzai!" "That night, for the very first and perhaps the last time, I heard the brave words — all they had left in their bodies — seemingly jerked out by some great force." He later learned that sixty of the ninety men in the assault had been killed. (American soldiers of the 383rd Infantry Regiment found fifty-eight bodies.) Then the former first baseman, an independent spirit by Japanese standards, proceeded to Shuri with three others.

We knew American tanks and soldiers would overrun this field in the morning, so we decided to dash the 300 meters in one breath, having discarded all our bundles. Some hesitated to abandon their gas masks because they might reveal military secrets, but I convinced them I'd thrown mine out long before. We all carried hand grenades for suicide . . .

I went first again [after taking refuge from a blazing machine gun in a rain-filled bomb crater]. The flares had lost some of their power as dawn neared, and some morning mist had formed: a heavenly gift, I thought as I ran with all my remaining strength . . . I stumbled four or five times but no machine gun fired. We'd stayed in the crater so long that maybe the enemy tired of waiting or thought we died there . . .

I ran up Shuri Road and flattened myself against the hillside. I couldn't stop grinning when the others appeared too, but those professional soldiers still worried about leaving their gas masks behind, which they seriously thought might get them court-martialed. I was reassuring them that we could take all we wanted from dead bodies when American trench mortars started firing, seemingly a hundred at once, into the field we'd just crossed and extending onto the road. They made their weird hissing sound, like escaping steam.

We jumped into a long, tunnel-like trench at the foot of the hill. My eyes got used to the dark after about ten steps and I nearly fell over in surprise: this was being used for serious casualties. They were lying in twos for the full length of the trench, 200 or 300 meters — so many that there was no place to step . . . Noticing us, someone pleaded, as if with his last breath, "Hey, please kill me."

That started a chorus. "Hey, kill me quick. Please!" Some must have been dead already because there was little movement as we picked our way around their heads, but someone grabbed my leg. "There are rifles in this trench," he said in a fairly strong voice. "Shoot the ones still alive. We can't stand just waiting to die. Please. *Please!*"

But I couldn't do it, not even to answer their earnest pleas . . . Leaving the trench . . . I prayed for the peace of their souls. Then a shell fell right on the road. Shuri was still a kilometer away. We'd be trapped by tanks unless we hurried, so we decided to run along the foot of the road — which, when I started down the bank and landed on it, felt like a balloon . . . It turned out to be a makeshift cemetery, with rows and rows of corpses covered by a thin layer of soil.

As a series of last-second miracles saved Matsuki from American bullets, he would encounter more grievously hurt soldiers begging for help or an end to their misery. If Kojo had to fight tears when confronted by his former trainee with the fresh amputation, such sights understandably shook all the nonprofessional soldiers who saw them. And few were spared the sight. The forced abandonment of masses of wounded during the retreat dealt another fearsome blow to morale.

The blow struck hardest at veterans of victorious campaigns in China and elsewhere. There buddies would dash to injured men, carry them back, and do all in their power to see that treatment was obtained. But even those with no previous combat experience were silently mortified by failing the wounded now, no matter how necessary it was. Four litter bearers were carrying a wounded man when a flare suddenly ignited directly over them. They dropped their burden and ran into a neighboring field. "We all hated being tied to a stranger at a time like that. We didn't feel sorry for the stranger. We didn't think about helping him. We only thought about saving our own lives." A warrant officer lamented that "there was no room in comrades' hearts to delay and care for the injured because we were losing too badly; it was too dangerous. When the next man went down, an animal instinct of survival prevailed."

Early in April, an older recruit had grieved over his first witnessed death. A lieutenant snapped that it would be impossible for friends to care for the dying from then on. "Hundreds — no, thousands — of you will be blown off the earth. Be resigned to that fate." Still, friends had been able to offer some sort of care, if not medical, during April and May. Now good men were pained and shamed by the desertion of injured troops and by the Army that reduced them to that.

Most of the wounded who had been left behind in great numbers did not live to spread their gloom. But those determined to join the withdrawal were the worst off. Aside from their injuries, they were traumatized by fear of being left behind. Yet soldiers from other units were as likely to show them indifference or coldness as compassion.

Masao Murata, a third-generation actor of that name, had been performing with a respected theater in Japan when he was drafted a second time, after a four-year stint in Manchuria. That put the staunch patriot in the Mixed Independent 15th Regiment and took him to Sugar Loaf, where a grenade gashed his back and right hip at dawn on May 16, the day before Dick Whitaker was hit in the hand. When Murata's unit was ordered to retreat, he was "abandoned," in his own word, with two dried biscuits. No one was available to dress his wounds. They became infected and grotesquely swollen. His departing comrades assured him that someone would return to fetch him, but how could they do so when they were retreating? Of course no one returned. The loss of a sense of unity and common purpose set off a dismal cycle. The struggle for survival was beginning to extinguish all other motives and actions and to make the wounded and the ill a liability and burden.

Almost all serious wounds made brave men frightened ones, the transformation aided by Japanese medical care. A colonel on the other side of Shuri from Sugar Loaf made a selection for *kiri-*

komi — suicidal hand-to-hand combat — at that same time. The elect unit used to shout "Banzai!" going into battle, but a chatter of teeth now echoed inside their cave. Most of the twenty men the colonel picked were seriously wounded and chilled with fear. Murata too had thought more about what he owed the Emperor than about his own welfare until his injuries punctured his courage, allowing fear to attack for the first time. The difference between wounded and fit men was widened by the most terrifying fear of being left behind.

While Whitaker's first wound was being treated at the battalion aid station north of Sugar Loaf, Murata crawled down from his hill and wandered alone for three days. On the fourth, he met two heavily bandaged soldiers — good luck, because he could ask where they'd been treated. The field hospital they cited — more good luck, for not all soldiers of another unit volunteered such information — was a cave dug into the side of a nearby hill. Murata dragged himself there but was turned away when he identified his unit: that facility did not serve the Mixed Independent 15th Regiment. The doomed man begged through his pain. His bloated hip remained untreated. Still, he was refused admission and directed to another hospital on the next hillside. Then an officer happened by who recognized the talented actor from his appearance at an evening of entertainment for the troops just before L-day. That officer allowed him in.

Murata felt great relief when his hip was lanced and bandaged. Told to move on, he began limping from the cave between rows of softly moaning patients without hands and legs — who gave the former actor an inspiration. The officer who admitted him and the medics who treated his wounds were not in sight. He asked some patients to move a bit and managed to squeeze in among them, then joined the moaning. He even managed to get a bowl of thin rice soup when nurses distributed food. (Patients in better condition got a rice ball laced with barley.)

The next morning, a medical officer told the patients they would be leaving after dark because Americans were advancing on the cave. The nonambulatory were to take "the appropriate action." But no means for suicide were distributed, and Murata stood at the head of the procession leaving the cave at nightfall. A stick given him by a nurse served as a cane but his useless right leg caused so many falls in the rain and slimy mud that he soon found himself at the rear, "walking" on his buttocks and hoping the dirt wouldn't finish him off by reinfecting his hip. Part of a field artillery unit passed him, struggling to carry parts of their gun. Murata fervently wished his wound were in an arm so that he could join those living souls — or *any* group. (He didn't guess this one was headed for almost certain death at Mabuni, site of General Ushijima's new headquarters cave.) Alone again and crawling only at night, he took forty-eight hours to cover three miles to a village midway to his destination. (Three miles in forty-eight hours was a good pace for the thousands who had to crawl; the same distance took other wounded three to four nights.) He kept going another two nights, his mouth now too blistered to touch his hardtack. But of all his tortures, the greatest were thirst and the thought of dying alone.

By now, all medical facilities except a few in the extreme south were in no better condition than those visited by Murata and by Captain Kojo at Kochinda. Their demoralized personnel were also near the end of their line.

Since the Japanese had no means of evacuating their wounded even if a hospital ship had magically arrived, all casualties had been treated on the island, the luckiest in the Haebaru Army Hospital where young Ruriko Morishita worked as a nurses' aide. Ikuo Ogiso, a medic from the mountains north of Tokyo, was attached to a smaller facility, the 2nd Field Hospital. Highly motivated Ogiso had been promoted to private first class by officers who appreciated his diligence and dedication. In June, however, all medical efforts came to an end.

A wing of Ogiso's hospital, already moved from the north to a village elementary school six miles below the landing beaches, was again moved farther south. It took great effort for him to find the designated cave in the dark, under a blanket of enemy bombs and shells. A villager's instructions to look for a stand of pine trees didn't help; no tree of any kind remained. Ogiso's despair grew when he did reach the cave, although he was hardly new by then to appalling medical facilities. It was disgusting to spend more than a minute in the foul hole with the walls and ceiling oozing moisture. Two days later, thirty patients were delivered to the "hospital," habitation of which would have been a danger even to men in impeccable health. There were no sanitation arrangements. Soon over two hundred gravely wounded soldiers were crammed into rock and mud thick with excrement. Few horror movies can hint of the noisome squalor of life in the dungeonlike grotto. It was lit by the flames of occasional oil lamps that cast weird shadows of stalactites on soldiers "who were lying almost on top of each other, all looking like creatures suffering the torments of hell." Sounds of weeping, groaning and shrieking — as some wounded became deranged — echoed from the walls and through the "nauseating, suffocating" smell of their sweat, blood, pus and wastes. Industrious, resolute Ogiso wondered whether he was in hell itself.

The luckiest patients lay where they could wet their throats by holding their mouths open to catch drops from the ceiling. The others remained racked with thirst on top of their excruciating wounds, swarming with flies and maggots. "Each time the bandages are changed, white maggots as thick as a child's little fingertip dropped from the gaping wounds — hundreds of them, all sucking the bloody pus." With no time to pick them off with tweezers, aides used gauze soaked in creosol. Proper medical supplies were so quickly exhausted that "the word *treatment* became a euphemism . . . All we could do was to disinfect the wound, place medicated gauze over the spot and bandage it." Soon bandages could be changed only every second day, then every third, although patients whose turn was postponed wept with pain. When the borax ran out, the eyes of a gaunt, blinded soldier, thought to be a graduate of the prestigious Imperial University, were washed with plain water.

Five Army "comfort girls" pleaded for refuge and were taken into the cave. Their Sisyphean labor to dispose of the human wastes had almost no effect, with two hundred gravely ill men jammed side by side. Soon the tiny space held an inconceivable 270 people. The horror paralyzed the medical officer, Lieutenant Mizoguchi. A pediatrician in civilian life, Mizoguchi had gone into a stupor at his first sight of the unoccupied cave. Now he lay immobilized there, his eyes closed and body rigid. (Ogiso would later be told that the lieutenant waded into the sea to drown himself below the site of the 32nd Army's last headquarters cave.)

In *his* civilian life, Private Ogiso had also been an actor.* But now, with only a medic's sketchy medical training, Ogiso became a de facto surgeon, cutting open and sewing up and amputating the limbs of a stream of wounded men because no one else could. Amputation was by saw, without anesthesia or antiseptics. Other wounded begged for admission but, as at other facilities, they were turned away unless they belonged to units served by that wing of the hospital. Inside, tetanus patients, doomed for lack of serum, had to be separated; a trellis partition was constructed beneath the lower bunks. "It was worse than a pigsty built over the quagmire of blood and pus." There

---

*Masao Murata was in theater; Ogiso made movies. During the early years of the war, while slogans such as "One hundred million, one mind" girded the home front, enthralled young Ogiso succumbed to Garbo, Dietrich, Cooper, Gabin, Chaplin and other "gods and goddesses" whose films he saw again and again. He was among the 25 — of 6000 — applicants taken by the Japan Film Art School in 1943. The following year, he began acting with a small company and continued until he was drafted.

was no medication for gangrene cases either, who "tossed about in unbearable agony" as their limbs turned dark and swelled grotesquely. They screamed for days — "It hurts! Please kill me!" — before going rigid. A patient who blew himself up with a hand grenade also killed the man next to him.

If cave medicine hadn't been one of the battle's dirty secrets, it might have provided the starkest measure of the inequality in the two sides' resources. Since mid-April, Americans had seen no Japanese plane challenge hundreds of their own on constant bombing and strafing runs. General Buckner's men took command of the sky as they had taken command of the sea from the first.* What they couldn't know was that the imbalance in medical treatment was even greater. Ninety percent of the Japanese on Okinawa would die before they ever knew.

The way of bushido *is to die — but in this battle where we and the enemy stand on different dimensions of metal and supplies, it completely loses its meaning. Something is now beginning that has had no precedent in Japan's military history: death without meaning.*
— Shigemi Furukawa

The road [to Itoman in the deep south] was full of . . . injured soldiers on crutches of sticks, crawling soldiers with their legs blown off going east and west as they hoped to escape to safety.
— Norio Watanabe

I hoped to die instantly. That's what I thought about day in and day out, not about how to live.
— Kenjiro Matsuki

The withdrawal was a trauma for the nonwounded too. Many trudged south in a daze, dumb with accumulated horrors, bereft of a hope that any effort now could produce even momentary tactical success. The retreat from one besieged position to the next was a jumble of corpses, groans and caves turned into crematoria by American fire. The "victory" of blocking the enemy had ended; the remaining goal of fighting to the last man to give the mainland more time and its people more inspiration was much less appealing. Kenjiro Matsuki sensed that "the battle had virtually ended and what followed was guerrilla warfare — a mop-up of us remnants." His decimated unit "walked in silence, like sheep heading for a slaughterhouse." The ambulatory patients of the main branch of Ogiso's

---

*The sky above the American fleet, still thick with kamikazes, was a very different matter.

field hospital — evacuating "inch by inch" in the driving rain and thick mud — seemed "the chilling sight of defeat itself."

Some ignored the danger of court-martial and threw away their ammunition and helmets, unable to carry the weight. A few comforted themselves with a wild rumor that they were going south to be picked up by submarine and taken home to Japan. Others still talked of the massive Japanese landing, now promised by some officers for late June. But the sight of other units as wasted as their own further unnerved them.

Bad led to worse. When the weather cleared, retreating units became prime targets. One transport company was caught by salvos from an American battleship. It had set out with 150 vehicles and arrived with fewer than thirty. A large explosion greeted men about to enter a southern village. For a split second, a brilliant bluish light silhouetted the soldiers of a platoon. "When we reached the spot where the soldiers had been we saw nothing, nobody — our fighting men had disappeared from the face of the earth like a dream!"

An exhausted soldier of the 15th Independent Mixed Regiment was dragging a badly wounded leg on June 1 when he ran into Colonel Seiko Mita, his regimental commander. The de facto leader of Sugar Loaf's magnificent defense was walking "as if he'd lost his mind." Mita later got hold of himself and told everyone in his entourage to continue fighting if he could carry a rifle — but at that point, the wounded soldier was shattered to see that the regiment of some five thousand was down to about twenty men. With the stragglers scattered elsewhere, the 15th Independent Mixed Regiment was at 1 percent of its fighting strength.

Within a week, the first deserters would slip away, some in civilian clothes, a few with the look of "wild dogs," as one frightened soldier saw them. By the middle of the month, the worst-off units would be a rabble "skulking in holes and trenches," in a journalist's words, "wandering through the countryside looking for food and water." Although some twenty-five thousand Japanese, a full division in number, were still coming, going and hiding in the remaining patch of friendly land, many from broken units hardly knew the names of their fellow soldiers or officers. They were becoming the loneliest of crowds. Some would show their despair by turning on civilians and even soldiers from other units, fighting them for food and shelter. They were not provided even with that in their new positions.

The Japanese reorganization, chiefly a consolidation of regimental and battalion rumps, was largely a paper operation. In the field, it was far too late for anything but last-minute preparations except where units had been stationed earlier — most important, teams of the 9th Division in the last high ground two miles short of the southern tip. Even those unfinished works were critically short of supplies. Elsewhere, field commanders lacked the time, resources and energy to fortify or properly provision their new positions.

Apart from that last mountain spine and the ridges leading to it, much of the south was too flat for defensive strongpoints. Fields were scorched, houses demolished, flares lit up the night. And although the limestone and coral held even more caves than up north — as the American cave flushers were discovering — they were still too few and small for the remnants of Ushijima's army, not to mention a far greater number of civilians equally eager for shelter. Besides, the northern caves were so different from the unimproved ones in the south that it is misleading to use the same word for both.

Men who had grown to hate those old sanctuaries now looked back at them with longing. The major installations of the outer and inner Shuri Line had had the comfort and security of concrete, electricity and ventilation. Even the lesser ones had the luxury of leveled floors, drainage and provisions. Shigemi Furukawa, the schoolteacher now in the 81st Independent Antiaircraft Artillery Battalion, noted the difference, starting with the disappearance of a town that had delighted him earlier.

> The town of bright, red-roofed houses shining beautifully in the sun from the hill to the beach no longer existed. Instead, there were mountains of rubble, scorched lumber, scorched earth. Our company marched through and went into . . . our last stronghold.
>
> This cave sloped down from its mouth. With no drainage whatever, it was a slimy morass underfoot. Worse still, the mouth was the only entrance, so there was no ventilation. Accumulated carbonic acid gas was always on the point of extinguishing the lamp.
>
> Even for soldiers whose sole weapon was endurance, living with the oil, smoke, gas and wet — and with all the odors of human existence — brought unbearable suffering. Life in that cave took us to the brink of insanity. After two or three days, I thought I'd prefer to go out and die rather than remain in such hell. "To die like this, pushed inch by inch to the wall by the enemy — I can't stand it." Although nothing green grew outside any longer, those imprisoned in the agony of that miserable cave began to long for the sun and some air before we died.

Furukawa would endure two more months in that cave and worse ones — not so much places for fighting from as for cowering in. Other than having the luck to survive, he was no exception; most southern caves and holes in the ground, carved out by eons of rain, subterranean streams and tides when the coral was still on the ocean floor, were equally craggy and creepy. A few days of frantic digging in early June managed to slightly improve a selection of them, but many remained pitch-black dungeons. Their fetid atmosphere — air so thick as almost to lose its transparency — suffocated the packed occupants. Rank moisture dripped from stalactites that left ceilings too low to stand even when their tips were chopped off. The floors were pools of mud and slime or rocks and coral too jagged for sitting or lying on without pain. But although every surface was wet, drinking water was rarely available or was polluted by the waste of dozens of men who relieved themselves on rocks bordering the underground streams. Those not too wounded to move dared not even dash outside any longer.

The new 32nd Army headquarters cave was better than most, partly because of its position on a tall cliff above the village of Mabuni. The long, twisting cave was near the summit of Hill 89, as the approaching Americans would name the cliff. It had a spectacular view of the Pacific from the mouth facing the sea. But even this improved natural cave was a far cry from the elaborate tunnel beneath Shuri Castle.

Out in the field, the shortage of ammunition was surpassed by a more critical shortage of water. A man wounded near Kakazu felt his body "didn't have a drop of water in it; I was skin and bones like a dead man. I became a slave to the desire for water. Water! Water! Water! I was crazy with thirst." That was in April, and in a medical cave. When the days turned fiercely hot in June and water provisioning became as erratic as all other, thirsts became unbearable, especially when the fear of slaughter became intense. While the great American logistical operation was delivering water, however foul-tasting, in trucks that drove almost to the front, Japanese were ceaselessly tormented even in sectors temporarily free of fighting.

Their food was also much worse now, although hunger was less insistent than thirst. Those with sacks of rice often had to cook it in the muddy liquid of stagnant puddles, soldiers taking turns blowing at the pine needles that served for fuel until their eyes burned and their lungs were bursting. Carbon monoxide caused cooks to drop utensils without being aware of it. The K- and C-rations disdained by Americans represented enormous luxury to soldiers who found the leavings on nocturnal forays. As for arms, the best-organized units had managed to arrive with some of their machine guns and light mortars. But others had only rifles, some of which were too fouled by mud to shoot more than several rounds without jamming.

Some men lived for weeks in those holes where ten minutes would have seemed the human limit. The mud grew thicker and thicker with their wastes, in which they slept, squeezed together and almost submerged. The overcrowding went from impossible to unbearable to inconceivable. Some men literally suffocated to death. "So this was how we were to breathe our last — trapped in a hole without air, without water, without the space to kneel and pray during one's final moments," one soldier ruminated. "I had expected all along to perish when the Americans came. But I'd visualized a very different death for myself; I'd hoped to die under an open blue sky with puffy white clouds."

Still more people pressed through the openings and into the holes to escape the rain of metal outside. The shelling of the few square miles still in Japanese hands naturally became more concentrated, rendering pigeons and military dogs "utterly useless" as messengers, in the measure of a soldier in a communications unit. Even Americans who blessed each shell thought the dawn-to-dusk bombardment "awesome" at a time when the word retained much of its original meaning. "All we cared about was to devastate, since one less buddy to be killed was everything," an infantryman remembered of those weeks. "And devastate we did — 155s, 75s, heavy mortars coordinated with the naval guns landed together and ripped the land apart." One of the rare Japanese who wanted to surrender carefully chose a place that promised the best chance without his being shot by the enemy or his own side. But he found it impossible to walk ten steps on the first road leading there. Another was convinced that low-flying Grummans and Chance-Voughts, their pilots now hardly troubled by antiaircraft fire, were "determined not to miss a single ant" with their bombing and strafing.*

Such determination helped turn the fighting itself far more lopsided than at the Shuri Line, where the losers exacted their heavy toll. Just as Japanese field commanders feared, their units, virtually unsupported by artillery fire, were far less effective than before. When they did sortie from their refuges, they were less skilled at maneuvering and concealing themselves, and made themselves easy targets by running from their makeshift positions when those positions were shelled by American tanks. Most Japanese saw themselves as the objects of a round-up. "This went beyond any concept of war,"

---

*This was closer to reality than to the hyperbole of the terrified. When Samuel Hynes's squadron began night flying in May, "any light — a truck's headlights, a fire, a lighted doorway — was to be fired on . . . [One night] I looked around for something to attack, somebody boiling a pot of tea or lighting his way to the toilet, but I could see nothing."

Hynes flew a plane nicknamed the Pregnant Turkey from Kadena Airfield, which Tadashi Kojo had originally been assigned to defend. Toward the end, he found almost nothing on which to unload his four 500-pound bombs, eight rockets and belts of machine gun ammo. After the last strike, on June 19, against "some trivial target" on the island, the squadron joker assured the intelligence officer he'd scored a direct hit on a three-hole privy.

an analytically inclined gunner observed. "This was sheer one-sided destruction and killing."

Those were conditions that begat dissension. If American service-men still engaged in interservice and even interunit rivalry, it was far more likely among the men facing annihilation. Japanese soldiers had to be part of a unit to share food. Straggling groups from Kojo's 22nd Infantry Regiment would share none of theirs with men from a sister regiment, the 32nd, of the same 24th Division. Only a small percentage were truly demoralized at this stage, but an infection of spirit began that would speed their inevitable end and also greatly increase civilian casualties.

Many caves housed remnants of several units, a circumstance that helped spread the infection. The dire conditions and prospects dis-solved the cohesion that had bound together fighting units — as small as infantry companies, in some cases. One man watched his company "disintegrate in morale, discipline and even sanity."

Previous losses had been heaviest among the bravest and best. Now the survivors, those slightly wounded or ill, felt the fight go out of them. Some feared fellow soldiers — who, for example, would rage against all cooking because smoke might escape from the mouth of the cave and reveal its position. Cliques shouted death threats to one another. "Since the unit ceased to exist," observed one wretched sol-dier, "there wasn't a shred of law or order among us. No one outside one's little group cared what happened to anyone else."

The inevitability of death did not eliminate fear of it. More than the Americans, most Japanese felt they were alive only through a series of amazing reprieves: squatting a centimeter or second away from a bullet, being shielded by a fellow soldier's body, knowing someone with access to medical treatment. Tens of thousands thanked God or their lucky stars for their miracles, for bodies housing the strongest wills still wanted to live. When the field hospital disbanded where Masao Murata, the former actor with the wounded hip, had been given his skimpy treatment, he crawled toward a village near the cliff where he had waited to crush the feinted American landing on L-day, twelve weeks earlier. Four days later, he was near collapse, hav-ing had no food other than the rice soup he had wangled in the hospital. Then another stroke of luck: he found a well and drank his fill. And another: villagers who came to draw water that night rec-ognized the mud-covered heap. They took him to a tomb and fed him horse meat and white rice, "very rare those days." His feast after his fast brought severe diarrhea. Still, he savored a day of blissful peace from enemy fire, gazing at a blue sky — until a child reported

Americans headed their way. Soon he and the civilians heard the
enemy soldiers call "*De-te koi, de-te koi!*" The civilians hid Murata behind a group of urns in a corner of the tomb and spread a kimono
over him.

> The Americans called again for us to come out. The Okinawans
> obediently did. Soon [one of the women] came back and told me
> the Americans were taking them away as prisoners. "So I'm going,"
> she said. "There's rice in the pot and meat in the bowl — please
> don't throw away your life."
>   Then three American soldiers entered with automatic weapons.
> I was never, never so very terrified as at that moment. They were
> stripped to the waist, their tattoos quite visible. I felt my hair stand
> on end. Although my mother was a devout Nichiren Sect Bud-
> dhist, I am an atheist. For the first time, I fervently chanted to my-
> self, "Mother, please save me!" . . . My knees started shaking vio-
> lently. I had to push one down with the other to keep them from
> rattling the urns. I hadn't quite succeeded in controlling them
> when my diarrhea started again . . .

The Americans' search seemed to last hours. They slashed rice
sacks with knives and twice shone a flashlight into Murata's corner.
Finally they left and he escaped into the hills with a hope of making
his way to the north to join a Japanese force supposedly still operating there. The unswerving patriot continued to believe Japan would
win the war until, when he was taken prisoner, he saw American
supply depots. But like much of the 32nd Army in June, he could
hardly be called a fighting man.

Murata's terror of a lonely death helped explain the increasing incidents of Japanese frenzy. Extreme stress gripped the many separated
from their dead or otherwise departed comrades. Just as the Americans surmised, those desperate loners, uncertain of what they would
do at their own fatal moment, did change their minds from one second to the next. In this sense, Whitaker's perception of the weak but
unpredictable remnants as "maniacal" was accurate and his fear of
them was justified.

As for the majority still with their units, the central experience was
waiting for the onslaught to approach their positions. Many saw their
final action hours before their caves were actually straddled. Sent out
to seek hand-to-hand combat with the enemy, some rushed tanks
as "human mines" made up of a dozen or more hand grenades
wrapped in a blanket. All knew the futility of those tactics, but their
officers felt compelled to try something — anything — active. Their
last orders were much like those given near a village some two miles

north of the 32nd Army's final headquarters at Mabuni. "Tonight we go out and to the top of Gushichan Heights," an artillery officer declared on June 10. "I assume you are ready. The time has come to give your life for the country and the Emperor. To honor this battery, you will fight to the end; is that understood? That's all."

The caves filled with dread, more so than when the units had been accomplishing their feats at the Shuri Line. No matter what dangers had been previously faced, no one was prepared for a superior's announcement that the time for the inevitable end was at hand. In larger caves, teeth could actually be heard chattering while calmer souls cleaned their weapons without comment. Older men removed photographs of their wives and children from their belongings and stared at them. Their tears irritated younger soldiers, who clicked their tongues. "How can you fight in that frame of mind?"

The very few who returned from such sorties usually met disgust from their officers. "How dare you come back alive?"

Even fewer tried to save themselves by fleeing the battle entirely. Norio Watanabe's independence of spirit put him in this tiny group. Watanabe, the Osaka sports photographer who opposed the war and perceived the chief purpose of his military training as destroying his ability to think, was with an antiaircraft battery now reduced to almost nothing. His entire being felt the futility and stupidity of fighting further, but he had to keep this to himself. Bombs and shells had pulverized friends in front of his eyes. He had seen whole gun crews blown to bits, in one case so thoroughly that a gob of innards hanging from a cave's ceiling support was the only residue. Escaping from a particularly bloody shelling one night, Watanabe climbed a hill near his cave in order to be alone. The military oddball was also unusual in having married for love, not by arrangement; perhaps this elevated his longing for his wife and three children beyond the yearning felt by most men facing death. But because the moment was so imminent, it was time to dispose of his personal possessions. He put a match to a letter from his adored wife — the single letter delivered to him during an entire year on Okinawa — and to photographs he had taken of his cherished daughters. He thought of his father, who had died one spring just before a last look at the cherry blossoms, and of his mother, who afterward had had to work far into the night to raise her children. He knew his own wife and children missed him sorely. Tears wet his cheeks as flames consumed the letter and photographs. His only consolation was a thought that loss of this "miserable war" was Japan's best hope to free herself of the Emperor cult that had dragged her into it.

After Watanabe climbed back down the hill, his battery was further devastated by enemy fire and suicide charges. But to his amazing good luck, his squad leader happened to have attended an American university — and to Watanabe's astonishment revealed that he intended to escape. Better to be shot for deserting, the thoughtful superior explained, than to die like a dog fighting for an ugly cause.

In early June, Watanabe and four trusted fellow soldiers laid plans to island-hop to Formosa. Some dropped out or were killed before they started. The others left with an Okinawan guide and crept south in search of a canoe, more afraid of discovery by fellow soldiers than of American bombardments. Their efforts ended in a series of twists strange even by the standards of the grotesque demise of the 32nd Army as a whole. They wandered, staggered, fled from terrifying danger, repaired discarded canoes and saw them stolen, were split up by yet more dangers, tried other unsuccessful ways to surrender. Eventually a chance meeting with another group planning escape, including members of the Naval Base Force, put Watanabe in a canoe in the East China Sea. Another miracle saved him when a near typhoon swamped and nearly splintered the fragile craft. He landed on Kume Island, some fifty miles east of Naha, the birthplace of Masahide Ota, the fervent member of the Blood and Iron Scouts for the Emperor.

Watanabe's bizarre adventures would continue on Kume, where a small number of other deserters soon landed. But their total number was tiny. He was still the rare Japanese exception.

The stiffest resistance in early June took place on the Oroku Peninsula, which gently extends into the East China Sea just below Naha. This was the site of the abandoned headquarters of Captain Kojo's 22nd Regiment, adjoining the much more elaborate tunnel complex housing the headquarters of Admiral Minoru Ota's Naval Base Force. Including Okinawan conscripts, the admiral's command was about nine thousand troops, all but a few untrained or poorly trained for land warfare. As the fighting neared, units were detached and sent to critical points in the shredding line, but most remained in place, many guarding Naha Airfield. Then Admiral Ota complied with a request from General Ushijima to join the general withdrawal.

In late May, the naval garrison, now at about half its original size, destroyed most of its equipment and weapons too heavy to carry. The evacuees trudged about five miles south to the village of Nagusuku, roughly parallel to the crossroads village of Makabe through which great numbers of Japanese units, including Kojo's, staggered to their final positions. The planned position of Ota's force turned out to be so exposed that some of his senior officers pleaded to return to their original fortifications, arguing that they belonged to the Imperial Japanese Navy. Until then, the admiral had been a model of rarely achieved interservice cooperation. No doubt influenced by the general demoralization, and without notifying Ushijima, Ota permitted about half his troops to return to the peninsula. He went with them.

On the American side, 10th Army headquarters debated whether to take the peninsula by pushing through its hills from inland, as the conservative General Buckner would have preferred, or by an amphibious landing. Fortunately for the troops involved, the more audacious approach was chosen. Part of the 6th Marine Division, including units that had just cleared Naha, landed in the predawn darkness of June 4 and advanced quickly. Dick Whitaker's 29th Regiment followed the same morning.

The first three days on Oroku were relatively easy even for the units assigned to take Naha Airfield (although Whitaker's second serious wounding occurred there, on June 6). Most of Admiral Ota's armament was waiting in hilly areas farther inland: chiefly hundreds of machine guns and light cannon transferred from antiaircraft positions and stripped from wrecked planes. Those machine guns — one to every three of Ota's force, according to Marine estimates — and a variety of land mines were particularly effective even for troops scarcely trained in their use. The motley units held up the advance, eventually of eight Marine battalions with tank support, for over a week. American casualties mounted surprisingly to a greater proportion even than at Shuri, although the total, 1608, was far smaller. This was more evidence of how a better-equipped defense would have rent the Americans — as it was preparing to do on the Japanese mainland.

As it was, the Naval Base Force shared the fate of the rump of the 32nd Army as a whole: it was hopelessly beaten before even beginning to fight. Ota's troops, green though they were in combat, would have caused much more punishment in the same battle before the general withdrawal. Now most of their armament and supplies had been destroyed or dispersed elsewhere instead of being available for use against the veteran American units. Marines finally forced the survivors of the hill clashes down into an area of mudflats and paddies bordering the Naha inlet. When those survivors were surrounded, Japanese-speaking Americans shouted inducements to surrender. Some answered by requesting permission for a kind of cease-fire so that they could kill themselves "in peace." Permission was granted. Approving Marines applauded the more spectacular performers, including a pair who sat on a large demolition charge and set off the fuse. Others used more conventional grenades or bullets on themselves. Scores who couldn't decide what to do were easily cut down, bringing the total Japanese dead on the peninsula to about five thousand.

Ota sent his last message to Ushijima on the night of June 11: "Headquarters under heavy enemy tank attack . . . Those at our position will all die honorably . . . Thank you for your past kindnesses . . . Wish you a victory." He ordered his senior doctor to make certain that three hundred badly wounded troops suffered no further and had an honorable death. A medical team walked down long rows of wounded in the underground complex, methodically injecting outstretched arms until the only sound was the team's own sobbing.

A Marine unit made a special search for Ota's headquarters, found it on June 13, and called its site Admiral's Hill. In addition to the bodies in the medical center, hundreds of suicides lay in the tunnels and corridors. Two further days of search in the underground maze were required to find the admiral himself. He and five senior officers lay on sleeping platforms in a room near the center of the complex, their uniforms freshly pressed, their hands behind their heads. Each had his sword, a naval dress saber and a slit throat. Ota's death poem expressed a kind of contentment.

> How could we rejoice over our birth
> but to die an honorable death
> under the Emperor's flag.

Elsewhere in Japanese-held territory, the gravely wounded were also dying by their own hands or their fellows'. In caves like that of the medic Ikuo Ogiso, the American ratio — ninety-seven of every hundred wounded saved — was almost reversed. The agonies of Ogiso's 2nd Field Hospital clinic continued until senior officers disbanded it too. Those able to limp or crawl were told to make their way back to their units. The orders for the others were to be more final.

Ogiso wanted anything but to convey them; however, seemingly catatonic Lieutenant Mizoguchi, the medical officer, neither moved nor answered his questions about what could be done to save their scores of nonambulatory patients. Finally, Ogiso assumed this duty too, producing absolute silence with the order that those unable to return to their companies should kill themselves. "Then the injured started to stir. One missing a leg crawled out. Another broke apart his bed to make a cane and tottered out. To my astonishment, serious cases who until now were considered immobile demonstrated a frightening tenacity to stay alive by crawling inch by inch toward the exit through the mud of blood and pus on the ground."

Ogiso set forth the three choices for the more than eighty who remained. The majority chose potassium cyanide. He helped them lie with their heads northward — a direction the living avoided because it was the customary positioning of the dead — and filled his syringe. Gunfire could be heard advancing toward the cave as he gave the injections, one by one. Death was almost instantaneous. "They breathed their last very quietly, unobtrusively. When one was done, the next very gently extended his arm toward me."

Many of the others yearned for a last breath of clean air after existing in the cave. Ogiso had them carried outside to a sky unexpectedly brilliant with stars after so much rain. Their heads were also pointed northward. A jar with a few swallows of water was placed in each helmet and left in easy reach — with three hand grenades because the cave's dampness had probably spoiled a good percentage of them. Ogiso told them to perform the act when the enemy appeared.*

He had no doubt that the turn of all the living was imminent. The relentless elevation of death as the highest virtue made him feel he was acting in the only way he could. But decades later he would think of that day, look at his hands, "which carried out the . . . order faithfully and with total certainty, and feel an urge to throw myself on the ground and weep."

In more torrential rain, Ogiso set out with other medical personnel for a new refuge. Several branches of what was still called the 2nd Field Hospital reunited there from their scattered locations throughout the south. Frequent requisitions for reinforcements for fighting units soon reduced the staff of some 250 to about a quarter of that. But Ogiso wasn't selected, and the chief medical officer, a former ophthalmologist who remained more professional doctor than military commander, did not order the rest out on pointless attacks. Ogiso's continued survival surprised him. While others sent out as messengers to the 24th Division's headquarters cave, two and a half miles away, failed to return, he survived his stints of running and crawling under the rain of bombs. Then the hospital unit's cave was surrounded, and the chief medical officer ordered him to report their end in a final dash to headquarters. Knowing he would be shot the minute he inched from the mouth, Ogiso was nevertheless about to obey when a compassionate lieutenant saved him. The lieutenant

---

*Superiors shot some badly wounded soldiers who declined suicide. In the village of Gushichan, about two miles north of the 32nd Army's final headquarters cave, a noncommissioned officer saw to this as the enemy approached. Even some starkly vivid Japanese memoirs of the hardships on Okinawa omit such details because their writers felt it would have been too cruel to reveal to families that their sons, husbands and fathers died at the hands of their own superiors.

reasoned that division headquarters had probably been destroyed; Ogiso should therefore pretend to have made the trip and safely returned.

Apart from his miraculous luck, Ogiso's experience was more or less typical of those in the medical services. Before its official disbanding in early June, the 2nd Field Hospital had become more a mass tomb than a medical facility. Then, just when the 32nd Army needed medical care most for its tens of thousands of gravely wounded, it simply dismantled — but not even that prompted any significant questioning of "the system" in which the suffering Japanese were locked.

22 · Civilian Suffering

In the desperation of the enemy's position, civilians have become vagrants who represent an additional difficulty for the defenders . . . [serving] to disrupt the enemy's communications, organization, and morale. Reports have been received to the effect that Japanese soldiers have been shooting civilians who made efforts to surrender. It is probably true that civilians would welcome an opportunity to surrender themselves to our forces if the Japanese gave them an opportunity to do so. The Japanese thus far have shown no inclination to give them that opportunity.

— From the 6th Marine Division's Field Intelligence Report, June 17

The thing about a phosphorous grenade is that you can't get it off the skin, so it just keeps burning into a person. You can't use water on it, just Vaseline, but the Okinawans didn't have any — or anything else. So lots of them just burned and burned. Mostly I remember the women burning. To me, phosphorous weapons are dirtier than napalm and they should be banned. It's just too cruel a way for civilians to die.

— An American medical corpsman who treated many Okinawans

Wandering and sleeping here and there in mountain caves and riversides, crying and weeping, [the civilian refugees] are near death, overwhelmed by hideous fatigue.

— A Japanese doctor

I was surprised to find that life wasn't cheap in the Orient. I saw the faces of ordinary human beings, people brought up on more hard times than me, and I'd had my share. Ordinary human beings racked by malnutrition and dysentery, carrying even worse-off wounded on their backs. I realized they had the same wants and loves as me. They wanted to live and wanted their children to live — and had to watch them die. Over the years, the pictures of those people have grown and grown in my mind.

— A gung-ho Marine

What on earth is the Emperor doing? Does he have any idea of what's happening to women and children? Why doesn't he make a move to stop this hideous war?

— Thoughts of Norio Watanabe

ABOUT a hundred thousand civilians remained behind the Shuri Line when the major assault on it was mounted on May 11. Their confidence in the 32nd Army and

446

their inability to think of an alternative kept them there even after the strict orders on May 13 to evacuate to the scarcely defended, little bombarded Chinen Peninsula on the west coast. The Japanese withdrawal in effect pronounced sentence on those noncombatants.

The result wasn't unexpected. Ei Shimada, governor of the Prefecture of Okinawa, attended the May 22 conference at which General Ushijima announced his intention to withdraw. Okinawans had no love for Shimada's immediate predecessor, who had returned home to Japan on "official business" on the eve of the invasion and did not return. But unlike many Japanese officials sent down from Tokyo, Shimada himself sympathized deeply with the Okinawan people, and voiced a passionate plea at that underground conference. He begged Ushijima not to abandon his main fortifications. He even called the plan "foolish" because it would condemn scores of thousands of civilians to death, whatever its military value.

At a later conference after the withdrawal, Shimada would go further and accuse the Army of having caused needless slaughter. Ushijima would reply that his primary mission was to prolong his defense in order to give more time to the mainland for preparing to meet the enemy invasion. It is true that he had been ordered to wring every day out of the battle and that he followed those orders admirably — and brilliantly in the withdrawal itself (although Colonel Yahara, his operations officer, was directly responsible for most of the planning). And it is hard to imagine a more impressive display of dignity and composure than Ushijima's in the face of impossible odds. More than a great Japanese general, he was a great general. Nor did he betray the Okinawan people, since Japanese planners had treated them as expendable from the beginning — "a sacrificial stone," as a celebrated Japanese military historian put it, "in the game of Go." More than supreme courage, it would have taken revolutionary initiative, the vision of a rebel prophet, for Ushijima to surrender when the Shuri Line was broken instead of prolonging the mutual killing.

But had he found the strength for this, he would have been a greater man and in the long run a greater general.

However, of all candidates to fail his superiors and break his samurai code, Ushijima was among the least likely. The exemplary general gave Japan four extra weeks by protracting the efforts of some of his forty thousand surviving soldiers — and causing the deaths of almost three times as many civilians. For decades after his death, it was said on Okinawa and repeated by Japanese and American writers that this filled him with remorse. "The Okinawans must resent me terribly," he was quoted as reflecting in his final moments. But this supposed flash of guilt may well have been invented by a sympathizer of Japan trying to make him a nobler person than he was, to preserve respect for samurai traditions and Japanese militarism despite the agony they caused. Or the story was a wish by one who grieved for Okinawa: native suffering might be more bearable if Ushijima had regretted how much his strategy had contributed to it. In any case, the current evidence indicates that, for all his good nature and soldierly virtue, the stoic general thought no more about Okinawans at the end than at the beginning.* The island remained the stage, not an actor, in his Japanese drama of defense of personal honor with sacrificial service.

However more honorable, dignified and likable Ushijima was than the long line of Japanese exploiters from Satsuma and elsewhere, his notion of right and wrong left no more room for native considerations. The campaign's final stage was about to surpass the sum of the island's suffering during the previous three and a half centuries.

Most Okinawan leaders contributed by following their old pattern of docility and submissiveness to Japanese authority. Scores of thousands might have been saved had they heeded the American leaflets continually rained on them: wear white; keep apart from military units; give themselves up. But the majority of civilians, still convinced that the bestial Americans lusted for their death, were too bewildered by events to do more than grope for safety in the same eight square miles where the remnants of the Japanese Army were hiding and charging.

Within days of the withdrawal to the island's southern tip, the battle became the civilian slaughter Governor Shimada had predicted. Had the 32nd Army held to its promise and remained in its main bastion for the final stand, it would have been destroyed to the last man, but a large number of civilians would have been spared because most were apart from the Army and relatively safe. Now the two were mixed, streaming together on the roads leading south and seeking cover in the same places, the civilians almost as doomed as the troops.

Noncombatant suffering in the north had remained within what might be called expected limits. This was true even in central sec-

---

*The last message to Tokyo of Admiral Ota, commander of the Naval Base Force, gallantly commended the Okinawan people's cooperation and self-sacrifice and requested "special consideration" for their "future prosperity." Ota's words, like those attributed to Ushijima about Okinawan suffering, would ring hollow after the war, when treatment of the island generally ranged from callous to shameful.

tions, where civilians were quickly interned and fed, however minimally. But there was no way civilians in the south could stay alive once they mingled with the troops. Prodigious as it had been before, American fire from land, sea and air became more intense on the compressed target of the southern end. Civilians were thunderstruck by the Americans' capacity to keep delivering bullets, shells and bombs: almost seven million shells alone in June, roughly fifty for each surviving Okinawan and Japanese.

Dodging that fire, hordes of desperate natives limped and crawled south without the slightest idea of a destination. Older Okinawans who had rarely left their villages were lost in unfamiliar territory. Some caught snatches of sleep as they plodded, waking when shells fell or a plane appeared overhead, then lapsing back into a wobbling doze. Almost everyone was hungry, thirsty and weak enough to bend or reel under the smallest bundles. They scattered in panic when bombardments began, some clawing to the top of rises, from which they stumbled or rolled down the far side until stopped by bushes. Thousands lay in the open, too exhausted to move or stand.

The muddy ribbons of road were choked with evidence of World War II's cost to civilians. The army of refugees was much larger than the shrunken 32nd Army. Their meager belongings — scraps of clothing and a piece or two of pottery piled in baskets on their heads or hung on shoulder poles — made their condition seem more pathetic. An Okinawan schoolteacher on his way from Kochinda, site of the field hospital Captain Kojo had visited during his evacuation, to Kyan on the southern coast found that words were inadequate to describe the "utter horror . . . Dead everywhere . . . *everywhere* . . . It was hell."

Most of the traveling was still risked at night, in rotting shoes or none at all. The first days of the evacuation were carried out under a steady deluge that filled trenches, ditches and all manner of craters with muddy water. When American flares were lit, the rain glittered like silver arrows. Occasional car or truck headlights picked out ghostly faces ravaged by exhaustion and fear. Villages were piles of stones and ashes of the artifacts of centuries of farming life. Charred trees stood like sentries from the nether world; rotting animal carcasses stank; the flesh and fat of people hit by shells "sizzled in the darkness, emitting now blueish, now reddish flames." Groups with no destination wandered on and off the roads, some turning back north in their confusion. A native novelist watched women and children disappear among some bushes "only to re-emerge a few moments later, striding resolutely in the opposite direction, as though headed for a new destination."

During the day, the bodies that littered roads and fields bloated under the searing sun that replaced the rain. Elderly couples sat in the mud, using their last strength to hold hands while awaiting their end. A Japanese soldier saw a mother and her child squatting in a field, their hands covering their faces, until they vanished in the flash and smoke of a shell burst, one of thousands of direct hits on unintended targets. Women screamed as their children died in flames. A few fathers — most were still with the Home Guard — joined the category of the crazed. One spent his last minutes in a pool of blood in the middle of a road. Split in two at the hip, he stared with horror at scraps of his wife and three children hit by a naval shell.

Some families made their way to their tombs to await death with their ancestors. Many were led by children, some with younger children on their backs. Boys and girls of five and six carried infants. Others whimpered with exhaustion as they were dragged by parents or others too weak to carry them. Orphans wandered alone or crouched in terror. Wretched suffering was so ubiquitous that families came to ignore others starving to death before their eyes.

Jo Nobuko Martin, a Himeyuri nurses' aide from the Haebaru Army Hospital, noticed during the evacuation a civilian male advancing along the ground, "the moving lines of soldiers and civilian refugees [towering] above him like an angry wave." One leg was gone. The man had just emerged "like a submarine" from a deep puddle by stretching his other leg forward and supporting himself with both arms. The water came up to his hips as he contrived to advance, thrusting the filthy bandages of his "good" leg ahead. A small bag hanging by a strap from his neck thumped on his chest with each jerk forward. "How many miles had he traveled like that and how many miles had he yet to cover?" the teenager, later the protagonist of an autobiographical novel, asked herself. No one stopped to help the man.

The emotional circumstances came to match the physical ones. It began to dawn on people that the Army's sworn "protection" had been a hoax.

Since L-day, the evidence of civilians' eyes had contradicted everything predicted and promised in the official version of the war. Enemy warships filled the ocean, enemy planes packed the sky, enemy guns, tanks and flamethrowers scorched the land — and the awaited counterattack never came. Of course there had been doubt during those eight weeks since the landing, most of all among those who had witnessed Japanese soldiers taking civilian food and other isolated episodes of military misbehavior. However, even victims of mistreatment almost universally suppressed their questions. Hope of eventual victory had made every terrible event bearable during April and May.

The hope was rooted in the great defensive line on which so many natives too had toiled. Even more than among the troops, citadel Shuri, the heart of the old kingdom and of the defense, had comforted and inspired Okinawans. "'As long as Shuri holds, as long as Ushijima and Cho command the Army, victory is ours,' we would tell one another — and believe it." The evacuation of the fortress that was never to be surrendered dealt a critical blow to trust in the 32nd Army. Still unable to contemplate defeat, most ordinary citizens lost faith in victory.

Families on the road met other families gripped by the same disillusionment. They heard terrible accounts from despairing witnesses, learned of massive civilian deaths in other sectors, and realized their suffering had been in vain — which undermined their faith all the more rapidly. The Emperor cult and admiration for death whose only purpose was upholding honor had hardly taken root among the ordinary folk. Further sacrifice could no longer be justified in any way that made sense to them.

The 32nd Army's condition, now exposed to view, further shocked and demoralized civilians. Troops passed piles of uniformed corpses without making a move to bury them. Soldiers disguised in civilian clothes after the withdrawal dismayed Okinawans previously unable to imagine Japanese cowardice. (Some members of the military police hid under kimonos.) Some tried to organize suicide stands; a larger number pushed on numbly. Individual stragglers were the starkest evidence of the military breakdown, even more disheartening than depleted units like Captain Kojo's. The most appalling were the gravely wounded men who had left the disbanded medical facilities, not wanting to kill themselves there. Their orders were to rejoin their units, whose direction and location were unknown to them and virtually unknowable. Injuries to both legs were common. The strongest of the cripples inched relentlessly forward, stumbling or crawling or pulling themselves with their arms. But many could not move, needing the last of their strength to support themselves on homemade crutches. The weakest, having come a short distance on one road or another, could not sit and lay prostrate, waiting for oblivion.

Civilians could not fail to see even unwounded troops succumbing to despair. One band sat motionless across a road from a burned-out army truck, although every child knew by then that even wrecked military vehicles were a favorite target of enemy planes. Many such groups seemed beyond caring.

Okinawans did not have to know how much Japanese soldiers

needed firm leadership to perceive that the Army was stumbling toward disintegration. All could see for themselves that some units were like collections of ragged individuals, not fighting forces. More and more soldiers became disoriented, miserable stragglers. Men who knew they had only weeks or days to live often resorted to rape. (The Okinawan woman reported to have been raped by American and Japanese soldiers on the same day was all too indicative of the civilian predicament.) When civilian morale began to crack, a rift between natives and the Army also opened.

The two categories had generally got on well before the evacuation of Shuri, in part because of the sense of shared danger and in part the continued Okinawan trust in Japanese victory. But it was almost inevitable that centuries-old dislike and antagonism would re-emerge as the common objectives began breaking down, and that the majority came to sense, if not yet vocalize, that the 32nd Army was going to lose.

The claim that Japan was a divine country, destined to rule the world, was now seen as myth. Civilians lost their admiration for the formerly invincible *Yamato* men, and the two groups began competing for food, shelter and impossible salvation. In the end, military mistreatment of civilians would grow from isolated instances before the withdrawal from Shuri to a small but clear pattern. Long-standing prejudice against the "little brown monkeys" surfaced without control as more and more troops lost their leadership. Shorn of the restraints of their community and higher authority, some became savage to natives. Never mind that Okinawans were Japanese citizens; this category of soldiers, themselves desperate, knew them as racially non-Japanese, therefore inferior.

> We discovered the inner face of [Japan's] war when we went to Okinawa. The first to be killed there were those with the least strength, the shy, the meek, the quiet. Japanese soldiers came to Okinawa and told the people, "We are here to defend you, so do as we say . . ." Whom did the Japanese end up defending, whom did they kill? They killed the very people they were pledged to defend.
> — Toshi Maruki, *The Hiroshima Murals*

> My condition was so bad after the evacuation — and my men's condition — that I had no energy even to think about incidents of civilian abuse I saw.
> — Tadashi Kojo

> I saw an Okinawan woman who sought refuge in a well. She gave birth to a baby there, standing up. These horrible things happen and our hands did them. No one is saintly during a war.
> — Fred Baxter

At the same time, civilians cared less about the outcome of the battle and the war. As they trudged the perilous roads amid the masses of dead and half-living, they could think of little beyond their own survival. Their priorities were safety, water and food, roughly in that order. When the supplies on their backs were gone, they chased rumors about food. Sweet potato leaves became a luxury, like frogs, toads, locusts, snails, slugs and lizards. Families resident in the far south were better off: most had a cache of edibles even after their houses were leveled. Refugees from elsewhere agonized over whether to steal from the locals' fields and larders. As the weeks passed, the takers were less troubled by conscience, and those who couldn't bring themselves to steal became too weak to care about nourishment.

Nursing children were first to succumb to starvation. When moth-. ers' breasts ran dry, some melted mashed sweet potatoes in boiling water, but the babies vomited up the liquid. Soon the little ones looked like "yellow clay dolls," then stopped crying and turned cold. A few mothers continued carrying them at their breasts but otherwise showed no emotion; they too were on the edge of starvation, although the grandparents were usually next to die. Families argued about eating sago palms, which they knew would poison them but only after a few days. Others debated whether to leave their caves to try to scavenge something in the fields, the effort of which might kill them faster by consuming their remaining energy.

Water, always scarce in the south in summer, became all but unavailable when May's rain turned to June's heat and drought. Some refugees drank their own urine. When lucky ones found water, they turned joyous, as if their problems were solved. But few knew the locations of springs, most of which had been sequestered by Japanese units. By mid-June, Ushijima's troops, with and without orders from superiors, commandeered the hiding places of many areas — making safety, the first priority, impossible for civilians.

After dragging himself south, everyone had to find shelter from the typhoon of bombs and steel, as Okinawans called it, that whistled and screeched everywhere around them. True shelter was possible only underground, in caves that belonged to their communities no less than the wells. In fact, many caves were the sites of the wells, the same fresh water that formed them serving as the only local supply. But many were seized by soldiers who ejected civilians already there, refused admission to new arrivals, and labeled protestors "anti-Japanese," including those who refused to surrender their last supplies of food. Over three hundred families in one Makabe area alone were driven from four substantial community caves in early June, after which they sought the almost useless protection of trees, pigsties, rock walls and the ruins of houses — or simply stayed in the open. Jo Nobuko Martin set the scene in her autobiographical novel.

> More and more shells were bursting around us so we decided to seek shelter. We happened to find a cave in a hillside near the village. We were greeted by an officer who had just come out of the cave, sword in hand. He began brandishing the sword at some farmers who had gathered nearby.
>
> "Get away from here!" he bellowed. "Dirty, stinking farmers! Are you trying to attract the enemy's attention? They'll smell you! Get out!"
>
> The farmers ran at the sight of the officer's sword. [A friend] and I ran with them, but we promptly returned to the cave. After all, we weren't dirty farmers. Surely some kindly officer would invite us into the cave for safety? While we stood waiting . . . the farmers began coming back too. Desperation had made them bold. It was their cave, after all, and they could no longer stay in the village, where shells were now exploding constantly. The officer reappeared, brandishing his sword. The farmers scattered again, only to return in a few minutes. Smoke was rising in the village; the village was burning. The fire and the bursting shells were driving these men back to the cave, despite the officer with the sword. How would it end?

The most common Japanese excuse was that Okinawans' comings and goings in search of food would reveal their hiding places. But soldiers who drove them to perish under the bombardments knew the cave mouths would be found anyway, not least because all vegetation around them had been charred to nothing. And the excuse of those who took food intended for dying children was despicable hypocrisy: "Who's more important, your family or the Emperor?" The small minority of inhumane soldiers began to dominate. Some were starving when they forced villagers to pay in food for "information" about what regions were safe from the enemy. Others fired into hamlets and looted when their inhabitants rushed away to escape bullets they assumed were American. And when Americans arrived right outside cave mouths, many soldiers turned their weapons on civilians inside and made them hostages, threatening death if they tried to leave, hoping their presence would deter the enemy from blowing up the caves. Or they killed and raped them. "Is this cold, cruel refusal our repayment for [Okinawans'] consistent good will, devotion and kindness?" a Japanese soldier agonized.

Needless to say, not all Japanese were cruel. Kindhearted soldiers often couldn't help Okinawans because their officers or comrades shouted them down. But many others befriended them, performed good deeds, made sacrifices. A female student named Momoko Yonaha was one of thousands they saved; when she reached for a suicidal hand grenade on the beach of the very southern tip, soldiers took the trouble to stop her despite their own desperation. A few survivors of the 32nd Army would return to Okinawa after the war to live among the gentle people who had sacrificed beyond the call to save them. Many would grieve for civilians together with their dead comrades; some grieved even then, recognizing that of all those enduring pain and suffering, Okinawans, "the real victims of this war," bore the greatest share.

But most of the Japanese soldiers remained locked in their ignorance, fear, upbringing and code of war, all of which tended to make them indifferent to Okinawan suffering even when they weren't adding to it. No doubt civilians would have been treated better on the mainland (although there too, many soldiers were arrogant to civilians). But one of the poisoned darts of the war started by Japanese officers was that the only battle fought on supposedly Japanese soil was actually fought on Okinawan. After centuries of Japanese effort to instill Ryukyuans with their own militaristic appetites, the military government in Tokyo assumed the role of Okinawa's protector, and caused the island some of the most severe destruction, person for person and house for house, ever suffered by any people. At the same time, elements of the Army were expropriating civilians' only means of protection in the last eight square miles it controlled. The failure of Ushijima's staff to take account of the civilian disaster in June was rooted in Japan's colonialist attitudes and policies.

The antagonism that flared up in the extreme stress of the imminent collapse also fired accusations of Okinawan "spying." That charge, grounded in the notion that any contact with the hated enemy was betrayal, wasn't new. The accusations began when the first civilians allowed themselves to be taken to American detention camps on L-day.

Even without charges of spying, soldiers executed civilians who tried to surrender, which was considered crime enough. Incidents became numerous after the fall of Shuri: shooting, strangling, clubbing and tossing hand grenades at natives, including hundreds of women and children, whom Japanese had detected moving toward the American lines with the apparent intention of surrendering. Possession of an American leaflet with instructions on how to do that was often taken as proof of treachery. Discovery of that scrap of paper sometimes led to the brutal torture of civilian helpers.

It may be said in mitigation that Japanese killed not only Okinawans who wanted to surrender but also fellow soldiers. American combat diaries had many entries like a Marine's on June 13: "The Japs were offered but refused to surrender and threw grenades at two of their brothers who had turned in and carried leaflets of surrender." But the Japanese murders of civilians were more repulsive. As in their conquest of Manchuria and China, some seemed more controlled by racial prejudice — which was no American monopoly — than by any rational motive, even in the new meaning of "rational" in severe battle.

As military disaster loomed during the final weeks, civilians were the handiest scapegoats for those driven to believe that *someone* was responsible. At least a hundred documented executions for espionage took place, all without trial — no instance of actual espionage is known — and most in spontaneous outbursts of vengeful frustration. They included at least seven beheadings, dozens of killings of women by hand grenades and several saber and spear slashings, some of "traitors" tied to trees. Many victims were minors. In Shuri, a feeble-minded female "spy" was executed with a bamboo spear.

When the enemy stormed the little offshore island of Ie Shima, a third of its forty-five hundred natives died, roughly twenty times the number of American combatants killed there. Many natives committed suicide to avoid capture. But two teenage boys survived hand grenade blasts that killed the rest of their families and were found, badly wounded, by American soldiers. The boys recovered in a hospital tent, from which they escaped when some Americans pressed them to go to their village and bring back some good-looking girls. Japanese soldiers from a detachment of stragglers later found the pair and took them to their lieutenant. "You were captured by the Americans," he declared. "You gave them military secrets!" He shouted an order; swords instantly dispatched the boys. Later, Americans told six young natives in a detention camp to take a letter to the same lieutenant, asking him to come down from his mountain retreat and surrender. The swords flashed again. The six executed for "treachery" died singing a patriotic song.* One Okinawan historian believes the known killings are but a few of a terrible number, of which little documentation exists. Performed in secret, most will never be known.

* Ie Shima's suffering mirrored Okinawa's in being caused by both sides. Three months before L-day, the Japanese forced some 3000 natives to evacuate. Weeks *after* the official end on Okinawa, the Americans removed all remaining civilians to improve security on the island's airfield, already gearing up for the coming invasion of the Japanese mainland. By that time, the surviving population were mainly women and children, some of whom tried to defend their demolished homes with stones and spears. Almost every building was rubble when civilians were returned to their island before the end of 1945.

Postwar Japanese governments have made it less likely that the facts will ever be uncovered. Ministers honored their own war dead in ceremonies at the Yasukuni Shrine, but well after the war, the Ministry of Education ordered mention of Japanese murders of Okinawan civilians deleted from textbooks. Still, the outlines are known and there is no other way to summarize them: members of the 32nd Army robbed food, refuge and life from tens of thousands of Okinawans, chiefly women and children, they had supposedly come to protect. A small but significant number bayoneted and beheaded innocents, poisoning, choking, drowning and injecting babies to silence them, tossing hand grenades into caves whose civilian occupants had decided to surrender.

Atrocities were proportionately greater on lesser Ryukyu islands whose smaller garrisons were commanded by junior officers — and where native suffering began well before L-day in some instances. Japanese commanders ordered the thirty-two thousand residents of the Yaeyama Islands, a small chain about 265 miles south of Okinawa, to evacuate to even more remote islands in advance of an American attack that never came. The people of the Yaeyama group had long avoided the almost uninhabited, mosquito-infested minor islands for fear of malaria. About half of the thirty-two thousand contracted it in 1945. Nearly four thousand died.*

On Zamami Island in the Keramas, natives were ordered to take their own lives after the American landing the week before L-day. One hundred and seventy-one people obeyed, most using razors and knives. On Tokashiki, largest of the Keramas, parents and children talked together, women and girls combing and pinning each other's hair, while preparing to obey the orders of the garrison. Then about 150 farming and fishing families used hand grenades distributed by the local policeman. A little river in a valley below the suicide mountain turned red. But some adults remained alive, crying out to God for help or to distant relatives to inhabit the island after they were gone. Finally, the strong clubbed the weak to death, the young axed the old, mothers suffocated their children.†

---

*Claiming there is no legal proof of its culpability, Tokyo has paid no compensation to the families. Some 30,000 Japanese soldiers stationed on outlying islands also fared badly even where Americans did not bomb or land. Well over one in ten died of malaria and malnutrition.

†Regaining consciousness to see some of his family still alive, a 16-year-old boy decided he and his brother must finish the job — with their hands, since they had no grenades. "We had to do it because of love. Mother was the first one we laid our hands on. I remember I screamed. It was a terrible sound. I'd never made a sound like that before. I know I can never make it again. When I was finished, my brother and I looked around us. Our parents and sisters were all dead."

Then the brothers marched out with sticks in order to die honorably fighting the

Few Japanese servicemen were killed on Tokashiki, but the mass suicide claimed 325 civilians and garrison soldiers beheaded at least ten more. Ninety percent of the over three hundred Korean laborers who had worked on the island under brutal Japanese orders and beatings also died, many beheaded for allegedly stealing food.

On Kume Island, Japanese soldiers bragged to grateful, admiring natives about how they would defend them — and then murdered twenty-six, roughly twice the number who would be killed by American units when they landed in late June. The dead included a year-old baby. Once more, the excuse was "spying": a lesson had to be made of civilians whom Americans sent to the hills to try to persuade military units to surrender. The warriors bayoneted some "traitors" so that they would bleed to death slowly.* Norio Watanabe, who had landed on Kume after fleeing Okinawa, learned of the atrocities there when members of the garrison killed the husband of a beautiful young woman who had befriended him. "I couldn't understand the reasoning of the Navy men who were killing villagers as spy suspects. Instead of fighting the Americans who landed, our men, full of dark suspicion and anguish to protect their own lives, kill the friendly, cooperative villagers! No amount of justification can forgive their deeds."

But Watanabe, who had always known the folly of war with America, remained the exception — willing to grieve for the murdered women and children — even decades later. Those were the kinds of episodes the Ministry of Education assiduously excluded from the school curriculum. As with the rest of Japan's atrocities in China and elsewhere, as much effort went into denying as acknowledging them, let alone seeking forgiveness.

Meanwhile, Okinawans began killing themselves in June because one facet of Japanese propaganda retained its power. No longer willing to die for a lost military or national cause, most civilians remained morbidly afraid of the enemy. The simple, isolated people had seen for themselves that their trust in Japanese superiority had been a terrible mistake — but the immensely powerful Americans continued to seem the monsters Tokyo had described. Some natives so feared American torture that they felt relief when their relatives cut their own throats. While newspapers on the Japanese mainland

---

Americans — as, they'd been told, all the Japanese soldiers had done. But on the way, they bumped into some of those Japanese soldiers. "They had betrayed us!"

*There is some evidence that this garrison also killed several shipwrecked Japanese soldiers who washed ashore and whose deaths were recorded as suicide. This would have been due to intensified interservice rivalry as the Japanese cause fell apart.

wrote of Okinawan children "dying gloriously on the battlefield," weeping parents were holding them tight as they exploded a grenade to bring relief to the whole family — or used kitchen knives, tree limbs and rocks on their babies' bodies. In some instances where the grenades had killed the parents, Japanese officers and soldiers finished off survivors.

Still, the majority of civilians did not choose death but were killed by starvation, disease, individual Japanese cruelty and, most of all, indiscriminate American firing. Most of the dying was accompanied by more emotional torment than at Hiroshima or Nagasaki, where it was usually over far more quickly, and for a smaller number of civilian victims. More Okinawans had more time to see the protracted agony.

Fourteen-year-old Shitsuko Oshiro pleaded with soldiers to let her into a cave. They relented after her promise to leave at the end of the bombardment that was in progress, then admitted an older woman — but gave her angry orders to stop her baby's crying. Unable to, she took him out.

"After a while, she came back alone. I don't know what she'd done with the child . . . She wouldn't say anything and nobody would ask her."

Nineteen people in a cave the size of a small bedroom left not a square centimeter for a middle-aged mother and elderly woman with two small children. Those four looked "awfully tired" even to the awfully tired. Japanese troops had forced them from another cave and they had nowhere to go. They settled under a nearby tree until shell fragments killed both women. But the baby still sucked at her mother's breast and the older child snuggled to her body in the pouring rain. When a teenage boy left the stifling cave to relieve himself days later, he found them newly dead alongside their mother. "I felt so bad I didn't know what to make of human lives."

Thirst-crazed Japanese soldiers searching for water entered a village's last standing house. A cloud of flies feasted on a collection of stinking corpses with stomachs punctured and innards oozing. "It's the same wherever we'd go, there's no safety anywhere," the remaining residents replied to a question about why they hadn't left. And: "If I die, I'd like to do it in my own home." That would be soon: more shells began falling as the soldiers left.

* * *

One of Captain Kojo's men recognized someone in the carpet of civilian bodies bordering a southern road. It was once-beautiful Yasu, daughter of the farmer in whose house the captain had quartered in his first position at Kadena Airfield. Bleeding to death from a shrapnel wound, young Yasu asked about the once-dashing captain.

Near the entrance to a cave at Itosu, a teacher and his wife sat on a rock almost submerged in muddy water. Skin and bone, they nevertheless retained an air of refinement while remaining motionless for days, she with her head split open and full of wriggling maggots, he using his last strength to sustain a flow of comforting words to her. A principled Japanese soldier inside the cave, himself too near his end to feel much sympathy for others, gave the couple the considerable gift of a drink of clean water just drawn from a nearby spring. The teacher tried desperately to raise the soldier's canteen to his wife's lips. Unable to forget them, the soldier volunteered to rush outside and fetch his unit's water again two days later. The couple were face down over the rock, dirty water washing their heads.

Middle-aged Eishun Higa and his family saw a woman floating face down in a pond near a road leading to a village sugar mill. A baby girl of about a year on the woman's back was moving her hands and head. When Higa's wife said something to him about the poor dead soul, the woman suddenly raised herself from the water. "I'm not dead, I'm still alive. I was hit by white phosphorus and can't see. Please take my child and adopt her . . . If you see a friendly soldier passing, ask him to shoot me as soon as possible."

Higa told the woman to come out of the pond and try to survive. But she, unaware that water was no treatment for white phosphorus burns, said she wanted to stay where she was and die as soon as possible because she couldn't see and her burn-covered body hurt too terribly.

Just then, a heavy rain of shells began falling at the pond, killing Higa's sister-in-law and just missing his children. They ran to seek cover.

A bullet ripped through the thigh of fourteen-year-old Koei Kinjo the moment he stepped outside to relieve himself. Some of the people packed inside the cave lectured him severely for his recklessness; his father was furious.

Days later, they were joined by a young man with a bad throat wound that leaked water when he tried to drink. The new arrival developed tetanus and bit "anything he could lay his hands on, whether it was a man or a stone. He would groan and squeal in an eerie, melancholy voice — and bite." The men worried that he would hurt someone and his wild squealing give away their position. Since he was beyond saving, they choked him to death in the hope of saving the others.

At dawn one day, a wild-eyed civilian with two pitiful daughters asked permission to join Norio Watanabe in a goat shed. Watanabe tried to convince the family to save themselves. "You must have seen [the Americans'] propaganda leaflets," he urged the father. "So give yourselves up, let them take you prisoner."

The father's desperately beaten look suddenly turned to fury. "What a terrible thing for you to say, Mr. Soldier. I'd rather die than become a prisoner." He produced a grenade obtained from another Japanese for use on himself and his children, then declared that he had had three daughters but had just killed one.

The eldest had been carrying the youngest of the two surviving ones on her back when a shell fragment ripped off half her face. "She tried to cry but only whistles came out. I lost my mind and strangled her with my own hands. *With my own hands!*" he repeated, sticking them out and watching them tremble.

Watanabe, who had three beloved daughters of his own on the mainland, was stunned. "Who told those people they'd be killed if they became prisoners? Who told them to fight on until death, civilians like soldiers? I wanted to tell the father that the Japanese military men who called Americans beasts were themselves more beastly. 'Don't be deceived!' I wanted to shout to him — but Okinawans were naïve and I couldn't reason with him."

An American sergeant rose from his foxhole one mid-June morning to see the bodies of about eighty Okinawan women at the perimeter of the 7th Army Division infantry company with whom he had spent the night. In an attempt to find safety — or flee callous Japanese or help kind Japanese — the women had unknowingly touched the trip wire strung around the position and set off the machine guns. The soldiers, who had seen similar results on previous mornings, got on with their business. Making no notes about the women, the sergeant got on with his: helping compile the Army's official history of the campaign. "It was an Army history, so we didn't include much about civilians."

* * *

Mitsutoshi Nakajo got no food in his cave because he was sixteen and considered an adult. Only children were fed from a supply of rotting rice balls. Then they too got nothing: the soldiers confiscated everything because they had to do the fighting. "They said they were going on a surprise attack . . . but we knew they just wanted to live and get back to the mainland."

The next day, they announced they were going to dispose of all children under the age of three in order to keep them from attracting the enemy's attention. The five children in this category included Nakajo's younger brother and niece. He pleaded with the senior officer to let them leave the cave with him. Saying that the family would become spies and give away their position, the officer posted guards at the mouth to prevent any exit. "Then four or five soldiers came to us and took away the children one by one, including my brother, and gave them the injection."

The following morning, the soldiers told the Okinawans they were going to dispose of the adults too — the only civilians alive in the area, they said — in order to save them from being captured by the Americans and crushed under their tanks. "We knew they were going to kill us all just to take our food. We were so shocked we didn't know what to say."

While they were talking among themselves, trying to think of how to prevent their execution, Americans blasted the cave, freeing the civilian hostages.

Toyo Gima moved from Makabe's huge Thousand People Cave, filled with great numbers of soldiers, to a slightly smaller one where civilians predominated. A boy of four or five was crying near the mouth because he couldn't find his mother. An angry soldier, warning that the cries would attract the enemy, asked where the child's parents were. When no one replied, he and fellow soldiers took the boy deeper into the cave.

There, Gima saw "this unbelievable thing" — men tying bandage around the boy's neck. Then the soldiers complained that the cloth was too thick and ripped it into smaller strips. "All the civilians who saw it were crying. I actually saw them put the string around the boy's neck, but it was so horrible I couldn't watch it to the end."

Seeking water during a lull in a bombardment of her village, nineteen-year-old Haru Maeda heard a younger sister and brother calling. Maeda found them both wounded, carried them inside her cave, and heard what happened to their mother. A Japanese soldier, they said, had entered their little house and asked her a question. The mother tried to answer politely but her Japanese was weak. The soldier swung his sword. Her head landed in the lap of Maeda's sister-in-law. Maeda's sister ran away with her younger brother on her back. Soldiers caught up with them and stabbed her until she let go of the boy, then slashed a wide cut in his stomach.

In the cave, intestines now spilled from them both. Maeda ran for water for them. On her way, she saw the body of another brother, her youngest, lying on the road, together with two boys from another family. They had been disemboweled. Then Maeda saw her sister-in-law's father. He was sitting cross-legged against a tree, holding his money and his chopped-off head. She found another sister dead and her uncle's body at the well.

Returning to her wounded brother and sister, she held their hands and tried to make them comfortable while they "trembled all over, chattering their teeth . . . one of them was really in pain, trembling and crying loudly until the last moment." Before that last moment — three hours away for one and four for the other — they asked Maeda what she would do after they died. She told them not to worry; she'd join them very soon. She tried to do that with a piece of string around her neck but stopped pulling before the end. "I couldn't kill myself after all. I tried it three times but quit when the string got too tight."

Then she went to see her mother's body, which the soldiers had dragged a short distance from the house. Unhinged by the sight, she screamed questions and accusations. The soldiers replied that they couldn't help what they'd done because they were in combat.

No sampling of civilian suffering in June can convey its scope. Long lost amidst other concerns of the war, it was far greater than what the two armies bore. And although most atrocities were committed by desperate individuals and small groups, some larger units contributed. On June 19, troops of another battalion of Captain Kojo's 24th Infantry Division made a midnight escape from a menaced cave to a temporarily safer one already occupied by villagers from Maehira, two miles above the 32nd Army's final headquarters. The approach of daylight and American troops made the units rush to complete their transfer. In an apparently premeditated raid on the second cave, they butchered over a dozen villagers, including women and children, with their swords.

23 · Young Okinawans Hold to Their Duty

What was it that Okinawans were supposed to gain and lose in the throes of war? . . . Who is going to be defended from whom in the "national defense?" . . . The colossal ego of leaders on both sides, who threw thousands of men into an inferno of steel and fire for the capture of a few square kilometers of scorched earth, is too great for the average citizen to comprehend.

— Masahide Ota, well after the war

THE EVACUATION of the Shuri Line left most conscripted Okinawans somewhere between the civilians and the military diehards in their outlook. Once the island's defense was seen as lost, older men tended to turn their attention from the fighting to finding their families, dead or alive. But many of the unmarried, especially among the elite represented by Masahide Ota and Ruriko Morishita, the nurses' aide nicknamed Miss Victory Day, remained more dedicated than many Japanese soldiers, their youthful energy driven by a consuming desire to prove their patriotism.

Until the general withdrawal, Ota, of the Blood and Iron Scouts, remained based in the cave of the communications soldiers near the 32nd Army's underground headquarters at Shuri. By the last week of May, when the Shuri defenses were finally crumbling, the morale of the Japanese officers was also flagging badly. Scavenging for food one night in the caves and cellars of leveled Shuri, the starving former Normal School students found a container filled with awamori, the Ryukyuan liquor with a higher proof and greater kick than sake. Although alcohol was strictly prohibited, their platoon had become so disorganized and demoralized that no officer stopped the boys from swilling. (Their own officer, the disagreeable intelligence lieutenant, lived apart, in the headquarters complex.) Still, Ota, the tough young Kume native, refused to be disheartened by the drastically deteriorating conditions. He did not permit even the deaths of more than half his unit, which regularly occurred on the roads as they tried to deliver their messages, to weaken his morale.

But the order to leave their cave deeply saddened the remaining members of the group. However furious the bombardment had been, however enormous the danger and fragile the hope of surviving it, the conscripted students yearned to remain in Shuri, heart of Okinawa, repository of its national treasures, home of their school years. Sacred Shuri should not have been abandoned, especially since surrender of Army headquarters and the main fortifications was tacit admission of defeat.

But of course they obeyed the evacuation order, which for them came on May 27, the eve of Ushijima's skillful retreat. Assigned to help prepare the new 32nd Army headquarters, they were the first boys to leave. Before they went, however, Ota was startled by the approach of a girl. Himeyuri girls had been living in the same student cave since the beginning; the music teacher who composed the song in memory of the dead — and who would soon be dead himself — worked at the Himeyuri, not at the Normal School. But boys and girls were forbidden to talk, just as before the battle. The girl who approached, a pupil one year behind Ota in the same Kume elementary school, now broke the rule. "You boys all think it's your destiny to die before you're twenty," she whispered. "But death is the end, the end of everything. So you take care of yourself. Please don't die." Ota believed the younger girl shouldn't have talked that way; it was right to sacrifice one's life for one's country. He felt sullied by her solicitude — but couldn't help feeling flattered too.

Soon after those first and last words he ever heard from a girl student, the boys headed for their new base near the 32nd Army's relocated headquarters on a cliff above Mabuni in the far south. Weakened by severe diarrhea, probably from drinking contaminated water, Ota couldn't carry the sacks he'd been given. When he fell, a Japanese sergeant assigned to the group unsheathed his sword. "Stand up or I'll kill you." He swung and missed. A classmate shouldered Ota's burden in addition to his own, and both carried on.*

The sergeant's sword didn't dismay the boys; they believed the tough veteran was motivated by desire to accomplish the evacuation successfully. But later during the march, young Ota felt his first involuntary resentment of the Japanese, prompted by the sight of officers wearing civilian clothes over their uniforms. As always, the enemy's dreaded observation planes flew overhead, particularly the slow-moving L-5, nicknamed *tombo,* dragonfly, because of its looks.

---

* At their destination, the boys were saddened and angered to discover that some of the sacks of "vital documents" they had been ordered to guard with their lives in fact contained officers' personal effects.

Ota's messenger work had given him all too much experience of the pilots' ability to report every detail of movement on the roads. As soon as the Americans saw through the ruse of the clothing disguise, he reckoned, all civilians would become open targets. Shocked and angered, he perceived that this sacrifice of the very Okinawans the Japanese were supposedly defending was linked to a further deterioration of their military discipline.

It was worse in the far south — so bad that when Ota and a fellow communications soldier delivered a message to a cave and found it empty except for supplies and uniforms, they indulged a youthful impulse to put on captains' uniforms. Only the general breakdown of discipline allowed them to ignore the risk of being shot for impersonating an officer. Sleeves flapping, they left the little supply depot in late afternoon to return to their own cave — and almost stumbled into the arms of an American band directly outside.

Ota had seen only one live American previously: a pilot who parachuted from a plane shot down in the 10/10 air raid. Bound to a large tree in the courtyard of 32nd Army headquarters in Shuri, the pilot assured a crowd of gogglers that more American planes would soon arrive to rescue him. News of his capture spread like fire, attracting students eager for a peek at the animal — who, however, utterly failed to live up to expectations. The dreaded enemy was disappointingly human, obviously very tired and not much older than the teenage students themselves. "He's so young!" "Look how handsome!" Sentries used threats and fists to scatter those reacting in that unexpected manner, but the fascinated students returned. They found it impossible to hate the helpless individual who seemed to belie the common knowledge that Americans were beasts. His eyes weren't even blue. ("Blue-eyed devils" was standard in Japanese propaganda.) Someone ventured a timid "Hello." The young captive answered with a weak smile, prompting youthful grins in return and fury in a Japanese guard. "How can you smile at your enemy? Unpatriotic brats!" Several onlookers caught too near the prisoner were badly beaten.

Worse was dealt to students who made friendly advances. Ota's best friend, the Normal School's top student, was passionate about English and wanted to test himself. Use of the language had been forbidden for years; even baseball terms such as "strike" and "out" had been given obligatory Japanese equivalents. In the dead of night, the two sneaked from the school with food and water for the grateful pilot, who seemed tortured with thirst. Ota's friend exchanged a few words in English with him. The next day, he was viciously lashed by military policemen, then drafted into the Army. The boy was later killed in the fighting on Okinawa — months after the pilot, who escaped, perhaps with help, but was shot when recaptured.*

Now, eight months after seeing the pilot in Shuri, Ota was far beyond thoughts about the nature of the American people as a whole. He simply knew that the purpose of those on the island, devils or not, was to shoot Japanese soldiers — which they did like ducks. His terror therefore doubled when he and his friend almost ran into the group of duck shooters as they left the supply cave. Preparing their camp for the night, the huge, half-naked killers somehow failed to see the self-promoted Japanese "captains." The boys tore off their new uniforms and hid in yet another cave — where, to their surprise, they found an old classmate who had deserted his unit to look after his mother and young sister, refugee civilians. The 32nd Army's final collapse was still two weeks away, but Ota's classmate, a Normal School karate champion, had seen the light. "We're going to lose this war," he said. "So come with us and try to save yourselves. There's no point in still trying to fight." Ota was too astonished to answer anything but exactly what he thought: "What's happened to you? You've gone crazy!"

He and his friend made their way back to Mabuni, from where the survivors of his unit continued to take optimistic reports to towns and villages not yet in American hands, spending most nights in caves near the crumbling front. Approaching one such cave as a murderous artillery barrage began tearing the area, Ota was warned by Japanese soldiers to scram or they would shoot. But civilians called from inside the entrance, "This is *our* cave, not theirs. Come in!" Certain the shells would kill him in minutes, Ota did push in.

By evening, the infernal enemy approached the cave's mouth, but the soldiers inside told the civilians to pay them no attention. "We'll kill them, nothing to worry about." One by one, they crawled out of the cave and were shot dead. The last living soldier continued the reassurances: "I'm the only one left but don't worry; I'm responsible for you and I'll make sure you're safe." Shot too the moment he put his head outside the cave, he crawled back in, spurting blood and moaning. "Water, oh please water. I'm dying. It hurts."

Suddenly, he raised his head and shouted something thrillingly different: "*Tenno heika. Banzai!*" That was the first time Ota heard the

---

*Another American pilot who parachuted into Naha during a later raid in February was executed by an intelligence officer several days after the fall of Sugar Loaf in May. A third shot down and severely burned in March, a month before L-day, was beheaded about a week after the second. Little is known about other American pilots presumed captured. At least one was killed in Tokyo, where many fellow inmates of POW camps were also executed, some in savage reaction to the Emperor's surrender proclamation in August 1945.

stirring tribute to the Emperor — may he live "ten thousand years" — supposedly affirmed by all dying servicemen. The bloody man proclaimed it three times, filling Ota with such powerful, painful admiration and hope that he had to fight an overwhelming urge to weep. But just as suddenly, the soldier switched back to his fearful despair and whispered an offer of money to the confounded Ota if he would help him, *please* help him. "I have a bankbook, a bankbook! Please!" Next he tried to crawl back out of the cave; Ota had to pull him back by his ankle. Then the defiant *Tenno heika. Banzai!* again — but weakly. He died ten minutes later.

Ota stayed put until the middle of the night, then slipped out of the cave and through the American lines. In late June, he was back in Mabuni in time to see more terrible things in a forward section of the last 32nd Army headquarters cave where Generals Ushijima and Cho were still in command, deeper inside. The cave was packed with bleeding, rotting, half-crazed men milling about in confusion and despair. Ota forced himself not to acknowledge the implications of the unholy scene but noticed several women, Okinawan or Korean, some ten meters deeper inside, near General Ushijima himself. Several staff officers were changing into civilian clothes, evidently hoping to save themselves or infiltrate to the north to fight again. (Colonel Hiramichi Yahara, Ushijima's talented operations officer, was among those who would try to escape disguised as civilians.) A captain sprawled on the ground grabbed Ota's ankles. "I'm going to die here but please let my family know about me, please *tell* them." Never having seen the officer before, Ota asked his name. The captain was unwilling or unable to answer. The demoralization was such that no one else seemed to notice his display of broken nerve.

But young Ota salvaged his own nerve. After all, he assured himself, this is only a battle. The rest of the war still lay ahead; glorious Japan will not be defeated.

As he left the new headquarters cave, he realized he was now on his own. His Blood and Iron unit no longer existed; individual Japanese soldiers had no more power over him except the power of their bullets. Like fishermen's nets, American tanks, planes and troops were sweeping everyone toward the island's southern tip, leaving only the sea open for swimmers and nonswimmers alike. Something other than rational thought took command of Ota. It was like pure will or submission to destiny. He waded into the water and began swimming. He had no destination or plan except to escape from the enemy. The end seemed to come by itself after a few strokes. He went under and blacked out.

He woke up lying on some rocks. Hundreds of Japanese bodies, some lashed together, many bloated like jellyfish, bobbed on the sea and covered much of the beach near his own useless body. He had no idea what had washed him ashore or when, although it seemed days since he had slipped under the water. A lucky wave probably saved him, or a passing soldier — but none paid him any attention now. He crawled a few yards, the limit of his ability. Certain he could not live long in his condition, he in fact existed for weeks hidden with packs of dazed, crazed soldiers between giant boulders strewn along the beach. He slept during the day or watched arrogant enemy soldiers at work — or, as it seemed to him, a terrible kind of play. Stripped to the waist, Americans on the cliffs above (almost certainly replacement troops, for those who fought the battle were being evacuated for rest, rehabilitation and retraining during the last week of June) took their time picking off the mutilated rabble below. Famished, half-dead Japanese played target in this sport of victors by not waiting until dark to crawl from the protection of their rocks to hunt in the sand for a shellfish or clam. Ota himself was starving.

Ruriko Morishita, the sixteen-year-old nurses' aide, also refused to react to the evidence of defeat and demoralization. When key strongholds in the Shuri Line had begun falling, the Okinawa Military Hospital sent scouts south from Haebaru to compete with others from fighting units searching for new sites. The hospital officers secured caves for each major ward, none large enough to accommodate the three together. The first evacuation group left on May 20, a week before the general withdrawal. Miss Victory Day followed five nights later with the last group.

The high ridge into which the old hospital's caves were cut was a blackened lump. In Haebaru itself — Meadows of the Southerly Wind — hardly anything grew. One evacuee found it incredible to see no patch of green; there was only reddish mud churned into craters and piles by the deluge of shells. The ravages of Okinawa's typhoons seemed trifling in comparison to the destruction he saw.*

---

*Okinawans' admiration and dismay at the enemy's ability to alter nature itself would be deepened by their first sight of "instant" roads and airfields built even while the fighting progressed. This started on the day after L-day, when Americans jumped into huge construction machines as soon as areas behind the lines were judged relatively safe from Japanese artillery. Even in April, a pilot reported that much of the captured land "looked more like a construction site or highway project back home than a battlefield." By June, Army engineers and Navy Seabees were well advanced in their transformation of selected areas into a "little America" and an arsenal for the invasion of the mainland.

But Okinawans and Japanese noticed little of this: when not underground, they had to keep their heads far down. A prewar project to build a north-south highway the length of the island was estimated to require ten years. Natives would gasp when they saw that American know-how and machines had completed much of this job during the two months

Conditions during the evacuation surpassed those in the Haebaru caves. The thought of being left behind was enough to drive some of the seriously wounded to join the exodus. One soldier with paralyzing lockjaw used all his strength to turn in his bunk, a shelf cut into a wall of his cave, and plop past a lower shelf and into a litter that elderly Okinawans happened to be carrying along a tiny passage below. Although surprised, the Okinawans carried him from the cave without complaint. However, the shock of falling into the stretcher put the soldier's body into a violent tremble. Gesturing a prayer with his functioning hand, he begged heaven for help.

No mechanical help was available. Promised trucks failed to arrive for the patients and the residue of medical supplies. The army of broken bodies set out in their rags, some expecting death, others still fantasizing about victory and an imminent return to Haebaru. The shelling and recent downpours had turned the dirt roads into a crazy quilt of quagmires. Some of the young nurses' aides tried to carry patients on litters or on their backs, but the weight would have been too much even for healthy girls on a paved road; there was nothing to do but set down the burdens after a few gasping hours and stumble on without them. Groaning men struggled to push their crutches through the mire. Even the few who knew the way became lost in a torrential rain that made the night impenetrable. Others gave up when their strength was exhausted — and all had to stop at dawn to find a hiding place for the day. Some groups took three phantasmagoric nights to complete the trek to the new caves, six miles south.

Ruriko Morishita worried less about the wrecks she was helping, even the hundreds who expired during the evacuation, than about the larger portion of the two thousand-odd patients left at Haebaru. Before leaving, she asked a military medic what would happen to those gravely wounded, nonambulatory patients. "They'll send trucks for them after you evacuate," he assured her. "Don't worry, we'll get them to you when we find safe caves for them." Believing this as firmly as what she was told about the war in general, Ruriko in any case had neither the time nor strength to think otherwise. Still, she worried.

The truth was that Ward Three received a supply of potassium

---

since the landing. For most, the revelation would come when they were in custody. "Which is the width and which the length?" one prisoner would joke as his truck raced him to a camp at over 60 miles an hour along what had been the "excellent network of poor roads."

But the blasting, bulldozing and grading were done with almost no notice or consideration of native concerns. The remains of villages were knocked flat to accommodate American projects; their rubble sometimes added to the crushed coral for making new roadbeds. Whole hillsides of tombs were destroyed and paved over without a word of protest, since no one aware of the sacrilege was anywhere in sight.

cyanide to solve the problem more simply and honorably. But the Okinawan pediatrician serving as the ward's chief doctor ignored his oral order to administer it.*

Ruriko knew nothing about the promoting and abetting of suicide among those left behind. When rumors of poison being handed out and administered to patients in Wards One and Two reached her new cave, she assumed that hundreds had killed themselves or were killed — but by that time, her more immediate difficulties had made Haebaru's seem less devastating.

Ward Three's new cave lay half a mile below the crossroads village of Makabe, about a mile and a half north of the southern tip and three miles east of Mabuni and Hill 89, site of the cave of the 32nd Army's last headquarters. Centuries of rain water had carved the entrance, a vertical hole in the ground. The water went on to gouge a relatively large chamber at the bottom, then spread to create wings, like the tentacles of an octopus. The Cave of the Virgins, as it would become known, was among the area's best.

Twenty-four medics, thirty-six military nurses, and thirty student aides — the virgins, including Ruriko — arrived there after completing the exhausting evacuation, which took many more lives. It was fitting that no medical supplies remained: the new "ward" had no accommodation for any wounded. Nor, for that matter, for the ninety members of the staff, inasmuch as this cave, like all neighboring ones, was jammed with local civilians. Ward Three's senior medics ordered them to leave. "Military units have priority. We need this place for ourselves." Natives who had taken refuge crawled out to their imminent slaughter, like thousands of others in the doomed eight square miles — but because of what awaited the Cave of the Virgins, the chances of this group were no worse than if they'd been allowed to remain. Still, Ward Three's head military nurse, an Okinawan who joined the 32nd Army when the 10/10 air raid destroyed her public health offices, would have years of nightmares about her role in helping to "murder" fellow Okinawans.

With no wounded to care for, the medical staff turned to thoughts of their own unlikely survival. They had gone from a military unit to a cluster of prey waiting for an unspecified but easily pictured end. Perhaps because there were no exhausting duties to attend to, exhaustion suddenly overwhelmed them, striking down even Miss Victory Day. Ruriko and her fellow aides slept in a wing separate from

---

*There is no reason to doubt this man's quiet, dignified statement that he refused to kill his patients. But there must be some skepticism about surviving Japanese Army doctors, almost all of whom would claim, years later, that they did the same. Doses of poison were also provided for critically wounded medical personnel, including the young aides.

the military nurses'. The cave's dankness nurtured incipient tuberculosis. Most of the girls ran high fevers; all were painfully weak.

They left the cave only when ordered by the Japanese medics — chiefly to fetch water. Ruriko began to wonder whether all the cave's inhabitants shouldn't share the risk of running outside. Weren't they all Japanese? But her unspoken disappointment in her immediate superiors led to no questions about the war's rights and wrongs, even when the caustic Japanese medics lectured the aides about their own importance. "We're here protecting you Okinawans, so of course it should be your job to bring our water." Those superiors also ordered the aides out at night to hunt for sugar cane, weeds, anything to assuage the constant hunger. Their most troubling order was for the aides to sneak to other caves, search for unexpelled civilians, and requisition their food.

The 32nd Army disbanded all civilian corps on June 18, about three weeks after Ruriko's arrival in the new cave. Messengers delivered the order — "Henceforth, act on your own" — to the Cave of the Virgins the following day. There were now ninety-six people in the cave, including officers. Each aide was given about a pint of brown rice and two bags of hardtack. At a farewell party that evening, one of the girls chanted *naniwabushi*, highly popular stories performed in a singsong voice. A teacher displayed his dancing skills and there were many choruses of school carols and farewell songs before the gathering ended in the old pledge: "Whether I float as a corpse under the waters or sink beneath the grasses of the mountainside, I will willingly die for the Emperor." Some soldiers cleaned a machine gun, preparing to fight their way out. The aides made ready to exit and disband — some, like Ruriko, with great reluctance. They remained convinced that Japan would soon rise again.

At dusk, they heard American voices. The clearest, which sounded female, called, "*De-te koi, de-te koi!*" again and again. It produced little reaction in the cave. The silence was laden with tension but not fear. All had seen too many corpses to be terrified by death. Ruriko was only slightly surprised to feel so little emotion — and to hear a voice outside speaking Japanese.

"Are there any civilians in this cave? If so, cease your useless resistance and come out. Otherwise, we'll throw bombs in there."

The minutes seemed like days. Ruriko tried to coax two friends to retreat to the cave's more uncomfortable innards. Suddenly a Japanese nurse moved toward the exit, having decided at the last moment that she must find her father, an Army doctor serving elsewhere on the island. A student aide also wanted to leave. Ward Three's former Okinawan pediatrician had earlier gone to the cave that housed the hospital administration, leaving a Japanese Army doctor and senior medic in charge. Those two ordered the errant women to stay put, and posted an armed guard at the entrance. No promises of safety could be trusted, they repeated. The Americans will rape all women. The beasts will cut off people's ears and noses, draw and quarter them, flatten them under bulldozers, tear them apart.

A shattering explosion interrupted the angry words. Thick white smoke — impenetrable, suffocating — filled that part of the cave. Terrified voices cried, "Gas! Poison *gas!*" Some screamed for water, others for help. "Mother, I can't breathe! Help me, please!"

Scores died in minutes. Ruriko survived but couldn't breathe. A wounded orderly told her to urinate on her trousers and hold them to her mouth — but that protection against the "poison gas" of course provided no oxygen. (Almost all the dead, including the aide who wanted to find her father, were apparently killed by suffocation rather than the explosion itself, which was probably of white phosphorous hand grenades.) The cave resounded with even more desperate screams of "Mother! Father!" Ruriko's best friend lay beside her, moaning about herself and her poor parents, who, she now realized, had probably died in the same unbearable pain. Ruriko's sole way to help her was to admonish that such talk only made it worse. Her friend's reply came in gasps: "Sisters, I'm going now — ahead of you. Oh, how it hurts. Long live the Emperor!"

Those words somehow filled Ruriko with the desire not to expire in that terrible place. She resolved to leave and breathe real air — but could not move. Some giant force strangled her until she lost consciousness, terrified yet happy that the agony was over.

When she came to — probably saved by her urine-soaked trousers — she tried to talk and discovered she could not produce a sound. The cave reeked of rotting flesh. Yoshiko, another aide, also regained consciousness to find her hand tightly held by a third friend. Yoshiko moved the hand up and down while calling the third girl's name, but got no answer. Staring hard into the darkness, she saw she was holding the hand of a headless corpse. Yoshiko managed to get up and look down at the bodies at her feet — where something moved. "Someone's alive!" she tried to shout, but she too had lost her voice to the white phosphorous smoke. Soon she saw that the living person was Ruriko, also vainly trying to talk.

Ruriko felt "no sadness, no emotion — only numbness." Heaps of dead friends, agony twisting their faces, lay nearby. More died during the next two days. On the third, four of the thirty nurses' aides remained alive. The stench drove them out that evening.

Led by a teacher who had also cheated death, the four young

women dragged themselves outside the cave, where American fire quickly killed the teacher and two girls as they tried to crawl away. Ruriko escaped the bullets and took shelter in another cave, which she left four days later with another handful of survivors. None knew that the Americans had declared the battle over, the island secured. In fact, they saw no Americans at all. Apart from flares that lit up the night, Okinawa seemed empty.

Still dazed from the explosion in the Cave of the Virgins, Ruriko crawled about — not very far, in her condition — in scorched fields. She became separated from the others, then merged with still others for protection and sanity, kept crawling, sometimes fell asleep in midstep. The flat area had no outcroppings of coral and no crops remained for cover. Between crawling and hiding, she was shot three times. She would later assume Americans had aimed at her legs because, having won the battle, they weren't hunting for more lives. (It could not have been because they took pity on a female: no one could be expected to discern the sex of the filthy refugee in her ragged military uniform.) When she woke up the last time, American soldiers were standing over her little group of fugitives. One girl pulled the pin of a hand grenade to save herself from torture. She was near enough so that Ruriko Morishita, very weak from her wounds and malnutrition, knew she would surely die at last. She closed her eyes and waited. The grenade was a dud.

She too was one of the lucky: 123 of the 155 Himeyuri girls would soon be dead, together with scores of nurses' aides from the five less prestigious high schools. And some thirty-seven hundred soldiers and thirty-eight hundred civilians died in and around the village of Haebaru, where the southerly wind blew on the once tranquil meadows.

24 · Mopping Up

*In every case, the goal was to get rid of the Japs. They were simply capable
of too much, too many devious ways and tricks. We were professional killers
who knew not to take a chance.*
— Norris Buchter

*Did I tell you about the Nip who ruined our swimming hole by playing tap-
tap on his head with a grenade?*
— Buzzy Fox, letter home, July 5, 1945

All the beautiful white hospital ships — Solace, Relief, *and* Comfort —
*were gone. There were just too many wounded men; they couldn't handle
the casualty traffic. So I sailed off for Saipan on an APA. Goodbye Okinawa, and up yours.*
— William Manchester after his severe wounding by a screaming meemie

THE THIRD mountain spine tra-
versed Okinawa's width some three miles from the southern coast,
two miles from General Ushijima's new headquarters on the cliff facing the Pacific. The 32nd Army's last strongpoints were manned by
fresh units or survivors of battles farther north who had four or five
days for frantic preparations before the Americans' arrival.

The ragged heights presented another forbidding barrier to attackers. Two mountains in the center, Yoza-dake and Yaeju-dake,
were towering island formations, clearly visible from far at sea. Massive escarpments with hills and ridges between the mountains made
the terrain almost as formidable as at the Shuri Line. Although lack
of water kept defenders from establishing positions on the peaks,
sister regiments of Kojo's 22nd in the 24th Division used protective
formations lower down, still with excellent lines of sight on the approaches. As at Shuri, efficient defense systems based on interlocking
fire from a mass of hills awaited the Americans. The last of the Japanese antitank guns and heavy artillery zeroed in on streams, open
ground and passes where the attackers, including large numbers of
green replacements, were most vulnerable. The defenders were far
too few and too depleted to stop the advance, especially of tanks, but
they had more than enough arms to rip apart unlucky units assigned
to take the hardest objectives.

Also as before, the Army divisions faced some of the most difficult mazes of hills, in this case on the eastern, Pacific half of the mountain barrier protecting Ushijima's headquarters. Many were so steep that they had to be scaled by cargo nets under cover of darkness or smoke screens. In some sectors, Japanese newly arrived from the Shuri Line were too disorganized and discouraged to fight a fraction of their previous tenacity. American replacements who arrived just in time to mow them down and burn them out with relative ease considered them cannon fodder. But defenders elsewhere used combinations of cliffs, steep slopes and escarpments, and hundreds of protective crags, crevices and niches in the coral and rock to stand off the attackers for days. Faces stiff with exhaustion, heads bound in bands emblazoned with GOT TO WIN!, many Japanese still able to function as proper soldiers fought superbly. At their best, or worst, the far less elaborate defenses were almost as effective, and the fighting nearly as brutal, as at the "land battleships" farther north. One company of the American Army's 96th division lost 75 of 175 men in a single day on Yoza-dake. A Marine company lost seventy men and all its officers in taking one hill. One group of soldiers tried to crawl away at night from an ambush of Japanese fire that pinned them down. The survivors escaped on the eighth night of consecutive attempts.

The loss of old comrades dismayed some Americans more than before. Weaker than ever with skin and stomach problems, nervous strain and cumulative exhaustion, veterans were sustained by a growing hope that they and their buddies might beat the casualty odds. To be hit so late in the game, having survived so much, seemed the cruelest fate. Yet the day-by-day chance of being killed or wounded actually increased. Having dropped significantly after the taking of the Shuri, the sum of American casualties grew again at the last mountains. Properly supplied and reinforced, the 32nd Army would have made them another Shuri Line in terms of American effort and pain.

Kunishi Ridge, just south of the village of Kunishi, stood a kilometer to the west of Yoza-dake, two kilometers in from the East China Sea. The two-thousand-yard-long outcropping was almost smooth and steep enough to have been constructed to the defenders' specifications. The hardest fighting took place there, although the difference was marginal up and down the line. On June 9, units of the 1st Marine Division forded a little stream that marked the start of the assault on the ridge. As at Sugar Loaf, they had to cross a large open valley to reach the objective, which was serviced by a single road covered by defenders dug in at all the best places. The unit there, also from a sister regiment of Kojo's 22nd, had more surviving armament than any other and a detailed fire plan for the exposed areas that had to be crossed. Overlapping bands of machine gun fire raked the critical places. The Marines could make no progress the next two days; after borrowing a Japanese tactic to take the crest with a night attack, they found defensive fire from concealed guns on adjoining hills so intense that they could neither advance nor retreat. Reinforcements had to be brought up in tanks. No fewer than twenty-one were destroyed during assaults and counterassaults similar to those at the Shuri Line. Progress down the sides of the hills was yard by yard against caves, tunnels and mortars. It took three more long, hard days — five in all.

So it went at the other strongpoints in the last line, on and off the twin peaks of Yoza-dake and Yaeju-dake. A large mass known as "the Big Apple" blocked the approach to Yaeju-dake with deadly artillery fire. The fierce battles for Hills 69 and 95, the western and eastern anchors of that last mountain barrier, were sagas in themselves. Forbidding retreat, Ushijima had ordered the positions to be defended to the death.

> *Back at our holes, we "saddled up," ready for the daily patrol and daily killing.*
> — Stuart Upchurch

> *The 1st Division was understrength both in numbers and in physical constitution, while Mezado [Maesato] loomed on its right flank, an obstacle as formidable as any yet faced.*
> — Fletcher Pratt, The Marines' War

For Marine units, the action in the far south was very spotty. The unlucky ones continued taking heavy fire from steep coral formations as they inched around to rake the hidden enemy with bullets and napalm or made crawling advances under machine gun and mortar fire. At the same time, others drove toward the southern coast almost unopposed. But the nightmare of nighttime continued; in fact, it became worse because more dislodged Japanese prowled from dusk to dawn. Americans didn't know that many were hunting for food and water rather than for the enemy, but their terror wouldn't have diminished if they had known. The crunch of hobnailed boots on a road or coral rise triggered wild bursts from them.

The surprises also continued. Hurrying down a dirt road to rejoin his outfit, an infantryman named David Chipp saw a cluster of Marines frantically running north — without helmets, rifles and in one case trousers. Chipp was understandably bewildered. Could it be a counterattack? But he saw no Japanese and surely no combat Marines would flee in such terror even from a whole regiment of them.

"A damn ammo dump's been hit," a lead man explained while racing past as if in a sixty-yard dash. "Run like hell!" Chipp dived for a coral cliff alongside the road.

> It was everyone for himself. The first . . . shells flew over the top of the precipice and into the gully below me. My body was numb; my mind was a blank. I clung to the jagged edges of coral protrusions as tightly as I could. My hands were cut and bleeding. I felt no pain. The various projectiles hissed, swished, screamed, whined, whistled, wobbled, and looped overhead . . . I was oblivious to all around me except for the noises of the destructive shells. I was petrified!

Fear endured even without the surprises. When another infantry-man named Charles Leonard threw his last grenade into a shallow cave, a great cloud of smoke gushed out, together with gobs of burning white phosphorus. One landed on his sleeve, melted through in an instant, and emitted a nauseating smell as it began burning into his flesh. Leonard yanked the bayonet from his rifle. Using it to scrape at the phosphorus, he turned his attention from the cave, and out charged a Japanese soldier with *his* bayonet. Leonard managed to kill him with four quick rounds before the bayonet, advancing under its own momentum, wounded him superficially. The dead body slumped to the ground. Leonard shot it four more times and continued jerking on the trigger even after his clip ejected past his ear.

Manifestations of camaraderie and of bad luck also continued. A platoon leader wounded on Sugar Loaf badgered hospital personnel to discharge him. He needn't have gone back to the line, maybe even shouldn't have in his condition, but his men were still there. Finally certified fit for combat, he resumed command of them on June 17. That night, a hand grenade and coral fragments smashed his face to pulp.

Asato village was a mile north of the last mountain barrier, near the site of the decoy American landing on L-day. On the morning of June 19, an Okinawan boy named Shin-ichi Kuniyoshi was in a hill-side cave above the leveled hamlet, playing a typical part in the collapse of the 32nd Army. Fourteen-year-old Shin-ichi had been so hungry so long that his skinny body looked like a child's. But aged by the fighting, his dirty face might have belonged to a thirty-year-old.

Before the battle, Shin-ichi stood out among Okinawan youth because his father, who had come to identify with Japanese ambitions and discipline while working on the mainland, imbued his children with his own pride in having served at a time when the Imperial Japanese Army still rejected about 80 percent of Okinawan draftees.

That Army's exploits during the early years of the war enthralled Shin-ichi and his inseparable friend Miyagi, who dreamed of becoming officers. Shin-ichi's father was called up again, this time as one of the twenty thousand in the Home Guard, Boetai; his oldest brother, a soldier in Manchuria, would be captured by the Soviet Army when it entered the war a week before its end — and kept in Siberia for five years of slave labor. A second and third brother, one a sailor in the Imperial Navy and the other a kamikaze pilot, were soon to be killed in action. Resigned to losing her three elder boys, Shin-ichi's mother wept and pleaded, but the exciting game of war won the ninth-grader's heart. A month before L-day, he and Miyagi volunteered to serve with the 32nd Army, vowing to die for Japan.

They trained for three weeks to become communications soldiers in a less prestigious unit than Masahide Ota's. The perilous work delivering messages could not dim their patriotism or their admiration for the Imperial Army. Only one incident was troubling. In May, Shin-ichi found himself with a unit that went without water for several days because of extraordinarily intense American shelling at the Shuri Line. Shin-ichi of course obeyed when a soldier ordered him to dash to a nearby well, but felt the soldier himself should have taken that great risk. His own unit, however, was like a family, with a gentle sergeant named Inagaki as a surrogate father to the forty-six boys. On nights when Inagaki considered the shelling too terrible, he risked his own life — in failing to follow a superior's orders — by not dispatching them with their messages. Still, most of the boys were killed as they raced or crept from cave to cave or charged American troops and tanks. Six survived.

Now, near the end, Shin-ichi and Miyagi crouched in the Asato cave with a group of lost soldiers they barely knew. The American killers assigned to that sector of the last mountain line were about to approach. The cave was relatively solid, with a well-concealed entrance. American tanks and soldiers started from three hundred yards away, at the bottom of the hill. There was something admirable as well as terrible in their methodical advance, cave by cave, job by job. Survivors from a dozen blown caves nearby took refuge in this one, doubling its inhabitants since dawn to fifty or sixty soldiers. The enemy's flamethrowing tanks were everyone's greatest worry. Against them, they had small arms, grenades and a light machine gun. At 6:30 A.M., the roar of their exhaust announced the time had come.

But the tanks missed the cave's almost-hidden vertical mouth and continued up the hill. Squeezing in with soldiers directly under the entrance shaft, Shin-ichi tried to keep his body covered while firing up at the legs of American infantrymen who were following the tanks. Their shots were futile because of the angle, but the enemy's fire down into the cave was effective. Corpses piled up under the entrance. Brave men crawled from the cave's farther reaches to replace them.

At seven o'clock, they heard "Okay!" in a clear, urgent American voice. A minute later, a blinding explosion knocked them flat. When Shin-ichi came to, he supposed his eardrums had been shattered. His arms were pinned in excruciating positions and his chest was being pressed into the cave floor by an insupportable weight. Unable to move his head, he guessed that six or more corpses made up the pile crushing and suffocating him. Miyagi's pleas and moans echoed from the walls along with others, but he couldn't move to help his friend.

Miyagi's voice lasted longest. When it went silent, Shin-ichi began to moan, perhaps just to hear a human sound. He couldn't free either arm to use his hand grenade on himself, but supposed the weight of the bodies would kill him soon.

Hours later, a voice from deep in the cave asked who was calling for help. Hope and relief animated Shin-ichi's answer, and his mood rose another step from utter despair when he heard steps moving slowly toward him. At last the terrible weight on him was lightened — also exceedingly slowly. Finally free to roll over, he saw the unit's gangling young commander above him. Both eyeballs hung low on his cheeks, forced out by a metal fragment wedged in his forehead. Dripping blood and exhausted from his effort, the lieutenant dropped to the ground. "You can still fight so take my pistol, it's got three rounds," he wheezed. "Use two against the enemy and the last one for yourself. But first try to get to headquarters and report what happened to us here."

When the lieutenant died, it was Shin-ichi's turn to feel his way in the dark. The corpses had apparently saved him from more than cuts and bruises. He found Miyagi's body and tried not to weep. "I'll get back at them for this, I promise on my life. I'll kill as many as I can."

The litter of civilian and military corpses at the cave's mouth was decomposing when Shin-ichi climbed over it. The front line had pushed well south of the cave, but many enemy soldiers were in sight, stacking ammunition and supplies. Shin-ichi returned to the dark and waited with the bodies.

Sneaking out again shortly after dusk, he encountered more of the enemy almost immediately. Some were in foxholes, others pitching tents to radio music. But sentries patrolling every fifteen yards or so failed to see him. The headquarters cave the lieutenant cited in his last order was on Yoza-dake, about a mile and a half due east. Shin-ichi believed he could find his way even at night, traveling on his belly: enemy shells pounding the mountain would serve as a guide. First he had to pick the safest spot to slip through the enemy line, then the safest trail. Head in the dust, inching forward on his elbows, he made about a yard a minute. The first streaks of dawn found him in the middle of an American encampment, exhausted.

The only consolation was that this area was naturally free of enemy fire, the first relief he remembered from daytime shelling, bombing or strafing. But more crawling was impossible in the light; he was finished unless he found cover immediately. Raising his head just enough to look around, he saw clusters of Japanese corpses. Shin-ichi inched into a drainage ditch, covered himself with bodies, and completed his camouflage before full daylight. All he had to do was look like another corpse until sunset, in about sixteen hours.

Larger problems kept him from dwelling on the appalling stench of the real corpses roasting in the sun. The hardest was to fool the beasts by not moving a muscle. Okinawa's mean daily temperature in late June is over 85 degrees; daylight temperatures of course rise higher, especially in the far south. That late June's abnormally hot sun on that particular land table scorched him unmercifully. The terrible stiffness, the torturing thirst! Involuntary pleas for his mother sounded in Shin-ichi's head. He hadn't eaten or drunk for days. The agony of the thirst was greater than that of maggots wriggling from the corpses into his fresh cuts, his nostrils, his mouth and anus. The adolescent didn't move for the full sixteen hours — and triumphed.

When it was dark enough to continue, the stunning bombardment of Yoza-dake kept him headed in the right direction through all detours around American positions. Animal instinct alerted him to the enemy's breathing and body heat. Only the unrelieved thirst — this large plateau had long been known for its lack of water — became unbearable.

Suddenly, someone jumped on his back, frightening him almost out of his mind. "You carry me to Yoza. On your back." The Japanese soldier who hissed those frantic words was missing a leg; the stump was a mush of blood, raw flesh and crushed bone.

Shin-ichi was under five feet tall and weighed less than a hundred pounds. However, there was nothing to do but try to manage the burden, knowing he would never make Yoza now. Standing or slouching to carry the soldier was a sentence to death from an enemy rifle. But this was an order from a superior — who had a pistol pointed at Shin-ichi's head.

The dead weight caved in his knees. After twenty yards in a field full of Japanese corpses, the famished boy knew he could not take another step. "Sir," he whispered, "I have to go. I have a bad case of the runs." His pistol unmoving, the soldier ordered him to "take care of your business right here." Setting him down and making to open his trousers, Shin-ichi tried to calculate how much his tormentor's missing leg would slow his movements; whether the soldier was willing to bring on his own certain death by firing. He held his breath and dashed behind the man in a flash — then raced away and dived to the ground after a hundred yards.

He found his way again and headed for the flares lighting Yozadake like a hundred moons. It was clear to him that he was more likely to die of thirst than of exhaustion. But he reached the mountain before dawn and had the luck not to be hit by a shell on his crawl to the headquarters cave. Some thirty soldiers inside, hardly believing he had come through the enemy lines from Asato, praised him generously. Reporting to the senior officer, Shin-ichi was dizzy with pride and happiness. As if that were not enough, the soldiers treated him to as much as he wanted of all they had. He drank his belly full and feasted from bags of hardtack in the cave. For the moment, the boy could ask for nothing more.

25 · American Atrocities

We were not in favor of giving the Japs a chance to surrender, but orders are orders.

   — An American Marine in a letter to his parents

It got to the point — I shouldn't say this — that Japs wouldn't surrender to Marines. If they wanted to surrender, they'd go to the Army. Ninety-nine percent of Marines would shoot them, and that includes me. You know why? You hated them for what they did to your buddies, so many of them. Besides, they tried to pull so many dirty tricks with their hands up — you could never trust them. So they weren't worth the really great risk, which you didn't want to take anyway. I didn't.

   — Another Marine, forty years later

Nobody wanted to take prisoners to begin with — nobody who had had a buddy killed, which was almost everybody. And nobody wanted to go somewhere to do it — leave his living buddies to walk the prisoners back behind the lines. Why take the risk? When they first started surrendering, we shot as many as we took.

   — A third Marine, also later

I shot one in the back as he was trying to escape. One day, I shot one who was trying to surrender.

   — A fourth Marine, one of many later dedicated to reconciliation

We had barbaric people too. You don't make a bracelet of Jap teeth without ripping them out of Jap heads.

   — A fifth Marine, 1983

There was something in some of the people I really didn't understand, real sadism or something. Myself, I only saw actual torture once. One of us had a knife at a sweating Jap's throat while he was interrogating him — and then just ran the blade right through. I was a green replacement. I didn't know what made the American do that, so I didn't say anything. But after I fought for a while myself, I realized there was no reason for that kind of crap. Well, there was a reason but it can't be accepted. Because the minute you do accept it, we become like Japs or Nazis and there are no winners, just all losers.

   — A sixth Marine, 1986

IN MID-JUNE, a week before the official end of the campaign, Japanese began surrendering in sizable numbers. Until then, the average had been four men daily. Many American companies fought for eight or ten weeks without taking a single prisoner. Many saw no enemy soldiers at all apart from dead — certainly never saw one try to surrender or allow himself to be taken unless he was physically or mentally disabled by bombs or artillery shells. But the 32nd Army's teetering morale began going over the edge in some units whose last lines of communication were gone. White flags, or substitutes, became a common sight.

On June 12, the day after Admiral Ota's final message to General Ushijima, 159 members of his Naval Base Force surrendered from among those who hadn't killed themselves before the Marine spectators on the Oroku Peninsula. That was by far the largest number until then. The daily average rose from the four in mid-June to fifty during the third week of the month, soaring to 343 on June 19 alone, a huge number by Japanese standards. One four-man patrol captured 150 prisoners after their officers bowed, surrendered their swords, shot some Okinawan women who had been accompanying them, and killed themselves. In all, almost three thousand Japanese were taken prisoner during the second half of June, about a third of the number killed during the same period.

The final count would come to seventy-four hundred, slightly less astounding than it seemed because about half proved to be conscripted Okinawans. Still, it was more than in the rest of the Pacific War, and many Americans *were* astounded, and justifiably frightened, especially by sudden appearances of droves of Japanese. A Marine fire team approaching the cliffs above the southern coast in late June was startled by four enemy soldiers who emerged from the bush carrying two wounded in stretchers. The Marines gestured for the four to drop their gear and strip. When they were in loin cloths and little able to work a trick, the Americans approached with C-rations, water and smokes. Suddenly, up to a hundred more poured from "nowhere" and surrounded the Americans — who included Lenly Cotten, the eighteen-year-old who had arranged to be shipped to combat by getting himself arrested west of the Mississippi. Cotten had seen Japanese blow themselves up with grenades held to their chests. Since this crowd was well armed, he thought his end had come. "There we were, completely surrounded; they could have finished us like Custer. They didn't seem to know what they were going to do, and *we* sure as hell didn't know, only that dying was their honorable thing and taking an American along was even better. But they'd probably sent out those first six to test us — to see whether we'd torture them. After an age, they gave themselves up, the whole bunch."

Such surrenders were new in Japanese history. Although the percentage remained very slight in relation to those killed in action, the absolute count leaped to nearly a thousand — probably half of them conscripted Okinawans — on June 20 and 21. That was the number of prisoners taken. The number shot will never be known.

Some Americans believe it was many. "You had no mercy for them whatever by the end of the campaign," one explained. "Nine Marines in ten would shoot them. If you saw a Jap trying to surrender, you'd let him have it fast." Other participants have disputed such contentions. Another infantryman remembered his outfit as "pretty damn tough; it was all hate and kill. But when we took a prisoner, he stayed alive." The truth between the extreme claims cannot be measured except to say that the killing of prisoners was widespread in some units.

Many officers condoned, even suggested it, until surrenders came in dozens on the very last days. "Your company commander would say, 'Take these people [Japanese prisoners] to regimental headquarters and be back here in five minutes,'" a third infantryman explained. "Regimental headquarters was thirty minutes away. He was telling you to get rid of them." "We gave our prisoners every excuse to run so we could finish them," another veteran added. "Nobody wanted to escort them five hundred yards through scary terrain where *he* could be shot. Nobody wanted to go *five* yards with them. For what?"

A weary platoon of Owen Stebbins's G–2–22 Company was cleaning out a sugar cane field south of Naha in early June. One of its combat veterans was calculating whether to jump across a little brook or get his feet wet when a young replacement's terror-frozen face instantly sent him into a higher level of alert. The veteran — Irving Ortel — shot almost at the same instant as he looked down and saw a Japanese arm reaching through some reeds to grip the replacement by an ankle. No one will ever know whether the wretched man was trying to hurt the American or surrender or both. "Later, I realized that's what the Jap might have been trying to do: surrender. But what I did *then* was what anyone with experience would have done: shot him that second. Killing him was instinct by that time. You had to do it. You were shot if you didn't shoot. You killed and didn't think twice about it."

"When they started surrendering," another man remembered, "we were supposed to take them back to the MPs at the command post or to some guys who came up from regimental headquarters. But we never took a lot of them back. We shot them — me too. We did it because . . . what we'd all been through all that time, understand? It was that terrible combat. Then it was Japs pretending to surrender so they could shoot *you*. One dressed in civilian clothes suddenly whips a pistol from behind his back and tries to get us with it. I saw plenty of things like that, but one was enough for everybody. So not many prisoners arrived back at command posts until the very last days."

A member of an Army transportation company encountered a group of Marines who urged him to shoot the prisoner he was escorting to the rear. The soldier, who had gone AWOL from his unit in order to participate in combat, took the suggestion but his carbine jammed. The Marines advised him to take his time and clean his weapon — which he did, then killed the man. The same soldier assumed a truckload he saw of Naval Base Force prisoners was being driven to a convenient place for shooting. They seemed white with fear.*

> Okinawa was a killing field. In the 82 days of battle for that island, an average of about 2500 people died every day. Under those conditions, with death everywhere, I seemed to have gone into a sort of trance. It was as if I had left my body and was looking at myself in a movie. I just did not feel anything.
>
> — Peter Milo

Shooting a man who had his hands up or may have wanted to put them up wasn't necessarily an atrocity. No American infantryman, whatever his previous moral tenets, had any question that unless every Japanese who prompted the slightest doubt about his intentions was killed, he would kill Americans. That cliché expressed an unrelenting reality on Okinawa. It did not necessarily reflect racial hatred or any hatred; many simply knew the job had to be done. On top of that, however, most riflemen were exhausted, frightened and full of grief for their own losses when they pulled their triggers on the unarmed, or seemingly unarmed, men. Some felt ambivalent about the

---

*It is worth repeating that Japanese who wanted to capitulate faced perhaps a greater risk of being killed by Japanese bullets than American, and General Buckner's men came to realize that when they saw Japanese throw grenades at other Japanese who carried surrender leaflets. One Japanese lieutenant who had graduated from an Ivy League college gave himself up with one of his sergeants. Soon a sniper started firing, apparently more at them than at the Marines to whom they surrendered. The Japanese calmly took the fire until one of the Marines told "you dumb bastards" to take cover, whereon they did what they were ordered and were saved.

enemy. Some had twinges of respect, admiration, perhaps sympathy for them. William Manchester was among those who hated other people more, including Frank Sinatra and everyone else who was free of danger and actually enjoying the war, "whereas the Japanese were right where we were, in the mud and shit, getting pounded by artillery." But most of the time, the feelings of almost every American in the line were clear: the bond with their comrades in arms went hand in glove with loathing for those who shot and shelled them. Whatever they felt about Japan in general, they detested the Japanese who killed their individual loved ones. "I didn't hate Japs before," one remembered. "It came the minute I saw my first buddy lying there in parts — the guy I lived with every day, the guy I loved. I started hating the bastards, a hatred I feel to this day. *I saw my buddy get killed!*"

It made no difference that killing was among both sides' most obvious goals and that there was nothing personal in it; the death of friends was a shattering personal tragedy for all Americans (as, of course, for all Japanese). A flamethrower who worked with various platoons, Evan Regal knew most of his company's sixty-nine KIAs (of its original 256 men). "The Japs had to be killed anyway because of how they fought; there was no other way. But what made you *want* to do it was your friends. When you saw their corpses day after day, your hatred — oh God, *hatred* — built day after day. By June, I had no mercy for a single Jap who wanted to surrender."

Any inclination to be merciful was further reduced by the aspiration to emerge whole: hidden hope that rose in proportion to the approach of victory. When the ocean below the southern coast became visible from the high ground, Americans had a real chance to "make it," and many resolved to do so, no matter what. That was just when the number of Japanese prisoners surged, along with the pressure for their quick disposal.

More than emotional reasons argued for this. To escort a prisoner to the rear was truly to expose oneself to additional danger. No one wanted to gamble on leaving the security of his unit for a single step through land dotted with unknown caves and "spider holes." Such risk was taken to help a buddy back to an aid station — but not for a Jap whose fellow Japs had killed so many of yours and who was aiming to get you. Not for a sneaky rat who might, even at this stage and even after being searched, die happily by pulling a grenade from his loin cloth and blowing you up along with himself. Every combat American had seen or heard of such performances of the final duty. Their common goal was to dispose *quickly* of the Japs who might try.

Ordinarily mild Norris Buchter had learned that "they were simply capable of too much, too many devious ways and tricks. You didn't want to get within grenade-throwing range of them, so you sometimes shot them as fast as you could."

There were also sound practical reasons — not mere excuses — for torching all Okinawan huts, as Americans continued to call the native houses. Since enemy snipers hid in some, large numbers were burned to the ground without regret or guilt. And there were provocations for many unreported incidents of American cruelty. In early April, a Marine fire team used cigarettes to burn the letters USMC on the chest of a dazed Japanese soldier they'd captured, then broke his leg by dropping the stretcher on which they were carrying him to the rear, as ordered by their officer. The group had found the "son of a bitch" next to two murdered children and a woman he'd raped before slitting her throat.

Beyond this, there was the extenuating circumstance of the Japanese way of fighting. They charged through their own artillery fire on their way to American positions. They cared less for themselves, as Americans saw it, than for their Emperor and spilled any amount of blood for him — and on their own impulses. In the third week of June, a Korean laborer emerged from a cave near the southern tip and told the American team that had blasted it that a dead Marine was inside. Reluctant to enter in case some of the Japanese were still alive, the Americans gave the Korean a wire to tie to the corpse. They pulled it out. One of the team saw an old friend who had grown up nearby in Georgia and trained with him on Guadalcanal. His ears and penis had been cut off, his face smeared with excrement. It was hard to keep men from taking revenge against so barbarous an enemy. The Marines who were driving the truckload of Naval Base Force Japanese to possible shooting had just taken some territory where American captives had evidently been shot. "Okay," one of them said, "the Japs don't take prisoners and we won't either." Some sprayed cave mouths with full submachine gun magazines after promising safety to all who came out with their hands up — but even they weren't necessarily war criminals (although not all other Americans considered them fully normal either). But if there was a rationalization for some of the brutal acts, there was none for others. War spawned many unqualified atrocities on Okinawa, as almost everywhere. "Once you kill somebody, the first one, it's much easier after that," Ed Jones remembered. "When they came out of the caves, it was like target practice, like a turkey shoot."

Some of the most revolting acts involved the enemy dead. One machine gun squad moved about with a makeshift little pipe, which it

used for directing their urine into the mouths of Japanese corpses.*
"I like to think we went to Okinawa with American standards and
morals," a man in that squad remembered in shame and disgust.
"But it was a crazy world there and we did crazy things."

In some cases, it was a short step from desecrating corpses to hankering for them, although most of that hankering was a normal reflex of fear or rage rather than an expression of anything pathologi-
cal. On one of the last days of the official campaign, a platoon leader
asked for volunteers to clean up a cave that had been vainly showered
with surrender leaflets the previous day. Noises disclosed that enemy
soldiers were still inside, but Lenly Cotten was "one of the 'crazies,'"
in his own description, "looking for a little more excitement now that
the real fighting had dulled down." He and other volunteers lowered
themselves into a theaterlike cavern that fronted the cave. While taking prisoners there, Cotten saw one Japanese fail to put up his hands.
He fired a burst of his BAR at the man's feet and saw him dash
deeper into the cave. Cotten started after him, but thought better of
it and called for a satchel charge. Just then he heard the pin of a
Japanese grenade being driven in and turned to race away, but
couldn't move fast enough over the coral. The grenade exploded
precisely where Cotten had been standing and sent fragments of steel
and coral into most of his body. (He spent eleven months recovering
in hospitals.)

At almost the same time, a platoon mate threw the satchel charge
inside the cave and the dazed Japanese emerged, probably with rup-
tured ear drums. Another volunteer fell on him with his Kabar knife.
"He was a buddy," Cotten remembered. "He had lost one friend
after another since April, and he himself had had a dozen minor
wounds. I myself was pretty much dazed after the grenade, but I still
felt pretty happy when I heard the Jap had been slashed to death.
'Nice going, they got that son of a bitch.'"

---

*One of E. B. Sledge's officers took pleasure in urinating directly into the mouths of
Japanese corpses, and once pulled down a corpse's trousers so that he could shoot off the
head of its penis with his carbine. "As he exulted over his aim, I turned away in disgust . . .
It was the most repulsive thing I ever saw an American do in the war. I was ashamed that
he was a Marine officer . . . Mac was a decent, clean-cut man but one of those who apparently felt no restraints under the brutalizing influence of war — although he had hardly
been in combat at that time."

That incident also illustrates that most Americans, although they rarely protested, were
disgusted by such acts even after they had been brutalized by combat. And that a disproportionate number of the disgusting acts were performed by new replacements or noncombatants, as opposed to bone-weary infantrymen who had seen too much killing and
other forms of horror during their long stints in the field. The soldier who cleaned his
carbine at the suggestion of Marines and shot his prisoner a second time was an artist. He
still felt so bad about his act after returning home to Flushing, New York, that he made a
lithograph of the scene.

Later, Cotten's happiness was replaced by memory of the "poor bastard" and regret for war's madness and cruelty. He was one of the majority on Okinawa who killed frequently without being killers — whose killing was more sane than sadistic. But almost inevitably, a small percentage of Americans was more thrilled by killing than by winning the battle or the war. Almost inevitably too, the percentage of disturbed psyches grew during the campaign. Every combat infantryman knew men — sometimes heroes — who took unnatural pleasure in the pain it was his duty to cause.

> *I've a Jap Imperial Marine coat, one for myself and one for [uncle] Eddie. We captured a Nip Q[uarter] M[aster] dump and they are brand new so Eddie doesn't have to worry about any stink in them.*
> — Buzzy Fox, letter home, June 15, 1945

> *As I look back, the first thing I can recall is the old saying that, no matter what goes on, someone will always figure a way to make a buck. I guess it's just a plain old American custom. Things were pretty quiet in the north . . . and the agile mind of one of our battalion officers quickly went to work. It seems we had taken over . . . the headquarters for the Japanese Imperial Marines. The place was loaded with hundreds, maybe thousands, of the Nip Marine insignia. So this enterprising officer dug up some sewing machines, got some cloth and put everyone he could find to work making Japanese Imperial Marine battle flags. I must confess they were a hell of a lot better than the ones from the Nip Army. Then he took the flags out to some of the hundreds of U.S. Navy ships off Okinawa. My God, did he clean up!*
> — Lee P. Stack, a tank officer

> *It is inconceivable to me that Americans in Europe would value some old sock or filthy cap just because it had belonged to a German, yet that is what is regularly done with Japanese souvenirs. The curiosity attached to the Japanese prisoner is such that many Americans are amazed to find that some of them are reasonably well built, that others have had enough education to say "Thank you" in English (which is usually interpreted as "He speaks fluent English!") . . . I think the answer . . . is that the Americans are unable as yet to appreciate the Japanese as human beings.*
> — Donald Keene, later a distinguished scholar of Japanese literature, to a friend on Okinawa, September 1945

There was also the strange lust for souvenirs. If the Japanese determination to die defied explanation to most Americans, an American passion for largely worthless Japanese artifacts also bordered on the bizarre. In a campaign that demanded every ounce of an infantryman's energy to stay alive, everyone knew that one of the most perilous things he could do was to go on a souvenir hunt. A disproportionate number who left their units for this sport — usually in twos and threes, often without informing their platoon leaders — were later found with their torsos riddled or throats slit. Some were killed by souvenirs themselves that had been booby-trapped: grenades fixed behind pictures on hut walls, Japanese rifles wired to explode when picked up. Others were shot by own fire, as with a young artilleryman named Pringle, who was rummaging in the shell of a house when a patrol of replacement infantrymen heard the noise, challenged and fired immediately. (Pringle had his mouth open to reply to the challenge; a bullet passed his lips, tore out several teeth, broke his jaw and exited through the back of his neck. He survived, but others needlessly hit by American rounds increased the killed-in-action statistics.) Yet no amount of risk deterred multitudes from hunting. Veterans violated fundamental rules of the combat wisdom acquired with such pain. Otherwise sober, cautious men ventured into caves for a possible find, an action ordinarily not attempted without careful back-up at the entrances.

Veterans of previous campaigns launched the competition for trophies on L-day. When the unknowing Zero landed at Yomitan Airfield that afternoon, Marines rushed to strip the pilot the moment they shot him — and the hunt was on. Americans devoted an inordinate amount of their free time to "collecting" — often, as one observer put it, "before the enemy hit the ground."

Samurai swords led the list. Other prized items included Japanese battle flags, especially large ones signed by all members of a given unit, and waistbands, each made by a loving mother who solicited contributions of a stitch each from a thousand women in the soldier's neighborhood. Americans valued them all the more, believing all the contributors were virgins. Many kamikaze pilots wore "thousand-stitch belts" on their final flights. But terrible risks were also taken for the most doubtful treasure: letters, teeth, belts, bones, underwear, yellowed snapshots, dirty caps, watches, rifles, combs, rice bowls, fresh fingers, fingers for pickling, *anything*. Infantrymen who traveled light and lean would proudly unwrap something from their packs to show to others: an ear. "Got me a souvenir!" It did not have to be military. The most humble Okinawan home usually had family photographs on the walls, the subjects uncharacteristically stiff in uniform or their best kimonos and blouses. They too were booty. One man found two photograph albums, a track suit and a pair of shoes — of an Okinawan track star, it happened — in the rubble. He grabbed them. (The albums would lie unopened under his bed for nearly four decades.) Others looted Okinawan offices of records and documents for which they had no conceivable use.

Dedicated collectors removed leg wrappings from reeking corpses — and were irritated when some items proved less valuable than their promise. One ordinarily admirable married man complained in a letter home that a wedding ring he'd taken turned out to be brass and "tarnished my whole finger." Much of the looting was carried on with a kind of innocence based on a presumption of superiors' rights. An officer observed an American soldier searching the body of a Japanese he'd just killed. "He took his trench knife and slit his pockets and several items tumbled out, including a wallet." The looter examined the wallet. Much to his surprise, it contained some American identification cards and currency and several snapshots of an American girl. "'Why those dirty bastards!' he declared indignantly. 'They even rob our dead!'"

Souvenir hunters broke yet more rules by lugging their stuff into battlefields, sometimes disposing of every possible item of their own gear to lighten their burden. Those who had to jettison articles during combat emergencies did so with great reluctance. This irrational passion for loot derived partly from life assertion. The "collectors" were displaced, frightened young men. The objects were proof of their visit to and survival in the nether world of combat against the "fanatic" Japanese. But it also derived from the view of those Japanese as less than fully human. The otherwise worthless souvenirs had the value of being from another species, another planet.

A good proportion of American letters home was devoted to the booty and to resentment when it was confiscated. "You risk your life getting the darn things," one veteran complained, evidently unaware of the folly he was revealing, "and then some jerk takes them away from you." Many front-line fighters were convinced that rear-echelon troops lifted their treasure for themselves. Some items were confiscated as contraband firearms, others because they were evidence of the officially prohibited mutilation of corpses — as when infantrymen rushed from the safety of their foxholes at first light to yank gold teeth from the enemy infiltrators killed during the night.* Here too, letters home reveal an almost innocent greed, as when a machine gunner informed his mother of his rights to a Japanese corpse he shot one May night.

> I waited for daylight because that Nip was "my man" and whatever he had on him belonged to me . . . When daylight came I pounced on him [but] all the son of a gun had was a flag and a fountain pen and of course a grenade but I let him have that . . . That same night my buddy in the next hole got a Jap doctor and he got a

---

*The majority of Americans refrained from such activities for more than one reason. A captain on Guadalcanal was shown a bag of gold teeth by a platoon sergeant who worked over every corpse he could find. "How in the name of heaven," the captain reacted, "can you put your hand into a stinking Jap's mouth?"

pistol, saber and watch. I already had my saber and 2 watches so I wasn't envious. I was glad though he had at least the common decency to carry a flag even if he didn't know that it would add to the Armed Forces collection. I only hope now that my box gets safely to [my wife]. I have a private ownership slip signed by my C.O. in it but some of those post office commandoes really do a job rifling your souvenir boxes. You get together with [my wife] and see if there is a flag, a pocket watch, a wristwatch, a cigarette lighter, gold teeth, a pen and a lot of little odds and ends.

Souvenirs became the currency for which cigarettes, fruit juice and other delicacies and valuables were swapped, including pornographic photographs.* As soon as the fighting was finished for them, American infantrymen hitchhiked to other units to sell or exchange some of their acquisitions. Demand for ears increased on land and in the fleet. One man who had "relieved" a Japanese doctor of his sword — "which goes big out here and it's a mighty proud thing to own" — hoped to sell enough prizes to buy a little car when he returned home. At that point, he also had four Japanese rifles, two of which he would give away or trade and one that he would sell for $50, then just under a month's salary. The fourth rifle was stolen, though he had taken the precaution of sleeping with it so that he could take it home.

Trophy hunting merged with sadism when gold teeth were pried not only from corpses but from badly wounded but living Japanese.† Some were stabbed, bayoneted or shot as they lay on the ground. Although it was not true in every case, the most zealous collectors of ears and skulls were the most likely to commit atrocities.

Several days after the "comic" incident when a Japanese sneaked up on Whitaker's buddy while he was squatting to relieve himself, the company was still on the Oroku Peninsula. Whitaker and the others came upon a handsome little house that promised some comfort for a night. Its rice-paper door and windows were surprisingly intact. The men quickly knocked them out to provide clear fields of fire from inside.

---

*The Navy was the source of the best supply of porno, through photographers who evidently had access to negatives in a rear base. In mid-May, a sailor traded a dozen dirty pictures for a stained little Japanese flag and what a witness to the transaction took for a small quantity of opium.

†Ernie Pyle prettified souvenir hunting like the rest of combat. "One of these days Mrs. Leland Taylor of Jackson, Mich, is going to be the envy of all her friends," he filed from Okinawa in April. "For she is about to come into possession of four pairs of the most beautiful Japanese pajamas you ever saw. These are daytime pajamas . . . the kind that some American hostesses wear at cozy cocktail parties. Mrs. Taylor's husband, who is a Marine corporal and known as 'Pop,' found these pajamas in a wicker basket hidden in a cave . . . Pop carries the basket around on his arm from place to place until he gets a chance to ship them home." As usual, the supply of charming detail concealed the real story.

Toward morning, Whitaker lay half-awake on a mat, calculating whether it was safe to light a cigarette. It had been one of the nights when he got little of the sleep his body craved, in this case less because of fear of waking up with his throat being cut than because he'd stood watch many hours and sensed he was due for another turn.

Whitaker's new assignment as a runner for the company commander meant that he hardly knew Charles Oates, the man now on watch. He did know that Private Oates had himself been a runner for their previous company commander, Captain Robert Fowler. And that Fowler's death had upset him deeply — with good reason. Incorrigible young Oates was thought to have been an orphan and known to be a problem. His buddies felt he'd gone "a little Asiatic," meaning sadistic or willing to court too many risks in his eagerness to kill. (The irony in this tag for fellow Americans with a penchant for atrocities seemed to be unintentional.) Then Fowler took him under his wing, and Oates, who had bucked orders from everyone else, settled down under his surrogate father — until the captain was hit in the field and bled to death from a wound in the spleen.

Now Oates touched Whitaker in the dark of the house and turned back to the door to stare at something. Without so much as a whispered word, Whitaker silently crawled to a knocked-out window and saw a thick morning mist rising from a nearby canal. Three Japanese soldiers were approaching through it, moving slowly and with extreme caution. When they were a hundred yards away, Whitaker saw they were in loin cloths, apparently unarmed. He thought they possibly intended to give themselves up, although he knew that was not a certainty.

Shuffling forward in half-steps, the Japanese saw Oates in the doorway. He gestured for them to keep coming. Then Whitaker noticed Oates was holding a chrome-plated Colt .44 behind his back. It had been a gift to the stricken, grieving problem kid from beloved Captain Fowler as Fowler lay bleeding to death. It came with a fancy Western-style holster.

The Japanese kept approaching. Whitaker knew that stripping almost naked often signaled a wish to surrender but that loin cloths could conceal grenades. He also knew never to trust a pistol alone. Again without a word, he dropped to the floor, slid to his mat and picked up his submachine gun, preparing for what the Japs might attempt. He covered them while they continued inching forward and Oates continued beckoning from the doorway. When they were twenty yards away, Oates dropped to a crouch and fired away as if in a Western movie.

At the time, the three bodies sprawled on the ground meant nothing to Whitaker. He and his buddies had seen so much death (*"so much in so many ways"*) that they weren't worth thinking about. If he had thought then, he'd have reckoned that the three were Japanese who deserved to die. What stayed with him was only how Oates saw to that. If he had followed the rules, he'd have stopped the Japanese and searched them, awakening the other Americans in the process. If he simply wanted to kill, he could have stopped them, turned them around and shot them in the back, to which the other Americans wouldn't have objected. Or simply mowed them down. But the "Jap killer," as he became known after Fowler's death — a significant term among Marines who were all Jap killers — wanted to avenge the death of the captain he respected and loved, and had to do it with Robert Fowler's gun.

That was different from the nasty *job* of killing. Oates's way also differed from the combat wisdom acquired by other veterans, which did not bode well for him. A week later, he was missing from his unit. Nothing was heard of him for several days, until a flamethrowing tank found his body. Whitaker and the others guessed he had died on a private, extracurricular mission to kill more Japs.

Atrocities against natives fell into more distressing categories, which shouldn't be mentioned without stressing the 10th Army's overriding respect for the Geneva Convention and specifying that most units were frequently told — in some cases constantly admonished — to try to save innocent lives. For most troops, the lectures were superfluous. They didn't want to kill unarmed civilians. In many cases, they risked their lives not to — by throwing smoke instead of phosphorous or fragmentation grenades into caves, for example. This was done for the sake of native families inside, but it allowed any soldiers mingled with them the luxury of shooting back.

It is also worth repeating that many Americans performed acts of humanity far beyond the Convention's requirements. Voluntary mercies and kindnesses to civilians abounded, from individual fighters emptying their packs to feed children to units adopting older children as mascots to corpsmen — the same who saved Japanese wounded — delivering Okinawan babies under extremely difficult conditions.* The photographs of GIs and Leathernecks passing out candy bars,

---

*And not only corpsmen. Sergeant J. R. Aichie was walking down a southern road one evening when an old woman "scared the hell" out of him. Emerging from some bushes, the woman tugged at his arm and eventually led him to a tomb, where a young woman was in labor. A machine gunner with no experience of obstetrics, Aichie did what he could. Word spread of the machine gunner "doctor." By the end of the campaign, Sergeant Aichie helped deliver four more babies, all of whom he would see on postwar trips to Okinawa.

cigarettes and cans of food didn't lie; the American public wasn't wrong to be convinced of their men's magnanimity. Far from shooting civilians when they could avoid it, most Americans continued to be generous in their instinctive, artless way. One Okinawan kid hiding in a cave with his mother and grandmother hadn't eaten for four days. Terrified of the approaching Americans, his mother stopped him from slipping out early in the morning to scavenge for food. When Americans appeared and called from the mouth of the cave, the civilians finally went out, convinced they would be tortured and killed. A Marine gave the boy a can of food. His mother begged him not to eat it, but he was too hungry to obey. Forty-five years later, his voice still broke when he told the story.

A kid in a nearby cave watched the approach of two enormous shoes. The "giant" who wore them was a flamethrower. The boy said a trembling goodbye to his parents but the giant handed him a Hershey bar.

In June, Marines found another boy, whom they took for an Okinawan, in a Japanese uniform and told him he'd surely be killed unless he took it off immediately. The beneficiary of that advice happened to be a twenty-year-old Japanese soldier small enough to have prompted the Americans' concern. And American bravery helped Okinawans more than their gullibility. While some soldiers and Marines poured napalm into caves and tossed in grenades to ignite an inferno, others — sometimes the same men — risked their lives to get civilians out when they realized who was burning inside.

But there were also many shameful acts. If a balance sheet between atrocities and generosities is ever drawn up, an outsider who has never suffered the pressures of combat will not be fit to do it. But ignoring the atrocities completely, as virtually every military account does, is too good to war and its phony legends. If Secretary of the Navy James Forrestal could "never again see a U.S. Marine without experiencing a feeling of reverence," as he said after watching a film of the 1944 landing on Saipan, Okinawa fighters themselves knew better.

It was no atrocity to steal natives' chicken, pigs and cattle. Although prohibited, that wasn't considered a crime; no one could have expected men who had been withdrawn from the line for a brief rest not to grill some fresh meat instead of trying to swallow more C-rations. It also wasn't an atrocity to throw phosphorous grenades into caves where civilians were hiding with enemy soldiers. This is what would prompt some Okinawans, including honorable civic leaders who were not anti-American, to charge that the poison gas used on some caves was a violation of the Geneva Convention. Well after the war, still haunted by the huge number of civilian deaths, they asked interested American visitors to investigate. What had actually happened was that the explosives unintentionally *released* poison gases that caused thousands of agonizing deaths in the confined spaces. Most lethal was an acrid yellow smoke from the petric acid used in Japanese munitions stored within the caves.

However, rape does qualify as an atrocity, and there was much of it. Violation of civilian women was among the most common crimes, although many units had no knowledge of it. Some fully believed their officers' warnings that "anyone who touches an Okinawan woman will be shot on the spot" — or needed no such threats. But other individuals and groups behaved differently, and American military chronicles ignore their crimes.

On April 7, six 6th Division Marines entered the house of a village on the coast of the Motobu Peninsula. A mother and her fourteen-year-old daughter were hiding beneath the house, as most women except for the very young and very old hid from the invaders whenever possible. To those two, the loud, sunburned Americans seemed like "red giants" and "red ogres." The men dragged mother and daughter into a little yard and took turns.

Later that month, eight Americans took four women from the tiny offshore island of Aka to sea in a little landing craft and gave them the choice of succumbing or swimming. They yielded but drowned anyway when the men threw them overboard. Those eight, who were black, helped give blacks in general a reputation among Okinawan women as the most persistent rapists, "who never gave up no matter how you ran," as one put it. But fear of whites was only marginally less, especially in some northern villages of a few hundred inhabitants where scores of assaults almost certainly took place.

That Okinawa's sexual code was far less rigid than Japan's made those violations no easier to bear. Partly because of the shame and disgrace, partly because the Americans were victors and occupiers, fewer than ten cases were reported by 1946, almost all of them accompanied by severe bodily harm or unconcealable maiming. In all, there were probably thousands of incidents, but the victims' silence kept rape another dirty secret of the campaign.*

*An Okinawan historian commissioned by the prefectural government to investigate the battle's effects on the civilian population is too professionally careful to be quoted without hard evidence — of which there is little about rape just because it was such a painful subject. However, his estimate exceeds ten thousand. The vast majority were not in the south, where most Americans were too busy and exhausted to think much about women, but during and after the far easier northern campaign, especially by troops landed for occupation and mop-up duty while the bitter southern fighting raged in May and June. The easiest prey, with the least chance of hiding, were evacuees from central and southern villages, such as the Sonans.

The secret was kept from absent husbands and fathers as well as from the American authorities. Few revealing pregnancies occurred, stress and bad diet having caused most Okinawan women to stop menstruating. Some women who did become pregnant managed to abort. A smaller number of newborn infants fathered by Americans were suffocated.*

Other episodes were more mistakes than atrocities, although the outcome was the same for the civilians. A medical corpsman spied movement in the darkness of a night he would never forget. "Hey, there's bushes out there that weren't there before!" The squad threw dozens of hand grenades and heard a chorus of moaning until dawn. Then they discovered that all the dead and dying were women, "nurses or something, in the baggy pants they wore." One was very beautiful. One of her arms had been blown off and both legs were dangling on small pieces of skin. "She was still alive, somehow hanging on — but there was no hope for her. She was mercy-killed."†

It was another short step from this confused picture to the grimmer one of random killing. One infantryman remembered pumping bullets into "straw houses" on the northern edge of otherwise leveled Naha. "There was some return fire from a few of the houses, but the others were probably occupied by civilians — and we didn't care. It was a terrible thing not to distinguish between the enemy and women and children. Americans always had great compassion, especially for children. Now we fired indiscriminately."

On the other side of Naha, an infantryman bet a mortar man he couldn't put a round down the chimney of "a typical little house" about five hundred yards ahead of them. "We bet a dime and I gave him three tries. His second round went straight down that chimney and exploded, *wonk!* We didn't know if anybody was inside and it didn't matter anymore, just didn't matter."

There was no doubt whether another typical little farmhouse was occupied: several medical corpsmen used their carbines to force a family into it before setting it alight. Then they fired round after round at its windows and doors while it burned to the ground. Another corpsman from the same unit who watched didn't know whether the civilians had done anything to provoke the atrocity. "But

---

*Rapes by Japanese soldiers were also hardly reported; the victims were intimidated by the mood of national emergency as much as by the perpetrators themselves. Japanese with previous service in Manchuria or China were held to be expert rapists. Many Okinawan women accepted that once war came to the island, they would inevitably be next in line, first for abuse by the dominating Japanese, then by the victors seeking spoils.

†The heavy bombing that badly damaged the leper colony on Yagaki Island, just offshore, was also probably a mistake. It stood near hidden Japanese pens for suicide boats, and Americans who discovered that installation probably assumed its easily visible Red Cross markings were another Japanese trick.

those men never needed provocation for their brutality. They were the worst kind of redneck, bullying everyone, always looking for trouble — and so tough that even our officers feared them."

Those particular officers — civilian doctors until recently — were not forceful military leaders. The horrified corpsman who watched was confident that nothing so blatantly evil could have been done in combat units, which had much better discipline and much less need for "excitement." In those combat units, not everyone who killed a civilian unnecessarily was sadistic; many simply didn't care. Eugene Sledge and others were infuriated by the death of an old woman in a hut. She had used sign language to beg Sledge to shoot her because she had a large, gangrenous wound in her abdomen. Sledge would do no such thing, but another Marine pulled his trigger. The others felt passionately even in the throes of battle that their job was to shoot Japanese, not old women: "Japs shoot back!" But far from everyone could still make that distinction.

The worst atrocities toward civilians were still to come. Days before the official end of the campaign, Okinawans were sheltering in caves about three miles above the island's southern tip, together with some of the remnants of the 32nd Infantry Regiment, a sister of Captain Kojo's 22nd. On the afternoons of June 18, 19, and perhaps 20, some sixty civilian men who had been flushed from those caves were, according to testimony recorded by Okinawan historians, rounded up and shot by Marines. Maybe those Marines were on the verge of battle fatigue. Maybe they were consumed with revenge. In any case, eyewitnesses reported those sixty were murdered in three neighboring sites.

In one sense, more than two thousand times that number of civilians were murdered. Most of the American firepower that caused the greatest civilian pain was unintentional. Willful atrocities against unarmed natives remained far fewer than those by Japanese, unless one accepts a Marine infantryman's later reflection that war itself is an atrocity. That proposition, still easily dismissed by patriots of individual countries, may one day be accepted as common sense. Meanwhile, the notion that civilian suffering was "accidental" need not be swallowed, since the barest knowledge of war attested to its inevitability.

26 · The Military Toll

Enemy morale may be analyzed as follows: 1) Japanese troops — These ap-
pear to be determined generally to die fighting and to see that all about
them die fighting, or by suicide once fighting becomes hopeless. It is signifi-
cant to note, however, that the Japanese soldier is fighting in a situation
that is already hopeless and suicides and counterattacks daily become
stronger . . . The enemy's situation, which is hopeless and grows more hope-
less each day, increases the possibility of isolated surrenders by Japanese
troops.
  — From the 6th Marine Division's (secret) Field Intelligence Report of
     17 June, a week before the 10th Army declared Okinawa "secure"

This morn we are packing sea bags, hammocks, etc. We received fresh eggs,
potatoes and butter. What's the Corps coming to? . . . Really delicious . . .
We heard rumors that Gen. Simon Bolivar Buckner Jr. was killed on the
front today . . . Tomorrow we move up to the front lines.
  — From Melvin Heckt's diary, June 18

All along the beach all you could see were Nip shoes and clothes. They must
have discarded them when they were forced to swim — where to no one
knows. But they figure drowning was better than to be captured by the
American "cannibals."
  — Buzzy Fox, June 25

Gᴇɴᴇʀᴀʟ ʙᴜᴄᴋɴᴇʀ had writ-
ten to General Ushijima on June 10, two weeks after the evacuation
from the Shuri Line. Dropped by air, the message took seven days to
reach Ushijima's new headquarters in the cave high on the cliff above
the Pacific coast.

> The forces under your command have fought bravely and well,
> and your infantry tactics have merited the respect of your
> opponent . . . Like myself, you are an infantry general long
> schooled and practiced in infantry warfare . . . I believe, therefore,
> that you understand as clearly as I that the destruction of all Japa-
> nese resistance on the island is merely a matter of days.

Buckner's invitation to end the useless bloodshed — useless, of
course, in American eyes — is said to have prompted laughter from

Ushijima and Cho, whose samurai background and long training in Imperial Army traditions made the notion of surrender hilarious.* But both officers knew Buckner's "matter of days" was no figure of speech. Cho busied himself writing cables to bolster the mainland's defense with the benefit of lessons learned about the latest American tactics and methods. He also tried to arrange for staff officers able to teach those lessons to smuggle themselves back to Tokyo. Ushijima attended to his more ceremonial final duties as commander. They included a farewell cable the following day to his direct superior on Formosa, the commander of the 10th Army Area (not to be confused with the American 10th Army opposing him on Okinawa). Ushijima reported that the "overwhelming tide of the enemy's material strength, which won control of the land, sea and sky," had brought the battle to "the brink of total disaster." He confessed that he had failed to defend Okinawa — despite "superhuman" efforts from every soldier and "devoted cooperation" from native citizens — because of his own lack of wisdom and virtue.

> For the Emperor and people of Japan, I have no adequate words of apology for the state of the fighting. It has come to the point where we are about to deploy all surviving soldiers for a final battle — in which I will apologize to the Emperor with my own death. Yet the regret for not having accomplished my enormous responsibility will torment my soul for thousands of years to come.

Ushijima also promised that those facing the final mortal combat were fully determined to join the heroic spirits of tens of thousands already fallen on Okinawa. He prayed for the Imperial family's "continued, even greater prosperity" and the sacred nation's eventual victory. "We shall, all of us, transform ourselves either into demons to protect the nation and destroy the enemy who is attempting to invade our mainland or into a Divine Wind to ride the skies and join the battle for ultimate victory."

The general also expressed profound gratitude to higher authorities and other units for their cooperation and guidance (of which he had had so little). High-ranking samurais traditionally left a poem or two when forced to depart. Although the various national crises had pushed that custom into some disuse, Ushijima observed it, composing two *jisei:*

---

*Although no one on the 10th Army staff seriously expected Ushijima to capitulate, it was hoped the open message might prompt mass surrender by less resolute Japanese. Tens of thousands of leaflets were dropped on enemy territory during the following week. The new ones focused on Ushijima's refusal to negotiate and appealed to his subordinates to surrender rather than become victims of their commander's selfish intention to doom his entire Army to destruction.

> Even as I expire, bullets and arrows depleted,
>> Dyeing heaven and earth [with blood],
> My soul will, my soul will
>> Return to protect the holy nation.

and:

> The island's green grass,
>> Wilting without waiting for autumn,
> Will revive with the return
>> Of the holy nation's Imperial spring.

General Buckner did not know of Ushijima and Cho's reaction to his surrender proposal. The day after they dismissed it with laughter, Buckner traveled from his headquarters in the north to follow the progress of his forces at first hand, from forward positions. Kamikazes were still crashing into ships, though the Floating Chrysanthemum operations had been considerably reduced in order to conserve planes and pilots for the mainland campaign. And American casualties remained severe in the faster but still deadly advance on land: almost three thousand that very week, to be followed by even more the following week. June casualties alone, when the battle was supposedly over except for the mopping-up, were a third of Iwo Jima's stunning total. "The end" as described in morale-building newspaper stories had almost nothing in common with how it appeared to sweaty infantrymen, who knew each grueling, terrifying day might be their last. But after seventy-eight such days — forty-eight more than the number originally estimated for the job — the end was in sight, especially to the commanders. Buckner had just told another press conference that most of what remained to do was mopping-up. At last his optimism was justified.

That afternoon of June 18, he chose to observe a component of the 2nd Marine Division that had been withdrawn for seven weeks to Saipan after making the feinted landing on L-day. The fresh 8th Regiment of that 2nd Division had recently been returned to Okinawa and committed to spearhead one thrust of the final push to the southern tip. This boost to the firepower and morale of the exhausted units mopping up elsewhere was a kind of coup de grâce for the even more exhausted defenders on the west coast, including the remnants of Tadashi Kojo's battalion.

But isolated Japanese artillery units in that area were still unloosing sporadic heavy fire. Fit, tough Buckner had ignored urgings to postpone a visit so close to the fighting. Accompanied by the commander of the newly committed regiment and other high officers, he came up to a forward observation post easily in sight of the cliffs and rocky beach at the island's southwestern tip, one major ridge north of where Tadashi Kojo's men were about to spend their final hours as an organized force. In a few weeks, the confident, hardworking victor, seemingly cast for his part, would be back in the States as one of the U.S. Army's handful of leading generals, surely preparing for a larger command in the invasion of the mainland.

The observation post, like most, was no more than a few square yards cleared of scrub, this one on Maesato Ridge. Artillery spotter glasses, supplemented by a second pair captured from the Japanese, had been set up on a leveled patch of land. They were positioned between two large boulders roughly a yard apart — protection against the remains of the Japanese 1st Heavy Field Artillery Regiment on the next hill farther south.

That battery had taken typical punishment on its retreat to the final hill. In previous positions, its crews had sent puffs of smoke from empty caves to deceive American naval and artillery gunners, but at best the inevitable could only be postponed. Day after day of concentrated fire terrified the men and destroyed their weaponry, the pride of the Army — some guns, before they fired a round. Now only one of a dozen guns was left — "miraculously spared," as one of its crew saw it, and maintained by parts salvaged from the wreckage of the eleven. Survivors of their gun crews took turns manning it.

Just after 1 P.M., a member of the skeletal unit scanned the hill to the north and focused his binoculars on the surprising sight of some apparently high-ranking enemy officers. The Americans seemed to be looking east, through their own binoculars, in the direction of General Ushijima's headquarters on the opposite coast. After almost an hour at the vantage point, General Buckner was ready to leave. Things were going so well, he told the others, that he thought he'd move on to another unit. Before he completed his goodbyes, an expert Japanese artillerist ordered the last gun to fire at the tempting target of important officers. The rest of the battery hurried into the cave, "knowing very well we'd get a 'return gift' of a thousand shots back from them for every shot from us."

The gun fired five rounds. American artillerymen were surprised by the accuracy; heavy gunfire usually required more adjustment on a target. The Japanese crew had no way of knowing just how accurate they were. A shell hit one of the protective boulders and a shower of chips, together with metal fragments, pierced Buckner's chest and abdomen.* Bleeding heavily, he could not be evacuated to an aid

---

*Most accounts specify splinters of coral but an artilleryman manning the spotter glasses insists splinters of rock did the greatest damage.

station. A medical corpsman accompanying the group tried desperately to staunch the flow, but Buckner died ten minutes later.

To footsloggers who had known all along that nearness to the end of the campaign was no protection from death, this was confirmation. "If you ask me," said one from the newly committed 8th Marines, "a guy who's the commander of a whole army just shouldn't have been at the front like that."*

The young staff at 32nd Army headquarters cheered when the news of Buckner's death reached their cave by radio from Tokyo. An Okinawan eyewitness is said to have seen Cho fling up his hands in pleasure. Only Ushijima, reportedly perplexed by the glee, remained silent and later said a prayer for his opposite number. That may be no more than rumor spun into myth, which also surrounds the deaths of the two Japanese leaders. What is certain is that Buckner was World War II's highest-ranking American killed in action. With so much death everywhere, his seemed to some "not inappropriate." And it was a matter of inches, in the battlefield way. None of the officers accompanying him was scratched. Like so many of his men, the commander had been dealt a dose of combat's vast store of random bad luck.

> *Our strategy and tactics were all utilized to the utmost and we fought valiantly; but they had little effect against the enemy's superior material strength.*
>
> — From Mitsuru Ushijima's last message to Imperial General Headquarters

> *A simultaneous shout and a flash of a sword, then another repeated shout and a flash, and both generals had nobly accomplished their last duty to their Emperor.*
>
> — A supposed eyewitness to the deaths of Ushijima and Isamu Cho

> *The hill, shrouded in the smoke of battle, was burning like an erupting volcano, red in the setting sun.*
>
> — An Okinawan schoolteacher describing Hill 89 on the following day

Buckner's death occurred on the day of Ushijima's apology for failing to accomplish his mission. The reply of the Japanese headquarters on Formosa came the following day: a letter of commendation extolling the 32nd Army's great efforts and extraordinarily brave fighting. Ushijima issued a general order to his Army that same June 19:

---

*Desire for revenge among other Americans may have been responsible for some of their alleged atrocities against civilians. The 60 reported murders on June 18, 19, and 20 came immediately after Buckner's death on the eighteenth. All were in the same vicinity; some right in Maesato, below the observation post on the ridge.

I appreciate and congratulate your brave efforts for the past three months in carrying out your duties. But now we face the end, as it has become extremely difficult to continue our efforts. Each of you should follow the orders of whoever is highest in rank in your group and continue to resist to the very end, then live in the eternity of our noble cause.

Although the last directive was cast in typically vague phrases, no translation was needed. The order was to "sacrifice yourself."

The cliff containing Ushijima's cave, Hill 89 to the Americans, rose about four hundred yards south of the village of Mabuni. This was just over a mile south of the last Yoza-dake–Yaeju-dake–Kunishi Ridge mountain line and two miles from the island's southern tip. By the next day, June 20, the hill and village — to which headquarters guards were sent as final combat troops — controlled only a small pocket, into which almost the entire remains of the 32nd Army had been squeezed. American Army and Marine forces had taken the entire opposite (western) coast, down to Kyan Point (Suicide Cliff) at the East China Sea side of the tip. The pocket stretched about five miles along the Pacific coast but was only a few hundred yards in width along most of that distance. It was attacked from the north by the Army 7th Infantry Division, which had been first to encounter the outer edges of the massive Japanese defensive works south of L-day's landing beaches. With rest periods, the 7th had been fighting since the landing, most notably at fortified approaches to the Shuri Line such as Skyline Ridge and at the far eastern sector of the grim line itself. Now, a month later, so little was left of Japanese territory that Army commanders hesitated to call for the usual massive concentrations of airpower and naval gunfire support, for fear of hitting their own men.* The weary soldiers had to eliminate the last resistance by hand. "This they did," a historian wrote, "with flame, demolitions and tanks, whittling the pocket down, breaking it up into several smaller ones, stamping these out in turn as a man would stamp out so many snakes, until there were no more Japanese to kill."

On that June 20, Ushijima received his last message — carried by a brave soldier — from the headquarters of the 24th Division, which was holding out in a pocket about a mile northwest. Meanwhile, units of the American 7th Division fought their way up Hill 89. The prominent coral formation rose over two hundred feet, almost

---

*One Marine battalion that had fought to the southern end watched an Army unit advancing toward the same coast, flushing out and shooting Japanese soldiers singly and in small groups. The Marines grew tense as doggie mortar shells landed nearer and nearer. Finally, a furious Marine officer told the Army officer in charge that *his* big mortars would have a go at *their* troops unless the dangerous fire stopped immediately. It did.

straight from the sea. Its jagged pinnacle was studded with crags and crevices: perfect protection for Japanese snipers, mortarmen and a few machine gun squads with operable guns. Desperation stiffened their resistance. Flamethrowing tanks used nearly five thousand gallons of napalm to burn them out. When the summit was finally taken, on June 21, only the area around Ushijima's headquarters remained.

The cave had two entrances, one facing land and the other the sea, both slightly below the flat summit. A Japanese prisoner of the 7th Division's 32nd Regiment agreed to take Ushijima a last appeal to surrender. He approached the landward mouth and called out the American message. An explosion from inside sealed that entrance. A subsequent explosion, set off by Americans who found an air shaft, killed ten officers and men: the first casualties among the 32nd Army staff, who had been drafting orders while an average of over twenty-five hundred people had been killed on the island during each of the eighty-two days since April 1.

> The commanders of the Okinawa Defense Forces ended their lives as warriors but could not escape criticism for dragging not only their line soldiers but also the unfortunate civilians into the war. It did not matter to others that they had acted "under orders."
> — Masahide Ota

Ushijima received a farewell message that day from the Minister of the Army and the Chief of the General Staff. He sent a last report, later called "pathetic" by one Japanese writer, to Imperial General Headquarters and broke off radio communication. That evening, American grenades exploding overhead rumbled the cave during a farewell party for surviving members of the Army staff and assorted members of the command staffs of the demolished infantry and artillery units. Ushijima wore his full dress uniform, Cho a white kimono. They toasted their guests with sake while dining on miso soup, fish cakes, canned meats, rice, cabbage, potatoes, pineapple and tea. The two generals also savored the last of a bottle of Black and White that Cho, his affection for Scotch intact, had brought with him from Shuri. Deeper inside the long, twisting cave, headquarters personnel sang "Umi Yukaba," a solemn ancient poem about sacrificing life for the Emperor which had become close to a national anthem.

At three o'clock, just before moonrise, most of the assembled officers left with most of the remaining men for a final "die in honor" attack up the hill. They had pledged themselves to push the enemy off and down, but a more realistic assessment of the American strength all around them had forced abandonment of an earlier plan for the generals to die at the summit while watching those same last units proceed to retake Mabuni village below. An hour later, just after four o'clock, all was ready for a shorter sortie by the two generals. Cho was solicitous. "Well, Commanding General Ushijima, as the way may be dark, I, Cho, will lead the way." Ushijima's professional serenity remained intact. "Please do so. I'll take along my fan since it's getting warm."

The generals rose. Ushijima picked up an Okinawan fan. Colonel Yahara was notably absent. The sober strategist's request to join his commanders in their final act had been denied. Instead, Ushijima and Cho ordered their chief operations officer to escape and make his way back to the mainland to inform Imperial General Headquarters about American tactics and techniques. "If you die, no one will be left who knows the truth about the Battle of Okinawa. Bear the temporary shame but endure it. This is an order from your military commander."* Driven by a kind of reversal of his lifelong romanticism, Yahara's sometime antagonist Cho was particularly eager for young staff officers not to deprive Japan of the benefit of their experience and potential as leaders of guerrilla warfare on Okinawa, which they could do only by refraining from suicide. Although some staff officers nevertheless remained with the commanders now, two dozen or so had already obeyed Cho by sneaking from the cave.

While attempts were made to distract the Americans above, the two generals left the unsealed, seaward, mouth of the cave, a large natural fissure in the rock. Ushijima imperturbably fanned himself as they walked a few yards to a small ledge overlooking the Pacific Ocean. "These are calm minds facing death," a witness later reported. "The generals who pass a row of subordinates have the air of immortals passing by." A sister-in-law of an Okinawan major in the 32nd Army, one of the few native officers of higher rank, had prepared the white sheets and underwear required for the ritual. One sheet was placed over a quilt on the ledge. Sensing movement below, Americans lobbed more grenades in the direction of the small party. Ignoring them, Ushijima and Cho bowed in reverence to the eastern sky. James and William Belote complete the story:

> Both knelt on the sheet, facing the ocean since room was lacking
> on the ledge to perform the ceremony facing north toward the Imperial Palace. Silently each opened his tunic, baring his abdomen.
> At General Ushijima's side stood his aide, Lieutenant Yoshino,
> holding two knives with half the blade wrapped in white cloth.
> The adjutant, Captain Sakaguchi, stood on Ushijima's right, saber
> drawn. Yoshino handed a blade to Ushijima, who took it with both

---

*Soon captured by American forces, Yahara would face severe criticism from some Japanese for failing to kill himself despite his orders.

hands and with a shout, thrust. Simultaneously Sakagushi's saber fell on his neck as prescribed, severing his spinal column. Ushijima's corpse lurched forward onto the sheet. Then General Cho took his turn and the ceremony was repeated.

That, at least, is how the deaths are recorded in most chronicles, which may owe something to imagination. Although the generals did die, surely by suicide, the traditional story, passed from writer to writer, relies heavily on the testimony of a Japanese military policeman, who later admitted he wasn't where he claimed to be but had heard the version from others. The cook who prepared the bountiful final meal was supposed to have been watching from the entrance to the cave, but he has also been reported as having heard pistol shots. And photographs of the corpses taken several days later show blood at their temples.

Shooting would have violated the samurai code, the notion of which enraged some Japanese officers after the war. "You son of a bitch, you've demeaned their families and insulted the samurai way," one screamed to an Okinawan whose research led him to question the conventional version of the generals' death. Some who uphold that version insist the death photos proved nothing because Americans faked them. After all, a multitude of high-ranking Japanese officers elsewhere committed *seppuku* exactly as described on the ledge overlooking the Pacific. And the shots may have been fired by seven staff officers — some accounts specify nine — who "blew their brains out" at the same time. Still, some of the most knowledgeable students of the campaign suspect that Ushijima's serene end may have been "prettified" to bring honor to his death and the samurai code.

Barring an unlikely revelation by a new eyewitness, the answers will never be known and the doubts never settled. Too many of the extant accounts derive from tainted sources and too many offer contradictory details. Those narratives don't even agree about what the principals were wearing; some put Cho also in full dress uniform rather than the white kimono. They differ on whether moonlight was shimmering over the sea during the farewell meal or whether the moon hadn't yet risen — perhaps because there is even disagreement about the date. Americans believe the suicides took place in the early morning of June 22; some Japanese, on June 23.

What is known for certain is that American soldiers of the 7th Division found the corpses several days later. They were where orderlies had buried them, either in shallow graves below the ledge or in the headquarters cave; there was disagreement on this point too. (Yahara had planned for burial at sea because the cave floor's coral was too hard for digging graves.) Cho had written his own epitaph on a silk mattress cover. The founding member of the savagely nationalist Cherry Blossom Society declared that he was departing "without regret, shame or obligations." The war launched with much aid by the Society had taken up to twenty million lives and brutalized hundreds of millions more. The invasion of the Japanese mainland would add enormously to that number. The patriot was satisfied that his honor was intact.

General Buckner's funeral at an Army cemetery had been attended by high-ranking officers. The general's three-star personal flag flew next to the Stars and Stripes. Solemn riflemen fired a volley and a commemorative artillery barrage shook the ground. Although there were no such honors for Ushijima, Japanese prisoners of war were permitted to spend a few moments paying respect to him and Cho soon after Hill 89 was firmly secured. Wooden memorial poles for the two had been dug into the coral beside their graves. A year later, Ushijima was posthumously promoted to General of the Army, the second and last in Japanese history. The first was the revered soldier-statesman of the Meiji era to whom he had often been compared: Saigo the Great, of Kagoshima.

This was the only Pacific campaign that took the lives of both sides' commanding officers. Their close subordinates kept falling. The day after Buckner's death, a Marine colonel who had warned the commander not to come to the front was shot by a sniper and died an hour later. That same June 19, Brigadier General Claudius Easley, assistant commander of the Army's 96th Division, was pointing to the location of a Japanese machine gun when two of its bullets hit him in the forehead. For once the losses at the top reflected those at the bottom. Total 10th Army casualties on land soon came to over seventy-two thousand — nearly as many as Japanese soldiers (excluding the Okinawan conscripts) in the 32nd Army. Of these, 7613 were killed and missing in action. About thirty-three thousand wounded — seriously enough to be out of action more than a week — and an almost equal number of nonbattle casualties, chiefly victims of battle fatigue, accounted for the others. As the most recent military historian of the battle points out, secondary sources often suggest that about six thousand American lives were lost, compared with 100,000 Japanese killed and captured. "This indicates a highly favorable American loss ratio of 1 to 17 [but] the overall impact of Okinawa" — not including the Navy's unprecedented losses of nearly five thousand killed and five thousand wounded — "was less positive than these triumphant figures suggest."

American casualties were fierce. In this sense, Ushijima's forces performed brilliantly, but only at the cost of ten times the number of the American KIAs. The 10th Army estimated it killed two thousand Japanese on June 19, the day after Buckner's death, three thousand on June 20, and four thousand on June 21: figures hard to imagine except from death camps. The equivalent of half a combat division died during those three days, not including many barely trained Okinawan teenagers drafted into the Home Guard at the last moment. Those three-day losses also represented nearly half the total of Japanese dead during the thirty-six hellish days on Iwo Jima. When *Toyama maru*, the ship transporting the entire 44th Independent Mixed Brigade, was sent to the bottom the previous June with the loss of fifty-six hundred men, the disaster seemed enormous. The soldier-passengers terrified by the explosions of the four torpedoes could not have imagined a greater percentage of them would survive the sinking than the proportion of the 32nd Army as a whole that would survive on land.

Book IV

27 · Expiration of the 32nd Army

The Okinawa campaign ended on 21 June 1945 after 82 days of battle. Torrential rains and difficult terrain, together with stubborn opposition by a fanatic enemy fighting from an intricate cave system, contributed to make this campaign one of the most severe in the history of the United States armed forces.

— From a confidential report entitled "Principal Lessons Learned in the Okinawa Operation"

The strength of willpower, devotion and technical resources applied by the United States to this task, joined with the death struggle of the enemy . . . places this battle among the most intense and famous in military history . . . We make our salute to all your troops and their commanders engaged.

— Prime Minister Winston Churchill to President Harry Truman, June 22, 1945

When the last Japanese were compressed into a small pocket at the south end, the great "turkey shoot" began . . . some of the old hands from our battalion raced to the area . . . I suspect there were as many American casualties as Japanese with all those bloodthirsty people looking for targets.

— Thomas Hannaher

Just before the flag-raising on the southern end, we were sitting on cliffs about 150 high, shooting at Japs in loin cloths. They were either trying to swim around to attack us from the rear or trying to save themselves. There were bodies all around. It was target practice.

— Irving Ortel

I always wanted to live, no matter what. To be captured, to be sent to heavy labor in America, never to go home again — even that would have been all right. But of course I never said this to anyone.

— One of four Japanese to survive in his unit of 169 men

IN THE UNFORTIFIED flat sectors of the far south, the days after the fall of Kunishi Ridge were a kind of open season on disarmed, diseased Japanese, still over ten thousand burrowed in trenches, ditches and caves. Like the teeth of a comb, platoons of infantrymen walked at arm's length across fields or scrubby rises, clearing out the last ones like animals, as one Marine remembered.

Americans had no reason to know or care that many enemy soldiers who popped up from tiny holes had been there for days, often without food or water. Or that they were terrified of their inevitable death. If the Japanese had been demoralized and desperate before, now many were frenzied; what the Americans did care about was that the cornered "animals" in that condition were still trying to kill them. "We knew we were coming to the end, of course. But in a way, that only made you more eager to live — to do anything to make it to the end after coming that far. Every day you hoped like hell it was the last day. Thirty days was like three years."

Flushing out a cave, Ed Jones thought he saw a Japanese behaving "funny." The man reached into his loin cloth when he was ten feet away and pulled out a grenade. But Jones blew his head off "and a buddy's too who leaned close to him." Such incidents grew in number during the 32nd Army's terminal days. Almost every American in the final attacks saw a buddy's bullets, or his own, stop the sudden charge of an isolated, desperate Japanese.

Some now attacked with knives and sticks. Combing out a cornfield with his team, a friend of Dick Whitaker's named Lindsay was in the point position when a Japanese stepped from behind a tree and hit him hard in the head with a sword case. If he'd had the sword, Lindsay might have been beheaded. As it was, the frantic Japanese grabbed Lindsay's shotgun and raced away with it while a stretcher was rushed to T.P., as Lindsay was called. The Japanese was obviously terrified. To Whitaker and the others, he was more evidence that all of them were capable of anything.

Mopping up in another field of high grass, members of Whitaker's company were near enough to the southern coast to hear ships' p.a. systems urging the enemy to surrender. John Senterfitt, the man with whom Whitaker had crawled down from Sugar Loaf, was five yards to Whitaker's left. A sudden explosion there prompted a cry: "I'm hit!" Rushing to the drainage ditch into which Senterfitt had fallen, Whitaker saw a tangle of bloody flesh for his buddy's left arm. But Senterfitt managed to get to his feet and the corpsman who hurried over found nothing wrong with him. They discovered the explosion had come from a Japanese soldier blowing himself up in the ditch as the patrol passed — and spraying his blood so hard on the shocked Senterfitt that he thought he'd been wounded.

He and Whitaker would laugh over the incident but not at the time.

> It wasn't funny because we were all so strung out. The tension might have been even higher now because we were so hoping to make it out alive — it'd be crazy to be killed in those last days. But even more bizarre things were happening even more unexpect-

edly. The Japs were in a kind of frenzy under their incredible pressure. They were squeezed into the last pockets before the ocean, where they could kill themselves or make a banzai charge — I saw some rush out absolutely determined to kill one of us with a last grenade. And since we were skinny and exhausted — no real sleep for about twelve weeks — and a little hyper about the end, we were still very nervous about them.

The mutual killing continued. On June 17, two Marine colonels used a tank to reconnoiter a hilly sector where accurate mortar, machine gun and artillery fire had stalemated the advance. Tiring after a long period loading the 75mm gun, the visiting colonel changed positions with the tank commander. The latter, who was also commander of the battalion, gave his guest instructions on how to pick out targets through the vision cupola, but the new man wanted a better view of the larger area and cracked the turret hatch about three inches. A grenade fired from a Japanese knee-mortar concealed in nearby rocks entered that opening, detonated on the cupola and ripped the guest colonel apart from his shoulders to his buttocks. He emitted a single gasp as he died, one of 250 Americans during the final week.

General Buckner's command passed to Major General Roy Geiger, his deputy and until then commander of the Marine contingent on Okinawa. But a Marine was kept in charge only until Lieutenant General Joseph W. Stilwell of the U.S. Army — the astute Vinegar Joe, famed for his role as adviser to Chiang Kai-shek — was appointed the new 10th Army commander days later, when the campaign was over because organized resistance had collapsed.*

General Geiger declared the island secure on the afternoon of June 21. The following day, a small detachment from Stebbins's G–2–22 company raised a flag on the limb of a tree at Ara Saki, the extreme southern tip. It was the same flag that had been raised at the northern end two months earlier. The detachment included Medical Corpsman Joseph Bangert, who guessed the group was picked because the members had survived the eighty-three days since L-day. Bangert believed the 10th Army's public relations specialists were trying to repeat the success of the famous flag raising on Iwo Jima, which had become a national symbol. But the American public received the Okinawa photos almost as old news because it had seen a similar image earlier. Compared with Iwo, the campaign as a whole

---

*Stilwell, one of the American Army's least orthodox and most capable generals, would surely have fought a much more imaginative campaign on Okinawa.

remained underreported and nearly obscure to the end. Naturally, no photos showed the abandoned, sometimes bloody clothes that littered the area — of Japanese soldiers and civilians who had jumped from the cliff or set out on a swim with no destination.

Home-front Americans chalked up a victory somewhere in the Pacific, but the mutual killing did not end. Infantrymen wondered why territory so dangerous had been declared secure. Perhaps headquarters staffs truly felt that only mopping up was needed now; perhaps the brass wanted to boost civilian morale, or "some general shooting for another star" wanted publicity. Relaxation of caution brought predictable results. Robert Sherer, Dick Whitaker's company commander, for whom he was still a runner, was a former enlisted man who kept being promoted in the field as his superiors were wounded and killed. His experience and skill probably helped him be the sole company officer not killed or wounded badly enough to require evacuation. But the certified survivor — since L-day — became careless and opened a map as his team was advancing on a dry strip between rice paddies the day after the official "securing." A Japanese soldier appeared from nowhere with a hand grenade and everyone scattered wildly, Sherer into a ditch, where he remained unhurt. His luck held again on the day when he approached Whitaker unannounced from behind and Whitaker, with the usual spurt of adrenaline, spun around, finger on his trigger. He stopped squeezing an instant before the hammer fell on his Thompson.

A New Jersey Marine named Red Burdett got up to relieve himself beside a huge boulder the morning after the flag raising and almost bumped into a Japanese soldier. They turned and ran opposite ways around it. The Japanese had his rifle cocked when they met again at the far side, and shot Red dead. Later that day, Buzzy Fox, the frightened replacement to whom Father Kelly had assured survival because of his star athlete's reflexes, was cautiously advancing near a tank across a flat, scrubby tract of land. Suddenly the tank hit a mine and flew into the air. "I felt so sorry for the crew. To have come so far and no farther. Every moment was crazy."

But of course vastly more Japanese than Americans were killed during the 32nd Army's last days. Even the units that had had enough cohesion to fight well on Kunishi Ridge and other strongpoints of the final mountain line disintegrated into confused bands of sixes and sevens, twos and threes, with far more thought of putting off destruction than of fighting back. "We had them in big bowls," a veteran American infantryman remembered. "We had them on the beach. Men with enough energy and drive to shoot were picking them off like turkeys."

The remnants of the heavy artillery battery whose "lucky shot" had killed General Buckner were virtually obliterated by American guns firing in revenge. The next morning, the exhausted artillerymen were ordered from their last cave on Yaeju-dake to a village on the east coast, not far from 32nd Army headquarters. "The order was very cruel. It was nearly impossible to leave the cave, let alone gather at [the village]. It was tantamount to 'Kill yourself!'" — and many indeed died. The survivors scattered. Some of the seriously wounded shot themselves. Senior Private Hiroshi Uchihata and three others fled to a pine grove, taking refuge in a hole so small they could barely move. They covered it with branches and set up their last weapon, a machine gun.

Squeezing out to draw some muddy water for the group at twilight, Uchihata heard a sharp *psssst* and felt a hot stab at the back of his left knee. A chunk of metal, perhaps from a tank shell, had disabled him: a dreaded wound because it would keep him from moving with his fellows. American flamethrowing tanks that had burned part of the pine grove would return in the morning. Uchihata decided it was time to end his struggle without burdening the others.

He crawled back to his hole, then out again with four grenades. While he looked for a place to perform the act before it grew fully dark, a soldier named Hayase appeared and asked what he was doing. Uchihata explained, adding that he'd first like a drink of clean water from one of the springs that bubbled up at Mabuni beach. Hayase, his superior, asked to join him, perhaps hoping that Uchihata, who had learned the lay of the land while serving as a messenger for regimental headquarters, might somehow lead him somewhere farther and safer than the beach.

Making their way to the nearest cliffs, they found a steep path leading to the mixed patches of sand, rock and jagged coral at the shore below. Torrential rain began falling as they were about to descend. They sheltered under a palm for an hour, Uchihata repeating *Namu myoho rengeko,* a well-known chant of the Nichiren sect believed to have protective powers. Despite his decision, he wanted to live. Asking the gods for help as he'd never asked before, he refrained from mentioning the possibility of surrender to Hayase, although he was unable to keep it from his thoughts.

When the cloudburst eased, they used vines to climb down the cliff, Uchihata in agony from his leg. They entered the sea and swam from reef to reef parallel with shore or, where the water was shallower, walked and crawled in the same northerly direction, Uchihata leaning on Hayase for support. They had worked and fought in the dark for so long — Uchihata had driven on pitch-black nights before all his unit's trucks had been lost — that it wasn't difficult to see in the open spaces of the midnight sea. Without specifying their destination or talking of suicide again, they agreed to try to make their way to somewhere safe.

About an hour later, Hayase disappeared during one of their swimming legs. Since he hadn't mentioned suicide again and no rifle shot sounded from the shore, Uchihata assumed he had drowned.

On land again, Uchihata found a stick for a cane and limped among ragged groups of soldiers struggling north along the shore, along "the passport route." Others told him that Americans waiting at a break in the cliffs would not shoot men who approached with their hands held high. Still wondering what he would do when the time came, Uchihata was gladdened to recognize a corporal named Yamazaki, next to whom he used to bunk in Manchuria. But Yamazaki immediately asked for one of his hand grenades and Uchihata refused. He felt he himself might need them ahead — and also didn't want to give a grenade for someone's suicide, though he still thought he might use one for his own at any moment. Yamazaki disappeared without further conversation, Uchihata not having dared suggest they continue together and surrender. Never to see him again, in a POW camp or elsewhere, Uchihata later assumed he had found other means of suicide or had been shot.

After dawn, Uchihata heard a shout from atop a cliff. Looking up at a lone American there, he remembered an old prediction of a Japanese who had lived in America that Japan could never win against her might — and also his assurance that Americans were gentlemen. But although he observed the enemy rifleman refrain from shooting the herd of soldiers and civilians inching their way along the beach below, he could not bring himself to surrender.

His wound throbbing, he hid behind a huge rock, watching bloated bodies wash up on the beach and half-living Japanese scavenge for food. Knowing he would starve after eating the last of his hardtack, feverish Uchihata agonized over his decision one more day, then pulled himself up and, supported by civilians, "allowed himself to be rescued" by continuing toward "passport point." They did not say aloud what they were doing. "Surrender" and "prisoner" never crossed their lips. Uchihata would continue to believe he would never have given himself up were it not for his wound.

I saw so many caves blown, I couldn't remember any except for this huge one just north of the final ridge. It was the size of a large ballroom with tunnels branching off — probably held hundreds. After we thought all the civilians were out, we heard the soldiers singing their heads off and getting all sake-ed up. Then the grenades started going off down there. We thought

the Japs had been under such terrific bombardment they must have been kind of nuts anyway. We waited a couple of hours before we ignited the gasoline. By that time, they were probably all dead anyway.
— James Burden

"There he goes, shoot him," one soldier shouted excitedly. "Shoot him your-self," another remarked. "I don't want to clean my rifle today."
— From the notes of a lieutenant colonel observing the action on June 18

The Jap corpses were all bloated, with juices dripping down and maggots crawling into the mouths, nostrils, ears . . . They reminded me of turkeys and I couldn't eat turkey for four years.
— Ed Jones

Uchihata's unlikely survival was a matter of chance. More and more Japanese in caves like the ones he left were heard singing drunkenly before Americans tossed in their explosives. For those in-side, the dreaded indication that the enemy had actually appeared at their last refuge was usually the repeated *De-te koi*. Other Japanese heard movements of boots or wheels, coughs, voices speaking unin-telligible English — or nothing at all until a grenade exploded or a flamethrower's napalm shot inside. Some of the occupants almost al-ways died quickly of suffocation or, in some cases, heart failure. But first blasts rarely killed all occupants of the larger caves.

The survivors moved farther to the interior while more explosives were tossed in over the course of days. Some who had survived the worst of combat, even when their units were reduced to skeletons, now went berserk. American veterans who rightly called battlefield horrors "incomprehensible" even to boot camp and infantry school graduates would themselves have been hard pressed to comprehend the experience here. Human senses simply couldn't grasp it. The de-ranged men "would suddenly start screaming with their eyes unfo-cused, jibbering. They would either run out of the cave or deep into its interior, never to return in either case."

The doomed increasingly pre-empted all this with their own gre-nades, used on themselves. Increasingly too — with enemy fire so much reduced — Americans called not for single barrels of gasoline but for whole trucks to move up and douse stubborn caves. More bulldozers appeared to seal cave mouths with occupants inside. More Japanese officers deliberately stood up in the line of fire of American machine guns directly outside their shelters. They fell immediately.

Language provided moments of comic relief. At one large cave thought to contain natives, bullhorns insistently blared that no one with his hands up would be hurt. "We're sorry for you civilians, so please come out right now." Finally, women, children and old men did emerge. The cave mouth was on a slope below a small plateau. Gripping his weapon in one hand, a Marine Hercules stood above the mouth to snatch the civilians with the other and lift them, one by one, to level ground. "Up you go, Mac." "That's right, Mac, out you come." When a Japanese appeared at the mouth, the trigger fingers of the Marine fire team instantly tightened on their rifles and automatics. "Easy, Mac, no trouble — okay?" proposed the big Marine. "My name's not Mac," the Japanese soldier answered in startlingly clear English. "My name's Yoshio and I'd rather be in Texas, where I should be." To the astonishment of the watchers, who included General Lemuel Shepherd, commander of the 6th Marine Division, Yoshio explained that he had traveled from his San Antonio home to visit Japanese relatives in 1941. This was his first friendly contact with Americans since Pearl Harbor stranded him in Japan, where he had been drafted.

Other caves housed a few Okinawan teenagers raised in the States and caught on Okinawa when visiting *their* relatives in 1941. Their war had been especially unhappy, beginning with years of pressure not to reveal that half their hearts remained in America, along with half their families. The battle itself tore harder at their allegiances as they watched the fearful American damage to the home island they also loved. Okinawans with no American ties were also stunned by the fate of individual Japanese soldiers they knew and liked. Even those with little love for Japan were appalled by the final days of slaughter. Most of the ordinary, unassuming Japanese "Macs" with whom they'd been serving had become heaps of filthy corpses.

If all combat seems beyond the pale of human life, the campaign's finale drove the Japanese survivors even farther beyond. A few days after the deaths of Ushijima and Cho, about a third of the forty to fifty soldiers in a large cave nearby began killing themselves. Yards from where they blew themselves up with grenades, fellow soldiers continued shaving and trying to dry their wet uniforms. However, the most vivid evidence of catastrophe was no longer in caves but at the water's edge and shallows. Razor-sharp coral extending a hundred yards seaward made up stretches of the beach below the steep cliffs at Okinawa's far southern end. It was torture to take two steps on those poisonous needles and spikes, which ripped the soles of boots and feet like claws. Now thousands of Japanese tried to escape — anywhere — along the half-submerged fangs or to hide nearby like crabs. Hundreds were picked off by Americans on the cliffs above who, unlike the sentry observed by Hiroshi Uchihata, did shoot at those tottering targets.

At night, a steady succession of flares lit the coast brighter than a full moon, as one Japanese remembered his terror. By day, the crisscrossing rabble on the beach and farther inland were bewildered without the authority, clear-cut duty and group allegiance that had formed and nourished them since infancy. The minority willing to give themselves up wandered for days with no idea how to do it. Even Norio Watanabe, the Osaka photographer, felt that the surrender he yearned for would put a stamp of dishonor on him that "must remain all my life." Kuni-ichi Izuchi, who had been carrying the bones of his friend's cremated hand to return to his family, happened to be his unit's highest-ranking man of about a dozen remaining after June 18. He believed he might be able to save those few if he could muster the courage to suggest they become prisoners, an idea that was "unthinkable; one simply doesn't say such a thing in the Japanese army. The slogan 'Better to be smashed into pieces as a precious stone than survive as a roof tile' was etched deep into our consciousness." But Izuchi did include surrender among four choices he put to the survivors; his others were to try to reach the north by breaking through the Americans swarming over the last pocket at Mabuni, to kill themselves with hand grenades, or to try to reach the Chinen Peninsula by swimming out from Mabuni. The very first response was a plea against surrender. "Chief, I can't become a prisoner, it's too frightening!" Izuchi knew the fear was not only of dishonor but also of "slaughter," as he put it, by fellow soldiers outraged by the betrayal. He didn't argue.

The most damaging wounds of Kenjiro Matsuki's months of miraculous escapes from seemingly hopeless situations were six deep holes in his left leg and hip from a mortar shell. The former professional baseball player dragged himself to a cave where a dozen other soldiers were joined by twenty-one Okinawan nurses' aides. When one of the aides volunteered to go for water, she was hit almost immediately by the rain of shells outside. Then she asked for a grenade and blew up two seriously wounded Japanese soldiers together with herself.

The other twenty all decided to follow her example in order to escape rape and disgraceful death. No soldier tried to stop them until Matsuki finally told the girls that he had visited America and could promise the enemy wouldn't abuse them. "You're not soldiers. Please surrender to them."

After convincing the twenty, he tried to persuade a lieutenant to lead them out because he'd been hideously burned by a flamethrowing tank that incinerated the rest of his mortar platoon and couldn't last long without medical help. The lieutenant was from the same northern region of Japan as Matsuki, who was careful to keep his "hometown" talk from the others. That a private would dare address an officer, even one with those ties, on his own initiative, let alone urge him to surrender, testified to the degree that discipline had crumbled. The lieutenant's eventual agreement perhaps spoke of his background as a teacher and the excruciating pain of his swollen, purple face. Still keeping their plan secret from the others, Matsuki made a white flag from a piece of cloth and prayed for the girls. Yet he himself, the one Japanese in ten thousand who disbelieved the anti-American propaganda, could not bring himself to leave with them and the lieutenant. "To die rather than be captured was central to our education and national life. No matter what I thought personally, I didn't have the courage to go against that or what the old soldiers would have thought of me."

Matsuki eventually tried to swim behind the enemy lines but was too weak, and the American positions, now armed with nets in the water as well as machine guns overlooking the beach, were too strong. He fell asleep making plans to break through on land and awakened to American shouts and half a dozen rifles pointed at him. If his last grenades, one for the enemy and one for himself, hadn't been out of reach, he too, the gregarious athlete who had played ball with major-league all-stars, would have killed himself rather than surrender.

Captain Kojo didn't know that the evening of June 17, when 22nd Regiment headquarters was attacked and Colonel Yoshida sent him the traditional last message of a promise to fight to the end and a wish for good luck, also marked the effective end of the 32nd Army, although Commander Ushijima would make it official only two days later. But Kojo could not fail to interpret the situation within his view. He saw a coordinated attack by American planes, artillery and tanks on Yoshida's cave, less than a thousand yards away. That evening, the enfeebled captain ordered his radio section to destroy its equipment, then go out to attack the enemy. The radiomen followed orders, smashing the set they had guarded and maintained with great care since Manchuria. Then the six men shook hands in silence, without even the usual "See you soon" or "Take care and do a good job." "Only our eyes, boring into one another's, told our farewells to each other. Sooner or later, death will overtake us." Leaving their cave in the dark, the men had no idea of what to "attack"; their wild hope was somehow to infiltrate to the north. A small enemy ship just off the beach sent them "a torrential rain of machine gun fire." They fled with their remaining strength.

A heavy barrage of shells burst almost on top of them. They were in a field with no cover whatever, running blindly. Even after having been similarly shelled scores of times in the twelve weeks of battle, even knowing they had to die in days or hours, they were terri-fied — and by the very same uncertainty as grips green soldiers dur-ing their initiation to artillery bombardment. They could not tell where the shells would land; each round had a firing squad's power to petrify.

Yoshio Kobayashi was no better at running now than as a boy. "Even in desperation, even under the threat of death, slow runners are slow." But he escaped yet again* — and hours later gazed at the sky from a shallow foxhole. He thought of his home, which lay under the same starry sky. What were his parents doing? It struck him that strawberries must now be at their peak back in Hokkaido. He surren-dered to deep nostalgia.

After dark the next day, he and the other five men found the rem-nants of Kojo's force in two small caves at Maesato, one of them des-ignated battalion headquarters. Outside, corpses of a unit that had previously occupied the position filled a space of about eight meters between two huge rocks. Some of the bodies were still smoking, for although the boulders protected from most artillery fire, mortar shells were landing between them.

Kojo was there with his fifteen men. More mortar fire killed several the same morning. American tanks followed, their roaring exhaust announcing that they had stopped directly in front of the caves. The shape and size of the mouth of Kobayashi's cave protected the inte-rior from direct hits, but its walls were thin. Each shell that blasted the surrounding rock seemed like a giant club relentlessly pounded on metal buckets over the heads of the men. The tanks fired from noon until evening. Kobayashi felt certain he would lose his mind from the bludgeoning and the acrid smoke that drifted inside and had nowhere to escape — like the men.

Messengers from nearby caves, some severely wounded, crawled in that night with news that their units had been reduced to a handful of men or entirely annihilated. Conflicting concepts of duty tore at Kojo. He had no orders to leave his position, and now there was no one to ask. But he could neither feed his men nor supply them with arms or water or proper cover. The inability to offer them anything pained him deeply. Exposed as they were, the ragged survivors could be only targets, unable to fight back when dawn — surely their last —

---

*Running back across the same field at dusk the next day, Kobayashi was surprised to see a soldier sitting there, arms crossed, legs lazily stretched out. What a brave or stupid man to rest in such a deadly place! Then he saw a face split in half like a watermelon, and ran faster than ever.

arrived. For the first time in his life, Kojo took an unauthorized decision — with great difficulty but also with conviction. "I can do nothing for my men any longer," he told himself. "Therefore, I'm right to release them from my command, even without orders."

He summoned his messengers, announced he was disbanding the unit, and told them to pass the word to the others that they were to pair off and go out at midnight for a hand-to-hand attack. Survivors were to try to break through the enemy lines and find their way north — specifically, to the battalion of Captain Tsuneo Shimura, an Academy classmate of Kojo's, which had been bypassed during the American advance. Unable to join the withdrawal from Shuri because it was surrounded, Shimura's battalion — of the 32nd Regiment in Kojo's 24th Division — managed a short advance to some high ground roughly three miles north of the old capital, where it continued to hold a pocket, according to reports Kojo had seen. (The reports were generally accurate: some four hundred officers and soldiers of Shimura's force were alive.) Kojo gave each pair of men two hand grenades, which left one for the final pair, his adjutant and himself. Then he distributed the hardtack that was the last of the food.

"So this is it," thought Kobayashi, listening to his battalion commander's last order. "This is the end of me." The private repeated the order, gave the captain a last salute and ran back to his own cave to spread the word. Kojo watched the men leave, two by two, for the beach and their attempts to escape from there. His command was disbanded, his duties as a field officer finished.

Yoshio Kobayashi managed to escape to the beach after Kojo's order to disband. Three days later, when the American flag was raised at Okinawa's southern tip, he was two miles away, huddled in a cave with civilians and some soldiers from various units. Women and children shrieked in the dark when a white phosphorous bomb exploded like a thunder clap. Coughing uncontrollably, Kobayashi couldn't help inhaling quantities of poisonous white smoke. He had managed to acquire four grenades. He covered his face with a wet rag, gripped one grenade, thrust his head into the slime of the cave floor and endured the "slow torture" of Americans approaching, their caution stretching his self-control "beyond limit." "The enemy advances . . . The core of my head freezes in the face of certain death. Now! Now? The feeling is beyond my power to describe. Time crawls, yet there is not enough time . . ."

Kobayashi saw a ray of light, probably from an American flashlight, inching toward him from around a curve. "Soon now." He heard the patter and sensed the movement of other Japanese soldiers creeping farther into the interior of the cave. Knowing their movement was futile — the Americans would follow and trap them — he reached out to restrain whomever he could touch.

Now the enemy were directly in front of him, shouting and aiming their flashlights "like a spotlight on actors." The din of their grenades and automatic fire again rent Kobayashi's ears. His mind blank, he sat up and threw one of his grenades at an enemy soldier, who screamed terribly when it exploded. A fragment hit Kobayashi in the chest, making each breath agony. They were not proper breaths because he could only pant like a dog in August while blood poured down his mud-covered front. "Oh it hurts, it hurts," he chanted, half in delirium. But the light disappeared, perhaps because of his grenade. The Americans seemed to retreat from the cave.

There was no antiseptic or medicine, but a senior private first class named Maruyama offered to help. The bandage that Maruyama tried to place on the wound in total darkness was only a little triangle, but contact with his comrade's uninjured body provided a surge of comfort. Kobayashi felt like a sick child whose hand is taken by Mother.

His dread of being alone was worse than his physical agony. The others planned to sneak from the cave and strike out for the north that night. He knew that would mean a final parting from his friends: he was too badly hurt to join them. When his last few hours with them passed and the time for his abandonment arrived, a flood of sorrow and terror seemed to wash him from the face of the earth. He urged Maruyama to go. The senior private seemed dismayed to leave him but had no alternative. Giving Maruyama two of his remaining three grenades, Kobayashi asked him to place the other in his hand: "One's enough for me." Maruyama repeatedly entreated him not to be "hasty." He would return and wanted to find Kobayashi alive.

When the others had gone, Kobayashi dragged himself around the cave on all fours, hurting as much from "the overwhelming sense of desolation" as from his wound. In mud to his hips, lapsing in and out of consciousness, he supported his torso with his hands, face upturned to endure the pain and suffocation. Civilians were alive deeper in the cave, but here the only sound was a whooshing of bats. Unconscious, he became "ecstatic" with visions of his buddies returning to pat him on the shoulder in delight at finding him alive. Conscious again, he slithered in circles. When he could endure no more loneliness, his comfort came from knowing relief would arrive four seconds after he pulled the pin of his grenade. Then he realized the grenade was missing from his hand. Gasping with madness, he groped in the blackness for his salvation — yet remained terrified by every noise inside the cave, as if his life were still precious.

He didn't know that over twenty-four hours of near-delirium had passed when a girl returned to the cave and reported that his fellow soldiers had all been killed attempting to break through the American lines. (Caught too, the girl promised to lead the Americans to Japanese soldiers but ran away from their truck when it stopped.) Devastated by the death of his last friends, Kobayashi crawled farther into the cave. Civilians were cooking there. The sight of them brought immense relief at no longer being alone. An elderly man helped reposition Maruyama's filthy bandage on his chest. The generosity of an elderly woman's gift of a rice ball astonished Kobayashi until he learned that Maruyama had left her some rice on her promise to feed him after he, Maruyama, had slipped from the cave — to his death, Kobayashi now knew. As he shared his rice ball with the adolescent girl, he could not restrain his tears.

28 · The Civilian Toll

The peninsula was teeming with refugees, thousands and thousands of them. More were arriving every minute. We had landed in a geographical sack . . . into which the war was pouring survivors from all of southern Okinawa.
— Jo Nobuko Martin

The thing is horrible beyond human nature to bear.
— Prime Minister David Lloyd George, December 1917, about the carnage of World War I

Man becomes brave when armed. I was in high spirits from the moment I held it in my hand. I could be saved from starving to death. I could kill myself in a moment. The thought made me shudder with joy.
— An Okinawan given a hand grenade in late June

We saw civilians who didn't utter a cry with absolutely terrible wounds and maggots crawling all over them. What they endured! Such stoicism!
— Arthur Cofer

The civilians were in just terrible shape — wounded, starving, terrified. You never saw such fear on faces. But we still couldn't trust them because of the gung ho ones mixed in.
— Buzzy Fox

Scores of civilians were pulled out of caves and from under the rubble, many so badly injured that they died. A very high percentage required medical care. The old were particularly pitiful. Half starved, utterly exhausted, harried from pillar to post during the 80-day-old campaign . . . their faces were solid in misery.
— Major Roy Appleman, a prominent Army historian of the battle

A DAY OR TWO before or after the June flag raising — Dick Whitaker never knew the date — a much depleted Company F–2–29 advanced along the western coast where Tadashi Kojo had disbanded his command. Some men took a moment to admire the East China Sea's blue-green water shimmering in the sun. LSTs patrolled the coast, loudspeakers blaring appeals to surrender in Japanese. "The battle's over! Come out with your hands up! You'll be given food and water." Planes dropped yet more leaflets with the same messages. Whitaker's company pushed ahead slowly, rooting out Japanese from ditches, culverts, fields, shells of houses and caves. It wasn't apparent from the look of the haggard Americans, who still took occasional sniper fire and suicide charges from individual Japanese, that the end was in sight. "Absolutely everyone" Whitaker knew was exhausted. "Tense, anxious, jumpy, wasted away. Nights were still a physical and mental ordeal. Night noises would set off a cascade of fire and dawn would reveal new collections of dead Japs, goats, women, children."

The company's advance patrol had stopped at the edge of a cliff that dropped to the sea. The small group took note that those men ahead were focused on the unseen face of the cliff, some distance below the summit. When Whitaker reached them, he was told of a large cave mouth facing the sea. Although it was hidden from the cliff edge, he saw small-arms fire from inside directed at an LST close ashore. Still broadcasting in Japanese, the little ship was also using radio to report the mouth's location and activity to the Marines.

The men found some nearby air vents that led down into the cave. They threw in phosphorous, smoke and fragmentation grenades, called for napalm and sprawled on the ground until a fifty-five-gallon drum arrived on an amtrac. The liquid was poured into the vents and set off with another phosphorous grenade. More screams than usual followed because the cave, like many in the far southern end, was huge; some extended ten or more miles. The Marines were enveloped by the familiar smell of white phosphorus and burning human flesh. The LST radioed that soldiers and civilians, many hardly able to move their ghostly bodies, were teetering out of the cave mouth and down the cliff. The ship moved in to pick them up from the beach, where other Marines waited to help. Fox Company resumed its advance and civilians continued to be saved or killed.

Farther south, another Marine company took the last hill and came to a cliff from which civilians were leaping, as at Saipan. Some jumped alone, some in pairs and small groups; a few pushed one another. A platoon leader who had fought straight through from L-day watched in mixed relief and caution.

> It was like ants when their nest has been dug up. Mass confusion. Civilians running here, running there, looking for a place where their fall wouldn't be broken on the way down, for a rock down below where they could hit full. Women too. It was the end of a long rabbit hunt: you'd been flushing them out and they kept running for new cover ahead of you. Now you flushed them out again

and they were trapped, so they dove onto the rocks or went into the sea. We didn't shoot them but we didn't try to stop them either. Seeing civilians do all that didn't bother me one bit, not one iota. Maybe I was half crazy myself by that time, I don't know — but I had other worries. I'd seen a lot of horrors by then, including one of my own men killed only a few hours before. What I was worried about was whether one of those milling ants would turn around and try to blow us up.

In fact, far more civilians now were engaged in trying to blow up themselves than blow up Americans. Until the last day or two, the goal of most families fleeing the advance had been to find refuge. Now it was to avoid capture and agonizing death. Some natives dreamed of no more than a few moments of peace on a clean, quiet beach before they died.

Those who were confident that surrender wouldn't end in fatal torture remained very few. Accounts of relatively humane treatment in the detention camps circulated widely but were mixed with so many rumors and wild falsehoods that the desperate refugees had little reason to believe anything good about the hairy, sunburned Americans of the indiscriminately ferocious firepower. More than ever, civilians were on their own, each depleted family responsible for itself. Some Japanese soldiers, especially those who had been abroad, tried to persuade Okinawans to let themselves be captured rather than kill themselves. But a larger number continued warning them to expect American atrocities and a small number continued shooting "spies" and "traitors" who tried to surrender. "Don't be discouraged," a lieutenant told a group of terrified civilians. "Although Okinawa has fallen victim to the enemy's hands, we haven't come to any decisive, fatal pass." Families that had obtained or been issued hand grenades were envied. But even when members squeezed together for the explosion in small caves, the grenade often left a badly wounded survivor or two. Japanese soldiers sometimes finished the job with rifle butts, sticks or rocks.*

On a southern beach, two women, possibly nurses, tried to drown each other by forcing their heads under the water. To Ed Jones, it was "like a pathetic comedy after seeing all that death." Finally an American infantryman waded out and brought the women in.

The physical difficulty of accomplishing suicide by other means

---

*Okinawans also used knives, rakes, hoes and rocks on themselves and their families. Killing women and children with makeshift instruments wasn't difficult but most people in their severely weakened condition found killing themselves almost impossible. Many parents had to find other methods, including hanging, after dispatching their children.

increased the number who jumped from the cliffs. Civilian clothing and shoes were strewn along the beaches, together with uniforms. "It was as if people had gone in for a swim," an American observed. "Except that the clothes and shoes were bloody."

All around the island's southern tip, clusters of Okinawans hid in nooks under cliffs and behind boulders above the water's edge. Those with children were especially afraid when Japanese soldiers approached. The selfish and ferocious soldiers — demanding rice from the civilians' tiny stores, warning of orders to kill all "nuisances" to "military operations" — naturally made a sharper impression than the kind and the gentle. Now many soldiers appeared willing to surrender but commanders of units still operating as such ordered final banzai attacks. Those without rifles were instructed to use bamboo spears; those without spears, to gather stones. When attacks were actually launched up the steep cliffs, American fire from the top sent corpses tumbling down to join those decomposing on the beach.

Civilian suicides continued. A relatively well-groomed woman emerged from a cave at Kyan Point and tried to strangle herself with her kimono sash. Others reasoned that killing oneself because other family members were dead would leave no one to remember their tragedy. Antisuicide Okinawans argued that although death from one side or the other seemed inevitable, people must try to stay alive every possible moment. But even the most forceful opponents of suicide quaked when Americans reached their groups to herd and help them back up the cliff. Many were certain the Army trucks on top were to take them to tanks waiting to crush their bones.

Members of the Okinawan elite insisted "temporary" setbacks changed nothing important. The Kadena chief of police was among those who gave assurances that the 32nd Army was strong enough to carry on and that Lieutenant Colonel Naomichi Jin, Ushijima's air officer, had escaped to Tokyo to lead the air assault that would precede the Japanese counterlanding. (Jin was indeed among the staff officers ordered to escape instead of killing themselves.) Meanwhile, patriotic young Okinawans continued on their odyssey. Shin-ichi Kuniyoshi, the fourteen-year-old communications soldier, didn't know what day it was when he hadn't moved a muscle while maggots ate into his orifices during his sixteen hours of hiding among corpses. In fact it was only two or three days before the end of organized Japanese resistance. After delivering his message to the Yoza-dake cave, Shin-ichi was told that his unit had moved farther south. Picking a route through territory still in Japanese hands, he climbed down the mountain and walked the three miles in a few hours.

The new position was in Hill 89. Not knowing of Generals Ushijima and Cho's suicides there, Shin-ichi was happy to find five or six of his classmates in his cave, survivors of their original group of forty-six. They were surprised by the excellent Japanese of the surrender appeals broadcast by an American flotilla patrolling some three hundred yards from the beach below. "Japan has lost so cease your useless resistance. Come out with your hands up. Give up now, you won't be harmed." "*Won't be harmed,*" snorted Shin-ichi, knowing he couldn't expect a swift death from any American. But traitorous whispers of Japanese soldiers who were sharing the cave reached the boys on the morning of June 23, the day on which the 10th Army brass declared Okinawa secured. Although also ignorant of the suicides of Ushijima and Cho, those whisperers insisted that Japan had lost the war. Shin-ichi reasoned that even if this appallingly defeatist talk were true, it wouldn't answer the question of what he, *a Japanese soldier,* should do.

A strip of junglelike vegetation lay below Hill 89 and the adjacent cliffs. Massive boulders bordered the sea, interspersed with pockets of coral and sandy beach. Shin-ichi saw Japanese soldiers make their difficult way down the cliff, through the dense green growth and into the water. Some swam out to surrender to the American ships, others only far enough to drown themselves. More Japanese remained on shore and saved their honor by shooting those surrendering before they completed their swim.

Back in the cave, some boys wanted to save themselves, however slim the chances. Others insisted they must obey the final Japanese order for survivors to infiltrate to the north and fight to the last man. Skeletal Shin-ichi didn't want to swim anywhere or think of surrender. But despite his vow to his dead friend Miyagi, the depletion of his energy had drained his desire to continue fighting. He decided to join some other boys and a dozen Japanese who were gathering around an unusually trustworthy and decent soldier. They indeed went north, toward where Japanese units were supposedly fighting on, still strong and in high spirits.

Lacking a destination, most civilians stayed put during those final days; a scattering were saved by last-minute luck. On June 24, a dozen high school students sat arm in arm in a tight circle so that their three hand grenades would kill them all. Their teacher had a sudden change of mind. Having believed the Japanese propaganda as staunchly as others, he now told himself that no one could be as cruel as Americans were painted; humans were humans, after all, and it wasn't human nature to kill. Using all his powers of persuasion on himself and the girls, he managed to stop them from detonating the grenades at the last moment.

Two days later, a forty-one-year-old man left a cave after hearing a Japanese soldier's advice to be ready to die. Fully ready, the Okinawan tossed aside his last bag of rice, but the Americans outside only searched him and appropriated the paltry contents of his pockets for souvenirs. The same day, phosphorous and fragmentation grenades burned and blasted two families to death in a tiny cave a mile up the coast from Mabuni. But the American team heard an infant's cries as it was about to move to the next cave. The burned, blackened, wormy orphan was rushed for treatment and saved.

Almost as many refugees in the packed southern enclave died as survived — more than servicemen of both sides combined, if only because more were in the path of the armament. On the day of the American flag raising, a flamethrower seared most of the skin from a five-year-old, who sought relief by running toward the sea along the razor-sharp coral. Slightly smaller and younger than the napalmed Vietnamese girl whose photograph would become one of that war's starkest symbols of native suffering, this child was no less horribly burned. He was one of up to 100,000 civilians — the number merits repeating — who perished during June, most of them in the last ten days. There were too many for a precise count. Forty-five years later, native experts still disagreed, most confessing the toll would never be known partly because so many registry offices were entirely demolished, together with all inhabitants of villages who would have remembered their neighbors.*

Okinawans used to wonder why so little attention was paid to their numbers.† They felt it was altogether right for mainland families to stream to Okinawa to hold memorial services and search for the bones of their missing Japanese men. The annual expressions of international grief on the anniversary of the Hiroshima bomb were also appropriate — but how to explain the scant interest in the greater Okinawan losses? Enormous as the torment was in the Japanese cities, the bombs were less tragic for Japan than months of fighting were for Okinawa, which bore far less responsibility for having started the war.

---

*Native experts may be the most credible because their tendency to exaggerate the total is probably less pronounced than the Japanese and American tendency to underestimate. Washington's record in coming to terms with the hardest truths of the war has been less dismal only than Tokyo's. But some of the failure is due to "innocent" rather than intentional ignorance. Not even American fighters on the island who witnessed a portion of the destruction had any way to appreciate its scale. Until he was properly informed not long ago, a general in command of a fighting division believed that 22,000 civilians died in all.

†Their puzzlement slowly faded. While the atomic victims were categorized in minute detail by age, sex, occupation, distance from the epicenter, and many other categories, the Okinawan dead remained a kind of secret. A world well informed and regularly reminded about the Japanese deaths scarcely heard of the Okinawan. In the end, however, most survivors stopped expecting anything like equal treatment.

Forty-five years after Hiroshima and Nagasaki, the death tolls were also unknown. Estimates varied between a 1967 United Nations' figure of 78,000 in Hiroshima and 27,000 in Nagasaki to more than thrice that in later Japanese estimates. Some experts took 140,000 and 70,000 as a best final estimate of the disputed figures: a combined total some 25 percent higher than on Okinawa, where final guesses put the figure at about 150,000 civilians.* Of course the Okinawan deaths — and those of an additional 10,000 Koreans brought to perform heavy labor and camp services for the 32nd Army — were caused by conventional weapons, a crucial difference for some critics of nuclear arms. But if one innocent life is as sacred as another — if what shocks and dismays about Hiroshima and Nagasaki is the appalling number of their dead — the comparison with Okinawa must be pursued. The American forces alone fired 7.5 million 37mm to 8-inch howitzer rounds, 60,018 5- to 6-inch naval shells, 392,304 hand grenades, 20,359 rockets and just under thirty million machine gun, rifle and pistol rounds on and into the island. This staggering weight of metal — supplemented by the Japanese weapons — lacerated almost as much Okinawan flesh as the two atomic bombs seared Japanese. And the greater number of civilians slaughtered on Okinawa than in either Hiroshima or Nagasaki more often died in days or weeks rather than minutes, with that much more time to witness the agony of their families.

Gripped by images of atomic devastation, the international public doesn't realize, and most media commentators never knew, that it would have taken 150 atomic bombs to wreak on Japan the equivalent cultural and material devastation and to kill a comparable percentage of Japanese. A third of all Okinawans were probably killed, and most of the island's national and cultural artifacts were demolished. Few peoples have suffered a similar catastrophe.

The Japanese rightly feel their losses were enormous, both on the mainland and on Okinawa. It is only when compared with Okinawan losses that theirs seem less. "Look at it this way, the way the Japanese never seem to and Americans have never thought of," said a long-term American resident of Okinawa. "The relatives of Japanese soldiers killed and missing in action here have been visiting the island

---

*In a sense, the death of Ei Shimada, governor of the prefecture, belongs in this total, although he was Japanese. Having predicted disaster if Ushijima withdrew from Shuri, Shimada did what he could to help civilians during the mass evacuation south, then held his final conference on prefectural affairs 200 yards from the 32nd Army headquarters cave. According to one version, he died there on June 22; a stone memorialized him and 445 prefectural workers killed "in action." But some civilian survivors reported seeing him help wash the wounds of the injured in a nearby stream on June 24. As with Ushijima's death, the circumstances are not certain, despite accounts by supposed eyewitnesses.

for decades, expressing legitimate grief over the fate of their poor men. What they never seem to realize is that every Okinawan family was devastated far worse. No matter what happened to Japan, it was easier than what happened to Okinawa. Many Japanese talk about the atomic bomb with deep, moving pain while they're here, never thinking that Okinawans lost much more than two cities — just about their whole island."

The imprecise casualty figures make much of this speculative, like the estimates of psychological and other damage to "unwounded" Okinawans. One eleven-year-old trekked with her family during its evacuation south from Naha, passing babies sucking at dead mothers' breasts, seeing an aunt alongside her ripped apart by a shell. The girl clutched her most prized possession throughout this passage through bombs and carnage: her report cards as her school's top student. But the trauma of those six weeks destroyed her ability to read and write. So it went for lucky survivors — and the tragedy continued in the postwar period, even after a few schools were built amid the rubble.

29 · Aftermath

We went to Guam and the A-bomb was dropped, ending the war and avoiding a landing on Japan that would have killed most of us . . . I was in San Diego, on my way home, when I became 21 years old. And the privates of this war will rule the world.
— Thomas Hannaher

The battle here is over but Japan is still fighting. If we can decrease the enemy's power by even one or two men, that is our duty.
— A Japanese straggler

[Okinawa] seemed like a bypassed island. Thousands of men, hundreds of planes and shiploads of equipment were sent there to do the biggest job of the war. Then suddenly the job was called off and now nobody gives a damn what happens. The big shots and many little ones are running off to China and Japan for sightseeing and souvenirs. Those who cannot do so well for themselves are just taking it easy, except for a conscientious few who struggle on with their jobs in the face of general confusion and corruption.
— Donald Keene, September 23, 1945, six weeks after Japan's surrender

Without doubt, our military operations in Okinawa have caused far greater disruption, destruction and casualties than any previous violent historical episode in the archipelago, and cannot be regarded by the people as anything but a calamitous disaster.
— Commander Henry Bennett, U.S. Navy, on the impact of the invasion and occupation, February 1946

GENERAL STILWELL, the 10th Army's new commander, announced the campaign officially ended on July 2, nine days after Okinawa had been declared secure. By the time of a final surrender ceremony two months later, almost all the units that had done the securing were gone. The Marine divisions were relieved by Army troops within days of the June 23 flag raising and shipped out, some grasping at a rumor that their destination would be home. "There was always a lot of that kind of bullshit around and that's just what this was," pronounced Stuart Upchurch.

They weren't going home but to the Japanese mainland, via Guam, for rest, rehabilitation and retraining. Life was less than cushy on

Guam but the veterans savored each day. The first phase of the invasion of the home islands was scheduled for November 1, four months after their departure from Okinawa. They didn't know the date, but they knew their new fighting would be the most difficult of all. A majority of combat troops would almost certainly die or be seriously wounded during the landing or in later combat there.

Then the atomic bomb and Japan's surrender changed everything. The Hiroshima bomb was dropped on August 6; Emperor Hirohito announced the decision to surrender — in his first broadcast to the nation — nine days later. Excited new rumors flooded Guam: home by Thanksgiving, by Christmas, by Easter. But Dick Whitaker was delayed. In October, his regiment was shipped to China to help repatriate Japanese forces there. His battalion enjoyed the "sweet revenge" of watching samurai swords humbly stacked on tables, then embraced other pleasures. Quartered in the port city of Tsingtao, it had the regiment's highest rate of venereal disease.

Whitaker was demobilized after eight months in China. He arrived home in Saugerties on Memorial Day 1946 and watched the town parade with his parents on Main Street, along which he had walked to school for twelve years. He was still in uniform. There was little defiant trumpeting that the country was number one but much affection for "the boys." Whitaker's hand was pumped for hours. Friends hugged and kissed him. "It was," he remembered, "a good day to come home."

The spectators dispersed after the parade. His parents walked home; Dick went to George Broome's saloon. George looked the same and the bar stool felt the same. The first beer was on the house, the next was his. "The war was over. The circle had closed."

It had closed almost completely to outsiders, for just as Whitaker had never written home about the real hardships on Okinawa, he found himself unable to talk about them now. Combat veterans didn't know how to tell the story of their experiences. They didn't want to brag to listeners who had little reason to believe the grotesque reality of the battlefield. "What's the point?" gregarious Whitaker would ask to explain his near silence about the emotional apex and nadir of his life. "How can anyone *know*?" Paul Fussell suggests another reason for the fighters' unspoken conspiracy of silence. They had participated in an event that smeared a monstrous blot on the human race. The appalling outrages to decency so soon after those of World War I left them with a sense of shame for the species supposedly created in God's image. They were happy to be home and to forget them.

Only other combat infantrymen knew and none needed reminding. Veterans tended to swap funny stories about the screw-ups and ludicrous confusion. Meeting others who did know would give Whitaker an infusion of battlefield camaraderie's unique intensity for decades. But he didn't need any extra stimulus to feel a glow in 1946. Although he was saddened to see many more gold stars on the yellowing honor roll over Broome's fireplace, some beside the names of good friends, his own name there satisfied him deeply. After months of beer rounds and laughter, the saloon doors stopped swinging with the newly demobilized; all who had made it through the war were home. Now the party too was over, but Whitaker remained proud.

So did most Marines who returned from the edge without crippling or disfiguring injury. They had a lifelong reservoir of pride, even if others would never know what filled it. And a reservoir of self-confidence. Marc Jaffe, a Marine first lieutenant who had broken down with shock during his first fighting on an earlier island but returned to win a Bronze Star for gallantry below the Shuri Line, felt his life had been irrevocably changed. "Whenever I ran into physical or psychological hardships later, I thought of Okinawa. I knew that if I could survive that, I could survive anything." Jaffe and the others talked as little about the highs as the lows, but would never forget. Would they do it again, even with the excruciating fear and misery? You bet they would, especially when basking in their neighbors' grateful admiration and savoring the knowledge that they wouldn't *have* to do it again. "That was the peak." "My proudest moments." "I can't explain it but they were the best days of my life — when *I* was best."

The band that greeted Whitaker's troopship in San Diego set off cymbals in the hearts of her thousand passengers, all seasoned veterans. But no music played on the wrecked Japanese piers; the trickle of Japanese who returned from Okinawa in wretched defeat felt no uplift. Civilians, physically and spiritually shattered by the ruinous war, welcomed their own family survivors with joyful pity, but held the once vaunted Army as a whole in silent or angry scorn.* Moreover, many Okinawa veterans felt scarcely human when they returned — and that day was still far off for a good number of them. The war that was over for Whitaker and his fellows dragged on for the 32nd Army's survivors, the so-called stragglers — although that term is misleading about the thousands in the first months after the collapse of organized resistance. For those men, the flag raising and

---

*The Japanese people would continue hating the memory. In 1963, 18 years after the surrender, less than 1 percent of those surveyed by a television station remembered the war as the best period of their lives. Those who did were presumably superpatriots and ex-officers, now out in the cold of Japan's powerful postwar antimilitarism.

surrender ceremonies might as well have been on the moon. The 10th Army's classification of the island as secure would have meant nothing to the wasted, desperate fugitives even if they'd heard of it. A week later, a Marine laconically recorded a toll in his diary. "We shot three more Nips last night."

When the 32nd Army dissolved, few of its members were alive without some freakish act of providence. Their temperament and make-up may also have helped. The surviving 10 percent probably had a higher than average quotient of initiative and individuality, qualities that would now count heavily.

The inhabitants of the last cave of medic Ikuo Ogiso, the actor turned de facto surgeon, were more skeletons than soldiers, macabre beings with sunken eyes and uniforms stiff with mud and excrement. In late June, the chief medical officer ordered twenty-five nurses' aides from a less prestigious high school than Ruriko Morishita's to leave and surrender. Calling themselves *Yamato nadeshiko* — proud and virtuous Japanese women — all pleaded for permission to remain and die with the soldiers or to join them on a break-out to the north. But the medical officer remained adamant and the girls obeyed.*

After the girls left, about eighty men survived remorseless satchel charges and phosphorous bombs, but the fear of death drove some of them to run outside the cave to get it over with. The others burrowed deeper into the vast cave near the village of Itosu. The last message from division headquarters, passed down from General Ushijima's final message, had commanded all to continue fighting. Accordingly, Ogiso's chief instructed his men to form groups for sorties from the cave. More than ever, those last orders made the recipients feel they were living a bad dream. The major himself dissolved cyanide in the last of his alcohol and swallowed it — or was injected by an aide, as some near him believed; the cave was too dark for Ogiso to see.

The first groups left for their final attacks several nights after the 10th Army's declaration of the end of organized resistance, when combat Marines maintained their nocturnal vigilance but started building volley ball courts by day. Some "human bullets" managed to inch toward American positions until conventional bullets hit them.

---

*Ogiso's commander, a major in rank and a China veteran, nevertheless saw his "true mission as not that of a professional soldier who kills but that of a medical doctor who helps man to live." Thanks to him, twenty of the girls were eventually saved — "twenty precious lives," Ogiso would write with relief many years later, "mothers who now enjoy a peaceful life."

But six of the most respected and resourceful doctors and senior staff decided to remain in the cave until the Americans' guard was down. The conscientious Ogiso was invited to join them.

Their two months of underground existence formed a new order of human experience, combining elements of *Robinson Crusoe, The War of the Worlds* and Dante's *Inferno*. Like their ancestors, those cavemen devised ways of preserving fire in the wetness — "the most precious commodity in the world for us," an inhabitant of a nearby cave explained. One of the best methods used cartridge powder, empty cans and abandoned medical bandages woven into a slow-burning rope. Every fire was tended reverently, in fear of insanity without it.

Ogiso's cave was one of the prodigious southern ones that wove and twisted for mile after unexplored mile. A supply of rotting rice gave the men some days of lice picking and nostalgia between continued American explosions. Forced to move on, the gasping, tottering group explored huge reaches of treacherous swampland, jagged "mountain" ranges and secret passes unknown even by local Okinawans: a supernatural universe of eeriness, dread and pain. Ogiso supposed the fear he felt in the perpetual darkness resembled what human beings had felt thousands of years earlier. "The darkness and thick, sticky air coil around your skin . . . while a weird aura rises from the grotesquely shaped stalactites and water's slimy surface . . . To live shut up in this darkness all alone was beyond any normal human being's endurance."

Other Japanese encountered in the menacing vastness — for the groups remained almost totally apart, as if they belonged to distinct prehistoric tribes — looked like a subspecies. Accumulated spectacles of suffering in the gargantuan dungeon finally broke through Ogiso's training and self-discipline. A demented soldier's shriek of "Banzai to the Emperor!" while he flung himself to a watery death filled the patriot with deep anger at the once-revered deity. "Emperor, do you really know? In your name, in places like this, men are dying unnatural, violent, miserable deaths." Yet the survivors reassured themselves that they would be guides for the Japanese forces who would soon come to liberate Okinawa. How could Japan lose with ships like *Yamato* leading her superb Navy?

Months of the dampness without a hint of sunlight also begat physical affliction. A stomach disease kept Ogiso in unbearable pain. To end it, he armed a grenade and pulled the hissing metal to his chest. A doctor in his group kicked it away just in time.

When the group finally emerged in September, it joined a small army of stragglers who took underground refuge every day but spent nights limping through the countryside. Hundreds of Okinawans shared their roaming travel, some using the same caves as Japanese for rest stops, although the two nationalities usually remained separate unless they were engaged in barter. Most groups began by trying to obey the orders to penetrate to the north. One of the most persistent rumors — strengthened by total ignorance of what had happened to the Japanese forces in the north — was of units supposedly intact in a mountainous, heavily forested area called Kunigami, near the island's northern tip.

Shelling had so altered the landscape that finding one's way would have been difficult in the darkness even with a map. Most used the North Star to try to head for the mythical forest hold-out with its vividly imagined food, weapons and clean water. Kunigami, the name whispered as if it meant "deliverance" or "secret super weapon," was a last trump and hope. When party after party was slaughtered attempting to reach it by creeping through the American lines, some men thought of floating to the mainland on a raft. American sentries on beaches leisurely picked off swimmers who set out with baskets over their heads of debris intended to blend with the battle's heavy flotsam in the water.

But the majority of stragglers simply existed, their goal reduced to staying alive until they were rescued by the mythical Japanese counterlanding.* The more principled groups agreed among themselves that individuals discovered by an enemy patrol or unable to carry on because of injury would kill themselves so as not to burden the others. But those who kept the promise delivered a horrific blow to their friends. Fewer and fewer were left. Those lucky ones roamed fields smelling of the earth, whose fragrance they might be savoring for the last time, and of the decaying corpses they would soon join, perhaps before dawn, for they lived with constant dread of being shot at any second. "Thank God American sentries speak loudly even on duty," one man remarked, but that was scant protection. Crawling back and forth, fleeing American fire, losing their way in villages where all landmarks had been destroyed, the human wrecks slithered from their caves and burrows every night to haunt southern Okinawa, inadvertently crunching rotting skeletons in the dark and passing cave entrances eerily glowing from the phosphorescent explosive tossed inside. They met, dispersed, exchanged rumors, scavenged, watched their numbers inexorably decline.

---

*One group cautiously dug up a portable safe their unit commander had buried before killing himself. Neatly wrapped bundles of a thousand 100–yen bills were stacked inside. The men were ecstatic because the paper on which the fortune was printed was enough to cook a canteen of rice.

The nightly activity lasted three or four hours, from when the occupying Americans fell asleep in their tents to the first suggestion of dawn. Failure to find a new burrow — even one reeking with decomposing bodies — or to return to a known one by early light was virtual suicide. "I wanted to grab the sun and smash it down," remembered one straggler forced to endure the terror of several days above ground. Desperation deprived many of all desire to continue fighting. American leaflets proclaiming further resistance useless because Japan had capitulated were half-believed. Some read leaflets with the Imperial Edict of Surrender and wept. But others predicted that anyone who followed the American instructions for surrender — discard all arms; appear on specified beaches with a visible leaflet as a sign — would be tortured to death. And the believers didn't believe enough to act.

A majority used their remaining weapons only to save their lives, as when reckless Americans entered their caves. But others — or the same men at different times — became more determined to kill at least one enemy monster before the end. Chased into fields, some groups threw their last grenades at the pursuers and were filled with frustration when they did not explode or satisfaction when they produced American screams. Others tossed grenades into audiences at outdoor movies or ambushed squads sent out to find them. The bravest crept into tents and massacred the sleepers, sometimes stealing American weapons on the way.*

Americans lit grass fires to chase the desperadoes into a wall of automatic fire. A straggler who returned alive from a pass covered by a machine gun reported seeing "a red river" of Japanese blood. When American dogs missed a man despite coming close enough for him to hear their wet panting, the trembling Japanese wondered whether it was because he and other stragglers no longer smelled human after months of bestial life. Other terror-stricken groups sniffed the cigarettes of American search patrols inches away.

The small groups that were formed when the fighting units disbanded comprised men drawn together by aim and outlook. Their leaders led by ability rather than rank; the Army's rigid class system and class consciousness had entirely disappeared. In place of the unthinking obedient soldiers, one straggler observed, they "were naked

---

*The luckiest and most daring stragglers stole food with growing expertise, sometimes taking enough time to search American tents for cigarettes. One team made off with a portable USO phonograph with records of the most popular American songs. Others interrupted their forays to enjoy moments of the open-air movies without trying to disrupt them.

human beings who came together and dispersed by the force of human attraction and repulsion." Privates insulted officers to their faces. The same officers begged the privates to take them into their groups.

Exclusion from a group was a terrible fate. It usually meant no food as well as the anguish of isolation, that state so contrary to Japanese instinct. Some men joined groups headed for almost certain death at passes covered by machine guns, not out of nonexistent hope but for the last comfort of numbers. Friends promised each other to stay alive, but weaker ones gave up the exhausting work of hiding and allowed themselves to be killed. Other friends swore to each other never to separate whatever the circumstances, but of course did separate when they became lost in the dark or when bursts of enemy fire scattered them in terrified chaos.

It was great credit to all involved that some semblance of civilized behavior survived. Some of the most seriously wounded men begged to be killed to reduce the burden on the others. Some of those unable to join the forays for food would accept none, believing they had no right to it. But although acts of generosity and self-sacrifice were not uncommon among the new comrades, most groups regarded all others as greater or lesser rivals, sometimes quarreling savagely over hiding places and tactics. Some stragglers hated "the gigantic [Japanese military] power that thrust us into this utter misery" with all the intensity remaining in their frail bodies; others threatened to kill anyone who mentioned surrender. However, food precipitated most of the clashes. By September, an outsider who stole a morsel from a group's supply was likely to be instantly killed. Some groups fought others like bandit gangs for a cache of anything edible, sometimes with swords and to the death.

Food included seaweed, wormy sweet potatoes and worms themselves. Arriving at new caves, starving survivors would rummage feverishly among decomposing corpses. The rucksacks still on the backs of the bodies were putrid with rotting flesh and gore, but the men managed to swallow rock-like hardtack soaked in blood and further hardened when it dried.

By early 1946, a fair percentage of the survivors wanted to surrender but didn't know how. That also applied to the small minority of Okinawans still loyal to the Imperial Army, including Shin-ichi Kuniyoshi, the boy who had almost miraculously delivered the message to Yoza-dake. After the successful mission, the fourteen-year-old took up the life of desperate fleeing and hiding, together with the older Japanese. Now he was near collapse from exhaustion and the pain of maggots eating his flesh at every cut and scratch. As much as he was able to think at all, he realized that he wanted to continue living, but he had no idea how to give himself up. Perhaps the unluckiest Japanese of all were those who did know but feared retaliation by comrades, most often noncommissioned officers, who were convinced that their duty was to stay ready to join the Japanese counterlanding. Whatever the 32nd Army had endured before, the stragglers in their new form of servitude suffered more — and, if they survived, for longer than the campaign itself.

After Masahide Ota went under while trying to escape by swimming and was inexplicably washed ashore, he joined the stragglers. Making his way inland, the starving twenty-year-old pursued the instinct for survival with no real hope of ending alive. (A good half of the Normal School's four hundred students would survive, but only about a quarter of his class of 128.) He ran into a fiercely patriotic Japanese second lieutenant formerly assigned to guard duty at the 32nd Army's Shuri Castle headquarters and now furious at the traitorous Okinawans whose "betrayal" had cost Japan the battle. Declaring that "locals" had no right to be in that sensitive area, he prepared to protect Japanese interests and vent his revenge by shooting the trespasser. Ota saved himself by thinking quickly enough to produce an old document certifying his assignment to intelligence operations. The tattered scrap was miraculously still in his pocket and readable after his time in the water and crawling in the fields.

He sustained himself largely from American garbage dumps and the occasional tent into which he tossed a grenade to flush out its occupants before racing in to grab what he could. For companionship, he found an idealistic private named Shirai, a student of English literature, who, in defiance of everything, carried a Webster's dictionary with him throughout the battle. One night Ota's booty from an American tent included a copy of *Life*. He was surprised at how easily his friend was able to read an article accompanying photographs of bomb-ravaged Japan — and amazed when Shirai told him the war was over. Shirai begged Ota not to repeat the news to other stragglers, who would kill them for saying such a thing. Even more urgently, he implored the youth to surrender. "You're a student, not a soldier. If you can survive and get out of this mess, you must study English. Come to Tokyo. I'll help you if I'm alive." Those fervent words from a kindly, honest friend prompted a revelation that Ota would try to remember the rest of his life. He realized he had been a fool. Unable to read English, he did not know the supreme fact that the war was over — and wouldn't have believed it from anyone's lips; he would have remained a prisoner of his false beliefs. He suddenly knew he must stop fighting and start studying.

In the later stages of the campaign, I was assigned to guard a large compound of prisoners. It was boring duty. The inmates were behind barbed wire. Most were civilians but it was hard to tell. One of them blew himself up with a hand grenade.
— Thomas Hannaher

In the end, some Japanese agreed to be disarmed when surrounded by American pacification units, but not to be called prisoners. A few avoided the disgrace of capture by mingling with natives and learning their ways well enough to avoid detection by the American-employed Okinawans charged with weeding out Japanese soldiers from civilians. Several settled down, married local women and were never discovered. After a year, American search and pacification units found fewer and fewer stragglers. One discovered in 1972, nearly twenty-seven years after the formal surrender, was almost certainly the last.

Almost all stragglers taken alive in 1945 and early 1946 very quickly considered themselves lucky. Jittery, angry Americans continued shooting a few with their hands up, but most sent the defeated men to camps for what the prisoners saw as unimaginable kindness and generosity instead of the expected torture. They looked back from there at their straggling days as their grimmest payment for believing Yamato propaganda.

The greatest volume of surprise had come in late June, when the greatest number of Japanese surrendered. Loaded onto boats in the south, many regretted not having killed themselves before being taken out for drowning, as they were convinced. But when they reached large camps outside northern villages, the hundreds of stripped Japanese blinked in wonder at offers of water and cigarettes from the "demons" and "beasts." One soldier just rounded up asked for what he believed would be a final cigarette and got six, which he smoked in a row after his long deprivation of tobacco. Kuni-ichi Izuchi, the proudly patriotic artist, had killed many Americans and was certain they would hate him as he hated them. But he sensed a bond with his captors — inconceivable until then — from his first moments in camp. They seemed to understand that he had fought for love of his country just as they — a sudden revelation — loved theirs. He thought it amazing that he and the other captives were "treated as human beings rather than enemies." The 22nd Regiment's chief medical officer, the lieutenant who had grown close to Captain Kojo, was among those astonished by Americans' "humanistic" behavior. Kenjiro Matsuki, the former first baseman, was in a group of a hundred prisoners waiting to be run over and crushed by nearby tanks. They could barely understand when the wounded were asked to come forward so that they could be trucked to a hospital.

Others hardly believed the rations they were fed, far better than their own during the fighting. Many were reduced to tears at the sight of enemy medics trying to save their dying comrades: *American* doctors treating maggot-infested *Japanese* wounds. A surgeon in a hospital tent cut open a cast on the arm of a warrant officer in Tadashi Kojo's battalion and ordered a medic to make a new cast with the wrist up instead of down because, the doctor explained to the medic, Japanese held their rice bowls palm up. The warrant officer was "profoundly, unforgettably" moved by what seemed the surgeon's immense concern for human life. Izuchi was equally moved by distribution of quinine "as generously as if to Americans themselves" to malaria-stricken Japanese from Ishigaki Island (where the American pilots had been beheaded).

A whole work could be written about Japanese astonishment — which led to the first serious questioning of their indoctrination, then anger at the authorities who had managed it — during the first days in prisoner-of-war camps, where minimal rations were received as startlingly generous and normal behavior toward captives seen as magnificent.* Man after man found life as the hated enemy's prisoner better than as a soldier of the Empire, with kinder treatment from his superiors.

But those who hadn't had that revelation could hardly count on it. Although talk of the benefits of surrender spread among the stragglers, their old attitudes and habits, enforced by the diehards among them, kept many of them captives of Japanese militarism.

Tadashi Kojo disbanded the last of his battalion on June 21. In the middle of the night, he crept down to the west coast beach with his adjutant, his sword and a grenade. Small craft patrolled with loudspeaker messages and machine gun volleys. The two hid behind bushes and boulders, living on hardtack and watching ragged groups flee north, south and inland. A few even lit fires to cook sweet potatoes: what use was caution now? Kojo's plan was still to break through

---

*A former orderly to Japanese officers tested his judgment by arranging to become an orderly to Americans. Forbidden to give gifts to the enemy, those Americans would throw away barely used shirts and razor blades where prisoners would find them for their own use. The man took this as confirmation that many enemy officers were more charitable to Japanese soldiers than their own officers had been. Meanwhile, Norio Watanabe, the Osaka photographer who had fled Okinawa in a canoe, was being paid nine cents, then a princely sum to a Japanese, to take identification photos in his camp.

to a battalion of a sister regiment in the 24th Division; the latest operational reports he had seen said it had survived a siege by American Army units that later bypassed the obstacle. Now the remnants, reportedly joined by other Japanese from service and airfield maintenance units, were supposedly holding out not far from Kojo's former position at Kochi, and the commander was Captain Tsuneo Shimura, his Academy classmate.

Not all appeared lost to Kojo in the strange quiet following the end of the naval and air bombardments. The Americans seemed to pull most of their ground troops inland when the big guns stopped — unbelievably, for in the reverse situation Japanese forces would have combed the beaches to finish off the enemy. Still, the captain's probing established that enough sentries and patrols were operating to make it almost impossible for him to sneak through to the north. He reckoned it might be safer to round the southern tip and smuggle themselves up the east coast.

Pressed against the base of the cliffs or burrowed under boulders, hundreds of maimed Japanese hid along miles of coast or scurried on the beaches. The captain offered them occasional encouragement but years later would be most proud of his words to a young teacher with five schoolgirls he saw huddled behind some rocks just as a patrol began "cleaning" the area with bullets and flamethrowers. The teacher asked for a grenade and Kojo put off thoughts of fleeing from the Americans in order to concoct the right refusal.

"Why do you want a grenade?" he asked, knowing the reason.

"We must kill ourselves. *Please.*"

Kojo said he and his adjutant needed their one grenade for themselves — and the teacher didn't need it anyway because unarmed civilians definitely would not be harmed. Actually, he believed Americans probably did rape and torture, but he wanted the teacher and her pupils to try to survive. "So you must go up and surrender yourselves," he solemnly pronounced. "You are not military people and have no obligation to die for your honor. Do as the loudspeakers say."

The enemy patrol edged closer. When its hand grenades joined the bullets and flames, Kojo scurried for cover in one direction, the teacher and students in another. The sole of an American boot appeared between two rocks above him but its wearer's bullets missed from near pointblank range. He never saw the group again.

Kojo's adjutant was First Lieutenant Yatsugi, up from the ranks during combat in China, who had joined him as a replacement during the fighting at Kochi. The two climbed down a cliff several nights later and foraged for sweet potatoes. When Kojo hit a trip wire, flares revealed Japanese corpses caught there hours earlier and still bleeding from bullet holes. Enemy soldiers surrounded them as they tried to crawl away. A last-second dash took them back to the cliff, but they lost the trail and couldn't climb up. Yatsugi, panting wildly, asked for the grenade as the enemy approached, rifles glinting in the starlight.

"What for?" Kojo asked again.

"This is the end, Captain Kojo. I have to kill myself."

"And what about me after you use it? Stop chattering and follow me."

His angry tone belied a calmness grounded in trust that instinct would dictate whether he should use the grenade on himself and Yatsugi or the enemy. Yatsugi did follow to an even more miraculous escape from the cliff, but extreme danger re-appeared nights later in one of the breaks between the cliffs where machine guns completely covered stretches of beach. The guns chattered throughout the night at the human crabs stealing east and west. This one was in sight of Mabuni beach, below Ushijima's suicide ledge, where Kojo thought to make his penetration inland and north. He and Yatsugi swam seaward to circumscribe its fire, but Kojo was a weak swimmer even when not enfeebled and without the unhealed hole behind his ear. "We won't make it, let's go back," he shouted. "No," came the answer. "I'm going to keep trying." Kojo later guessed Yatsugi may have intentionally drowned. He never saw him again.

Alone now, the once haughty elitist joined the anonymous nocturnal creatures forming and leaving groups in response to their intuition about who could be trusted. Thirst tortured them even more than in June. Kojo's seemed as vast as the ocean that glared all day in the midsummer sun, but he learned to avoid the spring that bubbled up from the foot of the cliff at low tide. It was littered with corpses over which weaker-willed sufferers kept crawling in demented craving. American snipers up on the cliffs seemed to prefer the targets of those Japanese who took desperate dashes, since hitting them was a greater challenge.

One night, Kojo waited below the Mabuni cliff, straining for the sounds of American patrols above. Hearing none, he climbed the nearly vertical rise. That feat, nearly inconceivable even if he hadn't been so weak, inaugurated a two-month crawl to the enclave of his fellow battalion commander, twenty miles north as the crow flies. He ate almost anything. He slept in caves, tombs and in the open, occasionally on steep slopes, his feet braced against tree stumps to keep from falling. The sharper the incline, the less the possibility an American patrol would find him and shoot. He and temporary companions forced themselves to swallow raw rice and sweet potatoes, but one night attacked a jeep for a box of precious matches to cook a meal. Bullets sought them out night after night, "like rabbits during a hunting season." Enemy rifles came so close he could feel their muzzle blasts as they fired. Unlike the time with Lieutenant Yatsugi, Kojo trembled violently while waiting for certain death. He tried to decide whether to use a pistol he had found, knowing the return salvos after a single shot at an American would finish him in a second. The fearful tension of those episodes suppressed even his boundless hunger and thirst. Hours afterward, he remained too drained to open his mouth for a word to a fellow straggler.

His escapes did not help him penetrate beyond the Shuri Line, along which he kept crawling until his sweat turned unrecognizably greasy, probably after so much stress with so little nourishment and sleep. The lights of a plane above a field where he wandered alone prompted fantasies of his becoming a bird that could fly back to tell his wife and parents he was still alive. He had no explanation for the wild shooting from thousands of enemy guns one mid-August night, tremendous volleys that lit the sky with tracers. (Emperor Hirohito's surrender message was broadcast on August 16.) But the subsequent cessation of kamikaze attacks, until then the targets of a huge volume of antiaircraft fire from American ships, was ominous.

Japanese encountered in the dark challenged *yama* (mountain) and were answered with *kawa* (river); other passwords were *chu*, loyalty to the Emperor, and *koh*, devotion to the family. Some reported that the bypassed battalion he was trying to reach was still operational, inspiring news because its commander, Tsuneo Shimura, was an old drinking friend from Manchuria as well as an Academy classmate. Kojo waited out the severe late-August typhoon that delayed the formal surrender ceremonies by battering 5th Fleet ships en route to Tokyo Bay. He still had visions, no matter how absurd, of the arrival of the Combined Fleet. Believing he had no further duty nor right to command anyone but himself, he wanted only to keep going in order to die a warrior, an honor that beckoned much more brightly than life. The noble ideals absorbed during his Satsuma childhood sustained his will when exhaustion had seemingly destroyed his body. As his stinking, terrifying odyssey continued, he envisioned Tsuneo Shimura as the answer to everything.

Kojo finally reached his cave on some high ground about five miles north of Shuri in the dark of an early September night. Overjoyed to see each other alive, the two twenty-four-year-old captains held hands while Shimura announced he was going to surrender that morning. The war, he explained, was over; Japan had been defeated.*

---

*Shimura had been convinced of this days earlier by Koichi Ito, a third Academy classmate, who had commanded the only unit to achieve significant results during the ill-fated

Kojo went into shock. Staring at Shimura, he thought of his months of hunger, misery and frantic efforts to stay alive in order to reach his trusted comrade. When he fought off his faintness, he still could not formulate an answer. Shimura quietly elaborated that he felt he must obey the Emperor's will and an Imperial order. "You're right," Kojo replied at last. "You have three hundred men to feed and you should surrender. But I'm responsible only for myself. I'm going on alone." Part of him believed that Japan was defeated; a stronger part could not accept it.

He set out again before dawn with a naval warrant officer, a private met along the way, and with pistols and fervent good-luck wishes from Shimura. He did not question why he was not obeying the Emperor's order; he knew that *his* war had to end with his death. Inability to surrender had become an entirely personal matter, unrelated to national concerns. What point could there be in denying the entire meaning of his life by staying alive?

The new group's wandering led them to the former headquarters of Kojo's 22nd Regiment below Naha Airfield. From there, they dug through the rubble blocking the entrance to the elaborate adjoining tunnel of Admiral Ota's Naval Base Force. Kojo could not move in the dark without trampling corpses that covered the floor. Although beyond the bloated stage, they emitted a corrosive gas each time they were touched. The smell and flies were worse than everything previously endured. Lighting a precious match, he saw the bodies of radiomen and operations personnel slumped over their transmitters in compartments he had visited in April before leaving for combat. New slogans summoned from the blood-splattered walls: "Japan will never be destroyed!" "Japan will rise up like a phoenix!" His disabled senses failed to react. Degradation almost complete, he and the others ignored everything to rummage for cans of food.

More months passed in the dark of various caves. Later in the autumn, Okinawan civilians freed from their internment ventured into one of them. Kojo almost shot them for trying to persuade the men to surrender, but he realized other civilians would report them sooner or later. Sure enough, a jeep appeared before he had time to find another hiding place. The search party consisted of an American driver, two Nisei interpreters and a Japanese officer using an

---

May 4 counteroffensive. After the dissolution of the 32nd Army, iron-willed Ito had also disbanded his broken battalion and kept going on his own, despite severe dysentery. Then his regimental commander, still alive and also a straggler, ordered him to investigate whether the war was truly over. American officers took Ito to a prisoner-of-war camp to see Colonel Hiromichi Yahara, Ushijima's captured operations officer, after which he informed several Japanese enclaves, including Shimura's, of the Imperial order to surrender.

assumed Okinawan name. They spoke in a friendly way about the end of the war and the folly of further resistance. Kojo stood apart when a second visit convinced most inhabitants of the cave they would not be killed if they submitted. The men had an absolute right to surrender, but he had his own code.

However, something intrigued him about an enemy who conducted himself without the slightest hint of a victor's haughtiness or display of superiority, even in weaponry. Maybe the truck that accompanied the jeep hid a machine gun, but the curiously relaxed Americans didn't carry even pistols. Kojo had never seen a "blue-eyed devil" outside of combat. Could his image of arrogant murderers be wrong? A voice said the time to kill himself had come again: right now, putting an end to further thought. Another voice observed that he alone was still trying to be a warrior. The enemy now had different goals, seemingly related to an entirely different kind of life.

He was prepared for Americans flourishing guns and for insults to his honor. He would have shot anyone like that who entered the cave, then shot himself — but would such a display make sense now? The first party had asked the stragglers to please give up their weapons. Some now did; others had buried theirs. Kojo told himself it was the responsibility of the senior Japanese present to observe closely. He inched closer. Then, in a kind of daze, he handed his pistol to an American lieutenant outside — which the latter returned, asking how to unload it. Was he an enemy or a wiser man? Kojo's realization of how easily he could have shot the lieutenant forced him to accept that the war had ended. He returned the pistol to the American, who invited him into the jeep. After five months of nocturnal existence, the sunlight blinded. When the men were in the truck, all were driven to a military police post and cigarettes, then to a POW camp in the north.

The last substantial group of Japanese POWs was repatriated in the spring of 1947, two years after L-day. Kojo had had the luck to be released a year earlier, in late March 1946. He returned to bombed-out Tokyo and by train to leveled Kagoshima, where he spent almost a year in a nearly immobilizing depression in a corner of his parents' house. On top of the battle and war, he had lost his beloved wife Emiko, whose parents had been influenced by the severe social changes that turned Imperial Army officers from figures of admiration to objects of scorn. He himself shared the new antimilitarism. His first job — obtained with a fake "résumé" to conceal his professional military background — was as a laborer at an American airbase. Then he became a driver for an American lawyer high in the occupation administration but resisted that influential man's attempts to have him join Japan's new Self-Defense Force. Kojo badly needed a better-paying job to support a new family, but memories of Okinawa kept him a driver. "Japan doesn't need an Army," he replied. "Japan must never fight again."

Eventually, he did become a captain in the Self-Defense Force. His mental and physical strength slowly returned. Forty-five years after the battle, the ex-soldier, again scrupulously neat, walked with some of his old ramrod straightness. One of the smaller postwar ironies is the much better physical condition of the average Japanese survivor of sixty or seventy — thin, trim, square-shouldered — than the average American. Most also appear to be more prosperous, but not Kojo. Friends urged him to apply for a pension for his war wound, the explosion that permanently damaged his hearing. "I couldn't sell my ear to my country," he answered. "I have to feel I did my duty." (Postwar politicians who awarded themselves honors and rewards gave nothing to the relative handful of veterans who returned alive from Okinawa.)

Kojo belongs to a category of prisoner, which includes ardent antimilitarists, who never lived down the stigma of captivity, though his came only after the destruction of his battalion, Japan's surrender and his grueling months as a straggler. The son of Satsuma samurais retired from active service in 1970, but the old warrior in him lived on in his devotion to the memory of General Ushijima, Colonel Yoshida — commander of his 22nd Regiment — and "all who fought to the last and died in the fields or in the water in order to defend Okinawa." His loyalty was coupled with resentment of "those who survived and refer to the Imperial Army in flippant tones" and indignation that "the superb conduct and sacrifice" of "our great Army" and the Special Attack Forces at Okinawa are less celebrated than "the tragedy of Okinawan civilians represented by the [Princess] Lily Brigade or well-publicized atrocities committed on Okinawans by a few desperate soldiers . . . I don't understand the emotionalism of certain groups of agitators who . . . insinuate that Okinawans are the only victims. 'That's enough!' I'd like to plead. 'It's time to stop!'"

Yet the war changed Tadashi Kojo radically, not least in liberation from the narrow focus of the Imperial Army officer. Now the once-feared battalion commander takes great interest in the outside world. He has also returned to his boyhood literary interests, using the English he taught himself after the war to work as a translator after retiring from the Self-Defense Force. He is shy, charming, articulate, uncommonly attractive. If circumstances did not prevent him from traveling, he would love to visit America. From his present peaceful life, he looks back in horror and wonder at his former one as the rigid officer whose whole being was devoted to battle for honor and the Emperor.

> *Among those who narrowly survived the battle, there is a common feeling inexplicable to others . . . a certain feeling toward life that is shared only by those who have leaned over and peered into the abyss called death . . . I shouted in my heart: let no trees grow, no grass sprout on that hill [the site of Shuri Castle] until all the peoples of the world have seen this ruin wrought by the Battle of Okinawa.*
> — Seizen Nakasone, Okinawan schoolteacher

> *They say things go in circles, that everything gets back to where it was. So has Okinawa. It's back to where it was.*
> — Thomas Hannaher

> *One must face the fact that our operations and base developments have reduced seriously and permanently the future capacity of Okinawa to support human life by agriculture.*
> — Commander Henry Bennett, U.S. Navy

> *Washington virtually lost sight of the Ryukyus . . . An appalling indifference blanketed [Okinawa] . . . The island became an immense, neglected military dump, strewn with the war's debris. Towns and villages were rubble heaps; tens of thousands lived in caves, tombs and lean-to shacks, or took shelter in relief camps established by the military forces. They were expected to live at subsistence level until a formal peace should restore them to Japanese administration and permit American withdrawal.*
> — George Kerr

Okinawans look back with little hope that others will appreciate the battle's impact. Clarence Clacken's *The Great Loochoo* states that the resilient people "showed remarkable ability to stand up under physical and mental strain"; the survivors "suffered little physical deterioration except for filth, disease and lice infestations." The islanders indeed recovered enough to startle American veterans visiting in 1987. Having left an essentially preindustrial island of dirt roads and thatched roofs blown to bits, the veterans returned to skyscrapers, choking traffic, a crazy quilt of stores and shops. But much of the deeper destruction is irreparable.

The cataclysm that surpassed those at Hiroshima and Nagasaki left an aftermath of longer duration. This is a separate story, parts of which Okinawan historians have told, but to a world less interested in the obscure people's fate after the war than during. After most of the battle's explosives fell not on the two armies but on their hosts

— some experts have calculated that disposal of the unexploded bombs in residential areas will take over sixty years — decimated families clinging to life in the ruins of their villages endured horrible postwar years.* Perhaps the point is made by the fact that the civilians who visited Tadashi Kojo's cave in November 1945 came in search of food — from those wretched Japanese stragglers who were themselves barely alive. Okinawans ate almost anything in 1946 and 1947, including dogs.

The peace brought continued suffering. Postwar Okinawa's devastation was evident in inanimate structures alone. Virtually every inhabited settlement taken by American troops was found deserted or in ruins. During the occupation's early years, the prostrate people could rebuild only a corner of their wood-and-paper houses from scraps in the rubble. Tens of thousands lived in lodgings of cartons, tar paper and other American refuse — but no closer than a mile to the bases and billeting areas: the occupiers protected their security and health by excluding the natives. When Okinawans at last began building anew, they were desperate for housing but too poor to return to traditional styles. Instead, they turned to the cheapest, most accessible alternative: American military-base design. A proliferation of stark concrete squares, cheap and fast to pour, spread over the south like some Marxist vision of proletarian hovels. Soon the land of some of the world's most graceful architecture was filled with some of the most depressing, a sprawl of garages, cheap shops, junkyards and instant slums.

The grim settlements evoked little from the past. Perhaps Okinawan culture was in any case destined to be submerged in Japanese and American, in the way of small peoples controlled by mightier ones. But the battle's obliteration of so much of the old greatly hastened and extended the process.

The destruction of tens of thousands of family tombs was especially hard on Okinawans. The 32nd Army's fortification of a selection of them before the battle had disturbed some natives more than anything else in the defensive preparations. Those little homes where the living would join their ancestors' spirits were not mere symbols; Okinawans built and maintained them as practical structures for fulfilling life's cycle and purpose. Many viewed their use for military purposes as a profound violation. Their subsequent devastation during the fighting became inevitable: once American infantrymen learned that some were serving as pillboxes and machine gun em-

---

*Most were naturally overjoyed to find lost members alive, but some survivors who limped home months later frightened families that had already planted flowers for them. Relatives sprinkled salt to chase away those "ghosts."

placements, they used hand grenades and tank and artillery shells to demolish as many as possible.* "The poor Okinawans," General Stilwell put it with characteristic brevity and bluntness, "have had even their ancestors blown to pieces."

Okinawans did survive their holocaust with remarkably few nervous breakdowns, probably thanks to their unusually secure family and spiritual life. But after the threat to life eased, psychiatric illness soared to a higher rate than anywhere else in the Pacific. Experienced observers believe a significant cause was the destruction of the tombs that had remained at the core of Okinawan culture and belief until the battle. The people whose emotional health had been nourished by the security of ancient family roots could neither pay tribute to their ancestors nor complete their own lives by joining them. With so many tombs effaced and so many parents and grandparents dead, younger generations grew up unable to find their homeless family spirits, a shocking condition for both living and dead.

The occupation of 1945–1972 was characteristically American: often generous in personal ways and in response to individual cases of hardship, usually ignorant of and insensitive to native ways and needs. When Commodore Perry forced Okinawans to satisfy his "reasonable" demands almost a century earlier, he was certain they would appreciate the "lenity and humanity" of American laws. Now Americans who paid wages to civilian employees and distributed free rations — the only antidote to mass starvation — were similarly convinced of their traditional magnanimity, especially when billions of dollars were poured into the economy in support of operations for the Korean War and other anti-Communist measures. Some of the medical assistance and scholarship grants to top students were indeed admirable. But the twenty-seven years until the occupation ended brought far more shame than honor to Washington and the men in the field who followed or ignored official intentions.

Japanese-speaking naval officers, some former professors trained in Asian studies and occupation affairs, did good work during the

---

*American infantrymen learned to stay out of the miniature houses of limestone and concrete, where a single Japanese grenade in the enclosed space could do terrible damage. But their little "front yards" where families gathered to celebrate with their ancestors were choice places for the tents of artillerymen and others slightly to the rear. The low walls enclosing the yards offered some protection against shrapnel. The structures themselves could provide a "sensational" dry night while rain soaked everything outside. This was "living with the dead to stay alive," as Thomas Hannaher put it.

However, those dead were often disposed of. Their beautifully crafted ceramic urns were removed and their bones dumped or scattered, by men hunting souvenirs as well as seeking shelter. Bodies whose bones had not yet been cleaned and stored in the urns were similarly evicted. Thus thousands of unblasted tombs were also desecrated.

first year or so. But the quality of the occupation plunged when responsibility for it was transferred more fully to the Army, most of whose senior officers knew nothing about their jobs and hardly cared to learn: civil administration was considered a sidetrack from line duty and its promotion. Pentagon officials changed almost as rapidly as occupation personnel. Okinawan duty was considered undesirable enough to be threatened as punishment for "goof-ups" elsewhere in the Pacific. The island became notorious among Americans as a place of exile from the Japanese mainland — a veritable Siberia, as George Kerr called it, known as "the Rock" and "the end of the line" — for incompetent colonels and civilian bureaucrats, rather as Tokyo had sent down second-rate administrators for decades before the war.

Soon only a few overseas eccentrics gave a damn about the remote possession. Resuming their civilian lives in the postwar boom, veterans in the States knew nothing about the abysmal conditions on the island. The vacuum of public interest and accountability allowed the generally negligent and incapable performance of the Army's secondary occupational functions to go unnoticed. The occupation force was composed not of combat troops who had seen at least a portion of the 1945 calamity but of "callow youth," as one of their officers called them, who were "demanding [their] creature comforts from the armed services." Or from the Okinawans, just under a hundred of whom they robbed, raped, otherwise assaulted and murdered during the first six months of 1949 alone: predictable distractions of occupation troops banished to the impoverished island.

Those youths felt condescension or scorn for the primitives eking out an existence without commerce or currency. Especially during the first years after the war, when family land was the sole source of self-support and the Army paid no compensation for its appropriations for the military use, scavenging natives lived in miserable poverty, some in areas ravaged by malaria, all in deep shock and bewilderment.* The island became a heap of war surplus and smelly junk. A witness described an Assistant Secretary of the Army as "flabbergasted with what he saw" during an unannounced inspection in 1949. Some of the worst outrages were remedied, but native hardship remained severe until the late 1950s.

Destitute Okinawans looked back at the war as confirmation that the island's salvation lay in pacifism. Not all regretted having fought for Japan, especially some of the young and the elite. But the handful

* An American soldier with the Corps of Engineers went for a look at Naha when he arrived in 1947. All he could see was rubble, "just piles and mounds of stone and concrete fragments . . . divided into large sections by what appeared to be roadways that had been bulldozed through the ruins."

of exceptions proved the rule of enormous regret and corresponding mistrust of everything military. If most Japanese turned fervently antimilitarist after the war, most Okinawans, whose losses made the 32nd Army's destruction seem almost slight by comparison, did so with stronger feeling.

The proportionately greater damage was followed by slower reconstruction. While Japan was gearing up for economic recovery in the 1950s, Okinawa remained in pathetic poverty, partly owing to the unconcerned, incompetent American generals who conducted a more rigid and repressive occupation than on the mainland, where neon was installed and diplomatic niceties with the Imperial Palace reintroduced. The real business of Okinawa's governors was to run America's defense installations, not to care for the natives. Thus traditionally peaceful Okinawa fared worse during the occupation than the historically militarist mainland, which American personnel had no notion of running as one big military base. Those least responsible for the war that hurt them most were also most punished afterward.

The Americans who returned in 1987 did so to attend the unveiling of a monument to the dead of the 32nd Army and the 6th Marine Division. Japanese and American veterans' associations had erected the spire — not the world's first nonpartisan, multinational memorial to battlefield loss and suffering, but most participants thought it was, which added to their emotion. Located in a Garden of Remembrance, the graceful, three-sided monument was six years in the planning and construction; Okinawan politics, playing on antimilitarist sentiment, had delayed its siting. It was eventually erected on an American base about a kilometer north of Sugar Loaf Hill.

The theme of the American fund-raising campaign for this first such monument on foreign soil was reconciliation. "We hope, as at our Gettysburg, our wounds will be healed by recognizing gallantry on both sides," wrote Edward (Buzzy) Fox, the campaign organizer. "Everybody said we could not do it and now we have raised an international beacon to the world showing that peace is possible; war a waste." Some came chiefly to visit cemeteries. James Hall found the grave of a buddy who had been killed in April 1945. "I visited my fallen comrade and it was as if time stood still," he wrote. "I can only . . . [say] that something that has been a part of my life for all this time has been put to rest." But the climactic moment came at an evening banquet. The Japanese and American contingents, which had previously sat apart, were asked to shake hands. This was very hard for some veterans, especially those who had forced themselves to return to the island of their misery. They were the men likely to feel the greatest relief when they did reach out to touch the former enemy. A few almost wept in the arms of men whom they had only wanted to kill, kill, kill. "I should have done this years ago," one American said. "I have lived a life full of needless hate. It is gone now and I feel at peace with myself and the world."

One of the ironies of war, or of the human condition, is the deep satisfaction battlefield survivors often feel when they become reconciled with former foes. Grateful for this chance "to show the world that two former enemies can really 'bury the hatchet,'" the American participants were buoyed with a feeling of purification and even joy. It was not simply that "it's better to eat together than to fight each other," as one put it, but the fulfillment of an inner yearning to make peace, to find understanding, to cast off hate. A man who had lost his right leg and his best friend during the battle drank and laughed with Japanese veterans who were also missing limbs, and almost all their comrades. "This was a wonderful event and I am so happy I could be there."

Some 6th Marine veterans had bitterly opposed the blasphemy of a joint memorial with the once detested "Japs," but recognition of its appropriateness grew in the 1980s. Stuart Upchurch, the tough former machine gunner, made the trip with Paul Panella, a replacement Upchurch looked after when Panella was wounded just after the taking of Sugar Loaf. Upchurch then wrote an open answer to William Manchester, the distinguished writer and veteran who had declared reservations about the memorial because he, who had also been wounded on Sugar Loaf, could never forget Japanese atrocities.

> Mr. Manchester speaks of atrocities. Atrocities were committed by both sides. This subject should best be left alone. The burning of Tokyo was taking war to innocent civilians . . . At Okinawa, who demolished the capital city of Naha that was never a military object? Who killed 150,000 Okinawans? We had the big guns and the ships and the planes. I don't think we ought to compare atrocities. War is an atrocity unto itself . . .
>
> The war is over . . . The hostilities caused by the politicians on both sides have ended. Let the hate sold by the propagandists die. You served your Country well, Mr. Manchester, but I think you've served yourself ill. The idea at the Garden of Remembrance is a fine idea. It is clean and pure. It was for remembering your friends that should have drawn you there. You would have felt closer to them than ever. I know I did. Let go the hate. The teachings of both Christ and Buddha were represented at the ceremony. Both teach the fine art of brotherly love. And that's really what this world is supposed to be about, isn't it?

A few of both nationalities cried openly, and more wept silently. If only they — and their people, their governments — had known forty years earlier what they now knew!

> *Okinawa lies in the midst of military bases.*
> — Current Okinawan quip

The monument's third side is dedicated to the Okinawan dead. "As it is in all wars, the soldiers are paid to fight and die, but the hapless island people were total victims," an American veteran acknowledged. Recognition of the scope of the civilian tragedy came late and only partially to veterans of both armies. But some glimpsed the whole truth in the late 1980s, largely through remembering their own dead and through their later contact with Okinawa; perhaps also in thoughts of their mortality as they approached their seventies. (Only two of the flag raisers on the southern tip were alive in 1990.) The men who had endured combat — and the wives to whom they confided — came to feel Japanese and Okinawan pain more keenly than the general population, who never knew even the American costs.*

The dedication of the memorial included explicit recognition of those who paid the greatest price in 1945 and afterward. Among the speakers was James Day, the corporal who had lost his best friend on Sugar Loaf and went on to be a Marine general in command, well in the postwar period, of all American forces on the island. In this "largest and longest major battle in history," Day noted, "more than 115,000 Japanese and American military men either were killed . . . or remained missing. But compared to the at least 150,000 [civilian

---

*By then, veterans' associations spent a fair part of their time returning souvenirs, many members regretting their youthful appetite for them and happier to return items, many worthless to them, than they'd been when taking them in 1945. Okinawan families who had lost everything during the battle were profoundly grateful for the smallest scraps. Forty-two years after the battle, an ex-Marine sent back a postcard that a soldier serving in Manchuria had mailed from there to a buddy's five-year-old daughter on Okinawa. The card said the father had died bravely and often spoke of the daughter, who, forty-eight years old when she saw it again, was overcome with emotion.

It took the Virginia Military Institute longer to give back its booty and more pressure had to be applied by highly placed veterans until a fifteenth-century Buddhist bell, which a Marine general had given the school as a trophy of war, was returned in 1991. A few other irreplaceable national treasures — of the handful of undamaged ones — continued to serve as decoration for American homes and gardens, but individual Americans, increasingly preoccupied with their moral record as they approached the end of their lives, were more eager than institutions to put things right. Joe Bangert, the medical corpsman, summoned a priest just before he died in 1988. One of the matters that most troubled him in his iconoclastic life was shooting a stand of "moving trees" that turned out to be not Japanese soldiers but Okinawan nurses. Bangert's wife realized how much the incident had been on his mind for over forty years. "He told me he knew war was hell but he never thought he'd kill a woman. It bothered him terribly."

deaths], the military losses almost pale in significance. It is a stark documentary to the folly of mankind. It is a stark documentary to the foolishness of war."

Such confirmation from generals as well as privates might seem to provide a decent ending to the Okinawa story, if not yet to the "foolishness of war." But there is still little justice or fairness in evidence. For all the recent decline in overt racism, for all the growing recognition that all nationalities live in one world where what's bad for *them* must in the long run be bad for *us,* some of the Pacific War's underlying causes endure. Americans still cherish their sense of moral superiority, recently reinforced by their pride in military superiority. Stiffened by a "Japanese fighting spirit" no longer directed to conquest but still central to the national ethic, Japan nurtures an equally firm notion of her superiority. And neither superior nation has yet done right by Okinawa after doing so much unavoidable and avoidable wrong.

In 1971, Berlin was the only other major area under occupation as a residue of World War II. When the Ryukyus reverted to Japan the following year, maintenance of America's bases was central to the deal, which included additional secret arrangements for the two powers to trade Okinawan favors. (Japanese officials assured American generals they could have far greater freedom of action there than on the mainland.) To Americans, those bases have great emotional as well as military significance. Many veterans were understandably angered by the return of Okinawa's dearly bought 875 square miles to the former enemy. After the loss of so much American blood, the Pentagon's wish to remain is understandable.

But by this measure, the loss of incomparably more Okinawan blood there makes the Okinawans' wish for the Pentagon to leave more reasonable. Native anti-Americanism is a political, not personal, phenomenon; most Okinawans tend to like Yanks in general, and perhaps feel easier with them than with Japanese.* But they abhor the beast in their midst: the largest concentration of American military force outside the continental United States. A native's comment to a Marine public information officer sums up their attitude: "We like you but we wish you weren't here."

Resentment of the swollen American military presence is neither universal nor entirely pure. Since the bases provide much income for the island — third only to subsidies from Tokyo and tourism — not all Okinawans want them closed. Some owners are happy to receive

---

*A survey in 1982, ten years after revision, found that over 40 percent of Okinawans felt awkward with Japanese from other prefectures; less than 5 percent had formed friendly relationships with them, although this figure has surely increased since then.

rent for the land — more, some say, than farming could generate. (Under the terms of the military alliance, Tokyo pays that rent for Washington.) Some shopkeepers enjoy selling to American servicemen even while decrying their behavior. The number of hypocrites making profit and political hay is no smaller than that of champions of Japanese nationalism and militarism before the war. To some extent, their protests are a substitute for self-improving deeds and a distraction from hard questions about economic prospects without the rental revenue from the bases and related income from American offices and personnel.

But the majority genuinely long for the departure of the military colossus. The incidents of rape and murder declined dramatically after the earliest postwar period,* but muggings, taxi robberies and delinquency by base teenagers continue. Live firing exercises still cause brush fires, bullets ricochet from ranges into adjoining civilian areas, errant parachute drops damage property, sugar fields are scarred by B-52s making emergency landings, and jet screams interrupt classes of schoolchildren whom the great bombers no more benefit than does the Great Wall of China. American domination of precious water resources has of course ended, but hillsides pockmarked by artillery fire and ridges sliced for helicopter landing pads continue to send streams of red silt into the sea. Seabees no longer destroy ancient burial grounds, but there is no way to restore those already bulldozed under or to return precious topsoil scraped away for use as fill in military construction. Many Okinawans try to ignore the American presence. It remains dominating. Few of the servicemen who constitute it are more interested in native ways than those who landed on L-day.

Statesmen and strategists have cogent arguments to justify this intrusion on national life. Okinawa was needed as an American coaling and supply station in Perry's time and became even more needed as the staging area for the invasion of Japan. Next she became a key outpost in the global containment of Communism, more vital than ever when plans were made to close bases on the Philippines. She is within aircraft-striking range of the Asian continent and strategically located to intercept Russian lines of communication, especially sea lanes connecting the naval bases at Vladivostok with many potential destinations. (The collapse of Communism hasn't ended Pentagon interest in such matters.) Okinawans who want their island left to

---

*The numbers soared during the late 1940s, when all Okinawans were hungry, defenseless and intimidated. Women's postwar rule was "Flee when you see an American soldier."

other uses may fail to perceive its place in the larger picture. And Washington and Tokyo may indeed better appreciate foreign menace than Naha does — but these are the same kinds of strategic considerations that led to the catastrophe of 1945. In any case, it is Okinawan land those other capitals are using, and no small portion of it. Forty-five American installations alone — not including those of the Japanese Self-Defense Force — occupy 20 percent of the island's territory. Mile after mile of base fences flank the major roads; vast housing estates and runways cover the most fertile soil. It is as if one of the four Japanese home islands were appropriated, or ten of the most valuably located American states — for a foreign power's mistrusted military use.

That proportion assumes greater significance in tiny Okinawa, where every usable acre — the installations take up some sixty-three thousand — is precious. (The population has grown to about 1.3 million in 1991.) America controls many of the best tracts of land in the most level areas of the center and south. A huge proportion of the island's richest farmland is buried under landing strips. A sympathetic American analyst warned in 1946 that much of the damage was likely to be irreparable: "Even if some of the airfields or roads are abandoned after they have served their purpose, there will be little prospect of restoring fertility to the hard coral-filled strips for many years." Rather than abandoning the airfields during the next forty-five years, the military authorities lengthened them and thickened the concrete. Malice is almost absent from this abuse of power; the abusers are convinced that they are good and generous people, respected and liked. (An official publication proudly announces that "Marine installations [alone] occupy about ten percent of the island's total land area . . . from one tip to the other.") But to the natives kept at bay by passes and gates, the miles of military golf courses on the chronically overpopulated island seem like absentee-owned feudal estates. The expanses of clipped base lawn are symbols of oppression, not good clean fun. What American would tolerate anything similar in his county or country?

The military presence might be less onerous to Okinawans if they saw some benefit in it. The overriding lesson of 1945 was that far from protecting them from anything, military bases on their land invite destruction. And that the destruction will be greatest at the bases, not at the command centers of the foreign powers. And that civilians will suffer most. Prophetic dissidents had warned that maintenance of Japanese armed forces on the island would invite invasion by foreigners with whom the inhabitants had no quarrel. The typhoon of bombs and steel was catastrophic proof that fortifications brought death, not the promised salvation. Now Okinawans fear that Washington's bases may again engulf them in war.

Their pleas carry as much wisdom for their land as do the global calculations of the Pentagon and White House. It is supported by the historical evidence that foreign planning for Okinawa has always been for foreign interests, at the island's certain expense. "What, again, is Okinawa designed to defend — and for whose benefit?" asked a scholar at the University of the Ryukyus. "What do we really mean when we say, 'to defend the country?' Who is defending whom and from whom?" That typically oblique protest — Okinawan politics are generally soft-edged — masks real anguish. Even before the disintegration of the Soviet Union, Okinawans long felt more threatened by the Japanese-American security treaty than by any danger from Moscow. Their longing for a "base-free" peace derives from more than nostalgia for their long history of nonaggression. The big bombers' jet screams make them shudder. The advanced military hardware provokes dread. The great powers' continuing exploitation of Okinawa's geographic position makes the people insecure on their own island.

> *I think the reason [for defeat on Okinawa] was the lack of unity in Army-Navy operations. Okinawa was actually supposed to be defended by three divisions. I was concerned. Umezu [General Yoshijiro Umezu, chief of the Army General Staff] thought two divisions were enough at first, but later, when he felt there were not enough forces and wanted to send one division of reinforcements, there was no longer any means of transporting them there.*
>
> — Emperor Hirohito in March or April 1946, regretting Japanese losses but making no mention of Okinawan

As for the Japanese, a few generous, far-sighted veterans took the lead in building the memorial and reconciling with their former American enemies. "The years have flown — half a century," reads the inscription on their side of the monument. "Recovered are the hills and rivers, grass and trees have grown in. As we remember our friends long gone, Let us ring out the bell of peace! O souls of the brave, please rest in eternal peace!" But for all the work of this small corps of internationalists, for all the sentiment for the dead among tourists who visit Okinawa and among the rest of the Japanese people, the government gives living Okinawans little peace. On the contrary, it has taken pains to shunt American military activities from the mainland to the island. Most natives wanted reversion to Japan in the hope that it would bring a significant reduction in the size and number of the bases "so that the island would become . . . a little better to live in." That was a dream.

Japan isn't primarily to blame that Okinawans remain the nation's poor southern relatives.* But Tokyo's continued concentration of the defense establishment on the island reveals its attitude toward the racially non-Japanese inhabitants. Okinawa's 0.6 percent of Japanese territory is crammed with almost 75 percent of the regular (as opposed to contingency) American-used bases and installations in all the forty-seven prefectures, and is staffed by almost three quarters of all American personnel.

The people whose museums display weapons only in antiwar exhibits want Japanese bases as little as they want American, but they are involuntary hosts to a hugely disproportionate share of Self-Defense Force installations. Japanese and American veterans returning as tourists are struck by what they see as the irony of their flags flying side by side from very tall flagpoles. But this is less irony than old history carried forward: use of the island by others — as an expendable or sacrificial strategic outpost, a steppingstone, a dumping ground. The present impositions are far less oppressive than Satsuma's and without the naked presumption of the Perry party that planted the Stars and Stripes as if they had discovered the island. But the old mentality endures in America's placement of her new big guns where they frighten the locals, and in Japan's collaboration, using Okinawa as a bargaining chip, instead of trying to make real restitution. Restitution is required in very great measure. The near hundred-day delay of U.S. forces on the island saved the mainland from stupendous destruction. But in 1992, outsiders were still exploiting the weakness that had allowed predecessors to make a pawn of Okinawa since the early 1600s. Instead of changing that, the typhoon of steel and bombs wedged the pawn more firmly between the rock and hard place of Japanese and American imperialism, with their power politics and militarism that are alien to Okinawa's nature and destructive of her land.

Still, Okinawans enjoy compensations. Tourists who arrive expecting just a more southern Japan quickly feel they are in a different world with a much softer ambience. The mainland makes many uncomfortable because of the persistent tendency of Japanese, however polite, to be uncomfortable with foreigners — but visitors are likely to feel much more at home in the old Kingdom of the Ryukyus. The

*Per capita income, 60 percent of the mainland's at reversion to Japan in 1972, has increased to 75 percent since then. But Okinawa Prefecture remains the poorest of the 47, with the highest unemployment rate.

difference is almost tangible from the moment one steps from one's plane and sees the easier smiles and more rhythmic gaits. People still rise late and keep "island time." It matters little to them that the person for whom they squeeze in to make room in their bars is a foreigner. The economic achievements are visibly less impressive than on the mainland; the hospitality and happiness quotients are noticeably higher.

Okinawa continues to have most of the troubles of island communities dominated by a richer, more powerful neighbor, including a mixture of dependence, resentment and resignation to inferior status, punctuated by ineffectual talk and rare flashes of anger. But to the extent that any generalization of this kind is valid, it is still, or again, a sunnier, emotionally healthier place than either of the superpowers. Its passionate little band of Japanese and American admirers is held there not by sadness over the destruction but love of the tolerant, artlessly welcoming social climate, the innate sense of human community that puts all at ease. It is a friendly island as well as a beautiful one where the scars have healed and the tawdry postwar sprawls are not in view. Despite the predictions of Americans who observed the devastation in 1945, Shuri Castle is being rebuilt for reopening in 1992.

Masahide Ota, the warlike member of the Blood and Iron Scouts for the Emperor who had a revelation when the friendly Japanese soldier read to him from *Life* magazine, gave himself up on November 27, five months after the battle's official end. In his internment camp, he whittled a bamboo stick into a "pen" and used his morning coffee as ink to write *shinsei*, "a new birth," and *saisei*, "rebirth," over and over. Following that self-admonition and his sudden passion to learn English, the former Normal School student worked his way into Tokyo's Waseda University and to graduate school at Syracuse University.

Ota went on to become a professor at the University of the Ryukyus, a prolific writer in Japanese and English, a forceful critic of the battle tactics that caused the profound damage to the island Japan claimed to defend. The ardent promoter of Okinawan identity disagrees with those who have buried 1945 as "a nightmare of the past," insisting that its lessons are relevant to the present. More than anything, he sees those lessons in the indoctrination that deceived him and in illusory national needs that crush bodies, spirits and human interests. "I decided to devote my whole existence not to empty words such as 'the will of the state' or 'in the interest of the state,' but . . . to live a life based on my human desires and aspirations, a life filled with my own individual being . . . Every one of the Okinawan people learned the preciousness and dignity of human life through the terrible consequences of the battle."

Ota was elected governor of the prefecture in November 1990. Although he enjoys the company of Americans and visits America often, his platform embraced antimilitarism in general and the drastic reduction of the American bases in particular. He recently wrote that "the *Okinawa no kokoro* [Okinawan mind] gives supremacy to human life and dignity; it gives value to friendly trade with neighboring countries, to hospitality based on mutual understanding, to peaceful coexistence." That self-advertisement is essentially accurate, perhaps because natives continued to think of themselves as Okinawan whether they were governed by Japan or America. Their attitudes are rooted in old island ways rather than in the presumption that underlies the American and Japanese urge to perform world missions.

Perhaps their fundamental virtue is simply being a "little" people who cannot dictate anything. But littleness may be a blessing in a world shaped by ambitious giants. A week or two in the Land of Constant Courtesy reassures visitors that they speak the same emotional language as people born halfway around the globe. And it raises questions about the wisdom and sometimes the sanity of the powers with magisterial callings.

30 · The Atomic Bombs

The Battle of Okinawa was the . . . most brutal military engagement between American and Japanese forces in the war . . . The immense cost of capturing the island, in human and material terms, did undoubtedly have a considerable influence on the decision to use atomic weapons. American leaders were left in no doubt that the losses in American lives increased dramatically the closer they came to the Japanese homeland. The experience of Okinawa convinced them that invasion was too high a price to pay.
— Ian Gow

If the defense of the Japanese home islands, with their immensely greater area and enormously greater population, was going to take on the character of the defense of Okinawa, where and when and at what cost was it going to end?
— James Jones

The U.S. Army is sure to attack and indeed has the power to do so. The sooner the enemy comes, the better for us, for our battle array is complete.
— Tokyo Radio on June 28, discussing the loss of Okinawa

We hated the Japs but nobody had the slightest desire to go there and fight them because the one thing we knew was that we'd all be killed. I mean we really knew it. I never used to think that, I used to say the Japs would never get me. But there was no question about the mainland. How the hell are you going to storm a country where women and children, everybody would be fighting you? Of course we'd have won eventually but I don't think anybody who hasn't actually seen the Japanese fight can have any idea of what it would have cost.
— Austin Aria

I lived through Okinawa somehow but the great battle of the mainland lay ahead. How long could my luck hold? Then the dropping of the A-bomb put a brand-new light in my life. I'd be going home, after all. And I did!
— Thomas Hannaher

FOR THE AMERICANS who had fought on Okinawa, the emotional end came not when they were shipped out from there but a month later. The handful who had waded ashore on L-day and were still standing when their units left had spent about a hundred days on the island. Together with the replacements for their departed buddies, those exhausted few were crammed back into LSTs and troopships for another rough ride to rear bases for rest and retraining. The commander of the 6th Marine Division warned that the campaign had been "in many ways a prelude" to future fighting, but no one needed a statement of the obvious to discount the rumors about going home. Few were able or willing to contemplate the next operation on the Japanese mainland. Norris Buchter's combat friends, all "too tired and too tense to think of the future," were typical. "We'd never really slept during the months on Okinawa, even when we supposedly slept. After those months constantly on edge, all we could think of was the relief of getting off the island to anywhere we could sleep a whole night through."

The trip to the largest rear base on Guam took a week. Skinny, nineteen-year-old James Day, who had won a Bronze Star for heroism on Sugar Loaf, was soon back on Guam in a work party, loading ships for the initial landing on the home island of Kyushu. The corporal had been heaving heavy cargo about a month when he heard the news about Hiroshima. His elation was immense.

Dick Whitaker was also on Guam, preparing more comfortably for the invasion of invasions. Still a runner for his company, he spent most of his time doing easy errands or happily cooling his heels in the Quonset hut of battalion headquarters instead of training in scorching fields. Whitaker had felt and seen no joy when the flag went up on Okinawa's southern tip because the ceremony had freed no one he knew from further fighting. But he and his friends erupted wildly when "the poop" about the odd thing called the atomic bomb was translated into the one essential fact for them. "It was instant pandemonium. We whooped and yelled like mad, we downed all the beer we'd been stashing away. We shot bullets into the air and danced between the tent rows, because this meant maybe we were going to live, and not as cripples."

Whitaker's reaction was universal. A wounded comrade remembered that the end of the fighting on Okinawa brought no real relief because "everyone knew it was just the last steppingstone to the really terrible stuff waiting on the Jap home islands. Everybody knew if he hadn't been hit so far he soon would be because we were going from the Oki slaughter to a much worse one." For them, Hiroshima was salvation.

The general concept of Operation Downfall, the invasion of the home islands, had been approved in the autumn of 1944, at roughly the same time as Okinawa was chosen over Formosa as that last steppingstone. Two days after L-day, the Joint Chiefs of Staff instructed

General MacArthur to begin detailed planning for the first landing on southernmost Kyushu. President Truman gave final approval for the operation on June 18, the day of General Buckner's death. Although few on Guam knew the new D-day was set for November 1, eleven weeks after the Hiroshima bomb, everyone knew it would be soon. It was no secret that the stream of bombers taking off from Guam's airfields was softening up the landing areas. (Prelanding naval bombardments of the Japanese coasts, most notably by three of America's four *Iowa*-class battleships, with 16-inch guns, and by the Royal Navy's *King George V,* also started in mid-July.) It was no secret either to Okinawa veterans that all the bombardment in the world wouldn't keep American infantry blood from pouring in a confrontation with a deeply dug-in, utterly resolute defense bound to be much stronger than Okinawa's. One man lay badly wounded in a San Francisco naval hospital when he heard the news. "My whole body shouted, 'Thank God for the A-bomb!' Because otherwise I'd have been sent out to more combat as soon as I was patched up — and killed sooner or later. Those were the odds. I was overjoyed."

The sympathy of Okinawa veterans for the atomic victims was much lessened by their conviction that the alternative would have been their own deaths or crippling wounds. Certain that only "the beautiful bomb" saved them, they would feel pity, contempt or anger — which turned to resignation over the years — for noncombatants who would later brand its use unnecessary and immoral. Almost every American who fought in the Pacific, as well as those who would soon be sent there from Europe, saw the atomic bomb as a "miracle of deliverance," in Winston Churchill's phrase. E. B. Sledge, the devout private sickened to the depths of his soul by the horrors on Okinawa, noted that those still more or less whole afterward viewed the next phase "with complete resignation that we would be killed." Frazzled veterans of all island battles wondered why they'd survived so far only to have to die on Kyushu or Honshu. That was why the end of the fighting on Okinawa produced the scant American emotion — not even a beer ration — while the news of the atomic bombs caused elation. Some of the toughest veterans broke down and cried with relief before celebrating.

Their joy clearly doesn't determine the morality of using the atomic bombs. Nor can the ethical quandary be settled on these pages — or, probably, on any other pages; certainly the libraries of previous writings haven't settled it. All that can be done here is to ask whether the Battle of Okinawa can throw any light on the tortured question, remembering that the sum of civilian and military deaths probably exceeded those in Hiroshima and Nagasaki combined and that the cultural devastation was far greater and longer-lasting.

This comparison does not supply the answer. No amount of death and destruction on Okinawa can morally justify the hideous devastation of the bombs if dropping them was unnecessary. But the Okinawan experience may focus attention on critical issues by dissipating some of the historical haze in which the Hiroshima and Nagasaki tragedies are commemorated. The earlier Okinawan tragedy is understandably blurred by the ghoulish images of seared, irradiated Japanese civilians. The new weapon produced far more dreadful ruin than anything previous and did it in two discrete, dramatic events, each with one plane, one bomb and one obliterated city. It posed a greater threat to the future than the heaviest concentration of bullets, mortar shells, torpedoes and conventional bombs. Here was stark evidence that humanity might destroy itself. Still, those images which have permeated much of the debate about the atomic bombs convey only a fragment of the Pacific War's misery.

Defenders of the bomb claim that President Truman made his fateful decision at least partly under the influence of the casualties on Okinawa. Even knowing the ferocity and unexpected duration of the campaign, Truman was shocked by answers to his pointed inquiries about the final casualty figures. But whether or not the World War I artilleryman knew the full impact of combat suffering — he almost certainly knew little about the civilian carnage — is not the point, any more than whether his chief purpose was more to frighten Moscow than to hasten the end of the war.* Since bad decisions can be made for good reasons, the question is not why that one was made but whether it was right.

Evidence quickly established the correctness on a subsidiary point made by Okinawa veterans. The occupation force sent to the mainland after Japan's surrender included the 4th Marine Regiment, which had been reconstituted despite its near annihilation by the victorious Japanese in 1942. After an emotional meeting with gaunt prisoners of the old 4th who had surrendered on Bataan and Corregidor, its current members saw what one called Tokyo Bay's "unbelievable concrete and firepower," which would have faced them in an aborted invasion.

Americans in other units of the occupation force who visited their planned landing sites were silenced by the sight of high sea walls

---

*Although some theorists have forcefully argued this contention, the historical evidence for it is too shaky to merit inclusion in a discussion of the rights and wrongs. What *is* clear is that the decision was made with insufficient care and enlightenment. The ancient Japanese capital of Kyoto was removed from the target list only because the secretary of war happened to know its cultural significance.

backed by gun-bristling fortifications more formidable than the Shuri Line's. One insisted that clusters of dreaded heavy cannon now flying white flags from their barrels would have "blown us out of the water." Hyperbole aside, the weaponry prepared for *ketsu*, the operation to crush the American landings, was prima facie evidence that the casualties were certain to be much higher against Japanese defending the familiar terrain of their sacred home islands than they had been on distant possessions and conquered territory. "I don't think many of the Oki vets would have been around to talk to you without the beautiful bomb" is not much of an exaggeration. Robert Stewart saw plans that had his 2nd Marine Division, the one that had gone into reserve after making the decoy landing on Okinawa, among the invasion's spearheads. Those plans made no mention of the division after D-day plus 4. "In other words, our losses would have been so great my division would no longer have been a serviceable division after the fourth day," Stewart observed.

One infantryman noted that his canceled landing site near Nagasaki, eighty miles northwest of Kagoshima, had "enough ammunition to keep its hundreds of guns firing for months." But more than heavy coastal artillery and unprecedented stocks of shells chilled Okinawa veterans who later saw those potential killing grounds. There was also a large supply of bamboo spears with knives tied to their ends. Since all men of fighting age were gone from the area, the observers supposed women and children would have used the makeshift weapons. "Who the hell could have shot those women and kids?" asked one. He paused. "I guess we'd have had to."

His speculation about the spears was also correct. The day after the raising of the American flag on Okinawa, the Imperial Army took command of volunteer corps that functioned in mainland residential neighborhoods and places of work. Their members were chiefly civilian men under sixty-five and women under forty-five, but students were also mobilized into fighting corps — great numbers of them because so many war plants previously employing student labor had been destroyed or idled for lack of raw materials. The Tokyo police referred to this as "the final people's movement." The calls for the hundred million Japanese to "die proudly" were more insistent than ever. (Mainland Japan's population was actually closer to seventy-five million in 1945; the commonly used figure of a hundred million included citizens living in colonies.) Never mind the absurdity of bamboo. Perhaps, as with the kamikaze phenomenon, sacrificing lives in a futile cause was part of the goal and the reward. A scholar of the period caught the mood from diary entries of students.

High school girls in remote Shimane Prefecture worked out with carpenter's awls and were told "to guard their honor like samurai without shame" against invading troops. [Fifteen-year-old] Yukiko Kasai recalled her teacher's warning: "When [the Americans come], we must be ready to settle the war by drawing on our Japanese spirit and killing them. Even killing just one American soldier will do. You must be prepared to use the awls for self-defense. You must aim at the enemy's abdomen, understand? The abdomen! If you don't kill at least one enemy soldier, you don't deserve to die!" Kasai added wryly that the Japanese would have looked ridiculous facing the American flamethrowers and machine guns with such tools — but she dutifully took part in the drills anyway . . . One reason for persisting . . . was that no one wanted to be blamed for quitting. Another was that people were not fully aware of the grim situation in Okinawa, the Pacific or even the Japanese cities unless they happened to be there.

The principal resistance, naturally, would have been military. The Japanese war machine was finished by Allied standards but four million men remained under arms. (Ushijima had had about ninety thousand, not counting the Okinawan Home Guard.) Although they could not possibly achieve victory, they had ample means for inflicting terrible punishment on the invaders while saving their honor by fighting to the end. Sailors' blood would have flowed heavily. Japan still had thousands of planes — the tally varies from three thousand to sixteen thousand — many of which were carefully hidden and designated for kamikaze use. Some five thousand additional men were being trained to fly them. Had they been sent up, with their shorter distances to cover, the toll they inflicted would have been stunning, supplemented by a panoply of new and old suicide weapons.* Allied naval brass, knowing the Japanese had been concentrating on the defense of the mainland for months, braced for kamikaze attacks that would have been much more intense than those at Okinawa.

Unlike the earlier kamikaze concentration on warships, the chief targets this time — in an effort to shatter American morale with the maximum possible casualties — would have been the troops wading in to land. As usual, the greatest toll would have been farther inland, where "the incomparable Japanese infantry," as an American analyst assessed it, would have been supported by vastly more artillery than on Okinawa. American anticipation of the bloodbath was evident in

---

*The radio commentator who said he looked forward to an early landing "just to sense the thrill when we strike a deadly blow to the enemy" and promised "worldwide amazement" at Japan's array of "special attack" weapons was not entirely bluffing about the available weapons.

the forty-two divisions they allotted to the invasion. Seven had fought on Okinawa.

The planners calculated the landing alone would cost a hundred thousand American lives. The full securing of the home islands was expected to cost ten times that number, or four times the combined losses of Hiroshima and Nagasaki. General MacArthur, whose estimates of casualties in previous battles had been uncannily accurate, made a careful study of the mainland operation at President Truman's request and predicted one million men would be killed or wounded in the invasions of Kyushu and Honshu alone. (MacArthur's estimate may have been low because the Japanese, as on Okinawa, managed to muster more divisions in critical strongholds on the home islands than American intelligence supposed.) Final victory might easily cost more American casualties than in the entire war until then, in both the Atlantic and Pacific theaters.

In 1582, to return to a reference early in this account, a Japanese feudal leader staked the entire course of his fierce war for territorial supremacy on the result of a single battle at Tennozan. The name came to stand for one great battle for everything, do or die, winner take all. The battle for Leyte had been a Tennozan. The Okinawan operation was a Tennozan that dwarfed the Battle of Britain in size, scope and ferocity, according to the military historian Hanson Baldwin. But the ultimate Tennozan would have been the most spectacular operation in modern military history, the most ambitious project in peace or war ever undertaken by Americans. In the end, it would have involved thousands of Allied ships, tens of thousands of planes, and more than five million men. The greatest sausage machine in history would have ground on for years — MacArthur predicted ten years in the likely event that guerrilla forces retreated to the mountains — with effects that "stagger the imagination," said Samuel Eliot Morison.

The predictability of the veterans' renewed love of the bomb when they saw what it saved them from at mainland landing sites is no reason to dismiss arguments for its use. Of course it killed many people, but the equation, if there is one, must include the people it saved, to the extent that saving now seems likely and the number can be estimated. Although the American fighting men who cheered Little Boy and Fat Man did not care as much about others' survival as their own, consideration of the larger issue must include possible Japanese losses.

The ratio of Japanese combat deaths to American was well over 10 to 1 on Okinawa. It might have been marginally different during fighting in the enemy's heartland rather than on isolated islands, where Japanese garrisons were often cut off from reinforcements. Civilian deaths assuredly would have been much higher, if only because the mainland had many more civilians with a commitment to die for Emperor and country. The best estimates of probable total Japanese deaths in a mainland campaign are around twenty million; if civilian suicides and suicidal resistance had generated hysteria — a likely prospect in light of the experience on Guam and Okinawa — the toll would have been higher. The country would have been leveled and burned to cinders. Postwar life, including economic recovery, would have been retarded if Russia, a full Allied partner during the ground combat from 1945 to 1947 or 1948, would have insisted on dividing Japan like Korea and Germany.

Any estimate of lives saved by the atomic bombs must include hundreds of thousands of combatants and civilians in China, Manchuria and other territories still fought for and occupied, often viciously, by Japan. There would have been tens of thousands of British casualties among the 200,000 set to invade the Malay Peninsula — to retake Singapore — on September 9, a month after Nagasaki. Six divisions, the same number as at Normandy, had been assigned to that operation. It was expected to take seven months of savage infantry fighting, over half the time required to defeat Hitler's armies in Europe.

The total number must also include European and Eurasian prisoners of the Japanese, chiefly from English, Dutch and other colonial military and civil forces. Okinawa was the most important prelude to the climax because its terrain most closely resembled the mainland's, but non-Japanese elsewhere in Asia would have suffered even more during the new Tennozan. After the fall of Okinawa, Field Marshal Count Hisaichi Terauchi issued an order directing his prison camp officers to kill all their captives the moment the enemy invaded his southeast Asia theater. That would have been when those 200,000 British landed to retake Singapore, less than three weeks after the Japanese surrender. There was a real chance that Terauchi's order would have been carried out, in which case up to 400,000 people would have been massacred. Even more were doomed to die soon after of "natural" causes. The Japanese treatment of their prisoners grew more brutal as the military situation worsened and their hatred swelled.* Laurens van der Post, who had been a prisoner for

* Perhaps paradoxically, the old Japanese notion that mercilessness is the swiftest route to a merciful peace may be cited in support of an argument that the atomic bombs were humane in the long run by quickly ending the war and the Japanese hatred of white destroyers — which would have grown together with the destruction of Japan by bombing and shelling.

more than forty months, was convinced that the majority of the half-million captives in the hellish camps could not possibly have survived the year 1946. Dying every day in droves throughout the summer of 1945, nearly all would have perished of disease and starvation in the months that followed.

Those numbers make the atomic bombs seem an unimagined deliverance, even if the price was the horrible death of 200,000 men, women and children. The natural wish to dismiss that measure as too dreadful can be satisfied only by denying the more dreadful military and political realities of 1945. On the other hand, the figures are an eternal indictment if an invasion was unnecessary. That is the real question. Did even those 200,000 have to die at Hiroshima and Nagasaki? Wasn't Japan beaten anyway?

No secret intelligence was needed to appreciate the country's appalling condition before the bombs were dropped. Practically speaking, her merchant marine and Navy lay at the bottom of the Pacific. America alone, without the Royal Navy, had twenty-three battleships, ninety-nine carriers and seventy-two cruisers on hand in August. The Imperial Navy's numbers were one, six and four. Enough fuel was available only to sustain a force of twenty operational destroyers and perhaps forty submarines (supported by suicide boats and other small craft) for a few days at sea, just as not enough food was available for civilians who showed their ration cards in empty shops. The average Japanese adult existed on under thirteen hundred calories a day. Many of the shops themselves were gone. Relentless saturation bombing, easier than ever with the new bases on Okinawa and Iwo Jima and the feeble opposition from Japanese interceptors, had leveled Japan's major cities.

As many as thirteen million people were homeless. Malaria and tuberculosis were rampant, especially in the shantytowns rising in the ashes of the blackened, bombed-out cities. Groups of schoolchildren, barefoot in winter as well as summer, were sent to forests to root out pine stumps needed for the war effort. The trees themselves were long gone. In Tokushima, home city of many of the six thousand troops lost on *Toyama maru* nine months before L-day, metal was already so scarce that the bells of shrines were melted down, together with charcoal braziers, sole source of heating for remaining wood-and-paper homes. While huge numbers of Soviet troops mobilized to attack Manchuria — just as Tadashi Kojo feared a year earlier when his regiment was shipped to Okinawa from the Siberian border — there was no hope of supplying the defenders even if the merchant fleet hadn't been obliterated: the country's industry and military production were in shambles. Exhausted, despairing, slowly starving Japan was in no shape for further fighting.

Many in high positions knew the facts. The cabinet of Hideki Tojo had resigned on the day the fall of Saipan was made public, eight and a half months before Okinawa's L-day. Everyone who knew the elliptical statements of Japanese politics understood that such a change of government after a military blow of that force was an admission of defeat and of desire to end the debacle.

His successor, Kuniaki Koiso, wanted a truce in his way and tried to obtain it, partly with a flimsy attempt to negotiate with Washington and London through Chiang Kai-shek. His replacement tried harder. The partially pacificist cabinet of the third wartime prime minister, an elderly baron named Kantaro Suzuki, was installed the day after the sinking of *Yamato*. Suzuki's necessary noises would soon include the proposition that Okinawa's loss had improved Japan's strategic position while dealing a crushing spiritual blow to America: "Now is the time for every one of the hundred million . . . to become glorious shields for the defense of the national structure." But the clearest signal of his real intentions was the appointment of Shigenori Togo as foreign minister. A career diplomat who had been repelled by the trickery at Pearl Harbor, Togo went on to become one of Japan's most forceful critics of the war and the military establishment.

Whatever the Emperor's earlier satisfaction in the expanding Empire, he was now a committed supporter of the peace faction, inasmuch as those scattered individuals represented a faction and the Emperor's guarded hints could be construed as real support. Soon after the war, Hirohito would say he believed Okinawa was the final battle; if Japan lost it, she would have "no choice but unconditional surrender." On June 22, 1945, the day before the flag raising, he summoned six leading members of the Supreme War Council to the Imperial Palace. Expressing deep concern about the state of the war, he probably suggested diplomatic feelers should be made to try to end it. The government renewed earlier efforts to persuade Moscow to use its "good offices" for negotiations with the Allies. Since Stalin was already moving huge forces from Germany to join in Japan's final destruction, Tokyo's efforts ended in failure. But the unknowing peace advocates pursued Moscow more and more urgently while Hirohito sought to encourage talk of peace in confidential meetings with former prime ministers. The *jushin*, as this small group was called, were in tacit alliance with other elder statesmen — even a few military leaders such as Admiral Mitsumasa Yonai, the Minister of the Navy who hadn't opposed *Yamato*'s sortie as vigorously as he would have wanted to because he was already preoccupied by the larger question of how to stop the war.

Other peace advocates included Marquis Koichi Kido, the Lord Privy Seal and Hirohito's closest political adviser. Among other peace efforts were three in Sweden and Switzerland. While they were under way, cabinet members marshaled evidence that the country could not continue fighting and the Emperor's confidential advisers urged more directly, and to more receptive ears, that the war was lost and must be stopped. The forbidden word *peace* was even pronounced in public. Could the slaughter of innocent civilians in Hiroshima and Nagasaki have been justified in such circumstances?

> *Japan was finished as a warmaking nation, in spite of its four million men still under arms. But . . . Japan was not going to quit. Despite the fact that she was militarily finished, Japan's leaders were going to fight right on. To not lose "face" was more important than hundreds and hundreds of thousands of lives. And the people concurred, in silence, without protest. To continue was no longer a question of Japanese military thinking, it was an aspect of Japanese culture and psychology.*
>
> — James Jones, *WW II*

> *The capture of Iwo Jima, less than eight square miles of volcanic ash, had cost 25,849 Marines, a third of the landing force. Okinawa's price had been 49,151 . . . If the Japanese could draw that much blood in the outer islands of their defense perimeter, how formidable would they be on the 142,007 square miles of their five home islands, where they would be joined — as they had been on Saipan — by every member of the civilian population old enough to carry a hand grenade?*
>
> — William Manchester, *The Glory and the Dream*

> *The cabinet expected the volunteers to be home-front equivalents of the kamikaze pilots, who went into battle with meager weapons fully prepared to die. The civilian units were routed out weekly at 3 a.m. to worship at shrines and drill with bamboo staves, the residue of General Araki Sadao's prewar fantasy that "if we could have three million bamboo spears, we would be able to conquer Russia easily." . . . Civilians may have been fed up and the volunteers may have felt foolish training with spears and awls, but nearly everyone on the home front kept up the fight to the very end.*
>
> — Thomas R. H. Havens, *Valley of Darkness: The Japanese People and World War Two*

> *The sooner [the Americans] come, the better . . . One hundred million die proudly.*
>
> — Japanese slogans in the summer of 1945

> *Up to this moment, we had shaped our ideas towards an assault upon the homeland of Japan by terrific air bombing and by the invasion of very large armies. We had contemplated the desperate resistance of the Japanese fight-*

ing to the death with samurai devotion, not only in pitched battles but in every cave and dugout. I had in my mind the spectacle of Okinawa Island . . . To quell the Japanese resistance man by man and conquer the country yard by yard might well require the loss of a million American lives and half that number of British — or more if we could get them there: for we were resolved to share the agony.

— Winston Churchill, on being informed at Potsdam of the results of the final test of the atomic bomb

The atomic bomb attacks and the Soviet entry into the war, thus deteriorating our position, shocked us. But we can take some countermeasures against them. We still have enough fighting strength remaining. Furthermore, don't we have large army forces still intact on the China continent and in our homeland? It might be the view of some clever fellows to surrender with some strength left instead of being completely destroyed . . . But those fellows advocating that idea are nothing but selfish weaklings who don't think seriously about the future of the nation and only seek immediate benefits.

— August 11 diary entry of Admiral Matome Ugaki, commander of the Fifth Air Fleet on Kyushu, which carried out kamikaze and conventional attacks on the American fleet off Okinawa

This is a great problem for me . . . as commander in chief. Although an Emperor's order must be followed, I can hardly bear to see us suspend attacks while we still have this fighting strength. I think many things remain to be done after consulting with those brave men willing to die.

— Admiral Ugaki discussing the possibility that Japan might surrender after the destruction of Hiroshima and Nagasaki

It can have been justified only if factors such as the attempts at negotiation and the Imperial household's growing opposition to the war were irrelevant because they were doomed to futility. And although this is another unanswerable question, the evidence, strongly supported by the Okinawan experience, points in that direction.

Japanese who wanted to end the war were frightened, however high their positions. Prime Minister Koiso had to undertake his peace initiatives in great secrecy, probably in fear of his life. Prime Minister Kantaro Suzuki, an admiral and hero of the Russo-Japanese War of 1905 as well as a baron, could not make direct approaches for negotiation without courting another attempt on his life too. (The seventy-eight-year-old Grand Chamberlain was weakened by a bullet still lodged in his heart from the time of the extreme ultra-nationalists' most ambitious coup attempt, that one in 1936.) In any case, all the would-be peacemakers were on the periphery of real state power. Japan remained dominated by the Supreme War Cabinet's military faction, the very kind of "Manchuria Gang" activists and sympathizers who had terrorized and assassinated opponents in the 1920s and

1930s and dragged the country into a war whose abandonment they now considered impossible. While civilian leaders had begun to whisper the hitherto shunned thought that the fighting had to stop, they had scant hope it would. The Lord Privy Seal put it in a nutshell in early June, when the 32nd Army faced annihilation on Okinawa. In a secret memorandum to the throne, Marquis Kido ventured that Japan had lost the war, "regrettable though it is." But the overriding determinant was the military faction's will to "fight to the death" nevertheless. He had to advise the Emperor that any peace move was "almost impossible."

To fight to the death was indeed what the military zealots were determined to do, and with the most ferocious resolve. To men such as War Minister General Korechika Anami and Commander of the Combined Fleet Admiral Soemu Toyoda, death for honor and Japan was more than ever life's purpose. Captain Kojo's failure to consider another alternative until he had no men to command and no military function — but knowledge of his Emperor's order to capitulate months earlier — suggests the diehard military state of mind. No thought of surrender entered Kojo's thoughts. Although the political generals could not have entirely avoided its mention in Tokyo, it represented to them the worst conceivable eventuality, incomparably worse than death.

The public record is long and full on the real rulers' refusal to consider negotiation until after a "decisive" Tennozan on the mainland. So far, the old guard insisted, the war had been a series of indecisive skirmishes; now was the time to lure the Americans to their annihilation in the final battle on Japanese soil required to preserve national honor. Some 150,000 dead Okinawans were proof of their determination to continue sacrificing any number of civilians. "Even if the Japanese people are weary of the war," Toyoda insisted, "we must fight to the last man."*

None of this was bombast or vacillation, as with the intimidated peace faction. None of it changed until the atomic bomb — and only barely after both bombs had done their work. Even then, some of the key generals insisted the country continue fighting in the ashes. Among the other decision makers, opinions changed so slowly with such distant prospect of the eventual acceptance of common sense over *bushido*, the way of the warrior, that continued resistance was

---

*It is relevant that a few of the "last men" themselves opposed this notion. Millions of Japanese, including civilians, still could not conceive of any end to the war other than victory or death. Just before the Emperor's speech telling his people to accept defeat, Tokyo shopkeepers sharpened knives, expecting an order for the entire nation to commit suicide.

inevitable. Other personal concerns and national factors were secondary. That is why Japan's weakened condition and developing peace faction is unconvincing evidence that Hiroshima and Nagasaki were unnecessary.

The Army's and the nation's commanders were almost certain to prevail, if necessary by assassinating any "weaklings" who dared speak openly about ending the war. Most of the documentation of the country's wretched condition is therefore largely inconsequential. For it proved further fighting was senseless in *Western*, not Japanese perception; at least the perception of the Japanese rulers who mattered. The handful of leaders who wanted to negotiate peace had almost no chance of performing the unprecedented feat of convincing the Imperial Army diehards to abandon the powerful code and passionate ethic under which they had striven until now. When they failed, servicemen and civilians would have fought with even more self-sacrifice than on Okinawa.

That they were defeated before the start wasn't the point for the Manchuria Gang — even less than it had been for the admirals who sacrificed *Yamato* in their war for face and honor. The supplies in Japan's armory were adequate for more years of suicidal delaying actions on this hill and at that escarpment. Superior American firepower would have provoked more murderous savagery on both sides, and deeper cultural devastation of Japan. Calls would have been made for ever greater sacrifice, although they already specified that every life must be given for the country. That is why many Japanese civilians as well as American infantrymen cheered the bomb. Not surprisingly, the Japanese kept their approval to themselves. Almost half a century later, few feel able to voice their belief that the terrible weapon liberated them; yet nonmilitarist Japanese, of whom there were surely millions, now and then whisper a confession that they believed they were doomed before Hiroshima and Nagasaki saved them.*

Okinawa demonstrated the extreme unlikelihood, to put it as conservatively as possible, of surrender by the Japanese who held the country in their grip, no matter what the odds were against successful defense. The foregone outcome of the battle for the island neither

---

*One young woman, deeply grateful to the bomb for "doing the trick" of saving her, never thought of surrender until then because it was unimaginable. She and almost all her classmates had been training to fight; to fail to attend her school's special class in the use of the bamboo spear was to court arrest for an unpatriotic display. She could not express her joy because she lost many friends in Hiroshima, which was near her village, and because it would have "looked indecent." But she had no doubt that the atomic bomb gave her leaders a way out. Now she could hope that "maybe there was a future of a kind instead of no future . . . Thank God!"

made the Japanese fight less resolutely nor diminished the casualties for either side or for Okinawan civilians. And the capitulation that was inconceivable to the Mitsuru Ushijimas and Tadashi Kojos was less acceptable to those military leaders in Tokyo, who were extremely reluctant — and in some cases simply unwilling — to consider surrender even after Hiroshima and Nagasaki.

The same evidence weakens the contention that the second bomb — whatever justification was offered for the first — approached wanton murder. War Cabinet minutes reveal that the generals were nearly as determined to continue after Nagasaki as after Hiroshima. They were stayed only when the Emperor spoke up, unprecedentedly, after decades of silence about decisions made in his name. Even after His Majesty announced his wish to prevent further slaughter by "bearing the unbearable" of surrender, it was touch and go during the six days after Nagasaki whether the hard-liners would prevent this. Some who wanted to continue the war planned assassinations and a coup, their trusted methods for furthering the Emperor's purported "real" wishes and the country's "fundamental" values. This makes dubious the argument that a demonstration bomb should have been used before either of the deadly ones. Such a warning, dropped off a Japanese coast, would have had less or no effect on the military powers.*

That is what the American fighting men believed in their gut, without knowing Japanese culture or history or, of course, the murders and mutinies by Japanese officers that were about to follow Hirohito's decision for peace. The American veterans were convinced there was no other way but to kill the Japanese, that all the rest was talk, that no one could understand — because it was otherwise not understandable — unless he had fought the singular enemy. They believed that even if the feeble peace faction did manage to turn tables on the militarists, the improbable relief would come only years into the invasion of Japan, when millions of lives would have been lost.

An almost visible line separated those who judged Japanese intentions through the prism of combat experience from people further removed, military as well as civilians. Fighting men, with their severely limited perspective from the lip of a foxhole, weren't necessarily right, but they weren't necessarily wrong either, though their opinion was deeply self-interested and unanimous.† Valid or not,

* Besides, only two atomic bombs existed, and no American was certain they could be successfully dropped on a target. A demonstration bomb that failed would have strengthened the grip of the military diehards.

† The single veteran of Okinawa I encountered who questioned the use of the bomb as possibly too harsh had arrived when the fighting was over and shuddered at American insensitivity to native needs and such practices as ignoring assaults on Okinawan women.

their points have virtually vanished from the media coverage, which is almost to say the national consciousness, on each anniversary of Hiroshima.

Not everyone who knew the cost of fighting the Japanese approved the use of the bomb. Admiral Ernest King, who had been persuaded to change the final major steppingstone from Formosa to Okinawa, and Admiral William Leahy argued that a more hermetic maritime blockade than the one in place during the summer of 1945, coupled with more intense bombing and naval gunfire, would have forced surrender within a reasonable time. Leahy called the atomic bomb "an inhuman weapon to use on a people that was already defeated and ready to surrender . . . [We Americans] had adopted an ethical standard common to the barbarians of the Dark Ages." A scattering of high-ranking officers — none from infantry units — agreed with those admirals. A few specified that there was no need for an invasion at all, let alone for atomic bombs: deprived of supplies and food, blockaded Japan would have surrendered sooner or later. Most of those few spoke out only after the war, when evidence became available of just how severely American submarines had crippled Japanese industry. They did not add that their argument also applied to the Palau Islands, the Philippines, Iwo Jima and the other murderous steppingstones. If blockades could have done the job, weren't the deaths there and at Okinawa also logically unnecessary?

In any case, their voices were the exceptions. Most of those with actual experience of Japanese behavior during the war — as opposed to those convinced of how Japan should behave — were certain that blockade and bombing could not work. The rule seemed to be that complaints about the atomic bomb's inhumanity increased in proportion to the critics' distance from the hell to which the weapon had put an end. "In general, the principle is, the farther from the scene of horror, the easier the talk," as Paul Fussell put it concisely.*

A blockade of the Japanese home islands might have worked. The Stars and Stripes and British ensign flew from nearly a thousand destroyers and destroyer escorts in August, and American yards were launching more every week. Stationed within sight of each other, they and the capital warships, supplemented by thousands of planes, could have sealed off the home islands. But it is hard to understand

*The less one knew about the Pacific War in general and such battles as Okinawa in particular, the greater one's doubts and the more likely one's disapproval. This is not to say that participation in Pacific combat was essential for reaching solid conclusions about the bomb; only that the very persuasive arguments *against* usually leave unmentioned the mortal costs of the alternatives, ignorance of which was likely to strengthen moral opposition.

how this would have been more humane or saved more lives. On the contrary, it is almost certain that the majority of Japanese would have voluntarily or compulsorily — in either case, agonizingly — persisted even after mass starvation rather than surrender.

It is also hard to imagine that conventional air attacks would have been halted during that period. Wars don't work that way, which may be partly why not even the blockade's handful of advocates suggested suspension of the bombing. Civilian casualties in the eighty-odd Japanese cities fire bombed by early August were already far larger than those at Hiroshima and Nagasaki combined. On August 1, to take a minor example, the secondary target of Toyama, a city of 130,000, was burned almost to nothing; one report described it as 99 percent ashes. Under the overall command of Curtis LeMay, the Air Force general who had promised to beat Japan back to the Dark Ages, saturation raids reached down to cities of fifty-five thousand in population because too little was left of Tokyo, Nagoya, Kobe, Osaka, Yokohama, Kawasaki and other industrial centers to make mass attacks on them worthwhile. A key aide to General MacArthur called those conventional raids "one of the most ruthless and barbaric killings of noncombatants in all history." Radio Tokyo's term was "slaughter bombing."

Those who deplored the use of the atomic bombs would have stood on firmer moral ground if they had protested the fire bombing of those cities. Their horror at the barbarity of Little Boy and Fat Man might have been more telling had it extended to the killing of many *more* hundreds of thousands of civilians by conventional weapons. The latter killing was certain to continue under the passionately committed LeMay.* But even if LeMay could have been restrained, starvation, exhaustion and disease would have taken many times the toll of the two atomic bombs. That pertains to Japanese lives only. During the months or years when the blockade and bombing were doing their work, hundreds of thousands or millions of non-Japanese would have died, chiefly on the Asian continent. Deaths among the Allied prisoners of war alone would have far exceeded the number of atomic victims.

Of course Japan did capitulate, prima facie evidence that all the predictions about her refusal to do so was also talk. But in some ways, the surrender actually testified to the contrary: that only the atomic

---

*On the eve of the March fire bombing of Tokyo, which killed nearly 200,000, the general wired a colleague in Washington to be ready for an "outstanding show."

bombs could have achieved it without the years of "decisive battle" or mass starvation. For the unbearable was (barely) accepted only when the Emperor spoke up, and that moment came only after Nagasaki. The terrifying atomic devastation prompted his startling intervention, then tipped the balance among military commanders in favor of obedience. Churchill wrote that he thought "the Japanese people, whose courage I had always admired, might find in the apparition of this almost supernatural weapon an excuse which would save their honour and release them from their obligation of being killed to the last fighting man." (He omitted nonfighting men, women, and children.) Others might suggest that some other revolutionary device would have allowed Japan to save face — but in the end, the bomb provided that opportunity. Gazing at the immense American fleet, among the most graphic displays of conventional weaponry in history, Ushijima's 32nd Army had seen nothing to reduce their obligation to their code and country. The men loathed the American planes that pulverized them in complete mastery of the air and in virtual impunity from return fire, but they fought on defiantly without thought of surrender. They took unimaginable punishment from every available American weapon without cracking until the pitiful 5 percent of survivors had been deprived of supplies, fortifications and leadership. Brother soldiers would surely be even braver and tougher on the sacred home islands with their immeasurably better preparation; no accumulation of bombs, shells and bullets was likely to deter them from their commitment.

The nation in trance did not care about the odds against her. Something was needed to free her from her spell. It had to be something qualitatively different from the current mix of conventional arms and strategic circumstances — and perhaps it wasn't accidental that the people whose Emperor was descended from the Sun God — and whose nation, Nippon, is written with two characters that mean "origin of the sun" — saw the atomic blasts as "brighter than a thousand suns." This was more than a new weapon. The explosion was more than the equivalent of ten thousand tons of TNT. It was another order of force, greater and more authoritative. The miraculous apparition presented a way out for the land of the Rising Sun.

All this is of course speculative, but until nuclear bombs do become the scourge of mankind by killing more than previous weapons and fatally contaminating the planet, Okinawa's caves, killing grounds and anguish ought to be remembered. It ought to be suggested, at least for the sake of the ambivalent human record, that the first atomic bombs probably prevented the homicidal equivalent of over two hundred more of the same: the twenty million Japanese deaths if invasion had been necessary, in addition to all the other deaths, Western and Asian.

It is difficult to comprehend such figures and to remember the strains of 1945. Focusing revulsion on the bomb is easier. But if a symbol is needed to help preserve the memory of the Pacific War, Okinawa is the more fitting one.

BIBLIOGRAPHY   CHRONOLOGY   INDEX

Bibliography

TRYING TO STUDY a military campaign, one is quickly struck by the difference between the reality of close combat and most books about war. The books are of course indispensable for many facets of the study, such as strategy, historical and social background, analysis of the warring sides' philosophy of training and operations. But apart from novels, few contribute much to the understanding of what individual men think and feel while fighting. Since my principal interest was daily life at the front, together with the fate of civilians caught in the battle, most of my research was more journalistic than scholarly. More of my information, in other words, came from interviews with Japanese, Okinawan and American survivors than from written sources.

My greatest fear was and remains joining those who don't know the difference between combat and talking or writing about it: "armchair warriors," as John Bayley recently called them, who never performed feats of fighting but who "nonetheless become connoisseurs of them at second hand." To some degree, my worry is muted by the near unanimity of the people with whom I talked. For if it is hard to acquire a sense of the duress of combat from books, it is also hard not to see and feel the power of the memory while listening to the fighters. All my previous journalistic work convinced me of the truth of the conventional wisdom about no two people having the same memory of an event they witnessed together. But probably because battle is such a terrifying form of human conduct, subjecting the parties to such extreme pressures and pain, the survivors of the Okinawan campaign spoke with almost one voice about their experiences. That is to say, the recollections of the various categories and sub-categories of participants — Japanese, American and Okinawan; Marines and soldiers, artillerymen and infantrymen, men and women — were remarkably consistent. This seemed to be true even of people with sharply disparate social and educational backgrounds. It was also true that the least educated foot soldiers were often as eloquent as high school and university graduates, for what they said came from the gut rather than the intellect.

On and off, I questioned them for eight years, throughout the time I worked on the book. My introduction to stories of the fighting began about a year earlier, when Dick Whitaker, my closest neighbor on a lonely dirt road in northwestern Connecticut, mentioned some incidents he had witnessed and experienced during his tour on the island. (Whitaker began talking about the hardships and savagery only after years of cutting and splitting firewood together.) In all, I interviewed some forty Marines; a similar number answered a brief questionnaire I mailed to veterans of the 6th Division. In between, I made two trips to Okinawa and Japan for interviews and research there. I spoke to many Americans, especially at reunions of veterans, without taking notes. But the notes and tapes of most of my substantive interviews, together with some diaries and letters, are in my possession and available for review. As I said, they constitute the major part of my research.

Some books were also extremely helpful. I have already mentioned the most impressive, E. B. Sledge's *With the Old Breed at Peleliu and Okinawa* (Novato, California: Presidio Press, 1983). This memoir, undertaken so that the writer could leave his grandchildren a record of a Marine infantryman's experiences, rightly became an instant classic, much admired on Okinawa as well as among American veterans. Nothing I know comes as close to off-the-record observations and memories of combat in the Pacific. Samuel Hynes's *Flights of Passage: Reflections of a World War II Aviator* also belongs to the small category of war memoirs that ring utterly true. And William Manchester's *Goodbye, Darkness* offers vivid glimpses of combat's fear and filth; the book's puzzling inaccuracies do not invalidate some of the best descriptions in English of the fighting on Okinawa and in other Pacific campaigns.

Among the contemporary writers about war I encountered, the most successful in conveying the truth about combat — which necessarily includes debunking the myths and deceptions about glory in the bulk of war literature and cinema — include John Keegan and Paul Fussell. I did not read Japanese books similar to theirs, not because they do not exist — no doubt they do — but because I do not read Japanese at all; all the written materials I did examine were translated for me by Tamako Yorichika. The memoirs interested me most. Many are excellent, among them those by Shigemi Furukawa, Kuni-ichi Izuchi, Yoshio Kobayashi, Kenjiro Matsuki, Ikuo Ogiso and Norio Watanabe. Mitsuru Yoshida's extraordinarily moving *Requiem for Battleship Yamato* may be the best record of the monstrous waste, pain and horror of the fighting, perhaps because it makes no attempt to chronicle them but records flashes of observation and thought in a kind of impressionistic poetry.

As for Okinawa itself, America's almost resolute lack of interest in the land where she fought one of her hardest, proudest battles and now maintains her largest foreign military establishment helps explain why so much Okinawan suffering has gone unknown. But the few books about the island in English include George H. Kerr's *Okinawa: The History of an Island People,* a labor of love that is among the best products of the postwar occupation.

The following is not an exhaustive bibliography but a selection from books, articles and other written materials read and consulted.

After the Battle (Okinawa, a Marine Returns). London: Battle of Britain Prints, 1984.

Agawa, Hiroyuki. *The Reluctant Admiral: Yamamoto and the Imperial Navy.* Tokyo: Kodansha International, 1979.

Appleman, Roy E., James M. Burns, Russell A. Gugeler, and John Stevens. *Okinawa: The Last Battle.* Washington, D.C.: Department of the Army, Historical Division, 1948.

Bailey, Thomas A. *A Diplomatic History of the American People.* New York: Appleton-Century-Crofts, 1964.

Baldwin, Hanson W. *Battles Lost and Won; Great Campaigns of World War II.* New York: Harper & Row, 1966.

Barker, A. J. *Okinawa.* New York: Gallery Books, 1981.

Belote, James and William. *Typhoon of Steel, the Battle for Okinawa.* New York: Harper & Row, 1970.

Benedict, Ruth. *The Chrysanthemum and the Sword.* Boston: Houghton Mifflin, 1946.

Bennett, Henry Stanley. "The Impact of Invasion and Occupation on the Civilians of Okinawa," *U.S. Naval Institution Proceedings,* vol. 21 (February 1946).

Berry, Henry. *Semper Fi, Mac: Living Memories of the U.S. Marines in World War II.* New York: Arbor House, 1982.

Blair, Clay, Jr. *Silent Victory: The U.S. Submarine War Against Japan.* Philadelphia: J. B. Lippincott, 1975.

Boei, Cho, Kenshujo Boei, and Shitsu Senshi (compilers). (Defense Ministry, Defense Research Institute. War History Office) *Okinawa homen rikugun sakusen* (Okinawa Region Army Operation). Tokyo: Asagumo Shinbun Sha, 1968.

———. *Okinawa homen kaigun sakusen* (Okinawa Region Navy Operation). Tokyo: Asagumo Shinbun Sha, 1968.

———. *Rikugun koku sakusen* (Army Air Operation). Tokyo: Asagumo Shinbun Sha, n.d.

Braddon, Russell. *The Other Hundred Years War: Japan's Bid for Supremacy, 1941–2041.* London: Collins, 1983.

Brooks, Lester. *Behind Japan's Surrender.* New York: McGraw-Hill, 1968.

Buruma, Ian. *Behind the Mask: On Sexual Demons, Sacred Mothers, Transvestites, Gangsters and other Japanese Cultural Heroes.* New York: Pantheon, 1984.

Bywater, Hector C. *The Great Pacific War.* New York: St. Martin's Press, 1991.

Cary, Otis (ed). *War-Wasted Asia: Letters, 1945–46.* Tokyo: Kodan International, 1975.

Committee for the Compilation of Materials on Damage Caused by the Atomic Bombs in Hiroshima and Nagasaki. *The Physical, Medical and Social Effects of the Atomic Bombings.* New York: Basic Books, 1981.

"The Contribution of the British Pacific Fleet to the Assault on Okinawa, 1945."
    Supplement to *The London Gazette,* June 2, 1948.
Congdon, Don (ed). *Combat: The War with Japan.* New York: Dell Publishing
    Company, 1962.
Coox, Alvin D. *Nomanhan: Japan Against Russia.* Stanford: Stanford University
    Press, 1985.
Cortesi, Lawrence. *Valor at Okinawa.* New York: Zebra Books, 1981.
Costello, John. *The Pacific War.* London: William Collins & Sons, 1981.
Craig, William. *The Fall of Japan.* New York: Dial Press, 1967.
Dictionary of American Naval Fighting Ships. Washington, D.C.: Naval History Di-
    vision, Department of the Navy, 1976.
Dillaway, Newton. *The Lesson of Okinawa.* Wakefield, Massachusetts: Montrose
    Press, 1947.
Dower, John W. *War Without Mercy: Race and Power in the Pacific War.* New York:
    Pantheon, 1986.
Dower, John W., and John Junkerman (eds). *The Hiroshima Murals: The Art of Iri
    Maruki and Toshi Maruki.* Tokyo: Kodansha International, 1985.
Dull, Paul. *A Battle History of the Imperial Japanese Navy.* Annapolis: U.S. Naval
    Institute Press, 1978.
Fallows, James. *National Defense.* New York: Random House, 1981.
Feiler, Bruce S. *Learning to Bow: An American Teacher in a Japanese School.* New
    York: Ticknor & Fields, 1991.
Fosco, Maraini. *Meeting with Japan.* New York: Viking, 1960.
Frank, Benis M. *Okinawa: The Great Island Battle.* New York: Elsevier-Dutton,
    1978.
————. *Okinawa: Capstone to Victory.* New York: Ballantine Books, 1970.
Furukawa, Shigemi. *Okinawa no saigo* (The End of Okinawa). Tokyo: Kawade
    Shobo, 1968.
Fussell, Paul. *Thank God for the Atom Bomb and Other Essays.* New York: Summit
    Books, 1988.
————. *Wartime.* New York: Oxford University Press, 1989.
Fussell, Paul (ed). *Modern War.* New York: W. W. Norton, 1990.
Gilbert, Martin. *The Second World War.* New York: Henry Holt & Company, 1989.
Glacken, Clarence J. *The Great Loochoo, A Study in Okinawan Village Life.* Berkeley:
    University of California Press, 1955.
Gow, Ian. *Okinawa, 1945.* New York: Doubleday & Company, 1985.
Hara, Tameichi. *Japanese Destroyer Captain.* New York: Ballantine Books, 1961.
Haraguchi, Torao. *The Status System and Social Organization of Satsuma.* Tokyo:
    University of Tokyo Press, 1975.
Havens, Thomas R. H. *Valley of Darkness: The Japanese People and World War Two.*
    New York: W. W. Norton, 1978.
Hayashi, Saburo. *Kogun: The Japanese Army in the Pacific War.* Westport, Connect-
    icut: Greenwood Press, 1959.
Hersey, John. *Hiroshima.* New York: Random House, 1989.
Hough, Frank. *The Island War.* Philadelphia: J. B. Lippincott, 1947.
Howarth, Stephen. *Fighting Ships of the Rising Sun: The Drama of the Imperial Japa-
    nese Navy.* New York: Atheneum, 1983.
Hoyt, Edwin P. *Closing the Circle: War in the Pacific, 1945.* New York: Van Nos-
    trand Reinhold Company, 1982.
————. *The Kamikazes: The Dramatic Story of Japan's Desperate Suicide Missions.* New
    York: Jove Books, 1984.

Huber, Thomas M. *Japan's Battle of Okinawa, April–June 1945*. (Leavenworth Papers, No. 18). Ft. Leavenworth, Kansas: U.S. Army Command and General Staff College, 1990.

Hynes, Samuel. *Flights of Passage: Reflections of a World War II Aviator*. Annapolis: Naval Institute Press, 1988.

Ienaga, Saburo. *The Pacific War: World War II and the Japanese, 1931–1945*. New York: Pantheon, 1978.

Ikemiyagi, Shui. *Senjo ni ikita hitotachi: Okinawasen no kiroku* (Those Who Lived Through It: Records of the Okinawa Battle). Tokyo: Saimaru Shuppan, 1968.

Inoguchi, Rikihei, and Tadashi Nakajima, with Roger Pineau. *The Divine Wind: Japan's Kamikaze Force in World War II*. Annapolis: U.S. Naval Institute, 1958.

Ito, Masanori. *The End of the Japanese Imperial Navy*. New York: W. W. Norton, 1962.

Izuchi, Kuni-ichi. *Okinawa ryoshuki* (The Diary of a Prisoner on Okinawa). Articles serialized in a provincial Japanese newspaper, June–August, 1984.

———. *Waga Okinawa senki* (My Tale of the Battle of Okinawa). Articles serialized in a provincial Japanese newspaper, date unknown.

The Japanese Navy in World War II. Annapolis: U.S. Naval Institute, 1969.

Japan's War: The Great Pacific Conflict. New York: McGraw-Hill, 1980.

Johnson, Jesse J. (ed). *Black Armed Forces Officers, 1793–1971*. Hampton, Virginia: Hampton Institute, 1971.

Jones, James. *WW II: A Chronicle of Soldiering*. New York: Ballantine Books, 1975.

Karnow, Stanley. *In Our Image: America's Empire in the Philippines*. New York: Random House, 1989.

Keegan, John. *The Face of Battle*. New York: Viking Press, 1976.

———. *The Mask of Command*. New York: Viking Press, 1987.

Kennedy, M. D. *The Military Side of Japanese Life*. Westport, Connecticut: Greenwood Press, 1973.

———. *Some Aspects of Japan and Her Defense Force*. London: Kegan Paul, Trench, Truber & Company, 1928.

Kennedy, Paul. *The Rise and Fall of the Great Powers: Economic Change and Military Conflict from 1500 to 2000*. New York: Random House, 1987.

Kerr, George H. *Okinawa: The History of an Island People*. Rutland, Vermont: Charles E. Tuttle Company, 1958.

King, Norman H. "Civilian Casualties in the Battle of Okinawa, 1945," Ryukyu Islands Project, Research and Information Papers, November 1972.

Kobayashi, Yoshio. *San! Okinawa sen* (Alas, the Battle of Okinawa!). Tokyo: Ashi Shobo, 1985.

Kogun, The Japanese Army in the Pacific War. Quantico, Virginia: Marine Corps Association, 1959.

Krulak, General Victor. *First to Fight*. Annapolis: U.S. Naval Institute Press, 1984.

Leckie, Robert. *Delivered from Evil: the Saga of World War II*. New York: Harper & Row, 1987.

———. *Strong Men Armed: The United States Marines Against Japan*. New York: Random House, 1962.

Lee, Ulysses. *The Employment of Negro Troops*. Washington, D.C.: U.S. Army, Office of the Chief of Military History, 1966.

Lensen, George Alexander. *The Russian Push Toward Japan: Russo-Japanese Relations, 1697–1875*. Princeton: Princeton University Press, 1959.

Livingston, Jon, Joe Moore, and Felicia Oldfather (eds). *Imperial Japan 1800–1945*. New York: Pantheon, 1973.

Lorry, Hillis. *Japan's Military Masters: the Army in Japanese Life*. Westport, Connecticut: Greenwood Press, 1973.

Makiminato, Tokuzo. *Tetsu no Bofu* (The Metal Typhoon). Naha: Okinawan Times Publishing Company, 1970.

Manchester, William. *American Caesar*. New York: Little, Brown, 1978.

———. *The Glory and the Dream: A Narrative History of America, 1932–1972*. New York: Bantam, 1974.

———. *Goodbye, Darkness: A Memoir of the Pacific War*. Boston: Little, Brown, 1980.

Maretzki, Thomas W., and Hatsumi Maretzki. *Taira: An Okinawan Village*. New York: John Wiley & Sons, 1966.

Martin, Jo Nobuko. *A Princess Lily of the Ryukyus*. Tokyo: Shin Nippon Kyuku Tosho, 1964.

Matsuki, Kenjiro. *Matsuki Ittohei no Okinawa Horyoki* (Pfc. Matsuki's Tale as a Prisoner on Okinawa). Tokyo: Kobun Sha, 1974.

Miller, Don Ethan. "Brick Breaker," *Atlantic Monthly*, April 1987.

Millot, Bernard. *Divine Thunder: The Life and Death of the Kamikazes*. New York: McCall, 1971.

Minami, Hiroshi. *The Psychology of the Japanese People*. Tokyo: University of Tokyo Press, 1971.

Minear, Richard H. (ed). *Hiroshima: Three Witnesses*. Princeton: Princeton University Press, 1990.

Morison, Samuel Eliot. *"Old Bruin": Commodore Matthew C. Perry, 1794–1858*. Boston: Atlantic Monthly Press, 1967.

———. *History of United States Naval Operations in World War II*. vol. III: *The Rising Sun in the Pacific, 1931–April, 1942;* vol. IV: *Coral Sea, Midway and Submarine Actions, May 1942–August, 1942;* vol. XIV: *Victory in the Pacific, 1945*. Boston: Little, Brown, 1975.

Morris, Ivan. *The Nobility of Failure: Tragic Heroes in the History of Japan*. New York: Holt, Rinehart & Winston, 1975.

Morris, Ivan (ed). *Japan, 1931–1945: Militarism, Fascism, Japanism*. Boston: Heath, 1963.

Morris, Morton D. *Okinawa: A Tiger by the Tail*. New York: Hawthorn Books, 1968.

Morton, William Scott. *Japan, Its History and Culture*. New York: Crowell, 1970.

Moskin, J. Robert. *The U.S. Marine Corps Story*. New York: McGraw-Hill, 1977.

Nagatsuka, Ryuji. *I Was a Kamikaze*. New York: Macmillan, 1974.

Naito, Hatsuho. *Thunder Gods: The Kamikaze Pilots Tell Their Story*. Tokyo: Kodansha International, 1989.

Naka, Shohachiro, and Kenich Tanigawa (compilers). *Okinawa no shogen* (Okinawan Testament). Tokyo: Chuo Koron Sha, 1971.

Nakasone, Seizen. *Himeyuri no toh wo meguru hitobito no shuki* (The Himeyuri Monument and Friends — Notes). Tokyo: Kadokawa Shoten, 1980.

———. *The Tragedy of Okinawa*. Tokyo: Kacho Shobo, 1951.

Nalty, Bernard C. *Strength for the Fight: A History of Black Americans in the Military*. New York: Free Press, 1986.

The New Yorker Book of War Pieces. New York: Schocken Books, 1988.

Nichols, Charles S., and Henry I. Shaw. *Okinawa, Victory in the Pacific.* Rutland, Vermont, and Tokyo: Charles E. Tuttle Company, 1955.

Nichols, David (ed). *Ernie's War: The Best of Ernie Pyle's World War II Dispatches.* New York: Random House, 1986.

Nitobe, Inazo. *Bushido: The Soul of Japan.* Tokyo: Charles E. Tuttle, 1969.

Norman, Michael. *These Good Men: Friendships Forged from War.* New York: Crown, 1989.

Oechsle, Rob, and Masatoshi Uehara. *Aoi me gamita Dai Ryukyu* (Great Lewchew Discovered: 19th-Century Ryukyu in Western Art and Illustration). Naha: Nirai Sha, n.d.

Ogiso, Ikuo. *Ah, Okinawa!* (Ah, Okinawa!: A Secret Record of the Bloody Battle of Derangement and Bitter Resentment). Tokyo: Kobun Shuppan Sha, 1968.

Okinawa. Washington, D.C.: Department of the Army, Historical Division, 1977.

Okinawa: The Last Battle. Okinawa: Senkiroken Shashin Kanko-kai, 1948.

Okinawa kenshi: Okinawasen kiroku, 2 (History of Okinawa Prefecture: Records of the Battle of Okinawa, 2). Compiled and published by the Education Committee of Okinawa Prefecture, 1974.

Okuda, Koichiro. *Okinawa Gun Shireikan: Ushijima Mitsuru* (Mitsuru Ushijima: Commander of the Okinawan Army). Tokyo: Fuyo Shobo, 1985.

O'Neill, Richard. *Suicide Squads: W.W. II, Axis and Allied Special Attack Weapons of World War II: Their Development and their Missions.* New York: St. Martin's Press, 1981.

An Oral History of the Battle of Okinawa: Survivors' "Testimonies." Naha: Okinawa Prefectural Government, 1985.

Ota, Masahide. *The Battle of Okinawa, The Typhoon of Steel and Bombs.* Okinawa: Kume Publishing Company, 1984.

——. *Okinawa-sen to watashi* (The Battle of Okinawa and I). Tokyo: Iwanami Shoten, 1972.

Ota, Masahide (ed). A Comprehensive Study of U.S. Military Government on Okinawa (An Interim Report). Ginowan, Okinawa: University of the Ryukyus, 1987.

Pacific War Research Society. *Japan's Longest Day.* Tokyo: Kodansha International, 1968.

Perret, Geoffrey. *There's a War to Be Won: The United States Army in World War II.* New York: Random House, 1991.

Pfuhl, Richard. *Chasing the Sun.* St. Louis: Ten Square Books, 1979.

Piggott, Juliet. *Japanese Mythology.* New York: Peter Bedrick Books, 1983.

Pineau, Roger (ed). *The Japan Expedition 1852–1854: The Personal Journal of Commodore Matthew C. Perry.* Washington, D.C.: Smithsonian Institute Press, 1968.

Poolman, Kenneth. *Illustrious.* London: William Kimber, 1955.

Potter, E. B., and Chester Nimitz. *Triumph in the Pacific: the Navy's Struggle Against Japan.* Englewood Cliffs: Prentice-Hall, 1963.

Pratt, Fletcher. *The Marines' War.* New York: William Sloane Associates, 1948.

Pyle, Ernie. *Here Is Your War: America's Favorite Correspondent Tells the Story of Our Soldiers' First Big Campaign.* Chicago: Henry Holt, 1943.

Rand McNally Encyclopedia of World War II. Chicago: Rand McNally, 1977.

Reischauer, Edwin O. *Japan, the Story of a Nation*. New York: Alfred A. Knopf, 1974.

Reischauer, Haru. *Samurai and Silk*. Boston: Harvard University Press, 1986.

Rhodes, Richard. *The Making of the Atomic Bomb*. New York: Simon and Schuster, 1987.

Rooney, Andrew A. *A Few Minutes with Andy Rooney*. New York: Atheneum, 1982.

Ross, Bill D. *Iwo Jima: Legacy of Valor*. New York: Vintage Books, 1986.

Ryokan, Yoshiaki (compiler). *Hikoku — Okinawa sen (Showa no senso — Jaanarisuto no shogen, v. 5)* (The Tragic Tale of the Battle of Okinawa — War in the Showa Period series: Journalists' Testaments, vol. 5). Tokyo: Kodansha International, 1985.

Sakakibara, Shoji. *Okinawa: Hachijyu-yokka no tatakai* (Okinawa, The 84-Day Battle). Tokyo: Shincho Sha, 1983.

Sheehan, Neil. *A Bright Shining Lie*. New York: Random House, 1988.

Shukyo Jijo Kenkyu-kai (Religion in Japan). Tokyo: Foreign Press Center, 1980.

Silvera, John D. *The Negro in World War II*. New York: Arno Press, 1969.

Smith, Peter C. *Task Force 57*. London: William Kimber, 1969.

Smith, Stanley E. (ed). *The United States Marine Corps in World War II*. New York: Random House, 1969.

———. *The United States Navy in World War II*. New York: Random House, 1968.

Spector, Robert H. *Eagle Against the Sun: The American War With Japan*. New York: Free Press, 1985.

Spurr, Russell. *A Glorious Way to Die: The Kamikaze Mission of the Battleship Yamato, April 1945*. New York: Newmarket Press, 1981.

Statler, Oliver. *Japanese Inn*. Honolulu: University of Hawaii Press, 1961.

Stein, R. Conrad. *Battle of Okinawa*. Chicago: Children's Press, 1985.

Storry, Richard. *The Double Patriots: A Study of Japanese Nationalism*. London: Chatto & Windus, 1957.

———. *A History of Modern Japan*. New York: Penguin Books, 1960.

Tetsu No Bofu: Okinawa senki (The Typhoon of Steel: A Record of the Battle of Okinawa). Naha: Okinawa Times, 1950, 1980.

Tasaki, Hanama. *Long the Imperial Way*. Westport, Connecticut: Greenwood Press, 1970.

Thomas, Lewis. *The Youngest Science*. New York: Viking Press, 1983.

Thorne, Christopher. *Allies of A Kind: The United States, Britain and the War Against Japan*. London: Hamish Hamilton, 1978.

Togo, Shigenori. *The Cause of Japan*. New York: Simon & Schuster, 1956.

Toland, John. *The Rising Sun*. New York: Random House, 1970.

Tregaskis, Richard. *Guadalcanal Diary*. New York: Random House, 1943.

Tuchman, Barbara W. *Stilwell and the American Experience in China, 1941–45*. New York: Bantam Books, 1972.

Ugaki, Matome. *Fading Victory: The Diary of Admiral Matome Ugaki, 1941–1945*. Pittsburgh: University of Pittsburgh Press, 1992.

Urasaki, Jun. *Okinawa no gyokusai* (Okinawa's Fight to the Last Man). Tokyo: Nihon Bunka Sha, 1972 (Bunka Shinsho series).

U.S. Army Assessment Committee. *Japanese Naval and Merchant Shipment Losses during World War II*. Washington, D.C.: Government Printing Office, 1947.

U.S. Army Forces in the Pacific Ocean Areas. *Participation in the Okinawa Operation* (declassified July 25, 1990).

Ushijima, Mitsuru Kanko Iinkai (compiler). *Okinawa Shireikan: Ushijima Mitsuru den* (A Biography of Mitsuru Ushijima, Commander of the Okinawan Army). Ushijima Mitsuru Kanko Iinkai, n.d.
Vandegrift, A. A. (as told to Robert Asprey). *Once a Marine: the Memoirs of A. A. Vandegrift.* New York: Ballantine Books, 1964.
Van der Post, Laurens. *The Prisoner and the Bomb.* New York: William Morrow, 1971.
Varley, Paul H. *Japanese Culture.* Honolulu: University of Hawaii Press, 1984.
Vian, Philip. *Action This Day.* London: Mullee, 1960.
Warner, Denis and Peggy. *The Sacred Warriors: Japan's Suicide Legions.* Melbourne: Van Nostrand Reinhold Company, 1982.
Warner, Gordon. *The Okinawa War.* Naha: Ikemiya Shokai & Company, 1987.
Watanabe, Norio. *Nigeru hei: sango sho no hi* (Fleeing Soldier: A Memorial on a Coral Reef). Tokyo: Maruju Sha, 1979.
Werstein, Irving. *Okinawa; The Last Ordeal.* New York: Crowell, 1968.
Wheeler, Keith (and the editors of Time-Life Books). *The Road to Tokyo.* Alexandria, Virginia: Time-Life Books, 1979.
Wheeler, Richard. *A Special Valor.* New York: Harper & Row, 1983.
Whiting, Robert. *The Chrysanthemum and the Bat.* Tokyo: Permanent Press, 1977.
Willmot, H. P. *The Barrier and the Javelin: Japanese and Allied Pacific Strategies to June, 1942.* Annapolis: Naval Institute Press, 1983.
———. *Empires in the Balance: Japanese and Allied Pacific Strategies to April, 1942.* Annapolis: Naval Institute Press, 1982.
———. (ed). *The War at Sea: The British Navy in World War II.* New York: William Morrow, 1968.
Winton, John. *The Forgotten Fleet.* London: Michael Joseph, 1969.
———. *War in the Pacific: Pearl Harbor to Tokyo Bay.* New York: Mayflower Books, 1978.
Winton, John (ed). *The War at Sea: The British Navy in World War II.* New York: William Morrow, 1968.
Woodburn Kirby, Major-General S. *The War Against Japan.* London: H.M. Stationery Office, 1969.
Yahara, Hiromichi. *Okinawa kessen* (Okinawa, the Decisive Battle). Tokyo: Yomiuri Shimbun Sha, 1973.
Yanagi, Soetsu. *The Unknown Craftsman: A Japanese Insight into Beauty.* Tokyo: Kodansha International, 1978.
Yokoyama, Hoën. *Ah, Toyama-maru!* (Ah, Toyama-maru!) Osaka: Osaka Kyoiku Tosho K.K., 1978.
Yoshida, Mitsuru. *Requiem for Battleship Yamato.* Tokyo: Kodansha International, 1985.

Chronology

1452	First mention of Shuri Castle in Okinawan chronicles.
1853	Commodore Matthew Perry "opens" Japan, stopping at Okinawa.
1871	Tokyo claims Okinawa as Japanese; China responds by declaring it hers.
1875	Tokyo imposes sovereignty on the Loochoo islands, changing their name to Ryukyu.
1879	Japanese troops occupy Shuri Castle, abolish monarchy and annex the islands.
1931	Japanese forces stage an anti-Japanese incident, strike immediately in supposed retaliation and go on to conquer Manchuria.
1937	Japanese forces stage another incident as a pretext for invading China; Tadashi Kojo enters the Imperial Military Academy at age seventeen.
1940	Kojo graduates and is assigned to the 22nd Regiment in Manchuria; briefly returns to Chiba, near Tokyo, for a combat engineering course.
1941	Sixteen-year-old Masahide Ota of Kume Island enrolls in Okinawa's Normal School.
December 7	Attack on Pearl Harbor.
December 11	United States and Britain declare war on Japan.
April 1942	Japanese forces conquer much of Philippine Islands; Bataan Death March.
June 4–6	Battle of Midway.
1943	First Lieutenant Kojo completes school for battalion commanders, returns to Manchuria and is promoted to captain and the regiment's youngest battalion commander.
March 1944	Imperial General Headquarters activates the 32nd Army for defense of Okinawa.
April	First large shipments of Japanese equipment and supplies arrive on Okinawa. Kojo marries.
July 19	Prefectural government orders young and elderly Okinawans to evacuate.

October 3	U.S. Pacific Fleet admirals choose Okinawa over Formosa as next and last steppingstone to the Japanese mainland.
October 10	10/10 day—first American air raid on Okinawa.
June 29	Sinking of the *Toyama maru,* with loss of almost the entire 44th Independent Mixed Brigade.
July	Dick Whitaker enlists in the Marines and is sent to boot camp on Parris Island; Kojo's 22nd Regiment withdraws from Manchuria and is shipped to Okinawa via Japan; General Masao Watanabe spends his last days in command of the new 32nd Army on Okinawa.
August	General Simon Bolivar Buckner, Jr., assumes command of the American 10th Army; General Mitsuru Ushijima takes command of the Japanese 32nd Army. Kojo's 22nd Regiment arrives on Okinawa.
August 21	Three ships bearing some six thousand evacuees from Okinawa depart from Naha for Kagoshima. One is sunk by an American submarine; 1845 women and children die.
December– January 1945	Accidental explosion wounds Kojo; despite severe ear infection, he waits a month before being taken to a hospital.
February	American forces land on Iwo Jima.
March 9–10	Great fire raid on Tokyo by American incendiary bombs.
March 15	Fleet of American warships close on Okinawa.
March 26	Beginning of final week of bombardment prior to invasion of Okinawa. Kojo rejoins his battalion, although he is still weak and ill.
March 30	Emperor Hirohito meets with Admiral Oikawa, Imperial Navy's Chief of Staff.
April 1	L-day: U.S. landing on Okinawa; Dick Whitaker goes in on third wave; Masahide Ota, drafted as a communications soldier for 32nd Army intelligence, watches from Shuri Castle, near General Ushijima.
April 6	Start of Operation Heaven Number One; destruction of the battleship *Yamato* the following day.
April 6–7	First Floating Chrysanthemum (mass kamikaze attack).
April 12	Death of President Franklin Delano Roosevelt.

April 12–13	Second Floating Chrysanthemum.
April 15–16	Third Floating Chrysanthemum.
April 16	Yae-dake, highest peak in the north, taken by Americans.
April 18	Death of the journalist Ernie Pyle.
April 20	Commander of American operations in Okinawan north declares it secure.
April 24	Americans take Kakazu Ridge.
April 26	Kojo resumes command of his old 1st Battalion and joins the fighting on the Shuri Line.
April 27–28	Fourth Floating Chrysanthemum.
April 29	Emperor's birthday. At a staff meeting in 32nd Army headquarters General Cho's argument for offensive attack wins out over Yahara's defensive strategy.
May 3–4	Fifth Floating Chrysanthemum.
May 4	Ushijima schedules massive counterattack; Kojo's 22nd Regiment assigned to screen advances of two attacking regiments, then join the advance.
May 5	After heavy casualties the 32nd Army announces "temporary" suspension of the counteroffensive.
May 8	Germany surrenders; V-E Day in Europe.
May 9–10	Units of 6th Marine Division cross the Asakawa River.
May 10	Kojo ordered to pull back slightly from his position at Kochi, in the Shuri Line.
May 10–11	Sixth Floating Chrysanthemum.
May 12–19	Battle of Sugar Loaf Hill.
May 16	Kojo's 1st Battalion is decimated; he is preparing to kill himself when an American satchel charge rips the pistol from his hand. Kojo and a senior private make their way to Colonel Yoshida's headquarters cave; Kojo spends next twelve days in unofficial reserve in a signal center near Shuri.
May 17	Dick Whitaker's platoon charges Sugar Loaf and retreats. Whitaker is wounded on May 18.
May 22	Ushijima calls a conference with senior staff and highest field officers.
May 22–31	Massive withdrawal of 32nd Army from the Shuri Line.
May 23	First American troops cross the Asato River.
May 23–25	Seventh Floating Chrysanthemum.
May 24	Japanese raid on Yomitan Airfield.

May 25–27	U.S.S. *Mississippi* destroys Shuri Castle; Naha also destroyed.
May 27	Eve of Ushijima's retreat. Students from the Normal School, including Masahide Ota, ordered to evacuate; he and his classmates head for their new base near the 32nd Army's relocated headquarters in the south.
May 27–29	Eighth Floating Chrysanthemum.
June 3–7	Ninth Floating Chrysanthemum.
June 4	Whitaker wounded again.
June 6	Remnants of the 22nd Regiment retreat to the far south.
June 10	General Buckner writes to General Ushijima inviting surrender; dropped by air, the message takes seven days to reach the new 32nd Army headquarters cave.
June 11	Admiral Minoru Ota sends farewell message to Ushijima.
June 12	159 members of the admiral's Naval Base Force surrender.
June 13	Marine unit discovers Admiral Ota's headquarters, filled with hundreds of bodies of suicides.
June 18	General Buckner killed at the front. The 32nd Army disbands all civilian corps.
June 19	Ushijima gives final orders to resist to the very end; troops of another battalion of Kojo's 24th Division slaughter over a dozen civilians in an apparently unpremeditated raid.
June 20	American advance reaches Kojo's dwindling 22nd Regiment at Maesato village; the regiment makes its final stand; Ushijima receives his last message from 24th Division.
June 20–21	Nearly a thousand Japanese and conscripted Okinawans surrender.
June 21	American 7th Division captures hill of Ushijima's headquarters cave. Island declared secure; Kojo disbands the last of his battalion.
June 21–22	Tenth Floating Chrysanthemum.
June 22–23	General Mitsuru Ushijima, Commander of the 32nd Army, and Chief of Staff Isamu Cho commit *seppuku* on ledge outside headquarters cave.
June 22	Emperor Hirohito summons six leading members of the Supreme War Council to discuss possibilities for peace.

June 23	American flag raised on southern tip.
July 2	General Joseph Stilwell, Buckner's replacement, announces the campaign officially over.
August 6	A-bomb dropped on Hiroshima.
August 8	USSR declares war on Japan.
August 9	A-bomb dropped on Nagasaki.
August 15	Emperor Hirohito surrenders. Message is broadcast on August 16.
September 2	V-J Day. Japan signs surrender terms aboard the battleship *Missouri*.
October	Whitaker's regiment is shipped to help repatriate Japanese forces in China. Masahide Ota surrenders and resolves to achieve a rebirth in learning, pacifism and individualism, as opposed to serving state interests.
Late autumn	Kojo surrenders and is sent to POW camp.
March 1946	Kojo returns from Okinawa to his native Kagoshima, where he spends close to a year in severe depression. Finally lands a job as a laborer, then as a driver for an American in the occupation force. He will join Japan's Self-Defense Force as a captain in 1954.
Memorial Day 1946	Whitaker returns home to Saugerties, New York.
1947	Opening of first full store in Naha amidst rubble and wreckage left by the campaign. Most Okinawans continue to live in severe poverty.
1949	Vickery Report to the U.S. Department of the Army suggests appalling condition of Okinawa under American occupation.
1972	American occupation ends; Okinawa reverts to Japan (the large Okinawan majority in favor of reversion will shrink as its promises fade).
1987	Unveiling of memorial to Okinawans, Japanese and Americans killed during the campaign.
1992	Unveiling of reproduction of Shuri Castle.

Index

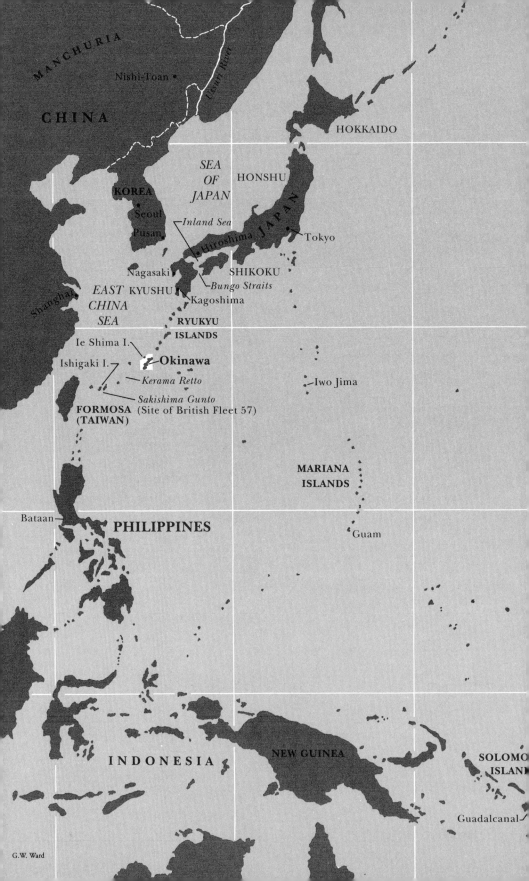